Gallipoli – The Road to Jerusalem

§

Kelvin Crombie

Heritage Resources

First published 2014

Heritage Resources
PO Box 565,
Mundaring WA 6073

www.heritageresources.com.au
sales@heritageresources.com.au

Crombie, Kelvin
Gallipoli – The Road to Jerusalem

ISBN 978-0-9873630-7-7

Printed in Western Australia
Typesetting by NQA Creative
Cover Design by Thamsanqa Mnangagwa, Minuteman Press, Midland, WA

Visuals front cover: Top - Anzac Cove, Gallipoli. Bottom - Surrender ceremony
Jaffa Gate, Jerusalem 11 December 1917

Heritage Resources

Table of Contents

Acknowledgements

There are two groups of people I would like to acknowledge for involvement in this project, those who were involved in the initial publication, and those involved in the present, updated version.

The initial publication of 1998 included the period of the Second World War and ended in 1948, while this present version ends in 1917. Those who contributed to the initial version in the period until 1917 included: Lindsay and Martha Bear, Grant and Jill Crombie, Peter Darg, Pat Ramsay, Murray and Rosemary Dixon, Owen Hoskin, Owen Eatwell, David Forbes, Prof Haim Goren, John Haldane, Wes and Gwen Hill, Bev Huch, Allan and Carol Jeffreys, Ray and Jill Lockhart, Alison Marchant, Jan Marriott, Bill and Rachel Millward, Wendy and Rod Monger, Sybil Parry, Ed and Helen Plenty, David Pileggi, Bruce and Heather Reekie, Jackie Reinhalda, Marie Shaw, Len and Bev Sherwood, Ruth Stark (z.l.), Kim Sutton.[1]

Thanks also to the following institutions: Australian War Memorial, Canberra ; Zionist Archives, Jerusalem ; Queen Elizabeth II New Zealand Army Museum, Waiouru ; Jabotinsky Archives, Tel Aviv ; Yad Ben Zvi Archives, Jerusalem ; British National Archives (formerly Public Records Office), Kew, London ; Rishon le Zion Archive Museum ; Imperial War Museum, London ; Beit HaGiddudim (Jewish Legions) Museum, Avihayil ; British Library, London and King's College, London.

1 Some of the above mentioned are no longer alive.

viii

In addition for this current edition thanks are also due to: Cyril Pritchard, Peter and Kathy Booth, Peter Cuthbertson, Brendan and Le-anne Johnston, Chris Moxon, Ian Lindsay, George Firth, Mark Durie, Mike Niebuhr, Alison Marchant, Bat Yeor and others. Also the Conrad Schick Library and Archive, Christ Church, Jerusalem ; Reid Library, University of Western Australia ; Middle East Centre (St. Anthony's College) Oxford.

Although quite an effort has been made to locate and access primary sources, time, space and resources did not permit me to fully achieve this. Numerous secondary sources therefore have been accessed.

To each and every author that I have accessed I give my heartfelt thanks. Great effort has been made to correctly acknowledge my source of infor-mation. Where this might have been overlooked I ask for forgiveness in advance, and also ask that where this has occurred I would be notified, in order to ensure the record is set straight.

I will be the first to acknowledge that no work of this nature can be done by one person. The subject matter is so big that it requires the expertise of many in the numerous fields and streams that it covers.

Special thanks are due to three people. The first is my late Mother, Dor-othy Crombie (nee Websdale). As a child growing up on a Western Austra-lian farm I developed an awareness for this subject matter. While others looked askance at my pre-occupation in this subject, Mum, although obvi-ously dubious at times, never discouraged me from pursuing it.

My wife Lexie, who has always kept a close and critical eye on my in-volvement in this subject. In 1992 I was all ready to write about how 'Aus-tralia saved the Middle East' by capturing Beersheba and so on, but Lexie would have none of it. She has always tried to keep my feet glued to the ground. Also my friend, Rev David Pileggi of Christ Church Jerusalem. Da-vid, an academic of the highest order, always encouraged me to base my work on thorough research.

Books of this nature are not written in a vacuum, nor are they the product of the author alone. To all of the above mentioned individuals and institutions and others not mentioned: Thank you.

Foreword

In 2005 as Australia's Governor-General, I was deeply spiritually moved as I stood in the ruins of Abraham's house in the biblical city of Ur (Iraq).

There I reflected on the paths of the three great religions created through Abraham's progeny – Jewish, Christian and Islamic.

I had a vision at that time that perhaps one day, the leaders of those religions would gather in Abraham's backyard and there in front of international television, proclaim to the world a new dawn of hope based on religious tolerance and brotherly love. I still hold to that hope.

Kelvin Crombie's *Gallipoli – The Road to Jerusalem* provides a masterly account of the Jewish diaspora's quest over millennia for a homeland; a homeland promised to them by Abraham in his covenant with God, partially achieved through the 1917 Balfour Declaration. This stated the British Government's desire to establish in Palestine a national home for the Jewish people. This was to be without prejudice to the civil and religious rites of any non-Jewish communities in Palestine, but an Israeli State was not finally realised until the United Nations resolution of November 1947.

By any measure of historical recording *Gallipoli – The Road to Jerusalem* is a masterly account, describing accurately and without prejudice, the long and often traumatic Jewish journey to nationhood. Crombie explains the central importance of a strip of land approximately 500 kms by 50 kms in extent, which in abutting the Eastern Mediterranean, had proven strategically essential to the prosperity of earlier civilizations, including Persian, Greek, Egyptian, Roman and Turkish.

In more modern times, Crombie describes in fascinating detail how Britain, France, Germany and Russian interests variously held sway, either in linkage with, or against the Turkish Empire. With the building of the Suez Canal in 1869 and its purchase by Britain, the quickest route to India and Britain's Indian Ocean colonies saw the canal assume a strategic importance to Britain matched only by that of the Dardanelles Straits enabling Russian access to the Mediterranean and Black Seas.

The closure of these straits by the Turks in 1914 with the complicit support of Germany, the declaration of *Jihad* by the Sultan of Turkey against all *dhimmis* (non-Muslim persons) except for Germany and Austria, saw Britain and Russia then declare war on Turkey and thus provide the catalyst for British support for an Israeli State.

The author then convincingly explains how the Gallipoli campaign that followed, whilst unsuccessful in its initial aim of opening the Dardanelles and capturing Constantinople, was ultimately successful through the gallant exploits of primarily British, Australian, New Zealand and Indian troops, at a cost of some 88,150 of their lives. General Allenby's subsequent capture of Jerusalem brought about the eventual defeat and break up of the 400 plus year Ottoman Empire, the establishment of the Jewish homeland in Israel and the birth of new Arabic nations of Iraq, Jordan, Lebanon and Syria, followed later by Saudi Arabia.

This is a marvellously written history for anyone interested in the Jewish journey. I commend it wholeheartedly and wait with eager anticipation for its sequel.

Michael Jeffery

Major-General the Honourable Michael Jeffery
AC, AO (Mil), CVO, MC (Retd).
Former Governor-General of Australia.

Introduction

The conception of this book in its original form[2] came during an ANZAC[3] Day service at the Commonwealth War Cemetery in Jerusalem in April 1992.[4]

Until that point I had been conducting *In Step with Allenby and the Light Horse* tours from Jerusalem to Beersheba, and speaking and writing on the subject of British involvement in the Eastern Mediterranean, for several years. These outlets provided me with a basic understanding of the role the Australian Light Horse, New Zealand Mounted Rifles and British forces played in the capture of Beersheba on 31 October 1917, and of the political dynamics behind the British Government's formulation of the Balfour Declaration (which also occurred on 31 October 1917.[5])

Yet it was only on that spring Jerusalem day on Mount Scopus[6] that I felt challenged to document the strategic role that the ANZAC soldiers had played militarily in aiding with Israel's modern rebirth. Although a previous publication dealing with British involvement in the region from 1798 onwards assisted with some foundational understanding,[7]this work was going to require a lot of extra research. Gallipoli at that point was only

---

2 *Anzacs, Empires and Israel's Restoration 1798-1948,* (Perth, 1998).

3 An acronym for Australia and New Zealand Army Corps. Each year Australians and New Zealanders remember their war dead on 25 April, the day in 1915 when their soldiers landed on the Gallipoli Peninsula in Turkey to fight their first battle as sovereign nations. British and French soldiers also landed on that day.

4 The Jerusalem War Cemetery is operated by the Commonwealth War Graves Commission.

5 Although Lord Balfour's letter to Lord Rothschild was written on 2 November, the actual Cabinet decision was on 31 October 1917.

6 Mount Scopus is contiguous to the Mount of Olives and forms a high ridge to the north of the Old City of Jerusalem.

7 *For the Love of Zion,* (Hodder & Stoughton, London, 1991).

moderately on the radar screen.

During the following years I researched the subject matter as best as possible, helped by a year's sabbatical in Australia and New Zealand in 1993, when visits were made to archives on both sides of the Tasman Sea. Gallipoli was now a little more on the radar screen.

Shortly after returning to Jerusalem in late 1993 I recall waking on one of my research and writing days, with this impression burning within: 'Gallipoli was integral in the process leading to the rebirth of Israel.'[8] This impression was so strong that I rushed down town to locate a copy of Alan Moorehead's book *Gallipoli*. My search, though, was unsuccessful. But then, somewhat by chance, I located a book entitled *The World Crisis*, which was Winston Churchill's autobiography of the First World War.

Later while reading this book, a passage virtually 'jumped out' of the page. In the context of the Gallipoli Campaign Churchill wrote:

> From the uttermost ends of the earth ships and soldiers are approaching the eastern Mediterranean in fulfilment of a destiny as yet not understood by mortal man... the arrival of the Anzacs in Egypt created the nucleus of the army ready to attack the heart of the Turkish Empire.[9]

This passage captivated me, especially those words, '*in fulfilment of a destiny as yet not understood by mortal man.*' What, I thought, did Churchill mean by those words? Could they, I then asked myself, have something to do with Israel's rebirth, a rebirth after almost 2000 years of national dispersion?

Some of the answers to that question came shortly afterwards when, while in the UK on business, I spent some time in the National Archives in Kew. The goal here was to locate the Minutes of the British War Cabinet of late 1914 into 1915, Minutes which Churchill had alluded to in his book.

---

8   Or words to that effect.
9   Churchill, W. *The World Crisis*, (New York, 1949), p. 249.

It was those Minutes which confirmed to me the centrality of the Gallipoli Campaign to the events which transpired over the following years, events which culminated first in the capture of Beersheba and the issuing of the Balfour Declaration, and then the capture of Jerusalem and Damascus.

Gallipoli was indeed an important link in the chain of events which led to the establishment of modern Israel – *and* the establishment of other nations in the Middle East. Gallipoli played a significant role in the formulation of all three Middle East political 'agreements' during the First World War, namely the McMahon-Hussein correspondence, the 'Sykes-Picot' Agreement, and the Balfour Declaration.

Following some six years of research and writing, interspersed with work commitments, *Anzacs, Empires and Israel's Restoration 1798-1948* was finally published in April 1998.

* * *

During the following years there was a desire to go over the subject matter again, 'to peel off another layer of the onion'. It was clear that there was a much bigger story yet to be told. Reading through other publications of a similar ilk, such as David Fromkin's, *A Peace to End All Peace* ; Donald Sanders', *High Walls of Jerusalem* ; Isaiah Friedmann's, *The Question of Palestine* ; George Antonius', *The Arab Awakening* ; Elie Kedourie's, *The Arab Labyrinth,* and other titles, helped me see that there were *many* layers yet to be uncovered.

The challenge I then felt was to take what I had been allowed to learn and see through my work as a local guide and researcher[10] and to somehow make understandable what in many ways is quite a complicated story.

Another challenge was to determine the best time for such a publication. An opportunity then seemed to present itself with the 100th anniversary of the beginning of World War One, in 2014, and of the Gallipoli Campaign, in 2015. Hence the arrival of this publication at this time.

It has been necessary, though, to divide this subject into two parts of a whole. This volume will conclude with the capture of Jerusalem in Decem-

---

10 Based at Christ Church inside the Old City of Jerusalem.

ber 1917, while the following volume, *Jerusalem – The Road to San Remo*, will follow the theme through to the League of Nations endorsed Conference in San Remo in April 1920, when Mandates were drawn up for the administration of the former Turkish Empire.

It was at San Remo, in Italy, on 25 April 1920 that the representative nations voted to offer the Palestine Mandate to Britain, and to incorporate within the Mandate the promise of the Balfour Declaration for the establishment of a Jewish National Home in Palestine.

Afterwards all 51 member nations of the League of Nations voted to accept the Mandates offered to Britain and France, Mandates which in turn led to the establishment of the Jewish nation of Israel, as well as the Arab nations of Iraq, Syria, Lebanon and Jordan.[11]

* * *

My main intention in this publication is not to over-emphasize either the military component (which would bore most people), or the geo-political (political), but to synthesize the two, showing how each complements and depends upon the outworking of the other.

There is, I believe, an intricate relationship between the military involvement of British, New Zealand, Australian and Indian soldiers in the Middle East during World War One and the political agreements which led to the ultimate establishment of the nations of Israel, Syria, Lebanon, Iraq, Jordan – and even Saudi Arabia.

Hopefully this publication can permit a slightly better understanding of the background leading up to the involvement of these soldiers in that region, and of how their involvement created the environment for the establishment of all those sovereign nations.

* * *

There is, in addition to the basic thrust of this book, one other subject which I have found necessary to present: the Armenian genocide.[12] Each year on

---

11   The area of Arabia was not part of the Mandate area, but it was the victory over Turkey which permitted the establishment of the sovereign nation of Hejaz under the Sherif of Mecca, head of the Hashemite tribe. Then in 1924/5 the tribe of Saud defeated the Hashemite tribe and later the Kingdom of Saudi Arabia was established.

12   The term 'Genocide' was only coined in 1944 by a Polish-Jewish lawyer named Raphael Lemkin. Lemkin was trying to convey the essence of what the Nazis were doing to the Jewish people, and thus combined two words, *Geno*

24 April Armenians around the world recall the beginning of the destruction of up to 1.5 million of their people.[13]

For some twenty years I worked adjacent to the Armenian Quarter in Jerusalem, and was aware that at the very time when I, as an Australian, was preparing to attend the ANZAC Service on 25 April, the Armenians were remembering a far more sinister loss of lives, which to them had its official beginning on 24 April 1915.

There is a connection between Gallipoli and the Armenian genocide, and although this publication by no means endeavours to present this event in its fullness, an attempt has been made to show the connections of the two events. The year 2015 marks the 100th anniversary of the Armenian genocide.

Initially this terrible event was going to be a peripheral part of this publication. That all changed, however, when I was sifting through hundreds of pages of 'boring' intelligence reports from Gallipoli and Cairo from the period of 1915 in the National Archives in London. While looking for something specific (and totally different), I came across numerous eye-witness accounts of the atrocities being meted out against Armenian civilians. These accounts were being given by people of sundry backgrounds, including Prisoners of War, and were written in Military Intelligence reports.

This was when I began to better understand the connection between my subject matter and the Armenian genocide. But I must emphasize that this issue, as important as it is, is not the central focus of this publication. What does present itself, though, is that the period of 24-25 April each year is central to the present national identities of Australia, New Zealand and the Armenians.

= race or tribe in Greek, with *cide* = a Latin word associated with killing. On 9 December 1948 the United Nations approved the *Convention on the Prevention and Punishment of the Crime of Genocide.*

Although realising that this word was not used until 1944, and that I do not presume to have a full understanding of what happened to the collective Armenian community in Turkey between 1915-1922, I will nevertheless use the term as it does seem to describe what was perpetrated against the Armenians.

Most nations and entities do not officially recognize the Armenian genocide, including Turkey, the United Nations and Australia (the exception being the New South Wales Parliament.) For further information about this event please see the sources mentioned at the appropriate section in the publication – and the many more written about the subject matter. (I am also mindful, as an Australian, that what happened to the Indigenous Australians could also be classified as a genocide, according to the criteria of the United Nations Convention of 1948).

13   While the Armenians claim some 1.5 million people were killed, the Turkish Government claims the figure to be 300-600,000 (Akcam,T. *A Shameful Act,* Preface), and also emphasize that the killing of Armenians was not a genocide, but was a result of their siding with Russia. Turkish historian Taner Akcam states a figure of about 1 million.

* * *

The central focus that I do want to present in this publication is the strong connection between the events associated with Gallipoli, to those associated with the capture of Beersheba and Jerusalem. These cumulative events provide the nation of Israel with a *legitimate right* to exist; as indeed there is a similar right for the surrounding Arab nations to exist. Both came out of the same situation – the defeat and dismemberment of the Ottoman Turkish Empire.

Additionally, that the initial foundation for these nations coming into existence - the defeat of the Turkish Army - actually had little to do with Jewish or Arab soldiers: the bulk of the fighting was carried out by, and the majority of the casualties were sustained by, Gentile soldiers from Britain, India, Australia and New Zealand.

One thing I will categorically state about this publication: it is not an exhaustive account of the many streams upon which it touches. Where possible I have provided details where the reader can go for further research and study on those streams through accessing the research and writings of experts in each of those fields. All this publication can offer is an overview.

Additionally, this publication most certainly does not provide the answers or solutions to the modern day Middle East imbroglio. Hopefully, however, it does provide a basic insight into some of the mechanics behind why there is unsettledness in the Middle East.

As an Australian who was priviledged to live in the Middle East for a quarter of a century, interacting with both Israelis and Arab people, and who worked as a local guide and researcher for a British institution for twenty of those years, this is my offering. I certainly do trust you will 'enjoy' what is offered.

§

The centre of the world

ANCIENT TRADE ROUTES

For some four millennia and more, the broad region stretching from Egypt (especially the Nile River) through to Mesopotamia (especially the Euphrates-Tigris Rivers) and Anatolia (especially the Bosphorus and Dardanelles Straits) has been a region of great contention. This region has been called the 'fertile crescent'; 'centre of civilisation'; 'centre of the world' and more. It was a political, cultural, economic and religious cross-roads. Anything or anyone travelling north-south or east-west, would of necessity pass through this region.

Major trade routes crisscrossed this region. From Egypt the *Via Maris* ('Way of the Sea'), hugged the Mediterranean coast through the Sinai Peninsula into the land of Israel. At the Carmel Range it diverged; one branch headed north along the Mediterranean coast past Haifa, Acre, Tyre, Sidon, Beirut, Tripoli and into Anatolia (Asia Minor or Turkey), and a second branch went north-east past Nazareth, the Sea of Galilee, over the Jordan River and into the Bashan (Golan Heights) and on to Damascus. A third branch continued eastwards along the Esdraelon (Jezreel) Valley over the Jordan River, and up the steep incline to the plateau above.

Here it met the route coming up from Arabia in the south, the 'King's Highway', which had steered its course from Jedda on the Red Sea coast, through Mecca, Medina, Rabbat Ammon (Amman), Deraa and then on to Damascus. From the major regional capital of Damascus, routes led

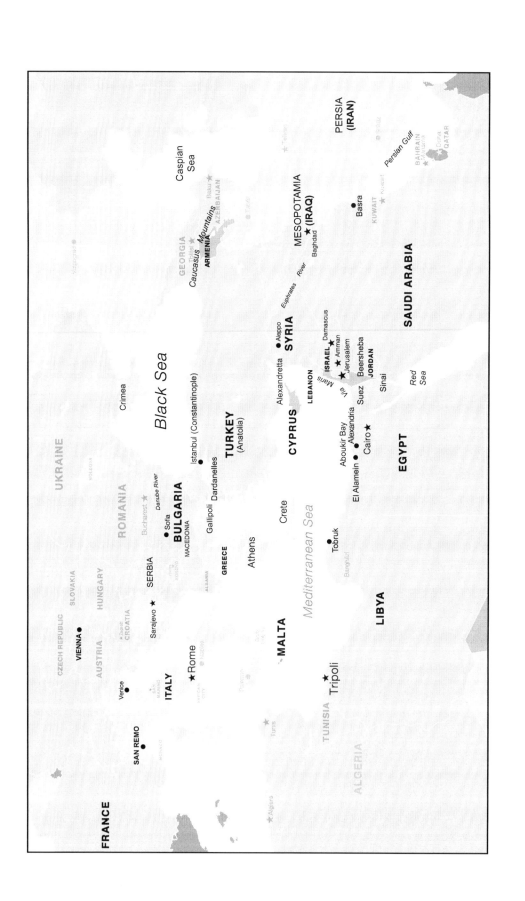

westwards to the Lebanon and Beirut, or north through Homs, Hama and Aleppo, and then either into Anatolia or north-east into Mesopotamia (modern day Iraq). Anatolia was itself a major centre for routes coming from further west in Asia, either overland, or via the Caspian and Black Seas. Produce also traversed by sea from the regions surrounding the Black Sea (modern day Turkey, Russia, Ukraine, Romania, Bulgaria, Georgia) through the strategic Bosphorus Straits (past the location of Byzantium/ Constantinople/Istanbul) into the Sea of Marmara (past a small village named Gelibolu – Gallipoli) and out into the Mediterranean Sea via the equally strategic Dardanelles Straits.

Some produce coming from India and from the Spice Islands was also shipped either to the Persian Gulf or Red Sea (and Gulf of Suez) and then transported overland from both locations to Levantine (Eastern Mediterranean) ports – and then on to Europe.

Such routes not only assisted with trade, but also relayed information, ideas and foreign armies seeking self-aggrandizement, glory and power.

ISRAEL – THE LAND BETWEEN EMPIRES

By geographical accident the most central land within this overall region was the land of Israel. 'The emphasis … upon this land' wrote Dr Jim Monson, 'must always be understood against the larger geographical context of the Eastern Mediterranean, Egypt and Mesopotamia. In light of these larger forces the country … is rather insignificant except as a land bridge between great empires.'[1] The land of Israel indeed was a 'land between empires'.

Vast empires rose and fell throughout antiquity in the regions where present day Turkey, Syria, Lebanon, Iraq and Iran now exist. Among these were the Hittite, Mittite, Assyrian, Babylonian and Persian empires. These were the 'northern empires'. To the west of the Isthmus of Suez lay another imperial bastion during those millennia: Egypt, which was the 'southern empire.'

---

1   Monson, J. *The Land Between – A Regional Study Guide to the Land of the Bible*, (Jerusalem, 1983), p. 13.

If during those thousands of years there was no strong empire in the north, then invariably Egypt reigned supreme over the region. Conversely, if during those years Egypt was weak, then one of those northern empires could have military, political and economic control over that vast area.

However, a major problem arose when both Egypt and a strong empire in the north existed at the same time. Invariably there was conflict, as only one could be in ascendance at any one time. During such periods of conflict one region in particular was caught in the middle, the land of Canaan, the land of Israel.

This land was coveted by the empires as it was a strategic buffer zone and it lay on the direct route of the armies of these empires. Such imperial rivalry did not augur well for the independence of any smaller nation in this strategic buffer zone. If such an independent nation did exist there it was at the behest of one of those major empires, or during a period of imperial passivity. Invariably such independence would not last for long.

THE SIGNIFICANCE OF ISRAEL AND JERUSALEM

The connection of the people of Israel (the Jewish people) to the land of Israel, and the city of Jerusalem, is closely associated with a man named Abram, or Abraham. It was to him, sometime in the second or third millennia BC, that the God named *Elohim*[2] introduced Himself when he lived in Ur of the Chaldees (modern day Iraq) and gave to Abram certain promises: that a nation would come forth from him; that this nation would possess the land of Canaan; and that all the nations on earth would be blessed through him.

God then confirmed these promises to Abram through the most sacred of ancient institutions, the cutting of a covenant. These promises, foremost of which was that the land of Canaan was entrusted to him and his descendants, were then transferred not to his eldest son Ishmael, but to his

---

2 The God of Abraham is given different names in the Hebrew Scriptures (the *Tanach* or Bible), often to describe any one of his attributes. Other names given are *Yahweh*, *Adonai* and *El Shaddai*. I will henceforth use the English derivation of God, or the God of Israel.

second-born son, Isaac, and then to Isaac's son, Jacob, who was also called Israel.

Many centuries later the descendants of Abraham were in slavery in Egypt. They then called out to the God of Abraham, Isaac and Jacob for deliverance from this cruel bondage. The God of Abraham heard their cry and sent Moses, who led the people of Israel out of Egypt and into the Sinai.

It was there in the Sinai that God entered into another covenant, this time with the people, or nation of Israel, and gave to them a Constitution for how to live in the land of Israel. According to ancient tradition, it was as if God was the suzerain king, and Israel was the servant or vassal. This Constitution is known as the *Torah* (in English, 'the Law'), and the central part of the *Torah* were the Ten Commandments. It was the desire of God that through Israel all the nations would come to know Him, His Constitution of how to live on earth, and of the character of His Kingdom.[3]

Moses' successor Joshua led the people of Israel into the land of Canaan, hereafter known as *Eretz Yisrael* – the land of Israel. However, a time came when the people desired to have a king to rule over them, like all the other nations. In due course God entered into covenant with a young man from Bethlehem named David, and ultimately David was accepted as the king of Israel. David then captured the town of Jebus (or Salem), in about 1004 BC, and renamed it *Yerushalayim* (Jerusalem). He made it the political and spiritual capital of the nation of Israel. There his son Solomon built a magnificent Temple, to which the people came in order to worship the God of their nation.

Following the reigns of David and Solomon, however the nation fell into gross disobedience to God's Constitution, and was split into two smaller kingdoms. During the following centuries as the nation struggled, prophets arose who continually called the people back to obedience to their God and His Constitution. These prophets also spoke of a forthcoming king from David's family who would reign wisely and justly, over Israel – and over the nations.

---

3 This Constitution, the *Torah*, was later written down and in time other Writings (known as *Chetuvim*) and the words of the Prophets (*Neviim*) were added, forming the *Tanach* – the Hebrew Scriptures or Old Testament of the Bible.

Many of those very same prophets foretold of a future great restoration of the scattered people of Israel from the ends of the earth back to the land of Israel.

EXILE TO BABYLON AND RETURN UNDER THE PERSIANS

According to the *Torah*, and in accordance with ancient customs, if the vassal nation Israel disobeyed the Constitution of the Great King, there would be consequences – pestilence, plague, famine and war. Gross disobedience would lead to exile from the land, albeit temporary exile, as possession of the land was founded upon the covenant with Abraham.

Such gross disobedience to God's Constitution led to the northern kingdom of Israel being conquered by the Assyrian Empire,[4] and the majority of the people taken into captivity and deported in 722 BC. Then in 586 BC the Babylonian Empire defeated the southern kingdom of Judah. The majority of the Judeans were then taken into exile to Babylon (modern day Iraq).

But in 539 BC the Persian Empire defeated the Babylonians and inherited the former Babylonian Empire - which included the land of Israel. Shortly afterwards the Persian emperor Cyrus permitted a remnant of the captured Judeans to return to Judah – and particularly to Jerusalem. Cyrus also gave permission to the returning Judeans to worship their God in their own way.

The edict of Cyrus, permitting the Jewish people to return, made geo-political sense. Being the 'northern empire' he would be concerned about his southern neighbour, Egypt. The Jewish people in 'the land between empires' could act as an ally in this buffer zone.

This returning remnant then began to rebuild Jerusalem and the Temple, and to restore the land from its destruction, deprivation and neglect. The return of Israel to their land, however, incurred the wrath of other peoples, who had moved into and usurped the land and property of the exiled Judeans. Despite such opposition the nation managed to survive, develop and even expand.

4　Many Israelites from the north had previously moved to the south, and many more fled south at the time of the Assyrian invasion. The tribe of Judah really was a composite of all the tribes of Israel.

Then, and especially in the following centuries, many of the people of Israel still awaited the coming of that wise and righteous king from David's family, the one they referred to as - Messiah.

GREEKS AND ROMANS

A new imperial power, Greece, then rose in the fourth century BC. In 334 BC Alexander (the Great) crossed from Europe into Asia at the Hellespont, the sixty-five kilometre long waterway which separates Europe from Asia, and which is today called the Dardanelles. Alexander would have crossed close to where a small Turkish village later existed named Gelibolu – Gallipoli.

Alexander's venture marked the first time that a European empire entered into the East, or the Orient. He soon defeated the Persians, and conquered their Empire. The Greeks then introduced western culture, language and religion into the East. However, the empire split in 323 BC following Alexander's death. One general, Ptolemais, took command of Egypt and another general, Seleucis, took command of Syria. These two regions henceforth were the 'northern' and 'southern' empires, and continually fought against each other – often in and around the land of Israel.

When the Syrian Greeks gained control over the land of Israel in 198 BC, they desired to bring all the various people groups into conformity to the Greek-Hellenic religion, culture and civilisation. Many Jewish people rebelled against this attempt to take away their national identity. Led by the Maccabees they ultimately rose in revolt and in the year 165 BC finally defeated the Greeks. This victory is remembered each year usually in the month of December, and is known as *Hanukkah*, the festival of lights, a remembrance of deliverance from an oppressive regime.

The Jewish people thereafter enjoyed a period of limited imperial interference during what was known as the Hasmonean period. Unfortunately though, civil strife erupted and shattered this period of relative tranquillity, raising the cry by many of the people for the coming of the king from David's family, the one they called the Messiah.

This period of Jewish quasi-independence was short lived for in 64 BC, the Roman Empire entered into the region and in 63 BC took control over the land of Israel, which then became part of the Roman province of Syria. This province was both geo-politically and economically important for Rome: trade continued to traverse the land, while the Euphrates River marked the boundary with the rival empire of the time – Parthia (part of modern day Iraq and Iran).

§

CHAPTER 2

Christianity rises – Israel exiled

BIRTH OF CHRISTIANITY

For many centuries the pious Jewish people had been anticipating the coming of the special ruler from the family of King David, the one they called Messiah (anointed one). Living under pagan Roman suzerainty (either through direct rule or through King Herod), increased this desire. About the year 4 BC a baby was born in David's town of Bethlehem, who at his circumcision[1] was given the name of *Yeshua* – Jesus.

As a grown man Jesus began an itinerant ministry as a rabbi, proclaiming a message about the Kingdom of God, and backed up his message by healing the sick and infirm, comforting the broken-hearted, and encouraging people to love those who despised and mistreated them.

He soon had a large following as many believed him to be the promised Messiah. But Jesus ultimately fell foul of both the Jewish leadership and the Roman authorities, and died a cruel death by crucifixion in Jerusalem about 27 AD.

The core of Jesus' teaching revolved around forgiveness. His life epitomised this very teaching. As he hung on the execution stake (the Cross)

---

1   Circumcision is the rite whereby a Jewish baby boy is made part of the covenant people of Abraham.

he prayed, concerning his accusers and enemies at his feet, "Father, forgive them, for they do not know what they are doing." (Luke 23: 34, NIV) Then he died.

To the astonishment of his followers, three days later he revealed himself as having risen from the dead - and those who confessed faith in him as Messiah increased. Just prior to the Jewish feast of *Shavuot* Jesus stood with his Jewish followers on the Mount of Olives and then departed into heaven. But before doing so he gave them his final instructions – to take his message from Jerusalem, to Judea, Samaria and to the ends of the earth.[2]

Shortly afterwards two angels appeared and informed his perplexed followers that this same Jesus would "come back in the same way you saw him go to heaven."[3] According to these words and an associated prophecy from the Hebrew prophet Zechariah[4] these Jewish followers fully expected Jesus to return to Jerusalem.

JESUS' MESSAGE GOES ALSO TO THE GENTILES

Initially all the followers of Jesus were Jewish. But then Gentiles (non-Jews), also came to believe that he was the promised Messiah. One Jewish man in particular was involved in taking this very Jewish message to the Gentiles – Saul, or as we know of him, Paul.

Initially the message went to Gentiles living in the land of Israel, and then into other regions of Roman Asia. Once while in Asia Minor (Turkey) Paul received a call to take the message to Europe. He boarded a ship at Alexandria Troas and sailed past the Hellespont (the Dardanelles) and landed in Europe[5]. Thereafter the message that Jesus came to deliver was taken first into Greece, and ultimately into the rest of Europe.

Within only a few decades entire communities in the Greco-Roman world were confessing faith in Jesus, and his teachings were written down in what became known as the New Testament.

---

2   See Acts 1: 6-8.
3   Acts 1: 11.
4   Zechariah 14: 4.
5   Acts 16: 9-11

ROMANS EXPEL JEWISH PEOPLE FROM ISRAEL

The Roman authorities ruled as suzerain overlords over the Jewish people, many of whom resented being in political, cultural and religious subjugation to a pagan power. The animosity ultimately spilt over into open revolt in 66 AD. The Romans recognized the danger in this revolt, as Parthia could easily link up with the Jewish nation and threaten Rome's hold on that strategic region. Consequently they sent in large forces and by 70 AD they had captured Jerusalem and destroyed the Temple. The only major building left standing was the Citadel. By 73 AD they had crushed the revolt. Many of those Jewish people who survived were sent into exile.

At the time of the Roman conquest one rabbi named Yohanan Ben Zakkai extricated himself from Jerusalem and went to the small village of Yavne near the coast. Ben Zakkai recognized that with the Temple destroyed and the people exiled, the Jewish nation could disappear. So he reconstituted Judaism in a way that the Jewish people could survive as a nation dispersed among the nations of the earth. Orthodox (or Rabbinic) Judaism rose from the ashes of the Temple.

Some decades later the Roman suzerains planned to rebuild Jerusalem and turn it into a pagan city to be named *Aelia Capitolina*. This act further antagonized the Jewish people who remained in the land and in 132 AD a second revolt broke out against Roman subjugation. This revolt was mostly led by Shimon Bar Kockba, who was erroneously proclaimed to be the messiah by the esteemed Rabbi Akiva.

This revolt too was harshly put down by the Romans. The old Jerusalem was completely destroyed and a new *Aelia Capitolina* arose in its place. Jewish people were forbidden thereafter to live in Judah, while the entire land was renamed *Syria Palestina* – in order to erase the Jewish connection to the land.[6]

Although Jewish people continued to live in the Galilee, by and large Jewish life had now been separated from Jerusalem and Judah; and by degrees Jewish life became synonymous with life outside the land of Israel.

---

6 The Romans fully understood the ancient antipathy between the Israelites and the Philistines, and purposely chose the name *Palestina* (Palestine), the Latin derivative of Philistia.

Separated by space they may have been, but the Holy Scriptures (the *Tanach*) and the traditions and writings of the elders (collectively known as the *Talmud*) ensured that the people never forgot Jerusalem and the land of their inheritance.

They always believed that one day Messiah (Mashiah in Hebrew) would come - and that in accordance with the words of the ancient prophets, the Jewish people would be restored to Israel.

ARMENIA, BYZANTIUM AND ROMAN CHRISTIANITY

The message of Jesus meanwhile continued to spread far and wide, penetrating into many regions. One of those was Armenia, a strategically located kingdom between Asia Minor and the Caspian Sea. About 300 AD the king of Armenia confessed faith in Jesus, and his entire kingdom then became Christian.[7]

Although initially heavily persecuted and outlawed by the Roman authorities, within two hundred years the numbers of followers of Jesus (now named Christians) had grown so much that they were a factor to be taken into consideration by the Roman authorities. It was within this context that Emperor Constantine in 312 AD accepted the Christian message, and in 323 AD legalised Christianity within the Roman Empire.

Constantine then integrated this new religion, institutional Christianity, into the life of the Roman state. He also sought to establish a new capital for this 'new Rome', and chose Byzantium on the shores of the strategic Bosphorus Straits which bridged Europe and Asia. There he built a new Roman capital which he named Constantinople.

By the year 380 AD Christianity was proclaimed as the official religion of the Roman Empire. At this same time the huge Roman Empire was divided into two administrative halves: the Western Roman Empire centred upon Rome; and the Eastern Roman Empire (henceforth known as the Byzantine Empire, or Byzantium) centred upon Constantinople. During the following centuries the two halves slowly diverged and in time became two distinct empires.

---

7   The subsequent history of the Armenian Church is somewhat complicated and outside the purpose of this publication.

Initially, Roman Christianity was identical in both halves of the Empire. However, as the political and cultural character of the two empires diverged so too did the religious character of the Roman Church in each half. The western church evolved into the Roman Catholic Church (centred upon Rome), and the eastern church developed into the Greek Orthodox Church (centred upon Constantinople).

The land of Israel, or Palestine as it was known to the Romans, was part of the Byzantine Empire. The two physical representatives of this religious system were the Church of the Holy Sepulchre in Jerusalem and the Church of the Nativity in Bethlehem.

THEOLOGICAL CHANGES

During these formative centuries when the life and teachings of Jesus went from being encompassed within a small Jewish movement to being the official religion of the Roman Empire, there was also a distinct adaptation in the theological beliefs of this movement.

Roman Christianity was heavily influenced by Greek rather than Hebraic thought, and many of Jesus' teachings were now being viewed through a Hellenistic lens rather than through a Jewish/Hebraic lens.

The leaders of the new Gentile Church were now all Gentiles, and progressively adopted a negative attitude towards the Jewish nation, which collectively did not accept Jesus as the Messiah. The Gentile Church then condemned the collective nation of Israel for the death of Jesus, the crime they called *Deicide* – the murder of God.

Further, the Gentile Church (mostly through the teachings of the Church Fathers as well as the various ecclesiastical councils) also claimed that the nation of Israel had forfeited its covenant position and privileges, and that these (particularly the positive promises or blessings) were now transferred to the Gentile Church, which became the 'new Israel'.

The Jewish people could continue to live under Roman Christianity, but as a second class group. They would be, as one church father named Augustine stated, a testimony to what happens to those who reject Jesus[8]. It

---

8 Augustine, *Contra Faustum*, Book 12.12, wwwnewadvent.org/fathers

is understandable that under such a system there was no hope at all for the Jewish people being restored as a nation in the land of Israel.

The Jewish people who then lived in the land of Israel under Byzantine rule were a tolerated minority who could exercise their own religion – Judaism. But they had little or no political influence. The only exception to their status was during the reign of Emperor Justinian in the fifth century AD, who held out hopes of them returning to their covenanted land and even of rebuilding their Temple.

The political reality, though, was that this would not happen, especially while the land remained under the control of the Byzantine Empire, and due to the theological position of the Greek Orthodox Church.

The attitude of the Western Roman Church towards the Jewish people was the same, if not worse. Throughout Europe, with but a few exceptions, the Jewish people were treated as second class citizens. They were often called "Christ killers", and were mercilessly persecuted by the Church authorities, especially at the time of Easter.

While either of the Roman Churches, East or West (or any nation associated with these two Churches), were in authority there would be no restored Israel. The Jewish people, meanwhile, continued to look for the coming of Messiah, who would establish a righteous form of government on earth, and who would reign from Jerusalem.

§

CHAPTER 3

The era of Islamic imperialism

BIRTH OF ISLAM

The Byzantine Empire was large and comprised of numerous smaller national entities which often resented the authority of the Byzantine rulers based in Constantinople. As such there were often conflicts raging throughout the Empire, creating weaknesses which could easily be exploited. The Persian Empire was one such entity that seized upon this weakness by invading and ravaging part of the Byzantine Empire, including Palestine, during the period 611-627 AD.

Another to seize upon the growing weakness of the Byzantine Empire was an ideology which grew out of western Arabia in the early seventh century AD, revolving around a young Arabian man named Mohammad. Mohammad lived in Mecca, the local religious centre for the many nomadic pagan tribes of Arabia. In the centre of Mecca stood the *Al-Kaaba*, a pagan temple in which were kept the idols of the many Arabian tribes.[1] The idol of Mohammad's tribe, the Quraish, was named Allah.

For some time Mohammad was exposed to the teachings of both the Jews and Christians, and this exposure may have influenced him to become interested in a monotheistic faith system and become dissatisfied with the

---

[1] Muslims now believe this was the place where Ibrahim (Abraham) prepared to sacrifice his son Ishmael. Laffin, J. *The Dagger of Islam*, (London, 1979), p. 11. The Bible states that Abraham prepared to sacrifice Isaac, traditionally on Mount Moriah – Jerusalem of today.

pagan belief system of his tribe.[2]

From 610 AD Mohammad stated that he had received special revelations from Allah via the archangel Gabriel, which were later recorded in book form in the *Koran* (*Quran*). The sayings of Mohammad were also recorded, known as the *Hadith*.

These revelations were basically an attempt at synthesizing the teachings of Judaism and Christianity with Mohammad's own pagan beliefs, and an attempt to equate Allah with the God of Israel. It was in this context that Mohammad proclaimed himself to be the final prophet and was bringing to completion that which had begun with Moses and Jesus.[3]

The majority of the people of Mecca rejected Mohammad and his teaching.[4] Finally in 622 AD, Mohammad went from Mecca to Medina, a migration (the *Hijrah*) which is regarded as the beginning of his movement, a movement henceforth known as Islam – which means 'submission'.

THE LAW OF THE SWORD

Initially Mohammad adopted a tolerant attitude towards those who would not accept his message, including the Jewish people, hoping they would all ultimately become adherents of Islam. A *Sura* from the Koran from this time reads: 'Let there be no compulsion in religion …' (Sura 2.256).

But the Jewish people in Medina claimed that Mohammad's message contradicted the Jewish Scriptures - which they also believed he was changing - and they rejected his message. In response, Mohammad, in about the year 623 AD, changed his previous tolerant attitude towards the Jewish people, and others who did not accept his message, and thereafter adopted the 'rule or verse of the sword.' This rule is best expressed in this verse from the Koran:

---

2   Laffin, J. *The Dagger of Islam*, (London, 1979), p. 10.
3   As recorded in Sura 3: 85.
4   For more on this period of Mohammad's life see Durie, M. *The Third Choice*, (Deror Books, 2010).

Kill the Mushrikun (unbelievers) wherever you find them, and capture and besiege them, and lie in wait for them in each and every am-
bush. But if they repent ... then leave their way free. (Sura 9: 5)[5]

This attitude might seem a contradiction to his earlier more tolerant attitude,
but this and other contradictions in his teachings were resolved through the
principle of *Nasikh* – progressive revelation. Whatever Mohammad said,
or presumed to hear from Allah after 623 AD, superseded or overrode what
was stated before.[6]

     An authority on Islam, Rev. Dr. Mark Durie, states:

Muhammad thus concluded that his coming had abrogated Judaism,
that the Islam he brought was the final religion, and the Quran the last
revelation. All who rejected this message would be 'losers' (Q3.85).
It would no longer be acceptable for Jews – or Christians – to follow
their old religion: they had to acknowledge, and becomes Muslims
too, like everyone else.

     Muhammad took this a step further. Not only was Islam the final re-
ligion, it was in fact the first! He announced that Abraham had in fact
been a Muslim, and not a Jew (Q3:67). Jesus also was a Muslim, and his
disciples had confessed 'we are Muslims' (Q3:52; Q5:111). Muhammad
also began to use the expression 'the religion of Abraham' ... to refer
to Islam **in contrast to** Judaism and Christianity...[7]

One of the first tangible results of this new negative attitude towards the
Jewish people was the assassination of individual Jewish opponents[8], and
then later the annihilation of the Jewish communities in Arabia. In one
location Mohammad oversaw the execution of some 800-900 Jewish men,
while the surviving women and children were led into slavery.[9]

---

5 Sura 9:5, cited in Gabriel, M. *Islam and the Jews*, (Lake Mary, Florida, 2003), p. 103.

6 Gabriel, ibid, p. 48.

7 Durie, M .*The Third Choice*, p. 109. Bold emphasis in Durie's quotation. Duries's comments then lead into Sura 2:135.

8 Durie, ibid, p. 110.

9 Gabriel, ibid, pp. 108-117.

The last Jewish tribe in Arabia to be subjugated was at Khaybar in 628 AD. Until Khaybar, Mohammad and his followers had adopted a policy of 'convert to Islam or die.' However at Khaybar, Mark Durie writes: 'a third choice was negotiated: conditional surrender. Thus did the Khaybar Jews become the first *dhimmis*.'[10]

This third choice was later also offered to some Christianized groups. The Jews at Kaybar and these other groups were permitted to live, provided they accepted: a second-class status; being subject to certain laws aimed at maintaining their inferior position; and paying a special tax known as *jizya*.

A world authority on Islam, and especially of dhimmitude, Bat Yeor states of this new principle:

> According to Muslim juriconsults some centuries later, the agree-ment (*dhimma*) made between Mohammed and the Jews of Khaybar formed the basis of the *dhimmi* status. The Prophet allowed the Jews to farm their lands, but only as tenants; he demanded delivery of half their harvest and reserved the right to drive them out when he wished. On these conditions, he granted *dhimma,* that is to say, his protection for their lives and safety.[11]

Mark Gabriel wrote that later Mohammad supposedly received another rev-elation calling for the destruction of all other religions[12], declaring: "There will never be two religions in Arabia."[13] The Hejaz region of Arabia was then purged of all non-Muslims.

The subjugation of the peoples of the Arabian Peninsula was the first stage of what could only be called, Islamic imperialism.

Islam henceforth adopted the principle of bringing all peoples into sub-mission to Islam. Conquered peoples were thereafter given three choices:

---

10   Durie, ibid, p. 113.
11   Bat Yeor, *Islam and Dhimmitude*, (Cranberry, NJ, 2002), p. 37, citing Ibn Ishaq, *Life of Mohammed*, (Oxford, 1955), pp. 525-25.
12   Surah 8.39, cited in Gabriel, ibid, p. 104.
13   Ibn Husham, *The Biography of the Prophet*, (Cairo), Vol 2, p. 326, cited in Gabriel, ibid, p. 114.

accept and submit to Islam; accept the status of a *dhimmi* and pay the *jizya* (tax) or die by the sword.

Bringing all peoples into submission to Islam is called *Jihad* – Holy War. The Islamic world-view is that the world is divided into two spheres, *dar al Islam* (the territory of Islam) and *dar al Harb*, (the territory of the non-Muslim) and the intention is to bring *dar al Harb* into *dar al Islam* – by *Jihad*. Bat Yeor has written:

> The aim of jihad is to expand the rule of Islam over all non-Muslim lands throughout the world. Hence the concept of jihad divides the world into two forever hostile camps: the dar al-Islam, that is the regions under Islamic rule; and the dar al-Harb, the land of war, because being still under non-Muslim control, it is targeted by jihad till its incorporation into the dar al-Islam.[14]

Bat Yeor recalled the words of a fourteenth century Islamic scholar, Ibn Khaldun, who wrote on this Islamic world-view:

> In the Muslim community, the holy war is a religious duty because of the universalism of the [Muslim] mission and [the obligation to] convert everybody to Islam either by persuasion or by force… [Jews and Christians have to choose] between conversion to Islam, payment of the poll-tax, or death.[15]

Another Islamic scholar Bat Yeor quotes is Majid Khadduri, who stated that: "The jihad was regarded as Islam's instrument to transform the dar al-Harb into dar al-Islam."[16]   The universal aim therefore of Islam was to conquer the world (*dar al Harb*) and bring it into *dar al Islam*.

---

14   Ye'or, Bat. *Understanding Dhimmitude*, (Kindle Locations 377-380). RVP Publishers. Kindle Edition, Christians and Jews under Islam and the Actualization of History.

15   Ibn Khaldun, *The Muqaddimah. An Introduction to History*, Vol. I, Trans. Franz Rosenthal (New York: Pantheon Books, Bollingen Series XLIII, 1958), pp. 473 and 480, cited in Ye'or, Bat (2013-06-07). *Understanding Dhimmitude* (Kindle Locations 927-928). RVP Publishers. Kindle Edition, Christians and Jews under Islam: A Specific Condition.

16   Majid Khadduri, *War and Peace in the Law of Islam* (Baltimore: Johns Hopkins Press, 1955), p. 64, cited in Ye'or, Bat (2013-06-07). *Understanding Dhimmitude* (Kindle Location 929). RVP Publishers. Kindle Edition, ibid.

CONSOLIDATION IN ARABIA

Following the conquest of Arabia, Mohammad and his followers began to consolidate their new-found religion. A foundational aspect is the belief that Islam is superior over all other faith systems in the world, and that it has superseded both Judaism and Christianity; that Mohammad was the last prophet in a line from Abraham, Moses, David, Elisha and Jesus; that Abraham was a Muslim: 'Ibrahim was neither a Jew nor a Christian, but he was a true Muslim …' (Sura 3:67-68), and that the promised son was Ishmael (and not Isaac).[17]

Emanating, therefore, from the above was the foundational belief in the subjugation of all peoples, through *Jihad*; and the establishment of the *dhimmi* system upon non-Muslims.

THE CALIPHATE

Following Mohammad's death in 632 AD the movement was thereafter led by successors, known as Caliphs. The first Caliph was Abu Bakr, his father-in-law, followed by Omar Ibn el Khattab. Some, however, believed that the rightful successor was Ali, the cousin and son-in-law of Mohammad, and these Muslims did not acknowledge Abu Bakr as the rightful Caliph.

The followers of Ali then became known as the Shia, or Shi'ite Muslims, who recognize Ali as the first Caliph, the first successor of Mohammed.

The followers of Abu Bakr, the majority of the Muslims, became known as Sunni. Ali became the fourth Caliph of Islam, and his followers were found mainly in the regions of modern day Iran, Iraq and Lebanon. The city of Karbala became important for Shia Islam.

ISLAMIC IMPERIALISM LEAVES ARABIA

With the subjugation of Arabia, the followers of Mohammad thereafter set out to bring other regions outside of Arabia into *dar al Islam*.

It was Abu Bakr who led this second wave of Islamic imperialism, in what would become one of the most brutal and all-encompassing expressions of imperialism in world history. From 633 AD the totalitarian system

---

17   See Mark Gabriel, ibid, pp. 193-206 for an in-depth analysis of this subject.

of Islam began engulfing one nation and culture after another, and in the process not only brought these regions into submission to the religion of Islam, but also imposed the Arabic language and culture upon most of these newly conquered regions.

The era of Islamic imperialism had begun, and in a short time they defeated the Byzantine forces in Syria, Egypt, and Baghdad, and later the Persian forces as well. A very strategic victory was the Battle of Yarmuk in 636,[18] which effectively ended Byzantine control in Palestine.

Jerusalem finally fell in 638 AD. The Second Caliph, Omar Ibn el Khattab came there shortly afterwards. He then issued certain clear rules for the treatment of non-Muslims and the relationship between Muslims and non-Muslims, known as the Covenant of Umar.[19] Pagans were offered two choices: submit to Islam or die. People of the Book, which included Jews, Christians, Samaritans and Zoroastrians were offered the three choices as initially pronounced at Khaybar.[20]

During the period when the Caliphate was based in Mecca (a period known as the Rushidun Caliphate 632-661), Islam spread into North Africa, the Levant and north and east to the Black Sea and Caspian Sea and regions further east including modern day Iran.

THE CALIPHATE MOVES AWAY FROM MECCA

Although the spiritual centre of this Islamic movement came from Arabia, it was often politically led by various regional empires. The third successor of Mohammad, Othman Ibn Affan, established his base in Damascus, where the Umayyad (Omayyud) Caliphate was established in 661 AD. This Caliphate ultimately saw Islam spread further along the North African coast, into Andalusia (Spain and Portugal), and also further east encompassing the regions of the Caucasus, modern day Afghanistan and further

---

18 Not far from where a village named Semack would later be located.
19 Bat Yeor, *Islam and Dhimmitude*, ibid, p. 42. For a full explanation of the Decree of Omar, see Gabriel, ibid, pp. 122-124.
20 Gabriel, ibid, pp. 108-117.

north still. It was geographically the largest empire in history until that time.

It was during this period that Caliph Abd el Malik built two large mosques, the Dome of the Rock and Al-Aksa, in Jerusalem. These large edifices were built on the very place where both the First and Second Jewish Temples had once stood.

Mecca and Medina were known as the Holy Places of Islam. Jerusalem was added, not because Mohammad went there but because of its centrality to both the Jews and Christians. A story was then given that in a dream Mohammad ascended from earth to heaven on a white horse from the very spot where the Dome of the Rock would later be built.

From 750 AD the Caliphate moved to Baghdad where the Abbasid Empire was centred. At one time, though, a group of Shi'ite Muslims called the Fatamids, took control over Egypt and ruled a large area of North Africa from 973 till 1173 AD.

Throughout this entire period Islam continued its system of expansion through *Jihad*, and more of those who survived conversion or the sword became *dhimmi* subjects. Control over the land of Israel throughout these centuries was mostly from either Damascus or Baghdad, and at no time under Islam was there any independent political entity in the land.

Despite being now part of *dar al Islam*, many of those living in the land of Israel were Christians, while quite a few Jews had managed to survive expulsions by the Byzantines and Islamic devastation.

In addition many Christian and Jewish pilgrims continued to go from Europe to visit the 'Holy Land'. These pilgrimages were not only important from the religious perspective, but also important for trade between the east and west, much of which was carried on by Italian city-states.

It seemed to be a *status quo* which was working to the satisfaction of all entities.

§

CHAPTER 4

New empires in the land between

SELJUK TURKS AND CRUSADERS

In the eleventh century a new Islamic force invaded the land of Israel – the Seljuk Turks, who originated from north of the Caspian and Aral Seas. Not being that concerned with international diplomacy, this regime began interfering with the Christian pilgrims visiting Jerusalem. When news of this reached Western (Roman Catholic) Europe there was a backlash of indignation, which in turn stimulated the raising of a 'Christian' army that would fight to oust the infidel from the 'Holy Land' and restore it to Christianity. A clash between Islamic imperialism and western European or Roman Catholic imperialism loomed.

Many factors contributed to the building of an army to recapture the 'Holy Land', and not all of those motives were by any means noble. There was very little resemblance between the motives of these Crusaders to the message and actions of Jesus whom they were supposed to represent. Such was evidenced even before the Crusader armies even left Europe: they rampaged through countless towns and villages and cruelly massacred thousands of innocent Jewish people.

The ultimate goal of the Crusaders was the capture of Jerusalem, and this they achieved in 1099. These mercenaries from Western Europe, though, continued their murderous spree there, massacring Muslims, Christian

Arabs (because they looked different) and virtually the entire Jewish community in Jerusalem. The terrible onslaught of Islam in the previous centuries had now almost been matched, albeit on a local scale, by the so-called 'Christian' Crusaders. It was now evident for all to see that there was in fact little correlation between the way the Crusaders acted as a collective entity and the life and teachings of Jesus.

During the period the Crusaders were in control of the 'land between empires', they engaged in considerable trade – exchanging western commodities for eastern ones. Much of that trade consisted of valuable spices and items which came from further east, from India, the Spice Islands, China and elsewhere, commodities which were highly valued in southern and western European societies. Most of this trade was carried out by Italian city-states, such as Venice and Genoa, which became in effect the middlemen in this lucrative business.

SALADIN AND THE MAMELUKES FROM EGYPT

The Crusader Kingdom was continually under assault by the various Muslim armies. For these Muslim armies the cause for which they fought, although heavily linked to economics, was based upon their ideology. Islamic ideology basically held that the land of Israel was *wakf* or Islamic territory, part of *dar al Islam*, the region belonging to Islam, and as such had to be brought again under the authority of its god, Allah. The champion for Islam in its battle against the Crusaders was Salah al-Din (Saladin).

Saladin, although originally from the Kurdish region, gained control over Fatamid Egypt in 1171. He then became the champion of Islam against the Crusaders, winning a decisive victory against them at the Battle of Hittim (near the Sea of Galilee) in 1187. By the time of his death in 1193 in Damascus he had gained the upper hand over the Crusader Kingdom.

The final victory of Islam over the Crusaders occurred at Acre in 1291. Thereafter Palestine returned to being part of *dar al Islam*, and under the control of the Muslim Mamelukes based in Egypt.

One important result of the Crusader period was the entrance of Western or Roman Catholic Christianity into the 'Holy Land.' Thereafter the Greek

Orthodox Church was constantly challenged for being the major representative of Christians in the region.

CONTROL BY THE OTTOMAN TURKISH EMPIRE

The Mamelukes, representing the 'southern empire', controlled the land of Israel for a little over two centuries. Meanwhile another Turkish force was moving into the northern region from the east – the Osmanli Turks. The Osmanli, or Ottoman Turks, ultimately captured Constantinople, the symbol of Christian Rome, from the Byzantines in 1453.

Although in many ways the Ottoman Turks were lenient to the non-Muslim residents of their empire, they nevertheless retained the standard Islamic attitude towards the *dhimmi* population, and Christians and Jews continued in their status of subservience.

But the Sultan Bayezid II was also a benefactor for the Jewish people. In 1492 the Roman Catholic Church and Spanish monarchy exiled all the Jewish people from Spain who would not agree to be converted to Roman Catholicism. Sultan Bayezid permitted many of these Spanish (or Sephardi) Jews to settle in his domain, especially in Salonika, Smyrna and Constantinople.

After conquering the region of Anatolia, the Ottoman Turks continued their move southwards, and in 1517 captured both the land of Israel and Egypt from the 'southern (Mameluke) empire'. Once again the 'land between empires' was under the dominion of a 'northern empire'. More Jewish people then entered into the Sultan's dominions, primarily moving to Jerusalem and Safed in the Galilee.

One of the first projects that the Turks carried out was the rebuilding of the walls around Jerusalem, during the reign of Sultan Suleiman I, from 1538. Apart from this grand project, the Turkish administrators did little else for the land, and more times than not the administrators who were sent from Constantinople were more interested in gaining personal wealth in the far off regions, than in developing them. Jerusalem and the entire region suffered further neglect and desolation under the Islamic Ottoman Turkish regime.

The Ottoman Empire now encompassed a vast region, from the northern and western regions of the Black Sea, through to Arabia; from the Euphrates River through to Algeria in the west. The ruler of this vast area was the Sultan of Turkey, who also doubled up as the Caliph of Islam; and Constantinople was both the political capital and also the seat of the Caliphate.

TRADE WITH THE EAST

The Turkish Empire inherited the ancient trade routes from the east to the west, and now the lucrative trade of porcelain, silks and spices from China, India, the Spice Islands (now Indonesia) was in its hands. They thereafter began openly challenging the monopoly of this trade which was often held by the Italian city-states.

The Italian monopoly by this time was already drawing considerable conflict from the other Europeans who now had to purchase the produce at exorbitant rates. Due to this combined monopoly, new and more economic means to trade with the East were sought by the Europeans.

It was this dynamic which was soon to have two dramatic effects upon world history: the discovery of a direct sea link to the East, and the diminishing power of the Ottoman Turkish Empire, both of which would in time impact the destinies of Gallipoli and Jerusalem.

§

CHAPTER 5

The age of discovery

EUROPEAN EXPANSION

This period of Ottoman Turkish imperialism coincided with the beginnings of European oceanic expansion as the seafaring countries of Portugal, Spain, Holland, England (Britain), and later France, sent expeditions away from their territorial waters. Their goal was to discover the route to India and the Spice Islands. For Christopher Columbus the lure of the spices drew him westwards, where he discovered the Americas. The Portuguese, who were envisioned by Prince Henry the Navigator, went eastwards via Africa.

Ultimately in 1498 Vasco Da Gama not only rounded the southern tip of Africa, but also landed in India. This marked the beginning of a new period in world history – the West was directly linked to the East – and the middle region, the Turkish Empire, progressively dropped out of the equation.

This discovery diminished the importance of the Levantine and Eastern Mediterranean ports, and of the power of the Italian city-states. The French capitalized upon this new dynamic and entered into an agreement, a *Capitulation*[1], with the Turks in 1535. Besides gaining numerous political privileges, there were also economic and other benefits from this

---

1   A *Capitulation* was a chapter in the trade agreements previously made between the Turks and the Italian city states.

'Capitulation' agreement. France, the traditional protector of the Roman Catholic Church in Europe, now became the official protector of all Christians, especially Roman Catholics, within the Turkish Empire.

THE TRADE WARS BEGIN

Initially Portugal commanded the newfound sea routes and monopolised the trade from the east, however, by the close of the sixteenth century Holland began to challenge this monopoly. By 1602 the Dutch had set up their own Dutch East India Company, with emphasis being given to trade with the Spice Islands (later named the Dutch East Indies). While seeking further areas of trade, or while being blown off course on their journey, many Dutch ships sighted and floundered upon the coast of a large land mass to the south, which they duly named *Nieuw Holland*, while two large islands further south-east they named *Nieuw Zeeland*. The Dutch, however, eager for trade and not for colonisation, recorded the existence of these lands, but showed little active interest in them.

In 1579 England entered into a Capitulation trade agreement with Turkey and her merchants then set up the Levantine Company in 1581 in order to trade in the Levant. But England at that stage was not a major sea-faring nation. All that changed, however, when she defeated the Spanish and sank her Armada in 1588. Thereafter, England began to challenge the monopoly held by the Portuguese and Dutch for trade to the east, and in 1601 set up the English East India Company.

Consequently the trade wars intensified and the Dutch ousted the English from the Spice Islands (East Indies). The English then concentrated their efforts upon India, where they entered into conflict with the Portuguese. An armed conflict resulted in an English victory in 1614, whereupon the English then entered into a trading agreement with the local Mogul emperor. Thereafter the English East India Company began to expand its activities and set up trading stations at strategic points of the sub-continent.

ENGLAND, FRANCE AND THE SUEZ CONNECTION

With the demise of the Spanish as a sea power in the late seventeenth century, France became more actively involved in the far eastern trade. Until this point France had been more concerned with the Mediterranean trade network, but now she set her sights further East – and entered into conflict with England, Portugal and Holland. The French East India Company was formed in 1664.

The search for the quickest and most convenient route to the East now intensified as the competition between these nations stiffened. It was the French who first saw the suitability of establishing a link between the Mediterranean and the Red Sea, via a squalid little port named Suez.

As by this stage all the other major European powers had vacated the Mediterranean in preference for the sea route around Africa, the French envisaged opening trading warehouses at Suez and transporting produce over the Isthmus of Suez to the Mediterranean, either via the Nile or directly overland to Alexandria. Such a proposal was submitted to the Turkish authorities in 1665, but it was turned down.

The German philosopher Gottfried Leibnitz then advised Louis XIV of France in 1671 that to truly establish French authority in the Eastern Mediterranean, he should reconstruct the ancient canal which had connected the Mediterranean and the Red Sea. Leibnitz predicted that the true commercial route to India would be found in Egypt.[2] His proposal, although unsuccessful, nevertheless revealed how the region of Egypt (and the nearby land of Israel) could very easily become of great importance in this quest for the riches of the East. By geographical 'chance' the Eastern Mediterranean was sandwiched between Europe and the East.

In the late seventeenth century the Turkish Empire was still relatively strong and in control of its destiny, and was not overly concerned about allowing European powers to have too much of a role within its territory. If, however, the Turkish Empire ever began to weaken, then such involvement might indeed occur – for it was by now apparent, due to these aforemen-

---

2 Tuchman, B. *Bible and Sword*, (New York, 1956), p. 164.

tioned proposals, that the true link from Europe to Asia was indeed through Egypt.

BEGINNING OF THE DEMISE OF TURKEY

Turkey began to weaken following its failure to capture Vienna in 1683. Soon afterwards Russia inflicted defeat upon Turkey and at the subsequent Treaty of Carlowitz in 1698, Turkey was forced for the first time to relinquish territory. 'Since then', wrote Michael Sturmer, 'the major European powers were divided over who would inherit the Ottoman lands and the power that went with them… The quest for the control of the eastern Mediterranean was to be the *leitmotiv* of European power politics ever since.'[3]

Endeavouring to exert some control over the Turkish Empire, Russia attempted, albeit unsuccessfully, to insert religious factors into the settlement, especially the return of the Church of the Holy Sepulchre to Greek Orthodox authority.

This matter of the status of the Orthodox Church concerned Russia. In the tenth century AD Russia had accepted Byzantine (or Orthodox) Christianity as the state religion. Then since the fall of Constantinople to Turkey in 1453 many Russians viewed Russia as having adopted the mantle of the Byzantine Empire and the Orthodox Church. They even viewed Moscow as the new Constantinople, and their king adopted the title Czar (Tzar), which was the Byzantine title for emperor.

Many Russians, therefore, believed they had certain titular rights to Constantinople and parts of the former Byzantine Empire, including the land of Israel and particularly the 'Holy Places' there.

RUSSIA BEGINS TO EXPAND

Clashes between Turkey and Russia increased following 1683. Such clashes intensified during the reign of Catherine the Great in the seventeenth century when Russia began to slowly expand southwards. Catherine fomented re-

---

3   Sturmer, M. 'From Moltke to Gallipoli: Strategies and agonies in the Eastern Mediterranean' in *Germany and the Middle East: Past, Present and Future,* edited by Haim Goren, (Jerusalem, 2002), p. 4.

bellion in the Turkish areas of Crimea, Morea and Georgia, forcing Turkey to go to war in 1769. Russia won this war convincingly.

The resultant 'Treaty of *Kucuk Kaynarca*' (which in effect became a Capitulation) of 1774 forced considerable concessions upon Turkey. Amongst these concessions was the right for Russia to henceforth protect Orthodox Christians living in *certain parts* of the Turkish Empire. Russia unofficially, however, expanded this right to all regions of the Ottoman Turkish Empire, including the land of Israel – and to also protect Orthodox rights in the 'Holy Places.'

Russia then annexed the Crimea in 1783. This was just another stage in that long and fervent quest of gaining access from the Black Sea to the Mediterranean through the Bosphorus and Dardanelles Straits, into the wider world beyond. Such access was vital for Russia if she was ever to be a serious competitor with the other European empires on the international stage.

TURKISH EMPIRE IN EUROPE CIRCA 1600

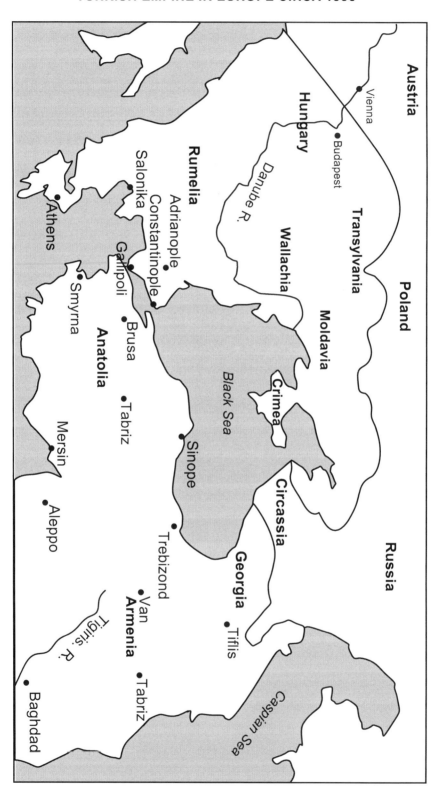

CHAPTER 6

§

Reformation and Restorationism

THE REFORMATION

S uch trading ventures and Russo-Turkish conflict weren't the only events taking place in Europe during this period. All over Europe and in Britain, men were challenging the authority and actions of the Roman Catholic Church. Collectively these men were known as Protestants.

By the 1600's entire regions and countries had broken away from the authority of the Roman Catholic Church. In addition, the Scriptures were printed in the vernacular language (instead of just in Latin), allowing more people to read the contents themselves.

Some of these Protestants now saw what they had not heard before: that Jesus was Jewish; that the covenants and promises were given to the Jewish people; and that God Almighty had not cast away national Israel as they had previously been taught.

When King Henry VIII officially broke away from Rome in 1535, the English Church entered into the Reformation (of which John Wyclife had been the herald), albeit in somewhat different circumstances to the Continental experience.

Henry's new Church of England, though, still needed much internal reformation. Those who felt it their duty to purify the English Church of all Roman and Papal vestiges were called the Puritans. Under Henry's son Edward (1547-1553) the Puritans furthered this internal reformation, but Queen Mary (1553-1558) reverted the English Church back to Roman Catholicism. These Protestant reformers, the purifiers, were then severely persecuted.

RESTORATION OF ISRAEL BEGINS

Many Puritans took refuge in Europe, including in Amsterdam and Geneva. Two of those in Geneva were Martin Bucer and Peter Martyr, teachers from Cambridge and Oxford. While in Geneva these British reformers compiled a new English Bible, named the Geneva Bible, in 1560. In the notes for Romans 11:26 they wrote: 'He sheweth that the time shall come that the whole nation of the Jews, though not every one particularly, shall be joined to the church of Christ.'[1] Here was a beginning of the restoration of the Jewish people to a place of significance in the Church – instead of their previous position as being the nation and people under God's curse, and without hope.

Under Queen Elizabeth I the Puritans continued the task of purifying the English Church, which was now a *via media*, mostly Protestant in theology but with Roman Catholic trappings, including episcopacy. Part of this process of reformation included the writing of theological materials.

One such work was a *Commentary upon Romans* by Peter Martyr, which was translated and printed in England in 1568. Martyr's commentary upon Romans 11 and especially verse 26, 'all Israel shall be saved', probably 'prepared the way' wrote Iain Murray 'for a general adoption amongst the English Puritans of a belief in the future conversion of the Jews.'[2]

The floodgates were opened. Numerous books, articles and pamphlets were written on the subject of the Jewish people, and their role in the revival which the Puritans then believed they were part of. Many also speculated on how the unfilled prophecies relating to the end of time and the Jewish restoration would occur. Mel Scult wrote concerning this new found interest:

---

1 Murray, I. *The Puritan Hope*, p. 41.
2 Murray, ibid, p. 42.

The English, more than any other people, became intoxicated with the new Hebraism of the Reformation … Their enthusiasm for the 'Holy Word' meant in part a heightened expectation of the destruction of Anti-Christ (i.e. the Pope) and the coming of Christ a second time. Expositions of the millennium took many forms and involved many people.

Some of these millennialists maintained that the conversion of the Jews was a pre-requisite for the second coming of Christ. The millennialists in question were quite unique in their confidence that the conversion was within the foreseeable future and that it was to include almost all the Jews.[3]

The second generation of Puritans after Bucer and Martyr took up the cause of Israel with a fervor not known until that point in the history of the Gentile Church. In 1585 Francis Kett, a Cambridge educated writer and physician, published a book entitled *The Glorious and Beautiful Garland of Man's Glorification Containing the Godly Misterie of Heavenly Jerusalem*, in which he had a section dealing with "the notion of Jewish national return to Palestine."[4]

Then in 1590, Andrew Willett stated in a treatise entitled *Calling of the Jews* that the term Israel in the Bible must be taken literally as referring to the people of Israel. Willett also stated that before the return of Jesus the Jewish people would be restored to their homeland.[5]

Willett took his lead from Romans 11:26 - 'all Israel shall be saved'. He did not agree that this was referring to a few individuals through history as some of the Reformers had believed, but 'the whole nation of the Jews.'[6] The whole nation of the Jews, he believed, must be 'taken in the litterall sense, for the nation and people of Israel.'[7] Willett further stated: 'Toward the ende

---

3   Scult, M. *Millenial Expectations and Jewish Liberties,* (Leiden 1978), p. 18

4   www.kettmiller.mysite.wanadoo

5   See M. Verete, *The Restoration of the Jews in English Protestant Thought 1790-1840.* Middle East Studies, Frank Cass Publishers, (London, January 1972), p. 15.

6   Quoted in Verete, ibid, p. 15.

7   Verete, ibid, p. 15.

of the world, before the coming of Christ, the nation of the Jews shall be called.'[8] But Willett would go no further when it came to the literal meaning of the prophecies relating to the return to the land of Israel.[9]

THEOLOGICAL FOUNDATIONS LAID

From the 1560's until the restoration of the Monarchy in 1660 (following the end of the Republican period of Oliver Cromwell) the concept of the restoration of the Jewish people, of their coming to accept Jesus as their Messiah and of their restoration to the land of Israel, permeated Christianity throughout Britain (and to a lesser extent also on the Continent).[10]

Although there were definite differences of understanding as to how all this would happen, especially on the matter of whether the Jewish people would come to acknowledge Jesus before or after they returned to the land of Israel, one matter was now firmly established in many British (and some European) churches: Israel and the Jewish people were no longer outcasts and peripheral, they were integral to the accomplishment of God's purposes on earth.[11]

Historian Iain Murray wrote concerning Puritan theology:

The future of the Jews had a decisive significance for them because they believed that, though little is clearly revealed of the future purposes of God in history, enough has been given us in Scripture to warrant the expectation that with the calling of the Jews there will come far-reaching blessing for the world. Puritan England and Covenanting Scotland knew much of spiritual blessing and it was the prayerful longing for wider blessing, not a mere interest in un-

---

8   Verete, ibid, p. 15.

9   Verete, ibid, p. 15.

10   For more details about the extent of interest in the Jewish people in Europe, especially Germany, see Clark, C. *The Politics of Conversion*, (Oxford, 1995); Crombie, K. *Three Sons of Abraham*, (Perth, 2013).

11   For a further in-depth analysis of this subject see Murray, I. *The Puritan Hope*, (Edinburgh, 1971); Verete, M. *The Restoration of the Jews in English Protestant Thought 1790-1840*. Middle East Studies, Frank Cass Publishers, (London, January 1972); Pragai, M. *Faith and Fulfilment: Christians and the Return to the Promised Land*, (London, 1985); Kobler, F. *The Vision Was There*, (London, 1956); Wilkinson, P. *For Zion's Sake*, (Paternoster, 2010); Tuchman, B. *Bible and Sword*, (New York, 1956); Crombie, K. *Three Sons of Abraham*, (Perth, 2013). Numerous primary sources can be viewed, primarily in the British Library in London.

fulfilled prophecy, which led them to give such place to Israel.[12]

Mel Scult provides a good analysis of the environment of that period, and the foundation it laid within the British Church for the period after 1660:

> By 1660 then we see that a new attitude toward the Jew had solidified in the minds of many English Protestants. Many of them no longer believed that the Jew was the devil or the anti-Christ, but was again God's Chosen people who are to play a key role in the drama of God's historical plan. They also believed that the positive prophecies of the Old Testament refer to Israel of the Flesh and not to the Christian Church ... and that Christians are very much in debt to the Jews who have been the keepers of the 'word' throughout History. Some maintained that those who persecute the Jews will eventually be held accountable for their actions.[13]

It was upon that theological foundation that much of Britain's future dealings with the Jewish people and the land of Israel must be seen. Although such attitudes themselves would be insufficient reason for the British Government to ever become the modern day Cyrus and facilitate the restoration of the Jewish people to their land, yet this attitude had so permeated much of British society by the mid-1800's that it, combined with geo-political factors of the time, would provide the right combination for just such a restoration to come about.

---

12 Murray, ibid, pp. 59-60.
13 Scult, ibid, p. 34.

CHAPTER 7

§

Britain, France and Eastern Empires

While the theological belief concerning Israel's restoration was taking hold in various parts of Europe and especially in Britain, the battle of the European powers for world-wide dominance was intensifying. The Russian and Turkish Empires were continuing to battle it out around the Black Sea region, while the emerging British and French Empires were now entering into a long period of serious confrontation.

Trade in the East, especially in India, was now gradually being caught up into this new political reality. From 1707 the once powerful Mogul Empire began a process of quick disintegration and several rival Indian dynasties as well as the English and French East Indies Companies vied to fill this vacuum. The French had steadily increased their activities in the first half of the eighteenth century, and at one stage stood to oust Britain from certain areas.

The first serious conflict between the two empires occurred between 1756-1763, in what is known as the Seven Years War, during which the French attempted to make strong military alliances with local Indian princes and thereupon to eradicate the British presence in India. At one point the French again raised the idea of cutting a canal from the Mediterranean through to the Red Sea and thereby establishing a quick route to India. The plan proceeded no further due to a British victory, and most of the former French holdings were taken over by the English East India Company.

This victory forced Britain to consolidate its holdings in India. The power of the East India Company thereafter became more far-reaching and India became essential for Britain's imperial designs. But the French never gave up the hope of conquering India. They merely embarked on other ventures, the most ambitious of which was probably the proposal to gain control over Egypt – the half way station between Europe and India.

In 1769 the Duc de Choiseul set the plan in motion, hoping to gain control over the Mameluke ruler (ostensibly under Turkish rule) named Ali Bey. Within just a few years though the venture faded out, as both De Choiseul and Ali Bey became politically obsolete. The French nevertheless did maintain a small trading station at Suez, which was then joined towards the end of the century by a British venture. France, though, never relinquished the idea of gaining a foothold in the region. In 1777 the French ambassador in Constantinople sent Francois Baron de Tott to Egypt and Syria 'in order to evaluate the possibilities of their occupation by France.'[1]

During the American Revolution, France endeavoured to oppose Britain not only in America, but also in India, where they encouraged uprisings by the local princes of Mysore, Hyderabad and Mahratta. Warren Hastings, the British Governor-General, ultimately prevailed against the opposing forces. Britain may have lost America, but she in turn gained India.

Even before the American Revolution and subsequent problems throughout the world, Britain was wary of the presence of rival European, especially French, activities in the Far East. With this in mind (as well as other factors) Captain James Cook set out in 1769 on a voyage of discovery and possession on behalf of the British Government. Part of this task was to determine if there was a large southern land mass, the legendary *Terra Australis*, and if in fact this was the same as *Nieuw Holland*. In the process of his voyage of

---

1   Goren, H. *Dead Sea Level: Science, Exploration and Imperial Interests in the Near East,* (London, 2011), p. 25.

discovery Cook rediscovered *Nieuw Zeeland*, and then sailed along the east coast of *Nieuw Holland*, claiming it for Britain in 1770.[2]

By the late 1770's Britain was recovering from the loss of the American Revolution as well as grappling with numerous domestic issues, including terrible social conditions brought on by the Industrial Revolution. The cities became crowded and living conditions worsened. Crime soared, although most misdemeanours could not be classified as crime as it was people merely attempting to survive within the decrepit social system then in existence in Britain; and the prisons became over-crowded.

Prime Minister William Pitt at this time was confronted by numerous problems, one of which was this deteriorating internal social situation. In 1779 Joseph Banks was asked to present himself to a Parliamentary Committee concerning a suitable location to send convicts. The Committee reported: 'That the Place which appeared to him best adapted for such a Purpose, was Botany Bay, on the coast of New Holland ...'[3] The final decision to send the convicts to New South Wales was announced by Lord Sydney on 18 August 1786.[4]

A second major concern for Pitt was the constant threat of France on the international scene. This concern was amplified by France's agreement with the Bey (or ruler) of Cairo in 1785. For the French this was 'a distant gambit to a possible invasion of India.'[5] A bigger problem for Britain then arose with the signing of an agreement between the French and the Dutch in the same year. Pitt was worried that through this agreement the Dutch might allow her East Indies ports to access by the French, as had actually happened at their colony in the Cape of Africa.

In view of the above stated factors, Captain Arthur Phillip departed Britain on 13 May 1787 commanding a fleet consisting of eleven ships carrying 1,030 people, including 736 convicts. These outcasts of British society would be the first of some 160,000 convicts who would be sent out in the

---

2 Lieut. Cook's Official Log, *H.R.N.S.W.*, Vol. I, Pt1, p. 157, cited in Clark, C.M.H. *Select Documents in Australian History 1788-1850*, (Sydney, 1950), pp. 25-6.

3 Banks on Botany Bay. 1779. (C.J., Vol. XXXVII, loc. cit), cited in Clark, ibid, p. 26.

4 Lord Sydney to the Lords Commissioners of the Treasury, 18 August 1786. *H.R.N.S.W.*, Vol. I, Pt 2, pp. 14-19, cited in Clark, ibid, p. 33.

5 Hughes, R. *The Fatal Shore*, (London, 1987), p. 59.

ensuing years, as well as being the foundation layers of two future nations – Australia and New Zealand.

Shortly after arrival at Botany Bay two French warships were spotted. This prompted Phillip to hasten to Port Jackson and to hoist the British flag thereby reinforcing British sovereignty over the eastern part of *Nieuw Holland* thereafter known as New South Wales.

Whatever geo-political interests France had at that stage in the region were soon to be swallowed up in the terrible events which engulfed France in July 1789 – the beginnings of the French Revolution. For the time being their attention was focussed elsewhere than Egypt, India and New South Wales.

Some years later though, in 1826, the Governor of New South Wales despatched Captain Edmund Lockyer to the southern coast of the western portion of the continent to establish a colony and claim it for Britain – in order to forestall France from taking the region. Captain Lockyer duly named this new settlement Frederick Town, later to be renamed Albany.

§

Napoleon's quest for
India – via Egypt

While the French were busy taking their message of Liberty, Fraternity and Equality throughout Europe following their Revolution of 1789, a young Baptist minister in Britain named James Bicheno penned these prophetic words:

"Now we are looking for the restoration of the scattered Jews … to pretend to determine, positively, how this ought to be brought about, would be arrogance; the probability being that the Turkish power being overturned in Palestine, by some invading enemy, that enemy will think it politic and necessary, for the promotion of its own schemes, to invite the Jews to take possession of their ancient patrimony, and to make one cause with themselves. For without the support of some powerful nation, how are the dispersed, disorganized Jews, to collect their numbers and unite their energies, so as to produce the effects predicted? We know God can work miracles; but we know also that he usually works by second causes.

I shall now only add that Egypt, it is probable, will be an easy conquest (Isaiah xi) and a thoroughfare for the returning sons of Abraham, to the country of their ancestors."[1]

At the time when Rev. Bicheno was writing the above, the French Government was actually planning to invade Bicheno's home country of Britain. An army was being assembled under the command of General Napoleon Bonaparte. The British were preparing for such an invasion, especially in the south of the country.

To hinder the French Mediterranean Fleet based at Toulon from slipping through the Straits of Gibraltar and joining with the French Atlantic Fleet based at Brest, the Admiralty despatched Admiral Horatio Nelson to the Mediterranean on 2 May 1798.

While the British Government was thus preparing as best it could for such an invasion, Bonaparte adapted his strategy. His new plan is revealed in the official British publication, *The Annual Register*, which wrote in its 1798 publication:

He [Napoleon] had often expressed in conversation even for several years before, that there could not be a nobler enterprize, or one more conducive to the interests of the human race, than to relieve India from the domination of the English, and to open the richest commerce to the whole world … he conceived the design of shutting it [India] out from England, by the possession of Egypt.[2]

Napoleon duly informed the French Government (the Directory) that in order to defeat Britain it would be necessary to firstly take Egypt.[3] By taking control of Egypt then the French could somehow get ships over the Isthmus of Suez and then sail to India – undetected by the British. In addition,

1   Bicheno, J. *A Glance at the History of Christianity and of English NonConformity*, (London, 1798), p. 28. Rev. Bicheno's son, James Ebenezer Bicheno, was colonial secretary in Tasmania, Australia, in the 1850's.

2   *The Annual Register*, (London, 1798), pp. 134-135. Copy in the National Archives, Kew, London.

3   *Correspondence de l'armee francaise en Egypte*, (Paris, Year VII) Vol. III, p. 235, cited in Herold, J. Christopher. *Bonaparte in Egypt*, (London, 1963), p. 14.

control over Egypt could preserve French trade in the Levant (the Eastern Mediterranean).[4]

DESTINATION EGYPT

Napoleon's fleet, comprising some one hundred and eighty vessels upon which were over 50,000 men left Toulon on 19 May 1798 – the largest force France had ever dispatched overseas. 'The path to Constantinople and India', wrote the British historian George Trevelyan, 'seemed open to the most ambitious spirit since Alexander the Great.'[5]

The departure of the French Fleet from Toulon alerted the British. Even before the French Fleet's true whereabouts became known, *The St. James Chronicle* (*or British Evening Post*) wrote:

> Curiosity and conjecture have been equally exercised with respect to the object of the expedition of Bounaparte [sic] up the Mediterranean, but nothing satisfactory or conclusive has yet been presented to the Publick [sic]. Even the overthrow of the Torkish [sic] Government, and the plunder of its capital, are considered as objects too trivial for an armament so formidable … and it has been assumed by many, that the conquest of India can alone bound the views, and satisfy the ambitions of the French Chief.[6]

When Admiral Nelson discovered the destination of the French he wrote to the First Lord of the Admiralty: 'I shall believe that they are going on their scheme of possession of Alexandria, and getting troops to India.' Nelson assured his superior that he would track down and destroy the French Fleet. He then set course for Egypt.[7]

En-route to Egypt the French Fleet captured the small yet strategic island of Malta on 11 June 1798. Then several days later they set sail for

---

4   Napoleon's secretary, Fauvelet de Bourrienne, later wrote that Napoleon also had a fantasy to emulate his great hero Alexander the Great who also invaded India. Herold, ibid, p. 3.

5   Trevelyan, G. *The History of England*, (London, 1948), p. 576.

6   *The St. James Chronicle* (*or British Evening Post*), from Thursday, July 12 to Saturday July 14, 1798. No 6349. No page number. Under heading: *The British Review*. Copy in British Library.

7   Nelson, Horatio, Viscount Nelson. *Dispatches and Letters*. Edited by Sir Nicholas Harris Nicolas, Vol. III, (London, 1895), p. 31, cited in Herold, ibid, p.50.

Egypt. Having been informed of Nelson's pursuit, Napoleon then altered his course, and the two fleets unknowingly passed each other. The British, though, did halt at and capture Malta.

HOPES OF A JEWISH RESTORATION RISE

Napoleon's venture to the East awakened the interest of many Jewish people. One Italian Jew wrote an anonymous letter which appeared in the leading French literary magazine *La decade philosophique, litteraire et politique*. This *Letter* then appeared in full in *The Courier* newspaper in London on 19 June 1798. It called for Israel's restoration as a nation among the nations of the world, a realization to be assisted by 'the invincible nation which now fills the world with her glory' – a reference of course to France. Speaking to his Jewish brethren, the writer stated:

> O my Brethren, what sacrifices ought we not make to attain this object? We shall return to our country, we shall live under our own laws – we shall behold those places where our ancestors demonstrated their courage and their virtues. Already I see you all animated with a holy zeal. Israelites! The end of our misfortunes is at hand. The opportunity is favourable – take care that you do not allow it to escape.[8]

The sentiment that France was going to be the nation which would restore scattered Israel to its homeland, was accepted by many in Britain. Although published in 1799 Henry Kett's book *History the Interpreter of Prophecy* stated what many Britons were already sensing in mid-1798:

> It certainly is not *impossible* that the French may offer them [the Jewish people] their ancient land … in order to render them subservient to their vast designs of universal conquest … I do not think this likely to happen. It seems to me *more* probable, that the French should choose to retain possession of a country so well adapted to their acknowl-

---

8   *The Courier*, 19 June 1798. British Library (Newspaper House). See also Kobler, F. *The Vision Was There: A History of the British Movement for the Restoration of the Jews to Palestine*, (London, 1956), p. 44.

edged views; and that thus this people may be the means of recovering the land from its present desolation …[9]

These and other writings in the period were indicative of a quite widely held viewpoint especially in Britain that scattered Israel would be restored to their ancient homeland through the assistance of a sympathetic European power. W. Whiston had expressed as far back as 1753 that an empire, even Britain, would be the restorer of Israel.[10] Even the highly influential *The Gentleman's Magazine* wrote in September 1799: '… it is surely no rash conjecture to suppose that they [the Jews] may be restored to their own land under the power and protection of a mighty empire.'[11]

THE FRENCH LAND IN EGYPT

The French Fleet arrived off the coast of Egypt on 1 July 1798 and the following day Napoleon attacked and captured Alexandria. The Mameluke ruler of Cairo, Murad Bey, then quickly gathered together a force to battle against Napoleon, whose troops then moved southwards towards Cairo. There, with the Pyramids as a backdrop, the French defeated a large Mameluke army on 21 July.

The Battle of the Pyramids was a turning point in the affairs of Egypt and the region. A European army had entered into the heartland of Islam (*dar al Islam*) and defeated an Islamic army. The Levant was now back on the geo-political 'radar screen'.

News of the French victories alarmed the British in India. The Governor of Bombay sent a letter to Earl Macartney, the British governor at the Cape Colony (Cape Town), appealing for help. Referring to the French as an enemy 'so notoriously and malignantly jealous of our Eastern Empire', he stated:

The object of this expedition appears … to be decidedly directed in its ultimate end against the British possessions in India & probably by

---

9   Kett, H. *History the Interpreter of Prophecy*, (London, 1799), p. 227. Copy in the British Library.

10   Whiston, W. *The Fall and Final Restoration*, (London, 1753), pp. 14-15, cited in Verete, M. *The Restoration of the Jews in English Protestant Thought 1790-1840*, Middle East Studies, (London, January 1972), p. 50.

11   *The Gentleman's Magazine*, September 1799, p. 738.

way of the Red Sea … The different ports in the Red Sea, will afford
more ample tonnage for the accommodation of this Army … it seems
very probable, that part of this Force would be left to annoy us this
side of India …[12]

NELSON DESTROYS THE FRENCH FLEET

It was the task of Admiral Nelson to seek and destroy the French Fleet before they could accomplish their goal of reaching India. The first part of the
French plan had already been achieved: they had landed their 'Army of the
Orient' in Egypt and had now, effectively, captured this strategic land-base
for their ultimate objective.

Napoleon had planned to get his ships from the Mediterranean Sea to
the Red Sea, either through locating ancient canals, or by building a link between the two. He had brought with him many engineers for this very task.
But before he could accomplish anything tangible in this project of connecting the two seas, Nelson discovered the French Fleet nestling securely in
Aboukir Bay to the east of Alexandria. On 1 August 1798 while Napoleon
and his men were celebrating their victory in Cairo, Nelson destroyed most
of the French Fleet.

In this 'Battle of the Nile', only four French ships managed to elude the
British net and escape. This was another crucial event as it was the first battle between European empires over the destiny of the Levant - the Eastern
Mediterranean. Although in the past European empires such as Greece and
Rome (and perhaps one could say, the Crusaders) had vied for control over
this region, this was the first time in the modern period that the Europeans
had contended over the strategic 'region between empires.'

TURKISH-BRITISH-RUSSIAN ALLIANCE

The French incursion into the region also resulted in the forging of a closer
political relationship between Turkey and Britain.

The Turks knew of the intended destination of the French Fleet as early
as May 1798. When the French explained to the Turks that their intention

---

12   Government of Bombay to Earl Macartney, 28 September 1798. WO 1/893, National Archives, Kew.

was merely to settle scores with the Mamelukes, the Turks (who were also upset with the semi-autonomy of the Mamelukes) were almost convinced by the French explanation. The Turks, however, could not understand why the French had not sent a fully-fledged ambassador to the Porte to explain their intentions? Diplomatic relations thereafter further deteriorated between France and Turkey.

France's true intentions for their eastern expedition are clearly revealed in a secret communique from Charles Talleyrand, representing the Directory, to Ruffin, the French *charge d'affaires* in Constantinople on 4 August 1798:

> All trade in the Mediterranean must … pass into French hands … and … Egypt, a country France always has desired, belongs of necessity to the Republic … The Directory is determined to maintain itself in Egypt by all possible means.[13]

Throughout this period the British and Russian ambassadors at Constantinople had been pressuring the Turkish Government to declare war against France. Yet the Turks only took drastic action when news reached them of the French defeat at Aboukir Bay.

Shortly afterwards the Russian Fleet left the Black Sea, passed through the Bosphorus (to cheers from the Turkish populace), through the Dardanelles and into the Mediterranean. In December 1798 Britain, Russia and Turkey signed treaties of alliance, each pledging not to make separate peace treaties with the French.

THE FRENCH STRANDED IN EGYPT

France's credibility rapidly decreased following the destruction of its Fleet and the Turkish declaration of war. Endeavouring then to garner support throughout the region Napoleon sent letters to various leaders, as far afield

---

13   La Jonquiere, C de. *L'Expedition en Egypt, 1798-1801*, (Paris, 1899-1907), Vol. II, pp. 607-08, cited in Herold, ibid, pp. 132-3.

as Acre, Damascus and Tripoli in Syria. The response in most cases was one of silence or opposition. France was becoming internationally ostracized.

Meanwhile in Egypt Napoleon set about the construction of a canal connecting the Mediterranean with the Red Sea via the Isthmus of Suez. From Suez he wrote on 29 December 1798 of his intentions to complete a survey of the Suez Canal.[14] There was of course no Suez Canal, but in antiquity there had been numerous canals which connected the Isthmus of Suez to the Nile River and thence to the Mediterranean Sea. When Napoleon departed from Suez in January 1799 he left behind a small group of engineers and surveyors. Due, however, to a miscalculation these surveyors wrongly deduced that the level of the Red Sea was higher than that of the Mediterranean and no actual digging of a canal began.

Napoleon's strategy to oust the British from India included establishing bases along the Red Sea, and establishing contact with opponents of British rule in India. He wrote to Sultan Fateh Ali Tipu of Mysore (the 'Tiger of Mysore') an Indian prince who opposed Britain, on 25 January 1799: 'You have already learned of my arrival on the shores of the Red Sea with an innumerable and invincible army, anxious to free you from the yoke of England ... I take the first opportunity of letting you know that I am anxious that you should send me information through Moca and Muscat as to your political situation. I hope you can send to Suez or Cairo, some able and trustworthy person with whom I can discuss matters.'[15]

The French invasion of Egypt had invigorated Sultan Tipu, who was supportive of the French. But this endeavour came to nought as he died shortly afterwards, killed in battle against the British. Napoleon's strategy for ejecting the British from India now became more improbable.

NAPOLEON INVADES 'THE LAND BETWEEN'

The Anglo-Russian-Turkish Alliance boded ill for Napoleon. The French consuls throughout the Turkish Empire were arrested, and Djezzar Pasha,

---

14   Johnston, R.M. *The Corsican: A Diary of Napoleon's Life In His Own Words*, (London, 1910), p. 89.

15   Napoleon I. *Correspondence de Napoleon I publiee par ordre de 'lEmperor Napoleon III*, (Paris, 1858-70), Vol. V, p. 278, cited in Johnston, ibid, p. 90.

the Turkish ruler of Acre, was commissioned to form an army to oust
Napoleon from Egypt.

When made aware of the intentions of Djezzar Pasha, Napoleon decided to invade 'the land between' and defeat the Turkish forces there. He
wrote to the Directory in Paris on 10 January 1799, boasting that by the time
they read his communique, he might be in Jerusalem standing upon the
ruins of Solomon's Temple.[16]

Napoleon explained his strategic reasons for the campaign to the
Directory as being: to consolidate the French presence in Egypt by conquering the Sinai Peninsula and forming a buffer zone between himself and the
Turkish forces; to force the Turks to explain their intransigence towards
him; and to deprive the British Fleet of using the province of Syria as a base
for operations and resupply.[17]

Napoleon's ultimate objective in his conquest of the province of Syria
was the capture of Acre, the most strategic port on the Levantine coast. His
intention thereafter was to capture Damascus and Aleppo, and then with
the assistance of sympathetic local rulers, to march upon Constantinople.
Having thus taken control over the Turkish Empire, he would follow the
footsteps of Alexander the Great and march on to India.[18]

Although unprepared for a long campaign, Napoleon's 13,000 man
army left Cairo on 10 February 1799. His first objective was to fortify Katia,
an oasis on the northern coastal route (the ancient *Via Maris*). From there
he would continue across the Sinai Peninsula and rout the remnants of the
Mameluke army which had fled to El Arish.

General Kleber captured El Arish on 19 February 1799, and then five
days later captured Gaza, the ancient gateway into 'the land between empires.' Following a sustained bombardment Jaffa was captured on 7 March,
to be followed by pillage, massacre and rape. The capture of Jaffa is best
known for a terrible massacre of between 2,500 - 3,000 Turkish prisoners by
orders of Napoleon himself.[19]

---

16   Johnston, ibid, p. 92.
17   Kobler, F. *Napoleon and the Jews*, (Jerusalem, 1975), p. 41.
18   Herold, ibid, p. 265.
19   Herold, ibid, pp. 276-78, citing several eye-witness accounts of this gruesome and hideous massacre.

HALTED AT ACRE

Napoleon's forces then captured Haifa on 17 March. The main strategic location though was Acre. This strategic port city was defended on land by Djezzar Pasha, known also as the 'Butcher', and at sea by Admiral Sir Sidney Smith of the British Navy.

Napoleon did not want to wait until his siege guns arrived, and attacked on 28 March. On that same day Admiral Smith landed 800 British marines to assist in the defence of Acre, and these British soldiers greatly assisted in stopping the French troops from entering the port city.

Unfortunately two days later Djezzar 'the Butcher' massacred some two hundred innocent Christian citizens of the town, obviously fearing they would collude with the French. Following another unsuccessful attack on 1 April, Napoleon chose to halt the offensive and await the arrival of his siege guns.

DECLARATION TO THE JEWISH PEOPLE

Djezzar Pasha requested help from as far afield as Damascus and Aleppo, and Napoleon needed to rout these forces before they arrived at Acre. This Turkish-led army comprising some 35,000 men crossed the Jordan River at the Bridge of the Daughters of Jacob in mid-April, and made their way down to the Esdraelon Valley where they assembled near Mount Tabor – within view of Nazareth and Har Megiddo (Armaggedon).

On 16 April General Kleber met this numerically superior force with about 2,000 of his own forces at the base of Mount Tabor. In the late afternoon Napoleon entered the fray and his timely intervention turned the tide in favour of the French, who were ultimately victorious over this large Turkish Army.

Basking in this spectacular victory Napoleon felt the time was right to reach out to the minority groups in the region who disdained Turkish rule, and who could become French allies. He then issued another of his proclamations, this time to the Jewish people.

The Paris newspaper *Moniteur Universal* wrote on 22 May 1799 that, 'Napoleon has published a proclamation in which he invites all the Jews of

Asia and Africa to gather under his flag in order to re-establish the ancient Jerusalem. He has already given arms to a great number, and these battalions threaten Aleppo.'[20] The declaration supposedly stated:

> Israelites arise!
>
> Ye exiled, arise! Hasten! Now is the moment which may not return for thousands of years, to claim the restoration of the civic rights among the population of the universe which have shamefully been withheld from you for thousands of years, to claim your political existence as a nation among nations, and the unlimited natural right to worship Jehovah according to your faith, publicly and most probably forever …[21]

Napoleon addressed his proclamation to the Jewish people as, wrote Barbara Tuchman, 'the rightful heirs of Palestine.' He also promised them the support of the French nation, which would help the Jewish people to not only regain their inheritance, but to 'remain master of it and maintain it against all comers.'[22]

DEFEAT OF THE FRENCH

All of Napoleon's victories and his proclamation to the Jewish people were worthless if he could not subdue Acre. He renewed his assault on 24 April 1799, which continued for several weeks. Their efforts, though, were constantly foiled by the combined Turkish-British force of Djezzar and Smith.

Napoleon made one last attempt on 10 May – and failed. Conceding defeat he then embarked upon an excruciating retreat back to Egypt across the harsh northern Sinai.[23] The dejected and exhausted French soldiers, and

---

20 *Moniteur Universal*, (Paris), 22 May 1799, cited in Schwarzfuchs, S. *Napoleon the Jews and the Sanhedrin*, (London, 1979), p. 24. The statement concerning battalions at Aleppo was, of course, a great exaggeration.

21 Sacher, H. *A History of Israel*, (New York, 1976), p. 22. Barbara Tuchman wrote: 'The original of this Proclamation has never been found. Its wording remained unknown until a manuscript copy in German translation came to light in 1940 in the archives of a Viennese family with rabbinical connections tracing back to Napoleon's entourage in the East. Until then only the fact of the Proclamation was known through two dispatches concerning it that appeared in May 1799 in *Le Moniteur*, the official organ of the French Directory.' Tuchman, B. *Bible and Sword*, (New York, 1956), p. 163. Simon Schwarzfuchs doubts the authenticity of this discovery. Schwarzfuchs, ibid, p. 24.

22 Tuchman, ibid, p. 163.

23 Richardot, Charles. *Nouveaux Memoires sur l'armee francaise en Egypte et en Syrie*, (Paris, 1848), p. 178, cited in Herold, ibid, p. 309.

accompanying Christians who were fleeing in dread of Djezzar's retribu-
tions against them, marched continuously until they reached Katia.

Once in Egypt Napoleon prepared for the pursuing Turkish army. In
mid-June 1799 the Turkish Fleet arrived off Aboukir Bay and Napoleon
made a successful surprise attack against it. One of the survivors from
the destroyed Turkish Fleet was a young Albanian officer named Mehmet
(Muhammad) Ali, who managed to swim to one of Admiral Smith's ships.[24]

Napoleon returned to Europe in August 1799. Before departing he
commissioned General Kleber to make peace with Turkey, but not to aban-
don the country. 'The Turkish Empire,' Napoleon wrote, 'is crumbling, and
the evacuation of Egypt would be all the more disastrous for France since
we would see that fertile country fall into the hands of some other European
power in our lifetime.'[25]

General Kleber then defeated a large Turkish Army which had
come from the north, at Heliopolis, on 20 March 1800. The French now
held the ascendancy in Egypt. Napoleon, meanwhile, had become First
Consul in France and again became involved in the affairs of the Eastern
Mediterranean.

Russia by this stage had withdrawn from its alliance with Britain and
Turkey, and Czar Paul and the French became aligned. Together they agreed
to contest British possessions in Asia, with the Russians prepared to march
against British India. Napoleon wrote to Czar Paul on 27 February 1801:

> The pride and arrogance of the English are unparalleled … The English
> have attempted to land in Egypt. The interest of all Mediterranean
> and Black Sea Powers is that Egypt should remain the possession of
> France. The Suez Canal, which would join the Indian Ocean to the
> Mediterranean is already surveyed; the work is easy and will not take
> long, it will confer incalculable benefits on Russian commerce.[26]

---

24   Also in June 1799 a small British military mission led by General George Koehler (1758-1800) arrived in Turkey
     'to give the Sultan technical assistance in driving Bonaparte out of Egypt. Koelher', wrote Haim Goren, 'had been
     allowed to consult the Ottomans on the Dardanelles but was not permitted to join the campaign in Syria.' Goren,
     ibid, p. 29.
25   *Correspondence*, ibid, Vol. V, p. 577, cited in Herold, ibid, p. 343.
26   *Correspondence*, ibid, Vol. VII, p. 40, cited in Johnston, ibid, p. 150.

Czar Paul accordingly set out to invade India with some 23,000 soldiers – but they never reached their destination as Czar Paul died in 1801. The Russian Army did, though, enter the Caucasus region and take possession of Georgia.[27]

While France and Russia were thus entering into an alliance, the British despatched an expeditionary force commanded by General Ralph Abercromby. This force landed at Aboukir Bay in March 1801 and defeated the French force arraigned against it.

The French hastened back to Cairo and Alexandria where the pursuing British besieged them. Finally, in September 1801, peace treaties were made and all the besieged French forces surrendered and were transported back to France. A formal peace treaty was completed in London on 1 October 1801.[28]

LONG-TERM CONSEQUENCES OF THE FRENCH EXCURSION

Napoleon's campaign to the Eastern Mediterranean marked the beginning of a new period of history in that region. It revealed to the Islamic world how easily a western 'infidel' power could penetrate into the heart of *dar al Islam*. It also revealed to Britain just how easily a rival power could sever her link to India and her Eastern Empire, which by 1801 included additionally the colony of New South Wales (later Australia) and New Zealand, and later again Malaya (including Singapore), Hong Kong and more.

Henceforth Britain would monitor every movement in the Eastern Mediterranean which could challenge its national interests in the Far East. Interestingly this geo-political move of 1798-1801 also included the Jewish people. Though their population in 'the land between empires' was not excessive, the very fact that Napoleon saw the connection between his own plans and the Jewish connection to the land of Israel, was signfcant for future events in the region.

---

27 Goren, ibid, p. 12.
28 Goren, ibid, p. 94. British troops remained in Egypt until March 1803.

NAPOLEON'S CAMPAIGN 1798 - 99

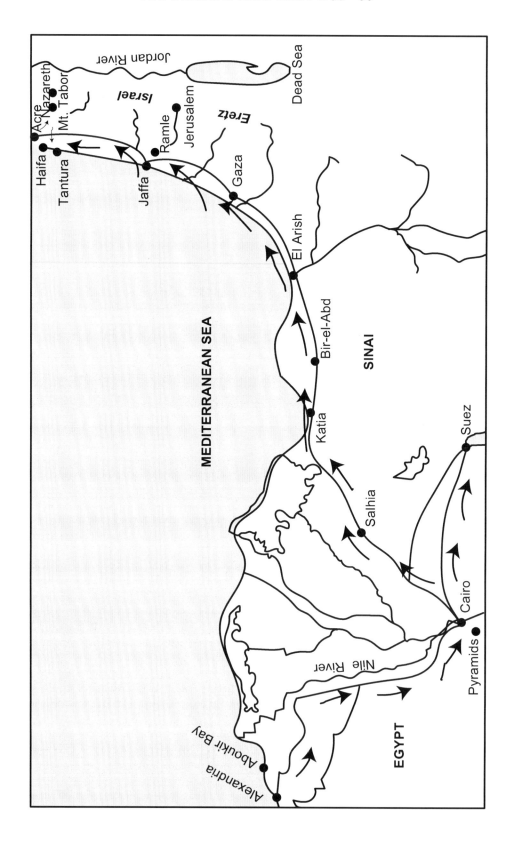

§

CHAPTER 9

Egypt and Evangelical hopes

BRITISH EVANGELICAL CHRISTIANITY

Ever since the outbreak of the French Revolution in 1789 many British evangelical Christians were excited by what they felt were 'the signs of the latter days.' Many books and pamphlets were published on the connection between the restoration of the Jewish people to the land of Israel (Palestine) within this bigger picture.

Most of the major British evangelical missionary societies were established in this the period of what Dr. Stephen Orchard called, heightened 'millennial expectancy.'[1] The Baptist Missionary Society was birthed in 1792; the London Missionary Society, in 1795; the Church Missionary Society, in 1799; and the Bible Society, in 1804.

British evangelical society was concerned with the welfare of the Jewish people, and of their national role in future events. The Non-Conformist London Missionary Society led the way, providing a platform for a Jewish disciple of Jesus named Joseph Frey (Levi) in 1801. Frey with the help and support of others then formed the Non-denominational London Jews Society (LJS) in 1809.[2] The goals of the London Jews Society very quickly grabbed

---

1   Orchard, S. *English Evangelical Eschatology, 1790-1850*, unpublished thesis (Cambridge, 1992), chapter 2.

2   The full name being: 'The London Society for promoting Christianity among the Jews'. This name has undergone several adaptions and changes during the following 200 years, and is currently named the 'Church's Ministry among

the attention of all levels of British society with William Wilberforce becoming a vice-President in 1810, and the Duke of Kent (Queen Victoria's father) being Patron for several years.

The message of the future role of the nation of Israel was now being spread throughout Britain by the emissaries of this Society, and later by other societies as well.[3] With the completion of the Napoleonic Wars in 1815 the LJS took its message overseas, to Europe and to the Middle East.[4]

The LJS spokesperson, Rev Lewis Way, was invited by the Czar to speak concerning the emancipation of the Jewish people before the European heads of state at the Peace Conference in Aix-le-Chapelle (Aachen) in October 1818. A clause relating to the Jewish people was included in the protocol of the Conference. Although little ultimately resulted from his speech, it revealed a subtle change in the atmosphere in Europe; and the depth of interest within British society towards the Jewish people. The Jewish people during this period were tasting for the very first time a degree of freedom - thanks in many ways to Napolean Bonaparte!

BEGINNINGS OF EUROPEAN INVOLVEMENT IN THE LEVANT

As early as 1823 the LJS had decided to establish a permanent base in Jerusalem. Yet Jerusalem was not receptive at that stage to the permanent presence of any non-Muslims who did not belong to one of the recognized *dhimmi* groups.

Each *dhimmi* group within the Ottoman Empire was called a *millet,* and Turkish *dhimmis* themselves were known as *rayahs.* Each *millet* community was entrusted with a degree of self-government. At that point Protestant Christianity was not officially recognized as a *millet* within the Ottoman Empire.

Jewish People', or CMJ.

3   From the 1840's other similar societies were formed, and men such as Presbyterian Rev Robert Murray McCheyne; Baptist Rev Charles Spurgeon; and Anglican bishop, J.C. Ryle took up Israel's cause.

4   The main emissary was Rev. Lewis Way, who undertook an adventurous tour into Eastern Europe in 1817, meeting with the Czar of Russia in the process.

There was a certain pecking order in the *millet* system, with the Greek Orthodox at the top, and the Jewish community at the bottom of the social ladder. The plight of the Jewish people is highlighted by one of the first LJS workers in Jerusalem, the Irishman Rev. William Lewis, who wrote in 1823:

> Here the Jews find no ease, though they love the land, for it is the land of their forefathers, and the land of promise … With respect to the foreign Jews, those who are not subjects of the Ottoman Empire, the difficulties … might certainly be a great deal diminished … by the residence of a Consular Agent or protector among the oppressed.'[5]

Lewis was the first to propose that Britain establish a consulate in Jerusalem, to provide diplomatic protection to the non-Muslims who had no protection under Islamic rule, particularly the Jewish people.[6] The Muslims were already in a superior position, although the Turks liked to keep the local Arab Muslims under some control, while the Roman Catholic and Greek Orthodox Churches had a degree of protection from the French and Russians.

While the Islamic Turkish regime held control over Jerusalem and the 'Holy Land' there would be no possibility at all of either the establishment of a British consulate which could look out for the interest of the Jewish people, nor of any lenient treatment for the non-Muslim communities.

Other Protestant missionary societies were also trying to establish their presence in the Levant at this time, many of them initially utilising Malta as their base. As early as 1819 the American Board of Commissioners for Foreign Missions had sent workers to the Levant.[7] They, like the British, were also not able to establish a permanent presence in the region.

---

5 *Jewish Expositor*, (London, 1825), pp. 16-17.
6 Other LJS workers, Dr. George Dalton and the Dane, Rev. John Nicolayson, stated the same. See *Jewish Intelligence*, (London, 1826), p. 76.
7 Established in Boston in 1816 primarily by Congregationalists. For further details about early American involvement in the region, see Michael Oren, *Power, Faith and Fantasy*, (New York, 2007).

RISE OF MEHMET ALI IN EGYPT

By 1805 Mehmet (Muhammad) Ali, who survived the battle of Aboukir Bay, had risen to become the leader of Egypt. Despite having been saved by the British, Mehmet Ali favoured the French, and understood that France's success in Egypt in 1798 had occurred due to Egypt's lack of modernisation, especially in the army. He thereupon set out to rectify this. On most occasions he turned to the French for assistance, which now became Egypt's European-backer.

The British were aware of this relationship, so when hostilities between the French and the British were renewed in 1807, and when the French and the Ottomans entered into an agreement, Britain feared there would be renewed French influence in Egypt - across their route to India. She then sent ships towards the Dardanelles and a force to Alexandria in 1807. These troops, however, were stopped from proceeding southwards by Mehmet Ali's forces.

At this point Napoleon and Czar Alexander signed the Treaty of Tilsit (July 1807), a treaty which thereafter threatened two empires – Britain and Turkey. Sturmer wrote, that 'both rulers pursued the dream of unhinging the British Empire and taking its most precious possessions in the East.'[8] One tangible result of this treaty was that Turkey was now further exposed to possible Russian penetration, and so turned to Britain.[9] The British departed Alexandria in 1809.

EGYPTIAN CAMPAIGNS IN ARABIA AND GREECE

The Sultan of Turkey (Egypt's titular ruler) recognized Mehmet Ali's abilities and military prowess and so commissioned him in 1811 to eradicate a harmful influence which had originated in central Arabia. This was *Wahhabism*, which had been initiated by Muhammad Ibn Abdul Wahhab and called for a purification of Islam. The powerful Saud tribe in central Arabia had ad-

---

8   Sturmer, ibid, p. 4.
9   Goren, H. *Dead Sea Level: Science, Exploration and Imperial Interests in the Near East*, (London, 2011), p. 95.

opted this teaching and had subsequently conquered parts of the Sultan's regions, especially the Hejaz which included Mecca and Medina.[10]

Mehmet Ali's forces complied and fought against *Wahhabism* and the House of Saud until 1818, when Mehmet's son Ibrahim (1789-1848) finally quelled the revolt. The success of this, and several other minor campaigns, gave many Arabs in the region the hope that Mehmet Ali could be a possible replacement for the somewhat despised Turkish regime.

Then in 1821 the Greeks rose in revolt against their Turkish overlords, and quickly began to overwhelm the Turkish forces. In desperation the Sultan again turned to Mehmet Ali for assistance. Mehmet Ali complied, and again sent Ibrahim to fight alongside the Turks against the Greeks. By 1825 Ibrahim's forces had gained control of much of Greece. As a reward for his assistance Mehmet Ali received assurances from the Sultan that he would receive certain lands to govern in recompense – including, so the Egyptian pasha believed, the region of Syria.

Russia was keenly observing events in the Eastern Mediterranean. Russia was the traditional protector nation of the Orthodox Christians in the East – which provided her with political leaverage, and she was not keen to see a new Orthodox Christian nation emerge - unless she was in control of it. Thus Russia had no choice but to enter into conflict against the Turks and Egyptians alongside the rebelling Greeks.

This situation now caused considerable geo-political angst for both France and Britain. Despite being apprehensive about fighting against Turkey, both also realised that if Greece triumphed, with Russian assistance, then Russia was likely to gain an ascendant position in the Eastern Mediterranean, and could gain control of the strategic Dardanelles Straits. Britain and France thereafter sided with Russia in the fight for Greek independence.

A Conference was convened in London and the three great powers agreed on 6 July 1827 to a request that Turkey offer complete autonomy to Greece under Turkey's overall suzerainty. The Turks refused to accept this

---

10   Antonius, G. *The Arab Awakening*, (Beirut, 1938), p. 22. The House of Saud was based at Nejd in central Arabia.

demand, and shortly afterwards a new Egyptian Fleet arrived at the Bay of Navarino on the Peloponnese Peninsula (of Greece).

An Allied fleet comprised of British, French and Russian ships and commanded by the British Admiral Codrington then attacked and totally destroyed the Turkish-Egyptian Fleets on 20 October 1827 in the Battle of Navarino. Thereafter the British Navy laid siege to Alexandria, forcing Mehmet Ali to withdraw his armies from Greece, which in turn seriously imperilled the Turkish cause there.

Although the conflict in Greece continued for several more years, the Battle of Navarino and withdrawal of the Egyptian Army basically sealed the issue, and Greece finally received full independence in 1832. This conflict marked the first tangible expression of a national group casting off the yoke of the imperial Ottoman overlord.

EGYPT NEARLY TOPPLES CONSTANTINOPLE

When Mehmet Ali tried to claim the areas 'promised' by the Sultan, his appeal was rejected on the grounds that the war against Greece had not been successful. As a consequence the Egyptian Pasha decided to take by force of arms that which he believed was rightfully his.

Utilising a supposed argument with the Pasha of Acre as a pretext, Mehmet Ali sent his French trained army into 'the land between empires' on 1 November 1831, under the command of his son Ibrahim. Like many previous Egyptian rulers, Mehmet Ali coveted the 'land between empires' as a buffer between himself and Turkey to the north.

Shortly afterwards Britain's Consul-General Campbell in Alexandria wrote to the Foreign Office:

> His immediate object is to establish his authority firmly in the Pashaliks of Acre and Damascus; after which to extend his dominion to Aleppo and Baghdad, throughout the provinces, where Arabic

is the language of the people, which he calls the Arabian part of the Empire.[11]

Ibrahim Pasha's Egyptian army followed the same route as Napoleon in 1799, across the northern Sinai coast, and captured Gaza. The army then met the remnants of the Egyptian Fleet at Jaffa and from there prepared for further advances. On 7 December 1831 the Egyptian army captured Jerusalem with very little opposition.

The main reasons why Ibrahim's forces succeeded so easily were because of the weakness of the Turkish forces, and also because in many places the locals welcomed him as a liberator from Turkish rule. Arab historian George Antonius states:

> He controlled the Holy Places of Islam; the Sharif of Mecca looked up to him rather than to the Sultan; the Sultan himself was unpopular with his Moslem as well as his Christian subjects…
>
> … The Moslems … were prepared to welcome this fresh challenge to the detested rule of the Turk. The Christians, envious of the fair treatment which Christians in Egypt enjoyed under Mehemed 'Ali, were no less expectant. The powerful Amir Bashir of Lebanon … played upon the feelings of the Moslems by skilfully dangling before them the alluring prospect of an Arab empire to be set up after the expulsion of the Turk from Syria. Based though it was on flimsy grounds, a belief arose and became widespread that an Egyptian conquest would bring freedom to the Arabs.[12]

According to Antonius, Ibrahim was imbued with a desire to see the Arab people again rule the region, although his father, Mehmet Ali thought more in terms of creating a hereditary empire – to ultimately include Constantinople as well. What Ibrahim did not realise at that time, though,

11   Campbell to the Foreign Office, January 1832, FO 78/213, National Archives, cited in Antonius, ibid, p. 25.
12   Antonius, ibid, p. 26.

was that there was no collective identity among the Arab peoples, and his ideas were premature.[13]

Ibrahim's next objective was the city which had defied Napoleon – Acre - the capital of the Turkish pashalik, or administrative region.[14] Following a sustained siege this strategic city was captured on 26 May 1832. Ibrahim now kept moving north towards Damascus. An LJS worker John Nicolayson recorded in his diary on 19 June 1832: 'This morning the surrender of Damascus to Ibrahim Pasha was announced … Thus he is advancing rapidly and everywhere the spell of Islamism is broken.'[15]

Thereafter the cities of Hama, Homs and Aleppo fell to the Egyptian Army – the Army of the 'southern empire.' The crucial conflict then occurred at Konya in Anatolia, which was won by the Egyptians on 21 December 1832. Ibrahim Pasha then continued his movement northwards – towards Constantinople. By the middle of 1833 he had reached Bursa – within striking distance of Constantinople.

At this crucial point the Sultan, Mahmoud II, appealed to Britain to send their Navy to Alexandria and the Dardanelles and thereby compel the Egyptians to withdraw. The British Government was at that time, however, pre-occupied with internal issues and its Navy was occupied in Holland. The Cabinet, with the exception of Foreign Secretary Lord Palmerston, was also unprepared to become embroiled in another conflict in the Eastern Mediterranean.[16]

Additionally, Britain at this time was attempting to establish better diplomatic relations with France, and with France being so closely aligned to Egypt, Britain feared that involvement on behalf of Turkey could bring her into conflict with France. As it happened, each Egyptian victory in its northern campaign increased France's prestige in the region.

---

13   Antonius, ibid, pp. 28-29.
14   Which included much of present day Israel and the regions administered by the Palestinian Authority.
15   LJS Report, (London, 1833), p. 155.
16   Ridley, J. *Lord Palmerston*, (London, 1970), p. 160.

The Turkish Government (known as the Porte[17]) was now desperate. She needed to find an ally otherwise she ('the northern empire') would be consumed by Egypt. Turkey turned to her arch enemy, Russia. In February 1833 several thousand Russian troops landed at Constantinople, and the Russian Black Sea Squadron was stationed at both the Bosphorus and Dardanelles Straits, both positions now being heavily fortified.[18] The Russian presence halted the Egyptian advance.[19]

The European powers were alarmed at the Russian presence in Constantinople and at the gateway to the Mediterranean at the Dardanelles, and they demanded a Russian withdrawal. The Russians in return demanded that first Ibrahim Pasha withdraw from the province of Syria. Ibrahim flatly refused – so the Russians stayed in Turkey.

In return for its assistance the Russians forced the 'Treaty of *Unkiar Skelessi*'[20] upon Turkey, which was signed on 8 July 1833. This Treaty provided for the presence of Russian troops in Turkey; the presence of the Russian Fleet in the Bosphorus and Dardanelles; and also that neither Russia nor Turkey would take any step in foreign affairs without consulting each other. There was also a secret clause (which the British ambassador Lord Ponsonby discovered through a spy) that in the event of a future war between Russia and non-Turkish belligerents, the Bosphorus would be open to Russian vessels, but closed to non-Turkish vessels.[21]

Once the terms of the 'Treaty of *Unkiar Skelessi*' became known both Palmerston and Ponsonby recognized the political blunder Britain had made by not supporting the Turks. This Treaty effectively gave Russia the same potential as France had in 1798 – the possibility of severing Britain's link to India and the Eastern Empire. 'There is nothing that has happened since I have been in this office which I regret so much,' Palmerston later wrote 'as that tremendous blunder of the English government. But it was not my fault;

---

17   The term 'Porte' is named after the *Sublime Porte*, the gate in the Sultan's palace through which the foreign diplomats entered.

18   Parkes, J. *Whose Land?*, (London, 1949), p. 180.

19   While based in Turkey the Russians did considerable mapping and reconnaissance of the region. One Russian, Lieut-Col Petr Lvov was also despatched to 'spy out' Syria, Lebanon and Palestine, and returned to Russia a year later with very comprehensive plans and information about the region. Goren, ibid, pp. 54-5.

20   Also spelled *Hunkar Iskelesi*.

21   Ridley, ibid, p. 160.

I tried hard to persuade the Cabinet to let me take that step.'[22] This episode, combined with Napoleon's excursion of 1798, became the foundations for Britain's future foreign policy decisions in the Eastern Mediterranean. It was all part of what is known as the 'Eastern Question.'

One other important side-effect was the concern about Russia's long-term geo-political ambitions. Henceforth British strategists were more concerned about the possibility of Russia also making a land assault on India through Persia, Bokhara, Afghanistan or Turkey. 'Thus', wrote Professor Haim Goren, 'Mesopotamia and the Persian Gulf began to play an important role in British strategic calculations and Palmerston calculated that this area was crucial for the defence of India.'[23]

22   Palmerston to Frederick Lamb, 22 May 1830, cited in Ridley, J. *Lord Palmerston*, (London, 1970), p. 160.
23   Goren, ibid, p. 10.

CHAPTER 10

§

Under Egyptian control

SOME FREEDOM FOR THE *DHIMMIS*

Once Ibrahim had taken physical control, Mehmet Ali abolished the pashalics of Acre and Damascus and created the province of Syria. Damascus was the capital, from where Ibrahim ruled as the pasha – or governor. One distinct change was to grant more protection and leniency to the non-Muslim entities, especially the Greek Orthodox and Roman Catholics, protected as they were by the Russians and French. Mehmet Ali realized, too, that it was important to maintain strong relations with all the European powers, especially Britain.

Mehmet Ali's real ambition was to create a united empire, encompassing initially Egypt and Syria and ultimately Constantinople as well, and to attain the tile of Caliph.[1] He was, additionally, a geo-political realist and understood the need to placate the European powers, especially Britain. Palmerston, though, was opposed to his ambitions, as he understood the role France was playing as Egypt's protector nation.

In July 1833 Mehmet Ali met with the British Consul-General Colonel Campbell in Cairo, who wrote to Lord Palmerston on 22 July 1833: 'His Highness [Mehmet Ali] assured me with great earnestness that his anxious desire was to give to British subjects every support in order to cultivate his

---

1 Antonius, ibid, p. 28.

relations with us, and to show his respect for His Majesty's government, and that every necessary order had been given by him in Syria to that effect.'[2]

The first tangible expression of this positive Egyptian attitude towards Britain was in October 1833 when the Protestant missionary John Nicolayson was permitted to settle in Jerusalem. Although being Danish, Nicolayson was employed by the British-based LJS – and thus became the first Protestant and British subject permitted to reside in the land of Israel.

The American Board workers also took advantage of Mehmet Ali's tolerant policies and from 1834 they became actively involved in the region, primarily at Jerusalem and Beirut. One of the pioneers in Beirut was Eli Smith, who was later to play a significant role in the birth of modern Arab nationalism.

Smith brought with him a printing press which had been in Malta. He and his wife Hetty then very quickly opened a small school for girls. Coincidentally Ibrahim also opened schools throughout the region for Muslim boys, part of the purpose being to equip them for future military service.

Additionally in 1834 the Roman Catholic Jesuit order returned to Beirut and the Lazarist fathers opened a College at Aintura in the Lebanon Mountains. Huge steps forward were being made throughout Syria for the education of the population.

There were, however, some negative effects from Ibrahim's tolerant policies. Much of the Muslim population resented the new liberties and privileges given to the non-Muslim communities, the *dhimmis*.

This was not their only resentment. Ibrahim imposed a more centralized and efficient form of administration, angering many of the more autonomous tribal rulers of the region. The reality of Syria was that people were more dedicated to their local sect or tribe than to a centralised form of government.

Additionally, in an effort to build up his armed forces so as to ultimately topple the Sultan, Ibrahim instituted conscription – a move which also

---

2   Campbell to Palmerston, 22 July 1833, in FO 78/227, National Archives.

upset many of the more localised tribal leaders. There was a local Peasants'
Revolt in 1834, and also a revolt by the Druze of Lebanon in 1838.

BRITISH CALLS FOR ISRAEL'S RESTORATION

These events, similar to the period of Napoleon's excursion into the Levant,
stirred the emotions of many people: diplomats concerned about the geo-political consequences; Jewish people concerned about the welfare of their
co-religionists, and Evangelical Christians who saw in these events signs of
the latter times.[3]

The number of people in Britain who held to the belief that the scattered people of Israel would be restored to their homeland (and that Britain
would be the modern day Cyrus nation to restore them) was quite substantial. From 1833 their collective voice became stronger and more pro-ac-
tive, among the Anglicans associated with the LJS and other evangelical
Christians from many denominations.

NORTHERN AND SOUTHERN ROUTES TO INDIA

During this period of geo-political excitement an Irishman named Francis
Chesney visited Egypt in 1830, and spent six months 'checking possible
overland routes connecting the Gulf of Suez with the Mediterranean, directly or via the Nile.'[4] Chesney concluded, wrote Professor Haim Goren,
that 'the idea … of connecting the Mediterranean with the Red Sea would
be realized.'[5]

Chesney's project was part of a growing realisation among strategists
that a quicker route to the East rather than around the Cape of Africa, was
necessary. The Mediterranean-Suez option became known as the 'southern route'. Later, in 1834, Chesney embarked upon a major expedition in
Mesopotamia endorsed by the British Government, named the Euphrates
Expedition.

---

3 LJS Report, (London, 1833), p. 161.
4 Goren ibid, p. 43.
5 Goren ibid, p, 44 & Footnote on p. 282.

The Euphrates option, known as the 'northern route', became favoured by most British strategists. This option would involve utilising a port in the Bay of Alexandretta, travelling overland via Aleppo and then sailing down the Euphrates River to Basra (Bussorah) and then through the Persian Gulf to India.

An alternative proposal for the 'southern route' was made in 1834 by Thomas Galloway, a railway engineer. Galloway had proposed to Mehmet Ali that freight could be off-loaded at Suez and be transported to Cairo by railway, and then from Cairo to the Mediterranean on the Nile. Mehmet Ali accepted Galloway's proposals – but the British Government vetoed the idea for several reasons: their endorsement of Chesney's Euphrates Expedition; the Turkish Sultan's opposition; and the tense diplomatic relations then existing in the region.[6] Basically, Britain was reluctant to back a project in a country, Egypt, which was aligned with a potential geo-political rival, namely France.

A BRITISH CONSULATE IN JERUSALEM

In 1834 John Farren, the British Consul-General in Damascus, visited Jerusalem, and afterwards wrote to the Foreign Office in London suggesting the establishment there of a British consulate, in order to: protect British subjects, such as Nicolayson and a Gibraltar Jew named Haim Amzalag; offer protection and assistance to British travellers, and to offset the French and Russian presence there due to the great number of Roman Catholic and Orthodox institutions.

Palmerston finally consented to this proposal, stating in 1836: 'I think it would be expedient to have an English Consular Agent at Jerusalem.'[7] Palmerston was still haunted by the error of the 'Treaty of *Unkiar Skelessi*', and would do all in his power to negate or neutralize that Treaty.

This decision was simultaneous with exertions by the LJS to receive official backing for building a Protestant church in Jerusalem. Such a project, though, ran counter to Islamic law (which Egypt was still bound to adhere

---

6 Goren, ibid, p. 90.
7 FO 78/295, National Archives.

to), which forbade the building of new churches (and new synagogues) in the area of *dar al Islam*.

The president of the LJS, Sir Thomas Baring, and newly elected vice-President, Anthony Ashley Cooper (Lord Shaftesbury) approached Palmerston on the matter. Palmerston then informed Campbell, and Ambassador Ponsonby in Constantinople, to seek the official permits necessary to commence construction. Although being supportive of the idea, Campbell stated that the only way he saw for this permission being granted would be for the establishment of the consulate in Jerusalem.

Palmerston now activated the decision he had previously agreed to, and the official policy was declared in 1838. William Tanner Young arrived in Jerusalem in 1839 as the first foreign diplomatic representative to reside permanently in Jerusalem. Britain was now becoming more actively involved in the affairs of Jerusalem and indeed of 'the land between empires.'

This move further excited the Evangelical party. Shaftesbury wrote: 'What a wonderful event it is… The ancient city of the people of God is about to resume a place among the nations, and England is the first of Gentile Kingdoms that ceases to tread her down.'[8] Shaftesbury was the acknowledged successor to William Wilberforce as the voice of Evangelical Christianity in Britain, so anything which he gave his consent to was bound to carry much weight. The December 1838 edition of the *Quarterly Review* carried a book review by Shaftesbury, in which he stated in reference to Napoleon's failed attempt on behalf of the Jewish people, that 'the affairs of the East are lowering on Great Britain.'[9]

Such sentiments were confirmed by the initial instructions given to Consul Young, whereupon he was instructed 'to afford protection to the Jews generally.'[10] These sentiments were confirmed by Young's initial observations when he reached Jerusalem, writing to Palmerston on 14 March 1839: 'There are two parties here who will doubtless have some voice in the future disposition of affairs – "The one is the Jew – unto whom God origi-

---

8   Diary entry, 29 September 1838, cited in Hodder, E. *The Life and Works of the Seventh Earl of Shaftesbury*, (London, 1886), p. 233.

9   *Quarterly Review*, December 1838, cited in *Jewish Intelligence*, (London, 1839), p. 38.

10   Bidwell (Foreign Office) to Young, 31 January 1839. FO 78/368 (No. 2), National Archives, Kew.

nally gave this land for possession, and the other, the Protestant Christian, his legitimate offspring." Of both these Great Britain seems the natural guardian.'[11]

Two keys factors were now more evident: Britain was becoming more tangibly involved in the affairs of the East, being centred upon Jerusalem; and this involvement was beginning to have an effect upon Jewish attitudes in Europe. At that time British Christians may have had a vision based upon the Holy Scriptures of an impending Jewish return to their homeland, and Britain may have had genuine geo-political interests in the region, but there had been no official British proclamation concerning such a Jewish restoration (similar to Napoleon's), and the Jewish people themselves were so locked up in Europe that there was little real opportunity for such a restoration.

RESTLESS EGYPT AGAIN ON THE MOVE

Ibrahim Pasha's rule established a sound administrative foundation in Syria, although it did cause some local disturbances due to the centralisation of law and order. As his regime stabilized it became more of a threat to the Sultan of Turkey.

Despite Egypt's lenient policies the British Government still preferred a weak Turkish regime, rather than a strong Egypt allied to France; and preferred that Turkey not be overly dependent upon Russia. Britain's policy remained the same – to keep the Russians away from the Bosphorus and Dardanelles and keep the French away from the Isthmus of Suez. Britain did not want to upset either France or Russia, but they still desired France's protégé, Ibrahim Pasha, to be expelled from Syria. From 1838 there were a number of British agents in the region encouraging local insurrection against the Egyptian regime.[12]

The situation escalated due to the decision of Mehmet Ali in 1838 to form Syria and Egypt into a hereditary kingdom. Turkey could not condone this move, as the region was 'legally' part of its Empire. At this time

---

11   Young to Palmerston, 14 March 1839. FO 78/368 (No. 3), ibid.
12   Goren, ibid, p. 97.

Ibrahim Pasha was battling the Druze in Lebanon, so the Sultan sent an army to battle against Ibrahim Pasha in Syria. The Turks were soundly defeated at the Battle of Nissib on 24 June 1839. Shortly afterwards the entire Turkish Fleet surrendered to the Egyptians at Alexandria. All seemed lost, and seemed more so when on 29 June 1839 Sultan Mahmud II died, and was replaced a few days later by Sultan Abdulmecid I.

The way seemed open now for Ibrahim's army to proceed on to Constantinople. Mehmet Ali counselled him not to proceed, fearing it would provoke the Europeans. The European powers, however, had already been provoked. If Ibrahim continued on to Constantinople, then Russia would intervene on behalf of Turkey. The French, not wanting further Russian involvement in the region, proposed to the British that they give warning against further Russian involvement by sending their Fleets to the Dardanelles.[13]

Meanwhile a number of Turkish ministers (viziers) in Constantinople agreed in July 1839 to recognize Mehmet Ali as Viceroy of Syria. Numerous Europeans leaders realized that this would seriously threaten the *status quo* of the Levant. Count Metternich of Austria preferred that the future status of the region be determined by the European powers.

Matters now climaxed. Palmerston, alongside Russia, Austria and Prussia preferred to expel Ibrahim from Syria. France stalled, for she stood to gain if Egypt was in control of that strategic region, and there was a strong ground swell of support in France for Mehmet Ali.

Sultan Abdulmecid was now dependent upon Britain, Russia, Austria and Prussia for the maintenance of his empire. He then issued a far-reaching reform, known as the *Hatti Sherif of Gulhane* ('Decree of the Rose Chamber'). Seeking to appease his European backers, Abdulmecid guaranteed better rights for non-Muslims in the Ottoman Empire. This reform was the beginning of the *Tanzimat* – the reorganization of the Turkish Empire.

The situation deteriorated in July and August 1839. France stated its reluctance to force Egypt to withdraw from Syria, and its opposition to

---

13   Ridley, ibid, p. 220.

Russian forces assisting the Turks against the Egyptians.[14] The Russians, looking to increase their power base in Turkey, aimed to oust Egypt from the region. War seemed inevitable.

In mid-1840 Palmerston and the European statesmen submitted a proposal to France for delivery to Mehmet Ali: that Egypt retain southern Syria up to Acre, and Turkey retain the region to the north of Acre. The French Prime Minister Thiers, however, rejected this proposal, while at the same time a French agent at Constantinople had attempted to persuade the Turks to compromise with Egypt and exclude the Europeans altogether. Such a deal, if successful, would have left France in a predominant position in the region.[15]

The British Cabinet, cautious not to offend France, procrastinated, which then prompted Palmerston to offer his resignation. If, he stated, his advice for taking a strong position was not accepted, it would lead to 'the practical division of the Turkish Empire into two separate and independent states, whereof one would be the dependency of France, and the other a satellite of Russia.' Britain's political and economic influence in the region, he further stated, would be seriously curtailed. Additionally, he continued, a division of the Turkish Empire would give rise to local insurrection, which would in time involve the European Powers.[16]

DAMASCUS AND RHODES ISLAND 'BLOOD LIBELS'

During this tense period two outbreaks of the medieval 'Blood Libel' occurred, on Rhodes Island and in Damascus. The worse of the two was in Damascus. A Catholic Capuchin monk, Padre Thomas, who was under French protection, went missing. As he was last seen leaving the Jewish quarter, the Jewish community was accused of murdering him and using his blood for the Passover. This false story provoked an anti-Jewish riot (or *pogrom*). Jewish people were killed, many were injured, and much property

---

14   Ridley, ibid, p. 226.
15   Ridley, ibid, p. 233.
16   Palmerston to Lord Melbourne, 5 July 1840, cited in Ridley, ibid, p. 233.

was harmed by this ludicrous outbreak of violence.[17] Then the authorities also placed sixty-four Jewish children in prison in order to attain information.[18]

The western world was shocked by these outbreaks of violence, as the 'Blood Libel' had not been a reality since the Dark Ages.[19]

Unfortunately the French Consul condemned the Jewish people and the French government supported his verdict.[20] But Palmerston was determined to assist the Jewish people as much as possible, and provided a Jewish delegation utmost support while they travelled to Damascus and Rhodes Island. This delegation was led by Sir Moses Montefiore, the scion of British Jewry. A French delegation was also sent out under the direction of Adolphe Cremieux.

Although influenced by political considerations, namely his desire to thwart all French ambitions in the East, Palmerston nevertheless also felt great sorrow for the welfare of the poor defenseless Jewish people.[21] He dispatched a Memo to his representatives in the Turkish Empire and in other areas where Jewish people resided, stating:

> I have accordingly to instruct you that, whenever any case is brought
> to your knowledge in which Jews resident within your District, shall
> have been subjected to oppression or injustice, you will make a dili-
> gent enquiry into the circumstance of the case and will report fully
> thereupon to Her Majesty's Ambassador at Constantinople ... you
> will, upon any suitable occasion, make known to the Local Authorities
> that the British Government feels an interest in the welfare of the Jews
> in general, and is anxious that they should be protected from op-
> pression; and that the Porte has promised to afford them protection

---

17 For further details see, Frankel, J. *The Damascus Affair: "Ritual Murder," Politics and the Jews in 1840*, (Cambridge, 1997).

18 *JI*, 1840, p. 174, quoting an Arabic Bulletin.

19 Hyamson, A. *British Consulate in Jerusalem in relation to the Jews of Palestine 1838-1914*, (London, 1939), Vol. 1, p. xxxvii.

20 *Encyclopaedia Judaica*, 5, p. 1250.

21 See Mordechai Eliav, *Britain and the Holy Land, 1838-1914: Selected Documents from the British Consulate of Jerusalem*, (Jerusalem, 1997), pp. 130-131.

and will certainly attend to any representations which her Majesty's Ambassador at Constantinople may make to it on these matters.[22]

Many people were horrified that such a case reminiscent of the Dark Ages could occur in this 'age of enlightenment.' The Jewish people in Jerusalem were also greatly perturbed concerning the possible ramifications upon them. The rabbis sent a delegation to George Pieritz, one of the LJS workers, and asked him to 'do what he could to rid them of this calumny; and requested him to go with one of their rabbies [sic] to Damascus for this purpose'.[23]

The influence of Palmerston and the British in this situation was taken seriously in Constantinople. En-route to the East, Montefiore received an imperial edict (*firman*) from the Sultan condemning the 'Blood Libel'. Montefiore passed this *firman* to Colonel Charles Churchill of the British Consulate-General in Damascus, who had witnessed this event – and who now sought for a solution for this problem of the vulnerability of the Jewish people in the region.

---

22   Palmerston to Ambassador Ponsonby, 21 April 1841, FO 195/181 (No 95).
23   Nicolayson Diary 16 March, 1840, Conrad Schick Library & Archive, Alexander College, Christ Church, Jerusalem. [Henceforth Schick Library]

§

CHAPTER 11

The Syrian Crisis of 1840

1840 – WAR & CALLS FOR ISRAEL'S RESTORATION

The embers of the Damascus and Rhodes 'Blood Libel' cases had barely simmered when Palmerston and the ambassadors of Russia, Austria and Prussia signed the 'Treaty of London' on 15 July 1840. An official ultimatum was presented to Mehmet Ali by the consuls of the four Powers at the end of July. It called upon him to:

- Withdraw from Syria and Crete within ten days. If he complied, then he would receive southern Syria (including Acre but excluding Jerusalem, as well as excluding Mecca and Medina) as a hereditary pashalik.
- If, however, he did not accept this request within ten days, then he would lose Syria.
- If after twenty days neither of these demands were met, then the Sultan, if he felt able, could dismiss him from his position as Viceroy of Egypt.

The French reacted angrily and announced the end of the Anglo-French Alliance. The situation thereafter deteriorated, and there was even talk of another European war. Palmerston maintained, however, that the French were only bluffing and would not go to war.

The European Powers now began formulating strategies for the future of southern Syria (Palestine) once the Egyptians were ousted. The LJS in particular was aware of the proclaimed belief amongst Jewish people that the year of their redemption was drawing near, and great things were anticipated in the Jewish year 5600, between September 1839 and September 1840. Shaftesbury wrote in his diary on 25 July 1840:

> Anxious about the hopes and prospects of the Jewish people. Everything seems ripe for their return to Palestine ... Could the five Powers of the West be induced to guarantee the security of life and possessions of the Hebrew race, they would now flock back in rapidly augmenting numbers.[1]

Shaftesbury desired a clause to be inserted into the final Treaty allowing for the restoration of the Jewish people to Palestine.[2] Several days later, on 1 August 1840, he presented his scheme to Palmerston, who, he wrote, was impressed by the proposal.[3]

Lord Shaftesbury's efforts were greatly aided by Erasmus Scott Calman, a Jewish member of the LJS work in Jerusalem, who was then in London.[4] Calman, at Shaftesbury's encouragement, wrote a Memorandum on 3 August 1840, in which he stated that his sojourn in Palestine had convinced him that Jewish people would return and till the land if there was security of life and possession. He wrote:

> A Proclamation like that of Cyrus would be echoed by hundreds of thousands of Jews in Poland, Russia and elsewhere, and by the rich as well as by the poor who would gladly exchange their present harassed and uncertain mode of life for the quiet and more certain one that

---

1 Hodder, ibid, p, 166.
2 Ashley to Palmerston, 25 September 1840, cited in Hodder, ibid, pp. 168-169.
3 Hodder, ibid, p. 167.
4 Friedmann, I. *The Question of Palestine*, (New Brunswick, 1992), p. xviii.

would result from the cultivation of the soil … They would be enabled to sit under their vine and fig-tree and none should make them afraid.[5]

Shaftesbury's proposal impressed Palmerston, who in turn then sent the following dispatch, on 11 August 1840, to Ambassador Ponsonby in Constantinople:

> There exists at present among the Jews dispersed over Europe a strong notion that the time is approaching when their nation is to return to Palestine; and consequently their wish to go thither has become more keen, and their thoughts have been bent more intently than before upon the means of realizing that wish. It is well known that the Jews of Europe possess great wealth; and it is manifest that any country in which a considerable number of them might choose to settle, would derive great benefit from the riches which they would bring into it.[6]

Palmerston needed to arouse the interest of the Sultan to the positive aspect of Israel's restoration, and exaggerated the financial condition of the Jewish people, as further evidenced in the same Memo:

> Whether Mehmet Ali accepts the first or the second offer which is to be made to him, in either case it would be of manifest importance to the Sultan to encourage the Jews to return to, and settle in, Palestine; because the wealth which they would bring with them would increase the resources of the Sultan's dominions; and the Jewish people, if returning under the sanction and protection and at the invitation of the Sultan, would be a check upon any future evil designs of Mehmet Ali or his successor.[7]

---

5 Memorandum by E.S. Calman, 3 August 1840, encl in Ashley to Palmerston, 25 September 1840, encl No 1 in Palmerston to Ponsonby, 25 November 1840, FO 195/165, No 261.

6 Palmerston to Ponsonby, 11 August 1840, FO 78/390, No 134.

7 Palmerston to Ponsonby, 11 August 1840, FO 78/390, No 134.

What Palmerston was proposing was the establishment of a buffer zone between Turkey and Egypt, in the land of Israel, and for this buffer zone to be occupied by the Jewish people. That this idea was commonly held is revealed by an editorial in the prestigious *Times* newspaper on 17 August, which also endorsed the concept of the restoration of Israel, writing:

> Let the four Allied Powers now publish to the four quarters of the
> world their determination to restore the Jews from all nations to the
> Holy Land, and to assist them in rebuilding the walls and temple of
> Jerusalem and assuredly, the multitudinous descendants of Abraham,
> already restless with the anxiety of desire, and excited by the antic-
> ipated fulfillment of this regeneration, would arise to the summons
> as one man... Let, I repeat, the Quadruple Alliance take advantage
> of this conjuncture, and issue a manifesto for the restoration and in-
> dependence of the Hebrew tribes, and by next spring the banks of
> the Euphrates would be once more thronged, and the long line of
> the European and African coasts be crowded by the gathering hosts
> of Israel. From the different ports on these shores they could be
> readily shipped, and, convoyed by the fleets that now cruise in the
> Mediterranean, be triumphantly landed on the strand of their long-
> lost Palestine – a more befitting occupation this, than the waging of a
> petty war to the hazard of all Europe's peace ...[8]

Shaftesbury and many Evangelicals were excited by these events, seeing in them a modern day Cyrus decree which would permit the restoration of Israel.[9] Calman's Memo was added to Shaftesbury's letter and both were sent to Palmerston on 25 September 1840, and then forwarded to Ambassador Ponsonby on 25 November 1840.

---

8 *Times*, cited in *JI*, (London, 1841), p. 35. Lieber, S. *Mystics and Missionaries, The Jews in Palestine, 1799-1840*, (Salt Lake City, 1992), p. 374.
9 Hodder, ibid, p. 168.

OUTBREAK OF WAR

Meanwhile French opposition to the Allied ultimatum increased, and by October 1840 they began increasing their Mediterranean Fleet. The French King Louis Philippe notified Queen Victoria of the negative mood in France towards the Allied position. There was, he stated, a strong group in France desiring a united Syria and Egypt, under French patronage. The King, though, assured Queen Victoria that he doubted France would go to war against the Allies.[10]

Yet war was imminent, especially when Mehmet Ali adamantly refused to comply with the Allied request. The campaign to oust him began in late September, and thereafter the Allied Fleet, led by the British, captured Haifa, Tyre, Sidon and Beirut. The campaign climaxed on 3 November 1840 when the mostly British Fleet bombed and captured Acre, the primary seaport along the Mediterranean coast.

The British commander, Admiral Sir Charles Napier, then sailed to Alexandria, without official authorization, and met Mehmet Ali. He encouraged Mehmet Ali to surrender; to return the Turkish Fleet; and accept the conditions of the 'Treaty of London'. If he complied, then his regime would retain control over Egypt, and in return to accept the offer of a hereditary monarchy in Egypt. Mehmet Ali accepted these conditions. One of those present at this crucial moment in history was Colonel Charles Churchill.

The Egyptian withdrawal from Syria then went into effect, with Napier even shipping out the Egyptian soldiers so they would not be subject to deprivations from the locals.[11] Nicolayson, who although a British subject, had remained in Jerusalem, wrote on 7 November 1840: 'Last night a firman arrived from the Turkish authority … to the Kadi here, which invests him with all authority, for the time, to require the surrender of the city, and to organize a provincial Government in the name of the Sultan.'[12]

Although temporary Turkish control was re-established over Syria, a final decision on the future status of the region would now need to be deter-

10   Lord Palmerston to Queen Victoria, 11 November 1840. Connell, *Regina v Palmerston*, pp 25-27, cited in Ridley, ibid, p. 239.
11   Ridley, ibid, p, 241.
12   *JI*, (London, 1841), p. 44.

mined by the European powers and Turkey. It would be at least six months until this final decision would be reached in London, in July 1841, with the 'Treaty for the Pacification of the Levant'.

BRITISH REACTIONS TO VICTORY

The conflict in 'the land between empires' engendered considerable interest in Britain. The Commission of the General Assembly of the Church of Scotland sent a Memorandum to the Foreign Office on 23 October 1840 in which they appealed for Israel's restoration.[13] Palmerston also forwarded this Memorandum to Ambassador Ponsonby on 24 November, strengthening his case as previously presented by Shaftesbury. In his letter to Ponsonby, Palmerston added:

> ... that the matters to which it relates excite a very deep interest in the minds of a large number of Persons in the United Kingdom, and the Sultan would enlist in his favour the good opinion of numerous and powerful classes in this country if he were immediately to issue some formal edict or declaration granting and assuring to such Jews as may choose to fix themselves in any part of the Turkish Dominions, but more especially in Syria, full security for their Persons and Property, and free liberty to go and come and ... probably contribute much to give confidence to such Jews as might determine to settle in Palestine, in consequence of such an Edict ...[14]

The LJS wrote in an editorial of its mouthpiece the *Jewish Intelligence*:

> The course of events, of late, in Syria, has been attentively watched by all those who are anxiously looking for the restoration of Israel, and awaiting the fulfillment of the sure word of prophecy ... It is true, that the Jewish nation were in no degree involved in the cause of conten-

---

13 'Acting Committee of the General Assembly of the Church of Scotland for Promoting Christianity among the Jews' to Viscount Palmerston, 23 October 1840, cited in *JI*, 1840, p. 35.
14 Palmerston to Ponsonby, 24 November 1840, FO 78/391 (no 248).

tion, and formed no part of the elements in collision; but who shall say what is the hidden meaning and intention of the array of emphatic events which has lately passed before our eyes in the East?...

The way ... seems to be opening remarkably for the restoration of the Jews...[15]

As if to encourage Palmerston in his thinking about making serious proposals for the future of the 'Holy Land', Consul Young who had temporarily vacated Jerusalem during the War, wrote to the Foreign Secretary soon after returning:

It is perfectly clear my Lord that without the aid of the British Forces the Turks could not have regained possession of Syria – and I would respectfully submit to Your Lordship my humble opinion, that without the continued aid of the British Government to advise, and assist in enforcing measures for the general good and tranquility of the Country – the Turks cannot govern Syria.[16]

EUROPEAN PROPOSALS FOR THE FUTURE

While the British were encouraging the Jewish cause, the other Powers during this period also submitted their agendas for the future of the 'Holy Land'. The French proposed the *internationalisation* of Jerusalem, with them and Russia taking the pre-eminent position. This plan, proposed by the French foreign minister Francois Guizot, was also called the 'Jerusalem Plan.'[17] Guizot also contacted Prince Metternich about this plan, in order to strengthen the Roman Catholic position. However, Metternich realized, as did Palmerston, that the object at this stage was to stabilize and not destabilize the Ottoman Empire. Metternich was aware of Muslim sensitivities on this issue, as the Sultan was the Caliph of Islam, and would never release one of the holy Islamic cities. The Turks, he believed, would never consent

---

15 *JI*, 1841, p. 34.
16 Young to Palmerston, 25 January 1841, p. 160, FO 78/444 .
17 Brugiere de Barante, *Souvenirs,* Vol 6, pp. 558-60, cited in Verete, ibid, pp. 142-3.

to Jerusalem becoming a free and Christian city, and certainly not a Jewish dominated one!

Metternich thought of setting up a 'Turkish Commissioner in the Holy Land' for the protection of Christian pilgrims and travelers. But the Russians opposed this idea, as the Russian foreign minister Nesselrode stated that the proposal 'did not appear to him a necessary or desirable measure, and that the Consuls in Syria were adequate to protect the Europeans whom commerce, piety, or curiosity might attract to that country.'[18]

The Russians never agreed to any of these plans, as they had their own. At this point they seemed desirous of fostering good relations with Britain, and weren't eager to endorse any purely French (or Roman Catholic) Plan. But Nesselrode did propose that the area of Palestine be made a separate *pashalik*, with independence for Jerusalem, which would be governed directly from Constantinople.[19]

BEGINNINGS OF PRUSSIAN (GERMAN) INVOLVEMENT

The new king in Prussia, Frederick William IV, who came to the throne in 1840, was also keen to enhance Prussian interests in the East. The Prussians envisaged a treaty between Turkey and the Europeans, guaranteeing control and direction by the Christians over the predominantly Christian areas of Jerusalem, Bethlehem and Nazareth. Under this arrangement, Russia would appoint the Orthodox representative, the French and Austrians would appoint the Roman Catholic representative, and the British and Prussians would appoint the Protestant representative.[20]

Later, in early 1841, Lieut. Helmuth von Moltke, the Prussian military attaché in Constantinople, proposed creating Palestine as a buffer zone between Turkey and Egypt, and placing it under Prussian protection.[21]

On 30 March 1841 the Prussian king dictated to his close associate Joseph Radowitz the address he wanted delivered to the Heads of State at

---

18 Verete, M. 'A Plan for the Internationalization of Jerusalem', in *From Palmerston to Balfour: Collected Essays of Mayir Verete*, (Frank Cass, London), p. 151.

19 Verete, M. 'A Plan for the Internationalization of Jerusalem', ibid, p. 151.

20 Wolf, L. *Notes on the Diplomatic History of the Jewish Question*, (London, 1919), p. 105; R. W. Greaves, 'The Jerusalem Bishopric 1841' in *English Historical Review*, 64, 1948, p. 336.

21 Eliav, M. *Eretz Israel and its Yishuv in the Nineteenth Century (1777-1917)*, (Jerusalem, 1978) [Hebrew], p. 48.

the forthcoming Peace Conference. This address revealed the King's intentions of taking advantage of the unprecedented opportunity offered by this present situation. The King stated that his idea 'was capable of general extension, not merely as a Prussian, but a German question; and again, not merely as a German, but a general Protestant question, when viewed in its connection with the entire Protestant Church.'[22]

There were so few Protestants and even fewer Germans in the 'Holy Land', that the King's ideas of establishing a purely German entity there were negligible, so he needed to unite with the British-based LJS work in Jerusalem.[23]

BRITISH INTERESTS

Many also saw this as an ideal opportunity of enforcing the stipulations of the *Hatti Sherif of Gulhane* and confirming protection for Christians in the East. The Earl of Chichester, the President of CMS, wrote to Foreign Secretary Palmerston on 25 March 1841 expressing the view 'that British Christians should have the same protection and religious liberty in the Ottoman Empire as other Christian Churches.' He proposed there be 'ecclesiastical authority' directing 'the Clergy of the Church of England in those parts.'[24]

Meanwhile Consul Young in Jerusalem sent an alarming dispatch to Palmerston on 4 June 1841, stating that the Greeks were constructing two new buildings 'to be at the disposal of Russia' and for use by Russians.[25] Similar observations were made concerning French aspirations and activities through the Catholics.

All of these proposals for the future status of Jerusalem and the land of Israel would need to be submitted at the upcoming Peace Conference scheduled to be held in London in July 1841. Some of those plans and proposals, however, had been compromised by Admiral Napier who had concluded an agreement with Mehmet Ali at the close of 1840.

---

22   Hechler, W. *The Jerusalem Bishopric*, (London, 1883), pp. 26-27. F. Bunsen, ibid, Vol. 1, cited in Skinner, J. *The Three Anglican Bishops in Jerusalem*, in 'Church Quarterly Review', July 1884, p. 328.

23   Hechler, ibid, p. 27.

24   Orchard, ibid, p. 205, quoting CMS letter book G/AC1, p. 405 letter of 20 March 1841.

25   Young to Palmerston, 4 June 1841, FO 78/444.

One of the main outcomes of the 'Treaty for the Pacification of the Levant' was the signing of the Straits Convention. This Convention, basically negated the secret clause in the 'Treaty of *Unkiar Skelessi*' of 1833 which gave Russia a strategic advantage concerning passageway through the Dardanelles and Bosphorus Straits.

The Straits Convention barred warships of all kinds from access through the Dardanelles and Bosphorus Straits, except they belong to an ally of Turkey. This Convention seriously curtailed Russia's ambitions of sailing her growing Navy into the Mediterranean.

ANGLO-PRUSSIAN JERUSALEM BISHOPRIC AND PROTESTANT CHURCH

After 1841 the active involvement of the European Powers in 'the land between empires' increased dramatically. Much of this change was due to the involvement of Prussia, which basically represented German interests.

King Frederick William IV of Prussia in 1840 envisioned the establishment of a world-wide Protestant church, with Jerusalem as its centre and starting point. Prussia's minimal involvement in the Syrian Crisis of 1840 provided the Prussian king with the opportunity to introduce Prussian-German interests into the 'Holy Land.'

King Frederick William was aware of the work of the LJS in Jerusalem. In June 1841 he dispatched his private envoy, Chevalier de Bunsen, to London to meet with Shaftesbury and the political and ecclesiastical leaders to ascertain the possibility of entering into an alliance with Britain, and through this to lay a foundation in Jerusalem. De Bunsen took with him three proposals from the Prussian King.

De Bunsen was well received in Britain, but ultimately only one of the King's three proposals was acceptable: to establish a joint Protestant Bishopric in Jerusalem. The British Government then passed a special Act through Parliament, the (Jerusalem) Bishopric Act, in quick time. A former rabbi, Michael Solomon Alexander, was then elected as the first Anglican-Protestant bishop of Jerusalem.

The establishment of the joint Anglo-Prussian Protestant Bishopric marked the tangible beginning point of German involvement in the 'Holy Land.' It also provoked considerable reactions from the other European powers. The Roman Catholic and Orthodox nations saw this move as an act of aggrandizement by the Protestant powers, and sought thereafter to neutralize this activity. Within just a few years both the Roman Catholic and Greek Orthodox churches restored their patriarchates to Jerusalem.

The Protestant presence was further enhanced with the completion in 1849 of an Evangelical Anglican church, named Christ Church. This church, whose construction violated the principles of Islam (which forbade the building of new churches and synagogues) was built by the LJS opposite the Citadel or Tower of David, and thereafter became the spiritual home for the British and German evangelical communities.[26]

Prussia also despatched a consul, Ernest Gustav Schultz, to Jerusalem in 1843. The other European countries later followed the lead initially made by Britain in 1838.

By the mid-1840's Palestine was being transformed into an enclave of Europe, an enclave whereby both Christian and Jewish communities were benefitting from the Capitulations and beginning to enjoy the benefits of freedom from their ages-long subjugation to *dhimmitude*.

---

26   Christ Church was filled with Jewish symbols and Hebrew inscriptions, resembling in part a synagogue. Permission was given to build Christ Church on the condition that it was the private chapel of the British Consul.

CHAPTER 12

§

Birth of Jewish and Arab nationalism

FURTHER PROPOSALS FOR THE RESTORATION OF ISRAEL

Colonel Charles Churchill wrote to Moses Montefiore on 14 June 1841 that he was 'most anxious to see your countrymen endeavour once more to resume their existence as a people. I consider' he continued 'the object to be perfectly attainable.' But, Churchill added, two things were necessary before this could happen. 'Firstly' he stated, 'that the Jews will themselves take up the matter universally and unanimously. Secondly, that the European Powers will aid them in their views. It is for the Jews to make a commencement.'[1]

A number of Jewish intellectuals took up the challenge before them during this period. One was Rabbi Yehuda Alkalai (1798-1878). Alkalai from Bosnia, had been much impressed by the Greek War of Independence, and the desire of some of the subjugated peoples of the Balkans to be freed from the clutches of the Ottoman Turks, and believed the natural resto-

---

1 Churchill to Sir Moses Montefiore, 14 June 1841, cited in Wolf, L. *Notes on the Diplomatic History of the Jewish Question*, (London, 1919), pp. 119-120.

ration of the Jewish people to *Eretz Yisrael* would precede their spiritual salvation.[2] He was also greatly outraged by the Damascus 'Blood Libel' affair.

Alkalai wrote *Minhat Yehuda* in 1843, which called for the 'adoption of Hebrew as a national language, purchase of land in Palestine, development of agriculture to form the basis for absorption of new immigrants, and encouragement of national unity.'[3] Although Alkalai's work never had a wide circulation, it was part of the increasing interest now growing within both Evangelical Christian and Jewish circles, for a national Jewish return to *Eretz Yisrael*.

While the work and publications of Montefiore, Adolph Cremieux and Alkalai were filtering out into the Jewish communities throughout Europe, evangelical Christians in Britain continued to inculcate an interest in the restoration of Israel throughout Britain.

COLONEL GEORGE GAWLER

Another Briton who, like Churchill, was concerned for Israel's future not just because of their part of the fulfilment of Biblical prophecy, but so that they could become free and equal world citizens, was a British officer and the former governor of South Australia named Colonel George Gawler.

Gawler was very concerned with the welfare of the Jewish nation and believed in their future restoration, but he was also a pragmatist. Gawler was perhaps the first to give practical suggestions as to how this proposed restoration would tangibly happen, and succeed.

Gawler returned from his position as governor of South Australia at the time of the crisis in 1839-40, and at the time when the official proposal by Palmerston for a Jewish restoration to Palestine was broached. He now set about devising a plan for this restoration to actually work practically.

The pragmatic Gawler propounded the idea that the Jewish people would again work the land. This proposal was quite novel at the time, considering that Jewish people in Palestine were not farmers; those in most parts of

---

2 *Encyclopaedia Britannica*, 1975, Vol, I, p.247.
3 www.zionism-israel.com/bio/alkalai.

Europe were forbidden to own land; and that in the 1840's most of the land of Palestine was barren, swampy and unproductive. Gawler, however, understood the similarities between the land of Israel and South Australia, and having achieved agricultural self-sufficiency in his brief term as governor, he knew the same could be done in Palestine.

The culmination of Gawler's thesis was presented in a book entitled *Observations and Practical Suggestions in Furtherance of the Establishment of Jewish Colonies in Palestine*, published in 1845.[4]

Gawler's overall perspective was a combination of the need for Jewish people to be restored to the land of Israel, and of the needs of the British Empire. Britain, he stated, urgently needed the:

> ... shortest and safest lines of communication ... Egypt and Syria stand in intimate connection. A foreign hostile power in either would soon endanger British trade ... and it is now for England to set her hand hard to the renovation of Syria through the only people whose energies will be extensively and permanently in the work – the real children of the soil – the sons of Israel.[5]

Another Briton who held strong views about Israel's future restoration was a politician named Benjamin Disraeli. Disraeli wrote two novels which alluded to Israel's restoration to her ancestral homeland, one being *Tancred*, which was published in 1847.

BIRTH PANGS OF ARAB NATIONALISM

While British geo-political interest in the Levant was slowly merging with the vision of a restored Israel, there were small beginnings of a future Arab national identity. Much of this had to do with the educational work of the second Anglican bishop in Jerusalem, Samuel Gobat, and the American Board missionaries in Beirut.

---

4 Gawler, Colonel G. *Observations and Practical Suggestions in Furtherance of the Establishment of Jewish Colonies in Palestine*, (London, 1845). Copy in the Southampton University.

5 Gawler, Colonel G, cited in, *British Projects for the Restoration of the Jews*, (London, 1917), p. 17. Gawler accompanied Montefiore to Palestine in 1849.

The Protestant schools which Gobat and especially the Americans estab-lished throughout Syria taught both religious and non-religious subjects. When the Americans adapted their printing press many materials were then produced in Arabic. The activities of the Protestant schools provoked the various Catholic institutions to also increase their educational work. The combined efforts resulted in a cultural revival among some Arab people, especially in and around Beirut, and primarily among the Christian Arabs. The Turkish authorities until this point were not encouraging education, and especially not in Arabic. They seemed more concerned in keeping the local inhabitants in ignorance, while emphasizing the Turkish language.

One Lebanese Christian, Butrus Bustani, went to Beirut in 1840 and joined Smith and the Americans. Bustani translated and wrote numer-ous books into Arabic. Bustani and Nasif Yazegi, alongside Smith, other Americans and Churchill, also formed the *Society of Arts and Sciences* in 1847. This Society encouraged the promotion of knowledge – although only Christian Arabs participated.[6]

In the following years other similar institutions opened, including the Syrian Scientific Society, which was composed of Muslim, Druze and Christian Syrians. Antonius wrote, that, for probably the first time:

> … in the 350 years of the Ottoman domination, a common ideal had brought the warring creeds together and united them in an ac-tive partnership for a common end. An interest in the progress of the country as a national unit was now their incentive, a pride in the Arab inheritance their bond. The foundation of the Society was the first outward manifestation of a collective national consciousness, and its importance in history is that it was the cradle of a new political movement.[7]

The foundations were now being laid for the renaissance of two national entities in the Eastern Mediterranean.

---

6 A similar Society, the Jerusalem Literary Society, was established in Jerusalem by Consul James and Mrs Eliza-beth Ann Finn in 1849.
7 Antonius, ibid, p. 54.

§

CHAPTER 13

The Crimean War

CLASH OF IMPERIAL AMBITIONS

While British and Prussian (German) interests slowly developed after 1842, those of France and Russia increased quite substantially. Both sought every opportunity to increase their position and prestige through their respective protected minority groups, the Roman Catholic and Greek Orthodox Christians.

By the early 1850's two ambitious personalities were ruling these nations: Napoleon III in France and Czar Nicholas I in Russia. Czar Nicholas had had ambitions for a long period. As far back as in 1844 Nicholas proposed to Palmerston that the Turkish Empire be partitioned with Russia taking Turkey and Britain taking Egypt and Crete, while Constantinople would temporarily remain a Turkish province.[1] Nicholas was also constantly agitating for the Sultan to further endorse and confirm Russia as the protector of Orthodox Christians in the Turkish Empire. Turkey, fearing the loss of her independence, refused to grant Russia the opportunity of any further encroachment upon her territory.

Napoleon III, like Napoleon Bonaparte, hankered after international fame – and also looked to the East. He was anxious to uphold the role as

---

1 Tuchman, B. *Bible and Sword*, p. 254.

protector of the Roman Catholics within the Turkish Empire. There was no doubt that such demands, somewhat neglected since the Napoleonic peri-od, would antagonize Russia, complicate matters for Turkey, and potentially embarrass Britain.

In 1847 a silver star in the Roman Catholic section of the Church of the Nativity in Bethlehem was stolen. The Roman Catholics blamed the Orthodox, whom they accused of attempting to usurp their rights in the Holy Places in both Jerusalem and Bethlehem. Such an accusation by the Roman Catholics against the Orthodox was construed by the Czar as an ac-cusation against him, as Russia claimed to protect the rights of the Orthodox (although the Treaty of *Kucuk Kaynarca* only provided a limited jurisdic-tion to exercise such rights). Nicholas appealed to the Sultan to intervene.

Napoleon likewise demanded Turkish intervention in the scandal in Bethlehem - in favour of the Catholics! The Sultan, caught between these two great Powers, conciliated by replacing the silver star at his own cost. This move upset the Orthodox and Russians, who felt slighted by the French-Catholic accusations.

In February 1853 the Russian envoy Prince Menshikov demanded that the Turkish Government intervene on their behalf. Russia simultaneously assembled troops along the borders of some of Turkey's European domin-ions and in her Black Sea ports. The British and French ambassadors imme-diately summoned their respective governments to send their fleets to the Dardanelles – as a warning to Russian aspirations.

Britain was initially ambivalent over the issue, and ultimately the French Fleet sailed alone. Palmerston, though, was adamant that Britain should oppose Russia, seeing Russia's intransigence as a threat to the stability of the Eastern Mediterranean. He wasn't alone. Sir Austen Layard stated in the House of Commons: 'We should not forget that, although Egypt is *a* high road to India, Syria and the valleys of the Tigris and Euphrates form *the* high road, and any power holding those countries would command India.'[2]

---

2   Layard, A.H. *The Turkish Question, Speeches delivered in the House of Commons*, 16 August 1853, and 17 February 1854, (London, 1854), cited by Sokolow, N. *History of Zionism*, (London, 1919), Vol. 1, p. 157.

Despite the presence of the French Fleet at the Dardanelles, Russia still threatened to invade the Turkish regions of Wallachia and Moldavia if her demands were not met. Palmerston and Lord John Russell thereafter increased their pressure upon the Cabinet, which finally agreed to dispatch the British Fleet to the Dardanelles. But when the weather fell foul, the British Fleet anchored within the Dardanelles Straits, which Russia construed as a violation of the Straits Convention of 1841 - and she thereupon invaded the Turkish provinces.

A peace conference was quickly convened in Vienna, where all the European powers agreed to a compromise agreement – except Turkey, which believed that any concessions granting Russia full protection rights over Orthodox Christians would adversely affect Turkey's independence. Turkey then declared war upon Russia.

Popular support in Britain was for supporting Turkey against Russia. The thought of Russia controlling Constantinople was repugnant to many Britons. This feeling increased following the destruction of a Turkish Fleet at Sinope on 30 November 1853. Shortly afterwards the British and French Fleets sailed into the Black Sea towards the harbour of Sebastapol in the Crimea.

Nicholas, looking for a pretext for war against Turkey in order to accumulate more Turkish territory and to attain his goal of controlling the Black Sea region as well as the Bosphorus and Dardanelles, now increased his demands. Despite increased efforts to bring about a peaceful solution, Britain and France were compelled to declare war on Russia on 28 March 1854. The Crimean War had begun.

The British and French objective was the capture of the Russian stronghold of Sebastapol by a combined force of some 60,000 men. As the ships carrying these troops steamed through the Dardanelles, past a small village named Gelibolu (Gallipoli), into the Sea of Marmara, under the guns of Constantinople, through the Bosphorus and into the Black Sea, Lord Palmerston and the generals saw the campaign as a *fait accompli* – that it would result in a quick and decisive victory.

The first landings occurred on 14 September 1854, but within two months half the British force was dead, wounded or sick with cholera. Despite some heroic victories, the anticipated quick victory at Sebastapol was not attained by the Anglo-French force.

CONSEQUENCES OF THE OUTBREAK OF WAR

The fighting may have been in the Crimea, but the consequences were felt far and wide, particularly in southern Syria - Palestine. Many of the destitute Jewish people who lived there relied upon funds (known as *haluka*[3]) from Jewish communities in Europe – much of which came from Russian controlled areas.

The situation became so desperate in the 'Holy Land' and particularly in Jerusalem, that many sought the assistance of British institutions, and especially the British consul, James Finn, and his wife, Elizabeth Anne. Consul and Mrs Finn exerted much effort on behalf of the Jewish community, and elicited support from the British ambassador at Constantinople, De Redcliffe.[4]

Lord Shaftesbury too was active, stating to the Foreign Secretary, Lord Clarendon, that 'the Sultan should be moved to issue a Firman granting to the Jewish people power to hold land in Syria or any part of the Turkish domains.'[5] Clarendon presented this request to Ambassador de Redcliffe. When the following year Moses Montefiore stopped in Constantinople en-route to Palestine, he received official permission to purchase small plots of land. When he arrived in Jerusalem in 1855 Montefiore purchased land outside both Jaffa and Jerusalem.[6] The Paris-based Rothschild family also became actively involved in the affairs of *Eretz Yisrael* at this time. They despatched an envoy, Dr. Albert Cohn, to Jerusalem with instructions to

---

3   The Hebrew word for distribution. Funds were collected in Europe and sent to Jewish leaders in *Eretz Yisrael*, who then distributed it among the needy.

4   De Redcliffe was Sir Stratford Canning. De Redcliffe also sought permission for the construction of a new synagogue on behalf of the Ashkenazi Jews of Jerusalem. Finn to de Redcliffe, 13 July 1854, FO 195/445 (No. 23), cited in Hyamson, A. *The British Consulate in Jerusalem 1838-1914*, Vol. 1, p. 225. Consul and Mrs Finn also purchased land outside the Old City of Jerusalem upon which they employed many destitute Jewish people in industry. This enterprise became known as 'Abraham's Vineyard.'

5   Shaftesbury's diary, 17 May 1854, cited in Hodder, ibid, p. 493.

6   In Jerusalem the area of Mishkenot Shaananim was constructed.

open a Jewish hospital, and other Jewish institutions so that Jewish people would not need to resort to the services of the British consul, and especially the 'Jewish mission' as the work of the LJS was referred to.

That Britain and France were helping Turkey provided them with the opportunity of bettering the lives of the non-Muslim communities within the Turkish Empire, particularly in the land of Israel. The Jewish community, which had been for many centuries at the lowest level, benefitted most.

CONCLUSION OF THE CRIMEAN WAR

The initial disaster in the Crimean War led to the downfall of the British government, and Palmerston took over as Prime Minister in February 1855. Shortly after Czar Nicholas I died and his successor, Czar Alexander II, was prepared for peace talks, which began soon afterwards in Vienna.

Palmerston was determined to cut Russia down to size so that she would never again threaten Turkey's stability and threaten Britain's link to India and her Eastern Empire. Russia, though, was not willing to accept Britain's harsh demands and the talks broke down and the war then continued.

In September 1855, Sebastapol was captured by French forces, and following further military set-backs, Russia in January 1856 finally agreed to the Anglo-French peace terms.

The peace conference began in Paris in February 1856. Britain's main desire was to minimise Russia's involvement and interests within the Turkish Empire and her demands were:

- The demilitarization of the Black Sea.
- The stripping away of any protection rights exercised by Russia over Orthodox Christians within the Turkish Empire.

Both of these key points were finally agreed to. The 'Treaty of Paris' was signed on 30 March 1856, and once again, peace and stability was restored to the Eastern Mediterranean, albeit only temporarily.

One of the most significant outcomes of the British-French assistance to Turkey was a new edict or *firman* issued by Sultan Abdulmecid named the

Hatti Humayan, which was part of the *Tanzimat* reforms which benefitted the non-Muslim communities of the Turkish Empire. Antonius wrote that the *Hatti Humayan* was important as it contained 'an explicit recognition of the complete equality of all creeds in the Ottoman Empire in matters of taxation, justice and the privileges and obligations of citizenship. In that respect it adopted and consecrated the principles introduced into Syria by Ibrahim Pasha, and gave the Christians a legal and absolute right of equality with the Moslems.'[7]

RUSSIA'S NEW APPROACH

Russia, deprived of its role as protector of the Orthodox Christians in the Turkish Empire after the Crimean War, then set out to establish a purely Russian presence in 'the land between empires.'

In view of the promises of reform held out in the *Hatti Humayan* for better conditions for non-Muslims, Russia despatched Boris Mansurov to Jerusalem immediately after the signing of the peace treaty to ascertain the possibility of establishing a purely Russian presence there, and of introducing a Russian shipping line to bring Russian Orthodox pilgrims to the 'Holy Land.' Mansurov, wrote the late Professor Alex Carmel, reported that:

> … Western institutions were making a greater impression upon the indigenous population than both the local Ottoman authorities and the administration of the Greek Orthodox Church together, and he perceived correctly that Russia's part in the rivalry was negligible. The local population saw no Russian monasteries, schools, hospitals or hospices, institutions which the other powers had been busy setting up throughout the country.[8]

Mansurov recommended that Russia set up a shipping line for the transport of Russian Orthodox pilgrims, establish hostels in various parts of the

---

7   Antonius, ibid, p. 57.
8   Carmel, A. *Activities of the European Powers in Palestine 1799-1914*, Asia and Africa Studies 19 (1985), (Institute of Middle Eastern Studies, University of Haifa), p. 67.

land to accommodate these pilgrims, and open a consulate in Jerusalem to cater for their needs. His plan was accepted by the Czar and a special 'Palestine Committee' was formed, the Czar himself becoming its patron. Negotiations then began in 1857 for the purchase of a large portion of land known as the Maidan, just outside the walls of Jerusalem.

The Grand Duke Constantine visited Jerusalem in 1859 in order to complete the purchase, as well as to purchase other strategic bits of real estate on the Mount of Olives and near the Church of the Holy Sepulchre, as well as in Jaffa. Russia's imperialist plans for the 'Holy Land' were now commenced in earnest. Building began shortly afterwards on the mammoth Russian Compound on the Maidan – the largest building project in Jerusalem probably since the Second Temple period!

Antonin Kapustin, the Russian representative overseeing this building project, wrote of his motives for being in Jerusalem:

> I have abandoned all ambition in life and followed with all my being one end – that of confirming and strengthening Russia's name in the Holy Land so that we should not be merely guests there, but to a certain extent rightful owners.[9]

The Russian Compound was indeed so enormous that many people, especially the Roman Catholic-French representatives, believed it was being built to become a Russian army barracks in the event of a Russian invasion. The Russians also purchased other large plots of land, including at Abu Kabir near Jaffa. There the Russian Orthodox pilgrims would spend the first night after arriving in the land and prior to their ascent to Jerusalem.

By the mid-1860's it seemed that Russia was in a good position for taking control over 'the land between empires' if and when the Turkish Empire collapsed – and this in spite of the fact that Russia lost the Crimean War!

---

9 Hopwood, D. *The Russian Presence in Syria and Palestine, 1843-1914: Church and Politics in the Near East,* (Oxford, 1969), p. 95.

FRENCH-ROMAN CATHOLIC INITIATIVES

Apart from the activities of the Rothschild family on behalf of the Jewish community, the French were also very active in the period after the Crimean War. Baron de Cauchy established the *Oevre des ecoles d'Orient*, the purpose of which was to further a Roman Catholic educational system throughout the Turkish Empire, and more especially in Palestine. This effort was assisted by utilising the Roman Catholic institutions already in existence. A. L. Tibawai wrote of this activity: '… apart from the usual opening of schools for boys and girls of their own sect, the French missions, often in alliance with the Propaganda Fide[10], formed seminaries for the Melkites, Maronites, Armenian Catholics and Syrian Catholics.'[11]

The most prestigious of all Roman Catholic initiatives after the Crimean War was the building of the Latin Patriarchate in Jerusalem, which was completed in 1864. Another prestigious French project was the reconstruction of the Crusader Church of St. Anna. This ancient church had been a gift to Napoleon III by the Sultan as a thank you for French assistance in the Crimean War.'[12]

There were many other French and Roman Catholic institutions established during this period, both in Jerusalem and indeed throughout the entire province of Syria. By the mid-1860's France was, alongside Russia, laying a solid claim to being the inheritor of the region if and when the Turkish Empire would fall.

BRITISH INTERESTS - THE PALESTINE EXPLORATION FUND

In contrast to French and Russian activities, British initiatives were quite unobtrusive, and mostly revolved around the operations of the consulate, the Protestant Bishopric and the various missionary societies, particularly the LJS and CMS.[13]

---

10 The main missionary seminary of the Roman Catholic Church, based in the Vatican.
11 Tibawai, A.L. *British Interests in Palestine*, (Oxford, 1961), p. 171.
12 Carmel, *European Activities*, ibid, pp. 49-50. The Church of St. Anna is located inside Lion's Gate and adjacent to the traditional site of the Pool of Bethesda and the *Via Dolorosa*.
13 Church Missionary Society, established by evangelical Anglicans in 1799.

Britain's military and geo-political strategists, however, were not idle, viewing each move played by the French and Russians (and even the Prussians) as a concern, and a potential threat to the link to her Eastern Empire.

In 1864 Angela Boudett-Coutts put up the finances for a project to establish a proper water supply in Jerusalem. The Army Ordnance Survey Department was asked to assist, and the War Office complied and released Captain Charles Wilson to head up the project. While assisting with this project Wilson was also to draw up maps of Jerusalem and its environs.

News of this venture stirred two prominent English churchmen, A.P. Stanley and George Groves, to form a society to help promote such worthwhile projects, as well as doing archaeological and scientific studies in the land of Israel. This new society was named the Palestine Exploration Fund (PEF), and was officially founded on 12 May 1865 in the Jerusalem Chamber of Westminster Abbey. Lord Shaftesbury was one of the founding members.

The operations of the PEF over the following years, on both sides of the Jordan River, provided considerable material to the growing number of students in Britain (and elsewhere) who were interested in the land of the Bible. Wilson was followed in turn by other influential men sent by the War Office, including Captain Charles Warren, Lieutenant Claude Condor, and a young officer named Horatio Kitchener.

One of the major contributions of these and other members of the PEF was the production of very accurate maps and descriptions of the land, which assisted later writers such as George Adam Smith when he wrote his important *Historical Geography of the Holy Land*. All these efforts greatly assisted many ordinary British people to become more familiar with the land of the Bible – and also helped British generals in a later war in the region.

THE BLACK SEA

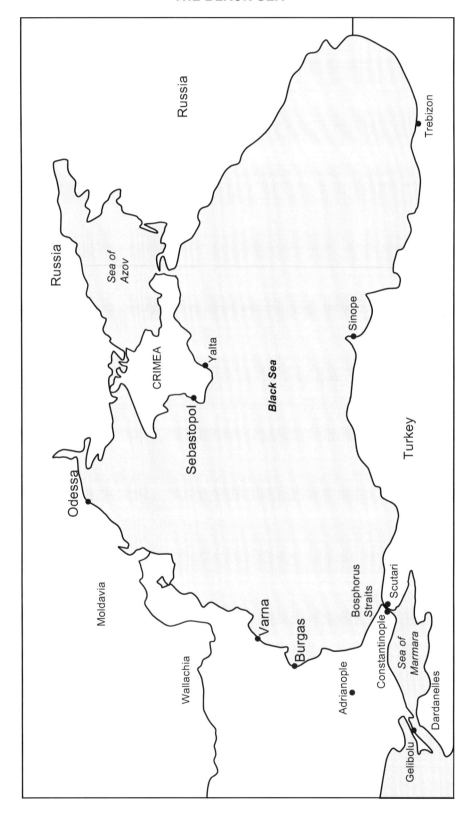

Russia

Russia

Sea of Azov

CRIMEA

Yalta

Sebastopol

Black Sea

Sinope

Trebizon

Turkey

Odessa

Moldavia

Wallachia

Varna

Burgas

Adrianople

Bosphorus Straits

Scutari

Constantinople

Sea of Marmara

Dardanelles

Gelibolu

§

CHAPTER 14

Lebanon crisis and nationalism

CRISIS IN LEBANON AND SYRIA

Although the minority groups benefitted from the lenient policies of Ibrahim Pasha and the Turkish reforms of 1839 and 1856, many Muslims were greatly upset by them, as they resented the minority groups gaining more status. These policies were a direct challenge to the system of *dhimmitude.*

During this same period the French continued to strengthen their influence in the Lebanon region, primarily through supporting the Maronite Christians. The British meanwhile were enhancing their position in the Lebanon region by supporting the Druze.

Tensions overflowed in the Mount Lebanon region of Syria in 1860. What began as a minor local dispute ended up becoming a major *pogrom* as Druze[1] and Muslims and Druze violently attacked the Maronite Christian community in the Lebanon region of Syria for three days. Many thousands of people, mostly Maronite Christians, were killed. The violence quickly spread and in Damascus Muslim mobs destroyed the Christian quarter and

---

1   A minority group encompassing numerous streams of belief, but are primarily an off-shoot of Ismailism, which itself is a part of Shia Islam. The Druze, like the Jewish people, also at times received a degree of protection from the British.

also killed thousands of people, including both the American and Dutch consuls.

France, the traditional protector of all Catholics in the Turkish Empire, called for an international Convention. The French call resulted in an international force, mostly French, which landed at Beirut on 16 August 1860. Napoleon III received a six month mandate to restore peace and order.

George Antonius wrote that: 'The upheaval of 1860, accompanied as it was by a savage massacre of Christians in Damascus and the Lebanon, had aroused the passion of religious hatred to a murderous pitch.'[2]

When Napoleon received a four month extension to restore peace in Syria, Britain became suspicious of French intentions. Lord John Russell, the Foreign Secretary, stated: 'We do not want to create a new Papal state in the East, and to give France a pretext for indefinite occupation.'[3] Britain then pressured the Turkish Government to establish a semi-autonomous Christian region within Syria, henceforth known as Lebanon, to be governed by a Christian.

Once this entity had been established the French forces departed in 1861. They left behind a safer and more stable environment for Christians, as well as an enhanced French reputation in the region, especially among the minority groups.

CHALLENGES FOR THE SULTAN

In that same year Sultan Abdulmecid died and was succeeded by Abdul Aziz. During his reign the Turkish Empire continued to spiral downwards with endemic corruption and dishonesty among the provincial administrators. Few Turks who governed and administered in the outer regions of the Empire held any genuine interest in the welfare of the people there, an attitude which in turn created an environment of distrust against the governing Turks.

---

2   Antonius, G. *The Arab Awakening*, (Beirut, 1936), p. 49.
3   Tuchman, ibid, p. 257.

The Turkish leaders in Constantinople realized that in order to maintain a hold upon their Empire they needed to appease the European Powers. This meant in turn being willing to grant more tolerance to the non-Muslim minorities, which then in turn upset many of the devout Muslims of the Empire.

RISE OF ARAB NATIONALISM

The events of 1860 forced many Christians in the East to leave the region, with many emigrating to the Americas, Australia, New Zealand and elsewhere. For most of these the massacres were an indication that it was impossible to live under Islamic control as a *dhimmi*.

Many of those who remained eagerly sought for ways in which they could live harmoniously with the numerically more Muslim (and Druze) communities. Those who remained realized that one of the most effective ways of combatting similar massacres was through educating the Muslim population about equality.

Some of these Christian Arabs realized that one day the Turkish Empire was bound to collapse, and the question they asked themselves was: 'What kind of a regime would we like to replace the Turkish regime?' If it was another Islamic regime, then their status as *dhimmis* would remain the same. But, if there could be a regime whereby both Christian and Muslim could be equal, under the same unifying banner, then there would be hope. That unifying banner would be the Arabic culture and language. Consequently the seeds were sown by Christian Arabs for the beginnings of the Arab nationalist movement.[4]

One of the most influential of these Arab nationalists was Butrus Bustiani. In 1860 Bustiani began a newspaper, the *Clarion of Syria* which was, according to Antonius, 'the first political journal ever published in the country, and was mainly devoted to the preaching of concord between the different creeds and of union in the pursuit of knowledge. For knowledge, he argued week after week in the earnest columns of his paper, leads to en-

---

4   Antonius, ibid and Hourani, A. *Syria and Lebanon*, (Oxford, 1956). See also the writings of Dr. Daphne Tschimchony of the Haifa University.

lightenment; and enlightenment, to the death of fanaticism and the birth of ideals held in common. A platitude, perhaps, but one that Syria had not heard before, and which contained the germ of the national idea.'[5]

Many of these Christian Arabs had been educated in the schools operated by western missionary societies, particularly those of the American Board of Commissioners. These schools taught secular subjects, one of which was that of nationalism as it was then being spread throughout Europe.

Perhaps the most influential conduit of this movement was the opening of the Syrian Protestant College in Beirut in 1866 – which taught in Arabic. This, and other Protestant activities in general, had provoked the various Catholic orders to also emulate their educational activities.

Although initially being the initiative of the Christian Arabs, Arab nationalism was later also adopted by Muslim Arabs as well.

DEVELOPMENT OF JEWISH NATIONALISM

One of the initial stimulants for the growth of Jewish nationalism was also a persecution: the Damascus 'Blood Libel' of 1840. This event provoked many Jewish people to recognize how vulnerable they were, surrounded by host communities which kept them in perpetual second class status, whether it was in Europe or in the East. Seldom could they adequately defend themselves.

The Napoleonic period had opened up the possibilities for small national groups being emancipated, as happened to the Jewish people when Napoleon summoned the Great Sanhedrin in 1807. Such nationalist hopes, though, were very much suppressed with the Congress of Vienna of 1815, headed up by Count Metternich, which restored the old order of the pre-Revolution/Napoleonic period.[6]

Those nationalist hopes, though, continued to lurk under the surface. They briefly came to the fore in 1830, but more so with the revolutions which swept Europe in 1848. It was very much as a result of the 1848 Revolutions that fires of nationalism began all over Europe, especially in Italy and

---

5 Antonius, ibid, pp. 49-50.
6 Jewish hopes of full emancipation were further dashed with the *Hep, Hep* riots in Germany in 1819.

many of the German states. Numerous Jewish people took note of this new movement.

Rabbi Yehuda Levi was one of the first to advocate that the Jewish people needed to return to their ancestral homeland. Other Jewish writers followed. One of these was Rabbi Zvi Kalischer from Prussia. Although Kalischer held a view that the redemption of Israel would begin with the Jewish people becoming active in returning to the land (to be followed by their ultimate redemption) since the late 1830's, it was not until about 1862 that he began to openly expound his viewpoint.

A small organization was founded in Frankfurt named the *Colonisation-Verein fur Paleastina* ('Society for the Colonisation of Palestine') to which both he and Rabbi Alkalai belonged.[7] This small work stimulated Kalischer into writing *Drishat Zion* ('Seeking Zion') in 1862, seemingly the first Jewish work on the subject of Jewish agricultural settlements in *Eretz Yisrael*.[8] Kalischer later formed the 'Central Committee for Settlement of the land of Israel', in Berlin, and encouraged the French Jewish philanthropic organisation, *Alliance Israelite Universalle* to undertake agricultural work in *Eretz Yisrael*.[9] The *Alliance* later established the *Mikve Israel* Agricultural College between Jaffa and Ramle, in 1870.[10]

Another Jewish man who wrote on the subject of Jewish nationalism at this time was Moses Hess. Hess, like many Jewish intellectuals, had turned away from Orthodox Judaism and was endeavouring to make his way in 'secular' German society. He was quite radical in his political views, even espousing a new concept known as socialism, and having a degree of influence upon Karl Marx. Hess, though, was forced to flee Germany during the 1848 Revolution, and settled in Paris, where he became more pragmatic in his political views.

It was here that he began to contemplate the place of the Jewish people in Europe, and came to the opinion 'that the Jews will always be a homeless

---

7 www.zionism-israel.com/bio/kalischer.

8 Colonel George Gawler had written a similar work in 1845.

9 www.zionism-israel.com/bio/kalischer. The *Alliance Israelite Universalle* was founded in 1860 by Adolphe Cremieux.

10 The first director was Karl (Charles) Netter.

people, never fully accepted by others, until they have their own country.'[11] Hess published his views in *Rom und Jerusalem* ('Rome and Jerusalem') in 1862.

Although his work had little immediate impact, within several decades, Hess's work would make an important impact upon two very significant Jewish nationalists: Leon Pinsker and Theodor Herzl.

11   *Encyclopaedia Britannica*, 1975, Vol. V, p. 17.

§

The Suez Canal

FERDINAND DE LESSEPS' VISION

A French diplomat named Ferdinand de Lesseps, who had grown up in Egypt and had been acquainted with Mohammad Said, the son of Mehmet Ali, heard in 1854 while living in France that Mohammad Said had just become the Viceroy (or Khedive) of Egypt.

De Lesseps then adopted Napoleon's vision of constructing a canal across the Isthmus of Suez, and supported by some French businessmen, went to Egypt and presented the plan to Said Pasha. Said Pasha was supportive and granted De Lesseps a concession on 30 November 1854 to form a company - the *Compagnie Universelle du Canal Maritime de Suez* (Suez Canal Company).

The French Consul-General was also very supportive of the proposal, which attracted the suspicion of the British. Palmerston wrote to Ambassador de Redcliffe in Constantinople that:

If ... the canal is meant to be one for seagoing ships, the expense would be enormous and the undertaking would never pay. But it would be injurious to England because, in any quarrel between England and

France, France being so much nearer to the Canal, would have much the start of us in sending ships and troops to the Indian seas.[1]

Turkey asked Said Pasha to drop the scheme, as they believed it would potentially grant Egypt further autonomy. Said Pasha in turn informed the Sultan's government of his determination to complete the project, stating it would benefit not only France, but also Britain, Turkey, Egypt, and the world at large.

Said Pasha's argument succeeded in changing the mood in Constantinople more in favour of the project. De Lesseps was then able to return to France in June 1855 in order to seek shareholders to join his Suez Canal Company. These positive moves increased Palmerston's concern, and he wrote again to De Redcliffe:

> It is quite clear that the scheme is founded on ulterior motives hostile to British views and interests and the secret intention no doubt is to lay a foundation for a future severance of Egypt from Turkey and for placing it under French protection. A deep and wide canal interposed between Egypt and Syria studded with fortifications could be a military defensive line which, with the desert in front of it, would render the task of a Turkish army very difficult.[2]

This potential conflict of interests with France was complicated by the fact that Britain and France were fighting together in the Crimea.

PROGRESS WITH THE SUEZ CANAL COMPANY

Despite numerous obstacles De Lesseps managed to foster support in France and Europe for the Suez Canal Company. Some in

---

1 Palmerston to De Redcliffe, FO 78/1156 (1854-1855), National Archives, cited in Lord Kinross, *Between the Seas*, (New York, 1969), p. 79.
2 Palmerston to De Redcliffe, FO 78/1156 (1854-1855), National Archives, cited in Kinross, ibid, p. 79.

Britain then finally began to see the importance of the scheme, mainly as a result of the Indian Mutiny of 1857.[3]

Although the British now realised the importance of having a faster route to India, many still opposed the construction of the Canal. One Parliamentarian, Benjamin Disraeli, saw the proposed Canal as a French effort to control the Eastern Mediterranean. Ironically, the official French position at this stage was somewhat ambivalent.

In November 1858 the subscription list for the Suez Canal Company was finally opened to the public. More than half of the 400,000 shares were purchased by French investors. Said Pasha was persuaded by De Lesseps to purchase the remainder of the shares, thereby allowing De Lesseps to finally register his Company.

Despite the lack of official Turkish recognition, De Lesseps enlisted Egyptian workers, and on 25 April 1859, work on the construction of the Suez Canal began at the point where the Red Sea would later enter the Mediterranean Sea.

Pressure from 21,000 French investors increased upon the French Government to make an official policy. French prestige, De Lesseps claimed, would be damaged in the East if British pressure forced the venture to fail. Turkey, in part due to British pressure, continued its official opposition, lest, as Lord Kinross stated, 'the Isthmus might make Egypt the theatre of conflict in any future European War.'[4]

In October 1859 the *Porte* stated that work on the Canal must stop. De Lesseps then met with Emperor Napoleon III and convinced him that the enterprise was sound, and for the benefit of France. Napoleon then announced his support for the project.

THE SUEZ CANAL OPENS

A new port, Port Said, emerged on the Mediterranean coast, while the towns of Kantara and Ismailia took shape along the course of the Canal. At the

---

3   This mutiny began as a local disagreement between Indian Sepoy troops and their officers, but spread to other parts of India. After finally suppressing the revolt the British Government curtailed the authority of the East India Company, and placed more of the administration of India under direct rule from Britain.

4   Kinross, ibid, p. 131.

southern end the old town of Suez began to take on new life. All these new towns had a distinct French flavour.

Said Pasha died in 1863, and the new leader or Khedive of Egypt was Ismail Pasha. Ismail was immediately confronted with the huge debt he inherited due to Said Pasha's purchase of the Company shares. Ismail decided to pay as much as he could of this outstanding amount from the Egyptian Treasury, thereby committing the Government financially as well as politically to the project.

Turkey finally gave conditional agreement to the construction of the Canal in April 1863. The conditions they laid down included: the Egyptians could no longer use forced labour; the Suez Canal Company had to surrender the lands ceded to her by the Egyptian Government; there needed to be international guarantees of the Canal's neutrality, similar to the Straits Convention.[5]

These conditions presented many difficulties to De Lesseps and Ismail. They turned to the French Government and Emperor for guidance. Emperor Napoleon, in 1864, again officially endorsed the project. Official British opposition, though, continued through Palmerston's successor, Lord Russell. He desired that no opportunity would be given for French colonists to settle on the lands owned by the Suez Canal Company.

Ultimately by 1866 most of the Turkish and British apprehensions were sufficiently satisfied and on 19 March 1866 the Sultan finally signed a *firman* authorizing the construction of the Suez Canal.

As the Suez Canal and the towns of Port Said, Kantara, Ismailia and Suez began to take shape the status of France in the region grew – while that of Britain decreased. Yet the long delays had created innumerable financial burdens for De Lesseps and the Suez Canal Company – debts which would seriously compromise Egypt itself.

In March 1869 the Prince of Wales visited the almost completed Suez Canal, and lamented that due to Palmerston's lack of foresight, this great work which was vital for Britain's link to India, had been achieved by the French. Some years later while passing through the completed Canal en-

5 Kinross, ibid, pp. 169-70.

route to India, he said to Lord Granville: 'The Suez Canal is certainly an outstanding work, and it is an everlasting pity that it was not made by an English company and kept in our hands, because, as it is the highway to India, we should be obliged to take it – and by force of arms if necessary.'[6]

The Suez Canal was officially opened in style on 17 November 1869. Numerous dignitaries came from all over the world for the opening, including Napoleon's wife, Empress Eugenie. Another guest was Crown Prince Wilhelm of Prussia. After the event the Prussian Prince visited Jerusalem, where he was gifted by the Sultan some property formerly belonging to the Templar Knights - adjacent to the Church of the Holy Sepulchre.

Interestingly, just a few years prior to this visit, a group of German settlers, named the Templers, came to Palestine and established agricultural and urban colonies in the Galilee (especially in Haifa) and Judea, especially Jaffa, Sarona and Jerusalem.[7]

FRANCO-PRUSSIAN WAR AND RISE OF GERMANY

Shortly after the Empress Eugenie returned to France war broke out with Prussia. King William of Prussia and Prime Minister Otto von Bismark had over the previous years united many of the German provinces. They felt that a war against France would unite the nation. Prussian and other German troops invaded France in 1869.

By 1870 the Prussian-led army had subdued imperial France, forced Emperor Napoleon and his wife into exile, and brought down the Second Empire. As one empire fell another rose. At the Palace of Versailles near Paris, the German Empire was proclaimed in 1871.

Defeat at the hands of Germany in the Franco-Prussian War ruined French prestige, particularly in the East. Conversely, as the prestige of France fell, that of Germany rose. A new imperial light had appeared, which was to radically alter and challenge the geo-political dynamics in Europe - and ultimately in the East as well.

---

6   Lee, S. *King Edward VII*, (London, 1925), cited in Kinross, ibid, pp. 233-4.
7   The Templer Society (*Tempelgesellschaft*) was a group from within the Lutheran Church who had an emphasis upon 'millennialism'. They were ousted from the Lutheran Church in 1858, and many then moved to Palestine.

BRITAIN PURCHASES THE SUEZ CANAL

The Turkish Government reprimanded Ismail Pasha for his apparent move towards independence, and for Egypt having taken large loans at a high interest rate from overseas in order to complete the Suez Canal. This could only jeopardize the financial stability of Egypt, making it increasingly reliant upon overseas investment.

Despite heavy usage of the Canal, the delays in construction and lower than expected profits led to De Lesseps and the Suez Canal Company entering into considerable debt. The shareholders were losing patience – they wanted some return for their investment.

The financial situation of the Egyptian Government continued to deteriorate and by 1875 had become critical, forcing Ismail to contemplate the sale or mortgage of the Khedive's shares.

The Suez Canal was now the major link between Britain and her Eastern Empire, and the vacuum created by France's defeat in the Franco-Prussian War allowed Britain to take more of an active role in the affairs of Egypt. So when Prime Minister Benjamin Disraeli became aware of the Egyptian financial dilemma he discussed the idea of Britain purchasing the majority shares of the Company with the Cabinet, which approved his idea.

De Lesseps meanwhile was encouraging the French Government to assist in purchasing the shares. France was reluctant, as Germany was threatening a renewal of the war, and so officially opted out of the possibility.

Disraeli then raised a loan of four million pounds from Lord Rothschild, and outbid contesting French consortiums. By November 1875 Britain became the major shareholder of the Suez Canal Company.

Until this point Britain had been more concerned with propping up the weakening Turkish Empire in order to ensure that no rival European power, especially France and Russia, would gain any control over the Eastern Mediterranean. Now Britain had become a major stakeholder in the region.

CHAPTER 16

§

Autocracy and
nationalist conflicts

ABDUL HAMID AND A NEW CONSTITUTION

The establishment of the Suez Canal, the increasing involvement of France and Britain in the East, and the apparent independence of Egypt from Turkey, were signs to the non-Turkish people that there was now an opportunity of casting off Turkish control.

In 1875 a revolt broke out in the Bulgarian region of the Turkish Empire. This revolt was brutally suppressed by the Turkish military. Russia, always seeking an excuse to fight Turkey, now saw an opportunity of supporting the Bulgarian struggle and of gaining Turkish territory in the process.

By 1876 many Turkish leaders knew that a change in how their Empire was administered was desperately needed. The viziers made a dramatic move on 30 May 1876 by deposing Sultan Abdul Aziz. He was ultimately replaced by Abdul Hamid.

Abdul Hamid appointed a liberal reformer named Midhat Pasha as the Grand Vizier (Prime Minister). Midhat announced a new constitution on 23 December 1876 – at the very time when representatives of the European

Powers were in Constantinople 'to draw up proposals for the better government of his empire.'[1]

In the new Turkish Constitution Midhat saw that two components were
necessary in order for the Turkish Empire to survive and prosper: a cur-
tailment of the autocratic powers of the Sultan, and the need for equality
between the numerous different groups and sects. No move to constitutional government could occur until these two radical reforms had been *truly*
instituted.[2]

However, as good as these principles sounded, they were problematic.
By that time many subject peoples, especially in European Turkey, had become so heavily influenced by nationalism that they wanted to completely
throw off the Turkish imperial yoke.

Sultan Abdul Hamid was not genuine about any form of constitutional
government, and by March 1877 he dismissed his reform-minded Grand
Vizier. Then the Russians, in support of Bulgaria, declared war on Turkey -
which provided Abdul Hamid with a pretext to suspend the implementation
of the Constitution.

RUSSO-TURKISH WAR 1877

The Russo-Turkish War concerned many Britons. It seemed like half the
people were anti-Russian – they realized that if Russia won they would take
control of Constantinople and the strategic waterways connecting the Black
Sea with the Mediterranean.

Fear of Russian expansion, though, was counterbalanced by abhorrence
at Turkish brutality against the Bulgar people. In a debate in the House of
Commons on 7 May 1877 William Gladstone even called for the ousting of
barbaric Turkey from European soil.[3]

Britain's official stance was confirmed once it became aware that the
Russian Fleet was approaching Constantinople. Disraeli sent a British
Fleet through the Dardanelles and Bosphorus. He also had reinforcements

---

1   Antonius, ibid, p. 63.

2   The *Tanzimat* in theory provided more equality for non-Muslims, but this was not always worked out in reality.

3   Barnett Smith, G. *The Life of the Right Honourable William Ewart Gladstone*, (London, 1880?), pp. 526-8.

brought from India – via the Suez Canal – to Malta. This show of force halted the Russian advance.

Before Russia halted her advance, though, she gained considerable concessions from the Turks, in the 'Treaty of San Stefano'. This Treaty angered the European Powers, as it gave Russia considerable influence in the region. Part of this added influence was a result of a direct request from the Armenian leadership. They asked, that if Russian forces were to leave the region of eastern Anatolia, that there would be reforms guaranteeing their safety and protection, especially from marauding Kurds and Circassians. If the Russians did have to leave this region, they wanted Russian soldiers to remain until such reforms had taken place.[4]

This request was inserted into the 'Treaty of San Stefano.' 'Russia' wrote Akcam, 'thus became a permanent supervisor and guarantor. But' he continued, 'Great Britain could not accept Russia's attainment of so much "sovereignty" over the Ottoman Empire …'[5] A second peace conference was accordingly called for to take place in Berlin.

Prior to the Berlin Conference, Disraeli met the Turks in secret. Foreign Secretary Salisbury had previously instructed Ambassador Layard in Constantinople, that it was vital for Britain to ensure that Turkey did not come under Russian control, and that it was essential that Turkey and Britain enter into an alliance - in order to keep Russia away from Britain's link to India. 'We shall have to choose' Salisbury stated to his ambassador, 'between allowing Russia to dominate over Syria and Mesopotamia or taking the country for ourselves, and either alternative is formidable.'[6]

Britain was aware of the vulnerability of the region and the potential of Russia gaining a pre-eminent position there. If Russia controlled Constantinople and the Bosphorus, the Russian Fleet could easily move through the Dardanelles, into the Eastern Mediterranean – and towards the Suez Canal.

---

4   Akcam, ibid, p. 38.
5   Akcam, ibid, p. 38.
6   Salisbury to Layard, 10 May 1878, cited in Temperley, H. *Near East: Disraeli and Cyprus*, English Historical Review, XLVI, (April, 1931) and Tuchman, ibid, p. 263.

Britain and Turkey concluded a formal alliance, in which Britain would support Turkey if Russia again moved against her. In exchange Turkey gave security rights over Cyprus to Britain. This so-called 'Cyprus Convention' was signed on 4 June 1878.

In the subsequent 'Treaty of Berlin' in 1878 Russia was stripped of some of the territories it had gained from the Turks, including eastern Anatolia. The Armenians were concerned that the concessions they gained at San Stefano would be lost, and communicated that 'they did not desire independence from Turkey but only an Armenian governor and a measure of autonomy in those areas where Armenians formed a majority.'[7]

The sixty-first article of the 'Treaty of Berlin' provided some guarantees of safety and reform for the Armenians, but fell far short of their desire for a degree of autonomy (similar to that of Lebanon).[8]

The concern of the European Powers in the Armenians was associated also, to a degree, to geo-political interests. But such an interest also encouraged some Armenian nationalists to contemplate establishing their own independent Armenian nation.

When the 'Treaty of Berlin' was signed Disraeli then informed the delegates of Britain's alliance with Turkey. The other nations then demanded their share of the spoils for offering their support of Turkey: France demanded Tunisia while Italy demanded Albania and Tripoli (Libya).

ABDUL HAMID'S DESPOTIC RULE

Following the revocation of the Constitution and the end of the Russo-Turkish War, Abdul Hamid ruled as an autocratic despot. Yet he could see his empire slowly slipping away. One way in which he endeavoured to strengthen his empire was by restoring 'the caliphate to its proper place.'[9] By doing this he also envisioned that the millions of Muslims under British, French and Russian rule would begin to revere him as the leader of Muslims throughout the world.

---

7 Akcam, ibid, p. 38.
8 Akcam, ibid, p. 39. The promise of reform, though, never eventuated, which in turn exasperated the Armenians.
9 Antonius, ibid, p. 69.

Abdul Hamid was quite an astute strategist, and understood that while much of his European empire was in turmoil and revolt, he could still shore up his Arab dominions – Syria, Mesopotamia and the Arabian Peninsula. He made various efforts to stamp out any form of Arab national consciousness, and had 'spies' throughout the region. Occasionally he would bring influential people from the provinces to live in Constantinople, where they could be observed and silenced.

Midhat Pasha, conversely, was banished to Syria where he became the Governor-General. While he was there a small secret society was busy laying the foundations for the Arab nationalist movement. Five young Christian Arabs, former students of the Syrian Protestant College, had founded a secret society in 1875 in Beirut.

This secret society grew and included several Muslims and Druze. This growth is explained by Antonius: 'Freemasonry on the European pattern had just found its way into Syria, and the promoters of the secret society were able, through one of their number to interest the recently-founded Lodge of its activities.'[10]

These men were dedicated to exposing the 'evils of Turkish rule, and exhorted the Arab population to rise in rebellion and overthrow it.'[11] After some time they began to expose their views by posting up placards and posters in Beirut, Damascus, Tripoli and Sidon. One such placard (the content of which was recorded by the British Consul-General in Beirut) was very damning of the Turkish regime which it accused of stifling 'the Arab tongue' and of 'transgressing the laws of Islam' and which contained four points in a programme:

1. The grant of independence to Syria in union with the Lebanon;
2. The recognition of Arabic as an official language in the country;
3. The removal of the censorship and other restrictions on the freedom of expression and the diffusion of knowledge;

---

10 Antonius, ibid, p. 79.
11 Antonius, ibid, p. 80.

4. The employment of locally-recruited units on local military service only.[12]

These points may have stirred the nationalist emotions of some, but the general population, educated along lines of affinity to their religious or tribal group, basically would not have been able to grasp this European concept of a unified nation state.

The Turkish authorities became so perturbed by these activities that they intensified the search for the members. The society then wound up its activities.[13] Although disbanded, that infant society laid foundations for future developments.

BRITISH RESTORATIONISM

The Russo-Turkish War created considerable interest throughout Europe, stimulating secular, Christian and Jewish writers and intellectuals to consider if indeed the time for the collapse of the Turkish Empire was impending – and that perhaps the time for the restoration of Israel had arrived.

In Britain a female novelist named Mary Anne Evans, who used the pen name George Eliot, wrote a novel named *Daniel Deronda*, which highlighted the concept of the Jewish return to Palestine. Other writers included George Cazalet and Laurence Oliphant, a former Member of Parliament and a friend of the Prince of Wales.

Oliphant had been particularly influenced by the war, and recognized that a partial solution to Turkey's economic weakness was to encourage Jewish immigration. With this view in mind, and with letters of recommendation from Lord Beaconsfield (Disraeli) and others, he travelled to Palestine in 1879 to 'spy out the land.'

As a result of his extensive journey through the land of Israel he concluded that the best possibility would be to establish Jewish agricultural colonies in Gilead, just east of the Jordan River. Oliphant then wrote up a plan and proceeded to Constantinople where it was agreed to in principle by the

12   British Consul General to Foreign Ministry, FO 195/1369, cited in Antonius, ibid, pp. 83-4.
13   Antonius, ibid, pp. 80-81.

viziers – but rejected by Sultan Abdul Hamid - 'for fear that it was a British intrigue.'[14]

Although this proposal was rejected by the Turkish Sultan, it nevertheless inspired many others with the concept of improving the state of Turkey in Asia by establishing Jewish agricultural colonies. Oliphant himself then settled in Haifa and continued with his vision from there, and wrote *Land of Gilead* in 1880.

DEVELOPMENT OF JEWISH NATIONALISM

One group of Jewish nationalists in Eastern Europe named the *Hibbat Zion* ('Love of Zion' – and whose members were known as *Chovevei Zion* - 'Lovers of Zion') was aware of and encouraged by Oliphant's endeavours. The *Chovevei Zion* were small clubs of nationalist Jews spread throughout the region, who met to discuss the issue of Jewish nationhood. Collectively this movement began working towards the establishment of a Jewish national entity in *Eretz Yisrael*.

The founder and leader of the *Hibbat Zion* was a Russian Jew named Leon Pinsker. Pinsker had been moved to action by a terrible *pogrom* in Odessa in 1871, and recognized that there really was no future for the impoverished and disenfranchised Jewish people in Europe. They needed to find their true emancipation – in the land of their forefathers. He found many willing adherents, and the *Hibbat Zion* movement developed from 1878. Pinsker's beliefs were later written in a small booklet entitled *Auto-emancipation*.[15]

Another Jewish writer of the time was Eliezar Perlman (later Eliezar Ben Yehuda), a writer for the Hebrew newspaper *Ha-Shahar* ('The Dawn') based in Vienna. Perlman believed that the Jewish people had all the attributes for nationhood – a common history, language (Hebrew) and culture – but they lacked the essential ingredient for nationhood: a national home.[16]

---

14 Oliphant, Laurence, Jewish Virtual Library, www.jewishvirtuallibrary.org
15 *Auto-emancipation* was originally written in German, and first published in 1882.
16 Sacher, H. *A History of Israel*, (New York, 1976), p. 263.

Ben Yehuda left for *Eretz Yisrael* in 1881, where he began a project of immense importance – the revival of the ancient language of Hebrew and its transformation into a language for everyday usage.

THE EGYPTIAN CRISIS

Egypt's financial crisis, precipitated by the extravagances of Said Pasha and Ismail Pasha, forced her to seek international advice. Britain and France complied by sending economic advisors, but when their economic advice was not adhered to, the British and French appealed to Turkey to intervene in the affairs of Egypt. The Turks complied by deposing Ismail in 1879.

The new Khedive, Tewfik Pasha, then adopted various policies aimed at stemming Egypt's slide into bankruptcy. One such decision was the reduction of the Egyptian Army, and of hindering those of peasant stock from becoming officers. This move was resented by numerous officers, and resulted in an insurrection led by Colonel Ahmed Arabi.

The proposed law was rejected, but the incident led to the formation of the Egyptian nationalist movement. Arabi then came on to the Egyptian cabinet. He then led a movement opposing the increase in foreign (especially British and French) involvement in Egypt, which culminated in a *coup d'etat* in September 1881. The nationalists adopted the slogan: 'Egypt for the Egyptians.'

Not only was Turkey disturbed by these events, but so too were Britain and France, lest this military dictatorship lead to further far-reaching consequences. They called for Tewfik Pasha to reduce the power of Colonel Arabi. Such a move further incensed the nationalist Egyptians, which caused the British and French concern for the welfare of their nationals living in the region, as well as the safety and security of the Suez Canal.

British and French warships were dispatched to the Eastern Mediterranean and towards Alexandria. Arabi retaliated by massacring fifty foreign nationals on 13 June 1882, and fortified Alexandria. British warships then fired upon these fortifications and landed troops, ostensibly to assist the Khedive.

The French Government, due mostly to George Clemenceau's influence, withdrew. Permission was then granted by Tewfik for British ships to sail along the Suez Canal, despite protests concerning its neutrality, and beginning on 19 August 1882 troops were then off-loaded at Port Said, Suez and other positions. Reinforcements from India arrived shortly later at Suez.

Colonel Arabi rallied his troops and several days later on 13 September 1882 fought a pitched battle against the combined British forces at Tel el-Kebir – and was defeated.

British troops occupied Cairo shortly afterwards. Arabi and his co-conspirators were arrested, and Egypt effectively was now under British control.[17] Although these troops were in Egypt to protect the legitimate ruler, Tewfik Pasha, Britain was primarily interested in protecting her strategic interests – the security of the Suez Canal and the link to her Eastern Empire of India, Australia, New Zealand, Ceylon (Sri Lanka), Malaya (Singapore) and elsewhere.

The occupation of Egypt (the 'southern empire') by Britain was a move of far-reaching geo-political significance. Britain's link to her Eastern Empire was now secure.

In 1882 the 'northern empire', Turkey, was allied to Britain. If, however, there ever came a time when that alliance was overturned and there was conflict between the 'northern and southern empires', then the security of the Suez Canal would once again be in jeopardy.

---

17 Arabi was not executed but deported to Ceylon (Sri Lanka).

THE SUEZ CANAL

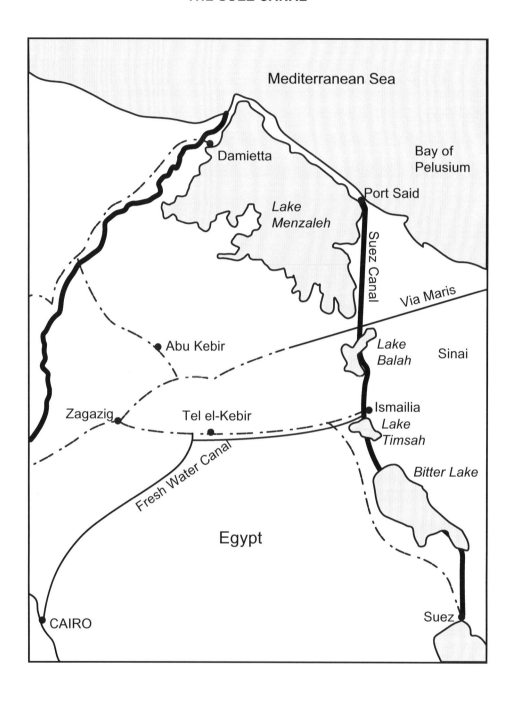

CHAPTER 17

§

Germany, Turkey and Zionism

TURKEY'S CONCERN BECOMES GERMANY'S GAIN

Britain's occupation of Egypt was another indicator to Abdul Hamid that he needed to make drastic changes in order to retain sovereignty over his vast empire. His first move was the modernisation of his army. He turned to Germany, which had no historical ambitions upon his empire, and in 1883 a military delegation headed up by Colonel von der Goltz arrived in Constantinople. The invitation may have come from Turkey but it fitted nicely into Germany's desire to expand in the East.[1]

One of Colonel von der Goltz's greatest achievements was through education. George Antonius stated: 'It was thanks to him that a system of military colleges came into being, whose standard was so far above the general educational level that it drew – from among the Arabs as well as Turks – many of the best brains of the coming generation. Of the men who were afterwards to play a part in the revolution which overthrew 'Abdul-Hamid's tyranny, and in the Arab Revolt a few years later, the graduates of those military colleges were the most prominent.'[2]

---

1   Also known as *Drang nach Osten.*
2   Antonius, ibid, p. 76. One of those men was Mustapha Kemal, who studied in the military school in Turkish controlled Salonika.

Accompanying the military mission were agents whose reports back to Bismarck provided details of 'conditions and prospects in Turkey.'[3] In following years, bankers and other commercial enterprises entered into Turkey. The most significant of these enterprises was the building of railways throughout Anatolia, particularly the line from Haidar Pasha (on the Asian side of Constantinople) to Konya. Germany had now arrived as a serious imperial contender in Turkey, not through the aggrandisement of territory, but through economic penetration.

THE RUSSIAN JEWS ARE COMING

The Russian Government was observing the outbreak of nationalist fervour throughout Europe and within the Turkish Empire, as ethnic and national groups were struggling for their historic national rights.

During this period of unsettledness Czarist Russia wanted to ensure that no such uprisings would occur within her vast territory. Then Czar Alexander II was assassinated on 1 March 1881. The authorities did not want this to be an opportunity for any civil or nationalist unrest and sought a scapegoat.

One of those implicated in the assassination of the Czar was Jewish, so the Russian authorities implicated the entire Jewish 'nation'. A number of government-inspired *pogroms* (murderous riots) then erupted throughout the *Pale* region (where most of the Jewish people were confined to live). Hundreds of thousands of Jewish people were affected.

The situation culminated with the publication in 1882 of harsh anti-Jewish laws. These laws made it difficult for the Jewish people to live according to their ancestral laws within Russia. There were now several choices for them: continue to live under the existing cruel regime, join one of the numerous movements which strove to change the existing Czarist system, or leave Russia. Hundreds of thousands of Jewish people decided to uproot and leave their homes.

---

3   Antonius, ibid, p. 76.

Many of these went to Britain, Canada, South America, South Africa, Australia and New Zealand. The majority, however, went to the United States of America, while a few thousand chose to go to their ancestral homeland – *Eretz Yisrael*.

While the vast majority of these would-be immigrants were refugees, there were also some *Chovevei Zion*. These were named the *Bilu*, an acronym for 'House of Jacob let us go up.' Their movement to *Eretz Yisrael* was the beginning of a new phenomenon – Jewish people going there, not to study the *Torah* and die, but to live and to establish a Jewish national entity. The non-religious character of this new movement, though, placed considerable strain upon the resources of the mostly Orthodox and impoverished Jewish community resident there.

Life from the outset was difficult for these new arrivals as there was no economic infrastructure for them, and the Turkish authorities were unwilling to assist them. Although several Jewish agricultural villages had been established, such as Motza in 1869 and Petach Tikva (Meleubis) in 1878, most of the existing Jewish community (known as the old *yishuv*) lived in Jerusalem, Hebron, Tiberias and Safed, and could not offer the new immigrants much help.

The *Bilu*, and later other refugees, endeavoured to establish agricultural colonies, but they mostly failed, due to Turkish bureaucracy, lack of finances, lack of local experience, and local Arab opposition. Previous approaches to wealthy Jewish philanthropists such as Baron Edmond Rothschild and Baron Hirsch, had failed. If help did not come then these would-be colonists would need to surrender their ambitions and leave the land of their forefathers.

Help finally came, primarily through Baron Rothschild, who financially undergirded the colonies. Rothschild, though, wanted to see financial returns for his investments in these colonies. This meant that to a large degree these pioneers surrendered some of their nationalist idealism in order to meet the Baron's economic expectations.

Ephraim Aaronsohn came with his family from Rumania and helped found a new colony, Zichron Yaacov, on the Carmel Range.[4] Some years later, his son Aaron was sponsored by Baron Rothschild to study agriculture in France.[5]

Another early arrival was Eliazar Margolin and his family, who settled at Rehoboth (Khirbat Deiran) in 1892 where his father purchased a small bit of land. Eliazar became the main worker on this farm, but also managed to become a good horseman, marksman and guide, and became part of the local Jewish self-defence group at Rehoboth.

In that same year the Ottoman authorities placed restrictions on land sales to Jewish people to hinder or stop their immigration.[6]

ABDUL HAMID MASSACRES THE ARMENIANS

These land sale restrictions were part of a policy of the Porte. Sultan Abdul Hamid had for several years noticed how independent nations such as Greece, Serbia, Bulgaria and Rumania had been formed from his empire. Most of these new nations had emerged through the direct intervention of the great powers, especially Britain, France and Russia. In addition, following the recent conflict, Russia had gained further territory in far eastern Turkey.

Abdul Hamid was now becoming increasingly suspicious about the national aspirations of any minority group within his empire. A potentially dangerous threat were the Armenians, who comprised some 10% of the population of Turkey proper, and who mostly lived in six provinces in eastern Anatolia.[7]

In the 1890's young Armenians who had received university education in Europe and who returned imbued with nationalist ideas, began to press for political reforms and a degree of autonomy for the Armenians. Two in-

---

4   Verrier, A. *Agents of Empire*, (London, 1995), ibid, pp. 104-5.
5   Verrier, ibid, p. 106.
6   Gouttman, ibid, p. 19.
7   Morgenthau, H. *Ambassador Morgenthau's Story*, (1918), www.net.lib.byu.edu, Chapter 22, p. 5. The provinces were: Erzurum, Bitlis, Van, Sivas, Diyarbakir and Harput.

dependent groups were then founded which sought for such autonomy, the *Henchak* party and the Armenian Revolutionary Party ('*Dashnaks*').[8]

Since 1878 Britain had been pressuring the Sultan to implement the reforms agreed upon at Berlin – but to no avail. The frustration continued to mount in the Armenian provinces, and resulted in a 'peasant's revolt' in 1894, which was encouraged by the *Henchak* party. The Sultan responded by unleashing his forces against the Armenians. Further pressure then mounted on the Sultan by Britain, France and Russia – but progress towards satisfactory reform was still thwarted. The Sultan's attitude is best summed up in his words to the German Ambassador: 'I swear that … I would rather die than accept reforms that would produce self-government [for the Armenians]'[9]

Finally on 26 August 1896 the *Dashnaks* took over the Ottoman Bank in Istanbul in order to draw attention to their plight. This move further provoked the Sultan, and only resulted in 'a large-scale massacre of Armenians…'[10] The main obstacle against him committing further atrocities was the strong opposition from Britain, France and Russia, who threatened to intervene unless the massacres stopped.

It is estimated that in the period 1894-96 between 80-200,000 Armenians were massacred.[11] This harsh Turkish policy against the Armenians was brought on by a Turkish Sultan and leadership realizing that its empire in 'Christian' Europe was slipping away. They needed a reason, a scapegoat for this demise of their once powerful empire – and that scapegoat was the collective *dhimmi* community, and particularly the Armenians.

THE ZIONIST MOVEMENT AND GERMANY

If the small Jewish nationalist movement ever wanted to attain some form of autonomy in *Eretz Yisrael*, it would require the active support and endorsement of a European power. Piecemeal colonisation of the barren and

---

8   *Encyclopaedia Britannica*, 1975, Volume 18, p. 1043; United Human Rights, www.unitedhumanrights.org.

9   Ambassador's report, dated 16 November 1894, quoted in Lepsius , Bartholdy, Timme, *Europäischen Kabinette*, p. 9; Bayur, *Türk İnkılabı Tarihi*, pp. 77– 78, cited in Akcam, ibid, footnote 112.

10   Akcam, ibid, p. 42.

11   Andrew Mango in his book *Ataturk,* states that various estimates of the number were given. Mango, A. *Ataturk*, Introduction, Kindle Books.

swamp-infested land itself would not move the Turkish authorities to grant any form of Jewish autonomy in the region of *dar al Islam*. In fact, even the support and endorsement of a European power was absolutely no guarantee that Turkey, being the custodian of Islam, would permit such autonomy.

A big step forward in the realisation of the ancient Jewish hope for a restoration to *Eretz Yisrael* took place in 1896. A secular Hungarian Jew, Theodore Herzl, who was then a journalist working in Vienna, published a book entitled *Der Judenstaat* ('The Jew[ish] State'), which declared that the only tangible solution for the plight of the dispersed and despised Jewish people, was the establishment of a Jewish State – in *Eretz Yisrael*.

Herzl had come to this conclusion as a result of observing the situation of Jewish people throughout Europe. He had been in Paris covering the trial of Captain Alfred Dreyfus, an assimilated French Jew who was accused (unjustly) of treason on behalf of Germany and publicly degraded at the *Ecole Militaire* on 5 January 1895.[12]

Herzl had witnessed much anti-Semitism in so-called enlightened France! He then began to understand that indeed the Jews were always going to be a 'ghost' nation living in Europe, and would never be fully accepted by the host nations. There was but one alternative – to have their own homeland. Herzl then began to work on the idea of establishing a Jewish state, which he outlined in *Der Judenstat*.

Herzl's vision of a Jewish State was quickly adopted by others, including Rev William Hechler, the chaplain at the British Embassy at Vienna. Hechler was of dual Anglo-German parentage, and his father had worked for many years for the LJS. For some years Hechler had been a tutor for the children of the Duke of Baden-Wurttemberg (who was the uncle of the German Kaiser). Through this work he was familiar with the German royal family.[13]

Hechler met Herzl and encouraged him to make contact with the leaders of Germany, and also to arrange a Congress to propound this vision. Hechler wrote to the Grand Duke of Baden:

---

12   De Haas, *J. Theodor Herzl*, (Chicago, 1927), Vol. I, p. 44.
13   He had also been commissioned to write a book on the Anglo-Prussian bishopric entitled *The Jerusalem Bishopric*. Hechler consequently was very well connected, both in Germany and in Britain.

I cannot help thinking, that if Germany and England were to take this movement and such a new state under their protection, and Palestine were declared to be a neutral country, something like Belgium, the Return of the Jews would become a great blessing to Europe, and put an end to the anti-semitic spirit of hatred, which is detrimental to the welfare of all nations.[14]

Thanks to Hechler, Herzl met with the Duke of Baden in April 1896. Then just two months later in June 1896 Herzl travelled to Constantinople and met with the Grand Vizier, providing a proposal that the Jewish people would resolve to solve Turkey's financial problems in exchange for Jewish autonomy in *Eretz Yisrael*.

Herzl then convened a Conference in August 1897 in Basel, Switzerland where several hundred Jewish leaders (and some Gentiles) mostly from Eastern Europe assembled together. At this first Zionist Congress the foundations were laid for what would ultimately become the Jewish State of Israel.

Despite the hype and enthusiasm for this vision it would need the support of a leading European power in order to become a reality. Germany seemed the logical power. Ever since 1871 the German Reich, or Empire, had slowly been establishing a solid power base in Central Europe. Sandwiched between France and Russia it was also a force to be reckoned with by the other leading powers, and was the only major European power which had not been at war with the Turkish Empire. The Sultan had been slowly moving towards rapprochement with Germany since 1878 and the Congress of Berlin.

The German leadership was also accessible – due to Hechler's contact with members of the German aristocracy. A meeting with Kaiser Wilhelm II would be the next step in their quest. As the German Emperor was due to visit the East in 1898, it was agreed to arrange a meeting between Herzl and the Kaiser during that visit.

---

14   Hechler to Grad Duke of Baden, 16 March 1896, cited in Ellern, H and B. *Herzl, Hechler, the Grand Duke of Baden and the German Emperor, 1896-1904*, (Tel Aviv, 1961), p. 6.

THE GERMAN KAISER AND THE SULTAN

The Kaiser's visit to the Ottoman Empire was ostensibly to open the new German Church in the Muristan area of Jerusalem's Old City, adjacent to the Church of the Holy Sepulchre. He was to travel to Jerusalem via Constantinople, where he was to meet the Sultan, and return via Damascus. But there were grander geo-political and economic goals behind the German Emperor's visit.

Already in 1898, the goal of economic penetration into the Turkish Empire had become central to Germany's foreign policy. Germany was seeking more concessions and contracts, the most ambitious of which was a railway from Konya through to Baghdad, and thence on to Basra and to the head of the Persian Gulf. 'Branch lines were contemplated at various points,' wrote Antonius, 'including one to Alexandretta, so as to provide direct communication between the Mediterranean and the Persian Gulf.' It was, Antonius continued, 'a bold and ambitious scheme, and a menace to British interests in the East.'[15]

The discussions in Constantinople between the Kaiser and the Sultan went according to plan and the Germans received the concession to construct the next stage of what became known as the 'Berlin to Baghdad Railway'. For the Sultan this railway would provide him with easier access to the extremities of his far-flung empire; and for the Kaiser it provided his young and energetic nation with enormous potential for economic expansion. Work on this strategic project began in 1899.

Herzl and his Zionist delegation arrived in Constantinople in order to have preliminary discussions with Turkish officials, and also with the German emperor.   In his meeting with the German emperor (who was accompanied by Minister Von Bulow) Herzl outlined his proposal for a Jewish protectorate in Palestine, and concluded, "… the scheme seems to me to be a natural solution." The Emperor responded, "And also to me."[16] Von Bulow responded that much depended upon the Turkish officials.[17]

15   Antonius, ibid, p. 77.

16   *The Diaries of Theodor Herzl*, edited and translated by Marvin Lowenthal, (New York, 1956), p. 272.

17   De Haas, ibid, p. 252.

At this point the Kaiser stated: "It will surely make an impression when the German Emperor concerns himself about this and shows he is interested ... Finally I am the sole supporter of the Sultan. He owes me something."[18] The Emperor then asked Herzl what he was to ask of the Sultan, to which Herzl replied: "A chartered company – under German protection." To this the Kaiser responded, "Good, a Chartered Company!" and bid Herzl farewell.[19]

This private audience with the German emperor could not have been more encouraging for Herzl. The Kaiser seemed positive towards the real benefits of Herzl's proposal: for the Jewish people, for the Sultan, and for Germany. The reality of *dar al Islam*, though, was soon to interfere with these optimistic attitudes.

Thereafter Herzl and his fellow Zionists were to work on preparing a formal document which was to be presented to the Kaiser in Jerusalem. As for the Kaiser, he now had his railway contract 'in his pocket' so he and his enormous entourage continued on their journey to the 'Holy Land.'

HERZL AND THE EMPEROR IN JERUSALEM

In October 1898, some 100 years after Napoleon's expedition to the East, the German emperor Kaiser Wilhelm II entered Palestine. He visited the German Templar colony in Haifa, and then continued on to Jaffa, where he stayed at the imposing *Hotel du Park* of Baron Platon von Ustinoff, also located in the German Templar Colony.[20] William Hechler was also present on this visit.

The Zionist delegation arrived in *Eretz Yisrael* on 26 October 1898, and Herzl's first visit was to Rishon-le-Zion, a Rothschild colony, where the reception was somewhat lukewarm. Then he visited Wady Hanein (Nes Ziona, and also known as Nahalat Reuben), which was a free colony, where he received 'a royal welcome.'

The Zionist delegation then moved towards Rehoboth (also known as Khirbat Deiran) where they were met by an honour guard composed of many

---

18 De Haas, ibid, p. 252.
19 *Diaries of Theodor Herzl*, ibid, p. 272; De Haas, ibid, p. 253.
20 Today Beit Immanuel, which is owned and operated by the LJS (CMJ)

of the young men of the new *yishuv*, one of whom was Eliazar Margolin.[21] Herzl recorded that he was deeply moved by the sight of these young vibrant Jewish men on horseback,[22] and the Jewish leaders from Europe had 'tears in our eyes.'[23]

On 27 October while the German delegation was en-route to Jerusalem, Herzl and his delegation stood on the road outside the Mikve Israel agricultural college. The Emperor recognized Herzl and beckoned him to draw near, and they had a brief conversation. The Emperor concluded by stating, "It is a land with a future."[24] Both the German and the Zionist parties then continued on to Jerusalem.

The Turks ingratiated themselves before the German emperor by having the moat which surrounded the Citadel at the Jaffa Gate entrance to the Old City filled in so that the German entourage could enter the city. The Kaiser entered on 31 October 1898 riding his huge white horse, and proceeded to the Muristan for the official opening of the new German Lutheran Church of the Redeemer.

Never in modern times had there been such an ostentatious show in Jerusalem, which the British press (especially the *Punch* magazine) noticed. Herzl, Hechler and the other Zionist delegates were left in no doubt that of all the European powers Germany held most sway with Turkey and was best suited to be their protector.[25]

The degree of Turkish sympathy for Germany is revealed when they gave several large tracts of land to the Kaiser, one on traditional Mount Zion and one on the Mount of Olives. In future years two huge edifices sprung up on these lands, the most imposing being the Augusta Victoria Hospice on the Mount of Olives. Many observers saw this huge edifice as being nothing more than a fortress ready to house a German army!

In the ensuing days Herzl's draft proposal was submitted to Grand Marshal von Eulenberg, who after editing the document, had it returned

---

21 Gouttman, ibid, p. 23.
22 De Haas, ibid, p. 255. Gouttman, ibid, p. 24.
23 *The Diaries of Theodor Herzl*, ibid, p. 281.
24 *The Diaries of Theodor Herzl*, ibid, p. 282; De Haas, ibid, p. 255.
25 *The Diaries of Theodor Herzl*. Ibid, p. 276.

to Herzl. Herzl then finally submitted the heavily edited document back to Von Bulow for final approval.

Herzl's last meeting with the Kaiser occurred on 2 November 1898, at his camp outside the city walls, where the future Probst's House would be located. The Jewish leaders hoped at this meeting to forge an alliance with imperial Germany. Herzl read out the Address to the Kaiser, which was then formally presented to the German emperor. At the conclusion, the Kaiser stated: "I thank you for these communications which have deeply interested me. The matter certainly calls for further study and discussion."[26] There was further discussion and then the meeting concluded.

Although Kaiser Wilhelm revealed some sympathy for the Zionist proposal, Herzl was aware that a distinct change had occurred since his previous more positive attitude during their first meeting in Constantinople. It would take some time before they became aware that the German leadership had no intention of sponsoring the Zionist programme.

Herzl first became aware of this from a newspaper article he read while in Naples – in which no reference whatsoever was made of the Zionist proposal of a Chartered Company for colonisation.[27]   Later Von Eulenberg stated:

To this day we have not been able to discover what was the real difficulty. The Sultan had declined the Emperor's advice regarding the Zionists so harshly, that it was impossible to pursue the matter further. We were anxious to remain on good terms. As a guest the Kaiser could of course go no further.[28]

Herzl himself was of the opinion that the change of attitude of the Kaiser was due to opposition to the Zionist proposal by Foreign Minister von Bulow. This view was somewhat challenged by the German Foreign Office.[29]

---

26   *The Diaries of Theodor Herzl*, ibid, p. 292; De Haas, ibid, pp. 258-59.
27   *The Diaries of Theodor Herzl*, ibid, p. 298; De Haas, ibid, pp. 266-67.
28   Eulenberg's Memoir, cited in De Haas, ibid, p. 272.
29   German Foreign Office, Abschrift III – O. 5357, cited in De Haas, ibid, p. 273-74.

Turkish and Islamic real-politic, though, dictated that the Kaiser, no matter how much he personally supported the Zionist proposal, could not pursue the German-Zionist protectorate proposal. The Kaiser's desire was to forge a close diplomatic and economic relationship with the Turkish Empire, and it would be impossible to also support and enhance the national aspirations of a minority group seeking some form of national autonomy within *dar al Islam*.

This episode effectively ended the hopes and aspirations of the Jewish nationalist movement for Germany's support and endorsement. The Zionist movement thereafter realised that they would need to look elsewhere for the accomplishment of their goal.

Firstly it was also decided that the Zionist organisation should attempt direct negotiations with the Sultan, with the negotiating item being an exchange: that Jewish financiers would pay off the large Turkish debt in exchange for a Jewish protectorate over Palestine. Although influential Jewish leaders, such as Baron Rothschild, scoffed at the idea, Herzl proceeded to Constantinople in 1901 and again in 1902. He believed that if the Sultan would provide a charter, then the Jewish financiers would participate in the idea.

Ultimately this ambitious proposal produced no tangible results. The Jewish nationalist movement had now hit a wall which was not going to move: a combination of a German refusal to act as a sponsor, and Turkish intransigence. If there was ever to be any form of Jewish national existence in Palestine there would have to be a scenario in which neither Germany nor Turkey were in authority; and there would need to be a protector empire which was sympathetic to the Jewish national aspirations.

CHAPTER 18

§

Challenges for the Sultan

CHALLENGES FOR ABDUL HAMID

The great desire of Sultan Abdul Hamid was to consolidate those parts of his empire that he still had control over. Internal tensions, however, mounted beneath the surface. Many intelligent young Turks, such as Ismail Enver and Mustapha Kemal, realised there was something better than the system of Government they then had.

Some of these thinkers were being influenced by such concepts as the Declaration of Human Rights which emanated from the French Revolution. Accordingly, in 1889 some students at the Military Medical College formed a secret society called the Ottoman Union. Later, wrote Mango, 'That society changed its name to Union and Progress in 1895.'[1]

Two streams were now moving within Turkish society; the one espoused by the young intellectuals, in and out of the military; and the official stream as espoused by Sultan Abdul Hamid, who sought to consolidate control over his vast Empire.

By 1900 this Empire was mostly restricted to Turkey-in-Asia, and was composed of:

---

1   Mango, ibid, Part 1, Chapter 2.

- The region of Syria (modern day Syria, Lebanon, Israel, Jordan and Palestinian Authority), which was divided into three *vilayets*: Aleppo to the north; Beirut in the west; and Syria in the east. In addition there were two smaller entities, the *sanjak* of Lebanon, which was detached from the *vilayet* of Beirut; and the *sanjak* (or *mutesariff*) of Jerusalem.

- The region of Mesopotamia (modern day Iraq) which was divided into the *vilayets* of Mosul in the north, Baghdad in the centre and Basra in the south.

- The region of the Arabian Peninsula. This region included: The *Vilayet* of Hejaz on the Red Sea side of the Peninsula, which was ruled by a Turkish *vali*, although much effective control was vested in the hands of the Grand Sherif of Mecca, the leader of the House of Beni Hashem. To the south was the *Vilayet* of Yemen, which had a somewhat tempestuous relationship with the Ottoman regime. On the Persian Gulf side there was only limited Turkish rule except at al-Hasa.

- The vast inland region, though, was completely out of Turkish control. Two large tribal dynasties, the House of Saud (based at Nejd) and the House of Ibn Rashid (based at Shammar) ruled over this region, and opposed any attempts by the Turks to impose centralised government upon them. They also fought against each other – and disdained interference from the Hashemites in the Hejaz.

- Britain had control over two small areas; Aden at the entrance of the Red Sea (taken possession of in 1839) and the Island of Perum at the entrance to the Persian Gulf (taken possession of in 1857).

- The Turks had gradually lost control over their African dependencies: Egypt to Britain in 1882; Sudan to Britain in 1888; Tunisia to France in 1881. They only had full control over the region of Libya, divided into the *Vilayet* of Tripoli and the *Vilayet* of Cyrenaica (Benghazi). Much of the hinterland of Cyrenaica was under the control of Senussi tribesmen.

THE IMPORTANCE OF RAILWAYS

The Turks were fully committed from 1900 to maintaining control as much as possible over their remaining dependencies, and kept a close eye on any potential independence movements. One of the ways they intended doing this was through the use of railways, which assisted with centralisation; by gaining quicker access to remote areas; for permitting the quicker despatch of troops to areas of need; as well as being of economic importance.

Apart from the 'Berlin to Baghdad' Railway, there were other major railways which the Sultan sanctioned 'in the provinces.' Moses Montefiore had initially suggested building a railway line between Jaffa and Jerusalem, and made this proposal to the Porte in 1856. Others such as Chesney and Laurence Oliphant also supported this scheme, but it eventually failed. It was revived in the 1880's by a Jerusalem Jewish man named Joseph Navon, and then following its endorsement by the Porte, a French company was granted the concession to construct the railway. The Jaffa to Jerusalem line was officially opened in 1892.

Abdul Hamid's most ambitious railway project was the building of a railway from Damascus to Mecca, to be known as the Hejaz Railway. This project was funded by the Porte, primarily through voluntary subscriptions. Most of the technical staff were German, and the chief engineer was Heinrich Meissner.

The purpose of the Hejaz Railway, as propagated, was for the quicker and more efficient transfer of pilgrims going to the Holy Cities for the *haj*. This image projected Sultan Abdul Hamid to his Muslim subjects as a benevolent ruler. Building a railway to the Hejaz, though, was also apt to incur strong opposition, as the Arabs of that region depended for their livelihood on transporting the pilgrims coming to the Holy Cities of Islam by camel, and it would also upset the coveted semi-autonomous existence of the Hejaz.

Abdul Hamid was already keeping a closer eye on the province of Hejaz. It is within this context that Hussein Ibn Ali from the House of Beni Hashem and a member of the family of the Grand Sherif of Mecca, found himself in Constantinople. Abdul Hamid was informed that Hussein was somewhat 'original and independent' in his thinking.[2] Consequently, the Sultan 'invited' Hussein and his family, including his three sons, Ali, Feisal and Abdullah, to come to live in Constantinople in 1893. This 'voluntary' sojourn would last fifteen years.

Work on the Hejaz Railway began in 1900, but then it became apparent that there was a logistical problem obtaining materials for the construction of the railway south of Damascus.[3] It was then decided to construct a spur from the Hejaz Railway, branching off at Deraa (south of Damascus) through to Haifa on the Mediterranean coast, and the construction there of a deep water port in order to bring the necessary materials for constructing the Hejaz Railway.

This railway line went from Deraa down the Yarmuk Valley to the village of Semack on the Sea of Galilee, and then south down the Jordan Valley to Beisan (Bet Shean), before heading north-west along the Esdraelon Valley (Jezreel Valley) via El Afule (Afula) to Haifa. It was officially opened in 1905.

The construction of this railway necessarily delayed the furtherance of the Hejaz Railway to Mecca. In addition, the construction of this railway opened up the possibility of constructing a connection through to the Jerusalem-Jaffa line.[4] The Hejaz Railway finally reached Medina in 1908 - a distance of some 900 miles (1500 kilometres) from Damascus.

In the same year that the railway reached Medina, Hussein Ibn Ali arrived back in Mecca. This happened because of tumultuous events happening then in Salonika and Constantinople.

---

2   Antonius, ibid, p. 72.

3   There were other projects then in progress or in discussion relating to railways from the Mediterranean coast up to the Hauran region and Damascus (including a railway from Beirut to Damascus).

4   This project began in 1913, with the line beginning from El Afule (Afula) through to Jenin. It was not completed, due to opposition from the French who feared competition with their monopoly of the Jaffa-Jerusalem line. The line was completed by German engineers during World War One.

§

The British-Jewish connection begins

THE JEWISH NATIONALISTS TURN TO BRITAIN

When Herzl and the Zionist movement were rebuffed by Germany, and while Herzl was about to make the first of his three visits to Constantinople, the Zionist movement was already redirecting its attention to Britain. The Fourth Zionist Congress was held in London in 1900. It was here that the Jewish Colonial Fund was established, to raise funds for the purchase of land in *Eretz Yisrael*.

Shortly afterwards, in 1902, there were further *pogroms*, especially in Rumania. Thousands more Jewish refugees were forced westwards, many of whom entered into Britain.[1] This influx created fears of cheap labour being available in the country. The British Government, led by Prime Minister Arthur Balfour, set up a Royal Commission to determine the best solution to this dilemma. Lord Rothschild was a member, and Herzl was also invited to give testimony on behalf of the Jewish people.

---

1   Also in 1902 Eleazar Margolin was forced to leave *Eretz Yisrael* due to financial insolvency. Lured by the gold rush at Coolgardie, Margolin moved to Western Australia, and later moved to Collie in the south-west district of that state.

Lord Rothschild, like many influential British Jews, opposed the 'wild' Zionist scheme. He did, however, see the potential of Zionism at this stage, as it could draw many of these would-be migrants to Palestine, thereby saving him and other more assimilation-minded British Jews any embarrassment. He agreed to meet with Herzl.

Herzl explained to both the British Government officials and to Rothschild that he desired a Jewish colony on British territory. As Palestine was still Turkish-held territory, he conceived the idea of having a half-way station somewhere on British controlled territory close by. He stated to Rothschild 'the idea of a Jewish Company for Sinai, Egyptian Palestine and Cyprus.'[2]

Herzl then discussed the proposal with Colonial Secretary Joseph Chamberlain. Chamberlain explained that any Jewish settlement on Cyprus was out of the question, as both the Greek and Muslim inhabitants would oppose such a proposal. Then, when Herzl showed Chamberlain the location of El Arish on a map (the most probable location in the Sinai for a colony) the Colonial Secretary showed interest in the scheme. For Herzl, any location on the borders of Turkish Palestine would suffice.

Here was an ideal opportunity, Herzl contended, to settle and hold that strategic piece of real-estate - the east bank of the Suez Canal – by colonists under British protection. The Suez Canal region was by now the jugular vein of the British Empire, its most important piece of real-estate, and this idea could act as a perfect buffer between Turkey to the north and the Suez Canal. The very concept was similar to the strategy of Cyrus emperor of Persia, with the Jewish people being an integral part of an empire's plans.

After some time Herzl said to Chamberlain: "Would you agree to our founding a Jewish colony on the Sinai Peninsula?" "Yes," he replied, "if Lord Cromer is in favour."[3]

Encouraged by Chamberlain's response, Herzl then met with Lord Landsdowne, the Foreign Secretary. Further discussions then had to wait

---

2 *Diaries of Theodor Herzl*, ibid, p. 369.
3 *Diaries of Theodor Herzl*, ibid, p. 376. Lord Cromer was the British viceroy in Egypt.

while he travelled to Constantinople for his last attempt to negotiate with the Turks about obtaining a charter for Jewish settlement in Palestine. His chances of success were minimal.

There were numerous difficulties associated with this scheme, such as, would it be a British colony, or a colony with statehood as the objective? Then there were legal complications, considering that Egypt (including the Sinai) was still, legally, part of the Turkish Empire. Any colonists in the Sinai would therefore need to become Turkish citizens, but living under Egyptian law.

Additionally there was uncertainty (even disputes) between the Turkish and Egyptian administrations concerning the exact boundary line separating the two regions. Despite all these complications, the British Government sent delegations to the Sinai to determine the feasibility of this venture. One matter of particular concern was the possibility of irrigating the region for a large number of people.

THE ANGLO-BOER WAR AND EAST AFRICA (UGANDA) OFFER

In 1899 the Anglo-Boer War erupted in South Africa as the British coveted the Boer (Dutch background) Republics of Transvaal and Orange Free State and moved to conquer them. The smaller and militarily inferior Boer Republics gallantly withstood the might of the British Army.

Almost immediately, Canada, New Zealand and all of the Australian colonies sent troops, most of whom were mounted infantry. The first Australian colony to send troops was Queensland, and included was an officer named Harry Chauvel. Among the hundreds of New Zealand troops was Edward Chaytor.

The British forces were led by Field Marshal Lord Roberts, whose Chief-of-Staff was Major-General Kitchener. Amongst the many thousands of British troops was Anglo-Irishman John Patterson; Edmund Allenby; Philip Chetwode and others who would later play prominent roles in the fighting in the Middle East. Another was Winston Churchill, who escaped from a Boer Prisoner of War camp in 1900 – and only several months later was seated in the House of Commons; while one of the commanders of the Boer forces was a brilliant general (and politician) named Jan Christian Smuts.

At the conclusion of the Anglo-Boer War in 1902, Colonial Secretary Chamberlain toured British possessions in eastern and southern Africa. While in East Africa he was informed that more settlers were needed. Chamberlain wrote a small note that this could be ideal for Herzl's Zionists. It was also at this time that it was becoming clear that a Jewish presence in the Sinai would not be favoured by the British authorities in Egypt, especially Lord Cromer.

Upon returning to Britain Chamberlain met with Herzl in April 1903 and explained the East Africa settlement idea. "I've seen a land for you on my recent travels," Herzl wrote about his conversation with Chamberlain, "and that's Uganda."[4]

The Foreign Office had already drawn up a draft agreement 'for the terms of the Jewish settlement', wrote Lowenthal, which 'was submitted to the Government.' The terms of the agreement were drawn up by an attorney and Member of Parliament named David Lloyd George.[5]

Despite opposition coming from Lord Cromer and the British authorities in Egypt, Herzl though was still very keen on the Sinai scheme. He said to Chamberlain concerning the presence of a Jewish colony in the Sinai: "We shall play the role of a small buffer zone."[6]

Events during the following three weeks, however, changed all of Herzl's plans and aspirations.

HERZL IN RUSSIA AND THE KISHINEV POGROM

For many centuries in 'Christian' Europe there had been terrible *pogroms* following the Easter Friday service, when priests and bishops would reinforce that the Jews had crucified Jesus.[7] Following the sermon on Easter

---

4 *Diaries of Theodor Herzl*, ibid, p. 382.

5 *Diaries of Theodor Herzl*, ibid, p. 407.

6 *Diaries of Theodor Herzl*, ibid, p. 383.

7 According to the Scriptures, especially the writings of the New Testament, there were six parties involved in the death of Jesus: God; Jesus (who said that no-one takes away his life but that he gives it up himself); the Jewish leadership; the Roman leadership as represented by Governor Pontius Pilate; every individual person, as Jesus died for the sin of all peoples; and Satan.

Friday in April 1903 in the Russian city of Kishinev mobs streamed into the Jewish quarter. Another terrible *pogrom* – or massacre – followed.

This was not the Middle Ages, this was 1903, and the Jewish people throughout the world were in shock. The Kishinev *pogrom* had a similar effect as the Damascus 'Blood Libel' of 1840. A young Jewish scientist named Chaim Weizmann was meeting with Nahum Sokolow, the editor of *Ha-Zephirah* newspaper in Warsaw at that time, and wrote:

> Forty-five men, women and children killed, more than a thousand wounded, fifteen hundred homes and shops destroyed and looted – this is the cold summary of the Kishinev pogrom …
>
> The wave of indignation and despair which swept over the whole Jewish community, from one end of Russia to the other, was augmented by the complex feelings of humiliation and impotence. The Kishinev pogrom was the reply of czarist Russia to the cry of freedom of its Jewish subjects.[8]

Following this wake-up call to the harsh reality of Jewish life in Europe, the Zionist movement needed some good news to succour their people. However, bad news continued, for on 11 May 1903 Lord Cromer informed the Zionist representative in Cairo that the Egyptian Government had rejected the Sinai colonisation scheme.[9]

Herzl was not giving up on his vision for a charter for Palestine and in August 1903 he visited Russia, in an attempt to alleviate the suffering and persecution of the Jewish people who lived there, and to ask for Russian support in Constantinople on behalf of the Jewish proposal for *Eretz Yisrael*. He twice met with the Minister of the Interior, H. Plevhe, who was generally deemed responsible for the Kishinev *pogrom*. Plevhe indicated that the Russians would act on behalf of the Zionist organisation in Constantinople.[10]

---

8   Weizmann, C. *Trial and Error*, (Philadelphia, 1949), Vol. I, pp. 79-80.
9   *Diaries of Theodor Herzl*, ibid, p. 384.
10 *Diaries of Theodor Herzl*, ibid, p. 401.

Herzl also met with the Minister of Finance, Sergei Witte, who stated in connection to the planned Jewish colony in Palestine: "How far from the Holy Places do you contemplate setting up your settlement? I think it would create alarm if people knew there were Jews close by." Such a comment was indicative of the 'special' regard many Russians still held for the Holy Places in the Holy Land - and disregard for the Jewish people.

In the end the Russians, like the Germans before them, had little real desire to assist in fulfilling the Jewish vision.[11]

Immediately after returning from Russia Herzl attended the Zionist Congress in Basel, and brought Chamberlain's East Africa[12] proposition to the delegates. Although a majority of delegates voted to send a delegation to spy out the land in question, there was also strong opposition from a smaller group, mostly of Russian Jews. For these delegates the Zionist movement and *Eretz Yisrael* were synonymous - there could be no other place for a Jewish national entity. For the first time the Zionist movement was on the verge of a split, and this great trauma seriously affected Herzl's health.

One of those who opposed Herzl and the East Africa project was Chaim Weizmann.

DEVELOPMENT OF ZIONISM AND 1905 REVOLUTION

Theodor Herzl died in 1904 and the Zionist movement thereafter passed into other hands. Until this point there were three main strands of Zionism: practical Zionism as espoused by the more pragmatic Russians and carried out by the colonists in the land already; political Zionism, as espoused by Herzl, and many idealistic Zionists from Western Europe; and cultural Zionism, espoused by Ahad Ha'Am (Arthur Ginzberg) which envisioned a Jewish cultural centre in *Eretz Yisrael*, as distinct from a political entity.

After Herzl's death practical and political Zionism merged their energies and efforts: together they would legally purchase land and establish agricultural settlements on the barren and mosquito infested lands and

---

11   In December 1903 Plehve asked the Russian ambassador at Constantinople to make a request in favour of Zionism. A month later the Ambassador informed Herzl's representative that he had not been able to do anything. This, wrote Lowenthal 'virtually ended the Russian "immortal game."' *Diaries of Theodor Herzl*, ibid, p. 414.

12   Also known as the Uganda proposal.

swamps of Palestine; while at the same time continue to agitate for a politically endorsed charter.[13]   During this same period there was a policy of extreme nationalism in Russia – and any group not regarded as being truly Russian was liable to be outlawed and persecuted. As had been the norm for several centuries by now, the Jewish 'nation' was singled out, and throughout the region of the Pale there were numerous small outbreaks of violence.

Non-religious Jewish people were drawn into one of several directions: to Zionism, assimiliationism, or political activism. Many espoused the ideas of socialism as being a remedy to the corrupt and hated Czarist regime - socialism in its purest form appealed to many young Jewish intellectuals and idealists.

Many of these people firmly believed there was a place in a new Russia for Jews to be accepted as *equals*. But the Kishinev *pogrom* of 1903 followed by *pogroms* associated with the 1905 Revolution radically challenged their perception.[14] Many now saw there was no future at all for Jews in Russia and opted alongside hundreds of thousands of other Jewish people to leave.

Associated with the unrest and the 1905 Revolution was a virulent outbreak of anti-Semitism. The Government, in an attempt to mask its imperfections and in order to provide a diversion for the dissatisfied masses, engineered numerous small *pogroms* throughout the Pale of Settlement region, culminating in a major *pogrom* in Kiev in October 1905.[15]   Many Jewish people took defensive action and formed self-defence units in the towns. One such unit was established in Poltava and was joined by Yitzhak Shimshelevitch (later Yitzhak Ben Zvi). The following year Ben Zvi helped found a socialist Jewish Zionist party known as *Poalei Zion* ('Workers for Zion'), and in 1907 made *aliyah* (immigration) to *Eretz Yisrael*.

There he joined another man named David Gruen (Ben Gurion). Ben Gurion came from Plonsk in Russian-occupied Poland. While a student in Warsaw Ben Gurion had been shocked by the 1903 *pogroms*, and also at

---

13   In the following years the Zionist movement was more-or-less synonymous with five men: Nahum Sokolow, Chaim Weizmann, Yitzhak Ben Zvi, David Ben Gurion and Vladimir Jabotinsky.

14   There were numerous reasons for the 1905 Revolution, one of which was Russia's defeat by the Japanese in the Russo-Japanese War.

15   When the pogrom broke out in Kiev on 18 October over a hundred Jewish people were massacred – but many were saved by a Jewish self-defence unit.

Chisinau and Bialystok in 1906, as well as by the rampant anti-Semitism he witnessed in Russian-Poland. He subsequently joined the recently formed *Poalei Zion* movement and made *aliyah* (immigrating to *Eretz Yisrael*) in 1906.

THE SECOND *ALIYAH*

Ben Gurion joined the thousands of other Jewish people streaming out of Russia, and in order to survive he began working on farms. He joined the local *Poalei Zion* movement as well as becoming part of a Jewish self-defence unit known as *Ha-Shomer* ('the guard').[16]

Despite incredible hardships these idealists of the second *aliyah* (1905-14) made the largest contribution thus far to the development of Palestine. Until this point other aspects of modernisation had been introduced into the land by the Protestant missionary societies, the German Templars, the various Roman Catholic and Orthodox institutions, and Jewish philanthropic agencies.

The Turkish administration had established only one new town in Palestine during their 400 year rule there, at Beersheba in the Negev region. They seldom encouraged any enterprise, especially among the Muslim population. Ironically, living conditions for much of the Muslim population only improved as a result of the activities of the various Protestant, Jewish, and other Christian welfare institutions.

The only modern farms until 1905 were those of the pioneer Jewish (especially Rothschild) colonies and the German Templars. Many European (and American) visitors to the region commented upon how the Jewish colonists had transformed former desolate and swampy land and made it productive. One such observer was a British archaeologist named Thomas Edward (T.E.) Lawrence. Following a tour through Palestine in 1909 Lawrence wrote to his mother and in reference to the land of Israel in the time of Jesus, he wrote:

Palestine was a decent country then, and could so easily be made so again.   The sooner the Jews farm it all

---

16   *Ha-Shomer* had been founded by Israel Shochet.

the better: their colonies are bright spots in a desert.[17]

One of the key components for the success of many of these Jewish colonies was the vision to transform the barren land and make it blossom and bloom. By the time of the second *aliyah* there were many such agricultural colonies spread throughout Palestine which were making the desert land 'blossom and bloom.'

Within this context one pioneer stood out: Aaron Aaronsohn. By 1906 he had distinguished himself in several agricultural colonies, and had ridden by horseback from one end of the land to the other.[18] In June 1906 he discovered an important strand of wild wheat, a discovery which rewarded him with international recognition. In 1909 he established the agricultural Experimental Station at Atlit on the Mediterranean coast near to Zichron Yaacov.

Another component in the vision to impart a common sense of purpose and destiny among the new immigrants was the common language of Hebrew.

Eliezer ben Yehuda was still persevering with his work of reviving the ancient Hebrew language in order to be a unifying factor for these scattered Jewish people in *Eretz Yisrael*. Ben Yehuda's vision was not well received by many Orthodox rabbis who believed the sacred language was not to be used for the secular and mundane. Yet ironically his work captured the imagination of others who were imbued with nationalist ideas.

In 1906 a young Turkish Army officer named Mustapha Kemal was stationed in Damascus and Jaffa as part of the Turkish Fifth Army. During his time in Palestine he surveyed much of the land, even down to Beersheba. This time away from his home helped Kemal gain a better awareness of his own Turkish national identity.[19]

He also began to give consideration to other nationalist movements, and while there he visited Ben Yehuda, in order, wrote M. Sukru Hanioglu,

17 *Selected Letters of T.E. Lawrence*, edited by David Garnett, (London, 1941), p. 27.
18 Verrier, ibid, p. 107.
19 Mango, ibid, Part One, Chapter 3.

'to understand ... how he had managed to reinvent the Hebrew language after millennia of disuse and make it a cornerstone of Zionist culture.'[20]

Mustapha Kemal was one of many young idealistic Turks of the time who realised the Ottoman system was badly in need of reform. At one time he returned to Salonika and established the 'Fatherland Freedom Society' – which collapsed once he returned to Jaffa.[21]

Other Turkish Army officers who held similar ideas, though, were putting together a plan in Salonika to bring about a thorough reformation of the Turkish Government.

---

20   Gabriel Mitchell, 'Ataturk, Ben Gurion, and Turkey's Road Not Taken', *The Tower,* Issue 8, November 2012, in www.thetower.com. Mitchell stated that Mustapha Kemal would 'mimic this feat in 1928 by changing the Turkish alphabet from Arabic to Latin characters.'

21   Mango, ibid, Part One, Chapter 3.

§

CHAPTER 20

The Dardanelles and Sinai

RUSSIA, CONSTANTINOPLE AND GALLIPOLI, 1903

Despite Abdul Hamid's attempt to stabilize the Turkish Empire, British strategists were concerned that Turkey would collapse. If so, two regions would be vulnerable to foreign penetration: Constantinople and the Dardanelles; and the Sinai Peninsula.

In January 1903 the British ambassador at Constantinople, Sir Nicholas O'Conor, submitted a letter to Prime Minister Balfour asking 'what course this country was likely to pursue if, as it might well happen, disorder and anarchy broke out in Constantinople, and if Russia, proclaiming herself to be acting in the interests of public order were by a sudden *coup de main* to occupy the city.'[1]

O'Conor had intimated that although the initial Russian occupation might be temporary, it would be very difficult thereafter to dislodge them from that position. He suggested to Balfour that this Russian initiative could be opposed by a 'British occupation of Gallipoli'.

O'Conor's letter was the basis of a Cabinet discussion held on 11 February 1903, where the issue under discussion concerned:

---

1   CAB 24/1, Report by Mr Balfour, 11 February 1903, in 'Committee of Imperial Defence, Russia and Constantinople', 11 March 1915, p. 3.

What difference would it make to the balance of power in the Mediterranean if Russia were to obtain, through the possession of Constantinople, free egress from the Black Sea through the Dardanelles, these remaining closed, as at present, against other Powers?[2]

Balfour stated that the decision of the Defence Committee was that such an action would not seriously affect Britain's interests. He also stated that schemes had been 'from time to time suggested under which 5,000 British soldiers and marines, supported by the fleet, are to hold the peninsular, thus making an effective counter-stroke to the Russian occupation of Constantinople.'[3] He added that such an operation would hardly be possible for logistical reasons, but that an occupation of the island of Lemnos could be possible, but this would only be a temporary solution.[4]

Balfour declared that if Russia decided to occupy Constantinople then it was not within Britain's ability to hinder this move; that Britain would work alongside both Turkey and other European powers, if need be, to hinder such a move; but that Britain would not work alone to stop such a Russian initiative.

W.G. Nicolson of the Intelligence Department of the War Office then presented a Memorandum in which he stated that: 'It is estimated that an army corps would be needed effectively to hold the Gallipoli Peninsular in the face of a Russian occupation of Constantinople.' Concerning where this force could be taken from, Nicolson concluded: 'It may ... be concluded, that 5,000 men could not be withdrawn at a critical time from any of the Mediterranean garrisons to occupy the Gallipoli Peninsular, even were it considered wise to risk its occupation by so inadequate a force.'[5]

The Director of Naval Intelligence, Captain H.S.H. Louis of Battenberg, also submitted a Memorandum to the Defence Committee in February 1903 on the issue of a Russian occupation of Constantinople and the Gallipoli

---

2   CAB 24/1, ibid, p. 2.
3   CAB 24/1, ibid, p. 3.
4   CAB 24/1, ibid, p. 4.
5   CAB 24/1, Director General of Naval Intelligence, 23 February 1903, ibid, p. 5.

Peninsula. Although Battenberg did concede that this would bring the Russian Fleet to within 440 miles of Malta and Port Said (the Suez Canal), as compared to 800 miles as it was then (with the closest Russian Fleet being in the north of the Black Sea), yet such a move did not seriously threaten Britain, although it 'would undoubtedly improve Russia's position in a war with England, and render our task correspondingly more difficult.'[6]

But, stated Battenberg, if Russia was allied with France, then the situation could be different. In that case the British would need to deal with the French Fleet first before tackling the Russian threat. In such a situation Britain would need to be in alliance with the German-Austrian-Italian Alliance, all of which could be involved in one way or another. Such, though, was highly unlikely due to the potential for a ramification of the conflict.

Battenberg concluded that Russia could attempt nothing, either in Egypt or elsewhere, until she had dealt with the British Fleet, and he was confident in the ability of the British Mediterranean Fleet to deal with both the French and Russian naval forces.[7]

All of the British authorities of 1903, therefore, acknowledged that in the likelihood of a Russian occupation of Constantinople and the Gallipoli Peninsula there would be no serious threat to Britain's objectives in the Levant. This evaluation was dependent, however, upon British consolidation in the region of the Suez Canal.

The sensitivity of the issue was revealed in August 1903 when a Russian Consul, Rostkovsky, was murdered by a Turkish soldier. The Russian Fleet, wrote Herzl, 'was then demonstrating before Constantinople.'[8] Although tensions ultimately simmered, this incident was an indication of the potential volatility of the region.

BRITAIN AND THE SINAI

The Zionist-Sinai scheme confirmed British concerns for the east side of the Suez Canal – her imperial jugular vein. Lord Cromer (The British Consul-General), had made an agreement with the Turkish authorities in 1892 that

---

6 CAB 24/1, ibid, p. 5.
7 CAB 24/1, ibid, p. 6.
8 *Diaries of Theodor Herzl*, ibid, p. 403.

the border of Sinai would run from Rafah on the Mediterranean coast down to Aqaba on the Red Sea. While legally remaining part of Turkey, the Sinai was administered by the Anglo-Egyptian authorities. It seemed to be a sound working scheme.

But in 1906 the Turks tested the degree to which Britain was willing to stand by this agreement. They staged an incident at Taba on the Red Sea, which was on the Egyptian side of the boundary line separating the administrative regions of Egypt and Palestine. Their stated desire was to gain more access to the Red Sea.

The Anglo-Egyptian Government, which viewed the Sinai as a buffer zone protecting the Suez Canal, immediately despatched warships into the Eastern Mediterranean, and forced the Turks to withdraw. Negotiations followed, during which the British ceded more territory to the west of Aqaba, and then a more formal 'international line' demarcated Turkish controlled territory from British controlled territory.[9]

From the British perspective, Professor Isaiah Friedmann wrote: 'This incident, combined with the construction of the Hedjaz railway, re-emphasized the strategic importance of the Sinai Peninsula and opened British eyes to the possibility of a serious invasion of Egypt from the east by Turkey.'[10]

British military analysts thereafter sought to determine the best form of defence of the Suez Canal, in the event of a Turkish-led invasion. Some maintained that the present *status quo* was sufficient and that no sizeable army could cross the Sinai. Others maintained that the 1906 incident disproved this theory, and that the only effective barrier was control of Palestine itself. Others still maintained that the most effective barrier was the maintenance and integrity of Turkey. This incident, though, did provoke some British policy makers to consider that there could be problems in the Sinai in the future if Turkey was aligned with another European power.

---

9   Britain was also concerned at this time of the possibility of the Turks constructing a branch of the Hejaz Railway to Aqaba. Mango, ibid, Part One, Chapter Three.
10   Friedmann, I. *The Question of Palestine*, (New Jersey, 1992), p. 2.

§

CHAPTER 21

European alliances and
a 'new' Turkey

EUROPEAN ALLIANCES FIRMING UP

The foundation and growth of the German Empire and its steady rapprochement both with the Austro-Hungarian and Ottoman Turkish Empires, unnerved the British, French and Russians. Britain and France entered into a 'Treaty of Agreement' in 1904 which removed a number of key confrontational issues between them.

Then in 1907 Britain and Russia finally realized the stakes were too high in their confrontations along the northern approaches to India (especially through Persia, Afghanistan and Bukhara) and they signed the 'Anglo-Russian Agreement'.

There was by 1907 the possibility of a Triple Alliance (an *Entente*) between the three former antagonists of the previous one hundred plus years. Interestingly at the same time as these realignments were taking place, another important realignment was occurring within the vast Turkish Empire.

THE 'YOUNG TURKS' REVOLT

Despite Abdul Hamid's efforts at centralisation, and despite the large amount of economic investment by the European powers (and America), by the first decade of the twentieth century the Ottoman Empire was economically, politically and militarily tottering.

Since its inception in 1889 the society, later known as the Committee for Union and Progress (C.U.P.), had gained momentum. More military officers had joined this movement which agitated for a serious reform in the way that Turkey was being governed. By 1908 the Committee of Union and Progress (C.U.P.), or colloquially, the 'Young Turks' party, had gained considerable strength. They were supported by influential Turks living in exile in Cairo and Paris, and the C.U.P. was composed not just of Turks, but also of Arabs and Jews and others.

On 23 July 1908 a group of young Turkish army officers belonging to the C.U.P. in Salonika, led by Ismael Enver (Enver Pasha), staged a revolt.[1] Sensing the seriousness of the revolt, Abdul Hamid proclaimed an amnesty the following day for many of his political prisoners, and more importantly, re-instituted the Constitution which he had vetoed some thirty-two years previous. Concerning this move Antonius wrote:

> … its revival was greeted with enthusiasm, and nowhere perhaps was the jubilation greater than among the Arab nationalists who, in the first flush of deliverance, had mistaken it for real liberty. There was rejoicing all over the empire, in which Turks fraternised deliriously with Arabs, and Moslems with Christians, in the genuine belief that the constitution would meet everybody's wants. Its incompatibility with cultural aspirations seems to have passed unperceived. The fact that it provided for the fusion of the different races into a single, Ottoman democracy with Turkish for its distinctive language was in itself the very negation of the doctrine of cultural identity.[2]

---

1 Mustapha Kemal was involved in this revolt, but at a second level of authority. Mango, ibid, Part 1, Chapter 3.
2 Antonius, ibid, p. 102.

One of the first decisions made by the C.U.P. was to depose the Sherif of Mecca and replace him with one whom they believed would further their purposes in the crucial *Vilayet* of the Hejaz. They chose Hussein Ibn Ali to be the new Grand Sherif of Mecca. By that time Hussein had been a 'guest' of the Sultan for some fifteen years. Abdul Hamid, however, cautioned the C.U.P. that this was not a sound move. He sensed that Hussein could be a danger to Turkish suzerainty in that strategic region.[3]

Interestingly in the same year that Sherif (or Emir) Hussein and his family returned to the Hejaz, the Hejaz Railway arrived at Medina. Additionally, on 2 September 1908, a small society named the *Al-Ikha al-Arabi al-'Uthmani* was formed in Constantinople. It was an Arab society dedicated, wrote Antonius, 'to protect the Constitution, unite all races in loyalty to the Sultan, promote the welfare of the Arab provinces on a footing of real equality with the other races of the empire, spread education in the Arabic tongue and foster the observance of Arab customs.' Its membership, Antonius continued 'was open to Arabs of all creeds.'[4] Soon branches were established elsewhere and a newspaper began to promulgate its ideas.

Until this point Germany had a very strong position in Constantinople, and one of the first moves made by the C.U.P. was to curtail this influence. Understanding the neglect of the Turkish Navy, they issued an invitation to the British to send a naval advisor to help them restore their Navy. Britain complied (partly because they did not want Germany to fulfill this position) and in February 1909 Vice-Admiral Douglas Gamble arrived in Constantinople.[5]

DESPITE THE C.U.P. TURKEY BEGINS TO CRUMBLE

Despite these internal Turkish moves, the countries surrounding the Turkish Empire sensed this to be an opportune time to strike – for their own nationalist and imperialist ambitions. Bulgaria declared its independence in October 1908. Then almost immediately afterwards, the Austro-Hungarian

---

3 Antonius, ibid, p. 103.
4 Antonius, ibid, p. 102.
5 Chris B. Rooney, "The International Significance of British Naval Missions to the Ottoman Empire, 1908-1914," *Middle Eastern Studies*, Vol. 34, no. 1 (January 1998), cited in www.mthdyoke.edu

Empire annexed Bosnia and Herzegovina – a move which aggrieved Serbia, which coveted these two regions in order to form a future large Slav state. The move also perturbed Russia, Serbia's protector nation.

Matters also deteriorated inwardly. According to the Constitution elections were held, but the mechanics of the election were controlled by the C.U.P. which ensured that its own candidates were elected. Additionally, the electoral boundaries had been so demarcated in order to allow the numerically smaller Turks to gain considerably more seats in the Chamber of Deputies than the more numerically superior Arabs. The Senate was directly appointed by the Sultan, and of the forty members, only three were Arabs.[6] The election results revealed that neither the Sultan nor the C.U.P. were truly dedicated to the democratic system.

THE REVOLUTION OF 1909

Tensions between Sultan Abdul Hamid and the C.U.P. meanwhile escalated, as both desired to be the ultimate authority in Turkey. More importantly there was mounting opposition to the liberal policies of the C.U.P. as encapsulated in the Constitution by Muslims, especially the Mohammedan Union, which called for 'a new Muslim orthodoxy, demanding the protection and the implementation of the *shari'a*, the sacred Muslim law of the Qu'ran.'[7]

A revolt broke out in Constantinople on 12 April 1909, with Muslim zealots and sympathetic soldiers shouting "Down with the Constitution!" and "Long live the *shari'a*!"[8] The rioters then attacked the offices of the C.U.P. and the city was in uproar.

A C.U.P. 'Army of Deliverance' was quickly mustered and entered Constantinople on 23 April and subsequently crushed the revolt and brought the Government firmly under C.U.P. control.

The Chamber and the Senate then deposed Abdul Hamid and installed his brother, who took the name Mehmet V. The new sultan had no ambi-

---

6   Three fifths of the citizens of the Turkish Empire were Arabs, yet from the 245 candidates in the Chamber, 150 were Turks and only 60 were Arabs. Antonius, ibid, p. 104

7   Balakian, P. *The Burning Tigris*, (Harper-Collins e-books,),Kindle, Part 2, Chapter 12.

8   Balakian, ibid, Part 2, Chapter 12.

tions like his predecessor, and was content to allow the C.U.P. to govern the vast Turkish Empire. Similarly the position of Grand Vizier (Prime Minister) also lost much of its effective power and authority. The C.U.P. in time adopted a system of administration not altogether different from that of the former Hamidian regime.

PROBLEMS FOR THE ARMENIANS AND ADANA MASSACRES

The dismemberment of the Turkish Empire in Europe 'fuelled' the Turks 'distrust and dislike of their Christian subjects' wrote Peter Balakian in his publication *The Burning Tigris*, 'in particular their Christian subjects inside Turkey – notably the Armenians.'[9]

This was the time when the C.U.P. had taken over control of the Government, and many hard line leaders within the C.U.P. were now in favour of strengthening whatever remained of their Empire. The C.U.P. adopted a totalitarian style of Government. One aspect of this period was the desire to confirm Turkish national identity.

Some areas of the Empire, however, had large minority populations, particularly the province of Cilicia, and the major cities of Mersin and Adana, where there was a large Armenian population. Following the issuing of the Constitution many of the Armenians began exerting their own nationalism, much to the disdain of the Muslims, who held to the belief that there could never be true equality between Muslims and non-Muslims.[10]

As a result of the counter-revolution in April 1909 tensions mounted in Mersin and Adana. Then on 15 April a massacre of Armenians broke out in Adana. The British consul Major Doughty-Wylie and several American missionaries did their best to stop the massacre and save Armenians, but the Turkish authorities refused to intervene.[11]

When the counter-revolution finally ended in Constantinople, several Young Turk regiments were ordered from Beirut and Damascus to proceed to Adana and restore order. 'Not long after the Young Turk regiments arrived in Adana on the evening April 25', wrote Balakian, 'the city went up in

9 Balakian, ibid, Part 2, Chapter 12.
10 Balakian, ibid, Part 2, Chapter 12.
11 Balakian, ibid, Part 2, Chapter12.

flames again. This time the killing was even more brutal and well organized because it was conducted by the new Young Turk liberation army.'[12]

The massacre of the Armenians also spread into the countryside, but in several locations the Armenian men were able to offer resistance and thus save their communities.

Consul Doughty Wylie later wrote an extensive report in which he predicted that between 15-25,000 Armenians were massacred in this killing spree during April 1909.[13] It was not just the huge number of Armenians who were massacred which was the concern, but it was the fact that it happened under the watch of a 'new Turkey.'

It now became more apparent to many that the 'new Turkey' was really not all that different from the 'old Turkey.' All the liberal voices within the C.U.P. which had been calling for 'some autonomy for the minorities of the empire' were now squashed. The emphasis henceforth was upon Turkifying the Ottoman Empire.[14]

The C.U.P. disbanded the *Al-Ikha* Society in Constantinople, and elsewhere. Those who were by now dedicated to a greater form of Arab representation, and even of Arab independence, went underground. Thereafter numerous societies were formed which promulgated these viewpoints. One of these was *Al-Fatat* ('Young Arab Society'), which although initially based in Paris, by 1914 had moved to Damascus.

OPPORTUNITIES AND CHALLENGES FOR THE JEWISH *DHIMMIS*

One observer to these events was a young Russian Jewish journalist named Vladimir (Zev) Jabotinsky who was then living in Constantinople. Jabotinsky was the editor of four Zionist newspapers, and was convinced by 1909 that 'where the Turk rules neither sun may shine nor grass may grow, and that the only hope for the restoration of Palestine lay in the dismemberment of the Ottoman Empire.'[15]

12 Balakian, ibid, Part 2, Chapter 12.
13 Balakian, ibid, Part 2, Chapter 12.
14 Balakian, ibid, Part 2, Chapter 12.
15 Jabotinsky, V. *The Story of the Jewish Legion*, (New York, 1945), p. 30.

While Jabotinsky adopted his viewpoint from observing the outcome of the 1909 Revolution, other Russian-born Jews were adopting a contrary viewpoint. In 1909 the *Poalei Zion* movement sent Yitzhak Ben Zvi to Turkey in order to better understand the workings of the empire under this new regime. He travelled throughout the region and made contact with many of the Jewish communities.

Upon his return he began declaring to the Jewish *yishuv* the importance of integrating as best as possible into the new Turkey. Inherent within the new Turkey was the possibility of Parliamentary representation, through which the Jewish people could make a difference. With this in mind Ben Zvi, and by now Ben Gurion, both contemplated running as candidates for election in the Turkish Parliament. They believed the best way forward for the Jewish people was to become fully engaged in the political life of the country – whereupon they could perhaps even be accepted as *equals*.

In order to better equip themselves for this future and to become fluent in Turkish, Ben Zvi moved to Constantinople, while Ben Gurion moved to Salonika in November 1911, but then later moved to Constantinople in 1912 to study law alongside Ben Zvi.

In the same year, 1912, the family of Mustapha Kemal also arrived in the Turkish capital. They had been forced out of Salonika.[16] This was due to the dismemberment of the Turkish Empire which had not been staved off by the Young Turks regime.

---

16 Gabriel Mitchell, 'Ataturk, Ben-Gurion, and Turkey's Road Not Taken,' *The Tower,* Issue 8, November 2012 cited in www.thetower.org

§

CHAPTER 22

The noose tightens

FURTHER DISMEMBERMENT OF THE EMPIRE

Despite the dramatic changes, the dismemberment of the Turkish Empire continued after 1909. Utilizing a flimsy pretext Italy declared war on Turkey in 1911 and among her war gains claimed the *Vilayets* of Tripoli and Cyrenaica (modern day Libya).

Turkish officers such as Enver Pasha and Mustapha Kemal volunteered to fight the Italians, with Enver claiming command of the Ottoman forces in Cyrenaica. Mustapha Kemal fought his first battle against the Italians in December 1911 outside the small Cyrenaican port of Tobruk, and was then later based near Derna for many months.[1] The relationship between these two senior Turkish officers during this period was often strained.

A treaty was concluded with the Italians in1912, and they retained the *vilayets* of Tripoli and Cyrenaica. The inland region of Cyrenaica was not subdued, and was left in the hands of the Senussi chieftain, Sayyed Ahmad al-Sharif, an ally of the Turks. The Italians also gained the Dodecanese Islands (including Rhodes Island).

While this campaign was being fought conflict began in the Balkans region. The Balkan League, comprising Bulgaria, Greece and Serbia declared

---

1   Mango, ibid, Part 2, Chapter 4.

war on Turkey in 1912. By October their forces had reached Tekirdag on the Sea of Marmara, and had cut off Gallipoli from Istanbul.[2]

Greece now added the northern region which included Salonika to its southern region – and many Turkish residents were forced to leave, including Mustapha Kemal's family. The loss of this region, known as Rumelia, was a major psychological blow to the Turks. Among the hundreds of thousands of Turkish refugees, there was a sense of humiliation, and a desire for revenge. Many of these refugees were resettled in the Armenian areas of Anatolia.[3]

Kemal and Enver Pasha came back from the Libyan campaign and went straight into action in this new conflict. Kemal found himself involved in the defence of Bolayir (Bulair) and his HQ was located at the village of Gelibolu - Gallipoli.[4]

Following the convincing victory by the Balkan nations, the C.U.P. lost its authority in the Turkish Government. But when the European powers attempted to enforce a treaty upon Turkey, Enver masterminded a coup in January 1913 and returned to power.

The new Government rejected the terms being imposed upon Turkey by the European powers, and so in February 1913 hostilities recommenced, in what became known as the Second Balkan War. Both Enver and Mustapha Kemal (from his position at Bolayir) in the Gallipoli Peninsula, were heavily involved in the fighting. Two other men to take leading roles at this time were Mehmet Talaat, who became the Interior Minister, and Ahmad Djemal, who was the Military Governor of Constantinople.

This new leadership of Enver, Talaat and Djemal, then sanctioned the recapture of the city of Edirne from the Bulgarians, which occurred on 21 July 1913. At the subsequent armistice with Bulgaria, Turkey managed to salvage some of her territory lost during the First Balkan War. It also meant there was a large population exchange in the region of eastern Thrace – and

---

2 Mango, ibid, Part 2, Chapter 6.
3 Akmac, ibid, Chapter 3. Arnold Toynbee states there were 413,992 Muslim Turks who were expelled during the Balkan Wars. Toynbee, A. *The Western Question in Greece and Turkey,* (London, 1992), p. 140.
4 Mango, ibid, Part 2, Chapter 6.

some 100,000 Greeks were forced to leave their homes. Muslim refugees from the Balkan countries took their place.[5]

The recent humiliating defeats generated a stronger sense of Turkish nationalism, especially within the C.U.P. This resulted in an attitude that a return to the "Ottomanism" of the pre-*Tanzimat* period was necessary and that it was necessary to put an end, wrote Ziya Gokalp, a C.U.P. stalwart, 'to "the illusion of Muslim-Christian equality."'[6]

Gokalp moulded an ideological foundation for the C.U.P. in which "he transferred to the nation the divine qualities he had found in society, replacing the belief in God with the belief in the nation: and so nationalism became a religion."[7] It was Gokalp who more than anyone else gave the C.U.P. a sense of a Pan-Turk national identity.

Within this developing ideology the emphasis was more upon what was best for the Turks, not what was best for the multiple peoples of the vast empire. In order to achieve this Pan-Turk (or Pan-Turan) goal, a 'Special Organisation' was established.[8] Thereafter the 'Special Organization' became "the foremost institution for both internal and external security for the Ottoman state."[9]

Already by mid-1913 the Armenian community was feeling the effects of this resurgent nationalism of the C.U.P. When no reforms transpired, and as more Muslim refugees from Rumelia were located in the six provinces, conditions for the Armenians deteriorated. Then the General Council of the Armenian Patriarchate resigned on 4 May 1913.[10] The Armenians, frustrated by the lack of protection offered by the Central Government, began agitating overseas for help, especially in Russia.

This initiative resulted in pressure being placed upon the Turkish Government to implement some reforms and administrative changes in the

---

5 Mango, ibid, Part 2, Chapter 6. Following this period and partly in order to separate the two leading military men, Enver and Mustapha Kemal, Kemal became Turkish military attaché in Sofia the capital of Bulgaria.

6 Kazım [Nami] Duru, *Ziya Gökalp* (Istanbul, 1949), pp. 61– 62, cited in Akcam, ibid, p. 88. Gokalp, who formulated an ideology for the C.U.P., also stated that the "Turks are the 'supermen' imagined by the German philosopher Nietzsche.... New life will be born from Turkishness.... "

7 Akcam, ibid, p. 89.

8 Akcam, ibid, p. 93. The actual date of its establishment is not known as most of the documentation was destroyed.

9 Kutay, *Birinci*, p. 36 cited in Akcam, ibid, p. 96.

10 Akcam, ibid, p. 98.

Armenian provinces. Despite the likelihood of a degree of Armenian autonomy or of a Russian protectorate, the Turks agreed. They procrastinated,
however, in implementing these promised reforms. Soon all possibility of
these reforms being instituted ended – with the coming of a new war in the
region.

THE SITUATION IN ARABIA

To add to Turkey's land loss in Europe, she also lost territory in 1913 in
Arabia. Abdul Aziz Ibn Saud ousted the Turks from al-Hasa, their only
territory on the Persian Gulf side of the Arabian Peninsula.

Turkey was now being replaced as the imperial power in the Persian Gulf
region by Britain, whose authorities in India had responsibility for British
interests in this region. They had made treaties with Arab tribal leaders
on the southern and eastern regions of the Arabian Peninsula, including
Ibn Saud. Initially these arrangements were to safeguard the sea route to
India, but by 1914 they had been taken also to preserve 'the rich oil-fields in
south-western Persia which had been conceded to a British company.'[11]

On the western side of the Arabian Peninsula another ominous sign
arose for the Turks. Since arriving back from his exile in Constantinople
the Grand Sherif of Mecca, Emir Hussein, slowly established 'un-official'
control over the Hejaz, and even challenged the House of Saud for control of
the vast inland region of Arabia.

In line with the C.U.P. goal of centralising control in Constantinople
the Turkish Government wanted to exert its authority in the Hejaz. In early
1914 a new stronger-willed Governor-General (or *Vali*) was sent out to bring
the semi-autonomous Sherif Hussein into line. This move was simultaneous to extra pressure being mounted to extend the railway from Medina
through to Mecca. Constantinople agitated to have complete control over
the *Vilayet* of Hejaz, while Sherif Hussein agitated to retain his semi-autonomous rule there. Conflict was inevitable.

---

11 Antonius, ibid, p. 122.

ARAB NATIONALIST MOVEMENTS

One group which was particularly interested in the events taking place in the Balkans and Constantinople was those Arabs agitating for a greater share in the governance of the Turkish Empire. In late 1912 a group of eighty-six men, of all creeds, formed a Committee of Reform in Beirut 'and drew up a scheme for the grant of home rule to the Arab provinces of the Ottoman empire.'[12] They agreed to work together with the Party of Decentralisation based in Cairo.

The basis of their scheme was for decentralised government, whereby certain aspects of administration would be local, while others would be centralised in Constantinople; that Arabic would be the official language of the Arab speaking areas and not Turkish; and that conscripted Arab soldiers would not be sent to non-Arab areas. Many Arab soldiers had previously served in the Russo-Turkish War as well as the Balkans Wars.

When this programme became public, the C.U.P. quickly banned and dissolved the Committee of Reform in April 1913. A general outcry against this move forced the Government to desist and they then permitted some reforms.

Then *Al-Fatat* issued a call for the various Arab nationalist parties to come to a Conference in Paris, which convened in June 1913. There was no reference to separatism or secession from the Turkish Empire, but they wanted to maintain 'the integrity of the empire provided the rights of the Arabs as partners were recognised and their cultural aspirations given free scope in a decentralised form of government.'[13] Their statement at the conclusion placed an 'emphasis on the Arab claim to full political rights and to an effective share in the administration of the affairs of the empire.'[14]

As could be expected the C.U.P. was opposed to this meeting and its conclusions, but was forced ultimately to come to terms with it. Three Arab delegates from this Conference were invited to Constantinople, and on 18

---

12 Antonius, ibid, p. 112.
13 Antonius, ibid, p. 115.
14 Antonius, ibid, p. 115.

August 1913 an imperial *firman* was issued 'purporting to enact the provisions of the Paris agreement.'[15]

But once again the Turkish leadership, on this occasion the C.U.P. resorted to political chicanery and diffused the agreements made so that they became of no real effect. At heart the C.U.P. had no desire to reform and no desire to decentralise: they were in effect an autocratic regime similar to the one they had replaced! By January 1914 the optimism of Paris had been squashed.

Officers such as Major Aziz Ali al-Mazri were now distraught by the corruption and treachery of the C.U.P. Al-Mazri was determined to do something to rectify the situation, and in early 1914 he formed a secret society composed primarily of Arab officers, named *Al-'Ahd* (The Covenant).

Branches were also established in Baghdad and Mosul. But al-Mazri was arrested in Constantinople on 9 February 1914, and tried on a number of fabricated charges. There was a general outcry, and ultimately he was pardoned by the Sultan and allowed to return to his native Egypt in late April 1914.

GENERAL LIMAN VON SANDERS AND ENVER PASHA

The Turkish Empire was tottering. To survive she needed to modernise her army, and form a strong alliance with a European power – or powers. In 1912 Admiral Arthur Limpus arrived in Constantinople as the third British Naval delegate, and later Turkey ordered the construction of three new battleships – from Britain!

This move could have indicated that Turkey was seeking a closer geo-political relationship with Britain. Britain, however, was allied to both France and Russia – and the C.U.P. (especially Enver) had Pan-Turk ambitions in regions controlled by the Russians.

Turkey's abysmal performance on the field of battle during the wars of 1911-1913 caused the leadership to admit that their army was badly in need

---

15 Antonius, ibid, p. 116.

of reform. The one army in Europe they believed which could help them was the German army.[16]

On 15 June 1913 General Liman von Sanders was asked if he would be willing to go to Turkey. The German Ambassador to Constantinople, Freiherr von Wagenheim, stated to him concerning this appointment, that it: '… would check British influence seeking to have British administration reformers called to Turkey.'[17] If Germany failed to comply with this request, Wagenheim stated, then Turkey 'may turn to other powers.'[18]

Von Sanders and the military mission of forty-two officers arrived in Constantinople on 14 December 1913.[19] There were immediate reactions to Von Sanders' presence in Constantinople, not least from the Russian, British and French legations.

Another important move shortly after he arrived was the rapid rise of Enver Pasha to the position of Minister of War – and then to being a General, in January 1914.[20]

One of Enver's first actions was to re-organize the 'Special Organization.' According to a C.U.P. member Kuscubasi Esref, Enver stated, 'that the only way out of the dismal position in which Turkey had found itself was to achieve a unity of the Turkish and Islamic worlds.'[21]

To achieve this goal they would need to eliminate the Christian population, especially in strategic regions, such as the Aegean coast and the Armenian provinces. Nurdogan Tacalan wrote:

The [Committee of] Union and Progress made a clear decision. The source of the trouble in western Anatolia would be removed, the Greeks would be cleared out by means of political and economic measures. Before anything else, it would be necessary to weaken and break the economically powerful Greeks.[22]

---

16   Mango, ibid, Part 2, Chapter 6.
17   Von Sanders, ibid, p. 2.
18   Von Sanders, ibid, p. 2.
19   By the end of the War, there were some 800 German officers, medical officers and other officials in Turkey. See Von Sanders, ibid, pp. 20-21. This number does not include German soldiers who fought alongside the Turks.
20   Mango, ibid, Part 2, Chapter 6.
21   Akcam, ibid, p. 102.
22   Nurdoğan Taçalan, Ege'de Kurtuluş Savaşı Başlarken (Istanbul, 1970), p. 65, cited in Akcam, ibid, p. 103.

When the harassment against the Greeks began, it had, as British historian Arnold Toynbee stated, all the hallmarks of a systematic operation.[23]
Unfortunately his observations proved to be correct, and from the middle of
1914 the non-Muslim communities began to experience the harsh reality of
the new C.U.P. policies.

BRITISH AND FRENCH INTENTIONS

Since her occupation of Egypt in 1882 Britain had basically surrendered her
active involvement in the province of Syria to other European powers, especially to France, Russia and Germany. By 1912 it would appear that if the
Turkish Empire indeed did disintegrate, then France of all the European
powers was in the best place to administer the province of Syria.

By 1912, however, rumours filtered into Syria that British agents from
Egypt were stirring up local sentiment against France. Indeed there were
some British administrators in Egypt (including Cromer's replacement,
Lord Kitchener) who were apprehensive about the prospect of having France
facing them on the east side of the Suez Canal. This group envisioned a form
of union between Egypt and Syria.

In view of growing geo-political tensions in Europe resulting from
the growth of Germany, the British Government was very keen to maintain
good relations with France. In order then to dispel any French concerns,
Foreign Secretary Sir Edward Grey informed the French in December 1912
that Britain had no strategic interests in the province of Syria. The French
Prime Minister told his Parliament on 21 December 1912 that, concerning
Lebanon and Syria 'the British Government has in a very friendly manner
declared to us that in these regions it has no intention of taking any action
nor has it any designs or political aspirations of any kind.'[24]

The British ambassador in Paris, Francis Bertie, wrote to Grey on 26
December 1912 that: 'Your assurances which Poincare quoted in the Senate

---

23 Toynbee, A. *The Western Question in Greece and Turkey*, (London, 1992), p. 140.

24 Stein, L. *The Balfour Declaration*, (London, 1961), p. 48. Stein concluded: 'This account of what Poincare said is
taken from his own extracts from his speech as set out in *Au Service de la France*, VI, 411-412. An editorial in *The
Times* of 23 December 1912, notes with satisfaction that Poincare had been able to say that there was no difference
between France and Britain concerning Syria. The passage in question is not, however, to be found in the official
report of the Senate debate on 21 December 1912, and it may be that, though Poincare describes his statement as
having been made to the Senate, it was made to the Foreign Affairs Commission of that body.'

that we have no designs in Syria have excited the appetite of the French newspapers. They appear to conclude that our disinteressement is equivalent to a free hand for France.'[25]

Despite Poincare's statement there were some ambiguities. Did Poincare, for instance, give the same meaning to Syria as did Grey? Did Grey infer the entire province and exclude southern Syria – Palestine? Was Grey in fact 'surrendering' Palestine, on the opposite side of the Suez Canal, to France in any future demise of the Turkish Empire? Subsequent agreements between the French and Germans over railway concessions, however, made the matter clear as far as the French were concerned.

FRENCH AND GERMAN CO-ORDINATION

By 1912 the so-called 'Berlin to Baghdad' Railway continued to progress further eastwards towards the Persian Gulf. One branch of this railway went to Alexandretta, near the Biblical city of Antioch, at the head of the strategic Gulf of Alexandretta – a region of geo-political interest to Britain, and also to France.

The main line went from Anatolia via Aleppo, in northern Syria towards Baghdad. In that year it was about to cross the Euphrates River near the ancient city of Carchemish then being excavated by British archaeologists, one of whom was a young Oxford graduate named Thomas Edward (T.E.) Lawrence.

France, sensing the dangerous proximity of the new German initiatives in the region to its own economic investments, initiated negotiations with Germany aimed at decreasing potential conflict between the two powers. An agreement was reached in February 1914 whereby Germany recognized the French zone of interest in Syria (which for the French included Palestine); and France recognized the German zone of interest in the eastern region, equating to Mesopotamia.

It was over the issue of railways, though, that Britain found itself opposing France. The French and the Turks proposed building a spur off the

---

25   Ambassador to Grey, 26 December 1912, FO: 800/43, National Archives.

Jaffa-Jerusalem Railway southward to Gaza and El Arish – and potentially towards the Suez Canal. This possibility was strongly opposed by Grey and many other British strategists.

One Member of Parliament, Sir Mark Sykes, highlighted his concerns in a speech before Parliament in March 1914, cautioning that French activities in Syria could result in Britain being faced with a 'European frontier in the Sinai Peninsula.'[26]

Despite the misgivings of Sykes, and others, France seemed the most likely inheritor of the land of Israel in 1914, come the eventual dismemberment of the Turkish Empire. Only where the Holy Places were concerned was she likely to share ownership – with Russia or some other international body. France, wrote Stein, 'was not slow to make it clear to her Allies that in any partition of the Turkish Empire her claims would extend to a Greater Syria, including Palestine.'[27]

By the middle of 1914 it seemed like the noose was slowly tightening around Ottoman Turkey's neck. But for the time being it continued to limp along, albeit now much assisted with a convenient crutch in the new German connection.

ABDULLAH MEETS KITCHENER AND STORRS IN CAIRO

Emir Hussein's second son Abdullah was the foremost Arab minister in the Ottoman Parliament. The Turks, who had not given up the idea of deposing his father as Sherif, tried to pacify Abdullah by offering him a number of prestigious positions. Abdullah refused them all.

In February 1914 while en-route from Mecca to Constantinople, Abdullah stopped in Cairo to visit the Khedive and while there he met Lord Kitchener. Also present at the meeting was Ronald Storrs, the Oriental Secretary at the British Agency. Abdullah mentioned the strained relations between the new *Vali* sent by the Porte and the Sherif, and asked Kitchener to ask Grey, that 'if an attempt was made by the Sublime Porte to dismiss his father from the hereditary office of Sherif of the Holy Places would you

26   Stein, ibid, p. 49.
27   Stein, ibid, p. 44.

use your good offices with the Sublime Porte to prevent any such attempt.'[28] Abdullah pointed out that his father had always done his best to look after Indian Muslim pilgrims. He further stated, that, 'in case the Turkish Government dismissed his father the Arab tribes of the Hejaz would fight for his father and a state of war against the Turkish troops would ensue.'[29] Abdullah continued:

> He hoped in such circumstances that the British Government would not allow reinforcements to be sent by sea for the purpose of preventing the Arabs from exercising the rights they have enjoyed from time immemorial in their own country round the holy places.[30]

Abdullah wanted to ascertain the attitude of the British Government in the event of open conflict between Turkey and the Hejaz. Kitchener stated that 'since England's traditional policy was one of friendship with Turkey, it was not likely that she would intervene.'[31]

While Abdullah was in Constantinople matters deteriorated in the Hejaz. The Turkish *Vali* attempted to usurp control, and had also fallen out with Hussein concerning the extension of the railway. The British Agency in Cairo reported that a messenger from Mecca had informed the Khedive that the 'Arabs are all with Sherif and will not tolerate Vali, whose recall they have demanded.'[32]

Constantinople was very concerned about this development, and especially when they learnt that Abdullah had met with Kitchener in Cairo in February. Kitchener meanwhile had received word from Constantinople 'that such audiences were displeasing to the Sublime Porte, always suspicious of Arab intrigue in the Hejaz and in Syria' - so he refrained from any further meetings.[33]

---

28 FO 141/460, Egypt 1914. File 1198, No 22, Kitchener to Grey, 6 February 1914. National Archives.
29 Kitchener to Grey, ibid.
30 Kitchener to Grey, ibid.
31 Antonius, ibid, p. 127.
32 FO 141/60, Egypt 1914. Telegram from British Agency in Cairo to Foreign Office, 21 March 1914.
33 Storrs, ibid, p. 122.

Kitchener actually received word from Grey who echoed the sentiments of the British Ambassador at Constantinople, Sir Louis Mallett. Kitchener agreed with Mallett that 'great care will have to be taken in dealing with the Arab question so as not to wound Turkish susceptibilities and arouse their suspicions.'[34] Grey and the Government were mindful that Turkey was closely watching each and every move in its Empire, and the last thing the British wanted was to push Turkey more into the arms of Germany.

Despite this serious geo-political factor, Kitchener reinforced to Grey that 'we cannot afford to lose sight of the interests which Great Britain must always take in the Holy places owing to the annual pilgrimage which is attended by thousands of Indian Moslems and also by many Egyptians.' The safety of these pilgrims, he stated, depended upon 'a good relationship between Turks and Arabs whose animosity has undoubtedly been roused by the recent Turkish policy of centralisation adopted during the last few years, and more especially by the proposal to push forward railway communications, which would cause great pecuniary loss to the Arabs who live on their camel hire.'[35]

While in Constantinople it became apparent to Abdullah that the Turkish Government was determined 'to push the railway on to Mecca which he saw would mean the economic death of the camel owning population of Arabia.'[36] It would also mean conflict.

In April 1914 Abdullah left Constantinople en-route back to the Hejaz. Upon his departure he was instructed not to return to Mecca via Cairo, and that if he had to, he was 'not to see Lord Kitchener or any representative of his.'[37] Abdullah, however, did stop in Cairo and asked Storrs to visit him, which he did.

Abdullah spoke at length of his recent conversation with the Grand Vizier, and how the Turks were insistent upon continuing with the railway line to Mecca and Jeddah. It was upon this factor that Sherif Hussein had

---

34　FO 141/60, No. 15883, Kitchener to Grey, 11 April 1914. National Archives.

35　FO 141/60, No. 15883, Kitchener to Grey, 11 April 1914. National Archives. There was indeed an intense tussle between the two rulers, which the Sherif finally won, and 'the vali was bidden to make his peace with the Sharif.' Antonius, ibid, p. 125.

36　Kitchener to Sir W Tyrrell, 26 April 1914, Grey MSS., Vol IX, cited in Storrs, ibid, p, 122.

37　Note by Storrs, British Agency, 19 April 1914, FO 141/460, ibid.

instructed Abdullah to approach the British Government for an agreement to assist them in stopping the Turks carrying this scheme into practice.[38]

Kitchener instructed Storrs to tell Abdullah: 'the Arabs of the Hejaz could expect no encouragement from us and that our only interest in Arabia was the safety and comfort of Indian pilgrims.'[39] At this stage Britain was committed to maintaining its long term geo-political relationship with Turkey – which it still viewed as a 'Friendly Power.'

But all that was soon to change, due to events in Europe.

---

38   Note by Storrs, British Agency, 19 April 1914, FO 141/460, ibid.
39   Kitchener to Sir William Tyrell, 26 April, 1914, cited in Kedourie, ibid, p.7

§

CHAPTER 23

World War One begins

WAR THREATENS

Although geo-political tensions simmered in Europe between the Triple Alliance (Britain, France and Russia) and the Central Powers (Germany and the Austro-Hungarian Empire) few anticipated that a great fire would erupt from these tensions.

The spark for that fire was the assassination of Archduke Franz Ferdinand, the heir to the throne of the Austro-Hungarian Empire, in Sarajevo on 28 June 1914, by a Serbian nationalist. Austria then demanded an official Serbian apology otherwise there would be retribution. Russia then sided with Serbia – her client nation. Germany then supported Austria. Britain and France were obliged to stand by Russia. In no time at all the fire was out of control.[1]

War officially began on 4 August when Britain and France declared War on Germany. David Lloyd George, the Chancellor of the Exchequer wrote: 'The 4th August is one of the world's fateful dates. The decision taken on that day in the name and on behalf of the British Empire altered the des-

---

[1] For one of the best analyses of how the War began see Barbara Tuchman, *The Guns of August*, (New York, 1962).

tiny of Europe.'[2] In fact the War was to alter the destiny of the world, and especially that of the Middle East.

KITCHENER BECOMES MINISTER OF STATE FOR WAR

Kitchener and Storrs were both in England when War began. Kitchener was then summoned to the Cabinet meeting that afternoon and was offered the position of Minister of War. He accepted, but Storrs was asked to return to Egypt. Kitchener informed him, wrote Storrs, 'that I knew what he wanted in Egypt.'[3] Upon his return he joined Milne Cheetham, who became the acting British Agent in Egypt, and then set out to establish what Kitchener 'wanted in Egypt.'

THE BRITISH EMPIRE VOLUNTEERS

Once Britain declared war, then the Empire was also legally at war. Moreover this legal binding did not require the colonies and dependencies to send troops overseas. This would need to be a voluntary decision made by the individual countries.

Almost immediately after Britain declared war, the nations of the Empire - Canada, Australia, New Zealand, India and Newfoundland – volunteered to send troops to help the 'Mother Country'. The soldiers from Canada and Newfoundland sailed first to Britain, and then in time crossed over to the war front in France and Belgium.

The Australian Government agreed to send an initial expeditionary force composed of 20,000 men – infantry and mounted (Light Horse) while the New Zealanders agreed to send 8,000 men – infantry and mounted (Mounted Rifles). The Australians were to be commanded by Major-General William Bridges, and the New Zealanders by Major-General Alexander Godley.

The soldiers of New Zealand and Australia had been inspected in May of 1914 by General Sir Ian Hamilton, the Inspector General of Overseas

---

2　Lloyd George, D. *War Memoirs*, (London, 1939), p. 42.
3　Storrs, ibid, p. 126.

Forces. After observing a 'series of practical field exercises' in New Zealand, Hamilton wrote: 'It is well equipped; well armed; the human material is second to none in the world; and it suffers as a fighting machine only from want of field work and want of an ingrained habit of discipline.'[4] These men were soon to get lots of field work and lots of discipline.

Many were the motives for the thousands of young men who volunteered. Professor Rodney Gouttman stated:

Some leaders of the non-Roman Catholic churches, to which the majority of Australians of the day adhered – at least nominally – first rationalized the war as a God-given chance to bring Australian civilization to the notice of the world through the suffering and baptism of fire that were often the precursors to nationhood. Australia's legitimacy needed to be proved on the battlefield, a trial that had not occurred when it federated into a single nation in 1901. These church leaders felt that this constitutional binding lacked, as it were, this military – and hence spiritual – dimension.[5]

Such nationalistic ideals, though, were not the main motive for most of those who enlisted. Albert Facey was one of the first Australians to join up, and, he wrote, 'we were fit, and another thing that appealed to us was that we would be travelling overseas and would be able to see what the other part of the world was like.'[6]

Hartley Palmer was a New Zealand farmer from Nelson, and he recalled of his motives for joining up: 'The British Empire wasn't in my thoughts: I didn't know a great deal about it. I wanted to have a trip around the world, and I thought it was a chance to have it. And I wanted to have adventure … Sailing off to war with all the other Nelson boys made it even more of an adventure.'[7] Another New Zealander, Tony Fagan, recalled: 'I was school teach-

---

4   Report of the Inspector General of Overseas Forces on the Military Forces of New Zealand, by General Sir Ian Hamilton. *The Times Documentary History of the War*, Vol. X, p. 487, cited in Pugsley, C. *Gallipoli: The New Zealand Story*, (Auckland, 1990), p. 45.

5   Gouttman, R. An *Anzac Zionist Hero*, (London, 2006), p. 35.

6   Facey, A.B. *A Fortunate Life*, (Melbourne, 1981), p. 234.

7   Shadbolt, M. *Voices of Gallipoli*, (Auckland, 1988), p. 29.

ing in Northland. When I heard about the war, I went down to Auckland and joined up. I suppose you could say I was looking for adventure.'[8]

Two Jewish men who signed up early on were Eliazar Margolin and Louis Salek. Salek came from Wanganui in New Zealand and was a stoker on a ship going between New Zealand and Australia. When War broke out he was in Australia, and 'hearing that the Australian army wanted accomplished horsemen' wrote Stephen Levine, Salek felt he 'fitted the bill because before going to sea he had spent all his spare time on horses with the Maori people up the Wanganui river.'[9]

Margolin enlisted on 19 September 1914. He joined the 16th Battalion, 4th Infantry Brigade and shortly after was made the commander of 'B' Company. Margolin then moved to Victoria for further training.[10]

The initial armada carrying 8,574 New Zealand soldiers and 3,818 horses left Wellington on 16 October 1914[11] and made its way towards Albany in Western Australia, where most of the Australian Expeditionary Force joined them. One of those Australians was Victorian Thomas Gardner who stated: 'There are over two thousand of us on board so it is rather cramped as we have a number of transport horses on board, and they take up a lot of room on the deck, so we can't get much exercise … I believe there will be about thirty ships at Albany.'[12]

INDIAN EXPEDITIONARY FORCE

Britain was apprehensive that Turkey would join the War with Germany. With this in mind they sent two ships *HMS Espiegle* and *HMS Dalhousie* to the Shatt-al-Arab (where the Tigris-Euphrates River enters the Persian Gulf) on 29 September. The objective was to protect the oil pipeline which went to Basrah (Basra).

The Indian Government, sensitive to the fact that Turkey was closely aligned to Germany, prepared an expeditionary force ready to land in

---

8   Shadbolt, ibid, p. 17.
9   Levine, S. 'The Flag Waved Free', in the *Jerusalem Post*, 23 May 1990.
10   Gouttman, R. *An Anzac Zionist Hero*, (London, 2006), pp. 34-35. He finally sailed on 22 December 1914.
11   Pugsley, ibid, p. 62.
12   Morice, J. *Six Bob A Day Tourist*, (Australia, 1985), p. 11. The horses were known as 'Walers'.

Mesopotamia as soon as Turkey entered the War on the side of the Central Powers.

Then on the day that the New Zealanders departed from Wellington, the first contingent of the Indian Expeditionary Force departed from Bombay (Mumbai). After departure, sealed orders were opened instructing them to proceed to Bahrain Island in the Persian Gulf, where they finally arrived on 21 October 1914.[13]

THE AUSTRALIANS AND NEW ZEALANDERS DEPART

The soldiers from Australia and New Zealand and their horses left from Albany on 2 November 1914. They were joined off the coast by the West Australians who had left from Fremantle.[14]

The monotonous voyage was interrupted by some adventure when *HMAS Sydney* intercepted the German cruiser *Emden* in the Indian Ocean. The convoy then continued on to Colombo in Ceylon (Sri Lanka), and from there towards the Red Sea, passing Aden and heading towards Suez. All those aboard anticipated heading first to Britain, to complete their training, and then on to France to fight the 'Hun.' Several events, though, altered this arrangement.

Prior to the outbreak of War Colonel Harry Chauvel had been appointed to the War Office in Britain, and was en-route from Australia when War broke out.[15] Upon arrival at the War Office Chauvel was informed on 19 August that he would command the Australian Light Horse Brigade, then being formed in Australia, and which would soon thereafter depart for Britain.[16]

Until they arrived he worked as the Australian representative on the Imperial General Staff. Chauvel felt that the quarters being prepared for the Australian soldiers upon arrival in Britain would be inadequate, and through his perseverance had Lord Kitchener command that the Australian

---

13   Verrier, A. *Agents of Empire: Anglo-Zionist Intelligence Operations 1915-1919*, (London, 1995), pp. 27-28.

14   The 10th Light Horse left in February 1915.

15   Henry George Chauvel had been born in New South Wales, but his family moved to Queensland in 1889, where he joined the Queensland Mounted Rifles in 1890.

16   Chauvel's personal account (partly written by Mrs Chauvel), p.2. PR00535.003 Series 3, Folder 1, Chauvel Private Papers, Australian War Memorial (AWM); Hill, A.J. *Chauvel of the Light Horse*, (Melbourne, 1978), p. 44.

(and New Zealand) soldiers would land in Egypt instead and complete their basic training there.[17]   Chauvel then sailed for Egypt on 28 November and arrived in Egypt on 10 December 1914, to await the first Australian and New Zealand contingent.

THE SECRET ALLIANCE AND CONTROVERSIAL WARSHIPS

Another determining reason for the change in the arrangements for the Australian and New Zealanders was due to events happening in London and Turkey in early August.   On 2 August as war threatened in Europe the Turkish leadership led by Enver, Djemal and Talaat entered into a secret alliance with Germany.

Then on 3 August Winston Churchill (the First Lord of the Admiralty), who was unaware of the German-Turkish agreement, commandeered two warships being constructed in Britain for the Turkish Fleet.   Although he offered full compensation, the Turks were incensed, as some of the financing for these two battleships was given by the populace.   At this time two German warships, the *Goeben* (commanded by Admiral Souchen) and the *Breslau*, were in the Mediterranean, being shadowed by the British Navy.[18]

The British Navy, anticipating that the German ships would head westwards and attack French convoys bringing troops from their North African colonies, waited - and subsequently missed their prey. The German ships had received orders to proceed east – not to Egypt, but to Constantinople.

The presence of the two German battleships was of paramount importance if Turkey was going to openly engage in War on the side of Germany. But when they failed to arrive, the Turkish leaders became apprehensive. Enver Pasha made a visit to the Russians with a counter-offer to that which they had just made with the Germans.[19]

Such an eventuality was not needed, for on 9 August the two German ships were at the entrance to the Dardanelles requesting permission to enter, which was duly granted by Enver Pasha. Upon arrival in Constantinople

---

17   Hill, ibid, p. 45.

18   The British Mediterranean Fleet could have sunk these two battleships on 4 August, but couldn't, as Germany had until midnight to respond to Britain's ultimatum, and War between Britain and Germany had still not been declared.

19   Moorehead, A. *Gallipoli*, (Illustrated Edition, South Melbourne, 1975), p. 22.

the German crew members donned Turkish *fezes*,[20] and were commissioned into the Turkish Navy. Ambassador Mallett and the Allied ambassadors, understanding that this violated the Straits Convention, protested.

Despite this incident, the official Turkish line of neutrality was maintained, although they did begin to mobilise their forces. General Von Sanders was given command of the First Army, which covered an area which included Constantinople and the Dardanelles.

Thus Turkey, prompted by Germany, was slowly preparing for involvement in the War.[21] This was clearly evident in the Dardanelles where Charles Palmer, the British vice-consul at Chanak (Canakkale) witnessed German soldiers being present when mines were being laid in the waterway.[22]

The area of Canakkale would soon become the focal point of military activity in Turkey. It would soon be associated with another, non-military episode. Taner Akcam draws attention to a conversation between Henry Morgenthau, the American ambassador and the German ambassador Wangenheim at this time, stating: 'With the outbreak of the war in August 1914, Henry Morgenthau warned him that the Turks would massacre the Armenians in Anatolia, to which Wangenheim replied, "So long as England does not attack Çanakkale or some other Turkish port there is nothing to fear. Otherwise, nothing can be guaranteed."'[23]

This forecast was ominous, for shortly after War was declared: 'The formation of the Special Organization units began' wrote Akcam. He continued: 'Three main sources of manpower were drawn upon for the task: Kurdish tribes, jailed convicts, and recent emigrants from the Caucasus and Rumelia.'[24] Within weeks these gangs were attacking unarmed villages on the Turkey-Russian border and indiscriminately murdering thousands of people, mostly Armenians, as testified by Johannes Lepsius.[25] Later Russian

---

20 A traditional hat or headdress of the Turks.

21 Von Sanders, ibid, p. 33.

22 Dolan, H. *36 Days – The Untold Story of the Anzac assault on 25ᵗʰ April 1915*, (Macmillan, Australia, 2010, Kindle Book, 2010), Chapter 1. Dolan states that Palmer relayed his observations to *HMS Indomitable* stationed off-shore.

23 HHStA III 171, Yeniköy, 26 August 1914. Telegram no. 494, in Ohandjanian, *Armenien*, vol. 6, p. 4402, cited in Akcam, T. *A Shameful Act: The Armenian Genocide and the Question of Turkish Responsibility*. (Henry Holt and Co.. Kindle Edition), p. 127.

24 Akcam, ibid, p. 134.

25 Lepsius, ibid, pp. 78-9, cited in Akcam, ibid, p, 139.

forces and Armenian volunteers fighting with the Russians retaliated with attacks upon Muslim villages.[26]

Also in August 1914, the *Dashnak* Party convened a congress in Erzurum 'to which,' wrote Akcam, 'standard sources concur, the CUP sent a special delegation. The CUP offered to grant autonomy to the Dashnaks in exchange for fomenting a rebellion inside Russia. However, the Dashnaks rejected this proposal, apparently deciding to avoid intrigues and perform their duty as Ottoman citizens.'[27]

The rejection of this overture was construed by the Turkish authorities as an indication that the Armenians were determined upon a revolt against the Turkish regime. The Turkish leadership then resolved to destroy the Armenian community.[28]

On 16 December 1914 the Armenian reform agreement was officially abrogated by the Turkish Government. The Armenians were never going to see the reforms they so desperately desired in order to live a peaceful semi-autonomous existence.[29] The previous work of the Armenian independence groups had come to nothing – and now the Turkish regime was going to seek revenge for what they construed as treason by the Armenians by going to the European powers for help.

THE FUTURE OF THE TURKISH EMPIRE

The British Government was aware of the close relationship between Turkey and Germany, and even though none was aware of the secret alliance, many suspected that ultimately Turkey would join the War on the side of the Central Powers. Some ministers, including Lloyd George and Churchill, proposed the formation of a Balkan confederation comprising Greece, Bulgaria, Rumania and Serbia. This bloc could both attack Turkey and ensure there would be no overland link between the Central Powers and Turkey.

26　Akcam, ibid, p. 140.
27　Akcam, ibid, p. 136.
28　Akcam, ibid, p. 136. For more on this Congress and its consequences see Akcam.
29　Akcam, ibid, Chapter 4.

Foreign Minister Grey saw numerous problems if Greece was involved in capturing the city of Constantinople. Many understood that Russia coveted control of this city, the traditional capital of the Orthodox Christians. As Russia was integral for the Allied war effort, and also quite vulnerable, nothing could be done to jeopardize Russia's alliance with the Allies.[30]

---

30 Fromkin, D. *A Peace to End all Peace*, (New York, 1989), p. 127.

TURKISH EMPIRE 1914 - 1918

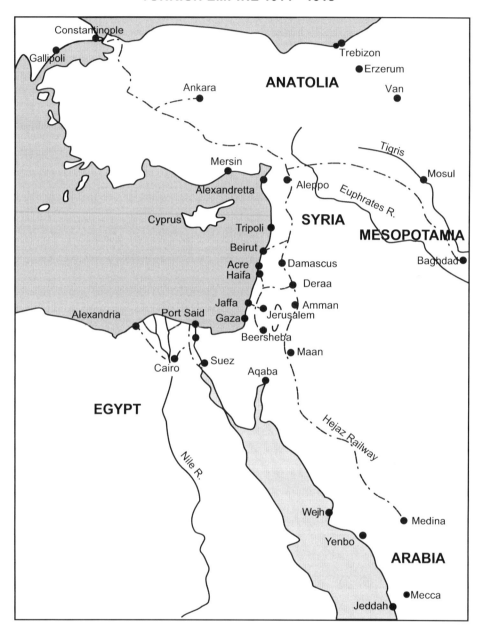

§

CHAPTER 24

Britain and Arabia

hile Grey was consumed with these important considerations, Kitchener and the British officials in Cairo were very concerned about Turkey joining with the Central Powers. One serious consideration of this happening was the possibility of a *Jihad* being proclaimed by the Turks.

Storrs stated: 'our constant preoccupation was the threat of Turkey on the Canal; less for its military effect than for the repercussion upon a Moslem Egypt.'[1] From information gleaned from the population Storrs stated that 'Germany is represented as the one great Power that has befriended Islam without acquiring one acre of Moslem territory.'[2]

One of the greatest concerns for Britain was the effect of having the Caliph of Islam, who was also the Sultan of Turkey, opposing them in War, as Britain administered millions of Muslims in India, Egypt and the Sudan.

In September 1914 Storrs wrote a private letter to Kitchener, 'suggesting that by timely consultation with Mecca we might secure not only the

---

1 Storrs, ibid, p. 131.
2 Storrs, ibid, p. 132. As later discovered the Turco-German plan also involved establishing German submarine bases and wireless stations along the Red Sea coast of Arabia. Storrs, ibid, p. 149.

neutrality but the alliance of Arabia in the event of Ottoman aggression.'[3] Kitchener responded on 24 September to 'H.M.'s Representative' in Cairo:

> Tell Storrs to send secret and carefully chosen messenger from me to Sharif Abdallah to ascertain whether "should present armed German influence in Constantinople coerce Khalif [Sultan] against his will, and Sublime Porte, to acts of aggression and war against Great Britain, he and his father and Arabs of the Hejaz would be with us or against us."[4]

Storrs chose a suitable messenger, 'an Egyptian named Ali Efendi',[5] and sent him to Mecca via Suez and Jeddah on 5 October 1914. Ali met with Abdullah as well as Sherif Hussein himself, and was given a letter to take back to Storrs. The content of that letter was forwarded to Kitchener and expressed a desire that Britain would promise that they will 'abstain from internal intervention in Arabia and guarantee Sherif against "foreign and Ottoman aggression."'[6]

Although Turkey was not yet officially at war against Britain, this communication from Kitchener placed Emir Hussein in a difficult position as to his future course. His son Feisal favoured standing by Turkey, while 'Abdullah thought otherwise.' Abdullah having had contact with the secret Arab societies understood the depth of potential support in Syria and Mesopotamia for taking a stand against Turkey.[7]

By the time Storrs received the answer back from Mecca, war with Turkey was imminent. Storrs in a telegram to Kitchener on 31 October reiterated that what Abdullah was stating was no different from what he had communicated while visiting Cairo earlier in the year.[8]

---

3   Storrs, ibid, pp. 148-49.
4   Telegram Kitchener to Cairo, 24 September 1914, No 219, FO 141/460, Egypt 1914. Also cited in Storrs, ibid, p. 149.
5   Antonius, ibid, p. 131.
6   Telegram Cairo to Foreign Office, 31 October 1914, No. 233, FO 141/460, ibid.
7   Antonius, ibid, pp. 131-32.
8   HM Agency Cairo to Foreign Office, 31 October 1914, FO 141/460, ibid.

Kitchener responded immediately and sent Storrs a telegram on 31 October to be delivered to Abdullah, which stated that: 'Germany has now bought the Turkish Government with gold, notwithstanding that England, France and Russia guaranteed integrity of Ottoman Empire if Turkey remained neutral in this war.' The Turkish Government, the telegram continued, had also committed various acts of war already, and added: 'If Arab nation assist England in this war that has been forced upon us (by) Turkey England will guarantee that no internal intervention takes place in Arabia and will give Arabs every assistance against external foreign aggression.'[9]

The British were already aware that the Turkish Army had been mobilised and German officers and advisors sent to Syria, and even the area near the Egypt/Sinai border. One of these officers was Kress von Kressestein.[10]

Kitchener concluded his message with a statement of much importance: 'It may be that an Arab of true race will assume Caliphate at Mecca and Medina and so good may come by the help of God out of all evil which is now occurring.'[11]

This message was then taken back to Mecca by the messenger Ali, who then returned to Cairo on 10 December 1914. Storrs communicated to the Foreign Office that the Sherif of Mecca was friendly towards Britain, but, 'pointed out that his position in the world of Islam and the present political situation in the Hedjaz made it impossible for him to break with the Turks immediately, though he was awaiting a colourable pretext.'[12]

Thereafter low key communications continued between Cairo and Mecca. All the while both parties kept looking for an appropriate 'colourable pretext' in order to justify taking their relationship to the next level.

---

9   Kitchener to Abdullah, 31 October 1914, Telegram No 303, FO 141/460, ibid; Storrs, ibid, p. 152.

10 Antonius, ibid, p. 137.

11 Kitchener to Abdullah, 31 October 1914, Telegram No 303, FO 141/460, ibid; Storrs, ibid, p. 152. Germany may have procured Turkey with gold, but Britain was about to do exactly the same if not more with the Arabs. See comments by T.E. Lawrence in Storrs, ibid, p. 153, footnote 1.

12 Storrs to Foreign Office, 10 December 1914, Telegram No. 310, FO 141/460, ibid. Also Storrs, ibid, p. 152. Sherif of Mecca also sent a private letter to Storrs through Ali Bey in which he emphasized the difficult situation the Sherif was in, trying to balance his responsibility to the needs of Muslims, as well as those of the Caliphate and of Turkey, of whom he stated: 'the Turkish Govt. has come to be nothing more than ENVER and his clique. We therefore are no longer bound to them with any tie. Notwithstanding this I am of opinion that it will be better now to put off action.' FO 141/460, ibid.

ARABIAN PENINSULA

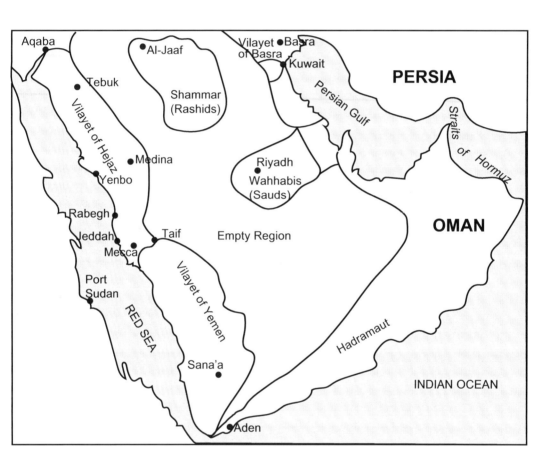

§

CHAPTER 25

Turkey officially enters the War

DARDANELLES CLOSED AND CAPITULATIONS ABROGATED

Despite the secret agreement between Germany and the Turks, there was little indication in August that Turkey would join the War, as the Central Powers were winning in Europe.

Then on 5 September the German forces in France received a major blow at the Battle of the Marne when they were stopped outside of Paris, and were retreating; while the Russians were more than holding their own on the Eastern Front. Suddenly the Central Powers realized it would be expedient to have more allies.

Thereafter the German leadership increasingly encouraged Turkey to make an official entry into the War. On 27 September 1914 the British Ambassador Sir Louis Mallett visited the American ambassador, Henry Morgenthau, and declared, "They have closed the Dardanelles."[1] Both men immediately understood that this was in effect a declaration of War, for according to international law, the Dardanelles were to be open in time of peace.

Now the British and French were separated from their ally Russia, and Russia was closed off from trading with the outside world. It would

---

1   Morgenthau, ibid, Chapter 9, p. 1.

now mean that for the Russians to export their surplus agricultural produce they could only use the Arctic port of Archangel, or the Pacific port
of Vladivostok – some 5,000 miles (8,000 kilometres) from central Russia.
This act could be disastrous for Russia – and very detrimental to the Allies.
Conversely it would be advantageous to the Central Powers.

The second act of the Turkish Government was the announcement on
9 September that the Capitulations would be abrogated as from 1 October
1914.[2] Until this point the citizens of the European nations, as well as
America, living and working in the Turkish Empire were protected by the
Capitulations.

Once they were abrogated it would mean that henceforth all foreign subjects would be subject entirely to Turkish laws and conditions. Ambassador
Morgenthau was immediately aware of the possible ramifications of this for
the many American institutions spread throughout the Turkish Empire.
He pulled off a diplomatic stunt by having Enver Pasha visit the American
operated Robert College in Constantinople, a visit which would engender
in the minds of Turks that the abrogation of the Capitulations did not automatically give them the privilege of interfering with American subjects
throughout the Empire.

Such may have been the case for the Americans, but this privilege would
not be accorded to other foreign nationals – especially those who would
soon find themselves at War with Turkey.

WAR ERUPTS

On 27 and 28 October 1914 the German battleships, by now given Turkish
names of *Yawuz Sultan Seliur* and *Midillu* and flying the Turkish flag, had
entered into the Black Sea. The Turkish Navy was now under the command
of the German, Admiral Souchen.   The French Ambassador in Russia,
Maurice Paleologue, recorded in his diary on 29 October 1914:

---

2 Mango, ibid, Part 2, Chapter 7; Fromkin, ibid, p. 69. Morgenthau, ibid.

At three o'clock this morning two Turkish destroyers entered the port of Odessa, sank a Russian gunboat and fired on the French mail boat *Portugal* doing considerable damage. Then they fled at top speed.

Sazanov[3] has received the news very calmly. He immediately applied to the Emperor for orders, and then said to me:

"His Majesty has decided that not a man shall be withdrawn from the German front… The defeat of Germany will necessarily involve the ruin of Turkey…"

Among the general public there is great excitement.[4]

Paleologue then reported that the following day the Russian Ambassador in Constantinople, Michael de Giers, asked for his passport. The Triple Alliance members still sought for Turkish neutrality, and some of the Turkish leaders were of a similar mind.[5]

The chances of success, though, were limited. The 'Turkish' ships then bombed the locations of Novorossisk and Theodosia in the Black Sea. Finally on 2 November Czar Nicholas declared to his people: '… We share with all the people of Russia the unshakeable conviction that the rash intervention of Turkey will only hasten that country's downfall and open Russia's path towards the solution of the historic problem which our ancestors have bequeathed to us on the shores of the Black Sea.'[6]

Turkey was now at War with Russia. Britain, because of her alliance with Russia, then declared War on Turkey on 2 November 1914.

Shortly after the declaration of war, Russia sent its forces over the border towards the major Turkish city of Erzerum,[7] while British and French warships bombed Turkish fortifications at the mouth of the Dardanelles.[8]

---

3   Sergei Sazanov was the Russian Foreign Minister from 1910-1916.
4   Paleologue, M. *An Ambassador's Memoirs*, edited by F.A. Holt, (New York, 1925), www.net.lib.byu.edu, Vol. I, Chapter 6, 29 October 1914.
5   Morgenthau, ibid, Chapter11, 2.
6   Paleologue, ibid, Vol. I, Chapter 6, 2 November 1914.
7   Mango, ibid, Part 2, Chapter 8. Later Enver left for the front line to command the Turkish forces.
8   Dolan, ibid, Chapter 1. Charles Palmer at this time had to flee from Chanak.

IMMEDIATE IMPACT IN EGYPT AND MESOPOTAMIA

Once the war began with Turkey, the situation changed overnight in Egypt. Martial law was proclaimed on 2 November. The complicated task of determining Egypt's future political status then began. The British Government then proclaimed Egypt a protectorate, headed up by a High Commissioner. Milne Cheetham held this position initially until a permanent High Commissioner, Sir Henry McMahon, would arrive. Hussein Kamel then became the Sultan of Egypt.[9]

The other immediate impact of the declaration of War was that the soldiers of the Indian Expeditionary Force landed on the Shatt-al-Arab. This landing marked the beginning of the Mesopotamian Campaign – which was to last a further four years and was to prove extremely costly to the British and Indian soldiers who served there.

The Indian Expeditionary Force, henceforth generally was known as the Mesopotamian Expeditionary Force (MEF), received invaluable assistance from Sir Percy Cox, the Chief Political Officer, Captain Arthur Wilson, and Mr. Bullard of the Levant Consular Service.[10]

The Indian forces captured Zain on 17 November 1914, and then headed towards Basra. Despite this Allied incursion Enver, the Minister of War, did not send Turkish reinforcements to Mesopotamia, as he was too occupied in battling the Russians in the Caucasus.

THE SULTAN PROCLAIMS THE *JIHAD*

With Turkey now having chosen her side, a potentially dangerous force entered into the War on the side of the Central Powers – Islam. The Sultan of Turkey was the Caliph of Islam, and his voice carried much influence.

One of the foundational principles of Islam is *Jihad*, the Holy War, which was always against the infidel – the non-Muslim. But on this occasion Islam (as represented by Turkey) was actually fighting with some of the infidel (the Central Powers) against other infidel (the Triple Alliance). Nevertheless it was anticipated that Muslims throughout the world would

---

9   In the winter of 1914 Thomas Edward Lawrence 'became a member of the Intelligence Branch of the Egypt Defence Force,' based in Cairo, and came into close contact with Ronald Storrs. See Storrs, ibid, pp. 187 & 193.

10   Verrier, ibid, p. 28.

rally to the call, especially Muslims living in regions administered by the Triple Alliance.

That Germany was encouraging this call to *Jihad* was evidenced by a frank statement by Ambassador Wangenheim to Morgenthau, when he said: "Turkey herself is not the really important matter … Her army is a small one, and we do not expect it to do very much. For the most part it will act on the defensive. But the big thing is the Moslem world. If we can stir the Mohammedans up against the English and Russians, we can force them to make peace."[11]

The Sultan made the call for *Jihad* on 13 November 1914. Morgenthau was on hand to observe its proclamation, which he said, was 'summoning the whole Moslem world to arise and massacre their Christian oppressors.'[12] Apart from the Sultan's official proclamation, another proclamation was issued which provided further details. Morgenthau in his book *Ambassador Morgenthau's Story* provides the entire text, part of which read:

> … the time has now come for the Holy War, and by this the land of Islam shall be forever freed from the power of the infidels who oppress it. This holy war has now become a sacred duty. Know ye that the blood of infidels in the Islamic lands may be shed with impunity --- except those to whom the Moslem power has promised security and who are allied with it [Herein we find that Germans and Austrians are excepted from massacre.] The killing of infidels who rule over Islam has become a sacred duty, whether you do it secretly or openly, as the Koran has decreed: 'Take them and kill them whenever you find them. Behold we have delivered them unto your hands and given you supreme power over them.' He who kills even one unbeliever of those who rule over us, whether he does it secretly or openly, shall be rewarded by God.[13] And let every Moslem, in whatever part of the world he may be, swear a solemn oath to kill at least three or four of

---

11 Morgenthau, H. *Ambassador Morgenthau's Story*, (New York, 1918), cited in www.net.lib.byu.edu, Chapter Fourteen, p. 2.

12 Morgenthau, ibid, Chapter Fourteen, p. 3.

13 Meaning Allah.

the infidels who rule over him, for they are the enemies of God and of the faith....'[14]

This pamphlet then decreed that there was to be a "little holy war" – which, Morgenthau stated, 'describes the battle which every Mohammedan is to wage in his community against his Christian neighbours', and a "great holy war" which was 'the great world struggle which united Islam, in India, Arabia, Turkey, Africa, and other countries is to wage against the infidel oppressors.'[15]

The 'danger of spreading such incendiary literature among a wildly fanatical people' wrote Morgenthau 'is apparent'. He and other diplomats 'feared the most serious consequences.'[16]   Although ultimately the call for *Jihad* did not have the desired effect outside the regions directly ruled by Turkey, yet the consequences for the minority groups, especially the Armenians, were soon evidenced.

Shortly afterwards there was a demonstration in Constantinople which affected various 'foreign establishments' and then ended, Von Sanders wrote, 'by breaking all the windows and mirrors of the hotel Toklatian, the proprietor of which was of Armenian birth and had recently become a nat-uralized Russian.'[17]

From this seed, the call to *Jihad*, there would ultimately result the most diabolical fruits - persecution and massacres especially of the Armenians, but also of other minority groups in the Turkish Empire.

14   Morgenthau, ibid, Chapter Fourteen, p. 4.
15   Morgenthau, ibid, Chapter Fourteen, p. 4.
16   Morgenthau, ibid, Chapter Fourteen, p. 5.
17   Von Sanders, ibid, p. 35. Sanders states it was 20 November, while Morgenthau states it was 14 November.

§

CHAPTER 26

Samuel's proposal for a Jewish 'State'

PROPOSAL FOR JEWISH STATE

The declaration of war by Turkey against Britain meant that now the traditional British attitude to Turkey, as an ally, was no longer valid. Ever since 1840, Britons had been agitating for an official British endorsement of the restoration of the Jewish people to their homeland. This goal could never be accomplished because of Britain's alliance with Turkey. But the 'moment Turkey entered the war' wrote Herbert Samuel, a Member of Parliament, 'the position was entirely changed. If Palestine was to be given a new destiny,' he wrote, 'Great Britain, with her important strategic interests in the Middle East, was directly concerned. The question' Samuel then raised, 'who was to succeed the Turk in controlling the country that bordered on the Suez Canal was one to which our Government would have to give serious consideration.'[1]

At the outbreak of War Herbert Samuel was not all that *au fait* with the Zionist movement, as he was very much an assimilated British Jew. He then made contact with Chaim Weizmann and discovered more about the work

---

1   Samuel, H. *Memoirs*, (London, 1945), p. 139.

and aspirations of the Jewish nationalist movement. Samuel came to the conclusion: 'The importance to the strategic interests of Great Britain stood out clearly. If Palestine, as was likely, were to be separated from Turkey, for it to fall under the control of any of the great Continental Powers would be a danger.'[2]

Armed with this perspective Samuel then sought a meeting with the Foreign Secretary, Edward Grey. They met on 9 November 1914, and Samuel records of his conversation:

> I spoke to Sir Edward Grey to-day about the future of Palestine. In the course of our talk I said now that Turkey had thrown herself into the European War and that it was probable that her empire would be broken up, the question of the future control of Palestine was likely to arise. The jealousies of the great European Powers would make it difficult to allot the country to any one of them. Perhaps the opportunity might arise for the fulfilment of the ancient aspiration of the Jewish people and the restoration there of a Jewish State.[3]

In his discourse Samuel alluded to the benefits for Russia if she played a leading role: 'the sentimental appeal to the Jews within her own territories' he stated 'would be so strong that it could not fail to have an immediate and a powerful influence on their attitude.'[4]

Samuel confessed to Grey that he 'never had been a Zionist' but that 'now the conditions are profoundly altered. If a Jewish State were established in Palestine' he stated, then 'it might become the centre of a new culture. The Jewish brain is rather a remarkable thing, and under national auspices, the state might become a fountain of enlightenment and a source of a great literature and art and development of science.'[5]

---

2   Samuel, ibid, p. 140.
3   Samuel, ibid, p. 140.
4   Samuel, ibid, p. 140.
5   Samuel, ibid, p. 140.

'I thought that British influence ought to play a considerable part in the formation of such a state,' he continued, 'because the geographical situation of Palestine, and especially its proximity to Egypt, would render its goodwill to England a matter of importance to the British Empire.'[6]

Samuel spoke of numerous practical matters associated with the establishment of this new Jewish State, and at the conclusion of his discourse, he wrote: 'Grey said that the idea had always had a strong sentimental attraction for him. The historical appeal', Grey, stated, 'was very strong. He was', Samuel continued, 'quite favourable to the proposal and would be prepared to work for it if the opportunity arose.' Samuel continued:

> If any proposals were put forward by France or any other Power with regard to Syria, it would be important not to acquiesce in any plan which would be inconsistent with the creation of a Jewish state in Palestine.[7]

Grey then asked Samuel 'whether I thought that Syria must necessarily go with Palestine. I said no, but on the contrary it would be inadvisable to include such places as Beyrout and Damascus, since they contained a large non-Jewish population which could not be assimilated.'[8]

Grey asked Samuel several more practical questions concerning the economic situation in Palestine, and in reply Samuel mentioned two other important factors, that the state 'should be neutralized, since it could not be large enough to defend itself, and that the free access of Christian pilgrims should be guaranteed.'[9]

Samuel concluded his conversation by stating:

---

6 Samuel, ibid, p. 141.
7 Samuel, ibid, p. 141.
8 Samuel, ibid, p. 141.
9 Samuel, ibid, p. 141.

I also said it would be of great advantage if the remainder of Syria were annexed by France, as it would be far better for the state to have a European power as neighbour than the Turk.[10]

In what would be a busy and enterprising day, Samuel then also spoke to another key member of the War Cabinet, David Lloyd George. 'He had referred in the Cabinet' Samuel commented, 'to the ultimate destiny of Palestine, and said to me that he was very keen to see a Jewish state established there.'[11]

At the very outset of the War, when the future destiny of the Turkish Empire was first being broached, the issue of a future Jewish State in Palestine was well and truly on the Cabinet drawing board.

WEIZMANN AND C.P. SCOTT

Samuel's activism was equalled at that time by Chaim Weizmann, a leader in the Zionist movement. Weizmann had visited Berlin just before War broke out, and several weeks later found himself in Paris, speaking with the esteemed Baron Edmond de Rothschild. Rothschild said to Weizmann: 'Yes … things looked black, but we would win the war. And this was the time for us to act, so that we might not be forgotten in the general settlement. He urged me, immediately on my return to England, to get in touch with British statesmen. It was his opinion – and I agreed with him – that the war would spread to the Middle East, and there things of great significance to us would happen.'[12]

Upon his return to Britain Weizmann met, by chance, one of the most influential non-politicians in Britain – C.P. Scott, the editor of the *Manchester Guardian*. Scott was sympathetic towards the Jewish people, and their national aspirations. The two met at a social function, and when Scott became aware of Weizmann's passion concerning a Jewish restoration to Palestine, he stated: "I would like to do something for you. I would like to bring you together with the Chancellor of the Exchequer, Lloyd George."

---

10 Samuel, ibid, p. 142.
11 Samuel, ibid, p. 142.
12 Weizmann, H. *Trial and Error*, (Philadelphia, 1949), Vol ii, p.148.

Then he added: "You know, you have a Jew in the Government, Mr. Herbert Samuel."[13]

Weizmann did not agree about Samuel being sympathetic with the Jewish national cause, an attitude which he soon realised was wrong.[14] Scott then became immersed in the issue of the Jewish national hope, and Weizmann supplied him with much information. On 12 November 1914 Weizmann wrote to Scott: "Don't you think that the chance for the Jewish people is now within limits of discussion at least? I realize, of course, that we cannot 'claim' anything, we are much too atomized for that; but we can reasonably say that should Palestine fall within the British sphere of influence, and should Britain encourage a Jewish settlement there, as a British dependency, we could have in twenty or thirty years a million Jews out there, perhaps more; they would develop the country, bring back civilization to it and form a very effective guard for the Suez Canal."[15]

True to his word Scott arranged for Weizmann to meet with Lloyd George. The meeting took place on 3 December 1914, at which Herbert Samuel and another Member of Parliament, Josiah Wedgwood were also present.[16] Weizmann wrote of this meeting:

I was terribly shy and suffered from suppressed excitement, knowing how much depended on this meeting. At first I remained a passive listener. They talked about the war in a way that seemed to me extraordinary flippant. I was very, very serious minded, did not quite appreciate English humor, and did not understand at first that behind this seeming flippancy there was a deadly seriousness. Lloyd George began to fire questions at me, about Palestine, about our colonies there, about the number of Jews in the country and the number who could go there. I answered as best I could. Then I had the surprise of my life when Herbert Samuel interposed some helpful remarks. I had been frightened out of my wits by his presence. It became clear

---

13   Weizmann, ibid, p. 149.
14   Weizmann, ibid, p. 149.
15   Weizmann, ibid, p. 149.
16   Wedgwood served in France in 1914. In 1915 he landed at Cape Helles in the Dardanelles Campaign aboard the *River Clyde* and managed to survive that carnage. He met members of the Zion Mule Corps at Gallipoli.

that every person in the room was favorably disposed, and an atmosphere was created which warmed and encouraged me. Lloyd George pointed out that I ought to talk with Balfour, as well as with the Prime Minister, Herbert H. Asquith. At this point Herbert Samuel said – I could hardly believe my ears – that he was preparing a memorandum on the subject of a Jewish State in Palestine, to present to the Prime Minister.[17]

Weizmann did meet Balfour soon afterwards, and he recorded that when he walked into Balfour's office at the Admiralty, Balfour stated: 'Well, you haven't changed much since we met."[18] Then, Weizmann stated, Balfour almost immediately said, "You know, I was thinking of that conversation of ours, and I believe that when the guns stop firing you may get your Jerusalem."[19]

The two men met later, and discussed among other matters, the progress of the War. Weizmann's hatred of the Russian regime filtered through, causing Balfour to ask, 'how a friend of England could be so anti-Russian when Russia was doing so much to help England win the war.' This statement permitted Weizmann to explain the atrocities being perpetrated by the Russians against the Jewish people in the regions overrun by the Russian Army – 'the pogroms, and the expulsions which made every Russian victory a horror for the Jews – this while hundreds of thousands of Jews were fighting for the Russian Army. It was news to him!'

'Then' Weizmann wrote, 'I spoke again of our Zionist hopes. At the close of our talk Balfour said: "It is a great cause you are working for. You must come again and again."[20]

17 Weizmann, ibid, p. 150.
18 They had previously met in 1906.
19 Weizmann, ibid, p. 152.
20 Weizmann, ibid, pp. 153-54. These atrocities are confirmed by the French ambassador in Petrograd, Maurice Paleologue in his *Memoirs*.

CHAPTER 27

§

ANZACs and Jewish refugees

ALLIED TROOPS IN EGYPT

As the Australian and New Zealand contingent (later dubbed ANZAC)[1] was heading westwards, Kitchener on 17 November informed the Australian Defence Department of the change in destination.[2] The ANZACs were to disembark in Egypt and complete their training.

The convoy arrived at Suez on 1 December and then proceeded on to Alexandria. Fred Jones wrote to his sister Iris: 'We arrived in Alexandria after good but rather monotonous voyage. It took 16 hours to steam through the Canal. The banks were lined with Indian troops guarding it against the Turks.'[3]

Following disembarkation at Alexandria, the ANZACs were entrained to their new camps: the Australian infantry at Mena near the Pyramids, the New Zealanders at Zeitoun, while the Light Horse Brigade was located at Maadi. Later Chauvel's 1st Light Horse Brigade moved to Heliopolis.

The scenery was quite different from what most were used to, especially the New Zealanders. Private P.M. Thompson wrote: 'We certainly did expect to find some grass, but not so this time – simply sand, sand, sand everywhere.

---

1 An acronym for 'Australia and New Zealand Army Corps.'
2 Gouttman, ibid, p. 41.
3 Letter of Fred Jones to sister Rita. MS 89/105, Auckland War Memorial Museum Library.

We are camped on the Sahara Desert.'[4] Thompson's view is supported by Australian Thomas Gardner who wrote home: 'We will be camped here for some time before proceeding to the Front, if we ever do. We are eight miles out from Cairo in the desert and do all our drill in the sand making trenches etc. When we are proficient we will go to the front. It all rests with ourselves. I will not care to live here very long as there is nothing to see but sand...'[5]

The arrival of these new soldiers was noted by Ronald Storrs who wrote in his diary for 14 December 1914:

> During the last fortnight the general appearance of Cairo has changed very much for the better. The streets are full of troops, the largest number of whom are Australians. These are at once feared and admired by the Egyptians, and are certainly well equal to any Territorials or Yeomanry we have yet seen. They are reported to be very lax in their discipline, and I have certainly seen one tram-load returning campwards at about 7.30 a.m. chanting with unimpaired freshness "We won't be going home till morning."[6]

Some Indian soldiers were also garrisoned in Egypt, while some British soldiers remained, most having been sent back to Britain.

TURKS EXPEL JEWISH PEOPLE

Of the 85,000 Jewish people who were living in Palestine at the outbreak of the War, many came originally from Russia, and were thereby protected by the Capitulations.[7] Many of those living in the four Holy Cities existed upon *haluka*, financial help sent by their co-religionists in Europe. The beginning of the War seriously affected the movement of finances from Europe to the Middle East, as Allied warships also blockaded the Levantine coast.

4   Diary of Pte. P.M. Thompson, Queen Elizabeth II army Museum, Waioru, cited in Pugsley, C. *Gallipoli: The New Zealand Story*, (Auckland, 1990), p. 72.
5   Morice, J. *Six Bob A Day Tourist*, (Australia, 1985), p. 23.
6   Storrs, ibid, p. 144.
7   Yaari, A. *The Goodly Heritage*, (Jerusalem, 1958), p. 348.

Another financial burden was that the cash crops being grown by the Jewish colonies could not be so easily sent to Europe. This added to the financial burden facing the Jewish people. One further complication was that one of the main centres of the Zionist movement was based in Berlin. The War effectively divided the Zionist movement.

Many Jewish organisations, particularly in America, came to the assistance of their co-religionists in *Eretz Yisrael* by sending financial support. In September 1914 the *USS North Carolina* anchored off Jaffa port and off-loaded some 10,000 pounds sterling in gold to be distributed among the destitute Jewish people. Two men involved in this work were Henry Morgenthau, the American ambassador in Turkey, and Otis Glazebrook, the American consul in Jerusalem.

With the revocation of the Capitulations those foreigners belonging to the nations of the Triple Alliance, were given a choice to either adopt Turkish citizenship or leave. Some of the Jewish leaders in Palestine, including Yosef Chelouche and Meir Dizengoff (the mayor of Tel Aviv), recommended that Jewish people accept Turkish citizenship. Ben Zvi and Ben Gurion, who had been en-route to Palestine when War began and who could not return to Constantinople, even volunteered their services to the Turkish governor to form a Jewish unit for the defence of Jerusalem.

Although many Jewish people did thereupon adopt Turkish citizenship, concerns for the general welfare of the Jewish people lingered. These concerns increased when an order came from Constantinople 'that all Ottoman subjects between the ages of 18 and 60 were to be drafted into the army.'[8] Some of the Jewish leaders understood full well what was likely to happen to Jewish men in the Turkish Army, and argued for exception. They failed.

It did not take long before the policies of the C.U.P. towards these Christians and Jews were revealed, as they were ill-treated in the Army. Verrier wrote: '… the final humiliation came when all non-Mohammedans were disarmed and drafted into labour battalions, to the mockery of low class Mohammedans who remained in the combatant units.'[9]

---

8   Yaari, ibid, p. 97.
9   Verrier, ibid, p. 110.

Djemal Pasha had moved to Damascus, where he became both Governor, and commander of the Turkish Fourth Army. He quickly began to enforce the revocation of the Capitulations. In early December another order came from Constantinople ordering all foreign nationals to be deported from Palestine. When an American warship, *USS Tennessee*, came offshore on 15 December the Turkish authorities, fearing it was a Russian ship, ordered the immediate rounding up of all Russian nationals.

Chelouche recalls that on 17 December the Turkish governor of Jaffa, Beha-a-Din 'sent out a large number of soldiers who spread all over the streets of Jaffa and Tel Aviv and indiscriminately rounded up all Jews of foreign nationality, adults and children, and locked them up in the Armenian monastery.' Despite protestations from Chelouche and Dizengoff, the Turks only increased their mistreatment of the impounded Jewish people.[10]

These grief-stricken people were then taken from the monastery, put into Arab boats and rowed out to an awaiting Italian ship which had received orders to take them to Egypt. The *Jewish Chronicle* reported that the Arab boatmen then brandished knives and extorted money from the passengers, even terrifying mothers by threatening to throw their babies into the water.[11] The correspondent of the *Evening Standard* stated:

> Moans, tears, hysterical shouts filled the air. Then without any warning, the steamer weighed anchor and left. It was late in the evening and you could imagine the horror of the situation.
> The boatmen tried to throw into the water all those who could not be placed aboard the steamer.[12]

These exiles were off-loaded at Alexandria – and more followed. In late December 1914 Djemal Pasha ordered the expulsion of all remaining foreigners. Many of these were taken aboard the *USS Tennessee* and also off-loaded at Alexandria. Among these were the family of an Australian

---

10   Yaari, ibid, p. 350.
11   *Jewish Chronicle*, 22 January 1915, p. 10.
12   *Evening Standard*, cited in *Jewish Missionary Intelligence (JMI)*, 1915, p. 46.

businessman from Melbourne named Lazar Slutzkin. Slutzkin owned a
large home in Rehoboth.[13]

The Aaronsohn family managed to remain, due to Aaron's renown.
In February 1915 he had an interview with Captain Decker of the *USS
Tennessee* and provided the American commander with details of what was
really happening in the land.[14] Interestingly there was a major locust plague
shortly after these events, and Djemal Pasha requested Aaronsohn's help in
stamping it out.[15]

By March 1915 some 10,000 Jewish people had been forcibly expelled to
Egypt. As most of these were of Russian nationality the British Government
now had the tricky problem of determining under whose political jurisdiction they came. Although some of these exiles were able to procure private residences, the vast majority were crammed into two makeshift refugee
camps named Gabbara and Mafruza.

For those Jewish people who remained behind in Palestine, life only
became more difficult. Djemal Pasha was deeply suspicious of any foreign
nationalist movement. Zionism and Arab nationalism both thereafter were
targeted. Chelouche stated that henceforth the Turkish authorities 'seized
men indiscriminately for forced labour, irrespective of their age, health or
family responsibilities.' 'The military authorities' he continued 'displayed
especial severity towards the Jews. Those who had become Ottoman subjects, including those who had paid for exemption from military service,
were taken … into the Army or made to do forced labour, and were subjected to particularly brutal treatment.'[16]

In such a situation it was understandable that those who remained
would be doing their utmost to demonstrate their loyalty to the Ottoman
Turkish Empire.

---

13   Interview with the late Mrs Ruth Stark (z.l.), granddaughter of Lazar Slutzkin, in Tel Aviv, 1996.
14   Verrier, ibid, p. 116.
15   Verrier, ibid, p. 116.
16   Yaari, ibid, p. 356.

CHAUVEL AND NEW COMMAND STRUCTURES

While the Jewish refugees languished in their camps, the Australian and New Zealand forces settled into their camps as best they could.   Harry Chauvel wrote to his wife on 24 January 1915: 'The 2nd Australian Contingent will be arriving in a few days & Cairo will be overrun again with Australians. I only hope they behave themselves … On the whole they have not behaved very badly but there are a few pretty bad eggs amongst them that it will be well worth to get rid of before we go anywhere else.'[17]

A few days later he again wrote to his wife: 'General Birdwood is to command us in France as far as I know but there may still be some changes.'[18] General William Birdwood was chosen to forge this colonial group into a cohesive military formation. As far as he was concerned when he went to take command, and as far as his charges were concerned in Egypt, they were destined for the battlefields of France and Belgium. Such thoughts were soon to change.

Another to take up a new command in January 1915 was Mustapha Kemal. While his nemesis Enver was commanding the Turkish forces opposing the Russians, Kemal was called back from his semi-diplomatic post in Sofia to take command of the 19th Turkish Division in the Dardanelles region.

---

17   Chauvel to his wife, 24 January 1915, ibid, Series 4, Folder 3.
18   Chauvel to his wife, 28 January 1915, ibid, Series 4, Folder 3.

§

CHAPTER 28

Conflicts erupt in the Turkish Empire

PREPARATIONS FOR ATTACK ON THE SUEZ CANAL BEGIN

In November 1914 the Turkish Fourth Army was formed in Syria, part of which would assault the Suez Canal. The Fourth Army was to be commanded by the Minister of Marine, Djemal Pasha.

Ambassador Morgenthau wrote in detail of Djemal Pasha's departure from Constantinople, where he was being hailed as the "Saviour of Egypt". Morgenthau then wrote: 'Djemal himself, just before the train started, made this public declaration: "I shall not return to Constantinople until I have conquered Egypt."'[1]

Djemal Pasha was indeed determined to become the 'Saviour of Egypt', but he was as equally determined to forge an empire for himself in the vast region of Syria, Mesopotamia and Arabia.[2]

The bulk of the preparations for the assault by the Turkish 8th Corps Suez Expeditionary Force were undertaken by a German officer, Colonel Kress von Kressenstein. Von Sanders, though, opposed the venture, stating, '… the undertaking was condemned to failure from the beginning. Egypt

---

1   Morgenthau, ibid, Chapter 15, p. 1.
2   Morgenthau, ibid, pp. 4-6.

cannot be taken by 16,000 Turkish soldiers.'[3] Nevertheless the expeditionary force began assembling and training soon afterwards at Beersheba.

PROPOSED ATTACK AT GALLIPOLI BY CHURCHILL

The defence of Egypt was now of paramount importance for Britain. At the War Council meeting on 25 November 1914 Churchill 'suggested that the ideal method of defending Egypt was by an attack on the Gallipoli Peninsula. This, if successful' Churchill continued, 'would give us control of the Dardanelles and we could dictate terms at Constantinople.' Churchill admitted that this venture would require 'a large force.' He added that if this was impracticable, then there could be a feint at Gallipoli while a real landing could be made elsewhere on the Syrian coast, perhaps even Haifa.[4]

Kitchener concurred that, 'later on we should probably have to make a diversion on the Turkish communication. The moment for it', he concluded 'had not yet arrived.'[5] At that same meeting Lord Fisher 'asked whether Greece might not perhaps undertake an attack on Gallipoli on behalf of the Allies.' Grey responded that this probably was not likely due to certain geo-political tensions in the Balkans.

The discussion about the defence of Egypt concluded with Balfour suggesting either capturing or filling in the 'wells some 30 miles east of the canal.' 'If those wells were held' he stated 'an enemy with a long tract of sandy almost waterless desert behind him would have great difficulty in advancing.' Kitchener squashed this suggestion, stating, 'he felt no anxiety about Egypt and the Suez Canal.'[6]

Meanwhile a further event occurred in the Dardanelles. On 13 December the British submarine B.11 entered through the Narrows, under the mines, and succeeded in sinking a Turkish battleship.[7]

3   Von Sanders, ibid, p. 43.
4   CAB 21/1, 25 November 1914, p. 3.
5   CAB 21/1, 25 November 1914, p. 3.
6   CAB 21/1, 25 November 1914, 4.
7   Dolan, ibid, Chapter 2.

WAR AGAINST RUSSIA

The land conflict between Turkish and Russian forces began in November 1914 near Koprikioj, between Erzerum and Kars, at the base of the Caucasus Mountains. The Turkish Third Army managed to halt the Russian advance. Filled with optimism, Enver Pasha then left for the battle front in early December 1914, intending on inflicting further defeat upon the Russian forces.

This situation fitted into Churchill's broader scheme. He had written: 'The Turks have barred the Dardanelles. It needs but a cry from Russia for help ... But as yet no cry has come.'[8]

This interruption in Russia's plans was unfortunate for at that time her forces were being badly beaten in fighting along the Eastern Front against the Central Powers. These set-backs created great concern for Britain. A further Russian defeat would only increase pressure upon Britain's forces on the Western Front.

To relieve pressure on the Russians Maurice Hankey (Secretary for the War Council) proposed on 28 December 1914, an assault upon the Dardanelles Peninsula, assisted by the Balkan states.[9] Lloyd George, the Chancellor of the Exchequer, submitted a Memorandum to the War Council on 1 January 1915 also indicating the advantages of attacking Turkey, most probably in Syria, which would draw Turkish forces away from fighting the Russians.[10] Churchill also chimed in and wrote to Asquith: 'I wanted Gallipoli attacked on the declaration of war ... Meanwhile the difficulties have increased.'[11]

The desperate situation forced the Russian Commander-in-Chief, Grand Duke Nicholas, to send Kitchener a request for assistance on 1 January 1915.[12] The British War Council discussed this Russian request, and at the Council meeting on 8 January 1915 General Sir John French presented a Memorandum whereby he 'expressed a strong preference for the employ-

---

8   Churchill, W. *The World Crisis*, p. 289.

9   Gilbert, M. *Winston S. Churchill*, Vol. 3: 1914-1916, *The Challenge of War*, (Boston, 1971), p. 230.

10 Lloyd George, D. *War Memoirs*, Vol. I, pp. 224-25.

11 Churchill, ibid, p. 325.

12 Churchill, ibid, p. 325.

ment of our armies in France.' Prime Minister Asquith also endorsed this perspective.[13]

Churchill, though, suggested they further examine a proposed 'attack from the south.' Kitchener then stated that the 'Dardanelles appeared to be the most suitable objective, as an attack here could be made in co-operation with the Fleet. If successful' he continued 'it would re-establish communication with Russia; settle the Near East question; draw in Greece and, perhaps Bulgaria and Roumania; and release wheat and shipping now locked up in the Black Sea.'[14]

After Russia issued its call for help she was attacked by the advancing Turkish Third Army, led by Enver Pasha. Enver, though, had over played his hand by ordering such an adventurous attack in the rugged Caucasus region in the midst of winter. This combination of harsh terrain and winter conditions resulted in his forces being badly defeated by the Russian forces, especially at Sarikamisch, beginning on 6 January 1915, prompting a retreat of Enver and the majority of the surviving Turkish force. The remnants of the Turkish Army in and around Sarikamish were finally captured on 17 January, thereby ending the Turkish thrust eastwards.

BEGINNING OF OFFICIAL ANTI-ARMENIAN POLICIES

The Turkish leaders, and especially Enver, were humiliated by this defeat, and sought a suitable excuse or scapegoat. They saw the Armenians as just such a scapegoat, accusing them of being traitors to Turkey and a potential fifth column, even though many Armenians were determined to prove their loyalty to Turkey.[15] Ahmet Refik, a Turkish officer and later a historian, wrote:

> In Istanbul, the propaganda work necessary to justify an enormous crime was fully prepared: the Armenians had united with the enemy, revolution was about to break out in Istanbul, they were going to kill

---

13 CAB 21/1, No 21347, 8 January 1915, p. 3.
14 CAB 21/1, ibid, 8 January 1915, 3.
15 Balakian, ibid, Part 2, Chapter 14.

the Unionist leaders, they were going to force open the [Bosphorus and Dardanelles] Straits.[16]

The fighting against Russian forces in this region provided the Turkish leaders with an ideal opportunity in which to implement their negative policy against the Armenians. In the early stages of the fighting, when every soldier was needed, no adverse orders were issued against Armenian soldiers fighting for the Turks. Now a change occurred.

'Anti-Armenian agitation' wrote Akcam, 'was coordinated by the War Ministry's "Second Department," the Department of Intelligence.'[17] By 25 February 1915 'all the Armenian men in the Ottoman army' wrote Balakian, 'were officially disarmed and thrown into labor battalions.'[18] The first stage was to destroy the Armenian men fighting in the army. Morgenthau describes the method:

In the early part of 1915, the Armenian soldiers in the Turkish army were reduced to a new status. Up to that time most of them had been combatants, but now they were all stripped of their arms and transformed into workmen. Instead of serving their country as artillerymen and cavalrymen, these former soldiers now discovered that they were transformed into road labourers and pack animals. Army supplies of all kinds were loaded on their backs, and stumbling under the burdens and driven by the whips and bayonets of the Turks, they were forced to drag their weary bodies into the mountains of the Caucasus.[19]

Most of these un-armed men were brutally killed. A German missionary, Jakob Künzler, who worked with the medical personnel at the Urfa missionary hospital, witnessed some of the killings. He wrote: "mostly knives were used, because the ammunition was needed for the foreign enemy."[20]

16   Refik, İki *Komite*, İki *Kıtal*, p. 44, cited in Akcam, ibid, p. 125.
17   Akcam, ibid, p. 125.
18   Balakian, ibid, Part 2, Chapter 14.
19   Morgenthau, ibid, Chapter 24, p. 1; Balakian, ibid, Part 2, Chapter 14.
20   Jakob Künzler, *Dreizig Jahre Dienst am* Orient (Basel, 1933), p. 54, cited in Akcam, ibid, p. 144.

The next stage in the policy against the Armenians was to disarm the community – thereby leaving it unprotected. This was done by ordering that all weapons owned by Armenians were to be surrendered to 'regional and local administrators.'[21]

Concerning this order Morgenthau wrote:

> Naturally the Christians became alarmed when placards were posted in the villages and cities ordering everybody to bring their arms to headquarters. Although this order applied to all citizens, the Armenians well understood what the result would be, should they be left defenceless while their Moslem neighbours were permitted to retain their arms. In many cases, however, the persecuted people patiently obeyed the command; and then the Turkish officials almost joyfully seized their rifles as evidence that a "revolution" was being planned and threw their victims into prison on a charge of treason.[22]

Many had no weapons to bring, and were then mercilessly tortured in order to elicit confessions. As news of this method spread, many Armenians purposely purchased weapons in order to avoid the brutal tortures of the Turkish officials.[23]

In the months of spring 1915 numerous attacks were made against Armenian villages. The signs were ominous indeed for the survival of this nation; and indeed for any unprotected minority group living within the Ottoman Turkish Empire.

WAR IN MESOPOTAMIA

Although the Dardanelles and Suez Canal were the most strategically important shipping zones in the region, the Persian Gulf was also of considerable strategic importance, especially in view of the recently discovered oil fields in Persia.

---

21   Balakian, ibid, Part 2, Chapter 14. Toynbee, A. *Armenian Atrocities: The Murder of a Nation*, (London, 1915), pp. 81-2.

22   Morgenthau, ibid, Chapter 24, p. 3.

23   There are various sources which describe this situation, including Morgenthau.

The Indian troops were already in the region, and following the declaration of War, these moved into action. Some 600 British Marines landed first and captured the fortress of Fao. The remainder of the Force then moved to a better landing position at Sanniyeh.

The first major Turkish assault occurred on 11 November, with further skirmishes in the following days. When General Bennett of the 6th Poona Division was informed that the Turks had abandoned Basra, he accordingly took possession of this strategic island city on 23 November 1914.

Possession of Basra gave the British Navy security of oil supplies, an invaluable asset so early in the War. The Turks, meanwhile, had moved north to the location of Qurna (pronounced Gurna), where the Euphrates and Tigris Rivers converge.[24]

The British-Indian force then moved north. The main attack began on Qurna on 6 December, and the Turks surrendered on 9 December. This victory gave the Mesopotamian Expeditionary Force force a strong defensive position north of Basra.

Until this point the British-Indian force had suffered many casualties, but their victories were quite substantial. Few realized at that point that another four years of sustained warfare lay before them during which they would sustain a very high casualty rate.

CHURCHILL'S INITIAL PLAN FOR GALLIPOLI ATTACK

Despite the defeat of the Turkish Third Army at Sarikamish, Churchill (at the behest of the War Cabinet) wasted no time in formulating a plan to attack the Dardanelles. He communicated with Vice-Admiral Carden, the Commander-in-Chief in the Mediterranean 'in regard to the possibilities of a naval attack on the Dardanelles.'[25] Carden's reply was communicated at the War Cabinet meeting on 13 January 1915. Carden, Churchill explained, stated that it 'was impossible to rush the Dardanelles, but that … it might be possible to demolish the forts one by one.'

---

24   *The Long, Long Trail*, www.1914-1918.net
25   CAB 21/1, 13 January 1915, p 8.

Churchill then presented Carden's plan, which called for an initial concentration of fire on the outer forts, then after they had been demolished, 'to deal with the inner forts, attacking them from the Straits and from the seaward side of the Gallipoli Peninsula.'[26]

'The Admiralty', Churchill informed the Cabinet, 'were studying the question, and believed that a plan could be made for systematically reducing all the forts within a few weeks. Once the forts were reduced' he continued, 'the minefields could be cleared, and the Fleet could proceed up to Constantinople and destroy the "Goeben."'[27] Lloyd George and Kitchener both liked the idea.

At the War Council meeting on 28 January 1915, the discussion about attacking the Dardanelles continued, Churchill stating that both the Grand Duke of Russia and the French Admiralty had answered favourably. Balfour presented six advantages for such an attack, concluding: 'It would put Constantinople under our control.'[28]

ATTACK UPON THE SUEZ CANAL

Having just suffered a major set-back with the defeat of the Turkish Third Army, Von Sanders opposed the planned Turkish attack on the Suez Canal scheduled for early February 1915 – but Djemal was determined to proceed. He had offered significant incentives for the would-be conquering Turkish soldiers.

As part of his preparations Djemal ordered the requisitioning of livestock and supplies from the already struggling agricultural sector in Palestine. Much of the infrastructure of the Jewish agricultural colonies was stripped away.[29]

The Turkish 8th Corps Suez Expeditionary Force left from Beersheba in late January 1915 and marched for seven nights towards the Suez Canal through the central Sinai route. The British were not anticipating an assault, as Von Sanders alludes: 'The scouting officers of the expeditionary corps saw

---

26   CAB 21/1, 13 January 1915, p. 8.
27   CAB 21/1, 13 January 1915, p 8. *Goeben* = German warship.
28   CAB 21/1, 28 January 1915, No. 21347, p. 6.
29   Verrier, ibid, p. 115.

British officers playing football when the leading Turkish troops were within twenty-five kilometres of the canal.'[30]

The Turks made their way to some large cisterns at Jif-jaffa, which was to be the staging post for the assault. Unfortunately for them the Royal Flying Corps (RFC) then discovered their advance.[31] That they managed to cross the Sinai carrying with them boats for crossing the Canal was quite an extraordinary accomplishment.

During the night of 2-3 February 1915 the first Turkish assault on the Suez Canal began. As the Turkish troops moved forward and entered the Canal in their boats, the mostly British and Indian force on the other side spotted them and opened fire. Panic struck the Turkish force as highlighted by Von Sanders: 'Part of the men already embarked jumped from the boats, others dropped the boats and rafts they were carrying.'[32]

About two companies of Turkish soldiers reached the west bank of the Suez, but they were confronted by Allied reinforcements, and they were either killed or captured. Then British warships began firing at the invading force still on the east bank from Lake Timsah and the Great Bitter Lake.

The Australian and New Zealand troops were held in reserve, but some saw action. Hartley Palmer wrote: 'The Turks tried to cross the canal right in front of the Motueka platoon of the 12th Nelson Company. No Turk got across. My platoon was 200 yards away and I never fired a shot. But I could hear all the shooting a short distance away. There was only one New Zealander killed, and that was Bill Ham, the first New Zealander to fall in battle.'[33]

Due to the constant arrival of Allied reinforcements, Colonel Von Kressestein was commanded to withdraw about four o'clock in the afternoon. The Turks withdrew to a base camp about ten kilometres east of Ismailia.

Thereafter the Turks decided to maintain a standing line from El Arish on the coast inland to Kalaat en-Nachle, and from there to constantly hassle

---

30   Von Sanders, ibid, p. 44.
31   CAB 21/1, 28 January 1915, p. 1. See also Von Sanders, ibid, p. 43.
32   Von Sanders, ibid, p. 44.
33   Shadbolt, M. Voices of Gallipoli, (Auckland, 1988), pp. 29-30.

the defences and shipping along the Canal. On the British side, they now saw that a surprise attack was possible on the Canal, so henceforth they devoted more attention to bolstering their defences at this strategic location.

DJEMAL PASHA SEEKS SCAPEGOATS

The Turkish defeat was a big blow for the prestige of Turkey – and especially for Djemal Pasha, who now had the embarrassing task of withdrawing his previous premature announcement of victory.[34] He now sought for convenient excuses for the defeat, and in particular for a scapegoat. As had become the norm throughout history, the Jewish people became one such scapegoat. At his behest Beha-a-Din, who had been given a new position of 'Secretary for Jewish Affairs' then outlawed Zionism, forbade all Zionist activities and closed all Zionist institutions. According to Yaari, infringements were punishable by death, and local Arabs were encouraged to ransack Jewish homes.[35]

Djemal had a willing accomplice in Jaffa in the person of the new governor, Hasan Bek, who together with his followers 'plundered, confiscated, carried out arrests, and beat up people right and left, making the town and the surrounding area desolate.'[36] Meir Dizengoff wrote:

It was forbidden to kindle a light in the house in night, lest it be used as a signal to the warships which sailed along the coast of Jaffa from time to time. Hasan Bek plunged the town in darkness by night and in fear by day.[37]

Djemal's anger at the Jewish people intensified and 'hundreds of young men', wrote Sacher, 'were marched off in chains to prisons in Damascus, others exiled to Brusa and Constantinople, yet others sentenced to a living death in the granite pits of Tarsus.'[38] Djemal Pasha had a particular loathing for the two brilliant leaders of the *Poale Zion* group – Yitzchak Ben Zvi

34 Bullock, D. *Allenby's War*, (London, 1988), p. 19.
35 Yaari, ibid, p. 357.
36 Yaari, ibid, p. 358.
37 Yaari, ibid, p. 358.
38 Sacher, H. *A History of Israel*, (New York, 1976), p. 90.

and David Ben Gurion. He had them expelled. These two men ended up in Alexandria, en-route to the United States of America where they anticipated setting up an office for *Poale Zion* – in order to recruit men to fight alongside the Turks against the Triple Alliance! For these men, as was the case with most Russian Jews who had experienced the *pogroms*, Russia was more of an enemy to the Jewish people than Turkey and Germany were.

PREPARATIONS FOR DEFENDING THE DARDANELLES

Following the victory at the Suez Canal, attention now switched to the impending attack upon the Dardanelles. Various Turkish entities were involved in the defence of Constantinople. The first portion to be defended was the strategic Dardanelles Peninsula. General von Sanders, commander of the First Army held this responsibility. He stated: 'As chief of the First Army on the spot I had made such preparations against an attempt of the Anglo-French Fleet to break through as would at least have made its prolonged stay off Constantinople very difficult.'[39] Von Sanders also held the belief that the two German warships, alongside Turkish ships, would then attack the weakened Allied fleet before it would reach Constantinople.

Von Sanders believed it was imperative that the Turks maintained control of the shores of the Dardanelles Straits, stating:

A decisive success could not be won by the enemy unless the landing of large forces in the Dardanelles was coincident with, or antecedent to, the passage of the fleet …

Perhaps there were certain chances for the capture of Constantinople by an Anglo-French fleet if at the same time large Russian forces were landed on one side of the Bosphorus and if this cooperation of the three allies accomplished the capture of Constantinople.[40]

By the end of 1914 Von Sanders had done his best to ensure the region from the beginning of the Bosphorus Straits to the end of the Dardanelles Straits

---

39 Von Sanders, ibid, p. 47.
40 Von Sanders, ibid, p. 48.

as they exited into the Mediterranean had been adequately prepared for any Allied offensive.

THE NAVAL PLANS PROGRESS

The Admiralty accepted Carden's plan at a meeting on 13 January 1915 'and decided to push on with the project.' Admiral Oliver who was present at the War Council meeting on 28 January stated: 'the first shot would be fired in about a fortnight.' One important consideration now was a staging point. The Naval C-in-C wanted Mudros harbour on Lemnos Island, but permission would need to be obtained from the Greeks, who at that stage were still neutral.[41]

Churchill also informed the War Council that he had 'communicated to the Grand Duke Nicholas and to the French Admiralty the project for a naval attack on the Dardanelles. The Grand Duke' Churchill related, 'had replied with enthusiasm, and believed that this might assist him. The French Admiralty' Churchill continued, 'had also sent a favourable reply, and had promised co-operation.'

Churchill concluded by asking 'if the War Council attached importance to this operation, which undoubtedly involved some risks?' The majority expressed they were favourable, and offered numerous reasons for their support.[42]

At the next War Council meeting on 9 February, Churchill explained that the attack was due to begin on 15 February – but this was later postponed until 19 February. Grey also informed the Council that the Greek Government had decided to withdraw from Lemnos Island (Turkey had never acknowledged Greece's sovereignty there), and Britain could take it over.[43] Kitchener then agreed to release the 29th British Division to be based at Lemnos for potential use in the Dardanelles.[44]

---

41 CAB 21/1, 28 January 1915, p. 4.
42 CAB 21/1, 28 January 1915, p. 5.
43 CAB 21/1, 9 February 1915, p. 5.
44 CAB 21/1, 16 February 1915, p. 1.

All now seemed ready for the conquest of the Dardanelles and Turkey to begin, and the naval assault was scheduled to commence on 19 February 1915.

While these Allied plans were being drawn up Mustapha Kemal arrived at Maidos (Eceabat) on the Gallipoli Peninsula to take command of the 19th Division – of which there was but one Brigade. Some time later the remaining two Brigades appeared – and were comprised primarily of Arab soldiers, many of whom did not want to be there.[45]

ARAB AND TURKISH INTRIGUES

Many Arab soldiers served with the Turkish Army, some willingly, and some unwillingly. Some were also involved in the *Al-'Ahd*. In the beginning of 1915 some members of the *al-Fatat* believed it was time to initiate their programme. In January they sent one of their members, Fauzi al-Bakri, to Mecca, with a message for Sherif Hussein. The essence of this message, Antonius states, was: 'the nationalist leaders in Syria and Iraq, including senior Arab officers in the Turkish army, favoured a revolt for the attainment of Arab independence; would the Sherif consent to lead it, and if so, would he receive a deputation in Mecca or delegate persons of trust to Damascus to concert measures?'[46]

Hussein soon afterwards became aware of the possibility that the Turkish leaders were hatching a plot to oust him from his position. He requested permission from the Grand Vizier to send one of his sons to Constantinople to speak about this situation. His purpose with this trip, though, was for his son to meet the representatives of the nationalist groups in Damascus enroute to the Turkish capital.[47]

Feisal visited Damascus on 26 March and during his one month stay there he met with numerous members of the *al-Fatat* and became more aware of the plans of the Arab nationalist movement. He was made aware that several months previous, *al-Fatat* had decreed that if there was clear

45 Mango, ibid, Part 2, Chapter 8.
46 Antonius, ibid, p. 149.
47 Antonius, ibid, p. 150.

evidence that the European powers were seen to have designs upon the Ottoman Empire, then they were to 'work on the side of Turkey.'[48]

Feisal was made a member of *al-Fatat* and then met with officers belonging to *al-'Ahd,* where he was also made a member.[49] He then continued on to Constantinople and arrived there on 23 April. Little did he know it then, but the following days were to be of tremendous significance for the cause to which he was now dedicated.

---

48   Antonius, ibid, p. 153. Antonious received these insights following discussions with Feisal and Dr. Ahmad Qadri who was also present at these meetings.

49   Antonius, ibid, pp. 155-6.

CHAPTER 29

§

Samuel's proposal before the War Cabinet

SAMUEL'S FURTHER PROPOSAL

While the above mentioned plans were taking place, Herbert Samuel continued his quest for gaining sympathy for a future Jewish political entity in Palestine. Samuel put together a Memorandum which was intended for the Cabinet, in which he 'examined the possible alternatives for the future of Palestine, and concluded that annexation to the British Empire, together with active encouragement of Jewish colonization and cultural development, would be the best solution.'[1]

Samuel initially sent the Memo to Prime Minister Asquith and several other ministers. Asquith wrote of Samuel's Memorandum on 28 January 1915:

> I have just received from Herbert Samuel a memorandum headed "The Future of Palestine." He goes on to argue, at considerable length and with some vehemence, in favour of the British annexation of Palestine, a country the size of Wales, much of it barren mountain and part of it waterless. He thinks we might plant in this not very promising territory about three or four million European Jews ... I confess I am not attracted by this proposed addition to our responsibilities ....[2]

---

1 Samuel, ibid, p. 142.
2 Earl of Oxford and Asquith, *Memories and Reflections*, (Boston, 1928), Vol ii, p. 59.

Samuel also sent the initial draft to David Lloyd George, who then forwarded it to Lord Reading, who wrote to Samuel on 5 February:

> I had a talk to L.G… He is certainly inclined to the sympathetic side. Your proposal appeals to the poetic and imaginative as well as to the romantic and religious qualities of his mind.[3]

Another who responded to Samuel was Lord Haldane, who stated: 'I have read your memorandum on Palestine with interest and sympathy. There may be possible questions with the French – as you quite foresee. But it is well worth considering as a possibility.'[4]

Samuel again spoke to Grey on 5 February, and he wrote about the Foreign Secretary's attitude:

> He is still anxious to promote a settlement of the question in a way favourable to Zionist ideas, but he is very doubtful of the possibility or desirability of the establishment of a British Protectorate. He does not know what views the French Government hold, and was rather disposed to sound them. I pointed out, however, that to do so would open up the whole question of territorial dispositions after the war; the disposal of Palestine could not be discussed without raising also the questions of Northern Syria and, probably, of African colonies. Grey is also very indisposed to assume for the British Empire the fresh military and diplomatic responsibilities that would be involved by this extension of frontiers. When I asked him what his solution was he said it might be possible to neutralize the country under international guarantee; to place the control of the Holy Places in the hands of a Commission in which European Powers, and the Pope, and perhaps the United States, would be represented; and to vest the government of the country in some kind of Council to be established by the Jews.

---

3   Samuel, ibid, p. 143.
4   Samuel, ibid, p. 143.

I expressed a doubt whether the Arab population, who number five-sixths of the inhabitants, would accept such a government. Grey said that a possible alternative would be, if it found necessary to continue the suzerainty of Turkey, to establish a regime somewhat like that of Lebanon, but with the governor appointed by the Powers. I pressed upon him the danger of any other Power than England possessing Palestine, and the risk that an international government might end in some European state becoming dominant. I pointed out that if Germany had possessed Palestine before the outbreak of this war, she could have prepared a most formidable attack on Egypt. He agreed that that was so.[5]

Before submitting his final version to the full Cabinet Samuel also spoke to people such as the present and former British Consuls in Jerusalem; the American Consul in Jerusalem, as well as several Jerusalem residents (obviously in London at the time); Chaim Weizmann and his colleague Nahum Sokolow; Lord Rothschild, the President of the Zionist Organisation in Britain; other leading British Jewish entities, and David Lloyd George again.

Samuel then wrote: 'Opinion was crystallizing in favour of something in the nature of a British Protectorate. But the more the situation was explored, the clearer it became that the idea of a Jewish State was impracticable. At some future time, perhaps, it might come about in the course of events; but so long as the great majority of the inhabitants were Arabs it was out of the question. To impose a Jewish minority government would be in flat contradiction to one of the main purposes for which it had been declared that the Allies were fighting.'[6]

SAMUEL'S MEMORANDUM TO THE BRITISH CABINET

As a result of considerable feedback, Herbert Samuel submitted his final Memorandum to the Cabinet in March 1915. Entitled 'Palestine' he begins

---

5 Samuel, ibid, p. 144.
6 Samuel, ibid, pp. 144-45.

by stating: 'IF the war results in the break up of the Turkish Empire in Asia, what is to be the future of Palestine?[7] Samuel then presents five possibilities:

1. Of the possible alternatives, the one most frequently discussed is annexation by France.
2. A second alternative would be to leave the country to Turkey.
3. A third alternative would be internationalisation.
4. Another alternative often suggested is the establishment in Palestine of an autonomous Jewish State.
5. The last alternative is a British protectorate.

Samuel then expanded on each of these five possibilities. Concerning French annexation he states: 'But the establishment of a great European Power so close to the Suez Canal would be a continual and a formidable menace to the essential lines of communication of the British Empire… We cannot proceed on the supposition that our present happy relations with France will continue always.'[8]

Concerning leaving the area under Turkish control he stated: 'Under the Turk Palestine has been blighted. For hundreds of years she has produced neither men nor things useful to the world. Her native population is sunk in squalor… Almost the only signs of agricultural or industrial vitality are to be found in the Jewish and on a smaller scale, in the German, colonies… The [Turkish] Governors who follow one another in rapid succession are concerned only with the amount of money they can squeeze out of the country to send to Constantinople. If it is possible for the Western nations to rescue Palestine from the Turk, it is as much their duty to do it as it has been to rescue the European provinces of Turkey. Besides, if Northern Syria goes to France and Mesopotamia to England, there seems to be no reason for leaving Palestine, detached and isolated, as a Turkish possession.'[9]

Concerning internationalisation, he stated: 'An international regime has invariably been a transition stage to something else. While it lasts it is a

---

7   Memorandum to the Cabinet, March 1915, MEC Archive, St Antony's College, GB 165-0252, Samuel Box 1.
8   Samuel Memorandum, ibid, p. 1.
9   Samuel Memorandum, ibid, pp. 1-2.

theatre of intrigues among the agents of the governing States, each seeking to establish for his country a claim to ultimate control. In this case internationalisation might prove to be a stepping stone to a German protectorate. Already Germany has been very active in Palestine ... In twenty years' time Egypt's neighbour, ostensibly internationalised, may have become so permeated by German influence as to furnish a strong case for German control ... Meanwhile, to govern the country through a Commission composed of representatives of several Powers would be to lay it under a dead hand. Continuous disagreements would be inevitable, and would result in nothing being done for the development of the land and the progress of the people.'[10]

Concerning an autonomous Jewish State, he stated: 'Whatever be the merits or the demerits of that proposal, it is certain that the time is not ripe for it.' Samuel alludes to how there had been much recent Jewish immigration into the land, but, he continued '... they still probably do not number more than about one-sixth of the population.'

'If the attempt were made', he continued 'to place 500,000 or 600,000 Mohommedans of Arab race under a Government which rested upon the support of 30,000 or 100,000 Jewish inhabitants, there can be no assurance that such a Government, even if established by the authority of the Powers, would be able to command allegiance. The dream of a Jewish State, prosperous, progressive, and the home of a brilliant civilisation, might vanish in a series of squalid conflicts with the Arab population. And even if a State as constituted did succeed in avoiding or repressing internal disorder, it is doubtful whether it would be strong enough itself from external aggression on the part of the turbulent elements around it. To attempt to realise the aspiration of a Jewish State one century too soon might throw back its actual realisation for many centuries more. These considerations are fully recognised by the leaders of the Zionist movement.'

Finally, concerning a British protectorate, he stated: 'Its establishment would be a safeguard to Egypt... A common frontier with a European neighbour in the Lebanon is a far smaller risk to the vital interests of the

---

10   Samuel Memorandum ,ibid, p. 2.

British Empire than a common frontier at El Arish.' Samuel then broached the question of strategic sea ports in the Eastern Mediterranean, of which Alexandretta was the most suitable. 'If on general grounds' he stated 'a base on the eastern shores of the Mediterranean is desired, and if political difficulties prevent the acquisition of Alexandretta, it may be worth considering whether Haifa would not serve.'[11]

Samuel then addressed the issue of the need for special consideration concerning the Christian Holy Places, as well as a need to ensure 'that Mahemmedan [sic] interests would be safe-guarded.' In regards to the Jewish people, he stated:

A British protectorate, according to the Egyptian Intelligence Department ... would be welcomed by a large proportion of the present population. There have been many previous indications of the same feeling. I am assured, both by Zionists and non-Zionists, that it is the solution of the question of Palestine which would be by far the most welcome to the Jews throughout the world.

It is hoped that under British rule facilities would be given to Jewish organisations to purchase land, to found colonies, to establish educational and religious institutions, and to co-operate in the economic development of the country.'[12]

It was very clear that Samuel had modified his views since his first draft. But his second draft expressed the reality of the situation: there could be no immediate Jewish national entity in Palestine. Such a concept would need to come as a result of a previous stage, and that previous stage could be none other than a British protectorate. It was to this end that Samuel, Weizmann and others now put their efforts. But the British Cabinet and Government, as it was in March 1915, was not at the stage of giving such a vision as a British protectorate and future Jewish national entity in Palestine serious consideration.

---

11   Samuel Memorandum, ibid, p. 3.
12   Samuel Memorandum, ibid, p. 3.

Lord Bryce, a former important member of the Cabinet wrote to Samuel on 8 March: 'I very much agree with your memorandum in principle, though there are still some minor points I should like to discuss with you, and I am extremely glad you have put the matter before the Cabinet.'[13]

Although there were some who were sympathetic and supportive of Samuel's proposal, some were not, including Asquith. He wrote on 13 March 1915:

I think I have already referred to Herbert Samuel's dithyrambic mem-orandum, urging that in the carving-up of the Turks' Asiatic domin-ion we should take Palestine, into which the scattered Jews would in time swarm back from all the quarters of the globe, and in due course obtain Home Rule. Curiously enough, the only other partisan of this proposal is Lloyd George, who I need not say does not care a damn for the Jews or their past or their future, but thinks it will be an outrage to let the Holy Places pass into the possession or under the protectorate of "agnostic, atheistic France".[14]

Samuel did not accept Asquith's analysis of Lloyd George, who was, Samuel stated, 'genuinely interested'.[15] Another at this initial period who seemed in-terested in the concept was former Prime Minister, Arthur Balfour. Chaim Weizmann wrote to Samuel on 21 March 1915 and stated: 'I had an oppor-tunity of talking to Mr. Balfour, who would help us, if the conditions with regard to France would be clear.'[16]

The conditions with regard to France would need to be clear, for at that stage, pending the collapse of the Turkish Empire, France was expecting to inherit the sceptre of authority in Palestine.

---

13 Samuel, ibid, p. 144.
14 Asquith, ibid, Vol II, p. 65.
15 Samuel, ibid, p. 143.
16 Samuel, ibid, p. 144.

§

Jewish refugees and Zion Mule Corps

B y March 1915 some 10,000 Jewish people had been expelled from *Eretz Yisrael* by the Turks. The vast majority of these people arrived destitute and penniless in Egypt and were soon in camps named Gabbari and Mafruza.

The status of these Jewish refugees in Egypt was unclear. The majority were Russian nationals, but almost to a man they despised the strongly anti-Semitic Russian regime. The confusion was expounded by one of the exiles, Dr Hirsch Loeb Gordon, who wrote:

> The Russian consul who came with us from Jaffa (Razumovsky), the one from Alexandria (Petrov) and the ambassador in Cairo (Smirnov) tried first to persuade and then to force the Russian Jews of military age to return "home" to defend the Czar. Horrifying police raids in the refugee camps were executed in the middle of the night, and able-bodied men registered and re-registered. Alexandria became a trap.[1]

---

1   Gordon, Dr. H.L. *The Jewish Legions in the British Army during the First World War (1914-1918)*, (New York, 1940), p. 2.

The status of the Russians was a quandary for the British, whose resources were severely stretched, without now having to house and feed thousands of destitute refugees. It sounded reasonable to despatch those of conscription age to their homeland, Russia.

JABOTINSKY AND TRUMPELDOR

This forced separation may have happened had it not been for the timely intervention of Joseph Trumpeldor and Zev Jabotinsky. Trumpeldor had been an officer in the Russian Army, and had distinguished himself at the siege of Port Arthur in the Russo-Japanese War of 1905, where he lost an arm.

Upon returning to Russia Trumpeldor, like many other Jewish people, was disillusioned with the social and political situation there, and so made *aliyah* to *Eretz Yisrael*. There he worked on the recently formed Kibbutz Degania on the southern shores of the Sea of Galilee. This first Jewish *kibbutz* (a collective farm) was adjacent to an Arab village named Samak (Semack, or Tzemach), and the railway line from Damascus down the Yarmuk Valley bypassed there.

When Djemal Pasha began expelling Russian Jews, Trumpeldor voluntarily departed in January 1915, and found his way to Alexandria. Here he was given preferential treatment by Consul Petrov (due to his recognized military career for the Czar) who ensured that Trumpeldor received a pension.[2]

Following his time in Constantinople Jabotinsky continued his work for the Russian newspaper *Russkiya Vyedomosti*, and had been in Europe when he heard of Turkey's entry into the War. Jabotinsky was then interested in the Muslim reaction to the Sultan's call for a *Jihad* against the Triple Alliance.

In his travels in North Africa he concluded that most Muslims were plainly not interested, and he concluded therefore that many Muslims had

---

2   Freulich, R. *Soldiers in Judea*, (New York, 1964), p. 18.

lost their faith in Turkey and the Sultan. Jabotinsky could see the imminent end of the Ottoman Turkish Empire.

Jabotinsky arrived in Alexandria in late December 1914. When passing through passport control he overheard one British official say to another: "A few days ago a boatful of Zionists, almost a thousand of them, arrived from Jaffa – the Turks kicked them out of Palestine."[3]

This news alerted Jabotinsky and he offered his services at the Gabbara barracks outside Alexandria. Others also offered their help, and Jabotinsky wrote how: 'Every morning a huge army wagon used to arrive, driven by an Australian soldier and led by two gigantic Australian horses, for the express purpose of giving the smaller children of the camp a "ride."[4] One other Australian soldier who would often visit, and whom Jabotinsky met, was Eliazar Margolin.[5] The convoy on which he was travelling with men of the 4th Australian Brigade arrived in Alexandria on 1 February 1915.[6]

JABOTINSKY AND TRUMPELDOR'S RADICAL PROPOSAL

The proposal of sending the Jewish refugees 'home' to Russia was gaining momentum. Jabotinsky then had an idea: establish a Jewish Legion from these men, and offer them to the British to conquer *Eretz Yisrael*. He sought out Trumpeldor, and propounded his idea to him. Trumpeldor agreed, and on 2 March 1915 a steering committee, comprising Jabotinsky and Trumpeldor as well as Chief Rabbi Pergolla and several other notables, was formed.

A public meeting was then convened at the Mafruza barracks, where a petition was drafted in Hebrew to (a) form a Jewish Legion, and (b) propose to Britain to use it for the liberation of the land of Israel. Trumpeldor wrote of that proposal:

We did not want to be relegated to transport services, or to be sent anywhere they pleased. We wanted to go into action, to be among

---

3   Jabotinsky, V. *The Story of the Jewish Legion*, (New York, 1945), p. 29.
4   Jabotinsky, ibid, p. 34.
5   Jabotinsky, ibid, p. 34.
6   Gouttman, ibid, p. 41.

the combatants and only in the Palestine theatre of war. We wanted to fight for Eretz Israel, upon its soil. Step by step, we would conquer the country from which we had been forcibly exiled; we would liberate our homeland and our comrades who had remained, under terrible conditions, to protect the Yishuv.[7]

THE IDEA PROPOSED TO GENERAL MAXWELL

Jabotinsky and Trumpeldor then submitted their proposal to General Maxwell. Instead of accepting it with enthusiasm, however, Maxwell suggested instead the formation of a unit for mule transport to be used on any front against the Turks. Maxwell proposed calling the unit the 'Assyrian Jewish Refugee Mule Corps.'

When this proposal was mentioned to the delegation leaders, there was shock and unbelief. Jabotinsky in particular was upset, and wrote: 'We civilians felt that General Maxwell's offer must be politely declined. The term he used in French, *corps de muletiers*, had a most unflattering sound in our civilian ears: what a shocking combination – Zion, the rebirth of a nation, the first really Jewish troops in the whole history of the Exile, and "mules".'[8]

Unable to be reconciled to this concept, Jabotinsky departed for Europe where he further agitated for the establishment of a Jewish Legion. While in France he met with Baron Edmond de Rothschild, who said to him: "You must continue at all costs! See that it becomes a real Legion when the time of the Palestine Campaign comes."[9]

FORMATION OF THE ZION MULE CORPS

The remainder of the delegation, led now by Trumpeldor, accepted Maxwell's offer. Trumpeldor stated: "To get the Turks out of Palestine we've got to smash the Turks. Which side you begin the smashing, north or south, is just technique. Any front leads to Zion."[10] The *Jewish Chronicle* recorded of this historic occasion:

---

7   Yaari, A, ibid, p. 429.

8   Jabotinsky, ibid, p. 42.

9   Jabotinsky, ibid, p. 51.

10 Trumpeldor Notes, under heading 'Via Gallipoli to Zion', Tel Chai Archives, cited in Schetman, J. *Jabotinsky –*

The formation in Alexandria of the Zion Mule Transport Corps – a Jewish legion comprised almost entirely of Palestine refugees – marks an era in the history of the Jews, as well as that of England. Never has England been known to depart from its policy of admitting none but British subjects or colonials into its army...[11]

Trumpeldor was disqualified from leading this formation, because he was not a British subject, and in view of his physical impairment. Maxwell now had to locate a British officer who was willing and able to lead this quite unusual unit.

At that time there was a British officer in Cairo awaiting a commission. His name was John Patterson, an Anglo-Irishman, who was better known as the 'Lion killer of Tsavo'. There was yet another aspect of his quite re-markable personality which suited Patterson for this position, of which he wrote:

From the days of my youth I have always been a keen student of the Jewish people, their history, laws and customs. Even as a boy I spent the greater part of my leisure hours poring over the Bible ...

It was strange, therefore, that I, so imbued with Jewish traditions, should have been drawn to the land where the Pharaohs had kept the Children of Israel in bondage for over four hundred years; and it was still more strange that I should have arrived in Egypt just at the psychological moment when General Sir John Maxwell, the Commander-in-Chief, was looking for a suitable officer to raise and command a Jewish unit.

Now such a thing as a Jewish unit had been unknown in the an-nals of the world for some two thousand years – since the days of the Maccabees.[12]

Rebel and Statesman, (New York, 1956), p. 205.
11 Jewish Chronicle, 30 April 1915, p. 11.
12 Patterson, J. With the Zionists in Gallipoli, (London, 1916), pp. 31-32.

Patterson took up his new command on 19 March 1915 and departed immediately for Alexandria to be united with his new formation. The *Jewish Chronicle* stated of him that 'no man could be better suited to the task of taking a Jewish army to Palestine.'[13]

Recruitment began immediately after his arrival. Within just a few days some 500 men had volunteered and on 23 March 1915 they paraded at the Gabbara camp and were then officially sworn into the British Army. Chief Rabbi Della Pergolla then addressed the recruits, explaining to them the meaning of an oath, the importance of keeping it, and impressed upon them, so Patterson stated, that 'the honour of Israel rested in their hands.'[14]

Shortly afterwards these excited men then 'dispersed in groups along the streets of Alexandria' wrote Trumpeldor, 'singing the songs of Eretz Israel. They joined company with English soldiers and sang with them the song that was then in vogue, "Tipperary"'[15].

Within a few days a new camp was established named Wardian, 'and from it could be heard' wrote Trumpeldor, 'words of command uttered vigorously and with precision in the Hebrew tongue.'[16] The camp soon had the 500 recruits as well as five British and eight Jewish officers (including Trumpeldor), as well as twenty horses and 750 pack mules. The uniform of the Zion Mule Corps was a standard British uniform, but embellished with the Star of David insignia.

The recruits included mostly secular nationalists, or Zionists. One of the religious recruits, Wertheimer, came from the ultra-Orthodox section of Jerusalem's Old City. He was accompanied to the camp by his father, who insisted that they, the ultra-Orthodox and non-Zionist Jews were also willing to lay down their lives for the liberation of *Eretz Yisrael*. There was a problem for men of his religious persuasion though – there was no *kosher*[17] kitchen in the camp.

---

13   *Jewish Chronicle*, 30 April 1915, p. 11.
14   Patterson, ibid, p. 35.
15   Yaari, ibid, pp. 429-30.
16   Yaari, ibid, p. 430.
17   *Kosher* – food prepared according to Jewish dietary laws.

The rigorous training began on 2 April 1915. 'Drilling and parades were the order of the day' wrote Patterson, 'horses and mules had to be exercised, fed and watered three times a day; the men had to be taught how to saddle and unsaddle them, load and unload packs; they had also to be instructed in the use of the rifles and bayonet.'[18]

The *Jewish Chronicle* correspondent one day visited the camp and afterwards wrote of noticing one sergeant 'drilling a squad of raw recruits. His words of command' the correspondent continued:

> … borne aloft by the breeze, though quite distinct, sounded strange at the moment. Were they taken from a new list of commands recently published and unknown to the writer? No – a little effort enabled me to recognize the words which proved to be Hebrew. The presence of a few men still wearing the Jewish garb, the Hebrew words of command ringing through the air and the continuous conversations held in Hebrew in the midst of a military camp soon transported me to a Biblical dreamland.[19]

Although Trumpeldor and others viewed this formation as the beginning of a road which would lead them to Zion, there was trepidation among the remaining Jewish people in Palestine when they heard of its establishment. They feared that such a formation would increase the suspicions the Turks already held towards them – that they, like the Armenians, were traitors. Many feared retribution. To forestall any possible retribution, many Jewish people marched through the streets of Jerusalem shouting their contempt towards these Jewish 'traitors' in Egypt.[20]

Ben Zvi and Ben Gurion were still in Alexandria at the time of this formation, and they too viewed its formation as potentially harmful. They were of the opinion that Turkey, allied to the Central Powers, would ultimately triumph in the War. Their attitude was opposite to that of Jabotinsky

---

18   Patterson, ibid, p. 42.
19   *Jewish Chronicle*, 30 April 1915, p. 11.
20   Sacher, ibid, p. 92.

and Trumpeldor, who believed the Allies would win and that it could only be beneficial to have Jewish units serving with the British, especially in the conquest of *Eretz Yisrael*.

The first step in that cause was soon to begin – on the Dardanelles Peninsula in Turkey, near a small village named Gelibolu.

RESTLESS SOLDIERS

While the men from Zion prepared for their next venture, the ANZAC and British soldiers were restless for action. A rather despondent Claude Pocock of the Canterbury Mounted Rifles wrote: 'Oh, I don't think we will ever get to the front.'[21] 'For the last month we have been merely filling in time' wrote Lieutenant William Johns of Pukekohe to his niece Iris on 20 March, concluding, 'they don't know what to do with us.'[22] Private Chadwick of the Lancashire Fusiliers wrote home: 'All the boys are looking as well as can be expected, but we are all fed up with this monotonous life.'[23]

The monotony was often relieved by visits to Cairo, and especially a place called the Haret el Wasser, or *Wozzer* to the troops. 'Getting to Egypt, seeing an Eastern city for the first time, was very romantic,' recalled Tony Fagan. 'I saw my first fighting there' he continued. 'It was the Battle of the Wazzir, the quarter of Cairo where all these brothels and booze dens were.'[24]

The battle Fagan referred to occurred on 2 April when the district was torched, primarily by New Zealanders (or so the Australians claimed!) in revenge for certain 'injuries' which they and their mates had received.

The monotony and boredom felt by these soldiers from Britain, Australia and New Zealand, however, was soon to end. In just a few weeks they would soon be seeing a lot more action than what the Battle of the Wazzir offered them.

---

21   Queen Elizabeth II War Memorial, Waiouru, New Zealand.
22   William Johns to his niece Iris, Auckland City Museum, MS 1392. 81/160.
23   Moorhouse, G. *Hell's Foundations: A Town, Its Myths & Gallipoli*, (United Kingdom, 1992), p. 59.
24   Shadbolt, ibid, p.17.

§

CHAPTER 31

The naval campaign begins

PROBLEMS IN TURKEY

The first few months of 1915 brought no succour to Turkey. Her Army was being sorely defeated in the Caucasus; Djemal had been defeated in Egypt; and the Allied blockade of the Dardanelles and the Levantine ports deprived Turkey of trading opportunities.

Much of the populace also understood that if the Allies began to advance through the Dardanelles, then both Bulgaria and Greece could join with the Allies and also converge upon Constantinople. Morgenthau summed up the mood in the wake of the impending Allied naval assault: 'Wagenheim and also nearly all of the German military and naval forces not only regarded the forcing of the Dardanelles as possible, but they believed it to be inevitable. The possibility of British success was one of the most familiar topics of discussion, and the weight of opinion, both lay and professional, inclined in favour of the Allied fleets.'[1]

Already in January preparations were being made to send the Sultan and the Turkish Government to Eski-Shehr in Asia Minor.

---

1 Morgenthau, ibid, Chapter 16, p. 3.

SPECIAL WAR COUNCIL MEETING

While the Anglo-French Fleet began assembling around the Greek islands of Lemnos, Imbros and Tenedos, there was an impromptu War Council meeting held on 16 February. It was agreed at that meeting to send the 29th British Division to Lemnos Island at the earliest possible date to form the nucleus of a landing force if needed. In addition the Admiralty was instructed 'to build special transports and lighters suitable for the convey-ance and landing of a force of 50,000 men at any point where they may be required.'[2]

Three days later, the full War Council met, and it was at this meeting that Kitchener dropped a bombshell: he intended substituting the Australian and New Zealand soldiers at Lemnos for the 29th Division, which could be sent later if needed.

Churchill expressed 'great disappointment' if the 29th Division was not sent out. He again emphasized 'the military advantages which success would bring' and stated his conviction that there should be 50,000 soldiers 'within reach of the Dardanelles, which could be concentrated there in three days.' Churchill did not consider the newly arrived Australian and New Zealand soldiers 'first-rate troops at present' and that they would require 'a stiffening of regulars.'[3]

Churchill's concluding remarks express his deepest emotions: 'We should never forgive ourselves if this promising operation failed owing to insufficient military support at the critical moment.'[4]

Kitchener stated that the 29th Division was being held back as there was a real chance that Russia would be defeated on the Eastern Front. If this happened Germany would introduce more troops onto the Western Front – therefore there was a great need of reinforcements there. Considerable discussion followed about the viability of despatching the 29th Division to

---

2 CAB 21/1, 16 February 1915, p. 1. This meeting began as in informal meeting but the decisions made were of such importance that it was recorded as a full meeting of the War Council. These decisions were conveyed to the Cabinet secretary, Lieutenant-Colonel Maurice Hankey.

3 CAB 21/1, 19 February 1915, p. 2.

4 CAB 21/1, 19 February 1915, p. 2.

the East, with Kitchener again emphasizing that he was prepared to send the 29th Division there - but not just yet.[5]

Balfour then suggested 'that the War Council ought to be informed what would be the precise political effect of an occupation of the Gallipoli Peninsula combined with naval command of the Sea of Marmora (sic)' and desired that the Foreign Office 'prepare a Memorandum on the subject'[6]

This critical meeting ended with a decision to prepare transports to convey the ANZAC troops to Lemnos and the 29th Division to the Mediterranean, if required.[7] Kitchener's veto for the immediate despatch of this Division would have serious long-term consequences.

THE NAVAL CAMPAIGN BEGINS

Two days before the scheduled beginning of the naval campaign a British plane took off from *HMS Ark Royal* on the very first aerial reconnaissance flight over the area. Two days later, on 19 February another flight took the plane over the region further to the north around Gaba Tepe.[8] Such reconnaissance flights were henceforth to play an important part in this campaign.

The Anglo-French Fleet began bombing the Turkish fortifications on both sides of the entrance to the Dardanelles on 19 February. Seddelbahir on the European side and Kum Kale on the Asian side received the bulk of the bombardment. The Allied ships remained just out of range of the less sophisticated Turkish guns.

In Petrogad the French ambassador Maurice Paleologue wrote in his diary on 20 February: 'Yesterday the Anglo-French fleet bombarded the forts which command the entrance to the Dardanelles. It is a prelude to a landing on the Gallipoli Peninsula.'[9]

On several occasions small parties of British marines were landed, but these, as Von Sanders stated, 'were unsuccessful because in spite of the bom-

---

5   CAB 21/2, 19 February 1915, p. 5.
6   CAB 21/1, 19 February 1915, p. 5.
7   CAB 21/1, 19 February 1915, p. 6.
8   Dolan, ibid, Chapter 2.
9   Paleologue, M. *An Ambassador's Memoirs*, 20 February 1915, Volume 1. www.net.lib.byu.edu/

bardment small Turkish bodies had remained in places not reached by the artillery fire and repulsed the landing.'[10]

Despite these unsuccessful landings, the Turkish high command never-theless expected the Allied fleet to break through.[11]

One of the best eye-witnesses to these events was Ambassador Morgenthau. He received a visit from the Austrian Ambassador, Johann Markgraf von Pallavicini, on 19 February, who was in a high state of agita-tion. Pallavicini believed that the Allies were sure to succeed, 'as did' wrote Morgenthau 'almost all the other important men in Constantinople.'[12]

At this point Enver Pasha made certain re-arrangements in the dis-position of Turkish forces, which in Von Sanders' view were prejudicial for proper defence. He ordered, for instance, Turkish troops to withdraw from the shoreline of the Dardanelles. Von Sanders objected, but Enver overruled him. So sure was Von Sanders that this move was destined to fail, that he went directly to the German Ambassador and the Chief of the German Military Cabinet – and they intervened in his favour. Enver's plan for with-drawal of Turkish troops from those strategic regions was halted.[13]

WAR COUNCIL MEETING

At the British War Council meeting on 24 February there was a lengthy discussion about the naval assault; the possibility of its failure; the effect of a land force in such a situation; the composition of such a land force; the political ramifications of a victory; the need of progressing with the expedi-tion in Mesopotamia or of withdrawing those troops and using them in the Dardanelles; and numerous other matters associated with the Dardanelles campaign.[14]

Churchill persevered in his request for the availability of a large land force in order to follow up the impending naval victory. Kitchener contin-

---

10   Von Sanders, ibid, p. 53.
11   Von Sanders, ibid, p. 53.
12   Morgenthau, ibid, Chapter 16, p. 10.
13   Von Sanders, ibid, p. 54.
14   CAB 21/1, 24 February 1915, p. 3.

ued to be apprehensive, and even though the danger of Russia collapsing had passed, he was still reluctant to send the 29th Division.[15]

It was finally agreed that General Birdwood, the commander of the Australian and New Zealand troops, would be sent to the Dardanelles to discuss the campaign with Vice-Admiral Carden, and that a decision concerning the disposition of the 29th Division would be deferred till the next meeting.[16]

The lack of harmony in the War Council concerning the Dardanelles Campaign became more apparent at the following meeting on 26 February. Once again considerable time was devoted to the composition and purpose of the land forces, and once again Kitchener demurred from immediately despatching the 29th Division. Churchill at this point stated:

… the XXIXth Division would not make the difference between failure and success in France, but might well make the difference in the East. He wished it to be placed on record that he dissented altogether from the retention of the XXIXth Division in this country. If a disaster occurred in Turkey owing to insufficiency of troops, he must disclaim all responsibility.[17]

Kitchener then stated in response that he thought that Russia could still fall, and that all seasoned soldiers needed to be available for the Western Front.[18]

It seemed that the impending Dardanelles Campaign was beginning with a serious impediment – lack of unity in the Cabinet. Such disunity could be compensated for if the Fleet managed to break through, and if those unseasoned soldiers could follow up by utilising raw courage instead of battleground experience.

---

15   CAB 21/1, 24 February 1915, p. 5.
16   CAB 21/1, 24 February 1915, p. 6.
17   CAB 21/1, 26 February 1915, p. 5.
18   CAB 21/1, 26 February 1915, p. 5.

CONSTANTINOPLE, BOSPHORUS & DARDANELLES

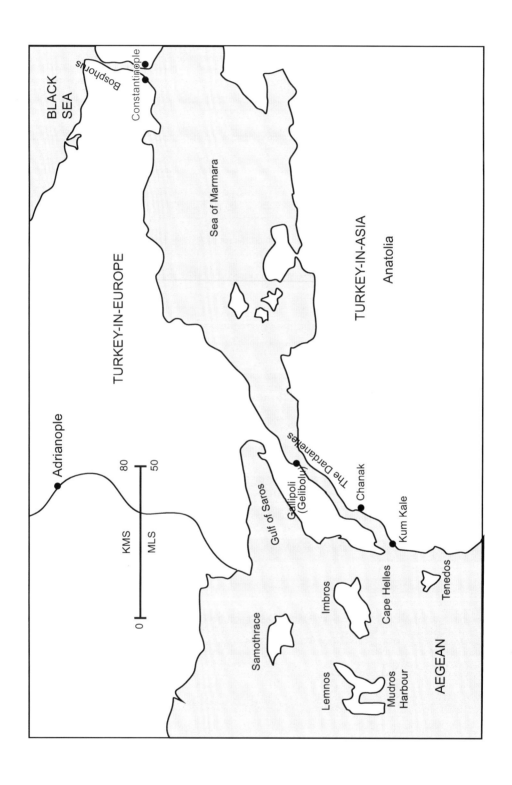

CHAPTER 32

§

Russia and Constantinople

RENEWED RUSSIAN INTEREST IN CONSTANTINOPLE

Although there had been serious differences of opinion concerning the use of ground forces, the matter of taking the Dardanelles and Constantinople was still much anticipated by the War Council. This very possibility now once again brought to the fore the political consequences of victory. The fall of Constantinople was of great interest to all those countries surrounding the Black Sea and Turkey. Now that the military campaign was in full swing, the War Council began to give further consideration to the future political status of Constantinople and Turkey pending its ultimate collapse. The War Cabinet meeting of 26 February concluded with Foreign Secretary Grey stating, 'that conversations on the subject with Russia had already taken place. Russia insisted that the *status quo* must on no account be guaranteed.'[1]

Ambassador Paleologue in Moscow wrote on 27 February:

The Anglo-French fleet is continuing its attack with the greatest vigour: all the outer forts are already silenced. The result is great public excitement in Russia, which expects to see the Allies off the Golden Horn any day now.

---

1 CAB 21/1, 26 February 1915, p. 7.

The Byzantine mirage mesmerizes public opinion more and more, and indeed, to such a pitch as to leave it almost indifferent to the loss of East Prussia – as if the defeat of Germany were not a condition precedent to the fulfilment of the Byzantine dream![2]

Then on 1 March Paleologue wrote that Sazanov had called British Ambassador Buchanan and himself to a meeting and called their attention to 'the excitement which the Constantinople question is rousing in all ranks of Russian society.' The hour for plain speaking had come, he said to the Ambassadors. 'The Russian people are now entitled to know that they can count on their Allies in the realization of their national task. England and France should say openly that they agree to the annexation of Constantinople by Russia when the day for peace arrives.'[3]

Paleologue had a personal conversation with Czar Nicholas on 3 March, in which the ruler of Russia stated very firmly that: 'The city of Constantinople and southern Thrace must be incorporated in my empire. You know that England has already expressed her approval' he continued. 'King George told my ambassador quite recently: *Constantinople must be yours.*' The Czar then informed the French ambassador that he agreed 'to everything your Government wishes.'[4]

Russia considered itself to be the inheritor of the Byzantine Empire, and therefore, they maintained, its former capital Constantinople rightly belonged to Russia. But similar ambitions for Constantinople were also held by the King of Greece and the King of Bulgaria.

The War Council meeting on 3 March 1915 was again mostly consumed with the Dardanelles Campaign, and in particular the future of Constantinople. Grey began the discussion by mentioning that Greece now wanted to be involved. His main point, though, related to Russia, stating: 'We are approaching a point at which we should have to say to Russia what

---

2 Paleologue, ibid, 27 February 1915.
3 Paleologue, ibid, 1 March 1915.
4 Paleologue, ibid, 3 March 1915.

we are willing to concede in regards to the Straits …' Grey later stated that some months before, Mr Sazanoff 'had been willing to agree to the neutralization of Constantinople. Now, however, he said that there was a growing feeling in Russia that they ought to control the Straits.'[5]

Grey insisted it was of vital importance 'to avoid anything in the nature of a breach with Russia, or any action which would incline Russia to make a separate peace.' It was reiterated that nothing could be done which would allow either France or Germany to benefit from this situation. Germany, stated Lord Haldane, 'would seize any opportunity to conclude a separate peace with Russia.'[6]

Lord Crewe even suggested that a treaty might be made in which Rumania was a party. Grey made a most profound response to this: '… treaties were apt to be disregarded in war.'[7] The broaching of this subject brought to the fore very deep opinions from all those present. The discussion concluded with Grey stating the content of his forthcoming message to the Russian foreign minister:

> You say that Russian sentiment will insist on the occupation of Constantinople by Russia. My personal opinion is that the British Government will not interpose a veto. But public opinion in this country will insist on all sorts of economic questions being settled. France will say that Syria must be earmarked for her. We ourselves have up to now asked for nothing, and have only declared a protectorate over Egypt. We should have to consider our claims in Asia Minor. British opinion, however, had entirely changed in regard to a Russian occupation of Constantinople, and he personally did not anticipate any veto to it.[8]

There was then considerable discussion as to the actual conquest of Constantinople.

---

5 CAB 21/1, 3 March 1915, p. 2.
6 CAB 21/1, 3 March 1915, p. 2.
7 CAB 21/1, 3 March 1915, p. 2.
8 CAB 21/1, 3 March 1915, p. 3.

RUSSIA CLAIMS CONSTANTINOPLE

On 3 March the Czar met for breakfast with Paleologue and stated to the French ambassador: 'My mind is entirely made up: the only solution to the problem of Constantinople and the Narrows is the one which I held out to you last November. The town of Constantinople and southern Thrace must be incorporated in the Russian Empire.'[9]

The Czar then elaborated further upon Russia's ambitions, and following Paleologue's insistence concerning French interests, he insisted that these would be safeguarded. When informed of this, the French authorities were aghast. President Poincare was then permitted to write a private letter to Paleologue expressing the view that this Russian demand could enable her to become a major naval power and could lead to the division of the Ottoman Empire. 'But', Poincare wrote, 'the possession of Constantinople would not only give Russia privileges as to the line of succession in the Ottoman Empire but would bring her within the concert of Western nations and might enable her to become a great naval power. This would entirely upset the equilibrium of Europe. So large an increase of strength could only be acceptable to us if we derive equivalent advantages from the war.'[10]

In view of Grey's communique to the Russian Government, the Foreign Minister Mr Sazanov presented an *aide memoire* to the British ambassador, George Buchanan, on 4 March, which stated:

Course of latest events leads His Majesty the Emperor Nicholas to think that the question of Constantinople and the Straits must be definitely solved in accordance with traditional aspirations of Russia.

Any solution would be unsatisfactory and precarious if it did not incorporate henceforth in Russian Empire the city of Constantinople, western shore of the Bosphorus, of the Sea of Marmora, and of the Dardanelles, as well as southern Thrace up to the Enos-Midia line.

Ipso facto and by strategic necessity, part of Asiatic shore included between the Bosphorus, River Sakharia, and a point to be fixed on the

---

9   Poincare, R. *The Memoirs of Raymond Poincare* (translated by Sir George Arthur), (London, 1930), Vol. 4, p. 52.
10 Poincare to Paleologue, 3 March 1915, cited in Poincare, ibid, p. 55.

Gulf of Ismid, islands of the Sea of Marmora, islands of Imbros and Tenedos, ought to be incorporated in the empire.[11]

Russia had spelled out loud and clear her requirements – pending of course an Allied victory at Gallipoli. But the message did conclude with these words:

> Special interests of France and of Great Britain in the region above described will be scrupulously respected.
>
> Imperial Government likes to hope that above considerations will meet with sympathy of the two allied Governments. Said Governments are assured of meeting with, at the hands of Imperial Government, the same sympathy for realisation of *desiderata* which they may form in other regions of Ottoman Empire and elsewhere.[12]

With Russia having made its demands clear, the matter now to be determined (pending the ultimate defeat of Turkey), was how the remainder of the Ottoman Empire would henceforth be governed - if Constantinople was to be in the hands of the Russians.

---

11   Telegram No 249, Sazanov to Buchanan, 4 March 1915, and conveyed by Buchanan to Grey on 5 March 1915. CAB 21/1, 10 March 1915, p. 8.
12   Sazanov to Buchanan, ibid, p. 8.

§

CHAPTER 33

Britain and France's response

BRITAIN'S RESPONSE

The Russian demands and their desire to meet the *desiderata* of her Allies in the future dismemberment of the Ottoman Empire placed a huge responsibility upon the War Council. The Council's meeting of 10 March 1915 was one of great long term significance, as it involved 'questions likely to arise after the fall of Constantinople.'[1]

Grey then gave a very lengthy preamble to the importance of the future of Constantinople, and particularly of Russia's demand for this city – and of further territory surrounding it. He provided a two-fold context. One was that Germany was pushing to make a separate peace with Russia and with France. Grey stated that France was as committed to defeating Germany as was Britain. But it was clear to all that a separate German-Russian peace would seriously impinge upon the Allies ability to win the War. The second important factor concerned Russia's principal desire from the War which was 'to obtain an outlet to the sea.'

Concerning this second point, Grey stated, Russia was cautious about encouraging other countries to enter the war, such as Greece, Bulgaria and Rumania, as each of these nations could challenge Russia for control of Constantinople and the Straits. Asquith then added 'that the

---

1 CAB 21/1, 10 March, 1915, p. 3. It was so important that Asquith invited Lord Lansdowne and Mr Bonar Law.

Russian *aide-memoire* referred to a *final* settlement, and not to an interim arrangement.[2]

Balfour kicked off the response and stated that he had no objection with Russia's demand, 'provided that the other Allies received similar assurances as regards their own wishes.' Lloyd George concurred, and added: 'It was vital for us, if we made concessions, to say what we wanted in return.'[3]

Both Asquith and Kitchener then broached the opinion that with Russia ensconced at Constantinople then it would be essential for Britain to have 'an additional naval base in these waters' and Alexandretta was stated by both as the best option.

Opinions varied somewhat as to exactly how and when to acquiesce with the Russian demand. Asquith then referred them all back to the conclusion of the Russian *aide-memoire* and of Russia's 'sympathy of desiderata' for the aspirations of the Allies in 'other regions of Ottoman Empire and elsewhere.'[4]

Lloyd George indicated it was now the time to formulate these *desiderata*. Churchill agreed. Concerning the matter of *desiderata*, Lloyd George made a very telling statement, saying that he 'felt considerable misgivings about the expediency of occupying Alexandretta. He suggested Palestine as an alternative, owing to the prestige it would give to us.' Kitchener immediately retorted that 'Palestine would be of no value to us whatsoever. He saw no reason why the French should oppose our occupation of Alexandretta, provided it was put to them in the right way. Alexandretta was beyond the French sphere of influence in Syria.'[5]

Lord Kitchener was fixated upon attaining Alexandretta. 'With Russia in Constantinople, France in Syria, and Italy in Rhodes', he stated, 'our position in Egypt would be untenable if any other Power held Alexandretta.'[6]

---

2   CAB 21/1, 10 March 1915, p. 3.
3   CAB 21/1, 10 March 1915, p. 3.
4   CAB 21/1, 10 March 1915, p. 4.
5   CAB 21/1, 10 March 1915, p. 5.
6   CAB 21/1, 10 March 1915, p. 6.

After other input, Kitchener reiterated: 'we could not count on holding Egypt if Alexandretta were in the hands of some other Power.'[7]

Churchill then asked a very telling question: '… if we were to give Constantinople to Russia, and Syria to France, and to receive nothing in return?' The conversation soon afterwards looked at the future of the Turkish Empire, prompting Lord Crewe to state: 'we ought to consider the expediency of leaving some territory to the Sultan of Turkey as the head of the Khaliphate. The Mohammedans of India, for example, had in no way diminished their reverence for the Sultan by reason of the war.' This comment elicited an immediate response from Kitchener, who stated, 'the location of the Khaliphate was solely a question for the Mohammedan world.'[8]

Following a lengthy discussion Grey proposed that the present arrangement concerning the future of Constantinople be kept secret 'otherwise the Balkan States might be alienated.' He also stated three other conditions: free passage through the Straits; Constantinople being a free port; that Arabia and the holy places to remain in Islamic hands.[9]

All those present would have understood that Arabia meant the Arabian Peninsula, which was composed of various tribes, and the holy places referred to Mecca and Medina.

The official reply sent to Russia (what became known as the secret 'Constantinople Agreement') stated that Britain agreed to the *proposals put forward in the Russian* aide-memoire, *subject to the war being prosecuted to a victorious conclusion, and to Great Britain realizing the desiderata referred to in the last sentence of the Russian* aide-memoire. *These desiderata will be put forward by the British and French Governments as soon as there had been time to consider them.'* The meeting also concluded with a statement that: *'The War Office* [was] *to prepare a memorandum setting forth the strategic advantage of Alexandretta.'*

---

7   CAB 21/1, 10 March 1915, p. 6.
8   CAB 21/1, 10 March 1915, p. 7.
9   CAB 21/1, 10 March 1915, p. 7.

THE FUTURE OF PALESTINE

Although there was thereafter considerable debate about the merits of claiming Alexandretta, it was the comments of Lloyd George and Kitchener which are of supreme importance. Within these comments lay the seed of a future direction.

Kitchener was only concerned with Britain's geo-political interests, and at this point saw Alexandretta of more importance than Palestine. Lloyd George was just as interested in Britain's geo-political interests, but he also saw and understood the deeper significance of attaining Palestine.

Lloyd George, Balfour and Grey were all acutely aware of the Jewish aspirations. All the Cabinet members, and many more, were also aware of Herbert Samuel's *desiderata* from the War, as explained in his Memorandum - a 'Jewish State' in Palestine – or at the very least a British Protectorate in Palestine, which would sponsor and support a Jewish national entity there.

PALEOLOGUE AND THE CZAR

On 8 March 1915 Paleologue wrote: 'In accordance with instructions in a telegram from Delcasse this evening I have told Sazanov that he may rely on the goodwill of the French Government as regards the questions of Constantinople and the Straits being solved in the manner desired by Russia.'[10]

Ambassador Buchanan conveyed the British compliance to Russia's demands to Sazanov. France, concerned by the Russian demands and realizing that with the continuation of the War her (France's) bargaining power could be weakened, wanted to deal with the matter urgently.[11]

On 15 March Paleologue wrote: 'The French Government has been considering the terms of peace to be imposed on Turkey by the Allies, and has instructed me to inform the Russian Government of the compensation France expects to receive in Syria.'

---

10   Paleologue, ibid, 8 March 1915. M. Delcasse was the French Foreign Minister.
11   Adamov, E. *German Translation of Vol VI of the series of documents from the Archives of the Russian Foreign Office*, published Moscow, 1924, No, 19. Grey, E. ibid, p. 230, cited in Stein, L. *The Balfour Declaration*, (London, 1961), p. 230.

The Czar at this time asked both Paleologue and Sazanov to visit him at his GHQ.[12] The following day, 16 March, Paleologue 'described in detail the full civilizing work France intends to undertake in Syria, Cilicia and Palestine.' Czar Nicholas then had Paleologue show him on a map, to which he then replied: 'I agree to all you ask.'[13] Stein, though, cites A. Pingaud who stated that the Czar made some reservations concerning Palestine and the Holy Places.[14]

At later meetings Sazanov made it clear that the Russians would not acquiesce to all the French demands, especially concerning the Holy Places, and that Russia would never agree to a Roman Catholic protectorate over 'Jerusalem, Galilee, the Jordan, and Lake Tiberius.'[15] The French ultimately believed they had received Russian support for Palestine *except the Holy Places,* but the Russian position wasn't quite so clear. What France ended up with was a 'vague assurance that Russia was prepared to let them have what they wanted in Syria and Cilicia.'[16]

Asquith then stated at the War Council meeting on 19 March that the French Ambassador to Petrograd, Paleologue, 'had laid claim to a very large part of Turkey in Asia as French desiderata in return for permitting a Russian occupation of Constantinople and the Straits. These desiderata', Asquith continued, 'included Cilicia, Syria and Palestine.'[17]

Asquith then mentioned a very significant Russian objection to the French demands: 'The Russians objected most strongly to the Christian Holy Places being in French hands.'[18] Herein lay another significant factor in determining the future status of Palestine, if and when Turkey lost control of that strategic region.

Grey at this point put forth two important questions for the War Council to consider:

---

12 Paleologue, ibid, 15 March 1915.

13 Paleologue, ibid, Vol. 1, 18 March 1915.

14 Paleologue, M. *An Ambassador's Memoirs,* I, p. 303. Pingaud, A. *Histoire Diplomatique de la France pendant la Grande Guerre,* (Paris, 1940), Vol 1, p. 253, cited in Stein, ibid, p. 244.

15 Poincare, A. *Au Service de la France,* (Paris, 1926), Vol VI, p, 118, cited in Stein, ibid, p. 245.

16 Stein, ibid, p. 245, referring to Adamov, ibid, No's 29 & 31.

17 CAB 21/1, 19 March 1915, p. 5.

18 CAB 21/1, 19 March 1915, p. 5.

1. If we acquire fresh territory shall we make ourselves weaker or stronger?
2. Ought we not to take into account the very strong feeling in the Moslem world that Mohammedanism ought to have a political as well as a religious existence?[19]

'If the latter question were answered in the affirmative' Grey continued, 'Arabia, Syria, and Mesopotamia were the only possible territories for an Arab Empire. If we took this standpoint we could say to our Moslem subjects that, as Turkey had handed itself over to the Germans, we had set up a new and independent Moslem State.'[20]

Grey's statement produced considerable debate. Lord Crewe stated that there were two views expressed in the India Office, one that Turkey in Asia should become stronger, and the other, 'that Turkey should be sacrificed and Arabia made as strong as possible.'[21]

Any mention of Arabia was sure to draw the attention of Kitchener, who then stated:

The Turks … would always be under pressure from their strong Russian neighbour, with the result that the Khalifate might be to a great extent under Russian domination, and Russian influence might indirectly assert itself over the Mohammedan part of the population of India. If on the other hand, the Khalifate were transferred to Arabia, it would remain to a great extent under our influence.[22]

The issue of Arabia allowed Asquith to read an extract from a Memorandum from Sir Theodore Morison (which was also circulated), 'in which he stated the apprehension of some leading Moslems that they would become like the Jews – a people having a religion, but no country – and in which he expressed a hope that the Khaliphate would obtain Syria and Mesopotamia.'

---

19   CAB 21/1, 19 March 1915, p. 5.
20   CAB 21/1, 19 March 1915, p. 6.
21   CAB 21/1, 19 March 1915, p. 6.
22   CAB 21/1, 19 March 1915, p. 6.

The mention of the Khaliphate again provoked Kitchener, who stated, 'if Mesopotamia was to be left undeveloped, it was all very well to leave it to the Arabs. But', he continued, 'if it was to be developed, we should only be creating trouble for ourselves by leaving it to them.'[23]

In relation to Mesopotamia Lord Crewe stated that all in the India Office were agreed that the *Vilayet* of Basra 'must form part of the British Empire.' Some, though, also favoured a protectorate over the *Vilayet* of Baghdad.[24]

Churchill then drew the question back to the matter of British *desiderata*, and stated, 'that in this question of the partition of Turkey in Asia the main difficulty was likely to be between England and France, leaving out the question of the Christian Holy Places, in which Russia also was concerned.'[25] Churchill suggested that the conversations with France be postponed. Grey then stated that, 'at present it was a question of making up our own mind, and not of discussing the matter with France.'[26] To this Churchill then responded, that 'the whole question depended on whether we intended to divide Turkey. Surely … we did not intend to leave this inefficient and out-of-date nation, which had long misruled one of the most fertile countries in the world, still in possession! Turkey had long shown herself to be inefficient as a governing Power, and it was time for us to make a clean sweep.'[27]

Prime Minister Asquith then drew the matter to a close by stating: 'the fact was we were not free agents. Russia intended to take a good slice of Turkey. France, Italy, and Greece each demanded a piece. If, for one reason or another, because we didn't want more territory, or because we didn't feel equal to the responsibility, we were to leave the other nations to scramble for Turkey without taking anything for ourselves, we should not be doing our duty.'[28]

Grey added: '… our reply about our desiderata should be, in the sense, that our first requirement was the preservation of a Moslem political entity, and that we are pledged to the maintenance of the Moslem Holy Places. The

---

23   CAB 21/1, 19 March 1915, p. 6.
24   CAB 21/1, 19 March 1915, p. 6.
25   CAB 21/1, 19 March 1915, p. 6
26   CAB 21/1. 19 March 1915, p. 7.
27   CAB 21/1, 19 March 1915, p. 7.
28   CAB 21/1, 19 March 1915, p. 7.

first thing we had to consider was as to what that entity should include. We might base our first reply by taking up this line.' Lord Crewe of the India Office then added, 'we must have a political capital for the Mohammedan State, and that this could not be at Mecca, as no one except Mohammedans could go there.'[29]

The telegram which Grey then sent to Sazanov on 19 March stated essentially that, 'after the Straits had been forced, and Constantinople had passed into the hands of the Allies, our first desideratum would be the establishment of a Moslem entity. It would have to include Arabia, and the question would arise as to what was to go with it. In the meantime, it would be premature to discuss the partition of Turkey.'[30]

THE DE BUNSEN COMMITTEE

After the dust had settled on the Russia and Constantinople issue, both Britain and France could then begin looking at their *desiderata*. The French ambassador to London, M. Cambon, informed Grey on 23 March that his foreign minister M. Delcasse was now anxious that 'there should now be an unofficial discussion, either verbally or in the form of private letters about French and British desiderata.'[31]

Writing to Sir F. Bertie, his ambassador in Paris, Grey stated that such discussions would best be between himself and Cambon. He also added: 'The Cabinet here had not yet had time to consider our desiderata … I said that we had already stipulated that, when Turkey disappeared from Constantinople and the Straits, there must, in the interests of Islam, be an independent Moslem political unit somewhere else. Its centre would naturally be the Moslem Holy Places, and it would include Arabia. But we must settle what else should be included. We ourselves, had not yet come to a definite opinion whether Mesopotamia should be included in this independent Moslem State, or whether we should put forward a claim for ourselves in that region.'[32]

---

29   CAB 21/1, 19 March 1915, p. 7.
30   CAB 21/1, 19 March 1915, p. 7.
31   Grey to Sir F Bertie, 23 March 1915, FO 371/2486, No. 34982.
32   Grey to Sir F. Bertie, ibid.

Although it would seem that both Russia's and France's *desiderata* in a dismembered Ottoman Turkish Empire were somewhat clarified, Britain was still to determine which regions she felt she should have control over in such a future dismembered Ottoman Turkish Empire. Britain's first move was to decide what were her *desiderata* before entering into negotiations with the French.

Accordingly on 8 April 1915 the Government set up a special Interdepartmental Committee headed up by Sir Maurice de Bunsen. The other members of the De Bunsen Committee were: Sir Mark Sykes (Kitchener's personal representative); General Sir Charles Calwell (Director of Military Operations in the War Office); Admiral H.B. Jackson (the Admiralty); George Clark (Foreign Office); Sir T.W. Holderness (the India Office) and Sir H. Llewellyn Smith (the Board of Trade).[33]

FRANCE INFORMS RUSSIANS

On 12 April 1915 France informed Russia that they accepted her terms, providing the War was carried through to completion. Already by this time, though, the Russian demand was common knowledge. In regards to Constantinople the *Jewish Chronicle* wrote on 12 March: 'The Russian Premier speaks of Russia's bright, historical future there on the shores of the Black Sea by the walls of Tsargrad…. M. Yves Guyot claims Palestine and Syria for France' the correspondent continued. 'The Turkish dominions are already on the dissecting table.'[34]

By the middle of April 1915 it appeared certain that soon the Russian flag would be flying over Constantinople, the French flag would be flying over Damascus, while the British flag would continue to fly over Cairo.

All of this was dependent, though, upon one major component – that the Dardanelles would be forced, Constantinople captured and Turkey defeated.

---

33 Sykes played quite a significant part in the forthcoming deliberations, as evidenced by an in-depth Memo from 3 May 1915 entitled 'Note by Mark Sykes on the proposed maintenance of a Turkish Empire in Asia without spheres of influence.' See Papers of Sir Mark Sykes, Middle East Centre, St Anthony's College.

34 *Jewish Chronicle*, 12 March 1915, p. 11.

CHAPTER 34

§

Naval failure and new plans

ANTICIPATED BREAKTHROUGH

Despite the difficulty of the Anglo-French Fleet breaking through the Dardanelles, the people of Constantinople continued to be fully expectant of this eventuality. In early March Morgenthau described the state of the city:

> At that time the exodus from the capital had begun; Turkish women and children were being moved into the interior; all the banks had been compelled to send their gold into Asia Minor; the archives of the Sublime Porte had already been carried to Eski-Shehr; and practically all the ambassadors and their suites, as well as the government officials, had made their preparations to leave.[1]

Arrangements had been made for Morgenthau's departure as well, but he refused to leave, believing that as a neutral ambassador he 'could forestall massacres and the destruction of the city.'[2]

---

1 Morgenthau, ibid, Chapter 16, p. 7.
2 Morgenthau, ibid, p. 7.

GENERAL HAMILTON DESPATCHED TO THE MEDITERRANEAN

It was becoming clearer to the Allied High Command that breaking through the Dardanelles was going to be more difficult than initially anticipated. This became even clearer following a failed landing of some 1,000 marines on both shores of the Dardanelles on 4 March.[3]

On that same day the first ANZAC soldiers arrived at Lemnos Island in preparation for future operations. This was the 3rd Australian Brigade, commanded by Colonel Sinclair-Maclagen, and composed of the 9th, 10th, 11th and 12th Battalions.

On 12 March while working at the Horse Guards in London, General Ian Hamilton was summoned to a meeting with Kitchener. When Hamilton entered the War Minister's room, Kitchener instructed him: "We are sending a military force to support the Fleet now at the Dardanelles, and you are to have Command."[4]

Once the shock settled somewhat, Hamilton was then informed who he would be commanding:

My troops were to be Australians and New Zealanders under Birdwood (a friend); strength, say, about 30,000. (A year ago I inspected them in their own Antipodes and no finer material exists); the 29th Division, strength, say 19,000 under Hunter-Weston—a slashing man of action; an acute theorist; the Royal Naval Division, 11,000 strong ...under a solid Commander—Paris); a French contingent, strength at present uncertain, say, about a Division, under my old war comrade the chivalrous d'Amade, now at Tunis.[5]

Kitchener, though, made it clear that no men were to be landed until the Navy had opened up the Straits. When Hamilton was about to finally take

3   Dolan, ibid, Chapter 2.
4   Hamilton, General Sir Ian. *Gallipoli Diary*, (New York, 1920), www.gutenberg.org, Vol. I, Chapter 1. No page number.
5   Hamilton, ibid.

leave, Kitchener said to him: "If the Fleet gets through, Constantinople will fall of itself and you will have won, not a battle, but the war."[6]

Hamilton was in Tenedos Bay by 17 March and joined a meeting aboard *HMS Queen Elizabeth*. The others present were: Admiral de Robeck; Commodore Roger Keyes; Admiral Guepratte (Commander of the French Fleet); General d'Amade; General Braithwaite (Hamilton's Chief of Staff); Admiral Wemyss and Captain Pollen.[7] De Robeck explained the difficulties of the campaign until that point, but stated his belief that the Navy would force their way through, believing that then, with the Navy en-route to Constantinople, the Army could land at Bulair, and would catch the Turks in a trap.[8]

Hamilton's instructions were then read out, but he said he would not make any further statement, until he had seen the lay of the land.

18 MARCH - HAMILTON SURVEYS THE GALLIPOLI PENINSULA

Early on the morning of 18 March Hamilton set out aboard *HMS Phaeton*, accompanied by Generals d'Amade and Paris, and Brigadier-General Sinclair McLagen of Australia, towards the Bay of Saros. It did not take him long to see and realize that it would be foolhardy to make his major landing at Bulair as the natural and man-made obstacles were too great for a landing force.

He contemplated the possibility of landing forces at Suvla Bay, but then realised that this was where the Peninsula was at its widest. He then wrote of the next area encountered:

All the coast between Suvla Bay and for a little way South of Gaba Tepe seems feasible for landing. I mean we could get ashore on a calm day if there was no enemy. Gaba Tepe itself would be ideal, but, alas, the Turks are not blind; it is a mass of trenches and wire. Further, it must be well under fire of guns from Kilid Bahr plateau, and is entirely

---

6 Hamilton, ibid.
7 Hamilton, ibid. Just prior to Hamilton's arrival Vice-Admiral Carden had a breakdown and was replaced by Vice-Admiral de Robeck.
8 Hamilton, ibid.

commanded by the high ridge to the North of it. To land there would be to enter a defile without first crowning the heights.[9]

Hamilton described the area from Gabe Tepe to Cape Helles as composed of cliffs, but with many small sandy beaches in between. As the ship sailed further south Hamilton and the others became aware of the naval battle then in progress, and they occasionally witnessed 'a huge shell hit the top of Achi Baba and turn it into the semblance of a volcano.'[10] About 1600 hours the *Phaeton* passed Cape Helles, and there they witnessed the naval battle before them.

18 MARCH – THE CRUCIAL NAVAL ASSAULT ON THE DARDANELLES

The Anglo-French Fleet planned one final attempt to break through the entranceway into the Dardanelles on 18 March 1915. The investment of fire on the Turkish fortifications began at 1030 hours and continued until 1900 hours, and during that period some sixteen Allied ships took part.

The ship on which Hamilton was cruising was one of dozens caught up in the frenzy of activity, including the mighty *HMS Queen Elizabeth*. Then suddenly the *Phaeton* had to make an abrupt movement, and the men aboard were almost cast overboard. The reason was the sudden exit of *HMS Inflexible* from the Straits, in obvious trouble. She had been seriously hit and was listing and the *Phaeton* was to draw near.[11]

As the *Phaeton* exited from the battle zone they witnessed the French battleship *Gaulous* limping out of the fire, and then later they received word that the *Irresistible* had also succumbed. The worst casualty, though, was the French battleship *Bouvet*, which hit a mine and sank within minutes – taking 639 French sailors with her.[12]

---

9   Hamilton, ibid, p. 19.
10   Hamilton, ibid, p. 19.
11   Hamilton, ibid, pp. 20-21.
12   Moorehead, ibid, p. 62.

THE FAILED ATTEMPT

Von Sanders reported concerning the fateful events of that day:

> In spite of the expenditure of enormous amounts of ammunition the hostile fleet accomplished no great results. The damage to the forts and batteries but little diminished their fighting capacity, though their ammunition supply had been reduced...
>
> The enemy suffered serious and weighty losses... the *Bouvet, Irresistible* and *Ocean* had been sunk and several other battleships were seriously damaged. Several smaller ships, engaged in salvage work, had been sunk. The fire of Fort Hamidje under Captain Wossidlo was mentioned as particularly effective. It may be assumed that the mine field in Erekkoj (Eren Keui) Bay laid at night by the Turkish mine expert, Lieutenant Colonel Geehl, contributed its share to the result.[13]

The Allied attempt failed, forcing a withdrawal. This climax was one of the ironies of history and warfare. Some days before, the small Turkish minesweeper, the *Nousret*, directed by a virtually unknown Turkish officer, Lieut-Colonel Geehl, had laid mines, which were undetected by the mighty Anglo-French Fleet on 18 March. Those mines halted the Allied advance towards Constantinople.

Ironically the Turkish fortresses were almost out of ammunition. An American journalist, George Schreiner, went to the Dardanelles on 18 March, and there General Mertens informed him just how low the ammunition supply was. They expected the Allied Fleet to return the following day – and they would have easily gained victory.[14]

Everyone was anticipating the arrival of the British and French warships. Throughout the Empire many were preparing for a revolution against the Young Turks leadership. 'Among the subject people' Morgenthau wrote, 'the spirit of revolt was rapidly spreading. The Greeks and the Armenians

---

13 Von Sanders, ibid, p. 55.
14 Morgenthau, ibid, Chapter 18, p. 4.

would also have welcomed an opportunity to strengthen the hands of the Allies.'[15]

HAMILTON'S ASSESSMENTS OF THE NAVAL FAILURE

Hamilton on 19 March cabled to Kitchener details of the previous day's proceedings, adding that he did not believe the Straits could be taken by the battleships, and that: 'The Army's part will be more than mere landings of parties to destroy Forts, it must be a deliberate and progressive military operation carried out at full strength so as to open a passage for the Navy.'[16]

Kitchener responded on 20 March: 'You know my view that the Dardanelles passage must be forced, and that if large military operations on the Gallipoli Peninsula by your troops are necessary to clear the way, those operations must be undertaken after careful consideration of the local defences and must be carried through.'[17]   Admiral De Robeck still felt he could press ahead. At a meeting on 22 March, however, the Admiral stated to Hamilton that: *"he was now quite clear he could not get through without the help of all my troops."*[18]

Hamilton began strategizing with Braithwaite and Birdwood how they were going to accomplish this mammoth task. Hamilton was already starting with a great disadvantage. He had no up-to-date maps to use, and limited intelligence. The proposal was even made of landing with the men then available, balancing out his shortage of manpower against the Turks having the time to dig in and prepare for a sudden Allied land assault.

This idea they had to surrender. Although the ANZAC Division was waiting in Egypt, they knew they must await the arrival of the experienced 29th Division before the actual operation could begin.

On 23 March Hamilton, together with Birdwood and General d'Amade stepped ashore on Mudros Island and inspected the men of the 9th Battalion,

---

15 Morgenthau, ibid, p. 5.
16 Hamilton, ibid, p. 22.
17 Hamilton, ibid, p. 23.
18 Hamilton, ibid, p. 24. Italics in the original.

3rd Australian Brigade, who were an advance force, and had them do a small attack.[19]

On that same day many of the troop transports at Gallipoli set sail for Alexandria, where they would await the 29th Division, and become acquainted with the soldiers of the ANZAC Divisions.

HAMILTON IN EGYPT

Hamilton with the Royal Naval Division reached Alexandria on 26 March and he went immediately to work, alongside Generals Birdwood, Godley, Bridges, Douglas and Braithwaite.[20]

At this point the tasks of the Intelligence Department became of supreme importance. Hamilton was fully aware of the difficulty of the task ahead of him and would require every ounce of valuable intelligence he could gather.

From this point forward the airmen of the Royal Naval Air Service played an increasingly important role, especially through the information they gathered from their reconnaissance flights over the Dardanelles. One man who also now began playing a pivotal role in the intelligence gathering was Major Charles Villiers-Stuart, of the Intelligence Department at ANZAC HQ.[21]

The Allied commanders were under no illusion of the difficulty now facing them at Gallipoli. Hunter-Weston stated that: "The Turkish Army having been warned by our early bombardments and by the landings carried out some time ago, has concentrated a large force in and near the Gallipoli Peninsula."

"It has", he continued, "converted the Peninsula into an entrenched camp, under German direction, made several lines of entrenchments covering the landing places, with concealed machine gun emplacements and land mines on the beach; and has put in concealed positions guns and howitzers

---

19 Hamilton, ibid, p. 27.
20 Hamilton, ibid, p. 31.
21 For an in-depth description of the role of the Intelligence Department and particularly of Villiers-Stuart, and for one of the best accounts of the beginning of the Gallipoli Campaign, see Dolan, 36 Days, ibid.

capable of covering the landing places and approaches with their fire."[22] In view of these serious considerations, Hunter-Weston suggested only two locations where a landing was feasible, at Suvla Bay and at Cape Helles.

THE TURKS PREPARE FOR AN ALLIED LANDING

General von Sanders had maintained from the beginning that the Turks needed to be prepared for an Allied landing on the Dardanelles Peninsula. On 24 March Enver Pasha asked Von Sanders if he would be willing to take command of a new army, the Turkish Fifth Army, that he was organising for the defence of the Dardanelles. Von Sanders accepted the command and left the following day.[23]

After landing and establishing his new HQ at the small port of Gelibolu (Gallipoli) on 26 March Von Sanders immediately set about preparing his scattered force on both sides of the Dardanelles Straits for the active defence of this strategic region. In addition he brought the 3rd Turkish Division from Constantinople.

The future of the Turkish Empire now depended upon the defence of this region. With this in mind Von Sanders and his staff had to determine the most vulnerable positions along a vast coastline for the impending Allied landing. He concentrated upon the area of the Bays of Besica (Bashika) on the Asian side, and three specific locations on the European or Gallipoli side, which were:

- The village of Seddulbahir (also spelled Sedd el Bahr) at the southern tip of the Dardanelles Peninsular. Behind this village lay the Eltsch-itepe or Achi Baba Ridge. From atop this ridge there was a commanding view over the shore line upstream from the Dardanelles Straits.
- The region of Kabatepe (Gaba Tepe). Of this position he wrote:

> From here a broad plain, broken only by a flat elevation, led directly to the town of Maidos on the straits. From the heights of both sides of Maidos the batteries of the fortress could be si-

---

22   Hamilton, ibid, p. 46.
23   Von Sanders, ibid, p. 56. According to Mango, ibid, it was 26 March.

lenced with certainty. North of Kabatepe (Gaba Tepe) the steep heights of Ari Burnu lay close to the coast with a well protected landing place. If the enemy directed his main attack on Maidos by way of Kabatepe it was necessary for him to hold the heights of Ari Burnu because they flanked the plain mentioned.[24]

- The region further north from Kabatepe on the Gulf of Saros (Xeros), the nearest town being Bulair. Here the distance from the coast to the Sea of Marmara was only between five to seven kilometres. If the Allied forces could gain control of this area, they could effectively cut the Fifth Army in two, and isolate the southern forces from the northern ones. In addition the Allies could hassle shipping going through the Sea of Marmara to the Turkish forces in the southern sector.

With these considerations in mind Von Sanders deployed his forces into three sectors: the northern sector at the Gulf of Saros; the southern sector between Kabatepe and Seddulbahir; and the Asiatic side of the Peninsula. He knew beforehand that his forces were thinly stretched, but success depended upon the flexibility of movement of these various forces.

In addition to these troop placements, he then devoted considerable effort to bettering the infrastructure and fortifications of the entire Dardanelles Peninsula. Mustapha Kemal during this time remained in the region of Maidos with his 19th Division.

THE ALLIED PLANS FOR LANDING AT GALLIPOLI

By 10 April Hamilton had developed his plan, which was basically:

- The French Division (under General d'Amade) was to land on the Asiatic coast near Kum Kale, and once having destroyed the Turkish forts there, was to move across the Straits and join the British force.
- The British 29th Division (under General Hunter-Weston) would land at Cape Helles on the European side. The 29th Division would

---

24 Von Sanders, ibid, p. 60.

land at five separate locations, code-named beaches S, V, W, X and Y. This would be the main operation, and would aim initially for the high point of Achi Baba, lying behind the village of Krithia. Together with the French Division they would move towards Constantinople.

- The Australian and New Zealand force (ANZAC, and under General Sir William Birdwood) would land some twenty kilometres north of Cape Helles near Gabe Tepe, code named beach Z, or Brighton Beach. This was to be a large feint, to draw attention away from the landings at Cape Helles. Their objective was the strategic Sari Bair mountain ridge, comprising the high points of Chunuk Bair, Hill Q and Koja Chemen Tepe (Hill 971). From this ridge the entire region, including the Dardanelles Straits, could be viewed and the enemy positions bombed. The ANZAC force would then move across the Peninsula and link up with the British and French troops as they moved towards Constantinople. Both of the beach landings would occur in day light following a heavy naval bombardment of the Turkish positions.

- There would be a diversion further north of the ANZAC landing, at Bulair, in which the Royal Naval Division (under General Paris) would participate – but they would not land. This Division was Hamilton's reserve force, ready to land following the first assault at the point he believed most appropriate for a decisive breakthrough.

INTELLIGENCE GATHERING AND ANZAC RE-ASSESSMENT

With a limited amount of time to plan, those in the Intelligence Department now had an extra responsibility. Additionally the airmen of the Royal Naval Air Service were now entrusted with more valuable work, and men such as Wing Commander Charles Samson and Harry Stain were constantly flying over the intended landing region.[25]

After each reconnaissance flight the information they sent back to the HQ created concern: during the night the Turks had been digging trenches

---

25 Dolan, ibid, Chapter 6.

and consolidating their positions throughout the Gallipoli Peninsula.[26] A flight by Lieutenant Pierce and Captain Collet over Gabe Tepe on 11 April confirmed this assessment.[27]

Hamilton concentrated upon the Cape Helles landing, and left the minor details of the ANZAC landing to the ANZAC commanders. On 14 April these commanders had their first sighting of the area they were to operate in. On that same day Major Villiers-Stuart went on his first reconnaissance flight with Captain Collet. Upon his return Villiers-Stuart, 'had explosive news' for those planning the ANZAC landing. The Turkish position in and around Gaba Tepe was much more heavily fortified, especially artillery batteries, than Hamilton had initially stated.[28]

General Bridges and his Chief-of-Staff General Brudenall White now had to begin processing this new material which Villiers-Stuart and the airmen were presenting.[29]

By 17 April it became apparent of the necessity to land in the dark before the Turkish artillery could get a clear view. Unfortunately on that same day the submarine E. 15 commanded by Lieutenant-Commander Brodie had been shelled and captured. The purpose of this submarine was to hassle Turkish troops movements at the time when the campaign began.[30]

The landing, especially in the ANZAC sector, was beginning to look more improbable, especially as aerial reconnaissance flights continued to reveal large Turkish formations, especially south of Gaba Tepe and inland near the village of Boghali.

WINGATE'S PROPOSAL

While plans were progressing for the Gallipoli campaign, discussions began again in London concerning the future of the southern region of the Turkish Empire. One of those in favour of encouraging the Sherif of Mecca to become involved was Sir Reginald Wingate, the Governor-General of the

26   Dolan, ibid, Chapter 7.
27   Dolan, ibid, Chapter 7.
28   Dolan, ibid, Chapter 7.
29   Dolan, ibid, Chapter 8.
30   Dolan, ibid, Chapter 8. Moorehead, ibid, p. 75. Charles Palmer was aboard the submarine and was captured.

Sudan, who communicated his views to Lord Cromer. In response Lord Curzon informed Cromer on 22 April that it was inadvisable to make 'promises and declarations' to the Arabs. Curzon asked Cromer 'what evidence had the Arabs shown that they would be able to administer an Arab state extending from the Persian Gulf to Egypt?'[31] Curzon became even more stinging, adding, how could Britain consider promising Basra and Baghdad 'to a people who are at this moment fighting against us as hard as they can and known to be in the pay of the Germans?'[32]

Wingate, however, understood that many Arabs detested being under the foot of the Turks. In April 1915 Wingate, 'was authorized to let it be known that H.M.G. would make it an essential condition in the peace terms that the Arabian Peninsula and its Muhammadan Holy Places should remain in the hands of an independent sovereign state. It was impossible to define at the moment how much territory should be included in this state.'[33]

As was to become more evident, Wingate and Brigadier-General Clayton, head of military intelligence in Cairo, were of the opinion that, a 'scheme of a pan-Arab union presided over, in some fashion, by an Arab caliph, and the whole under the aegis and protection of Great Britain … seems to be cogent and feasible.'[34]

Several significant streams were now beginning to flow in the East: one related to the Dardanelles in which Jewish nationalists would be fighting against the Turks, believing that all fronts led to Zion; another was composed of some Arab nationalists and some British strategists, who were just beginning to merge their different perspectives as to the future of a defeated Ottoman Empire, part of which would be the formation of an Arab national entity of some notion.

The Turkish regime, meanwhile, had other ideas when it came to non-Turkish entities within its vast empire – as the Greeks and Armenians were now beginning to experience first hand.

---

31   Kedourie, *The Chatham House Version and other Middle Eastern Studies*, (London, 1970), p. 15.
32   Wingate Paper, 134/5, cited in Kedourie, *Chatham House*, ibid, p. 15.
33   Storrs, ibid, p. 152.
34   Kedourie, *Chatham House*, ibid, p. 18.

CHAPTER 35

§

Persecution of Armenians
and Greeks

MORGENTHAU'S EVALUATION OF THE WITHDRAWAL OF THE FLEET

Few western observers had the first-hand experience of the internal dynamics of Turkey in this period as did the American ambassador Henry Morgenthau. Concerning this period he wrote: 'The withdrawal of the Allied fleet from the Dardanelles had consequences which the world does not yet completely understand.'[1] Morgenthau was referring to the beginning of what became known as the Armenian genocide.

The withdrawal of the Anglo-French Fleet gave the Turks the belief that they had defeated the superpowers. Now the Young Turk leadership felt they had the power to do as they wanted, without the restraints of the conscience of Europe watching over their shoulders – except the conscience of Germany and Austria, which did not seem to be much in evidence during this period.[2]

'In the first minutes of their pride,' Morgenthau penned, 'the Young Turk leaders saw visions of the complete resurrection of their empire.' This

---

1 Morgenthau, ibid, Chapter 22, p. 1.
2 Morgenthau, ibid, Chapter 22.

resurrection amounted to a desire to regain the glories of their once brilliant past, of four hundred years previous when the Turkish armies carried all before them into Europe – even unto the gates of Vienna.[3]

Morgenthau then described the motive for the establishment of the millet (and *dhimmitude*) system: 'The sultans … erected the several peoples, such as the Greeks and Armenians, into separate "millets," or nations, not because they desired to promote their independence and welfare, but because they regarded them as vermin, and therefore disqualified for membership in the Ottoman state.'[4]

Then, he continued, conditions improved for many of the *dhimmi* subjects, due to the Capitulations, involvement of the foreign powers, and finally the 1909 Constitution. The leaders of 'new' Turkey, unfortunately, then 'lost their democratic aspirations' and took on the idea of 'Pan-Turkism', whereby 'in place of equal treatment for all Ottomans, they decided to establish a country exclusively for Turks.'[5]

'When the Turkish Government abrogated the Capitulations,' he continued, 'and in this way freed themselves from the domination of the foreign powers, they were merely taking one step toward realizing this Pan-Turkish ideal.'[6]

The Young Turks goal 'for Turkifing the nation', Morgenthau continued, 'seemed to demand logically the extermination of all Christians – Greeks, Syrians, and Armenians.'[7] Morgenthau then outlined the policy of the Young Turks:

They would destroy all Greeks, Syrians, Armenians, and other Christians, move Moslem families into their homes and into their farms, and so make sure that these territories would not similarly be taken away from Turkey. In order to accomplish this great reform, it

---

3   Morgenthau, ibid, Chapter 22, pp. 1-2.
4   Morgenthau, ibid, Chapter 22, p. 3.
5   Morgenthau, ibid, Chapter 22, p. 4.
6   Morgenthau, ibid, Chapter 22, p. 5.
7   Morgenthau, ibid, Chapter 22, p. 7. It needs to be understood in the context of such statements, that just as there were many Germans who did not condone the actions of the Nazis, so too not all the Turkish Muslims condoned what their Government was undertaking concerning the Armenians.

would not be necessary to murder every living Christian. The most beautiful and healthy Armenian girls could be taken, converted forcibly to Mohammedanism, and made the wives and concubines of devout followers of the Prophet ... Armenian boys of tender age could be taken into Turkish families and brought up in ignorance of the fact that they were anything but Moslems... Since all precautions must be taken against the development of a new generation of Armenians, it would be necessary to kill outright all men who were in their prime and thus capable of propagating the accursed species ...[8]

Turkish historian Ahmet Refik, who was a Turkish army officer for many years, wrote in 1919 that, 'the annihilation of the Armenians had become one of the national objectives of the Unionists. They planned, by means of the annihilation policy, to avoid carrying out reforms in the six eastern provinces, and to solve the Armenian "problem" at its root.'[9]

Akcam cites Joseph Pomiankowski , military attaché in the Austrian Embassy in Istanbul between 1909 and 1919, who stated:

A great number of Turkish intellectuals have sincerely expressed the sentiment that the reason for the Ottoman Empire's loss in recent years— and more generally, over the last two centuries— of [many of] its provinces in Europe and Asia lies first and foremost in the excessively humanistic behavior of the previous sultans. What should have been done was either the forcible conversion to Islam of the population in the provinces ... or their utter and total extirpation.

'According to Pomiankowski,' Akcam continues, 'the Young Turk government used the war as an opportunity to undo the mistakes of previous sultans.'[10]

---

8 Morgenthau, ibid, Chapter 22, p. 7.
9 Ahmet Refik, İki Komite, İki Kital (Istanbul, 1919). Transliteration/ simplification by Hamide Koyukan (Ankara, 1994), p. 27, cited in Akcam, ibid, p. 112.
10 Joseph Pomiankowski, Der Zusammenbruch des Osmanischen Reiches, Erinnerungen an die Türkei aus Zeit des Weltkrieges (Zürich, Leipzig, Vienna, 1928), p. 162, cited in Akcam, p. 120.

The Young Turks leadership in 1915 was not bound by any restrictions placed upon them by Britain, France and Russia as had Sultan Abdul Hamid in 1894-96. Having just driven off the powerful fleets of two of those nations, the Young Turks felt they could carry through to completion the intended but unfulfilled goals of the 'red sultan.'

ARMENIAN NATIONALISM AND ATROCITIES AT VAN

The beginning of the war and the deep incursion of Russian forces into eastern Anatolia, renewed hopes for many Armenian nationalists for the establishment of an Armenian national entity in that region.

Many Armenians were serving in the Russian Army, and now some others deserted from the Turkish side of the border and joined them. Some nationalists within Turkey also now began to work against Turkey.[11]

This situation would, unfortunately, provide the Turkish leadership with a 'legitimate' reason to unleash their fury against the collective Armenian population.

When the Russian forces withdrew from the province of Van in the spring of 1915, the Turkish Army, wrote Morgenthau:

> … turned their rifles, machine guns, and other weapons upon the Armenian women, children, and old men in the villages of Van. Following their usual custom, they distributed the most beautiful Armenian women among the Moslems, sacked and burned the Armenian villages, and massacred uninterruptedly for days. On April 15th, about 500 young Armenian men of Akantz were mustered to hear an order of the Sultan; at sunset they were marched outside the town and every man shot in cold blood. This procedure was repeated in about eighty Armenian villages in the district north of Lake Van, and in three days 24,000 Armenians were murdered in this atrocious fashion.[12]

---

11   Akcam, ibid, p. 120.
12   Morgenthau, ibid, Chapter 23, p. 2.

Although the Turkish approach to the destruction of the Armenians had been slowly developing, it became blatantly obvious for all to see in April 1915, primarily in the region of Van. This region was governed by Djevdet Pasha, the brother-in-law of Enver Pasha, a man, wrote Morgenthau, who 'hated the Armenians and cordially sympathized with the long-established Turkish plan of solving the Armenian problem.'[13]

Djevat Pasha demanded on 17 April that the Armenian community at Van supply him with 4,000 able bodied men to become soldiers. The community leaders well understood that this was a ploy – these men would then be massacred, which would in turn deny the entire community of their protection.[14] They refused to fully comply.[15]

The lines had been marked out and the following day conflict began. The besieged Armenian force withheld the attacking Turks for five weeks until relieved by the coming of Russian forces. The Turks nevertheless took revenge upon Armenian villages in the region, and the Russians later cremated the bodies of some 55,000 Armenians.[16]

'The resistance at Van', wrote Balakian, 'became another pretext for the CUP to claim that the Armenians were disloyal during wartime.'[17] The revolt at Van gave these leaders justification in their eyes to completely destroy this ancient community.[18]

This perspective increased when news of atrocities enacted by Armenian revolutionaries against Muslims in the region of Van, reached Constantinople.

OFFICIAL AUTHORIZATION FOR GENOCIDE: 24 APRIL 1915

From the time the Allied warships approached the Dardanelles in February 1915 local persecution against Armenian communities escalated.[19] Matters

---

13 Morgenthau, ibid, Chapter 23, p. 2.
14 Balakian, ibid, Part 2, Chapter 14.
15 Balakian, ibid, Part 2, Chapter 14; Morgenthau, ibid, Chapter 23, p. 3.
16 Morgenthau, ibid, Chapter 23, p. 3.
17 Balakian, ibid, Part 2, Chapter 14.
18 Morgenthau, ibid, Chapter 23, p. 3.
19 *The New York Times* carried at least 145 articles on the atrocities against the Armenians in 1915 alone. See John Kifner, *The Armenian Genocide of 1915: An Overview*, in www.nytimes.com

intensified when on 24 April Mehmet Talaat, the Minister of Interior, is-sued an order for the arrest of some 235 Armenian notables and leaders in Constantinople and for their deportation from the city – on the pretext that there was a revolt in Van.[20] There had already been similar arrests in other cities, and soon afterwards there were many more. Later these men were murdered.[21]

Material was being accumulated in Constantinople to provide justifi-cation for the systematic destruction of the Armenians. According to his-torian Vahakn Dadrian, an Ottoman naval officer stated, concerning the accumulated propaganda being put together, that "the Armenians are in league with the enemy. They will launch an uprising in Istanbul, kill off the Committee of Union and Progress leaders and will succeed in opening the straits (of the Dardanelles)".[22]

Morgenthau knew many of these Armenian leaders, and when he asked Talaat Pasha about this event, he was informed that they were revolution-aries in cahoots with the Russians, and the uprising in Van had revealed what they were capable of doing.[23]

Where this move was heading is indicated by a letter sent to the Turkish Government by the International Association of Genocide Scholars in 2005, which stated:

"The scholarly evidence reveals the following: On April 24, 1915, un-der cover of World War I, the Young Turk government of the Ottoman Empire began a systematic genocide of its Armenian citizens — an unarmed Christian minority population. More than a million Armenians were exterminated through direct killing, starvation, tor-ture, and forced death marches. The rest of the Armenian population fled into permanent exile. Thus an ancient civilization was expunged from its homeland of 2,500 years."[24]

20 Lepsius, J. *Der Todesgang*, p. 189, cited in Akcam, ibid, p. 130.
21 Akcam, ibid, p. 130.
22 Dadrian, Vahakn N. *The History of the Armenian Genocide: Ethnic Conflict from the Balkans to Anatolia to the Caucasus*, (Oxford, 1995), p. 192, cited in Armenian Genocide, www.wikipedia.com
23 Morgenthau, ibid, Chapter 25, p. 1.
24 Southern Poverty Law Centre, *State of Denial*, Intelligence Report, Summer 2008, Issue No. 130, www.splcenter. org

Turkish historian Taner Akcam in his book *A Shameful Act,* states that after 1918 attempts were made to destroy or 'confiscate' many of the original documents detailing the official policy against the Armenians, but, he continues: 'While we are missing a significant portion of these papers, what remains in the Ottoman archives and in court records is sufficient to show that the CUP Central Committee, and the Special Organization it set up to carry out its plan, did deliberately attempt to destroy the Armenian population.'[25]

PERSECUTION OF GREEKS LIVING IN TURKEY

Simultaneous to the beginning of the genocide of the Armenian people, persecution increased upon the large Greek population. Already in mid-1914 about 100,000 Greeks had been relocated in Turkey.

When conflict became inevitable 'several hundred thousand' from the regions of Thrace and the region surrounding the Sea of Marmara and the Black Sea coast 'were sent to the interior of Asia Minor.' 'The Turks' Morgenthau wrote, 'adopted almost identically the procedure against the Greeks as that which they adopted against the Armenians. They began by incorporating the Greeks into the Ottoman army and then transforming them into labour battalions, using them to build roads in the Caucasus and other scenes of action.

These Greek soldiers, just like the Armenians,' Morgenthau continued, 'died by thousands from cold, hunger and other privations. The same house-to-house searches for hidden weapons took place in the Greek villages, and Greek men and women were beaten and tortured just as their fellow Armenians... The Turks attempted to force Greek subjects to become Mohammedans; Greek girls, just like Armenian girls, were stolen and taken to Turkish harems and Greek boys were kidnapped and placed in Moslem households. The Greeks, just like the Armenians, were accused of disloyalty to the Ottoman Government.'[26]

---

25 Akcam, T, *A Shameful Act,* Preface. Arnold Toynbee, in his book *The Armenian Atrocities: The Murder of a Nation,* (London, 1915), page 69, makes a very strong case that the persecution of most of the Armenians had little at all to do with the military situation.

26 Morgenthau, ibid, Chapter 24, p. 11.

Although exact numbers of Greeks who were uprooted and moved inland is not known,[27] they were not subject to wholesale massacre as were the Armenians, for at that stage the Greek Government had not committed to entering into the war and was, naturally, very concerned about the welfare of Greeks living in Turkey.

The signs were ominous for non-Muslim communities in Turkey. A comprehensive Allied victory could not come quickly enough for the *dhimmi* communities.

---

27 Morgenthau quoted the number as being between 200,000 to one million. Morgenthau, ibid, p. 12.

CHAPTER 36

§

The first landings: 25 April 1915

MOVING OUT

Troops of the Mediterranean Expeditionary Force (MEF) began leaving Egypt for Lemnos Island in early April. Eliezar Margolin and the men of the 4th Australian Brigade, commanded by Brigadier-General John Monash, moved out on 11 April.[1] En-route to Lemnos Island Monash made a note, 'that a probable result of this campaign would be the freeing of Jerusalem and Palestine from the Turks.'[2]

When the Zion Mule Corps left Alexandria harbour there was great excitement. 'Embarkation day came' wrote Yaari, 'and that night, before they set sail, the Jewish soldiers sang the songs and danced the dances of Eretz Yisrael, the girls who had come to see them off adding to the gaiety of the occasion.'[3]

One man who did not enter into the festivities was Wertheimer. When Trumpeldor asked him why he wasn't joining in, he replied 'that he was

---

1   Monash and the other brigade commanders only officially received this rank in July 1915, but it was back-dated to September 1914. Monash later went on to command 3rd Australian Division in France and then 1st Australia Corps, a remarkable achievement for a Jewish person of German background.
2   Cutlack, G.M. *War Letters of General Monash*, (Sydney, 1934), p. 28, cited in Gouttman, ibid, p. 45.
3   Yaari, ibid, p. 430.

afraid, - lest he should not acquit himself honourably if faced with a serious test, and so disgrace the Zion Corps and the Jewish people.[4]

When the Australian and New Zealand soldiers moved out, one man who was left behind was a disappointed Harry Chauvel. The MEF commanders didn't believe Gallipoli was a good environment for horsemen. 'I am afraid the Light Horse' Chauvel wrote to his wife 'are rather at a discount in the present war.'[5]

THE ANZAC FORCE

For the ANZAC Corps this was a special time in their individual and national destinies. It was the first time they were fighting as nations. The ANZAC Corps, commanded by Lieutenant-General Birdwood, was composed of two divisions: The Australian Division (commanded by Major-General Bridges), composed of the 1st, 2nd and 3rd Infantry Brigades; and the New Zealand and Australia Division (commanded by Major-General Godley), composed of the New Zealand Infantry Brigade and the 4th Australian Brigade.

Hamilton issued an order of the day addressed to the 'Soldiers of France and of the King.' He stated:

Before us lies an adventure unprecedented in modern war. Together with our comrades of the Fleet, we are about to force a landing upon an open beach in face of positions which have been vaunted by our enemies as impregnable.

The landing will be made good, by the help of God and the Navy; the positions will be stormed, and the War brought one step nearer to a glorious close.

"Remember," said Lord Kitchener when bidding adieu to your Commander, "Remember, once you set foot upon the Gallipoli Peninsula, you must fight the thing through to a finish."

---

4 Yaari, ibid, p. 430.
5 Chauvel to his wife, cited in Hill, ibid, p. 50.

DARDANELLES PENINSULA

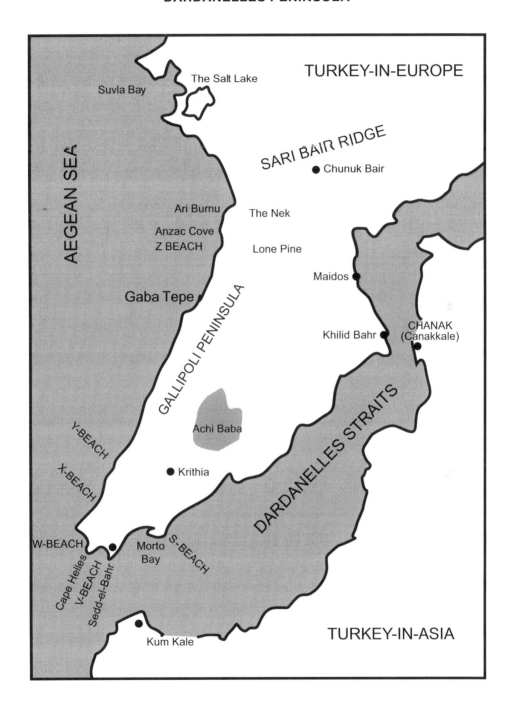

TURKEY-IN-EUROPE

The Salt Lake

Suvla Bay

SARI BAIR RIDGE

● Chunuk Bair

AEGEAN SEA

Ari Burnu

The Nek

Anzac Cove

Z BEACH

Lone Pine

Maidos ●

Gaba Tepe

GALLIPOLI PENINSULA

CHANAK
(Canakkale)

Khilid Bahr ●

DARDANELLES STRAITS

Achi Baba

Y-BEACH

X-BEACH

● Krithia

W-BEACH

Morto
Bay

S-BEACH

Cape Helles

V-BEACH

Sedd-el-Bahr

Kum Kale

TURKEY-IN-ASIA

ANZAC SECTOR

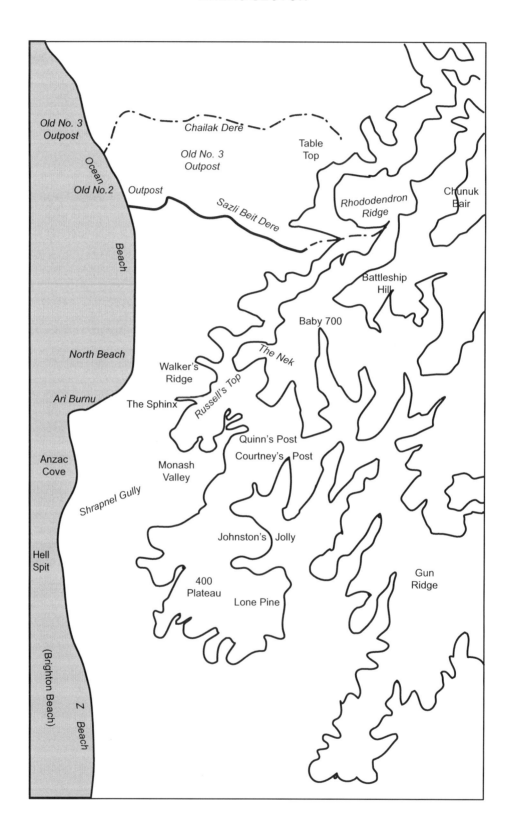

The whole world will be watching your progress. Let us prove our selves worthy of the great feat entrusted to us.[6]

CHANGE OF PLAN

On Lemnos Island the men trained and waited. Twice the date of the landing was changed, and each additional day gave Von Sanders and the Turks extra time to improve their defences. These changes were duly noted by the British aerial reconnaissance flights operating out of Tenedos Island.

Dolan in his seminal work *36 Days* states that the aerial photography 'was largely ignored' by the commanders of 29th Division.[7] Villiers-Stuart, Birdwood, Bridges and Brudenell White, however, took all such updated intelligence seriously. When it became apparent that the southern area of Z Beach (around Gabe Tepe) was heavily fortified, Birdwood convinced Hamilton to re-adapt his plans. Birdwood and Bridges were virtually entrusted with total control over organizing the landing in the ANZAC sector.[8]

The initial ANZAC landing force, the 3rd Australian Brigade, would land in the dark, with no preceding naval bombardment. Although fraught with certain dangers, such a landing would permit the men to quickly capture their objectives before the Turkish artillery and machine-guns had time to zoom in upon them, which would invariably have occurred had they landed in the daylight.

While the British and French landings would be preceded by a heavy naval bombardment, the ANZAC forces would be landed in the dark – and without a bombardment. The heaviest concentration of Turkish forces was at Cape Helles, where the British force was to land.

The ANZAC force would be landed over a 4000 yard frontage, from Gabe Tepe in the south to Fisherman's Hut in the north of their sector.[9] The objective was now to secure the region, and especially the dominating Sari Bair Ridge – before the large Turkish force known to be camped at the village of Boghali could arrive to bolster the Turkish force at Gabe Tepe. The

---

6 Hamilton, ibid, p. 59.
7 Dolan, ibid, Chapter 11.
8 Dolan, ibid, Chapter 11.
9 Dolan, ibid, Chapter 9.

1st Brigade of 1st Australian Division had responsibility for capturing the Turkish artillery at Gabe Tepe, while 2nd and 3rd Brigades were tasked with capturing the imposing ridge.[10] The New Zealand and Australia Division would land after the bridgehead had been secured.

While these plans were being adapted, the captured Charles Palmer provided information to his captors. Although Palmer mentioned where the landings would occur, he emphasized that the main thrust of the attack would occur at Bulair in the Gulf of Saros. This confirmed Von Sanders' perception and he had extra Turkish troops sent to this region.[11]

TOWARDS GALLIPOLI

The landing was finally scheduled to begin on 25 April. Led by the battle-ship *Queen Elizabeth* the force of the MEF began moving out from Mudros harbour in the afternoon of 24 April 1915. New Zealander Captain A.B. Morton wrote: 'We felt as we watched it with fascinated interest, that this indeed was the first line of a new page in the history of the Empire.'[12]

The troopship carrying the Zion Mule Corps struck a sand bar as it was leaving the harbour. All the men, animals and supplies aboard had to be transferred to another ship. In the midst of this task Captain Edmunds, the medical officer of the Australian Hospital stores, then approached Patterson. He was also to transfer his supplies, and asked Patterson for the loan of his transport vessels. Edmunds explained that these were the only medical sup-plies available for the Australian soldiers.

Patterson agreed and the transfer occurred. Later Captain Edmunds thanked Patterson for his help, informing Patterson that he had prevented a calamity on the first day of the landing. 'So I think Australia and New Zealand owe me one' Patterson later wrote, 'for the help I gave them on that strenuous night of 24 April, when I was buried up to my neck in work of my own.' Patterson then confessed: 'I felt very glad that I had risen to the occasion and put the needs of Australia and New Zealand before my own.'[13]

10   Dolan, ibid, Chapter 10.
11   Dolan, ibid, Chapter 10. Palmer had been convicted of spying and was sentenced to death, but evaded this sen-tence by providing this information.
12   Morton, A.B. Diary and Letters, MS 1310, Alexander Turnbull Library, Wellington, cited in Pugsley, ibid, p. 103.
13   Patterson, ibid, p. 63.

THE FIRST LANDINGS – THE ANZAC SECTOR

Early in the morning of 25 April the soldiers of the Australian and New Zealand Army Corps were woken and given a hot drink. They then made their way from the larger ships to smaller landing boats manned by sailors. 'I was scared stiff', recalled Albert Facey, 'I know I was – but keyed up and eager to be on our way. We thought we would tear right through the Turks and keep going to Constantinople.'[14]

Several hundred metres from the shore the row boats were cast adrift from the picquets or small steamboats, and the sailors began to row towards their designated landing area. As the lead boats struck sand banks close to the shore, Queenslanders from the 3rd Australian Brigade leapt into the water.

Unfortunately some of the ANZAC soldiers were not landed where anticipated. Birdwood later wrote: 'The boats did not go in the right direction. They didn't go due east but inclined left and landed a good mile further north than intended ... We hit difficult country at once in which I feared that the troops would be sure to lose their symmetry in the dark and this is exactly what happened.'[15]

Von Sanders had anticipated a landing at Z Beach and had many soldiers in that location. There were also about 200 Turkish soldiers of the 27th Regiment, 9th Turkish Division, in the hilly country to the north of the beach, and more around the region of Gabe Tepe – and these confronted the first ANZAC troops to come ashore. Although held up by the Turkish fire, many of the ANZAC troops managed to scramble up the sharp hills and began to head towards the main objective, the Sari Bair Ridge. The commander of the 9th Turkish Division, Colonel Halil Sami, requested reinforcements from Mustapha Kemal, whose 19th Turkish Division was at Bogali village. Kemal then personally led his 57th Regiment towards Ari Burnu.[16]

The forward Australian troops pushed the Turkish soldiers back. These retreating Turkish troops were then met by Colonel Kemal who spotted

---

14 Facey, ibid, p. 254.
15 Letter of Birdwood, 29 April 1915, in Birdwood Papers, 3 DRL 3376, Australian War Memorial (AWM), cited in Winter, D. 'The Anzac Landing – the Great Gamble', *Journal of the Australian War Memorial*, April 1984, p. 13.
16 Mango, ibid, Part 2, Chapter 8..

ANZAC troops just ascending Chunuk Bair. Kemal stated that he: 'ordered them to fix their bayonets and lie down. As they did so, the enemy too lay down. We had won time.'[17] The ANZAC advance was halted, and the Turkish soldiers then continued to pour fire onto the Australian soldiers landing below.

'We got in without any loss in our boat.' Gardner recalled of his landing. 'We had picks and shovels … and each of us had to take one and wade ashore. The bottom was stony and I slipped, nearly went under, but recovered myself and got ashore all right.'[18]

By 0530 hours some 4,000 men had been landed, and Turkish resistance was stiffening. Villiers-Stuart, who had landed with the initial 1,500 men, then informed Bridges, wrote Dolan, to send all further men to 'the sheltered cove rather than to the beach raked by relentless bursts of shrapnel.'[19]

The New Zealanders and Australians of the 4th Brigade, which included Monash and Margolin, were observing the landings from their ships offshore. Then it was their turn to land. 'Ours was the first New Zealand boat ashore,' recalled Tony Fagan 'about eight thirty or nine in the morning.' One of the first scenes he saw were two boats full of dead Australian soldiers which drifted past their boat. 'It stunned us all,' he continued 'those two boats of dead Australians. It was the first time I had seen death.'[20]

Those two boatloads were only part of the butcher's bill for that day. They were part of the 2,000 Allied dead from the opening day of the Dardanelles Campaign.

THE FIRST LANDINGS FRENCH AND BRITISH ZONES

The British and French warships bombarded the Turkish fortifications throughout 24 April. Then early in the morning the British and French troops began landing on the beaches.

The naval bombardment of Beach V, the village of Seddulbahir (Sedd-el-Bahr), had been so severe that no-one was believed to have survived

---

17   Mustapha Kemal's Report, January 1917, cited in Mango, ibid, Part 2, Chapter 8.
18   Morice, ibid, p. 34.
19   Dolan, ibid, Epilogue.
20   Shadbolt, ibid, p. 20.

on shore. In the early morning light soldiers from Dublin, Munster and Hampshire boarded their boats (steamers) and began making their way towards Beach V. Captain W.L. Weldon was aboard one of the transport ships, and recalled: 'As the steamers neared the beach the ships ceased fire, and once within 150 yards of the shore, the boats were cast adrift, when the soldiers got out their oars and raced each other to the beach.'[21]

Weldon, who could observe from his transport, then recorded: 'the minute the boats started to row the silence was broken by a terrific rifle and machine-gun fire from the entrenched and concealed Turkish positions.'[22] A disbelieving Weldon observed a massacre: '… the casualties were awful, they grounded and our men leaped out carrying their rifles with bayonets fixed, leaving behind dead and wounded behind them.'[23] One ship, the collier *River Clyde*, was then moved up to the beach and beached. The soldiers then began alighting down gangplanks – but were gunned down by the entrenched Turkish soldiers. All attempts to take this strategic location failed.

Another eye-witness was General Hamilton, aboard the *Queen Elizabeth*. He felt powerless, and the only thing he could do was ensure the battleships laid down some fire upon the village and Fort.[24] The men from the Lancashire Fusiliers who landed at Beach W near Tekke Burnu encountered similar opposition to Beach V. There too hundreds of young British soldiers lost their lives. Finally though they did manage to secure what thereafter became known as Lancashire Landing.

The Royal Fusiliers and some men of the Royal Naval Division captured X Beach with less opposition. When they had secured their position, they proceeded on to join the men at Beach W. The South Wales Borderers landed at Beach S near Morto Bay. When their position was secure they proceeded towards Beach V. Seddulbahir, however, remained in Turkish hands by the end of 25 April.

The final position in the British sector was Y Beach, which was taken by the Kings Own Scottish Borderers and the Plymouth Battalion of the Royal

---

21   Weldon, Captain L.B.. *Hard Lying*, (London, 1925), p. 63.
22   Weldon, ibid, p. 63.
23   Weldon, ibid, p. 63.
24   Hamilton, ibid, p. 64.

Marines. Their objective was the village of Krithia, which they captured, but then lost to a fierce Turkish counter-attack. These men were then forced back to the beach, and, much to Hamilton's chagrin, had to re-embark.

The French force landed at Kum-Kale and obtained their objectives, except one heavily defended position. They suffered, though, heavy losses. Some of Hamilton's advisors suggested the French remain on the Asiatic side, as this would strategically assist the Navy when the time came to access the Straits. But Hamilton felt restrained by Kitchener's explicit orders not to stay on the Asiatic side.

The Royal Naval Division (RND) was off-shore at Bulair. There, early in the morning Bernard Freyberg, a young New Zealand born soldier, swam about three kilometres to the shore and placed several flares to simulate the bivouac fires of disembarked soldiers. This was intended as a decoy to trick Von Sanders. He then swam back and was picked up by the small naval cutter.[25]

GENERAL VON SANDERS RESPONSE

General Liman Von Sanders spent the night of 24/25 April at Gallipoli. He wrote:

> At 5 a.m. of April 25th reports were received in rapid succession at army headquarters of extensive landings of troops made or about to be made. From the south, beginning on the Asiatic side, the 11th Division reported the concentration of hostile war vessels and transports in, and off, the large and small Besika (Baskika) Bays, threatening a landing.
>
> A little further north, at Kum Kale, the advanced troops of the 3rd Division were heavily engaged with French troops which had been debarked there under a heavy fire of numerous French war vessels.
>
> At the southern point of the peninsular of Gallipoli at Seddulbahir … , Tekke Burnu, at the mouth of the Sigindere (Zighin Dere) and in

---

25   On 28 April four battalions of the RND were landed at the Anzac sector, and later the entire Division was sent to the Helles sector.

Morto Bay the advanced troops of the 9th Division were contending with heavy British forces for the possession of the landing place. All of these stretches of coast and the country in rear were deluged with a frightful fire from the large calibre naval guns of the British.

At Kabatepe … and top one side of the formerly mentioned place of Maidos, and at Ari Burnu troops were being debarked from British war vessels and transports, while a semicircle of hostile battleships was deluging the shore and the ground in rear with fire from the heaviest calibers.

Nearest to us, in the upper Saros (Xeros) Gulf, numerous war vessels and transports were approaching the coast. Soon we distinctly heard a continuous roar of artillery fire from that direction.[26]

Although the Allied movements were at the very locations predicted by Von Sanders, the intensity of the operation surprised him and his staff officers. His initial problem was to determine where the major landings were taking place. To this end he himself made immediate passage to the Bulair region – where Freyberg's flares were burning.

Finally Von Sanders was convinced that there was to be no major landing at Bulair, so he despatched two of his divisions to other more pressing locations, primarily Seddulbahir and Kapatepe (Gaba Tepe).

HAMILTON'S DILEMMA

At 0050 hours on 26 April, General Hamilton was roused from his sleep by General Braithwaite, and called to a meeting. A message from Birdwood was read:

Both my Divisional Commanders and Brigadiers have represented to me that they fear their men are thoroughly demoralised by shrapnel fire to which they have been subjected all day after exhaustion and gallant work in morning. Numbers have dribbled back from firing line and cannot be collected in this difficult country. Even New Zealand

---

26   Von Sanders, ibid, p. 63.

Brigade which has been only recently engaged lost heavily and is to some extent demoralised. If troops are subjected to shell fire again to-morrow morning there is likely to be a fiasco as I have no fresh troops with which to replace those in firing line. I know my representation is most serious but if we are to re-embark it must be at once.[27]

Hamilton asked those present for their views. Admiral Thursby said it would take three days to get the men off the beaches, adding: "I think myself they will stick it out if only it is put to them that they must." Hamilton immediately sent a message to Birdwood informing him '… there is nothing for it but to dig yourselves right in and stick it out. It would take at least two days to re-embark you as Admiral Thursby will explain to you…'

A PS was then added to his order, a PS which became part of ANZAC folklore: 'You have got through the difficult business, now you have to dig, dig, dig, until you are safe. Ian. H.'[28]

General d'Amade came aboard in the morning and reported that their position would become tenuous unless they could capture a nearby village. Kitchener's initial instructions were to keep out of Asia, and Hamilton also realized he was not strong enough to maintain a force on both sides of the Straits.[29] He gave the order for D'Amade to withdraw, the intention being that the French troops would transfer across the waters to the British sector, and join the fighting around the Morto Bay area.

Hamilton later rued having made this decision, for had the French taken the village of Yeni Shahr, 'and kept our grip on Kum Kale' they would have greatly assisted the Fleet. Hamilton, however, had to accept the withdrawal, and the French soldiers arrived on 27 April at Seddelbahir.[30]

The *Queen Elizabeth* then made haste past Y Beach, where much to his consternation Hamilton observed the soldiers still being withdrawn from the beach. Then the battleships arrived off Gabe Tepe. Hamilton, and his

27   Hamilton, ibid, p. 69.
28   Hamilton, ibid, p. 69. The ANZAC soldiers were thereafter called 'Diggers.'
29   Hamilton, ibid, p. 72.
30   Hamilton, ibid, p. 75.

staff, understood that the task of withdrawing the ANZAC's would have been extremely costly, and hence he wrote:

> No doubt the panorama was alarming, but we all of us somehow ... felt sure that Australia and New Zealand had pulled themselves to- gether and were going to give Enver and his Army a very disagreeable surprise.
>
> Imagine, had these brave lads entrusted to us by the Commonwealth and Dominion now been crowding on the beaches – crowding into their boats – whilst some desperate rearguard was trying to hold off the inrush of the triumphant Turks. Never would any of us have got over so shocking a disaster; now they are about to win their spurs (D.V.)[31]

While observing the ANZAC positions, the Turks began their counter-at- tack, and the *Queen Elizabeth*, as well as other ships off-shore, responded with many salvos – which assisting in stopping the Turkish soldiers coming forward - and which also won the praises of many of the soldiers on land. This Turkish attack was thwarted, which much pleased the Commander-in- Chief, as too did the news that the 29th Division had just taken Seddulbahir.

THE ZION MULE CORPS LAND – AND THE WOUNDED EVACUATED

The fighting in all three sectors had been intense and bloody in the first twenty four hours, but the anticipated initial breakthrough had not been attained. Von Sanders then ordered more Turkish reinforcements to be sent to the danger areas.

The Allies then landed other auxiliary troops on 26 April. Among these were Patterson's Zion Mule Corps. As these troops landed they en- dured shelling from the Asiatic side. 'I watched my men very carefully' recalled Patterson 'to see how they would stand their baptism of fire, and I am happy to be able to say that, with one solitary exception, all appeared

---

31 Hamilton, ibid, p. 73.

quite unconcerned and took not the slightest heed of the dangerous position they were in.'[32]

The many wounded meanwhile were being evacuated. There was considerable chaos in this operation as the authorities were unprepared for the number of casualties. One of the wounded was Tony Fagan, who had been taken out to a troopship – which was already crammed with the wounded and no space could be found for new arrivals. 'Eventually we arrived at a ship which had some space' he recalled. '… There were 600 wounded aboard that boat, two doctors, no nurses, no medical orderlies, no anaesthetics, and there we lay. I wasn't touched', he concluded, 'all the way to Alexandria.'[33]

Ronald Storrs wrote in relation to these wounded:

> Alexandria had to witness, not a victorious return, but steady relays of Hospital Liners freighted with hopeless heroism; with glory, save of the spirit, unachieved. The schools and great hotels became an infinite series of sick bays round which we walked with books, newspapers and cigarettes, amid a crowd of suffering fortitude, and strange, terribly true stories.[34]

In such a situation it was a good thing that Captain Edmunds and his medical supplies had arrived at the ANZAC sector.

Despite the lack of a breakthrough, the French President Poincare recorded on 29 April that they had decided 'to send another Division under General Baillou to the Dardanelles; General Goraud will be in supreme charge of the contingent.'[35]

With another experienced French Division on the way it would only be a matter of time before the area was captured – to be followed by the capture of Constantinople and then the defeat of Turkey.

---

32 Patterson, ibid, p. 98.
33 Shadbolt, ibid, pp. 20-21.
34 Storrs, R. *Orientations*, p. 199.
35 Poincare, ibid, p. 90.

§

CHAPTER 37

Counter-attacks

TURKISH COUNTER-ATTACKS

Throughout the first days the Allied objectives remained the same – the capture of Krithia and Achi Baba in the Helles sector, and the capture of the Sari Bair Ridge in the ANZAC sector.

The Turkish objective in both areas was the same: to drive these foreign invaders off the Dardanelles and to protect their Empire. To this end they continued to mount counter-attacks, especially during 28-29 April.

The constant presence of the Allied battleships off Seddulbahir, however, forced the Turkish forces to desist from attempting to drive the Allied forces off the Peninsula during a day time attack.

They mounted their attack on three successive nights, but Von Sanders conceded, 'the purpose could not be accomplished.' The reason, he wrote, was because: 'In each case daybreak brought an overwhelming fire from the ships which compelled the Turks to withdraw to their positions.'[1]

Von Sanders then had no choice but to call off any further such assaults, and for his forces, especially near Seddulbahir, to go onto the defensive. His forces continued to adamantly defend the Achi Baba Ridge.

---

1   Von Sanders, ibid, p. 71.

The Allied battleships not only hassled Turkish troops but they also bombed Turkish towns in the Peninsula. One such location was Maidos, which Von Sanders stated, was completely bombed out. One building hit by shells was the hospital, and many Turkish wounded 'and some twenty-five wounded British became victims of the conflagration … Many peaceful inhabitants likewise perished.'[2]

ALLIED COUNTER-ATTACKS AND REINFORCEMENTS

The failure to break out prompted Kitchener to release the 42nd Territorial Division and an Indian Brigade based in Egypt. Hamilton was also informed that another French Division was also en-route. On 1 May he inspected the French positions, of which he recorded: 'The French have suffered severely but are in fine fighting form. They are enchanted to hear about their second Division. For some reason or another they have made up their minds that France is not so keen as we are to make a present of Constantinople to Russia.'[3]

Godley, the commander of the New Zealand and Australia Division, ordered a break-out on 2 May. It failed, and once again the casualties were high – some 700 in total.[4] One of those casualties was Eliazar Margolin who received a bullet in his upper arm, but he nevertheless remained in the line.[5] Later while fighting at Quinn's Post his life was spared when a bullet struck a notebook in his pocket.[6]

The ANZAC force suffered such heavy casualties that General Birdwood requested a thousand volunteers from the mounted forces in Egypt. Both Chauvel and H.A. Russell, the commander of the New Zealand Mounted Rifles Brigade, volunteered their entire brigades in order to keep them together.

---

2   Von Sanders, ibid, p. 72. Morgenthau though maintains that there were no civilians in that area at that time.

3   Hamilton, ibid, p. 86.

4   Hamilton, ibid, p. 90.

5   National Archives of Australia, Series B 2455, 'Personal Dossiers for 1st AIF ex-Service members', E.L. Margolin, K1143/1, Casualty Form- Active Service, cited in Gouttman, ibid, pp. 45-6.

6   Longmore, L.C. *The Old 16th: Record of the 16th Battalion A.I.F. in the Great War*, (Perth, 1929), p.57, cited in Gouttman, ibid, p. 46.

The failure of the 2 May break-out convinced Hamilton of the futility of attempting further break-outs from the ANZAC sector, and thereupon he began to plan a new counter-attack from the Cape Helles sector. He transferred men from the New Zealand Brigade and the 2nd Australian Brigade to Helles, who alongside a Brigade from the Royal Naval Division, formed a new composite Division. This force, together, with the 29th Division and French forces, prepared for a new assault aimed at the Allied 'Goliath' of Achi Baba.

Hamilton, though, was faced with a huge problem prior to this attack – the lack of ammunition. No matter how hard he tried to get Kitchener and the Ordnance personnel in Britain to understand the precariousness of his situation, nothing seemed to work. As dedicated as he was to the War Minister, Hamilton by this stage was becoming exasperated. Yet the battle needed to proceed, otherwise the Turks would bring in more reinforcements, which would in turn nullify the arrival of the new Allied forces.

On 6 May some 50,000 Allied soldiers left their trenches and attacked from 'sea to sea' along a line heading towards Achi Baba. They attacked over open country and against entrenched Turkish troops, who resisted this intense Allied assault. The majority of the attacking force was quickly pinned down and sustained very heavy casualties in the process. 'At 4.30' Hamilton reported, 'we dropped our high-vaulting Achi Baba aspirations and took to our spades.'[7]

The battle was renewed on 7 May, and despite general advances, the main problem now was the scarcity of artillery shells to support the advancing infantry. 'At night' Hamilton reported, 'several counter-attacks were delivered, in every case repulsed with heavy loss.'[8] Hamilton was now in a quandary, as he expressed: 'We are now on our last legs. The beautiful Battalions of the 25th April are wasted skeletons now; shadows of what they had been … but we must go on fighting to-morrow!'[9]

---

7 Hamilton, ibid, p. 95.
8 Hamilton, ibid, p. 96.
9 Hamilton, ibid, p. 96.

On the morrow, 8 May, the New Zealand Brigade was to advance through the line taken during the night and attack Krithia. 'The ships began to fire at 10.15' Hamilton wrote 'and after a quarter of an hour the flower of New Zealand advanced in open order to the attack.' Later some Australians were also committed, having been brought down from the ANZAC sector.

Every unit gave everything they had for this great attempt to break-out – and break into Krithia and Achi Baba. At darkness, Hamilton wrote somewhat despondently: 'The battle is over. Both sides have fought with every atom of energy they possessed. The heat is oppressive… On shore all quiet.'[10]

Now it became clear that effecting a break-out in both sectors was going to be very difficult, and Hamilton renewed his request for further Divisions.

THE ANZAC HORSEMEN ARRIVE

Chauvel and his fellow ANZAC horsemen left Egypt on 9 May and arrived at Anzac Cove on 11 May. Upon arrival Chauvel took command of No. 3 Section of the defences being held by the 4th Australian Infantry Brigade commanded by John Monash.[11] The entire area was precarious, and it was clear that one very determined Turkish counter-attack could push the beleaguered ANZAC force to the beach.

Shortly after he had landed Chauvel renewed acquaintance with his close friend General Bridges, commander of the 1st Australian Division. Then on 15 May Bridges was on his way to discuss matters with Chauvel when he was shot by a Turkish sniper and died shortly after.[12] Bridges' death was a personal shock to Chauvel as well as to all the military and populace in Australia. It also provided first hand experience to the newly arrived Light Horse of the daily dangers at Anzac Cove.

Another Light Horseman to land was Trooper Ion Idriess, who wrote: '… jolly glad to step on shore among huge stacks of ammunition and stores… Men were toiling among the heavy stacks of stores, men trudged

---

10   Hamilton, ibid, p. 98.
11   Hill, ibid, p. 52.
12   Hill, ibid, p. 53. Bridges later died on the hospital ship.

all over that tiny beach in ragged, clay-stained uniforms, their familiar Australian faces cheerful and grimy under sprouting beards.'[13]

REACTIONS AROUND THE WORLD

News of the Allied disaster was not initially broadcast around the world. What was known was that the attack on the Dardanelles had commenced, and most people were expecting a quick break through and the capture of Constantinople.

Ambassador Paleologue recorded on 12 May:

In the Dardanelles the Anglo-French are making methodical progress digging in each night on the ground won during the day.

Public opinion in Russia is closely following every detail of the fighting: it does not doubt the ultimate result and thinks it is near at hand. In imagination it already sees the Allied squadrons passing through the Hellespont and anchoring off the Golden Horn.'[14]

TURKISH COUNTER-ATTACKS

Von Sanders planned a major Turkish counter-attack for 19 May. It almost succeeded. They attacked in the ANZAC sector with some four infantry divisions, and each position in this sector was involved in the fighting, and the dismounted ANZAC horsemen had their baptism of fire.

The Turkish attack narrowly failed. But it cost them badly: some 10,000 Turkish soldiers were either killed or wounded. Their dead lay scattered in the area of no-man's land between the opposing forces.

Following the aborted 19 May assault it became apparent to both sides that thousands of men lay dead, and many hundreds of men lay wounded in 'no-man's land'.

In his first letter to his wife since arrival Harry Chauvel wrote on 23 May: 'I am writing in my dug-out which a … excellent batman has made very comfortable but the smell of dead Turks which lie in hundreds, if not

---

13   Idriess, I. *The Desert Column*, (Australia, 1973), p. 5.
14   Paleologue, ibid, 12 May 1915.

thousands, in front of our lines is awful, especially at night. There is some talk of an armistice to bury them but I am doubtful of it coming off.'[15]

Communication did occur between the two sides and arrangements made for an armistice in which to bury the dead. The Turkish representative in these negotiations was Mustapha Kemal.[16]

The details of the Armistice were then determined, and it began on 24 May, and ran for nine hours duration. Throughout this period there was an edge of uncertainty from both sides, but there was quiet and some 4,000 Turkish dead were buried.

For many of those present there was a surreal atmosphere, with members of the burial parties exchanging gifts and conversing in an assortment of languages. As soon as the armistice ended though, matters returned to normal. 'At 4.45 p.m.' wrote Moorehead, 'a Turkish sniper fired from somewhere in the hills. Immediately the Australians answered and the roar of high explosive closed over the battlefield again.'[17]

SUBMARINE THREAT

On 27 April Lieutenant-Commander Boyle passed through the Dardanelles in the submarine E. 14, and thereafter for three weeks bombed Turkish shipping in the Sea of Marmara, including one Turkish ship which was carrying 6,000 troops. When Boyle came out from the Dardanelles on 18 May he was given a victor's reception.[18]

Boyle was replaced by Lieut-Commander Nasmith on the E. 11 who then succeeded in bombing targets in Constantinople on 25 May – sending panic and consternation into the heart of the Turkish capital.[19] His successes earned him the Victoria Cross.

While these Allied submarine exploits were occurring news came through that a German submarine, U. 21, had passed through the Straits of Gibraltar, and was believed to be heading towards Gallipoli. The German

---

15   Chauvel to his wife, 23 May 1915, Chauvel Papers, ibid.
16   Moorehead, ibid, p. 125. Mustapha Kemal was much involved in the fighting before and during 19 May, and received numerous medals, including the German Iron Cross.
17   Moorehead, ibid, p. 127.
18   Moorehead, ibid, p. 138.
19   Moorehead, ibid, p. 140.

commander Hersing then fired his first shot at the Allied shipping on 25 May, sinking *HMS Triumph* near the Anzac sector.

This action caused Admiral De Robeck to order all the ships to leave the region, but the following day the *HMS Majestic* returned. But on 27 May she too was sunk near Cape Helles – in view of the soldiers ashore. These losses forced the Anglo-French battleships to withdraw to the area of Imbros and Lemnos islands, which in turn meant they could no longer offer the Allied infantry the same protection as before.[20]

POLITICAL CRISIS IN BRITAIN

The losses on the Western Front; lack of a breakthrough in the Dardanelles; and a severe munitions shortage, deeply concerned the opposition parties, which until this point had supported the Liberal Party's war effort.

On 15 May 1915 Lord Fisher, the First Sea Lord, tendered his resignation. Churchill, as the Lord of the Admiralty, was shocked. Fisher's resignation seemed to confirm what many had already suspected – that coupled with the problems in the handling of the war effort on the Western Front and on the home front, the Dardanelles Campaign had been poorly planned and executed.

Asquith in response called for a national unity government. He was supported in this endeavour by David Lloyd George, and the new government was formed on 19 May. A scapegoat for the failures, particularly at the Dardanelles, was needed. Kitchener was far too esteemed to go, and so the lot fell upon Churchill. He was replaced in the Admiralty by Arthur Balfour.

A new department, the Ministry of Munitions, was formed which was headed by Lloyd George. Lloyd George lost no time in his new task of increasing Britain's munitions and ammunition. In the process he became further acquainted with the former Russian scientist – Chaim Weizmann. Weizmann was asked to produce acetone, a vital ingredient for the production of ammunition.

---

20   Von Sanders, ibid, p. 77.

THE IMPETUS LOST

For Hamilton the loss of Churchill was another big set-back to his aim of securing the Dardanelles. He knew that Churchill had a grasp of the dynamics and complexities of the Campaign, and wrote: 'How will he feel now he realizes he is shorn of the direct power to help us through these dark and dreadful Straits? … What a tragedy that his nerve and military vision have been side-tracked: his eclipse projects a black shadow over the Dardanelles.'[21]

By the end of May both sides on the actual battlefield had seemingly tried and failed in all their attempts to dislodge the other. What had by now become the norm in France and Belgium was now doomed to curse Gallipoli as well: a military stalemate. Ambassador Paleologue wrote on 28 May in view of German successes on the Western Front: 'All the more anxiously is the public gaze turned towards the Dardanelles. Yet the Gallipoli expedition seems to me to have lost something of its power as a mirage and a diversion.'[22]

---

21 Hamilton, ibid, p. 110.
22 Paleologue, ibid, 28 May 1915.

§

CHAPTER 38

The Stalemate

NO RUSSIANS COMING TO THE RESCUE

The huge exertions of both sides in May forced serious re-evaluations to their strategies. Hamilton now realized that his hopes of success lay in receiving more munitions and forces. Until May he held to the hope that the planned Russian landing at the Bosphorus would take place, or even that one or more of the neutral Balkan countries (especially Bulgaria and Greece) would enter the fray alongside the Allies.[1]

But at the end of May Hamilton was informed that the Russian force would not be coming.[2] This changed the dynamics of his offensive completely. He now realised that without the involvement of the Russians, the scales were now tipped against him. This could be counter-balanced, though, by the presence of Greeks.[3] Greek involvement, however, was highly problematic at that point. Without the active involvement of either the Russians or the Greeks, then Hamilton's only real chance of success was to receive an entire new Army Corps.[4]

---

1   Hamilton to Kitchener, 17 May 1915, cited in Hamilton, ibid, p. 106.
2   Hamilton, ibid, pp. 118-19.
3   Hamilton, ibid, p. 120.
4   Hamilton to Kitchener, ibid, cited in Hamilton, ibid, p. 119.

TURKISH ATTACK ON QUINN'S POST

While Hamilton was contemplating his options the Turks made a concerted effort to capture one of the strategic positions in the ANZAC sector - at Quinn's Post. They attacked in force on 29 May, and Chauvel found himself in the midst of the fighting commanding the defence of that strategic position. It was primarily due to his leadership that the Turkish assault was not only halted, but a counter-attack succeeded.[5] He wrote to his wife: 'We had quite a stiff fight again on the 29th.'[6]

Hamilton visited the ANZAC sector the following day and walked through the 'Valley of Death' up to the HQ of 4th Australian Infantry Brigade. From there, he wrote: 'I could see the enemy trenches in front of Quinn's Post, and also a very brisk bomb combat in full flame where the New Zealand Mounted Rifles were making good the Turkish communicating post they had seized earlier in the day.'

Hamilton wrote concerning the morale of the men: 'The spirit of the men is invincible … I never struck a more jovial crew. Men staggering under sides of frozen beef; men struggling up cliffs with kerosene tins full of water; men digging; men cooking; men card-playing in small dens scooped out from the banks of yellow clay – everyone wore a Bank Holiday air … All the time, overhead, the shell and rifle bullets groaned and whined, touching just the same note of violent energy as was in evidence everywhere else.'[7]

THIRD BATTLE OF KRITHIA

Several command changes occurred in late May. Hunter-Weston was promoted to Lieutenant-General and placed in charge of all the British troops at Helles, which now became 8th Corps. Command of the 29th Division was given to Major-General Beauvoir de Lisle.

With the arrival of a second French division, 8th Corps (the Royal Naval, 29th and 42th British Divisions) and the French launched a new of-

---

5   Hill, ibid, pp. 55-56.
6   Chauvel to his wife, 30 May 1915, ibid, Chauvel Papers.
7   Hamilton, ibid, p. 116.

fensive on 4 June, in what was known as the Third Battle of Krithia. The ANZAC's were to attack as a feint in order to draw Turkish forces away from the Helles sector. Once again the Allied aim was to capture Krithia and Achi Baba.

Hamilton recorded: 'Chapters could be written about this furious battle fought in a whirlwind of dust and smoke … For the best part of an hour it seemed that we had won a decisive victory.' The Commander-in-Chief then described the great work of the French, and how the Manchester Brigade 'wrested two lines of trenches from the Turks; and then, carrying right on; on to the lower slopes of Achi Baba, had *nothing* between them and the summit but the clear, unentrenched hillside.' At that point all they needed was support – and they would have reached the top.[8]

The support never came as the other units were by that stage too battered, especially General Gouraud's French Division. The Manchester Brigade had to withdraw and surrender their hard fought territory – at the base of Achi Baba. The attack ultimately failed and the casualties for both sides amounted to some 10,000 men killed and wounded.

The failure of this major assault resulted in a furtherance of the stalemate during the months of June and July. Both sides dug trenches and consolidated their lines – sometimes within metres of each other. These weeks witnessed a continuous war of attrition, with constant artillery barrages, sniper fire and small incursions, punctuated by these occasional bigger thrusts.

THE ZION MULE CORPS

From the time they landed on 26 April the Zion Mule Corps had actively delivered ammunition and supplies to the front line of the Cape Helles sector. On one occasion volunteers were called for to take several ammunition-laden donkeys to the front line – under Turkish fire. No volunteers initially stepped forward, but then finally Wertheimer, the young man from the Old City of Jerusalem, came forward and took hold of the mules.

Trumpeldor was an eyewitness to what happened next:

---

8   Hamilton, ibid, p. 122.

When Wertheimer appeared with his mules on the stretch of open ground, the enemy's fire redoubled. Shells fell thick and fast, exploding with frightful detonations… The mules stiffened their backs and did not want to move. But the quiet, reassuring hand of Wertheimer held them and pulled them forward. He walked calmly, as if nothing were happening around him, and he paid no attention to the exploding shells. On either side of the open space the soldiers watched him with bated breath, saying in a whisper, 'Brave fellow, brave fellow.'[9]

Unfortunately while only several metres from the trenches Wertheimer was hit. His wounded body was retrieved and he was sent on a hospital ship to Alexandria, but he died shortly afterwards. Trumpeldor relates that later: 'A letter arrived from his father asking to be sent his late son's *tefillin*.[10] There was no suggestion of complaint or unrestrained grief. The man of *Chaluka* from Jerusalem had bravely shown his love for Eretz Yisrael.'[11]

The involvement of Zionists at Gallipoli did gain a certain amount of interest. On one occasion General Hamilton wrote in response to a query from the New York paper, *The Day*: 'It may interest you to know that I have here, fighting under my orders, a purely Jewish unit. As far as I know' he continued 'this is the first time in the Christian era that such a thing has happened. These troops were officially described as the 'Zion Mule Corps', and the officers and rank and file have shown great courage in taking water, supplies and ammunition up to the fighting line under heavy fire.'[12]

In July Patterson and Trumpeldor returned briefly to Egypt to recruit reinforcements for the ZMC. In Cairo the leading Jewish notables were summoned by General Maxwell to meet with and support Trumpeldor and Patterson. The leaders then permitted these two men to propagate the cause of the Zion Mule Corps in the synagogues. Some 150 Jewish men volunteered and after some brief training they ventured to join their comrades in arms in Gallipoli.

---

9   Yaari, ibid, p. 431.
10 Phylacteries, which are used when Jewish men pray.
11 Yaari, ibid, p. 432.
12 Patterson, ibid, pp. 213-14.

There were also many Arab soldiers fighting at Gallipoli – on the Turkish side. While some of these fought willingly, others were conscripted and found themselves at Gallipoli against their will.

THE PROBLEM OF LOGISTICS AND ATTRITION

Regardless of whether a soldier was Turkish, Arab, Zionist or Allied, whether they were there voluntarily or under duress, all the soldiers faced several common enemies: logistics and disease. Maintaining a constant supply of food, water and ammunition was a problem. But the biggest problem by far was disease.

Dead bodies were littered everywhere, particularly in no-man's land, and these decomposed in the hot summer sun, producing a sickening stench, as well as flies and inevitably - disease.

A major problem was also the cramped location where the soldiers had to fight. Such a life presented some interesting scenarios, one of which Chauvel wrote to his wife:

> I attended the weirdest Communion service you could imagine this morning – in a narrow gully all amongst the men's dug-outs – the parson in a spotless surplice with a dirty old felt hat – with two ammunition boxes for an altar and just the dust in the bottom of the gully to kneel on. It was the first Church of England parade we have had since we landed and was quite well attended in spite of discomfort...
>
> The Australian Light Horse are now cave-dwellers and I am living the life of a rabbit. I do hope it won't last much longer.'[13]

Unfortunately the life of a rabbit did not suit Chauvel, and several days later he was diagnosed with pleurisy and was shipped off to Alexandria. 'I am afraid the habits of a rabbit don't agree with my constitution' he wrote to his wife while on the hospital ship.[14]

---

13   Chauvel to his wife, 13 June 1915, ibid, Chauvel Papers.
14   Chauvel to his wife, 20 June 1915, ibid, Chauvel Papers.

MUSTAPHA KEMAL'S MOVEMENTS

Mustapha Kemal, like all the officers on both sides of the conflict, had fluc-
tuating fortunes during the Campaign. In June he was promoted to a full
Colonel, and then in the attack of 29/30 June his Division lost some 1,000
men – and he was blamed for the failure.[15]

On 20 July, when there was little activity Kemal sent a letter to Corinne
Lütfü, stating:

> Our life here [he wrote] is truly hellish. Fortunately, my soldiers are
> very brave and tougher than the enemy. What is more, their private
> beliefs make it easier to carry out orders which send them to their
> death. They see only two supernatural outcomes: victory for the
> faith or martyrdom. Do you know what the second means? It is to
> go straight to heaven. There, the houris, God's most beautiful wom-
> en, will meet them and will satisfy their desires for all eternity. What
> great happiness![16]

Presumably commanding such men would have certain advantages as they
would be more willing to be martyred for the cause – the preservation of
their Empire.

GOOD NEWS FOR HAMILTON

The cause of the Allies was the exact opposite – its defeat. This cause received a boost when at the War Council (now renamed the Dardanelles
Committee) meeting on 7 June 1915, Kitchener agreed to the sending of
three new infantry divisions to the Dardanelles. He wrote to Hamilton:
'Your difficulties are fully recognized by the Cabinet who are determined
to support you.'[17] This new force was part of the New Army, and would
become the 9th Corps.

Success, it seemed, was now a real possibility.

---

15 Mango, A. *Ataturk*, (John Murray, Kindle Edition), Part 2, Chapter 8.

16 Mango, A. *Ataturk*, ibid, Part 2, Chapter 8, citing from Özverim, Melda, Mustafa Kemal ve Corinne , Lütfü: Bir Dostlu
ğun Öyküsü (Atatürk and Corinne Lütfü: The Story of a Friendship), (Milliyet Yayınları, Istanbul 1998), pp. 56-7. Mango
did state that 'Mustafa Kemal did not associate himself with his men's beliefs.'

17 Hamilton, ibid, p. 127.

§

CHAPTER 39

The De Bunsen Committee Report

THE DE BUNSEN COMMITTEE REPORT

While the troops were still endeavouring to complete the victory on the ground, the British politicians had still to determine their *desiderata* for the Turkish Empire once it had been defeated.

The first step was to receive the report of the special Committee headed up by Maurice de Bunsen. The De Bunsen Committee completed its deliberations and submitted its report on 30 June. The purpose of the Committee was to determine Britain's interests in the region of the Turkish Empire.

In the section where the Committee stated the reasons for its formation (in order to determine British *desiderata* created by Russia's demand for Constantinople and other regions), the Committee stated two precipitating criteria:

(1) A revision of the Anglo-Russian Agreement of 1907 respecting Persia, and

(2) That when the fact that Russia was to have Constantinople at the end of the war became public, His Majesty's Government would state that they

had through all the negotiations stipulated that in all circumstances Arabia and the Moslem holy places should remain under independent Moslem rule.[1]

Of the two points the more relevant to our narrative is point (2). The British Government in India was very aware of the sympathy many of its Muslim citizens felt towards the Turkish Empire, and the presence of the Caliphate at Constantinople. Point 2 was the Committee's attempt to ensure there would be no Muslim backlash in India.

Ultimately the Committee proposed four schemes for the future Ottoman Turkish Empire, pending its defeat at Gallipoli which was still fully expected:

1. Partition among the Allied Powers.
2. The establishment of zones of interest in a mostly independent empire which would have effective European control.
3. Continuance of the Ottoman regime in the Asian part of the Empire, but with some territorial changes.
4. A decentralized independent Empire run on federal lines, and again with some territorial adjustments.

BRITISH *DESIDERATA*

One key component of the Committee's deliberations was the balance between (a) Britain's imperial interests, and (b) not adding more areas to the Empire, but of consolidating what they already had, in order 'to make firm and lasting the position we already hold, and to pass on to those who come after an inheritance that stands four-square to the world.'[2]

The Report then proceeded to state that the main object of obtaining *desiderata* was for the maintenance of the Persian Gulf; and of trade through that region. It was within this context that the Report, in Point 12, stated the need for Britain to fulfil pledges given or under consideration in the region,

---

1   CAB 42/1/12, located in De Bunsen Private Papers Collection, Middle East Centre, St. Anthony's College, De Bunsen GB 165-0078.
2   De Bunsen Committee Report, ibid, p. 2.

including Arabia (the Emir of Nejd was mentioned) and 'maintenance of assurances given to the Sherif of Mecca and the Arabs.'[3]

Several other sub-points were also of future importance:

(vi.) Maintenance of our strategic position in the Eastern Mediterranean and in the Persian Gulf, and security of our communications with the minimum increase of naval and military expenditure and responsibility.

(vii.) To ensure that Arabia and the Moslem Holy Places remain under independent Moslem rule. Dependent upon this, we should seek for a settlement which will appeal to, or at least not antagonise, Indian Moslem feeling, and will provide a satisfactory solution to the question of the Khalifate.

(viii.) A satisfactory solution to the Armenian problem.

(ix.) A settlement of the question of Palestine and the Holy Places of Christendom.[4]

Interestingly the Committee then made a distinction between the first six sub-points, which all related in one form or another to the Persian Gulf region, from the last three, which, it said 'are questions which could be discussed and settled in concert with other Powers…'[5]

The Persian Gulf region was becoming of increasing importance for Britain, and as Germany would not be a participant in any future dismemberment of the Turkish Empire, that region could be considered without Germany in consideration (which was not the case in the pre-August 1914 period).

FUTURE STATUS OF OTTOMAN TURKISH EMPIRE

Pending the ultimate defeat of Turkey, the Committee looked at four distinct forms of how the Turkish Empire could be structured, namely:

(a) The Kingdom of Turkey in Anatolia and the remainder of the Empire partitioned;

(b) Turkish Empire to remain nominally independent, but under effective European control, with various zones of political and economic interest;

---

3   De Bunsen Committee Report, ibid, p. 3.
4   De Bunsen Committee Report, ibid, p. 3.
5   De Bunsen Committee Report, ibid, p. 3.

(c) Ottoman Empire to remain intact in Asia;

(d) maintenance of Ottoman Empire as an independent state but the form of government to be modified by decentralisation on federal lines.[6]

The Committee favoured the last stated scheme, but, they stated, if this could not be achieved, they next favoured 'the division of the empire into zones of interest.'[7] Within the context of an independent Empire ruled along federal lines, the Committee stated: 'Turkey in Asia falls ethnographically and historically into five great provinces – Anatolia, Armenia, Syria, Palestine and Iraq-Jazirah.' The Arabian Peninsula was excluded from this analysis.

Each of these five regions, or provinces, the Committee stated, had its own distinct characteristics, which provided for the establishment of local government within those boundaries.

The Committee recognized that the Arabian Peninsula was a separate region altogether, and proposed that in any eventual demarcation of Turkey in Asia, a line should be drawn from Akaba through to Maan on the Hedjaz Railway, 'thence eastwards in a northerly curve to the limits of Koweit [Kuweit]' and that 'this would correspond roughly to a fair division between Arabia proper and those Arabs who belong to the districts of Damascus and Mesopotamia.'[8]

PALESTINE

The issue of Palestine was vexing, and ultimately it was dealt with at two levels: 1) What was geo-politically best for Britain, and 2) The Holy Places.

At the very beginning of the Report, the issue of Palestine was mentioned within the context of France's *desiderata*, when they stated:

> The French Government were more precise in announcing their counter-claims to Russia. They demanded Cilicia and Syria, in which latter term they included, though they did specify the precise form of their claim - whether annexation or protectorate or sphere of interest.

---

6   De Bunsen Committee Report, ibid, p. 4.

7   Kedourie, *Labyrinth*, ibid, p. 59.

8   De Bunsen Report, Paragraph 36.

It would appear that Russia is ready to accede to the French claim to Cilicia and Syria proper, but will demur strongly to the inclusion of Palestine.[9]

Geo-politically Kitchener and Fisher (although not on the Committee, their views were clearly stated) favoured Alexandretta being part of the British zone of interest. Their reasons, as Fisher stated in a letter to Kitchener on 11 March 1915, and Kitchener stated in a Memorandum dated 16 March[10], were that Alexandretta offered the closest port to the Euphrates River, and with this port under British control there could be a direct line of communication with the Persian Gulf.

Sir Mark Sykes, Kitchener's man on the Committee, however, well understood how this view would be seriously challenged by the French, and insisted instead upon the port of Haifa becoming Britain's port on the Mediterranean. If Haifa was included in the British area of interest, then there could still be access to the Euphrates (although somewhat longer); it would place Britain on the east bank of the Suez Canal; and it would potentially relieve any contention with France. Sykes managed to persuade Kitchener to adopt this viewpoint.[11]

As could be expected the issue of Palestine was placed in a separate category. Point 96 stated:

Still less do the Committee desire to offer suggestions about the future destiny of Palestine, but since that territory has been included within the geographical limits assigned to the British sphere in the two schemes, of partition, and of zones of interest, they desire to repeat that they see no reason why the sacred places of Palestine should not be dealt with as a separate question. They have felt free to deliberate on the assumption that the French claim will be rejected, since they are convinced that the forces opposed are too great for France ever

9   De Bunsen Committee Report, ibid, p.1.
10   Memorandum, 16 March 1915, Cab 27/1, & letter from Fisher to Kitchener, 11 March 1915, Kitchener Papers, 30 57/80.
11   Kedourie, *Labyrinth*, ibid, p. 60.

to make that claim good, but for the same reason they consider that it will be idle for His Majesty's Government to claim the retention of Palestine in their sphere. Palestine must be recognized as a country whose destiny must be the subject of special negotiations, in which both belligerents and neutrals are alike interested.[12]

Thus, as far as this Government appointed body was concerned, Palestine would geo-politically remain within Britain's sphere of interest, while the question of the Holy Places would need to be 'subject of special negotiations, in which both belligerents and neutrals are alike interested.'

    There was no indication at all in these words that Palestine would become part of any future Muslim dominated Arab national entity.

DEPARTURE OF SIR MARK SYKES

Even before the final De Bunsen Committee Report had been released, Sir Mark Sykes set out, at Kitchener's request, on a six month fact-finding tour of the East with the goal of determining, from a practical perspective, Britain's position in that vast region.

    Sykes took with him a draft copy of the De Bunsen Committee Report, which he was to show to the many relevant parties whom he was to meet on his upcoming journey.

---

12   De Bunsen Committee Report, ibid, p. 26.

§

CHAPTER 40

Under the cover of war

ARMENIANS 'LEGALLY' DEPORTED

One of the points raised in the De Bunsen Report concerned: 'A satisfactory solution to the Armenian problem.' At the time when these words were being written in Britain, the Turkish regime was about to implement its own solution to the Armenian problem.

In an article entitled 'Under the cover of war' historian Jay Winter stated, that 'the landing of British, French, Australian and New Zealand soldiers at Gallipoli, propelled Turkey further into a siege mentality which fuelled the zeal for exterminating the Armenians.'[1]

The policies of the Turkish Government had been progressing towards this unfortunate goal and the landing of troops on her soil provided her with a 'legitimate' reason for such activities against the Armenians – and other minorities.

On 27 May the Central Committee of the C.U.P. passed the 'Temporary Law of Deportation.' This Law allowed for the deportation of anyone who was deemed to be a security risk.[2] Although the Armenians were not specifically mentioned, it wasn't long before the Armenians in eastern Turkey bore the brunt of this new Law.

---

1   Winter, J. 'Under Cover of Darkness', in *America and the Armenian Genocide 1915,* edited by Jay Winter, (New York, 2003), p. 4.
2   Balakian, ibid, Part 2, Chapter 14.

Talaat Pasha wrote to the nominal head of government, the Grand Vizier, on 26 May concerning the implementation of this policy.[3] It was proposed that these 'security risks' would be deported to remote regions, primarily the desert region of Syria and Mesopotamia – hundreds of miles away. These forced deportations began in earnest at the beginning of June 1915.

THE MECHANISM OF GENOCIDE

The genocide of the Armenian community of Anatolia began through two avenues. The first, Akcam stated, was 'an official deportation order' which 'was sent to the provincial regions by the Interior Ministry. Specifically, the Department of Public Security and Dispatches within the ministry was responsible for overseeing all the practical matters involved in the deportations. The orders were sent to the government's local representatives (governors and prefects) in the provinces, who were expected to carry them out.' The second avenue, Akcam states, 'were separate, unofficial orders for the annihilation of the deportees, issued by the CUP Central Committee and conveyed to the provinces through party channels.'

'When the local governors', he continued, 'received deportation orders from the Interior Ministry they would forward them to the security forces in their area, usually to the gendarmerie, the body responsible for keeping provincial order (and part of the Interior Ministry). At the same time, the CUP would send the liquidation orders to the local governors. The messenger, usually a party secretary but on occasion Bahaettin Şakir himself, would travel from province to province transmitting a written document or conveying the order verbally. In cases where local governors resisted, they were removed from office.'

Once the deportation order had been received, then, Akcam stated further, 'the gendarmerie would summon the Armenians to a central point and then accompany them on their route. When the convoy reached the provincial borders, the gendarmerie was supposed to deliver the deportees to the

---

3   *Ati*, 24 February 1920, cited in Akcam, Preface, Footnote 15.

gendarmerie of the next province, however this was often the point where the Special Organization took over— set in motion by the secret liquidation order —and deportation became elimination. The Special Organization units, in cooperation with the gendarmerie, would join the convoys of deportees and set about their murder.[4]

Although the Turkish authorities tried to conceal these operations, news of them filtered out, often times through American consuls and missionaries, but also through others, including Germans.

Morgenthau alerted the American Government to these atrocities, as well as doing his utmost to persuade the Turkish leadership from desisting from their policy. In one meeting with Talaat Pasha, the Turkish leader informed him outright that he wanted to inform the American ambassador 'our position on the whole Armenian subject.' He then informed Morgenthau that their policy was based upon three factors:

1. The Armenians had 'enriched themselves at the expense of the Turks.'
2. The Armenians were 'determined to domineer over us and establish a separate state.'
3. The Armenians had 'openly encouraged our enemies. They have assisted' Talaat stated 'the Russians in the Caucasus and our failure there is largely explained by their actions.'[5]

Morgenthau had great difficulty persuading Enver Pasha to desist from the policy of extermination. In one meeting with the Turkish Minister of War Enver stated to Morgenthau:

You must understand that we are now fighting for our lives at the Dardanelles and that we are sacrificing thousands of men. While we are engaged in such a struggle as this, we cannot permit people in our

4   Akcam, ibid, pp. 161-2.
5   Morgenthau, ibid, Chapter 25, p. 8.

own country to attack us in the back. We have got to prevent this no matter what means we have to resort to.[6]

'There is sufficient evidence to conclude' wrote Akcam, 'that the deportation was to be understood as annihilation. A. Nuri, who was stationed in Aleppo, reported that Talât Paşa said: "The intention of the deportations is annihilation."'[7]

Walter Geddes, who worked in Smyrna, was travelling in central Anatolia in the spring of 1915 and informed Consul Horton in Smyrna, that 'Armenian communities across Anatolia were being evicted from their homes and marched into the desert by Turkish soldiers. Most never even reached their destination; they were butchered by the roadside or left to die in the heat and dust.'[8]

GERMAN ATTITUDES

There were many eye-witness accounts of the atrocities from non-Americans, including even German diplomats, missionaries and journalists.

German ambassador Wangenheim appointed Consul Mordtmann to monitor the Armenian situation. Following a conversation with Talaat Pasha, he informed Berlin that Talaat stated to him: 'What we are dealing with here … is the annulation of the Armenians.'[9]

One German missionary, Schwester Mohring, wrote a very graphic account of the horrors of what was happening which was published in the September 1915 version of the German newspaper *Sonnenaufgang*.[10] A German missionary, Dr Johannes Lepsius who was very concerned about the news of the massacres, also visited Morgenthau, who allowed the German to read through all of the reports from the American consuls, and other

---

6   Morgenthau, ibid, Chapter 26, p. 1.

7   "Tehcirin imha maksadina müstenit bulunduğu," first session (indictment), Takvîm-i Vekâyi, no. 3540 (27 Nisan 1335/ 27 April 1919), cited in Akcam, ibid, pp. 167-8. This testimony was from the legal proceedings in Turkey following the War.

8   Geddes Report, in Horton G. *The Blight of Asia*, cited in Milton, *Paradise Lost*, p. 84.

9   PA-AA /Bo. Kons./ B. 191, Report of Consul Mordtmann, dated 30 June 1915, cited in Akcam, Taner (2007-08-21). *A Shameful Act: The Armenian Genocide and the Question of Turkish Responsibility*. Henry Holt and Co. Kindle Edition, Preface, Footnote 8.

10   Letter by Schwester Mohring, published in *Sonnenaufgang*, September 1915, cited in Viscount Bryce, *The Treatment of Armenians in the Ottoman Empire 1915-16*, (London, 1916), pp. 566-69.

reports he had been sent.[11]   Lepsius soon after published *Der Todesgang des Armenischen Volkes* ('The Death Passage of the Armenian People'), in Germany.

The efforts of the Germans to get official condemnation of the atrocities were often thwarted by the inaction of Ambassador Wangenheim. On one occasion he said to Morgenthau: 'The Armenians … have shown themselves in this war to be enemies of the Turks. It is quite apparent that the two peoples can never live together in the same country.'[12]

Wangenheim did, though, submit an official note of protest on 4 July 1915, although it was not presented to the actual leaders, Talaat and Enver, but to the nominal leader, the Grand Vizier.[13]

BRITISH INTELLIGENCE REPORTS OF THE MASSACRES

Such blatant acts of brutality were reported by numerous witnesses to the British Intelligence offices, both on Lemnos Island and in Cairo. A cursory look at these reports will reveal just the tip of the iceberg. On 3 September 1915, from Cairo:

> Censored telegram 3/9/15: - The Turks are treating the Armenians atrociously. The Armenian committee addressed an appeal to the powers, especially the neutrals, and to the whole civilised community begging for help for the Armenians, who are being massacred wholesale. In some districts there is not a single Armenian left alive.[14]

The same report included a report from an Arab staff officer from ALEPPO who had defected at Gallipoli, who stated:

> The Armenians were being deported when informant left. There were thousands of them in ALEPPO living in churches, and in camp as big

---

11   Morgenthau, ibid, Chapter 26, p. 1.
12   Morgenthau, ibid, Chapter 27, p. 5.
13   See Morgenthau, Chapter 27, p. 6. Not long afterwards Von Wangenheim died.
14   Military Intelligence Office, Cairo, 3 September 1915, WO 157/695.

as that for an infantry division. They had lost everything they had, and were ill-treated...[15]

On 7 September a young officer named T.E. Lawrence recorded in the Military Intelligence Office in Cairo of the accounts provided by numerous informants:

Officers and men state that systematic massacres of Armenians have taken place at DIAR BEKAR, KHARPUT, URFA and DORTYOL. The women of DIAR BEKAR have been distributed among Mohammedan harems as far as Persia. An officer who is ex private secretary to Kiamil Pasha says that the ZEITUN people exiled at DEVI EL ZOR are dying off fast.[16]

Several days later on 10 September, the Cairo office carried a report from an American doctor, Dr Ward, who had travelled quite considerably through Syria in the previous months, and had tended wounded Turkish soldiers at Bir El Saba with the American Red Cross, following the aborted attack on the Suez Canal in February.[17]

After leaving Syria Dr Ward returned to Constantinople. In his report, it is stated:

Speaking of ASIA MINOR he estimates the number of Armenians massacred at between 200,000 and 300,000. It seems that the extermination of the Armenians is aimed at. The Turks justify their acts by saying that all the Armenians are traitors. The Germans and Austrians also take this view, including German missionaries who have worked for some time among the Armenians. The American Embassy has protested, but the Ambassador hardly feels justified in

---

15   Military intelligence Office, Cairo, 3 September 1915, WO 157/695.
16   Military Intelligence Office, Cairo, 3 September 1915, WO 157/695.
17   According to Dr. Ward, Kress Von Kressestein had informed him that the intention was to tie down 100,000 British soldiers at the Canal. Report of Dr Ward, cited in Military Intelligence Office, Cairo, 10 September 1915, WO 157/695. Ward also stated, that 'Djemal Pasha intends to carry on the campaign even if Constantinople falls, and may possibly set up an independent government there, with himself as the head.'

councelling [sic] the breaking off of relations with Turkey over this issue in view of the other interests entrusted to him, interests which would be left unprotected if he withdrew. Dr. Ward considers that the German and Austrian Governments, ought to protest against the persecution of Armenians, if they wish to avoid the charge of complicity.[18]

The Intelligence Department in Cairo carried a letter from a private citizen from Constantinople on 11 September, which stated:

The Armenian question in the interior has been a succession of horrors. From ISNID and all its surroundings right up the line many women and children have been sent away with only a few articles they could carry in their hands, almost wholly unprovided with money, as they weren't allowed time to realise anything. What is going to happen to them is a mystery, but only death and starvation appear to be before them. One heard of mothers deliberately drowning their babies in the fears of the horrors before them. This is much worse than the massacres. Can no one make a step on their behalf?[19]

ARMENIANS FIGHT BACK AT JEBEL MUSA

Amongst all the terrible stories of massacres and deprivations now filtering out of Turkey, there was one which was slightly different. The Cairo report of 10 September mentioned a telegram from a French Admiral to the High Commissioner in Cyprus, detailing how 6000 Armenians were fighting bravely against the Turks at Gebel Musa near Antioch Bay. The Admiral, the report continued, had supplied them with munitions and supplies, 'but they ask for the removal of 5000 old men, women and children to CYPRUS.'[20]

All the Armenians in the villages near Gebel Musa were ordered on 30 July 1915 to depart from the country. Having witnessed what happened to the

---

18   Report of Dr. Ward, ibid.

19   Extracts from a private letter from Constantinople, 26 August 1915, cited in Military Intelligence Office, Cairo, 11 September 1915, WO 157/695.

20   Military Intelligence Office, Cairo, 8 September 1915, WO 157/695.

Armenians in Zeitun and Diarbekar, they decided to refuse the order, and consequently congregated upon Gebel Musa.

The Turks, led by German officers (according to the Armenian leaders) then attacked with some 1,000 – 1,500 soldiers, and these numbers then increased. On 5 September the Armenians managed to signal the French ship *Guichen* and the following day the Admiral met with Pierre Dimlekian 'who asked him to take off the old men, women and children, adding that the able-bodied men could hold out for a long time' if they were given weapons and flour.[21]

Unfortunately more Turkish troops arrived on 8 September, prompting the French warship *Desaix* to seek, and receive permission to bomb Turkish positions. The *Desaix* commander also stated that he believed it was imperative to rescue and take on board the women and children shortly.

On 12 September five French ships were involved in embarking the Armenians, and the fighting men would also be taken, as they had by that stage run out of ammunition. A note at the end of the communication stated: '3,444 refugees have arrived on three French cruisers at PORT SAID. Many of them are wounded.'[22]

When they arrived the refugees provided vivid accounts of what was befalling the Armenian communities in Turkey, which was reported:

> Armenian Massacres – The refugees have told horrible stories about the wholesale massacring of the Armenian population, adding that scarcely 20% of the Armenian population still exists. Wives and girls are violated and children killed.[23]

A former European resident of Beirut provided further details which were recorded on 16 September:

---

21   Military Intelligence Office, Cairo, 14 September 1915, WO 157/695.
22   Military Intelligence Office, Cairo, 14 September 1915, WO 157/695.
23   Military Intelligence Office, Cairo, 15 September 1915, WO 157/695.

In conversation with the Governor of the Imperial Ottoman Bank, on 2 September, Talaat referred to the Armenians as "Bok Millet", i.e. an excremental race, and said that their disappearance would be no loss... There have been massacres at VAN but when the [they] took the town they put all the Turks to death in revenge. There had been fighting, followed by massacre at URFA : killing of men, rape and abduction on a large scale, drowning of refugees from rafts on rivers, wholesale starvation of great numbers of women and children and execution of political suspects without trial in many places along the TAURUS and south of it.[24]

The Cairo Intelligence Report of 19 September mentioned the arrival of Dr. Hoskin of the American College in Beirut at Dedeagatch (present day Alexandroupoli) on 10 September, and the British representatives there wrote: 'He confirms all the tales of Turkish brutality to Armenians.'[25]

One displeasing bit of information was presented by a Persian Armenian at Cairo on 26 September, which stated: 'The Jews of Constantinople are taking an active part in the persecution of the Armenians. They are violently pro-German and anti-British.'[26]

On 27 September the Intelligence Report from Lemnos stated:

[Another agent] reports that Rahmi Bey, the SMYRNA Vali, is disgusted with the treatment of the Armenians, and had agreed with Pertev Pasha, in military command, to protect them. The situation therefore is somewhat easier, but many arrests are still made. 600,000 Armenians are said to be homeless, and all along the Anatolian coast groups of homeless and starving are to be seen.[27]

The Egypt Intelligence Department report for the period 8-14 September summarised the Armenian situation:

---

24 Military Intelligence Office, Cairo, 16 September 1915, WO 157/695.
25 Military Intelligence Office, Cairo, 19 September 1915, WO 157/695.
26 Military Intelligence Office, Cairo, 26 September 1915, WO 157/695.
27 War Diary or Intelligence Summary, Imbros, 27 September 1915, WO 157/649.

Armenian Massacres – Detailed information, which is beginning to arrive concerning the Armenian massacres and the general policy of the Porte towards the Armenians, tends to confirm the impression that, if Talaat Bey did not really say "I will make any idea of Armenian autonomy impossible for 50 years," he has acted on that principle. The persecution of the Armenians has taken two forms:

- Massacres most prevalent in the provinces adjoining the CAUCASUS; also executions.
- Wholesale deportations into desolate areas of the non-combatant Armenian population. Compulsorily deported Armenians may therefore be expected to starve with greater or lesser speed. Complaints of the rape and abduction of girls and women thus deported have been very general. An American medical missionary, who knows Turkey well, gives the number of Armenians massacred, starved or executed, as close to 200,000. It is to be hoped that these numbers are exaggerated.[28]

TURKISH BRUTALITY IN SYRIA

Djemal Pasha was not distanced from the outrages against the Armenians and other minorities in his vast province of Syria. On one occasion he ordered Morgenthau to inform his consuls 'to stop busying themselves in Armenian affairs.' Morgenthau ignored this order and continued to send eye-witness accounts back to America.[29]

Djemal was Governor of a province where hundreds of thousands of destitute Armenians were being deported to – and most of these then perished in Syria. One eye-witness wrote: '… at Homs there was a concentration camp of about 30,000 practically all without shelter; that there had been a massacre at Diyarbekar.'[30]

---

28   Egypt command intelligence report for the period 8-14 September, WO 157/695.
29   Morgenthau, ibid, Chapter 26, p. 9.
30   Report from a Foreign Resident at Damascus, dated 20th September, cited in Viscount Bryce, ibid, p. 558.

The harsh Turkish treatment of the civilian population was also experienced throughout the province of Syria. Ever since Djemal took control he instituted a reign of terror against those suspected of harbouring nationalist tendencies, and against the local population. Djemal publicly hung twelve Arab notables in August, after which he stated that 'he would run "to hear the cries of those damned Jews, if a few of them were hung.'"[31]

Associated with the ill-fated attack on the Suez Canal in February, Djemal had requisitioned food and supplies for his Fourth Army, thereby depriving much of the population of the essentials of life. A severe drought then followed a locust plague, further depleting the meagre food supplies. Starvation now became rampant.

Once while driving from Beirut to Damascus Aaron Aaronsohn "had become nearly demented at the sight of hundreds of starving people wandering aimlessly about and dozens of dead bodies by the roadside. Next day", wrote Verrier, "he sounded the feelings of Ali Faud Bey, Turkish Chief of Staff of the IV Army, only to be laughed at for being affected by the 'crocodile tears of half a dozen beggar women'. At that time Aaron believed the number who had died of starvation to be 50,000; he could have little doubt that it was the set policy of the Turkish Government to let Christians, Jews and the disaffected Arabs die of starvation instead of being actually massacred."[32]

RUSSIAN ADVANCES

All of these unfortunate people were being murdered under the cover of war. During the summer of 1915 this war was taking place in the Dardanelles, as well as between Turkish and Russian forces along the border region separating the two empires, from the Black Sea coast inland towards Lake Van. The fighting in this region slowed down when snow began to fall in September, which hindered communications. Then later in 1915 the Grand Duke Nicholas took command of the Russian forces in the Caucasus region.

---

31   Verrier, ibid, p. 129, citing Djemal.
32   Verrier, ibid, p. 129.

The only hope for the remaining Armenian population was for Allied breakthroughs, at the Dardanelles and in eastern Anatolia.

All the while, as the fighting was taking place, the Turkish authorities often far away from the war zone, continued their programme of destroying the Armenian nation 'under the cover of war.' Under that cover, it is conservatively estimated that up to million Armenians had been killed by the end of 1915.[33]

---

33   Balakian, ibid, Chapter 14. Viscount Bryce, ibid, pp. 649-653. Viscount Bryce calculated that there were about 600,000 who were killed outright and 600,000 who were exiled (deported). As most of these were exposed to terrible conditions it would be expected that a very large percentage of this number also perished. The Turkish authorities claim that Viscount Bryce's book was for propaganda purposes.

CHAPTER 41

§

Sherif Hussein's bold request

FEISAL RETURNS TO DAMASCUS

During his stay of almost a month in Constantinople Feisal had numerous meetings, including with the Grand Vizier, Sa'id Halim; Talaat Pasha; Enver Pasha and the Sultan on two occasions.

All of the aforementioned stressed clearly that they hoped his father, Sherif Hussein, would wholeheartedly position himself on the Turkish side, and, wrote Antonius, 'to support it by giving his endorsement to *jihad*.'[1]

Armed with this clear Turkish stance, Feisal then returned to Damascus, where he arrived on 23 May 1915. Here he discovered that the leadership of *al-Fatat* and *al-'Ahd* had together 'drawn up a protocol defining the conditions on which they would be prepared to co-operate with Great Britain against Turkey.'[2]

They requested that Feisal take this proposal, also known as the 'Damascus Protocol', back to Sherif Hussein. The proposal included:

- The boundaries for a proposed future Arab kingdom (which included the entire region of present day Iraq, Syria, Lebanon, Jordan, Israel, PA region, Arabia, except Aden).
- The abolition of all exceptional privileges granted to foreigners under

---

1 Antonius, ibid, p. 157.
2 Antonius, ibid, p. 157.

the Capitulations.

- The conclusion of a defensive alliance between Great Britain and the future independent Arab state.
- The grant of economic preference to Great Britain.[3]

Six members of the Damascus nationalist groups then pledged with Feisal on oath 'to recognize the Sharif as the spokesman of the Arab race, and pledged themselves that, in the event of his securing an agreement with Great Britain on the basis of the Damascus Protocol, the Arab divisions in Syria would rise to a man.'[4]

SYKES ARRIVES IN EGYPT

Meanwhile another of the important architects for determining the future status of the Turkish Empire, Sir Mark Sykes, arrived in the region. He visited General Hamilton on 25 June and then by the middle of July he was in Cairo where he had discussions with both McMahon and Maxwell. McMahon's response to the suggestions of the De Bunsen Committee was, as Kedourie points out, that he opposed retaining the Turkish Empire in Asia (minus Constantinople and Basra) with the same administrative structure.[5]

McMahon also favoured the partition scheme, and that the port of Haifa would be more preferable for Britain than Alexandretta, otherwise if France attained Haifa, this would place her too close to the British presence in Egypt, as well as to the impending independent Arabia.[6] He stated that if partition was adopted, 'the Palestine portion of British territory should be included in the dominions of the Sultan of Egypt.'[7]

Quite understandably, McMahon had concerns for a potential French border contiguous to Egypt – and therefore preferred that Palestine would be attached to the 'southern empire.' The opinions of Maxwell were some-

---

3   Antonius, ibid, pp. 157-8.

4   Antonius, ibid, p, 158.

5   Kedourie, E. *In the Anglo-Arab Labyrinth*, p. 63.

6   Kedourie, ibid, p. 63.

7   FO 371/2476, 106764, Sykes despatch No. 11 to Calwell, War Office Cairo, 12 July, enclosed with McMahon's despatch No. 72, Cairo 21 July 1915, cited in Kedourie, ibid, p. 63.

what different, but as he would have less bearing upon subsequent developments, the focus will be upon those sentiments of McMahon. Both of these men, though, (as well as Sykes) considered that Palestine should in some way be attached to Egypt – and thus not be attached to 'independent Arabia.'[8]

RENEWED CONTACT BETWEEN SHERIF HUSSEIN AND CAIRO

Following Feisal's return to Mecca Sherif Hussein contemplated his next move.   It came when Storrs received a letter from Abdullah, written on 14 July, which arrived in Cairo on 18 August 1915.[9]

This letter and especially the accompanying Memorandum written in Sherif Hussein's name, surprised and intrigued both Storrs and McMahon, in view of the unrealistic demands it made. From the very outset Sherif Hussein implied that he represented 'the entire Arab nation', by stating: 'Whereas the entire Arab nation without exception is determined to assert its right to live, gain its freedom and administer its own affairs in name and in fact ...'

Hussein stated, as 'the Arabs believe it to be Great Britain's interest to lend them assistance and support in the fulfilment of their steadfast and legitimate aims to the exclusion of all other aims' and that it was 'to the advantage of the Arabs ... to prefer British assistance to all other' then 'the Arab nation has decided to approach the Government of Great Britain with a request for the approval ... of the following basic provisions...'[10]

Thereafter followed six points, which Storrs and McMahon accepted were merely beginning points for discussion:

Point 1. Hussein asked that 'Great Britain recognizes the independence of the Arab countries which are bounded: on the north, by the line Mersin-Adana to parallel 37 degrees N. and thence along the line Birejik-Urfa-Mardin-Midiat-Jazirat (ibn 'Umar) – Amadia to the Persian frontier; on the east, by the Persian frontier down to the Persian Gulf; on the south by the Indian Ocean (with the exclusion of Aden whose status will remain

---

8   Kedourie, ibid, p. 64.
9   Abdullah to Storrs, 2 Ramadan [14 July 1915], FO 141/461.
10   Emir Husain to Sir Henry McMahon, Mecca, Ramadan 2, 1333, [14 July 1915], cited in Antonius, ibid, p. 414; McMahon to Foreign Office, 22 August 1915, Telegram No. 450, FO 141/461.

as at present); on the west, by the Red Sea and the Mediterranean Sea back to Mersin.

Point 2. Hussein asked that 'Great Britain will agree to the proclamation of an Arab Caliphate for Islam.

Point 3. Hussein stated that: 'The Sharifian Arab Government undertakes, other things being equal, to grant Great Britain preference in all economic enterprises in the Arab countries.'

Point 4. Hussein asked, that 'the two contracting parties undertake, in the event of any foreign state attacking either of them, to come to each other's assistance with all the resources of their military and naval forces; it being understood that peace will be concluded only when both parties concur.'

Point 5. Hussein asked, that: 'Great Britain agrees to the abolition of Capitulations in the Arab countries, and undertakes to assist the Sharifian Government in summoning an international congress to decree their abolition.'[11]

Point 6. Hussein stated that, 'Clauses 3 and 4 of the present Agreement are to remain in force for a period of fifteen years. Should either party desire an extension, due notice of one year before the expiry of that period will have to be given.'

Hussein's letter ends with this quite elaborate statement:

> Therefore, since the entire Arab nation is (God be praised) united in its resolve to pursue its noble aim to the end, at whatever cost, it requests the Government of Great Britain to return an answer, whether negatively or in the affirmative, within thirty days of the receipt of this message, in default of which it reserves its right to complete freedom of action, just as we will consider ourselves absolved from the letter and the spirit of the declaration which we made earlier through 'Ali Efendi.[12]

---

11   What Hussein was effectively calling for here was the abolition of all vestiges of the Capitulations, and thereby the return of all non-Muslims to the state of *dhimmitude* – under Islam.

12   Emir Hussein to McMahon, ibid, cited in Antonius, ibid, pp. 414-5; FO 141/461. There are some minor differences in wording between the Memorandum as quoted by Antonius and that as translated by the Residency in Cairo and sent to the Foreign Office.

Storrs himself was quite amazed by the request, 'for' he wrote 'he [Hussein] demanded, with the exception of Aden, the whole of Arabic-speaking South-West Asia.' MacMahon, Storrs wrote, 'rightly refused to commit the Government to precise areas, particularly in Western Syria and Lower Mesopotamia ... '[13]

'It was at the time and still is', wrote Storrs some time later, 'my opinion that the Sharif opened his mouth and the British Government their purse a good deal too wide.'[14] Concerning Hussein's claim to be Caliph, Storrs also wrote: 'There was ... not even as much prospect of Arab Union then as there is now.'[15] Storrs, who understood the Arab world better than most, and who was to be as actively involved in the political deliberations thereafter as anyone else, expressed his deep reservations about Hussein's claims to be the Caliph:

... Husain, who had indeed through Faisal been in touch with the Syrian revolutionaries, claimed to wield a general mandate as King of the Arabs for a Spiritual Pan-Araby, to which he knew better than we that he could lay no kind of genuine claim. Of the great Arab people of North Africa some must repudiate his Sunni claims to the Caliphate: others, like Egypt and the Sudan, vastly preferred their own superior civilization. The Christians of the Lebanon could never acknowledge him, Mesopotamia was mainly Shia, regarding his Islam about as benevolently as Alva did the Protestantism of the Low Countries; to the South the Imam Yahya[16] recognized him as nothing at all, whilst with Ibn Sa'ud on the immediate East ... he had long been on the terms which were to lead to his final ruin and exile... When in addition we reflected that 90 per cent of the Moslem world must call Husain a renegade and traitor to the Vicar of God [the Sultan – being the legitimate Caliph] we could not conceal from ourselves (and with difficulty from him) that his pretensions bordered upon the tra-

13 Storrs, ibid, p. 152.
14 Storrs, ibid, pp. 152-53.
15 Storrs, ibid, p. 153.
16 Ruler of the Yemen.

gi-comic. Nevertheless, this partial sacrifice of his name before Islam, vital to our cause though also greatly to his interest, imposed upon us the real obligation of raising and maintaining his prestige to the limit of the impossible, so that for this and other reasons we were in the end committed far more deeply in bullion, in munitions of war, and in promises very hard to fulfil, than most of us had dreamed of in September 1914.[17]

Storrs realized the impossibility of meeting these demands, and saw them merely as a beginning point for discussion. In his note to the Foreign Office of 19 August 1915, (which was attached to McMahon's Memo to the same) he stated that 'the chief point of immediate decision [was] the expulsion of the Turks and the Germans and the maintenance of tranquillity and solidarity in Arabia.'[18]

McMahon, Storrs and most of the relevant parties in the Foreign Office all understood that the Sherifians had little serious influence outside of the Hejaz. The Indian Office, however, felt it wise to hold out enough encouragement to Hussein in order to bring him towards Britain, so that he would not return into the hands of Turkey.[19] In time of war it was important to woo prospective allies to your side.

Wingate was much involved and concerned about the connection with Mecca. On 14 August 1915 he wrote to McMahon, reminding him about some notes he had put together about the Sherif of Mecca and had sent to Clayton. He also sent an accompanying memorandum just presented by Sayed Ali Morghani, which he thought might interest McMahon 'in view of the present political situation.' In relation to this political situation Wingate wrote:

---

17   Storrs, ibid, p. 153.
18   FO 371/2486, 125293/34982, No 94, 26 August 1915, cited in Kedourie, ibid, p. 68.
19   See the various discussions as outlined by Kedourie, ibid, p. 68.

The contingency of the Turks, after the capture of Constantinople, seriously turning their attention to the Hedjaz is a serious one which has always to me seen as not improbable.[20]

MCMAHON INFORMS THE GOVERNMENT

The High Commissioner informed the Foreign Office on 22 August about Hussein's letter, in which, he wrote, the Sherif 'proposes what amounts to an offensive and conditionally offensive alliance.'[21]

It was very evident that McMahon understood the groundless claims of the Emir, when he stated: 'His pretensions are in every way exaggerated doubtless considerably beyond his hope of acceptance, but it seems difficult to treat them in detail without seriously discouraging him.'[22]

McMahon then informed Grey of his proposed response, which included: 'Discussion … of boundary details premature during war, Turks not having yet been expelled from much of area in question; and H.M.G. have observed with surprise and regret, that Arabs in some areas are still neglecting this supreme opportunity and working for Turks and Germans.'[23]

His letter to Grey concluded with a common feature throughout the subsequent correspondence, that of urgency: 'Early reply requested as Messenger must return immediately.' In the following several days this matter was discussed further in Cairo and London.

The issue of the Caliphate, naturally, was also one of immense importance, and it was understood by all parties that this needed to be handled very delicately. In referring back to Kitchener's statement of November 1914, the final wording suggested by the Foreign Office telegram of 25 August (drafted by Nicolson) to McMahon read: 'if Sherif with consent of his co-religionists is proclaimed Khalifa he may rest assured that His Majesty's Government

20 Wingate to McMahon, 14 August 1915, FO 141/461, No 1198/4. Contingency = 'a future event or circumstance which is possible but cannot be predicted with certainty.' Sayed was the Muslim leader in Sudan.
21 McMahon to Foreign Office, 22 August 1915, Telegram No. 450, FO 141/161, 7198/2.
22 McMahon to Foreign Office, 22 August 1915, ibid.
23 McMahon to Foreign Office, 22 August 1915, ibid.

will welcome the resumption of Khalifate by an Arab of true race, as already indicated in Lord Kitchener's communication of last November.'[24]

It so happened, however, that McMahon chose not to write these words concerning the Caliphate in his letter of response to Hussein of 30 August, his wording being more substantive.[25]

McMahon was at this time obviously mindful of the larger situation in the region, as too was Sir Reginald Wingate in the Sudan, who wrote to Clayton on 30 August 1915:

> If the Foreign Office concurred I should personally recommend the insertion of a pious aspiration on the subject of the Sherif's illustrious ideal of an Arab union, in other words something might be added to ensure his remaining definitely on our side, at any rate until our success in the Dardanelles enables us to give more authorative expression to our views.[26]

This is an important point made by Wingate, as he drew the connection between the Dardanelles campaign and the relationship with these Arab aspirations. Even at this point most military and political analysts anticipated an Allied victory at the Dardanelles, an event which would obviously be assisted if the Arabs were with Britain and not against them.

MCMAHON'S RESPONSE

McMahon sent a communique to Grey on 26 August, enclosing the full translations of Abdullah's letter and Hussein's Memorandum, and in which he also stated:

> The moment in my opinion has not arrived when we can usefully discuss even a preliminary agreement, and it might at this stage injure

---

24　Foreign Office to McMahon, Telegram No. 598, 25 August 1915, FO 141/461, 1198/3; FO 371/2486, 117236 and 118580/34982,McMahon's telegram no. 450, Cairo 22 Aug, Hirtzel's letter 24 August 1915, and Minutes, cited in Kedourie, ibid, p. 69.

25　Kedourie, ibid, pp. 69-70.

26　Wingate to Clayton, 30 August 1915, FO 141/461, No. 565. Wingate's message arrived after McMahon's letter was already complete.

the Sherif's chances of the Khaliphate to advertise his dealings with us by sending a son or other notable to treat with us.

I have also omitted any explicit mention of the Sherif as the future Khaliph as the terms of my message will be sufficiently clear to him on this point.[27]

McMahon then wrote his reply to the Sherif on 30 August, stating: 'it pleases us … to learn that Your Lordship and your people are at one in believing that the Arab interests are in harmony with British interests, and vice-versa.' 'In earnest of this' McMahon continued, 'we hereby confirm to you the declaration of Lord Kitchener … in which was manifested our desire for the independence of the Arab countries and their inhabitants, and our readiness to approve an Arab caliphate upon its proclamation.'[28]

Ignoring the words of the Foreign Office, McMahon then stated: 'We now declare once more that the Government of Great Britain would welcome the reversion of the caliphate to a true Arab born of the blessed stock of the Prophet.'[29]

On the matter of boundaries, McMahon never deviated from his wording as stated to Grey, stating: 'As for the question of frontiers and boundaries, negotiations would appear to be premature and a waste of time on details at this stage, with the War in progress and the Turks in effective occupation of the greater part of those regions…'[30] McMahon's letter was then entrusted to the trustworthy Arab messenger who journeyed with it to Mecca.

As this messenger was on his way another Arab messenger was soon to make his appearance at the opposite side of the Mediterranean - at Gallipoli.

---

27 McMahon to Grey, 26 August 1916, FO 141/461, No. 94.
28 McMahon to Sharif Hussein, 30 August 1915, cited in Antonius, ibid, p. 416.
29 This is how Antonius translates the Arabic, while in McMahon's communique to Grey on 25 August, he just states 'by an Arab of true race.'
30 McMahon to Hussein, 30 August 1915, as cited in Antonius, ibid, p. 416.

CHAPTER 42

§

Preparing for a final assault

PREPARATIONS FOR A RENEWED ASSAULT

Following the decision of the Dardanelles Committee on 7 June 1915 to send another three divisions to the Dardanelles there were again delays. The original plan was for these three divisions to land in early July, when there was no moonlight. This landing was then postponed until August, again when there was no moonlight.

This delay allowed the Turks to bring in more reinforcements of their own. Von Sanders knew that 'another great landing was imminent'[1], but now he had to determine where it would occur. He looked at the various options, and considered that the Gulf of Saros could again be a possibility, with an Allied landing there potentially cutting the Peninsula in two.[2]

The Allied plan, though, was to land the New Army divisions at Suvla Bay, north of Anzac Cove, on 6 August, with simultaneous diversionary attacks being staged at both the ANZAC and Helles sectors.

The idea of landing at Suvla Bay originated, Hamilton stated, with Birdwood, who believed that with another Division he could capture the Sari Bair Ridge. From there, Hamilton stated: 'the Turkish trenches opposite Birdwood can be enfilidated: the land *and* sea communications of the

---

1   Von Sanders, ibid, p. 79.
2   Von Sanders, ibid, pp. 81-82.

enemy holding Maidos, Kilid Bahr and Krithia can be seen and shelled and, in fact, any strong force of Turks guarding the European side of the Narrows can then be starved out …'[3]

The plan might be simple in theory, but the carrying out of it would be very difficult. 'The ground between Anzac and the Sari Bair crestline' wrote Hamilton 'is worse than the Kyhber Pass but both Birdwood and Godley say their troops can handle it.'[4]

While Hamilton waited for the arrival of the new forces and equipment, which would be commanded by Lieutenant-General Sir Frederick Stopford, he also knew that extra Turkish reinforcements were arriving. These included some 20,000 mostly Arab soldiers from Syria.[5]

His mood, though, was tempered a little when he heard that M. Venezelos had gained a big majority in the Greek elections, and there was now a greater possibility of Greek involvement in the campaign.[6]

Meanwhile the French 1st and 2nd Divisions mounted a big offensive on 21 June aimed at Kereves Dere, of which Hamilton wrote on 22 June: 'Gourard has done splendidly; so have his troops. This has been a serious defeat for the Turks; a real bad defeat …'[7]

This victory gave the MEF commanders more confidence for the future.

THE LAST PUSH BEFORE THE 9TH CORPS ARRIVED

The MEF had sufficient ammunition to launch one last major push before the arrival of the 9th Corps – also known as the New Army. This push began on 28 June at Helles, and this time while the British infantry attacked, the French artillery gave assistance. The initial result was even more than Hamilton had anticipated, and once again they believed that Achi Baba was within reach – had they had sufficient ammunition to complete the task.

---

3   Hamilton, ibid, p. 147.
4   Hamilton, ibid, p. 148.
5   Hamilton to French, 17 June 1915, cited in Hamilton, ibid, p. 140.
6   Hamilton, ibid, p. 142.
7   Hamilton, ibid, p. 145.

Simultaneous to this push, the ANZAC force attacked towards Gabe Tepe as a feint – which worked, as Von Sanders had to bring back some of the men due to reinforce the Helles sector.

The following day the French made further inroads, capturing the contested Quadrilateral position. This positive action was somewhat negated as General Gouraud was seriously wounded and had to be repatriated back to France.[8]

This battle continued to rage into early July, with the Turks mounting a large counter-attack on 5 July. Many of the Turkish soldiers involved in this new assault were fresh recruits - two Divisions had newly arrived from Adrianople.[9]

In the end both sides ended up more-or-less where they had started.

ARRIVAL OF GENERAL STOPFORD AND NEW FRENCH INITIATIVE

Lieutenant-General Stopford arrived on 11 July 1915, and he and Hamilton immediately went over the plans for the planned big offensive. Meanwhile the French Corps and 52nd Lowland Division fought another small battle on 12 July, gaining further ground in the Helles sector. This battle continued for several days, and the Royal Naval Division fought perhaps its last battle, as what remained of them would soon be withdrawn back to the ships.[10]

On 27 July Poincare recorded a meeting in which General Gourard expressed, that 'three or four more Divisions ought to be sent to the Dardanelles.'[11] The French leaders agreed, and then informed General Joffre, the French Commander-in-Chief.

Joffre preferred that the French Expeditionary Force only be sent after September following a major offensive being planned in France.[12] General Sarrail was released to take command of the French forces in the Dardanelles in anticipation of the later arrival of the extra Divisions.[13]

---

8   Hamilton, ibid, p. 160.
9   Hamilton was also informed on 5 July that 5,000 Russian soldiers had just sailed from Vladivostock to join the Allies at Gallipoli. Hamilton, ibid, p. 166. On 19 July, however, he was informed that these Russians were being sent elsewhere. Hamilton, ibid, Vol 2, p. 21.
10   Hamilton, ibid, Vol. 2, pp. 7-9.
11   Poincare, ibid, p. 173.
12   Poincare, ibid, p. 174.
13   Poincare, ibid, p. 176.

One very positive move in the French sector was the installation of some heavy guns at the strategic de Tott's Battery in the end of July, which enabled them to return fire upon the Turkish guns based on the Asian side.

PREPARING FOR THE AUGUST OFFENSIVE

Harry Chauvel returned from Egypt on 3 August and found his Brigade in the same position as when he left it. In fact life in general was just as he left it, as Hill records:

> The days now blazed with heat; the flies were, if possible, worse than in June, water was short and dysentery and septic sores were rife. Carrying water up to the position was exhausting but there was no way of avoiding such heavy work. Then, to add to their burdens, there were rumours of a gas attack; respirators had already been issued and troops were learning to use them.[14]

Another Light Horseman who arrived with Chauvel was Lieutenant Hugo Throssell, a reinforcement for the 10th Light Horse Regiment. Chauvel and Throssell arrived in time for the great offensive, the last Allied attempt to break out at Gallipoli. While there would be a significant feint in the Helles sector, most of the fighting would occur in the ANZAC sector. All of this fighting was diversionary in nature, as the Allies were to land the 9th British Corps (the New Army), at Suvla Bay to the north of the ANZAC sector.

Hamilton's overall plan was:

- The Lancashire and Lowland Territorial Division was to attack the Turkish lines protecting Krithia.
- 1st Australian Division was to attack Lone Pine and German Officer's Trench, aimed ultimately towards Gabe Tepe. This assault was a decoy to draw as many Turkish soldiers as possible to this area, and away from the Sari Bair Ridge.

14 Hill, ibid, p. 58.

- The 9th British Corps was then to be landing at Suvla Bay. This force included elements of the Yeomanry Division which was based in Egypt.[15]
- The New Zealand and Australia Division was to advance during the night of 6-7 August to the strategic Sari Bair Ridge and take Chunuk Bair, Hill Q and Koja Chemen Tepe (or Hill 971). British, Indian and Ghurkha troops were brought up from Helles to join the Anzac forces.
- Simultaneous to the capture of these heights, anticipated for early in morning of 7 August, there was to be an assault against the strong Turkish position of Baby 700 from Russell's Top. The New Zealand-ers, having now taken the higher points on the Sari Bair Ridge, were then to attack from the other direction, thereby catching the Turks in a pincer movement. This assault on Baby 700 would include the 3rd Light Horse Brigade attacking the Nek position, and the 1st Light Horse Brigade attacking from Quinn's Post.
- The British and French troops at the Helles sector would contin-ue their assault so as to draw the Turkish attention away from the ANZAC and Suvla sectors.

PREPARATIONS FOR BATTLE

Several months previously General Mustapha Kemal sensed that an impend-ing Allied assault would target the Sari Bair Ridge, and that these troops would come from the Suvla Bay area and along the seemingly impenetrable Sazlidere Ravine. Kemal's Corps commander, Essad Pasha, disagreed with his assessment.[16]

A small Turkish force was, though, placed in the region of Suvla Bay. This force was commanded by Major Willmer, who concentrated some of his men upon Hill 10 to the north of the Salt Lake, and Lala Baba to the

---

15   The remainder of the Yeomanry remained in Egypt and in November were involved in quelling the Senussi invasion of Egypt. Some of those at Gallipoli would later be involved in the capture of Jerusalem, especially the Worcester and Westminster Hussars Regiments.

16   Moorehead, A. *Gallipoli*, pp. 174-5.

south, between the dried up lake and the sea. The remainder of this force was located about five kilometres inland around a series of hills.[17]

This force of some 1,500 men was to defend the Suvla Bay area against any Allied invading force. The odds as it worked out were stacked heavily against them.

Meanwhile the Allied soldiers were fully aware of the seriousness of the upcoming battle. Private T. Oliver of the 7th Australian Battalion wrote to his mother on 3 August: 'Don't have any fear for me, I am ready for whatever comes and quite prepared to die for king and country…'[18] New Zealander William Malone wrote to his wife: 'I expect to go thro alright, but … if anything happens to me you must not grieve too much – there are our dear children to be brought up - … I am prepared for death and I hope that God will have forgiven me all my sins.'[19]

17   Moorehead, ibid, p. 175.
18   McCleod, G. Anzacs, (North Ryde, 1985), p. 58.
19   Letter dated 5 August 1915, Queen Elizabeth II Army Museum, ibid, cited in Pugsley, ibid, p. 263.

§

CHAPTER 43

The August offensive

8TH CORPS ATTACK KRITHIA

The great battle to determine the future of the Dardanelles Campaign began on the afternoon of 6 August. At Helles the soldiers of the 8th Corps advanced against the Turkish lines aiming once again at Krithia. Unbeknown to them, the Turks had just brought up two new divisions to the front line. Although the 8th Corps soldiers captured some Turkish trenches, the Turks mounted intense counter-attacks during the night, and by the morning of 7 August had regained those lost positions.[1]

Hamilton's analysis after the initial day was: 'Fighting is going on and we ought to be pinning the enemy to the South which is the main thing.'[2] The two forces thereafter clashed head on for one entire week in the Helles sector.

ATTACK ON LONE PINE

While the 8th Corps attacked towards Krithia, the Australian Division made its feint to the south of their sector as if heading towards Gabe Tepe. The main location they were to capture was located near Lone Pine.

---

1 Hamilton to Kitchener, No. M.F. 562, 17 August 1915, cited in Hamilton, ibid, Vol. 2, p. 50.
2 Hamilton, ibid, Vol. 2, p. 27.

The Australian infantry at 1730 hours in the afternoon charged out of their trenches and headed for the strongly fortified Turkish trenches, the first of which was covered over with pine logs. Thereafter some of the most desperate hand-to-hand fighting ever witnessed took place. The degree of intense fighting by the Australians is evidenced by the fact that seven Victoria Crosses were awarded for that assault.

Lone Pine was so important for the Turks that they sent whatever forces available to them in an effort to recapture it. They failed. Hamilton recorded that it was 'a desperate fine feat.'[3] That was an under-statement if ever there was one. In his telegram to Kitchener, he expanded and stated that the 'afternoon attack was successful and Lone Pine trenches were captured by a most gallant Australian assault. Throughout the day, and for three successive days the enemy made repeated attempts to recapture the position, but each time were repulsed with severe loss.'[4]

The master plan at least in the ANZAC sector seemed to be working. Theoretically there were now fewer Turkish troops guarding the Sari Bair Ridge. When news finally came through to the Turkish headquarters of this assault Von Sanders contacted his two divisions (the 7th and 12th) in the upper Saros Gulf to be prepared for an immediate march, which they did shortly later, to the Suvla Bay area. The 9th Division was also summoned towards the same area. It would take some time before all these reinforcements would arrive.

LANDINGS AT SUVLA BAY

In the early evening of 6 August the first echelon of some 7,000 soldiers from the 9th Corps under Lieutenant-General Stopford landed uncontested at B Beach south of the Salt Lake at Suvla Bay. As they moved inland the Turkish soldiers on Lala Baba sent up a flare, and then began to fire on the British soldiers who were heading in their direction.

---

3 Hamilton, ibid, Vol. 2, p. 27.
4 Hamilton to Kitchener, No. M.F. 562, 17 August 1915, cited in Hamilton, ibid, Vol. 2, p. 50.

A fierce fire-fight ensued and up to one third of the British soldiers were hit, but they succeeded in driving the Turks from the position. They were supposed to meet men from their third brigade, but when they never arrived, these soldiers remained put. The reason the third brigade never arrived was because they landed at the wrong location - in the dark the landing craft got lost among numerous small reefs When the moon rose about two in the morning some of the troops headed towards what they thought was their objective, Hill 10, but which wasn't. Other troops came upon Kiretch Tepe Ridge further north. Others remained on the beach in a state of confusion.

By morning Major-General Hamersley, commander of the 11th Division, realized the objects of the landing – the inland hills - had not been reached. Hamilton, at his GHQ on Imbros was frustrated at the lack of news. Later, when he heard how the initial landings had not fulfilled their objectives, he wrote that the failure was owed, 'to lack of energy and determination on the part of the leaders, and, perhaps, partly to the inexperience of the troops, had failed to take advantage of the opportunities …'[5]

Instead of rectifying the situation, the following morning confusion reigned, and no clear-cut decision made and order given. Hamilton was on Imbros and Stopford was on the *HMS Jonquil*. No-one on land took possession of the overall objective – which was the capture of the inland hills which would connect the Suvla and ANZAC sectors.

ADVANCE TOWARDS SARI BAIR RIDGE

The first advance towards the summit of the Sari Bair Ridge began at about 2100 hours on 6 August. The striking force was composed of men from the New Zealand and Australian Division, the 29th Division and 13th Division. Their initial objective was to be at the summit by dawn on 7 August, at which time there would be an assault upon Turkish positions in the Anzac sector, primarily in the region of Baby 700.

One assaulting force headed down the Sazlidere Ravine and some initially succeeded in reaching Rhododendron Ridge, but some of them also

---

5   Hamilton to Kitchener, No. M.F. 562, 17 August 1915, cited in Hamilton, ibid, Vol. 2, p. 51.

got lost. The second attacking force had to take a longer circuitous route and when their guides decided to take a short cut, they came to a standstill when confronted by difficult terrain and Turkish soldiers. One of those involved in executing this difficult night march was Eleazar Margolin of the 16th Battalion.[6]

A combination of factors therefore resulted in the New Zealand and Australia Division and associated troops not reaching their positions at the appointed time. Sari Bair Ridge was supposed to have been assaulted at 0300 hours but wasn't, as the terrain was more difficult and Turkish resistance stronger than anticipated. Then the Turkish reinforcements summoned by Von Sanders were just arriving on the scene.

'SUICIDE' AT THE NEK

The key attack upon the Baby 700 position at the Nek was scheduled to begin at 0430 hours on 7 August, immediately at the conclusion of a British Naval bombardment. The bombardment, though, ended seven minutes earlier than scheduled. The officers did not send the troops over the top during that interval, thereby permitting the Turkish soldiers time to return to their front-line trenches and man their machine guns.[7]

As the whistle went first one line and then another of Victorians from the 8th Light Horse Regiment went over the top and were systematically mown down by Turkish fire. Then it was the turn of the West Australians from the 10th Light Horse, and they too were mown down, although some, like Hugo Throssell, survived the carnage.

Finally the commander had the common sense to halt this suicide, and the last line remained in the trenches – and survived. In total some 234 young Australians lay dead, most just metres from the front line trenches.[8]

New Zealander Ken Stevens observed the attack from Old No 3 Outpost, and stated: 'We did not see one of them reach the enemy trenches which

---

6 Gouttman, ibid, p. 46.

7 There are numerous accounts of this sad episode, and where the fault lay in ordering the men to proceed with what was a certain suicide mission. One good source is John Hamilton, *The Price of Valour*, (Sydney, 2012).

8 Australian War Memorial, Charge at the Nek, www.awm.gov.au.

were only twelve yards in front of them.'[9] In an article that was later printed in the *Daily Express* in Britain, correspondent Captain Charles Bean, stated that 'for sheer self-sacrificing heroism there was never a deed in history that surpassed the charge which two Australian Light Horse Brigades made in the first light of Saturday, August 7, in order to help their comrades in a critical moment of a great battle.'[10] Lieutenant Colonel Meldrum stated, though, from a moral and military perspective, that there was: 'No greater record of crass stupidity.'[11]

While this massacre of the innocents was taking place the Allied troops on the heights could look down over the Suvla Bay and see the men of the 9th Army Corps landing below them. Some of these men achieved the objectives given to them, while others remained on the beaches, oblivious to the sacrifices taking place only kilometres away.

THE BATTLE FOR SARI BAIR RIDGE BEGINS

In the middle of the morning of 7 August the Gurkha soldiers had extricated themselves from the wild terrain and joined the New Zealanders on Rhododendron Ridge, and thereupon assaulted the ridge at Chunuk Bair.

As the Turkish 9th Division was approaching the position of Koja Chemen Tepe, a report came to Von Sanders that Allied infantry were ascending the same ridge from the northern side. The two sides then clashed atop the ridge.[12] The Turks, led by a German officer named Colonel Kannengiesser, managed to stop the New Zealanders and Gurkhas from gaining control. Von Sanders stated that this was the first crisis they had to overcome. It was imperative that the Allies did not 'retain possession of the summits of this massive height' wrote Von Sanders, who further stated:

---

9   Stevens, K.M. *Maungatapere: A History and Remembrance,* (Whangarei, 1973), p. 101, cited in Kinloch, T. *Echoes of Gallipoli,* (Auckland, 2005), p. 210.

10   *Daily Express,* 4 October 1915.

11   Waite, Major F. *The New Zealanders at Gallipoli,* (Auckland, 1919), p. 201, cited in Kinloch, T. *Echoes of Gallipoli,* (Auckland, 2005), p. 210.

12   Von Sanders, ibid, pp. 83-84.

It dominated the Anafarta valley to the north, and to the south afforded artillery positions towards the straits of the Dardanelles a long stretch of which was in full view.[13]

While the main Allied objective was the capture of that strategic ridge, the main objective of Von Sanders now was the retention of that ridge. Henceforth the safeguarding of that strategic position was entrusted to Mustapha Kemal.

HAMILTON COMES TO SUVLA

General Hamilton came to Suvla Bay late on 7 August, and was aghast at the lack of penetration inland of the forces. Following the capture of Hill 10 in the morning, the troops did not quickly pursue the retreating Turks due to lack of supplies, especially water. Hamilton desired the immediate capture of the strategic Tekke Tepe position.[14] He understood full well the need to capture the Anafarta Hills before the anticipated Turkish reinforcements coming from both Asia and Bulair arrived and beat them to it. Several vital water wells were also located in the vicinity.

Major Willmer meanwhile was desperate to receive reinforcements as quickly as possible from Bulair to bolster his meagre force of 1,500.

Hamilton was perturbed at the lack of preparedness of these New Army Divisions to make the extra effort to achieve this important goal. In his frustration he ordered the 32nd Brigade, 11th Division 'to advance *at once and dig themselves in on the crestline.*[15] Hamilton was keen to capture Tekke Tepe quickly, as he could see it was the key to the entire Suvla Bay sector. The key to capturing Tekke Tepe Ridge were two small mounds named Chocolate Hill and Hill 70.

In the late afternoon of 7 August the leading British forces moved towards these objectives, and Chocolate Hill was taken. The New Army soldiers, however, proceeded no further, as no orders or reinforcements arrived.

---

13   Von Sanders, ibid, p. 84.
14   Hamilton, ibid, Vol. 2, pp. 28-29.
15   Hamilton, ibid, Vol. 2, p. 30. Italics in the original.

After the first day none of the major objectives at Suvla Bay had been obtained. A small Turkish force had virtually brought a British force of some 20,000 men to a standstill. Alan Moorehead states of this situation: 'There is something so mocking about this situation, something so wrong, that one feels that it is not explained by all the errors and mischances that had occurred.'[16]

Early in the morning of 8 August the Turkish troops in Suvla Bay were congregated around the village of Anafarta Sagir. The key position was Tekke Tepe, and the indications were that there were no Turkish soldiers there. On that day Hamilton despatched Colonel Aspinall to Suvla, who communicated to Hamilton 'golden opportunities are being lost and look upon situation as serious.'[17]

Hamilton arrived at Suvla late on 8 August and was furious about the lack of progress and urgency. He finally managed to persuade General Hammersley to send the 32nd Brigade immediately and take the summit of Tekke Tepe before the Turkish reinforcements arrived. It was now a race against time – would the men of the 11th Division arrive before Turkish re-inforcements did?

CAPTURE OF CHUNUK BAIR

During the night of 7/8 August Godley managed to consolidate his force, and organized them into five columns. Early in the morning of 8 August these columns set out for three separate peaks of the Sari Bair Ridge. Captain Allanson and his Gurkhas almost obtained Hill Q, but just failed. His force was then fired upon from above, and had to endure the remainder of the day under constant sniper fire.

Two companies of New Zealanders under Lieutenant-Colonel Malone managed to attack and take Chunuk Bair. They then dug in, but throughout the remainder of the day came under intense fire from Turkish positions further above them on the Ridge. By the end of the day Malone and many of the New Zealanders had been killed.

---

16 Moorehead, ibid, p. 179.
17 Hamilton, ibid, Vol. 2, p. 30.

Chunuk Bair, the key to the success of the Gallipoli Campaign, which had been reached on 25 April and then lost again – was finally in Allied hands. Desperate hand to hand fighting then ensued, but the Allied soldiers managed to keep this strategic position. New Zealander Major Arthur Temperley wrote:

> The New Zealand Infantry Brigade was for 48 hours … at the throat of the Turkish Empire and had support been forthcoming at the right time and place and had certain events turned out differently, the Turkish Army would have been beaten, Constantinople would have fallen and the war might have been shortened by two years.[18]

On 8 August Von Sanders gave command of the Anafarta area over to Mustapha Kemal. This area comprised both the Suvla Bay and Sari Bair sectors, and he now had six Turkish divisions under his command.[19] Kemal immediately sensed the danger and made desperate moves. It was a race against time for both sides.

While Kemal was bringing reinforcements to the ridge, the Allied force was reinforced by Lancashire and Wiltshiremen and Gurkha's from the 13th Division, relieving the exhausted New Zealanders. It all depended now upon which force could attain and maintain the ridge the longest.

TURKISH COUNTER-ATTACK AT ANAFARTA

Kemal ordered a general Turkish attack, from Tekke Tepe through to the Sari Bair Ridge for the early morning of 9 August. As these Turkish soldiers were moving towards their positions, New Army troops of the 32nd Brigade were moving towards the strategic Tekke Tepe Ridge. As they approached, the Turks charged over the top towards them.

A wild melee followed as the Turks poured fire into the British troops. Hamilton observed these movements from the bridge of his ship, and stated:

---

18 'A Personal Narrative of the Battle of Chunuk Bair, 6-10 August 1915' by Colonel A.C. Temperley, (MS 0017), cited in Pugsley, ibid, p. 287.

19 Mango, ibid, Part 2, Chapter 8.

'… we could see the enemy advancing behind their own bursting shrapnel and rolling up our line … The enemy counter-attack was coming from the direction of Tekke Tepe and moving over the foothills and plain on Sulajik.'[20]

Although some of the men of the 11th Division made a stand, the Turkish counter-attack drove elements of the New Army back towards the sea. Hamilton's disappointment at a lost opportunity is revealed in his words: 'our occupation of the open key positions has been just too late! The element of surprise – wasted! The prime factor set aside for the sake of other factors! Words are no use.'[21]

LOSS OF HILL Q AND CHUNUK BAIR

On the morning of 9 August Brigadier-General Baldwin and four fresh British battalions were to advance towards Hill Q. A massive naval bombardment began at 0430 hours, and at 0523 hours these fresh troops sprang from their positions. Following fierce hand-to-hand combat they obtained their position – but later lost it to a fierce Turkish counter-attack.

During the night of 9/10 August New Army soldiers replaced the badly depleted New Zealanders. Then early in the morning of 10 August despite the tiredness of his men, Kemal had ordered a general charge against the British soldiers entrenched at Chunuk Bair. Kemal personally led the assault, and despite many of his soldiers being killed by Allied shelling, the Turkish soldiers overwhelmed the Allied troops, and pursued them into the valleys and positions below, especially one place called the Farm where hundreds of young British men died.

Mustapha Kemal recaptured the strategic Sari Bair Ridge. When Chunuk Bair was lost the last opportunity of an Allied breakthrough was lost with it.

HAMILTON'S PREDICAMENT

Every hour in which the initiative was not won, was an hour in which the Turks would bring forward reinforcements. This situation became even

---

20   Hamilton, ibid, Vol 2, p. 31.
21   Hamilton, ibid, Vol. 2, p. 32.

more desperate when Hamilton was informed on 10 August from the Helles sector that the Turks had withdrawn some of their troops and were sending them to the northern sectors of ANZAC and Suvla.[22]

Despite all of the stalwart efforts made in all three sectors, by 13 August Hamilton had to concede that the impetus had gone out of the Suvla attack. Hamilton accordingly advised Kitchener by telegram that evening that, 'the swift advance was not delivered, - therefore, the mischief is done.'[23] Kitchener in reply suggested that Stopford be replaced.[24] Hamilton implemented this order immediately, and the command of the 9th Corp (temporarily) was given over to Major-General Beauvoir de Lisle.[25] Another new commander was Major-General Frederick Maude who came to take command of 13th Division.

FURTHER ASSAULT ON 15 AUGUST

The third and final crisis which Von Sanders and the Turks needed to overcome began on 15 August when the Allies attacked along the northern region of the Suvla Bay region. The Allies brought up for this major offensive elements of the 29th Division, the Yeomanry Division (dismounted) from Egypt and the New Zealand and Australian Division. The strategic area of contention was the Kiretch Tepe Ridge (close to the coast), and, wrote Von Sanders: 'They were successful at first and advanced beyond the middle of the ridge.'[26]

The Allied force had a great opportunity, but once Turkish reinforcements arrived that opportunity too was lost. After two concentrated days of fighting, the Turks managed to halt the Allied advance, and they thereafter retained a strategic position on the Ridge.

Once again there were numerous casualties on both sides during this intense period of fighting. One of those was Albert Facey (who had already lost one brother killed) who was wounded and evacuated on 19 August on

---

22   Hamilton, ibid, Vol. 2, p. 41.
23   Hamilton, ibid, Vol. 2, p. 46.
24   Kitchener to Hamilton, 14 August 1915, cited in Hamilton, ibid, Vol. 2, pp. 46-7.
25   General de Lisle was commander of 29th Division, having replaced General Hunter-Weston. Following the unsuccessful Third Battle of Krithia in July, Hunter-Weston was sent home for 'medical reasons.'
26   Von Sanders, ibid, p. 86.

the ship *Ulysses*. He wrote: 'We couldn't help thinking of our mates that we left behind …'[27] Shortly afterwards while recovering at No. 1. Australian General Hospital in Heliopolis, he received word that his other brother had also been killed at Gallipoli. Light Horseman Ion Idriess was also wounded and was subsequently moved to a hospital in Egypt.

FINAL AUGUST OFFENSIVE AT SUVLA AND HILL 60

Despite the disappointments, Hamilton was still resolved to make the most of the New Army Divisions at his disposal, so one more attempt was to be made in the Suvla sector. The plan was for the ANZACs and Indian Brigade to attack the strategic Hill 60, while the 11th Division was to aim for Hetman Chair, and the 29th Division for Hill 70.

With these positions held, then the Allies would be in possession of the Anafarta Hills, from whence they could hinder any Turkish artillery fire on to the 9th Corps troops westwards, and from where they could themselves bombard the Turkish positions on the Sari Bair Ridge.

The attack began in the afternoon of 21 August, and apart from the Yeomanry being enfiladed by Turkish artillery, there was much optimism. The presumed capture of the strategic Hill 70 in particular pleased Hamilton, who was at Suvla at the time of the commencement of the attack.[28] The attack from the ANZAC sector managed to capture the locations of Kabak Kuyu and Kaiajik Aghala.

The following day Hamilton discovered that Hill 70 had not in fact been captured. This was a great disappointment.[29] Another major assault had been thwarted, and once again Hamilton had to admit as much to Kitchener, and at the same time request reinforcements. These were necessary he stated, as the casualties since 6 August (including sickness) amounted to some 40,000 of his men.[30]

The fighting in and around Hill 60 was intense. Eliazar Margolin and his men of the 16th Battalion were actively involved and by 28 August

---

27 Facey, ibid, p. 274.
28 Hamilton, ibid, Vol. 2, p. 56.
29 Hamilton, ibid, Vol. 2, p. 57.
30 Hamilton to Kitchener, No. M.F. 578, 23 August 1915, cited in Hamilton, ibid, Vol. 2, p. 58.

only 185 men remained in his battalion. The number of casualties resulted in Margolin being promoted to second-in-command under Lieutenant-
Colonel Pope.[31]

In his diary for 28 August Hamilton mentioned 'Cox's attack on Knoll
60 to the North-east of Kaiajik Aghala came off well. The New Zealanders
under Russell and the Connaught Rangers did brilliantly. Fighting is still
going on.'[32]

During this intense fighting at Hill 60 the 10th Light Horse – those who
had survived the massacre at the Nek - were once again in action. They
were involved in a very intense assault on 29 August where Lieutenant Hugo
Throssell showed exemplary bravery under fire. Throssell was later awarded
the Victoria Cross.[33]

That the fighting during these last battles of August was intense is testified to by Von Sanders, who recorded: 'On the 21st August the enemy combined all the troops recently landed on the new front in a grand attack on,
and on both sides of, the Anafarta plain. It led to severe and bloody fighting
but was repulsed by the Turks who had to use their last reserves including the cavalry. Various English papers stated the enemy's (British) losses
as about 15,000 killed and 45,000 wounded. Between the 22nd and 26th of
August we had to transport 26,000 wounded to the rear.'[34]

CONSEQUENCES OF DEFEAT

When it became apparent that no reinforcements were forthcoming,
Hamilton had to consider the possibility of relinquishing one of the three
sectors. But then General Byng arrived to take over command of the 9th
Corps, and news came in that Italy had at last joined the war effort by declar-
ing war against Turkey. Hamilton was again optimistic of better things.[35]
He again imagined the possibilities – that gaining three or four miles, he

---

31 Gouttman, ibid, p. 46.

32 Hamilton, ibid, Vol. 2, p. 67.

33 Like most of those who survived, Throssell was badly wounded. As the hospitals in Egypt and Malta were full, he like
many others had to be taken to hospital in England. After he recovered Throssell returned to Australia before returning to
join the Light Horse at Gaza.

34 Von Sanders, ibid, p. 90.

35 Hamilton, ibid, Vol. 2, p. 60.

wrote, would 'give us the strategical hub of the universe – Constantinople!' Gaining Constantinople 'would give us' he continued 'Asia; Africa; the Balkans; the Black Sea; the mouths of the Danube: it would enable us to swap rifles for wheat with the Russians; more vital still, it would tune up the hearts of the Russian soldiery to the Anglo-Saxon pitch.'[36]

Indeed an Allied victory in August would have altered the outcome of the War, as confirmed by Von Sanders: 'Secure communication between the Western Powers and Russia would have been established and Turkey would have been split off from the Central Powers. In that case it is more than probable that Bulgaria would have relinquished her neutrality and precipitated herself into such an unpromising military situation.'[37]

But the Allies did not succeed, and as a result there would be repercussions. Neutral nations were observing the outcome of this campaign. Serbia was already committed to the Allied cause, but other Balkan countries were not.

The most strategic nation was Bulgaria, which stood between the area controlled by the Central Powers and Turkey. While Bulgaria was neutral there was no direct supply and communication link between the two.

Despite all of the set-backs in August, one bright spot came from the French. Poincare recorded on 31 August: 'It has been decided that anyhow four Divisions shall be ready to start on the 20th September for the Dardanelles and that if necessary four more shall go as soon as possible.'[38]

With four, perhaps even eight, new French divisions on the way, victory at Gallipoli was still a strong possibility.

36 Hamilton, ibid, Vol. 2, p. 60.
37 Von Sanders, ibid, p. 89.
38 Poincare, ibid, p. 209.

SULVA BAY SECTOR

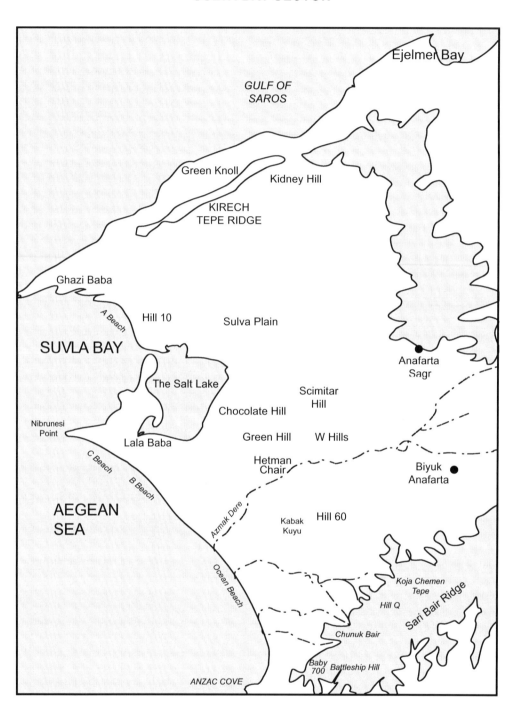

§

CHAPTER 44

Mesopotamia, Syria and Palestine

FROM AMARA TO KUT-EL-AMARA

Although there was much focus upon the Gallipoli Campaign, the operations in Mesopotamia, which were occurring simultaneously, were also of significant military and geo-political consequence. The British-India force under the overall command of General Sir John Nixon continued its northward journey from Basra towards Baghdad under the leadership of Major-General Charles Townshend. This British-Indian force captured Amara on 3 June 1915. Then after consolidating his forces, Townshend continued on to the strategic location of Kut-el-Amara, which he captured on 29 September.

With this victory the *Vilayet* of Basra had now effectively been captured – which had been the main objective of the Mesopotamian Expeditionary Force. But then, following the arrival of fresh reinforcements and supplies, Townshend proceeded under Nixon's orders northwards towards Azizie.

The Turkish High Command finally understood the gravity of the situation, and in October Field Marshal von der Goltz was sent to Mesopotamia to command the Turkish Sixth Army.[1]

THE ATTACK ON BAGHDAD

General Nixon then commanded Townshend to proceed north and capture Baghdad. Townshend was unsure and wrote as much to the Viceroy of India on 2 November, stating that his troops were tired and dispirited and were going down 'with every imaginable disease.'[2]

Nevertheless, with about 15,000, soldiers (albeit fatigued and under supplied) General Townshend set out in the middle of November 1915 for Baghdad. Just to the south of this ancient city the British-led force was met and brought to battle at Ctesiphon.

Although Townshend claimed victory, about half of his force were casualties. He then became aware that Field Marshal von der Goltz was approaching with an estimated 30,000 Turkish reinforcements – many of whom had come from Gallipoli.[3] Townshend only had about 4,500 able bodied soldiers remaining.[4] He chose to retreat on 25 November.

After suffering considerable casualties during the retreat, the Mesopotamian Expeditionary Force reached Kut-el-Amara on 3 December. From there Townshend evacuated his sick and wounded down river to Basra, most of whom arrived there several days later in a deplorable state.[5]

On 7 December 1915 the Turkish force prepared to attack the remaining British forces holed up in Kut-el-Amara. Herein began a siege which was to last some four months. All during that time Townshend awaited the arrival of a relief force.

---

1   Mustapha Kemal had hoped to get this command.
2   Knight, W. *The History of the Great European War*, (London), Vol. VII, p. 75.
3   Knight, ibid, p. 76.
4   Fromkin, ibid, p. 201.
5   Knight, ibid, p. 78.

PREPARATIONS FOR FURTHER ATTACK ON THE SUEZ CANAL

Following the ill-fated assault on the Suez Canal in February 1915 several other very small operations were carried out, but were ineffectual. In August 1915 Kressestein became chief of staff at Djemal Pasha's headquarters for the Fourth Army in Lebanon. But then at the end of August the headquarters were transferred to Jerusalem. Kressestein made further demands for German officers and assistance for the proposed future assault on the Suez.

Several small scale raids were made into the Sinai. One of those raids was led by Colonel Kressestein himself. But he realised that unless there was a general and supported plan from the Turkish high command, backed up by German personnel and equipment, then it would be fruitless to consider implementing any plans for future operations against the Suez.

A further major operation against the Suez Canal was not a priority for the Turkish High Command. They were more concerned at this time in defending the Dardanelles, and stemming the British-Indian force from further encroaching into Mesopotamia. Djemal Pasha himself was still licking his wounds from the ill-fated February assault, and seemed more content forging a power base for himself from Damascus.

DJEMAL PASHA'S POLICIES

Although employing harsh policies against the minority groups in Syria, particularly the Jewish Zionists and Arab nationalist leaders, Djemal Pasha at the same time was also developing a strategy.

By late 1915 Djemal had a semi-autonomous political entity in the vast region of Syria. Then in December 1915 Djemal, via the *Dashnaktsutium* (Armenian Revolutionary Federation), contacted the Russian Government with a proposal: that in return for his help in overthrowing the Ottoman Turkish regime, he would receive the region of 'Asiatic Turkey (consisting of Syria, Mesopotamia, a Christian Armenia, Cilicia, and Kurdistan as autonomous provinces.'[6] Djemal would become the Sultan of this region.

---

6   Adamov, E. *German Translation of Vol. VI of the series of documents from the archives of the Russian Foreign Office*, (Moscow, 1924), No's 50 and 52, cited in Stein, ibid, p. 255-7; Fromkin, ibid, p. 214.

Djemal Pasha offered to assist in toppling the Turkish Government; and agreed to recognize Russia's right to Constantinople and the strategic Straits, in return for endorsement of himself as Sultan of the region he proposed to govern.

The Russians seriously considered this proposal. When informed by Sazanov, both the British and French understood that it would mean Russia would gain its objectives (Constantinople and the Straits), but that they, as well as the Arab nationalists, would not attain theirs.[7]

What this situation did achieve, though, was to force the British and French to seriously discuss their *desiderata* for the region of Asiatic Turkey. In time, though, this proposal dissipated, and Djemal Pasha continued ruling his region with an iron fist.

THE *NILI*

Djemal Pasha's harsh policies forced some of his subjects to become more loyal to the Ottoman regime, while others felt they needed to work towards its overthrow. It was into this second category that a small group of Jewish nationalists in Palestine belonged. This group, led by the Aaronsohn family of Zichron Yaacov, became known as the *NILI*.

The *NILI* believed, wrote Verrier, 'that British support for Zionism might be strengthened if the intelligence which they were prepared to risk their lives in acquiring was made available to GHQ in Cairo.'[8] They decided they had to work towards a British victory over Turkey. Accordingly in August and September 1915 two members of the group, Alexander Aaronsohn and Absalom Feinberg 'had reached Cairo and Port Said respectively.'[9]

Although only one British intelligence officer, Leonard Woolley, was prepared to partner with these two men, yet this small beginning was the starting point of a partnership which by mid-1917 would be very important in assisting the British-led army in ousting the Turks from Palestine.

---

7   Stein, ibid, p. 256.
8   Verrier, ibid, p. 2.
9   Verrier, ibid, p. 2.

CHAPTER 45

§

The al-Faruqi deception

The failure of the August offensive and uncertainty concerning Bulgaria caused considerable angst for the British Government. Everyone was now paying close attention to the situation in the Dardanelles and the Balkans. One very keen observer was Sherif Hussein, who understood that a Turkish victory would jeopardize his position, and even his life. His only real possibility of survival was through forging a concrete alliance with Britain.

One person who found himself caught in the midst of these two pincers of the Dardanelles imbroglio and Arab aspirations was Sir Henry McMahon. He later wrote of this time:

> It was the most unfortunate date in my life when I was left in charge of the Arab movement... and I think a few words are necessary to explain that it is nothing to do with me: it is purely military business. It began at the urgent request of Sir Ian Hamilton at Gallipoli. I was begged by the Foreign Office to take immediate action and draw the Arabs out of the war. At that moment a large portion of the [Turkish] forces at Gallipoli and nearly the whole of the force in Mesopotamia were Arabs, and the Germans were then spending a large amount of money in detaching the rest of the Arabs, so the situation was that the

Arabs were between the two. Could we give them some guarantee of assistance in the future to justify their splitting with the Turks? I was told to do that at once and in that way I started the Arab movement.[1]

MOHAMMAD AL-FARUQI

The pressure from Hamilton was related to finding a solution to the dead-lock in the Dardanelles, a deadlock which could be helped if the Arab soldiers fighting for the Turks all deserted and changed sides.

This pressure from Hamilton was enhanced due to the information gleaned from one Arab soldier who deserted, named Mohammad al-Faruqi.[2] Al-Faruqi had been sent to the Gallipoli front by the Turkish authorities for purportedly conspiring against Turkish interests while based in Damascus. In July Djemal Pasha had sent one Arab Division, composed of many nationalist minded officers, to Gallipoli.[3]

Al-Faruqi had been in the firing line about ten days in the midst of the August battles when, 'on the pretext of arranging a truce for the burial of the dead' he surrendered to the British forces.[4] Al-Faruqi, though, had a motive for surrendering – he claimed to be a messenger for the Arab nationalists based in Damascus.

On 21 August 1915 the British Intelligence at Gallipoli made the following report: 'An Arab officer Lieut. SHERIFF UL FARUKHI, 34th Regt., 12th Division, deserted into the lines of the 11th Division and made a statement, which is here reproduced in an abridged form….'[5]

Al-Faruqi thereafter proceeded to give a detailed report of the disposition of all the Turkish forces on the Dardanelles Peninsula, even stating:

---

1 Wingate Papers, School of Oriental Studies, Durham University, File 141/4, cited in *Kedourie, E. The Chatham House Version and Other Middle East Studies*, (London, 1970), p. 14. McMahon made this statement at a Conference held in Cairo on 12 September 1916, which included Clayton and Colonel C.E. Wilson, Governor of the Sudan Red Sea province. It was called in order to appraise the 'Sharifian rebellion, which then seemed on the point of collapsing.' [Kedourie, ibid, p. 14].

2 Also spelt Al-Farukhi, El-Faroki, El Farugi and other renditions.

3 Antonius, ibid, p. 159.

4 Statement by 'Sherif El Farugi', Intelligence Office, War Office, Cairo, cited in FO 371/2486, No. 157740. See also, Kedourie, *Labyrinth*, p. 73.

5 Gallipoli Intelligence Summary, August 1915 (War Diary or Intelligence Summary), Imbros, 21 August 1915. WO 157/648.

'The Staff did not expect the new landings to be at SUVLA BAY.'[6] Until this point there was nothing particularly untoward in this statement. What followed though was to have significant historical importance.

The War Diary then stated:

> This officer also made a statement to the following effect: - He belongs to an organisation of Arab officers whose programme is to desert to us and then returning to Syria, to raise a revolt against Turkey. The head of this organisation is AZIZ el MASRI (believed now to be in Egypt) ... SHERIF el FAROKI appears to have played an important part in this movement. He claims to be a descendant of the Prophet and wishes to go to Mecca to see the GD. SHERIF. He gives the names of 11 officers, all holding Staff appointments of importance in the Turkish Army, including a Corps Commander, to whom he wishes the fact of his desertion and our willingness to assist the movement to be made known.[7]

In early October, at the time when Sherif Hussein's letter of 9 September was being read in Cairo, al-Faruqi was sent to Egypt to be interviewed by British military intelligence.[8] It would appear that Hamilton was of the opinion that the information which al-Faruqi carried was of vital importance for swinging the balance in the Gallipoli Campaign.[9]

Gilbert Clayton, the head of military intelligence in Cairo, in particular seemed impressed with al-Faruqi's story. Clayton wrote a Memorandum and attached it to McMahon's despatch to the Foreign Office on 12 October 1915.[10]

---

6 Gallipoli Intelligence Summary, ibid.
7 Gallipoli Intelligence Summary, ibid.
8 Antonius, ibid, p.169.
9 According to al-Faruqi 'both General Hamilton and the Military Authorities in Egypt thanked me greatly.' FO 371/2486, No. 157740, Statement, p. 8.
10 FO 371/2486, 157740/34982, attached to McMahon's despatch No. 121, Cairo, 12 October 1915.

AL-FARUQI'S INVOLVEMENT WITH ARAB NATIONALISM

While based in Aleppo at the beginning of the War al-Faruqi became a member of a secret society 'started by the Arab officers in the Turkish Army whose object was the independence and happiness of Arabs.'[11] This society was al-'Ahd. Al-Faruqi was later transferred to Damascus at the time when Djemal Pasha took over control of Syria and was preparing for his assault on the Suez Canal.

While in Damascus al-Faruqi became further involved in the workings of al-'Ahd, which now had branches in numerous locations, and was spreading the news that the 'English are our friends.'[12] He had previously been aware of a civilian society the 'Fetat El Arab' (al-Fatat) which had similar aims as the officer's society, and while in Damascus, so he stated, he made attempts to unite them.[13] The officers then joined al-Fatat, whose members 'had already paid allegiance to the Sherif of Mecca as Khalifa and renounced allegiance to "Rashad" the Sultan of Turkey.'[14]

The members of al-Fatat, he stated 'take an oath on the Koran that they will never divulge the secrets of the Society' and that there are three degrees of seniority within the Society. He was in the second degree.[15] The Central Office was based in Damascus and members communicated with each other through a particular cypher. The members of the Society, he continued 'have taken a solemn oath on the Koran that they will enforce their object and establish an Arab Caliphate in Arabia, Syria and Mesopotamia at all costs and under any circumstances, sacrificing for this object all their efforts and property and, if needs be, their lives.'[16]

'Our first action after joining' Fetat al Arab, al-Faruqi stated 'was that we sent an officer to the Sherif of Mecca and he paid him allegiance on behalf of all the officers in our party and renounced our allegiance to "Rashad".'[17]

---

11 Statement by Mohammed al-Faruqi, p. 1, FO 371/2486, No. 157740.
12 Statement by Mohammed al-Faruqi, p. 3, FO 371/2486, No. 157740.
13 Statement by Mohammed al-Faruqi, p .2, FO 371/2486, No. 157740.
14 Statement by Mohammed al-Faruqi, p. 3, FO 371/2486, No. 157740.
15 FO 371/2486, No. 157740, Memorandum, p. 2.
16 FO 371/2486, No. 157740, Memorandum, p. 2.
17 The Turkish Sultan.

It was at this time, he continued that: 'We also found out that the Sherif of Mecca was in communication with the High Commissioner in Egypt, and the English were willing to give the Arabs necessary arms and ammunition for the attainment of his object. That the English have given their consent to the Sherif establishing an Arab Empire, but the limits of his Empire were not defined. It was mentioned that the dominions of the Sherif shall include "the Sherif and those who follow him." When this phrase reached Damascus it was suggested that the northern line of limit of the Sherif's Empire should be "Mersina – Diarbekr" line.'[18]

Following disclosure of these details, the Damascus society sent representatives to Jedda about 'three months ago' al-Faruqi stated, 'with instructions that if England agreed to these limits they were to discuss and modify with them other articles of the agreement...' He then stated, 'I do not know what happened to this mission.'[19]

It was about this time, he claimed, that Djemal Pasha became aware of the existence of the two societies which were working against the Turkish regime, and arrested a number of civilians. In addition nine army officers were arrested, including al-Faruqi, and subsequently imprisoned in Aleppo.[20]

During his period of incarceration it was agreed among some of these officers that they would escape to the British at their first opportunity. Al-Faruqi had to wait until he was posted to Gallipoli, and then after ten days 'in the firing line' he crossed the line, carrying with him a message for the British.[21] Following his interrogation, and details of the message he was carrying, Hamilton had al-Faruqi despatched to Cairo where the full worth of the message he was carrying could be assessed.

CLAYTON'S ASSESSMENT

'El Farugi', Clayton wrote in his memorandum, 'maintains that the Young Arab party wields very great power throughout the Turkish dominions ...

---

18 Statement by Mohammed al-Faruqi, p. 4, FO 371/2486, No. 157740.
19 Statement by Mohammed al-Faruqi, p. 4, FO 371/2486, No. 157740.
20 Statement by Mohammed al-Faruqi, p. 5, FO 371/2486, No. 157740.
21 Statement by Mohammed al-Faruqi, p. 7, FO 371/2486, No. 157740.

and … many of its members [are] actively sympathetic towards the Allies, more especially Great Britain.

… the party have now come to the conclusion that the moment is approaching when action is imperative. They have therefore decided to approach England with the offer of active co-operation in return for a guarantee that England will support them in their attempt to secure independence.'[22]

Al-Faruqi told Clayton that the party realize 'that to carry out the idea of an Arab Empire in its entirely is probably outside the region of political policies at present' and he understands that 'England is bound by obligations to her Allies in this war.' His next statement is of some significance:

The more experienced probably are aware that England could hardly be expected to regard with equanimity the establishment of a powerful and united Arab Empire, marching with Egypt and on the flank of the highway to India. But they do ask that England should promise to assist them to obtain a reasonable measure of independence and autonomous Government in these Arab countries where England can fairly claim that her interests are greater than those of her Allies.[23]

Having stated this, he then adds: 'that a guarantee of the independence of the Arabian Peninsula would not satisfy them, but this together with the institution of an increasing measure of autonomous Government, under British guidance and control, in Palestine and Mesopotamia would probably secure their friendship. Syria is of course included in their programme but they must realize that France has aspirations in this region.' Concerning Syria, they would stress for 'the inclusion of Damascus, Aleppo, Hama and Homs in the Arab Confederation.'[24]

Clayton then adds al-Faruqi's own words: 'our scheme embraces all the Arab countries including Syria and Mesopotamia, but if we cannot have all, we want as much as we can get.'[25]

---

22   FO 371/2486, No. 157740, Memorandum, p. 2.
23   FO 371/2486, No. 157740, Memorandum, p. 3.
24   FO 371/2486, No. 157740, Memorandum, p. 3.
25   FO 371/2486, No. 157740, Memorandum, p. 3.

Al-Faruqi also stated that the Turks and Germans were aware of their claims and, 'have already approached the leaders of the Young Arab Committee and, indeed, have gone so far as to promise them the granting of their demands in full.' The Arab Committee, though, he claims, 'are strongly inclined towards England.' 'We would sooner have a promise of half from England' he stated 'than of the whole from Turkey and Germany'[26]

Al-Faruqi concluded: 'they are convinced that they can no longer remain neutral and, unless they receive a favourable reply from England within a few weeks, they have decided to throw in their lot with Turkey and Germany and to secure the best terms they can.'[27]

According to Clayton al-Faruqi, 'maintains that he is accredited by the Committee and that through him the reply of England can be given.' However in al-Faruqi's own statement, he says otherwise.[28] Whether al-Faruqi was qualified or not, Clayton concluded his Memorandum by stating that, 'together with the events of the previous year' and a study of the Pan-Arab movement, 'lead to the conviction that the proposals now put forward are of very grave and urgent importance.'[29]

This importance, Clayton continued, was exacerbated by the fact that the Allies were fighting against the Caliphate. The failure of the call to *Jihad* had been due mostly to Arab indifference. There were, however, 'indications that, as the successful resistance of Turkey continues, a feeling of doubt and uneasiness is spreading. The Sherif of Mecca recently approached His Majesty's Government with proposals very similar to these put forward by El Farugi, and defined the boundaries of the territories to which the Arabs lay claim.'[30]

The boundaries of the proposed Arab Kingdom were mentioned on several occasions, the northern limit being, according to al-Faruqi, 'the Mersina-Diabekr line.' What was of quite some significance though, was

---

26 FO 371/2486, No. 157740, Memorandum, p. 4.

27 FO 371/2486, No. 157740, Memorandum, p. 4.

28 In his Statement al-Faruqi states: 'I am not authorised to discuss with you officially our political programme, but if no agreement between you and our representatives who came to Jedda has yet been made I can, for the sake of shortening negotiations ... give answers to any questions you wish to make re the agreement and if necessary make modifications in its articles including the Mersina-Diarbekr line ...'

29 FO 371/2486, No. 157740, Memorandum, p.4.

30 FO 371/2486, No. 157740, Memorandum, p.5.

his allusion to the 'new empire' being 'headed by a Khalifa' but its 'basis will be national and not religious. It will be an Arab, <u>not a Moslem</u> Empire.'[31]

Whether the impossibility of what al-Faruqi stated dawned upon Clayton (or other British officials) it is hard to know. It is an impossibility for there to be a Muslim Caliph ruling an Arab as distinct from a Muslim Caliphate (Empire); especially if that Khalifa (Caliph) was the Emir (Sherif) of Mecca. The Emir of Mecca had already previously stated to the British that it was his desire for *all foreign privileges to be revoked.*[32] This would mean there would be no special privileges for non-Muslims in his Empire (which the Capitulations provided for) which means by inference all non-Muslims would live in, or return to, their rightful place within Islamic ideology as second-class or *dhimmi* subjects.

If al-Faruqi was truly representing the ideals of the Damascus-based nationalists then this formula was diametrically opposite to that espoused by the Sherif of Mecca - understandably so from one who would theoretically be the *Caliph* of Islam. Non-Muslims could have no other status than being *dhimmis*, or second-class subjects.

This contradiction of understanding is no more apparent than in al-Faruqi's final point in his statement: 'Christian Arabs, Druses and Neseiria will have the same rights as Moslems, but the Jews will be governed by a special law.'[33] In this new Arab Empire all, theoretically, would be equal – except the Jews!

CLAYTON'S APPRAISAL

Clayton then alluded to the recent correspondence from the Sherif, who obviously was somewhat impatient with Britain's procrastination.[34] Clayton's assessment was: 'A favourable reply to the Arab proposals, even though it did not satisfy their aspirations entirely, would probably put the seal on their friendship.'

---

31   FO 371/2486, No. 157740, Statement, p. 10.
32   Sharif Hussein to McMahon, 14 July 1915, point 5, cited in Antonius, ibid, p. 415. Italics mine.
33   FO 371/2486, No. 157740, Statement, p. 10. Neseiria may refer to the Nestorian Christians.
34   FO 371/2486, No. 157740, ibid, p. 5.

'On the other hand' Clayton wrote, 'to reject the Arab proposals entirely, or even to seek to evade the issues, will be to throw the Young Arab party definitely into the arms of the enemy. Their machinery will at once be employed against us throughout the Arab countries … Moreover, the religious element will come into play and the "Jehad", so far a failure, may become a very grim reality, the effects of which would certainly be far-reaching and at present the present crisis might well be disastrous.'[35]

Thoughts of a universally proclaimed and accepted *Jihad* haunted many British officials, not only those in Egypt and the Sudan, but also in India where there was a very large Muslim minority population.

The India Office was very concerned and involved in any discussion currently being held concerning Arabia. Although the Sherif of Mecca and the Hejaz was located on the western side of the Arabian Peninsula, its eastern side adjoined the Persian Gulf, and affairs in that entire region came under the jurisdiction of the India Government. The India Government had entered into, on behalf of the British Government, agreements with some of the local chieftains including the House of Saud based in Nejd.

RESULTS OF AL-FARUQI'S EXAGGERATIONS

By far al-Faruqi's most grandiose statement alluded to the potential strength of this movement:

> We, the Arab party, are a power which cannot be disregarded. 90% of the Arab officers in the Turkish Army and a part of the Kurd officers are members of our Society.
> In uniting with the civilian party, which comprises the natives, sedentary and nomad, and all sects … , we have become stronger morally and financially.[36]

If true, this was indeed a formidable force, and one which the British authorities would need to take seriously. But if the British did not take this

---

35 FO 371/2486, No. 157740, ibid, p. 7.
36 Statement by Mohammed al-Faruqi, p. 9, FO 371/2486, No. 157740.

claim seriously then there were, so al-Faruqi claimed, serious consequences: '… unless they receive a favourable reply from England within a few weeks, they have decided to throw in their lot with Turkey and Germany and to secure the best terms they can.'[37]

The British establishment in Cairo was impressed by al-Faruqi's bold assertions, evidenced when Clayton informed Wingate on 9 October that, 'I shall take the opportunity of rubbing in the fact that if we definitely refuse to consider the aspirations of the Arabs, we are running a grave risk of throwing them into the arms of our enemies.'[38]

The statement by al-Faruqi and Clayton's Memorandum were attached to McMahon's despatch to London on 12 October 1915. Whereas previously there had been just the correspondence with Emir Hussein to consider, now the al-Faruqi interview also came into serious consideration.

Al-Faruqi may not have been sanctioned by the Arab nationalist group in Damascus, and he was not even known to Emir Hussein, yet now his word was taken at almost face value by the head of British military intelligence in Cairo. In addition, through Clayton's Recommendation, McMahon and soon the Foreign Office personnel in London were also to be taken in by al-Faruqi's deception.

---

37 Memorandum by Clayton, p. 4, FO 371/2486, No. 157740.
38 Clayton to Wingate, 9 October 1915, Wingate Papers 135/4, cited in Kedourie, ibid, p. 77.

§

CHAPTER 46

Bulgaria and Salonika

THE IMPORTANCE OF BULGARIA

Despite the failure of the August offensive there was still the possibility of an Allied victory at the Dardanelles, because of three factors: 1) that all the Arab soldiers fighting with the Turkish Army would desert as al-Faruqi did; 2) that Bulgaria would surrender its neutrality and join the Allies; and 3) that the four French divisions would quickly arrive.

The Bulgarian border was only some 100 miles (160 kilometres) from Constantinople, and if only a portion of the possible 500,000 man Bulgarian Army marched eastwards, then the Turks would need to withdraw troops from Gallipoli in order to defend their capital.

The strategic and geo-political significance of Bulgaria was told in early September to Ambassador Morgenthau by a senior German, who stated: 'We cannot hold the Dardanelles without the military support of Bulgaria.'[1] The main reason for this statement was due to the strategic location of Bulgaria – it straddled the communication line from the Central Powers to Turkey.

---

1 Morgenthau, ibid, Chapter 21, p. 1.

The railway from Berlin went through Vienna and then through Serbia and on to Sofia, the capital of Bulgaria, before heading on to Constantinople.

Thus both Bulgaria and Serbia were of vital importance. Bulgarian neutrality also helped to buffer Serbia, an Ally, from the Central Powers. In the aftermath of the failed August offensive all eyes were now trained upon Bulgaria to see if this latest Allied failure would have a bearing upon her position. Germany was at this time exerting considerable pressure upon Bulgaria to join with the Central Powers; while the Allies were likewise trying to woo Bulgaria to side with them.

Bulgarian involvement in the war was much dependent upon her attaining the region of Macedonia, which she claimed was ethnically Bulgarian. In the First Balkan War of 1912 Bulgaria gained this region, only to be stripped of it after the 1913 War, with some territory going to Serbia and some to Greece. Bulgaria insisted that she have actual possession of Macedonia before becoming actively involved on behalf of the Entente.[2]

Thus if Bulgaria joined the Central Powers (and the Germans were trying hard to engineer this) then not only would there be dangers to Serbia and Greece, there would be dangers to the Allied troops in the Dardanelles. Additionally the only remaining supply route between the Allies and Russia, from Salonika port by railway to Nisch, would be broken.

FRENCH AMBIVALENCE

The four French divisions were scheduled to arrive at the Dardanelles after 22 September, and Kitchener was enthusiastic about what they could accomplish by a landing on the Asiatic side of Turkey.[3] When Marshal Joffre, however, read General Sarrail's Memorandum and saw that he had not laid out any clear plans for what these divisions were to accomplish, he hesitated.

Then on 14 September Hamilton received notification from Kitchener that the anticipated four French divisions would not be released, until 'the

---

2   Morgenthau, ibid, Chapter 21, p. 4.
3   Poincare, ibid, p. 212.

result of the approaching offensive in France is determined.'[4] Kitchener also alluded to the various opinions of the French leaders and commanders about the merits of this new expedition.

Hamilton, naturally, was disappointed, as these divisions would not arrive, even if the offensive in France was successful, until middle to late October. He well understood that a decisive victory in Turkey would dramatically alter the bigger picture, whereas a victory in France would only have temporary value. In his memoirs he then quoted Napoleon's famous words: 'Who holds Constantinople is master of the world.'[5]

Over the following weeks the French position constantly changed concerning these four divisions.[6] In the meantime General Gourard, who was in Paris recovering from wounds, visited Poincare and informed him that it was 'very dangerous to leave our two Divisions where they are without trying to silence the Asiatic guns.' Two extra divisions would be necessary, he stated, and these troops should arrive sooner rather than later.[7]

The need for quick action was soon afterwards impressed again upon Poincare by M. Jean Cruppi, a Deputy in the French Government, who had just returned from Russia and the Dardanelles. Cruppi met with French officers, and stated of their opinion: 'if we do not send reinforcements at once, our people are very likely to be thrown into the sea.'

Cruppi also informed the President: 'In Russia … all eyes are turned towards Constantinople, and they are waiting impatiently for us to take the town; there is a good deal of grumbling about our inaction.'[8]

Despite the French procrastination, Hamilton still expected the four French divisions to arrive at some time. This expectation was soon to change, however, when a new dynamic arose.

---

4 Kitchener to Hamilton, No. 7843, 14 September 1915, cited in Hamilton, ibid, Vol. 2, p. 76.

5 Hamilton, ibid, Vol. 2, p. 78.

6 Poincare, ibid, pp. 212-3; 228-9 & 232. Poincare was also informed that the Dardanelles expedition would not materialise because G.Q.G. would 'not look at it because Sarrail is to command.'

7 Poincare, ibid, p. 218.

8 Poincare, ibid, p. 223.

THE SALONIKA OPTION

One idea which had been bandied about for quite some time was the possibility of sending troops to the north of Greece, to the region of Salonika (Thessalonica). This would potentially hinder Bulgaria from surrendering its neutrality and joining the Central Powers; would encourage Serbia; and strengthen Greece.

Hamilton recorded a conversation he had with Colonel Napier, the British Military Attaché in Sofia (the capital of Bulgaria) on 21 September. Napier mentioned 'that we should transfer the troops on the Gallipoli peninsula to Salonika so as to hearten up the Serbians and Greeks and dishearten our enemies at Sofia.' Napier informed Hamilton that he had already made this proposal to the Foreign Office.[9]

Hamilton, though, remained steadfast that the only viable option in the East was the capture of Constantinople. He could see no military, nor long-term strategic purpose in beginning a campaign in Salonika, stating: 'We can't feed Russia with munitions through Salonika, nor can we bring back Russian wheat via Salonika …'[10]

Ominous signs now were being projected from Bulgaria towards the end of September. Unbeknown to the Allies, Germany/Austro-Hungary and Turkey had all entered into an agreement with the Bulgarians on 6 September. Paul Weitz, the correspondent for the *Frankfurter Zeitung* newspaper, later informed Morgenthau that the Turks had agreed to cede to Bulgaria a portion of its country including part of Adrianople (Edirne). This land was significant as it meant the railway line from Sofia to Dedeagatch (Alexandropoli) on the coast, was now entirely in Bulgarian hands.[11]

Enver later confessed to Morgenthau that this move saved Constantinople. 'We gave up a small area', he stated, 'because we saw that that was the way to win the war.'[12] Now not only could Turkey win the conflict against the Allies at the Dardanelles, it also now completely closed off the supply lines

---

9   Hamilton, ibid, Vol. 2, p. 86.

10   Hamilton, ibid, Vol. 2, p. 86.

11   Morgenthau, ibid, Chapter 21, pp. 5-6. On 17 January 1916 a regular train service between Berlin and Constantinople, known as the *Balkanzug*, began again.

12   Morgenthau, ibid, Chapter 21, p. 7.

through to Russia – and from this point forward the Russian war machine began grinding to a halt.

The fruits of these agreements were first noticed when the Bulgarians began a general mobilisation of its forces on 22 September. Several days later Kitchener informed Hamilton:

> On account of mobilization of the Bulgarian Army Greece has asked the Allies to send a force to Salonika in order to enable her to support Serbia should the latter be attacked by Bulgaria, as well as by German forces from the North. No doubt you realize that if by such action Bulgaria joins hands with the Central Powers they will have a clear road to Constantinople and Gallipoli, and be able to send large quantities of ammunition or troops, rendering your position very hazardous.[13]

Kitchener then disclosed that the French and the British were resolved to despatch the 150,000 soldiers requested by the Greeks. This meant, Kitchener continued, 'some troops will have to be taken from the Dardanelles to go to Salonika, but it must be clearly understood that there is no intention of withdrawing from the Peninsula or of giving up the Dardanelles operations until the Turks are defeated.'[14]

Such a withdrawal would necessitate a reduction in the area occupied by the Allies at Gallipoli. Kitchener then informed Hamilton: 'The projected dispatch of reinforcements of French and British divisions for Asiatic operations must be in abeyance until a decision in the Western theatre can be reached.'[15]

Kitchener stated that the two divisions to be taken from the Dardanelles were most likely to be the 10th and 11th Divisions, and the Yeomanry Division en-route to Gallipoli would now be diverted to Salonika.

---

13 Kitchener to Hamilton, No. 8229, 26 September 1915, cited in Hamilton, ibid, Vol. 2, p. 89.
14 Kitchener to Hamilton, No. 8229, 26 September 1915, cited in Hamilton, ibid, Vol. 2, p. 89.
15 Kitchener to Hamilton, No. 8229, 26 September 1915, cited in Hamilton, ibid, Vol. 2, p. 89.

The French would also need to withdraw a considerable number of men. In fact Poincare recorded on 26 September that following a conference with the Greek Prime Minister, Venizelos, the French would send one of the two Gallipoli divisions to Salonika, while other materials and men were being sent directly to the Greek port city.[16]

In the last days of September one French division and 10th Irish Division began departing the Peninsula. The withdrawal of the French division would seriously imperil the Helles sector, in view of the seasoned 29th British Division already being deployed at Suvla.

With Greece secure, the next question to face would be to what extent were the Allies going to support Serbia: and if they were to support her, would it be at the expense of Gallipoli?

BULGARIA AND THE CENTRAL POWERS ATTACK SERBIA

Following the Bulgarian mobilisation the Russians felt betrayed and insisted on the Allies giving the Bulgarians an ultimatum. This they did on 4 October. When the Bulgarians gave no reply the Allied representatives left Sofia on 5 October.

Bulgaria declared war on Serbia on 14 October, and launched her forces against her Balkan neighbour immediately, while the Central Powers attacked Serbia from the opposite direction.

Many in Britain at this point seemed more in favour of remaining at Gallipoli, while more in France seemed intent on boosting Salonika and supporting Serbia. The French position prevailed and more troops were sent to Salonika – but they had to basically sit and watch as Bulgaria and the Central Powers crushed Serbia.

This latest event was another blow for Russia. By the end of 1915 the novelty had worn off in Russia for the capture of Constantinople. In addition continued defeats on the Eastern Front began to gnaw away at the resolve of the Russian people to remain in the war.

---

16 Poincare, ibid, p. 240.

OMINOUS SIGNS FOR HAMILTON

From the beginning of October Kitchener began dropping hints to Hamilton concerning certain changes being muted by the Dardanelles Committee, and their dissatisfaction with Hamilton.[17]

Further problems arose for him when Kitchener informed him of a message from the Australian journalist Keith Murdoch to the Australian Prime Minister, with certain allegations about the improper conduct of the Gallipoli Campaign.[18]

It was obvious that the leadership in Britain were seeking a suitable scapegoat to blame for the recent defeats – and Hamilton seemed to be best candidate.

Despite these interruptions, Hamilton continued with his duties, and on 5 October he visited the Helles sector and inspected the lines of the 1st Newfoundland Battalion. 'This was', he wrote, 'the Newfoundlanders' first day in the trenches and they were very pleased with themselves. They could not understand why they were not allowed to sally forth at once and do the Turks in. The presence of these men from our oldest colony adds to the extraordinary mix-up of people now fighting on the Peninsula. All the materials exist here for bringing off the biblical coup of Armaggedon excepting only the shell.'[19]

Several days later, on 8 October, Hamilton was able to authoritatively inform Kitchener that after a thorough investigation there was 'no truth whatever in the allegation made by Murdoch.'[20] This, he hoped, would quell this storm. But on the same day a huge physical storm did considerable infrastructural damage, including washing away two of the piers at Anzac Cove, and causing much other damage.[21]

Another storm then followed, contained in a message from Kitchener on 11 October, who asked Hamilton: 'What is your estimate of the probable losses which would be entailed to your force if the evacuation of the Gallipoli

---

17 Kitchener to Hamilton, 5 October 1915, cited in Hamilton, ibid, Vol. 2, p. 99.

18 Kitchener to Hamilton, 5 October 1915, cited in Hamilton, ibid, Vol. 2, p. 99.

19 Hamilton, ibid, Vol. 2, p. 101.

20 Hamilton to Kitchener, No. M.F.A.B. 4491, 8 October 1915, cited in Hamilton, ibid, Vol. 2, p. 102 [246].

21 Hamilton, ibid, Vol. 2, p. 102-3. [246]

Peninsula was decided on and carried out in the most careful manner?' The message continued: 'No decision has been arrived at yet on this question, but I feel that I ought to have your views.'[22]

Hamilton was furious and stated: 'If they do this they make the Dardanelles into the bloodiest tragedy of the world! Even if we were to escape without a scratch, they would stamp our enterprise as the bloodiest of all tragedies!'[23]

This was not the only problem Hamilton now had to face. The accusations made by Murdoch had been taken much at face value by Asquith and some parts of Murdoch's paper were printed – before Hamilton had been asked to provide verification of the accusations made against the conduct of the campaign![24]

The end was inevitable. On 16 October Kitchener informed Hamilton that the War Council 'wish to make a change in the command which will give them an opportunity of seeing you.'[25]

The end was swift. Hamilton would be replaced temporarily by Birdwood until the arrival of General Charles Munro. By 17 October Hamilton had already departed from Gallipoli.

This was an ominous sign for the continuation of the campaign, and no further options remained for its continuation. Unless, of course, if Sherif Hussein and al-Faruqi could in fact engineer a withdrawal of the Arab soldiers fighting with the Turks, or at least the supposed 90% Arab officers who were supposedly prepared to come over to fight for the Allies.

---

22 Kitchener to Hamilton, 11 October 1915, cited in Hamilton, ibid, Vol. 2, p. 104. [249]
23 Hamilton, ibid, Vol. 2, p. 104.
24 Hamilton, ibid, Vol. 2, p. 108.
25 Kitchener to Hamilton, 16 October 1915, cited in Hamilton, ibid, Vol. 2, p. 113.

CHAPTER 47

§

The Sherif and McMahon

WINGATE ECHOES THE SHERIF'S CONCERNS

While geo-political changes accrued in the northern Mediterranean region their effects were felt in the southern region. Governor-General Wingate sent a telegram to Clayton on 5 October containing details just received concerning the present sentiments of the Sherif of Mecca.[1] These details emanated from a message which Sherif Hussein had sent to Ali Morghani (the Muslim leader in Sudan). Wingate stated of this correspondence that Hussein feared 'condemnation by Mohomedans [sic] should he destroy the unity of Islam.' Wingate also wrote:

The impressions I have received from this document are that the Sherif is increasingly apprehensive for his own position and in absence of news of our success in Gallipoli, is probably inclined to turn a more willing ear to overtures from Constantinople than formerly.[2]

---

1 This information came via a message from the Sherif to Said Ali El Morghani, which although unsigned and undated 'evidently emanated' wrote Wingate 'from the Sherif.' Wingate to Clayton, 5 October 1915, FO 141/461, Telegram No. 721.

2 Wingate to Clayton, 5 October 1915, FO 141/461, Telegram No. 721, and then forwarded by Clayton to Storrs on 5 October 1915, FO 141/461, No. 1198/10.

Sherif Hussein knew that if the Turks were triumphant at Gallipoli then they would be resurgent in the remainder of their Empire, and vengeful against anyone who had opposed them. Hussein was a known opponent of the Turkish regime. A British loss at Gallipoli would bring intolerable consequences for his semi-autonomy in Arabia. His only option, if such a British defeat was inevitable, would be to ingratiate himself with the Turkish leaders.

Conversely, a British victory at Gallipoli could also mean one of two things: first that the Turks would then try and consolidate their Asian possessions, which would again encroach upon his semi-autonomous rule in the Hejaz; or second, the entire Turkish Empire could collapse, and this being the case he wanted to ensure he gained as much territory as he could. Thus for the Sherif of Mecca this was an issue of self-preservation.

The British too were desperate. The failure of the August offensive and the entrance of Bulgaria into the War with the Central Powers were major set-backs. A defeat at Gallipoli would not only be a military disaster, but a political and propaganda disaster of the first order. Thus at this propitious time two entities, one the largest Empire in the world, and the other a virtual political non-entity were considering how they could complement (or use) each other.

THE ROLES OF CLAYTON AND STORRS

Both McMahon and Maxwell depended quite heavily upon their two lieutenants in the Arab department, namely Storrs and Clayton – who both exercised a certain amount of authority themselves. Clayton wrote to Wingate on 9 October: 'I shall take the opportunity of rubbing in the fact that if we definitely refuse to consider the aspirations of the Arabs, we are running a grave risk of throwing them into the arms of our enemies.'[3] He then wrote to Fitzgerald (Kitchener's private secretary) on 10 October:

---

3   Clayton to Wingate, 9 October 1915, Wingate Papers 135/4, cited in Kedourie, ibid, p. 77.

The Arab question is reaching an acute stage.

I gather from the Sherif, as does Clayton from Faroki that they feel, rightly or wrongly, that their time has come to choose between us and Germany...[4]

HUSSEIN'S INITIAL RESPONSE TO MCMAHON'S
LETTER OF 30 AUGUST

Colonel Wilson (the British consul in Jeddah) sent a message to Clayton conveying Sherif Hussein's initial response to McMahon's letter of 30 August. Wilson wrote that Hussein was upset that Britain was not willing to take seriously the issue of boundaries, and indicated that the result of this issue 'is anxiously awaited by Mohammedans generally.' He was also 'hurt at a hint conveyed in above-mentioned letter of High Commissioner that some of his Arabs still assist in Ottoman Government propaganda ...' – that is, were still fighting for the Turks.[5]

On the same day Captain Symes (Wingate's assistant), who had read Wilson's telegram, stated to Clayton: 'Wilson's [telegram] does not lay sufficient stress on the paramount importance Sherif attaches to immediate understanding on the Boundaries question in a manner satisfactory to Pan Arabic aspirations.'[6]

Clayton's superior, General Maxwell, then sent a telegram to Kitchener on 12 October, stating:

A powerful organisation with considerable influence in the Army and among Arab Chiefs, viz: the Young Arab Committee appears to have made up its mind that the moment for action has arrived. The Turks and Germans are already in communication with them and spending money to win their support. The Arab party however is strongly inclined towards England but what they ask is a definite statement of sympathy and support even if their complete programme cannot be accepted.

---

4   Storrs to Fitzgerald, 10 October 1915, PRO 30/57,47, cited in Kedourie, ibid, p. 77.
5   Wilson to Clayton, 10 October 1915, FO 141/461, Telegram No. 1934.
6   FO 141/461, Symes to Clayton, 10 October 1915, Telegram No. 37.

Sherif [of] Mecca, who is in communication with the Arab party, also seems uneasy and is pressing for a declaration of policy on the part of England.

If their overtures are rejected or a reply is delayed any longer the Arab party will go over to the enemy and work with them, which would mean stirring up religious feeling at once and might well result in a genuine Jehad. On the other hand the active assistance which the Arabs would render in return for our support would be of the greatest value in Arabia Mesopotamia Syria and Palestine.

This question is important and requires an early decision.[7]

Thus through McMahon's report to Grey, and Maxwell's sending the same report to Kitchener, it was apparent that the British Government was being pressured to make a quick decision.

What is interesting in this situation is the degree to which al-Faruqi's exaggerated statements were being taken at face value by both the civil and military leadership. As Kedourie rightly states, there was no such thing as '*a powerful organisation with considerable influence in the Army*'; and there was little by way of the 'Turks and Germans' being 'in communication with them and spending money to win their support.'[8]

In addition, the strong suggestion that 'the active assistance which the Arabs would render in return for our support would be of the greatest value in Arabia Mesopotamia, Syria and Palestine' was very misleading. Ultimately most of the fighting and *almost all* of the casualties sustained were British, Indian, Australian and New Zealand soldiers.

OFFICIAL RESPONSE TO MCMAHON'S MESSAGE OF 12 OCTOBER

On 13 October Kitchener informed Maxwell that the Government was 'most desirous of dealing with the Arab question in a manner satisfactory to the Arabs.' He also asked Maxwell to inform him of their specific requests, and the following day asked Grey to do the same of McMahon.[9]

---

7   Maxwell to Kitchener, 12 October 1915, cited in Kedourie, ibid, p. 78.
8   Kedourie, ibid, p. 78. Italics mine.
9   Kitchener to Maxwell, 13 October 1915, FO 371/2486, 150309/34982, cited in Kedourie, ibid, p. 79.

General Maxwell then sent a further telegram to Kitchener on 16 October, in which he seemingly gave credence to what al-Faruqi was claiming, that there was 'a large and influential party actually in the Turkish Army.' This party, Maxwell stated, would work against the Turkish regime if there was a 'reasonable basis for negotiation.'[10]

Maxwell's telegram, additionally, stated that if a suitable agreement was not soon made, then those Arab 'potentates' and the 'influential party' in the Army would 'throw in their lot with the Turks'.[11] The alarmist sentiment, though, went further, when Maxwell stated:

> We are up against the big question of the future of Islam ... I feel certain that time is of the greatest importance, and that unless we make definite and agreeable proposals to the Shereef at once, we may have united Islam against us.[12]

Maxwell concluded by stating that the time had come for some serious negotiations, in which the British would insist upon retaining the *Vilayet* of Basra, while the remainder of Mesopotamia would be open for negotiations. But, he stated, 'the Arab party will, I think, insist on Homs, Aleppo, Hama and Damascus being in their sphere.'[13]

SHERIF HUSSEIN'S NEXT LETTER – 17 OCTOBER

Sherif Hussein's response to McMahon's letter of 30 August arrived in Cairo on 17 October. The following day McMahon sent an appraisal of this letter to the Foreign Office, and then again on 19 October following a further translation of the Sherif's letter, which McMahon stated was 'couched in vague terms.' McMahon stated:

---

10   Maxwell to Kitchener, 16 October 1915, FO 371/2486, 152729/34982, No. 2030E, cited in Kedourie, ibid, p. 79. A copy of this communique was forwarded to the Foreign Office on 18 October 1915.

11   Maxwell to Kitchener, 16 October 1915, FO 371/2486, 152729/34982, No. 2030E, cited in Kedourie, ibid, p. 79.

12   Maxwell to Kitchener, 16 October 1915, FO 371/2486, 152729/34982, No. 2030E, cited in Kedourie, ibid, p. 79.

13   Maxwell to Kitchener, 16 October 1915, FO 371/2486, 152729/34982, No. 2030E, cited in Kedourie, ibid, p. 80.

The major part of the letter … may be summed up as a plain intima-
tion that the Sherif of Mecca and the Arab communities whose policy
and ideas he represents, are ready to side with us in the present war on
the condition that we accept their main demands and especially the
territorial boundaries defined in the Sherif's previous communication
forwarded to you …[14]

Meanwhile pressure was mounting on the British Government to come to
some final decision concerning the Arab situation.

The main concern of Sherif Hussein with McMahon's letter was what he
termed 'a lukewarmth and hesitancy' concerning 'our essential clause.' That
essential clause concerned 'the question of frontiers and boundaries.' This
question, Hussein continued, represents 'the demands of our people who
believe that those frontiers form the minimum necessary to the establishment of the new order for which they are striving.'

Following some further concerns, Hussein then concluded:

For these reasons, and the better to set your mind at ease, I may state
that the people of all those countries, including those of whom you say
that they are zealously furthering German and Ottoman designs, are
awaiting the result of the present negotiations, which depend solely
upon whether you reject or admit the proposed frontiers, and upon
whether or not you will help us to secure their spiritual and other
rights against evil and danger. Please communicate to us the decision
of the British Government on this point, for our guidance as to what
suits their policy, and as to what steps it behoves us to take.[15]

THE BRITISH GOVERNMENT'S RESPONSE

McMahon's two telegrams to London (which merely outlined the contents of
Hussein's letter), added to the previous appraisals of Maxwell and McMahon

---

14 McMahon to Grey, 19 October 1915, FO 141/461, No. 1198/17.
15 Sherif Hussein to McMahon, 9 September 1915, cited in Antonius, ibid, pp. 416-8; also McMahon to Grey, 19
October 1915, FO 141/461, No. 1198/17. Quoting from Antonius' translation of the Arabic rather than that of the
Residency in Cairo.

concerning the sentiments of both al-Faruqi and Hussein, probably created a false understanding of the real situation in the East. In short the Foreign Office and the Government were being pressured into making a quick decision based upon improper and misleading information.

It was during this period that the representations of al-Faruqi took on further prominence. McMahon wrote to Grey on 18 October:

> From further conversations with Faroki it appears evident that Arab party are at a parting of the ways, and unless we can give them immediate assurance of nature to satisfy them they will throw themselves into the hands of Germany ... In the one case they seem ready to work actively with us which will greatly influence the course of Mesopotamia and Syria campaigns while in other Arabs will throw in their lot against us and we may have all Islam in the East united against the Allies.
>
> Arab party say they cannot longer hesitate because they must act before Turkey receives further assistance from Germany. Matter therefore is urgent.[16]

McMahon, in his telegram to Grey on 18 October, also stated that following the talks with al-Faruqi:

> England accepts principle of independent Arabia under British guidance and control within limits propounded by Sherif of Mecca, in so far as England is free to act without detriment to the interest of her present Allies ...
>
> In regard to North-Western boundaries proposed by Sherif of Mecca, Faroki thinks Arabs would accept modification leaving in Arabia purely Arab districts of Aleppo, Damascus, Hama and Homs, whose occupation by the French they would oppose.

---

16 McMahon to Grey, 18 October 1915, FO 371/2486, 153045/34982, cited in Kedourie, ibid, p. 90. This very situation is, ironically, mentioned by Von Sanders, who made a statement regarding a telegraph that 'Secretary of State Mr. Chamberlain' sent to 'the Viceroy of India on October 21st 1915', which stated, 'The Arabs are hesitating and will probably join the Turks unless we offer them large inducements.' Von Sanders, ibid, p. 145.

He also accepts the fact that British interests necessitate special measures of British control in Basrah Vilayet.[17]

'If we consider letter of Sherif of Mecca in light of Faroki's views', McMahon wrote to Grey, 'I do not think either Sherif or Arab party are likely to regard any less wide assurances as acceptable.'[18]

What is ironical here is that Mohammad al-Faruqi was being quoted as an equal to the Sherif, yet the Sherif had never heard of al-Faruqi, and al-Faruqi was not representing any official body.

Several key members of Grey's staff at this point took hold of McMahon's telegram and correspondence. George Clerk (head of the war department at the Foreign Office), although sympathetic to Hussein's proposal, nevertheless understood the complications of implementing what Hussein wanted, due a) to the British position in Mesopotamia, and b) France's claims in 'the North-Western portion of Arabia as now defined by the Arabs.'[19]

Sir Arthur Nicolson (the permanent under-secretary), wrote a minute on 19 October: "I doubt if it will be easy in view of the conflicting rivalries and jealousies of the Arab Chiefs to set up 'an independent Arab State.'"[20] Their concerns, it seems, were not taken seriously.

Their chief, Sir Edward Grey, completed a telegram and had it approved by Kitchener and the India Office by 20 October, and then sent it to McMahon.[21] In his message Grey stated to McMahon:

You can give cordial assurances on the lines, and with the reserve about our Allies, proposed by you. Stipulation that Arabs will recognize British interests as paramount and work under British guidance etc., should not be included unless it is necessary to secure Arab consent, as this might give impression in France that we were not endeav-

17 McMahon to Grey, 18 October 1915, FO 371/2486, No. 153045/34982, cited in Kedourie, ibid, p. 91

18 McMahon to Grey, 18 October 1915, FO 371/2486, No. 153045/34982, cited in Kedourie, ibid, p. 91.

19 Minute by George Clerk connected to McMahon's telegram of 18 October 1915, FO 371/2486, 152901/34982, cited in Kedourie, ibid, p. 92.

20 Minute by Sir Arthur Nicolson connected to Clerk's Minute, 19 October 1915, FO 371/2486, 152901/34982, cited in Kedourie, ibid, p. 93.

21 Austen Chamberlain of the India Office, though, only became aware of this situation somewhat by accident, and he had no opportunity of soliciting the opinion of Lord Hardinge, the Viceroy.

ouring to secure Arab interests, but to establish our own in Syria at expense of French.

There is no difficulty in speaking without reserve about Arab Peninsula and Holy Places. The general reserve you propose is however necessary more especially for North Western Boundaries.

As regards Mesopotamia proposed sphere of British control, namely Basra Vilayet, will need extension in view of British interests in Baghdad province and area actually in our occupation. Our treaties with Arab chiefs will of course stand.

But the important thing is to give our assurances that will prevent Arabs from being alienated, and I must leave you discretion in the matter as it is urgent and there is not time to discuss an exact formula.

The simplest plan would be to give an assurance of Arab independence saying that we will proceed at once to discuss boundaries if they will send representatives for that purpose, but if something more precise than this is required you can give it.

You should keep Sir R. Wingate informed.[22]

McMahon, though, did not keep Wingate as involved in all these discussions as he should have done.[23]

In Grey's instructions to McMahon as outlined in his message of 20 October, there was an important statement that: 'we will proceed at once to discuss boundaries if they will send representatives for that purpose.' No representatives came from the Hejaz - but as far as McMahon was concerned he had the second best representatives at his disposal in Mohammad al-Faruqi and Aziz el-Masri.

It was at this point, on 21 October, that Grey spoke to the French ambassador in London, Paul Cambon, 'that representatives of the two Powers should meet together to discuss the frontiers of Syria.'[24] Shortly afterwards

---

22 Grey to McMahon, 20 October 1915, FO 141/461, 1198/21 Telegram No. 796.
23 Wingate for his part sent a telegram to Clayton on 23 October outlining some possible wording for McMahon's ultimate message to Hussein, but it probably was not utilised. Kedourie, ibid, p. 95.
24 Stein, ibid, p. 250.

the French nominated Francois George Picot as their delegate for these negotiations.

MCMAHON'S LETTER TO SHERIF HUSSEIN ON 24 OCTOBER 1915

There can be no doubt that McMahon felt pressured by the correspondence from Hussein, as well as the representations from al-Faruqi. Kitchener too was pressuring for quick progress, as he was aware that if the Arab soldiers could be drawn out of the War, it could alter the situation in the Dardanelles.

McMahon then *quickly* completed his letter to Hussein on 24 October and wrote to the Foreign Office and India Office on 26 October: 'In view of urgency of matter, I seized suitable opportunity which occurred today of sending reply to the Sherif of Mecca.'[25] He then gave a brief outline of his letter, and then sent the complete version later by a separate mail.

One quite amazing paragraph in his letter to Grey read: 'I now propose to communicate above terms in definite form to Faroki and Aziz el Masri, and facilitate their commencement of propaganda. I will report later how they propose to act.'[26] Mohammad al-Faruqi was now an advisor to the British, and a middle man between them and the Sherif of Mecca![27]

McMahon wrote to Hussein, concerning the future boundaries:

The districts of Mersina and Alexandretta and portions of Syria lying to the west of the districts of Damascus, Hama, Homs and Aleppo cannot be said to be purely Arab and should be excluded from the proposed limits and boundaries.

With the above modification, and without prejudice to our existing treaties with Arab chiefs, we accept those limits and boundaries, and in regards to those portions of the territories wherein Great Britain is free to act without detriment to her Ally, France, I am empowered in the name of the Government of Great Britain to give you the following assurances and make the following reply to your letter:-

---

25 McMahon to Foreign Office and India Office, 26 October 1915, FO 141/461, No. 644.
26 McMahon to Foreign Office and India Office, 26 October 1915, ibid.
27 In time though al-Faruqi's façade began to unravel and before long his true character as an imposter was revealed.

Subject to the above modification, Great Britain is prepared to recognize and support the independence of the Arabs within the territories included in the limits and boundaries proposed by the Sherif of Mecca.

Great Britain will guarantee the Holy Places against all external aggression and will recognize their inviolability

When the situation admits, Great Britain will give to the Arabs her advice and will assist them to establish what may appear to be the most suitable forms of government in those various territories.

...

With regard to the Vilayets of Baghdad and Basra, the Arabs will recognize that the established position and interests of Great Britain necessitate special measures of administrative control in order to secure these territories from foreign aggression, to promote the welfare of the local populations and to secure our mutual economic interests.[28]

McMahon's letter, written under pressure of time and based upon some false and misleading information conveyed to him by the Sherif of Mecca and al-Faruqi, was thereafter to cause some quite serious ramifications – from what it said, and from what it did not say.

WAS THE 'AGREEMENT' OR 'ARRANGEMENT' CLEAR AND TRANSPARENT?

One of the major considerations thereafter was the validity of the McMahon correspondence. As the Jewish people were later to discover, war time commitments were often made in the midst of a military confrontation between two parties who were fighting against a common enemy, and then not always adhered to afterwards.

In this instance it was those Arabs who desired some form of independence, and who realized that under Turkish sovereignty they would never attain such independence. There was only one real option: to fight along-

---

28   McMahon to Sherif Hussein, 24 October 1915, FO 371/2486, 163832/34982, letter of McMahon to Foreign Office 26 October 1915, No. 131.

side an entity which could conceivably defeat the Turks. That entity in 1915 was Britain.

Additionally, the qualifications of both the Arab entities were questionable. The Hashemite dynasty of the Hejaz, which was merely a vassal of Turkey, maintained that it had the following of many other Arab entities, but this was not true in 1915 or thereafter. The majority of the Arab population of Mesopotamia was Shi'ite, and would not wholeheartedly submit to the leadership of a Sunni 'King.' Additionally, the animosity between the Houses of Hashem and Saud was so deeply entrenched that it would be a virtual impossibility for there to be any long-term co-operation between the two.

The so-called 'agreement' had one very important condition attached, a condition which precipitated the entire arrangement: that the Arab peoples would rise against their Turkish overlords. According to the testimony of al-Faruqi and Sherif Hussein, the majority of the Arab officers serving in the Turkish Army were actively involved in the two nationalist societies, and would upon hearing of this arrangement, defect and change sides.

No-one understood the true situation in London as did the India Office. The Secretary of State for India informed Grey, who then wrote to McMahon, the following:

I have read with concern the terms of Sir H. McMahon's letter to the Sherif... my information is that the Sherif is a non-entity without power to carry out his proposals, that the Arabs are without unity or the possibility of uniting, and I disbelieve reality or efficacy of suggested Arab revolt in the army and elsewhere. Please observe that our friends Idrisi and Ibn Saud are believed to be hostile to the Sherif, and his friends the Imam and Bin Rashid are pro-Turk while one of his sons is actually on his way to support Bin Rashid presumably against Bin Saud.

Until therefore it is proved that the Sherif and Farugi both can and will carry out their promises I agree with the Government of India in deprecating the issue of any proclamation at Baghdad or in Egypt.

The next step should be to make clear to them that promises made by McMahon are dependent on the immediate action by them in the sense of their offers and will not be binding on us unless they do their part at once.[29]

Grey fully concurred with the comments of the Secretary of State for India, and added at the conclusion of his letter to McMahon: 'If the Arabs do their part we will fulfil the promises made through you but in the next communication made to them we should state that they should act at once.'[30]

From a British perspective, facing an embarrassing defeat in the Dardanelles (where many Arab soldiers were fighting), this change of allegiance would be welcome *immediately, at once.*

Thus the entire arrangement was dependent upon the immediate active involvement of the Arabs in the fight against Turkey – otherwise the agreement would not be binding upon Britain.

WHY NO SPECIFIC MENTION OF PALESTINE?

Throughout the deliberations there was little mention of 'Palestine'. The question could rightly be asked: 'Why was Palestine not specifically mentioned in the regions being written about in McMahon's letter to Hussein on 24 October 1915?'

In view of the fact that the Arab nationalist movement was a virtual unknown entity, McMahon, representing the greatest empire on earth, attempted to use terminology which was both vague and non-committal.

His words '… portions of Syria lying to the west of the districts of Damascus, Hama, Homs and Aleppo cannot be said to be purely Arab and should be excluded from the proposed limits and boundaries' are important. Although later much ink was spilled on the meaning of the word 'districts'[31] a basic understanding of the topography will reveal that Damascus was the most prominent town along a line running from Aleppo in the north, south

29 Grey to McMahon, referring message from Secretary of State for India, 11 November 1915, FO 141/461, 1198/29a.
30 Grey to McMahon, 11 November 1915, FO 141/461, 1198/29a.
31 See Kedourie, and Antonius for two representative approaches to the use and meaning of the word 'district.'

to Damascus, and the clear inference would mean anything lying to the west of Damascus. Perhaps McMahon could have said west of Amman, but Amman then was a virtual un-known locality. Besides, the 'Aleppo, Hama, Homs, Damascus' terminology had already been used previously, by al-Faruqi as well, so McMahon merely applied a common usage.

Even more important, in the context of Palestine, were McMahon's words: '... those portions of the territories wherein Britain is free to act without detriment to her Ally, France ...' Sherif Hussein was aware, as too was al-Faruqi, that France had desires, ambitions and a large stake-hold in the region of Palestine, and had for some time made it clear that in any dismemberment of the Turkish Empire, she desired Syria, which to her included Palestine.

Any leader in the region would have known that there was a considerable non-Arab, and non-Muslim population in Palestine: at the outbreak of the War there were some 85,000 Jewish people, as well as a considerably larger number of Christian Arabs, living there. Many of these Christian Arabs were then living a far better lifestyle that they had hitherto experienced under purely Islamic-control, due mostly to the Capitulations. They may still theoretically have had a *dhimmi* status, but they were living as if they didn't have it.

Of all the regions in the Turkish Empire, with the exception perhaps of the Mount Lebanon region,[32] and the Armenian regions, Palestine was probably the most un-Islamic. Britain, France, Russia, Germany, Italy, Austria and the United States of America all had enormous undertakings and commitments there, especially in Jerusalem; and in addition to the large Jewish population there was also a growing number of Protestant Christians as well.

Sir Arthur Hirtzel of the India Office wrote a Minute on 9 November 1915, in which he stated: 'The problem of Palestine has not been expressly mentioned in these negotiations. Jerusalem ranks third among the Moslem holy places, and the Arabs will lay great stress on it. But are we going to

---

32   Where there was a large population of Maronite Christians.

hand over our own holy places to them without conditions? Whatever may be the attitude of western Christianity in this subject, the very strong feeling of Russia will have to be reckoned with.'[33]

THE RAMIFICATIONS

The gauntlet had now been thrown down by the British Government. For this 'agreement' to become valid the Arabs now had to fulfil their commitment and produce *immediate* action by pulling the Arab soldiers out from fighting with the Turks – for this was the initial basis for the 'agreement' being made.

There does not appear to be complete clarity or transparency in this Anglo-Hejazi 'agreement', or as it could be termed, 'arrangement'. Cyril Falls correctly states of it:

Sherif Hussein was generally, but not completely satisfied with these stipulations. Like many other discussions conducted during the strain of war, these ended in agreement to take action for the common good, but with many details left over for future adjustment.[34]

One of those very definite 'details left over for future adjustment' related to the boundaries of the proposed Arab national entity. But in the meantime all eyes were upon the Sherif of Mecca to see if he could actually produce the works to match his words.

---

33 L/P & S/10/523, p. 4082/1915, cited in Kedourie, ibid, p. 106.
34 Falls, C. *Military Operations: Egypt and Palestine*, (London, 1930), Part. 1, p. 217.

§

CHAPTER 48

Defeat in Gallipoli

VISIT OF KITCHENER

General Sir Charles Monro arrived in the Dardanelles on 28 October 1915. Soon after arrival Monro concluded that the only feasible option remaining was withdrawal.

Kitchener initially opposed any thought of evacuation. The Dardanelles Committee, now renamed the War Committee, and which was composed of Asquith, Lloyd George, Balfour, Grey, Kitchener (and later Bonar Law), met on 3 November 1915 to discuss the issue. It was agreed that Kitchener should proceed to the Dardanelles and determine for himself the situation there.

During his visit Kitchener visited all three battle sectors and heard those advocating for withdrawal and those against. Apart from discussing tactics with the leaders Kitchener also made time to visit the soldiers. In the ANZAC sector men, mostly privates, surrounded Kitchener - as one New Zealand soldier recalled - and with hands in pockets and in a leisurely fashion they spoke about the great man as many would discuss a prize bull in an agricultural show back home.[1]

---

1   Burton, O.E. *A Rich Old Man*, unpublished manuscript, p. 117, cited in Pugsley, ibid, p. 339.

FARUQI AND SHERIF HUSSEIN'S COVER IS REVEALED

One factor which Kitchener may have had to consider concerning his final decision involved the timing of the supposed revolt of the Arab soldiers
serving in the Turkish Army, as per the declarations of al-Faruqi and the
Sherif of Mecca. One of the key components for rushing through the 'agreement' with Sherif Hussein was so that there could be a wide scale uprising by
the Arab officers and soldiers serving within the Turkish army. No-where
would that event have been more welcome than in the Dardanelles.

Sir Mark Sykes met on 20 November with al-Faruqi who 'declared that
there would be no Arab uprising'. Sykes later wrote to the Foreign Office
his impressions from his meeting with al-Faruqi. The uprising, al-Faruqi
insisted:

> ... was dependent on the Entente landing between Mersina and
> Alexandretta and making good the Cilician Gates or Amanus Pass;
> stipulating further that, until this has been done, the Sherif should
> take no action... The necessity of immediate and adequate action in
> the Gulf of Alexandretta was also urged by Faroki, who added that the
> Germans would forestall them if the Entente did not seize this oppor-
> tunity: the Arabs would in their own interests be obliged to reconsider
> the situation, once the Turks or Germans got into Syria.[2]

Instead of the promised local uprising, al-Faruqi, endorsing Sherif Hussein's
view, now wanted an Allied landing in the region of Cilicia (southern Asia
Minor), and if this did not occur, there would be no Arab revolt. This news
was completely contrary to the expectations which led to the 'agreement'
with Sherif Hussein, and was a final blow to any hopes of a saviour for the
Gallipoli Campaign.

It appears, though, that Kitchener may have been willing to give this
idea of a new landing some thought. On 4 December Paleologue wrote of
serious differences between the British and French. Kitchener was propos-

---

2   Sykes telegram to War Office, 20 November 1915, FO 882/13, No. 19, cited in Kedourie, ibid, p. 109.

ing a withdrawal from the Dardanelles and Salonika and a fresh assault in the north of Syria (in the region of Alexandretta). The new French Prime Minister, Aristide Briand, supported a withdrawal from the Dardanelles but opposed a landing in Syria or a withdrawal from Salonika.[3]

Despite this set-back concerning the Arab revolt, while in Cairo Sykes was influenced by those advocating that the Arabs could play a significant part in defeating the Turkish armies in the Asian part of their Empire. Clayton in particular emphasized this perspective upon Sykes.[4]

Hussein's response to McMahon's letter of 24 October arrived in Cairo in mid-November 1915. In it he accepted the exclusion of the *Vilayet* of Adana (which included the port of Mersin), but he refused to accept McMahon's demand for the exclusion of 'portions of Syria lying to the west of the districts of Damascus, Homs, Hama and Aleppo.'[5] He had several other objections, including the future of Mesopotamia, and also did not agree to surrender Alexandretta.[6]

Hussein also included a new stipulation, 'that of a guarantee against a separate peace.' He wanted firm assurance that the Arabs would not be left to incur the 'united forces of Germany and Turkey.' Further, he wanted an assurance that Britain would stand beside the Arabs and 'advocate their case' in a future peace conference.[7]

He concluded by stating that he would be 'unwilling to proclaim the revolt at once, without some further preparation, but in any case he must have those guarantees before he can make any move at all.'[8]

McMahon wrote back to Hussein on 13 December 1915, and reiterated his statement concerning the coastal regions of Syria, using different wording this time: 'on the ground that French interests were involved.' McMahon

---

3 Paleologue, ibid, Vol.2, 4 December 1915.

4 Fromkin, ibid, pp. 180-1. Sykes had written to Callwell on 15 November that he felt it would be expedient to block the Cicilian Gates in order to hinder the movement of Turkish troops into Syria and Mesopotamia, a matter likely to happen following Bulgaria's entrance into the War. Sir Mark Sykes Collection, Box 1, File 2, Middle East Centre Archive, St. Anthony's, GB 165-0275.

5 Antonius, ibid, p. 172.

6 Antonius, ibid, p. 172.

7 Antonius, ibid, p. 172.

8 Antonius, ibid, p. 172.

reiterated that Britain would not conclude any peace that did not provide for "the freedom of the Arab peoples."[9]

The final letter in this line of correspondence was Hussein's reply on 1 January 1916. In this letter he maintains his insistence upon maintaining the coastal regions of Syria, but decides to postpone dealing with the matter. 'He tells McMahon', Antonius records, 'that he is anxious to avoid disturbing the concord between France and Great Britain, and that he will therefore shelve the matter for the duration of the War.'[10]

This entire situation is akin to two entities who desperately needed each other, and were doing their level best to present a satisfactory picture to the other side; but neither side was being totally honest in the process. Britain didn't fully trust that the Arabs could achieve what they said they could; and the combined forces of Hussein and al-Faruqi could at no time fulfil their commitments and promises.

KITCHENER RECOMMENDS WITHDRAWAL

When he returned to Britain Kitchener at a meeting on 22 November, recommended withdrawal, initially just from the ANZAC and Suvla Bay sectors. Apart from the military disadvantages, the onset of winter also became a major factor behind the decision to withdraw. Many men were now becoming sick because of violent weather.

Colonel John Patterson was one of those who succumbed to illness, and was withdrawn sick in November. He recalled how:

> A night or two before I left Gallipoli we had a sudden downpour of rain which made the trenches raging torrents, and turned the dugouts into diving baths ... The men of L Battery, R.H.A., like all others, were flooded out in the twinkling of an eye, and I watched them, standing in their shirts on the edge of their dug-outs, endeavouring with a hooked stick to fish up their equipment and the remainder of

---

9   Antonius, ibid, p. 173.
10   Antonius, ibid, p. 174.

their attire from a murky flood of water four feet deep – all the time singing gaily: "It's a long way to Tipperary."[11]

Towards the end of November a severe blizzard hit the Peninsula, covering it with several inches of snow and causing the temperature to plummet to zero degrees. The ground, roughed up by constant bombing and trekking, began turning into slush and mud. Hundreds of soldiers began reporting in with frostbite, especially those who had not received their winter clothing. At Suvla Bay alone many men died from exposure and frostbite – and 6,500 men were withdrawn due to these effects. The prospects for remaining during the winter looked dim indeed.

With Serbia's defeat and Bulgaria's entrance into war, a direct supply line had now been established between the Central Powers and Turkey. This permitted the introduction of new and more powerful German artillery. The Australians at Anzac Cove were the first to experience this new reality when their positions at Lone Pine were shelled on 29 November – killing fifty-eight men and wounding 204.

The War Cabinet now took Kitchener's suggestion to heart, and decided on 8 December 1915 to withdraw – from all locations.

ENVER MEETS WITH VON FALKENHAYN

In December Enver, the Turkish Minister of War, met with the German Chief-of-Staff General Falkenhayn. Part of the discussion revolved around the possibility of entering into peace talks with the Allies. The Germans wanted President Wilson of America to be the broker for such talks. Upon his return to Constantinople Enver approached Morgenthau and requested him to deliver this request.

The reason for such a proposal at that time, so Morgenthau was able to detect from both Enver and the incoming German ambassador Graf Wolf-Metternich, was that with the impending defeat of Serbia, German now had an unhindered and direct rail link from Berlin to the East. This would en-

---

11 Patterson, ibid, p. 290.

able her to develop her geo-political and economic plan for development in the East; and she was willing to concede most of the territory she had conquered in Belgium and France to attain this end.[12]

THE WITHDRAWAL

The forces from the Suvla Bay and ANZAC sectors were withdrawn on 20 December and those at Cape Helles during 8-9 January 1916. Von Sanders admitted that: 'We of course knew nothing of the intended withdrawal and did not learn of it up to the last minute.'[13] Indeed while the landing and duration of the campaign had basically been failures, the withdrawal was an unmitigated success.

The last group to leave on 20 December from the ANZAC Cove sector was composed of 170 'die-hards' that Monash had chosen. Eliazar Margolin was one of those 'die-hards'.[14]

Everyone was astounded at the success of the withdrawal, including Chauvel, although, Hill stated: 'he was sad to leave the Gallipoli enterprise unfinished.'[15] This sentiment was felt by most departing Australians and New Zealanders. But Chauvel and many of those horsemen would have an opportunity in the next three years to put right that defeat, and to finish the campaign which had started at Gallipoli, in ultimate victory.

Many ANZAC's were disappointed to leave. Their mates lay dead and buried there. A "Special Order of the Day" was issued by Major-General A.L. Ball on 25 December, which stated:

No soldier relishes a withdrawal before the enemy. It is hard to leave behind the graves of 9000 comrades and to relinquish positions so hardly won and so gallantly maintained as those we have left, but all ranks in the Dardanelles army will realize that they were carrying out the orders of H.M. Government so that in due course they could more usefully be employed elsewhere for their King, their Country and the

---

12   Morgenthau, ibid, Chapter 28, pp. 1-3.
13   Von Sanders, ibid, p. 97.
14   Gouttman, ibid, p. 47.
15   Chauvel to S. Chauvel, 20 December 1915, cited in Hill, ibid,p. 63.

Empire. There is only one consideration: what is best for the common cause. In that spirit was the withdrawal carried out and in that spirit the Australians and New Zealanders … have proved and will continue to prove themselves second to none as soldiers of the empire.[16]

The withdrawal from the Helles sector took place during the night of 8 9 January. Von Sanders, interestingly, was planning a major assault against Helles at that time – but now there was no need for it.

Paleologue wrote from Petrograd on 12 January: 'The English and French troops have carried out the evacuation of the Gallipoli Peninsula without mishap … The failure is complete but disaster has been avoided.[17] Several days later, on 16 January he wrote:

The evacuation of Gallipoli by the Anglo-French troops is having a disastrous effect on Russian opinion. Everywhere I hear the same re-mark: "The question is settled now: we shall never get Constantinople… Then what's the good of going on with the war?"[18]

THE COST

The human cost of the Dardanelles Campaign was high on both sides. Von Sanders estimated that there were 215,000 Turkish casualties, of which some 66,000 were killed or died.[19] The Allied deaths were 21,255 British; 9,874 French; 8,709 Australian[20]; 7,594 Indian and 2,701 New Zealand and some 49 from Newfoundland.[21]

It is not difficult to understand why Australia and New Zealand look at this event with significance – considering their combined populations were only just over six million at the time, and this was their first major campaign as sovereign nations.

---

16 Adam-Smith, P. *Anzacs*, (Melbourne, 1991), pp. 181-82.

17 Paleologue, ibid, Vol. 2, 12 January 1916.

18 Paleologue, ibid, Vol. 2, 16 January 1916.

19 Von Sanders, ibid, p. 104.

20 Australian War Memorial, *Gallipoli*, www.awm.gov.au

21 Aspinall-Oglander, C. *Military Operations Gallipoli*. Volume II: May 1915 to the Evacuation, (IWM & Battery Press 1992), www.wikipedia.com

By comparison the Zion Mules Corps losses were small, with six men killed and fifty-five wounded. The numbers of casualties are significantly smaller, but the impact of their presence was very significant. The fact that a Jewish unit from *Eretz Yisrael*, wearing the Star of David insignia, fought together as a unit was in itself of great psychological importance for the Jewish people. Joseph Trumpeldor proved that Jewish people could fight (hundreds of thousands of Jewish men were already serving in all of the European armies). It yet remained to be seen if his adage that all fronts lead to Zion would still be fulfilled.

The British and French Governments on the other hand had been humiliated by what was regarded as a second-rate army and nation. It now remained to be seen what the Turks would do with their fruits of victory – and what the British and French would do in light of this great humiliation.

§

CHAPTER 49

Sykes in – Morgenthau out

SYKES BEFORE THE WAR CABINET

Following his exhaustive six month tour of the East, Sykes returned to Britain in early December 1915. He was called to meet with the War Cabinet on 16 December, where, in connection to the possible future Arab national entity Sykes stated: '… the Arab army officers want to establish an Arab State in which Christians shall be recognized as Arabs first, and not to go on religious lines.'[1]

Sykes then elaborated as to the distinct groups of Mohammedans, some of whom thought similar to the above mentioned, while others did not. There are, he stated, 'uneducated notables in places like Hama, Homs, Baghdad and Nablus who are bigoted, and who want to establish an Arab State which shall be a Mohammedan State, and a good many of the Ulema and religious leaders are on their side.'[2]

When speaking about French involvement in the region Sykes stated that the matter would 'require diplomacy' and it would need to be pointed out to the clerical feeling in France that if matters are not handled properly

---

1 War Committee, 16 December 1915, p. 2. Sir Mark Sykes Collection, GB 165-0275, Middle East Centre Archive, St. Anthony's College.
2 War Committee, ibid, 3.

there could well be a 'massacre of Syrian Christians in the same way that the Armenians were massacred.'[3]

Sykes was of the opinion at this stage that it was important for Britain to encourage the Arabs to rise up against the Turks,[4] although concerning their fighting ability he stated: 'I do not count upon them as a positive force … [even when] they are armed … they do not fight to win.'[5] Additionally, Sykes insisted that 'under no circumstances, should encouragement of the Arabs be at the expense of good relations with France.'[6]

A POTENTIALLY RESURGENT TURKEY

By the end of 1915 the British Government, through the De Bunsen Committee and the findings from Sykes' extensive tour of the East, had a much better idea of their *desiderata* in the Ottoman Empire.

However the initial impetus for determining their *desiderata* had now changed. As the Dardanelles Campaign had failed Russia would not be getting Constantinople, the Bosphorus, and the Dardanelles –at least not via a victory at the Dardanelles. The Dardanelles Campaign had, however, ignited a fire that was not going to be easily snuffed out. Additionally, although the promise of Sherif Hussein to ignite a revolt had turned out to be mostly illusory, nevertheless that initial impetus was also not going to be easily extinguished.

All the while behind the scenes the likes of Herbert Samuel, Chaim Weizmann and Zev Jabotinsky were working tirelessly to see some form of a Jewish national entity established in Palestine.

A major matter that now had to be seriously considered was that of a resurgent Turkey, basking in the glory of victory, and ready to stamp its authority throughout its realm. The upcoming year would witness a continu-

---

3   War Cabinet, ibid, p. 3.
4   Fromkin, ibid, pp. 180-1.
5   CAB 42/6/9 and 46/6/10, evidence of Lt-Col. Sykes on the Arab Question before the war Committee, 16 December 1915, G46 Secret, cited in Friedmann, ibid, p. 105.
6   Friedmann, ibid, p. 105.

ation of efforts by the Turkish leadership to liquidate all potential resistance movements within the Empire.

Freed of the Gallipoli Campaign, Turkey could now concentrate upon re-establishing its authority in other problematic regions of its Empire. It was within this environment that the British Government realized that the failure at Gallipoli ensured a continuing campaign against Turkey. The logical next step after Gallipoli was not going to be France and Belgium – it was going to be in the other regions of the vast Turkish Empire.

Four events henceforth developed in the Turkish Empire: a military campaign into the Sinai in order to defend the Suez Canal; a military campaign to expunge the humiliation of the surrender at Kut-el-Amara; a major effort to ignite the Arab revolt; and a diplomatic campaign to determine a clear course with France as to the future of Turkey's domain in Asia.

ANGLO-FRENCH DISCUSSIONS

Already on 21 October 1915 Grey had suggested to Cambon that the British and French should discuss the frontiers of Syria, in order to ensure there was compatibility between what Britain was discussing with the Arabs and with French aspirations.[7]

The Anglo-French talks began on 23 November 1915 with an initial meeting between Sir Mark Nicolson and Picot.[8] Francois Picot was a staunch advocate of a French presence in Syria – that was understandable as he was part of the French Syria movement which believed that France had a historic role to complete the work it had begun in the region of Syria in the time of the Crusades.[9]

Picot also had first hand experience in the region. In 1914 he had received a pamphlet concerning the desire of the Arab nationalists to attain independence in Syria. Picot tried to convince the French Government to work together with these Arab nationalists – but to no avail.[10] According to

---

7   Stein, ibid, p. 250. Poincare wrote in his diary on 27 October that these discussions could confirm what the French regarded as the Anglo-French accord of 1912. Poincare, ibid, VII, p. 206.

8   Stein, ibid, p. 251.

9   Fromkin, ibid, p. 190.

10   Barr, J. *A Line in the Sand*, (London, 2011), p. 21.

James Barr he then 'secretly arranged for the Greek Government to supply Christians in the Lebanon' with weapons.[11]

But when war broke out Picot left Lebanon expecting to return shortly after. This did not occur. But in the interim, the Turkish authorities found his correspondence and later arrested and executed many of those Lebanese with whom he was in contact.[12]

Upon his return to France Picot dedicated his time to working towards attaining France's historic goal in Lebanon and Syria, alongside a group of similar-minded people in the 'Comite de l'Asie Francaise'.

In these initial meetings Picot 'insisted', wrote Isaiah Friedmann, 'that Syria was a purely French possession … No French Government that surrendered this claim, he maintained, would survive a day.'[13] Their *desiderata* were very clear: if the Turkish Empire was to be partitioned, they wanted Syria and Palestine.[14]

Additionally, Picot believed that the 'British authorities in Cairo had exaggerated the strength of the Arab-Syrian movement, and he doubted its reliability.'[15]

Nicolson 'replied that the Allies were not taking undue risks, since any promises made to the Arabs were conditional upon their assisting the Allies.' Nicolson also mentioned the British desire to avert the *Jihad*, and, 'that there was a real possibility that the Syrian troops, 100,000 strong, would defect from the Turkish army.' Finally, Nicolson tried to impress upon Picot that 'with Arab rule, France had better prospects of establishing her influence than under a Turkish regime.'[16] Within a short time, though, there was a deadlock in these Anglo-French discussions.

SYKES JOINS THE NEGOTIATIONS

Picot then returned to Paris where he discussed with his Government how to proceed in view of the stalemate. Before Picot returned and resumed the

---

11   Barr, ibid, p. 21.
12   Barr, ibid, pp. 21-22.
13   Friedmann, I. *The Question of Palestine*, (New Brunswick, 1973), p. 102.
14   Fromkin, ibid, p. 191.
15   Friedmann, ibid, p. 102.
16   Friedmann, ibid, pp. 102-3.

negotiations on 21 December 1915, the War Cabinet met with Sykes. In view of Sykes' positive report concerning the potential Arab uprising, they realized there was an urgent need to come to an understanding with France over their respective *desiderata* (central to which, was the matter of boundaries). They asked Sykes to lead the negotiations with France.

Although representing the British Government in these important discussions, Sykes reported to Fitzgerald, Kitchener's secretary, and through him, to Kitchener himself.[17]

The need for a quick and decisive understanding with France was reinforced in late December 1915 when news came through via Armenian sources that Djemal Pasha was willing to enter into an agreement with the Russians.[18]

THE ARAB BUREAU

Apart from his involvement now in the Anglo-French negotiations, Sykes made another important contribution to future developments in the East. While on his journey Sykes wrote to London and suggested the formation of an interdepartmental centre in Cairo to collate all information, and to help determine policy concerning the involvement of the Arabs in the ongoing campaign against Turkey.[19]

Clayton encouraged Sykes to pursue this idea. Ultimately Asquith consented to its formation, but it was established as a sub-department of the Cairo Intelligence Department of the War Office which Clayton headed up.

David Hogarth became the director of this new department, named the Arab Bureau, and was responsible to Clayton. His deputy was Kinahan Cornwallis from the Sudan administration. Hogarth's expert on Turkish affairs was Wyndham Deedes, who had previously worked for many years in Turkey, and had also served at Gallipoli. Two other less known men who joined were Philip Graves and T.E. Lawrence.[20]

---

17   Fromkin, ibid, pp. 189-90.
18   Stein, ibid, p. 255.
19   Sir Mark Sykes Collection, GB 165-0275, Middle East Centre.
20   Fromkin, ibid, p. 171.

From the outset, this new entity espoused the views of Kitchener, Clayton and others, who all desired a closer relationship between the Arab speaking regions of the Ottoman Empire with Egypt.[21]

The Arab Bureau also continued to impress upon the policy-makers in Britain the opinion that Britain had to assist the uprising of the Arabs against the Turks, and for the removal of the Caliphate to Mecca. All these men were of the opinion that Turkey had forfeited its right to continue governing its Empire in Asia.

Following his discussion with al-Faruqi, Sykes had concluded that the Arab armies of Emir Hussein would not rise in revolt *until* British forces had begun to invade the region of Syria. A British-led invasion of Syria, though, could not proceed without prior co-ordination with its ally France – and hence the Arab Bureau was also impatient for serious discussions to begin with the French.

MORGENTHAU DEPARTS FROM CONSTANTINOPLE

While all of the above-mentioned activities were taking place Henry Morgenthau was embarking upon a new assignment. Entrusted with the important message of seeking a peace agreement, he prepared to return to America.

His final meeting with Talaat and Enver was on 14 January 1916. 'At this moment of their great triumph', he wrote, '- the Allied expedition to the Dardanelles had evacuated its positions only two weeks before – both Talaat and Enver regarded their country again as a world power.'[22]

At this meeting Morgenthau asked them about the Armenians, at which time the physical disposition of Talaat changed. '"What's the use speaking about them?" he said, waving his hand. "We are through with them. That's all over."'[23]

In fact it was not all over. The massacres continued into 1916 (and only ceased in 1922). Such atrocities against a non-Muslim entity were fur-

---

21 Fromkin, ibid, p. 171.

22 Morgenthau, ibid, Chapter 28, p. 3.

23 Morgenthau, ibid, Chapter 28, p. 4. Another important reason for Morgenthau returning to the US was to assist President Wilson win the upcoming election.

ther evidence that the very existence of the *dhimmi* communities within the Turkish Empire were very much at stake.

The American Henry Morgenthau had done what he could do for the Armenians and other *dhimmis* in the Turkish Empire. Now it was time for others to continue with this work.

§

CHAPTER 50

New structures in Egypt

ALLIED TROOPS WITHDRAW TO EGYPT

When the ANZAC and British troops returned to Egypt they were first to rest, and then prepare either for disembarkation for France or to face an expected Turkish assault upon the Suez Canal.

The veterans were greeted by recent reinforcements. Trooper Reg Walters, a 10th Light Horse Regiment reinforcement wrote: 'The original 10th Light Horse has arrived in camp from Gallipoli (or rather what is left of them). They look pretty weary on it.'[1]

Some of those wounded at Gallipoli were re-acquainted with their mates. 'With the old regiment at Ma'adi again' Idriess wrote in January 1916. 'It was real lonely wandering down the old familiar line looking for familiar faces, and saddening to find only an odd one here and there.'[2]

When the Zion Mule Corps veterans returned to Egypt, their future was uncertain. Trumpeldor had unsuccessfully pleaded for the retention of the unit, and it was formally disbanded. The ZMC was for Gallipoli use only. While the majority of the men blended back into the camps and life

---

1 Diary of Trooper Reg Walters, 10th Light Horse Regiment. (Unpublished, copy in author's possession). Hereafter 'Walters.'
2 Idriess, ibid, p. 50.

in Egypt, 120 men volunteered to re-enlist with the British Army, and then slowly made their way to Britain.

CROSSING THE SUEZ CANAL

There was some anxiety now about the security situation in Egypt. In December 1915 Senussi tribesmen in Cyrenaica, having been excited by the call to *Jihad*, and encouraged by Turkish and German officers, began threatening the Delta and Nile region. Walters wrote: '... we are expecting a general upheaval any minute in Egypt.'[3]   Maxwell, understandably, was concerned lest there be a pincer movement towards the Suez Canal from east and west, and established two separate forces to face this possibility.

The force sent to combat the Senussi was known as 'Western Frontier Force'. They fought skirmishes against the Senussi and were primarily based near Sollum or Mersa Matruh – locations more familiar with the British and Commonwealth soldiers during the next World War. One member of this force was Archie Newton of the Westminster Dragoons.[4]

Shortly after the ANZAC troops returned from Gallipoli they were moved to camps closer to the Suez Canal to form a first line of defence against an expected Turkish attack coming from the Sinai. Reg Walters wrote on 1 March 1916: 'We are right on the banks of the Suez Canal. Had a swim in the Canal going from Africa to Asia.'[5]

Maxwell planned to establish a three line form of defence on the Sinai side of the Suez Canal: one line at 11,000 metres east, the next at 6,500 metres east, and the third at the Canal itself. These defence positions would be supplied with fresh water piped from the Nile to Ismailia, where it was processed in a filtration system of plants, and then piped across to the east side of the Canal. In addition the railway to Ismailia was also improved.

---

3   Walters.
4   Eedle, S. *Archie Newton – His Service with the 2ⁿᵈ County of London (Westminster Dragoons) Yeomanry,* (Tewkesbury, 1997), p. 3.
5   Walters.

Much of this work was accomplished by the newly formed Egyptian Labour Corps (ELC).[6]

In January 1916 General Archibald Murray came out to join Maxwell, and then took over command entirely in March. Murray divided the Suez Canal into three sectors: sector one based at Suez; sector two based at Ismailia; and sector three based at Port Said. Most of the ANZAC soldiers were located in sector two, under the command of Major-General H.A. Lawrence.

In February 1916 Murray informed the Commander-Imperial-General-Staff (CIGS) General William Robertson, that he believed the best forward position to protect the Suez Canal would be at El Arish. Control of El Arish and El Kossaima inland, would seal the two main attacking routes from Palestine through the Sinai to the Suez Canal. Murray was permitted initially, though, to take control over the region of oases some forty kilometres east of the Canal. Walters wrote on 8 March 1916: 'Have now shifted camp across the Canal – 8 miles into Turkey-in-Asia on to the first line of defence.'[7]

FORMATION OF ANZAC MOUNTED DIVISION

While Chauvel oversaw the 1st Australian Division from his HQ at Serapeum,[8] Murray determined that the most effective way to secure the region of oases on the northern route near Romani and Katia (also spelled Qatya) would be by a combination of infantry and mounted forces. The most accessible mounted force were the ANZAC mounted troopers, and Chauvel was asked if he would be willing to relinquish his infantry duties, and take command of the ANZAC mounted forces.

Chauvel agreed, and on 16 March 1916 the Australian and New Zealand Mounted Division was formed. It was commanded by Major-General Harry Chauvel.[9] Henceforth this division was known as the Anzac Mounted Division (AZMD), and was composed of the 1st Light Horse Brigade (com-

---

6   Bullock, D. *Allenby's War*, (London, 1988), p. 23. The ELC began with 500 men, but at its zenith in June 1917 there were 185,782 men in its employ.
7   Walters.
8   Chauvel was temporarily in command of the 1st Division while General Walker was recuperating.
9   Hill, ibid, p. 66.

manded by Brigadier.-General C.F. Cox); the 2nd Light Horse Brigade (com-
manded by Brigadier.-General G. Ryrie); the 3rd Light Horse Brigade (com-
manded by Brigadier-General J.M. Antill) and the New Zealand Mounted
Rifles Brigade (commanded by Brigadier-General Edward Chaytor).
Attached to this mounted division were four batteries of the Royal Horse
Artillery (RHA), Machine-Gun Squadrons, Signals Troop, Mounted Field
Ambulance, Field Troop (Engineers) and a Mobile Veterinary Section.

At that time there was a reshuffle in the organisation of the British forces in the region, and those now entrusted with the safety of the Suez Canal
were named the Egyptian Expeditionary Force (EEF). The EEF was to protect the Suez Canal through the establishment of a secure buffer zone in the
Sinai. In conjunction with this aim Murray would construct a railway line
from the Canal to Romani oasis as well as a water pipeline for the garrison
he planned placing there.

The ANZAC soldiers weren't the only ones protecting the Suez
Canal. They were soon to be joined by thousands of British soldiers. One
of those was Robert Wilson, who on 19 January 1915 had just joined the
Berkshire Yeomanry in Reading.[10] Wilson was later transferred to the Royal
Gloucestershire Hussars Yeomanry.

This unit had previously been despatched to Egypt in 1915 and landed
at Suvla Bay as dismounted Yeomanry. They suffered heavy casualties in the
fighting at Chocolate Hill, and returned to Egypt in November 1915. There,
at Mena Camp they recuperated and retrained, and awaited fresh orders -
and fresh reinforcements. Lieutenant Robert Wilson was on his way as one
of those fresh reinforcements.[11] The fresh orders came in early 1916 when
they joined the ANZAC horsemen and crossed over the Suez Canal and in
to the Sinai.

As there still had been no Arab uprising, any further fighting against
the Turkish Empire would again have to be carried out by British, Australian
and New Zealand soldiers – just as in Gallipoli.

---

10   Wilson, R. *Palestine 1917.* Edited by Helen Millgate. (Tunbridge Wells, 1987), p. 18.
11   Wilson, ibid, p. 37.

§

CHAPTER 51

Conflict in Anatolia and Mesopotamia

TURKISH AND RUSSIAN CONFLICT IN EASTERN ANATOLIA

Many of the Turkish troops who had served at Gallipoli were then despatched to other fronts – some to Syria and Mesopotamia, but most to Europe and to fight against the Russians in eastern Anatolia.

The Russian commander, the Grand Duke Nicholas, was aware that with the completion of the Dardanelles Campaign, these Turkish reinforcements would soon reach the eastern Anatolian front. He needed to strike at the Turkish front line before they arrived.[1]

A fresh Russian assault began in January 1916 and resulted in the capture of the regional capital of Erzerum, reputed to be the best fortified city in Turkey, on 16 February.[2] The Turkish reinforcements sent to bolster the Third Army were insufficient to halt the advance of the Russians.

While further Turkish troops were pushed forward as quickly as possible, the Russians made further progress westwards. With winter now in its fullest force, though, the general Russian advance then stopped. From

---

1 Knight, W. *The History of the Great European War*, (London), Vol. VII, p. 114.
2 Knight, ibid, p. 114.

the Turkish perspective this was welcome as its forces were terribly sick and emaciated.[3]

In April 1916 the Russians captured the strategic coastal city of Trebizond, which permitted them to establish a forward line stretching from the Black Sea through to Erzerum and on to Lake Van.

The loss of Trebizond and especially Erzerum was a major blow to the Turkish leadership, and they began preparing for a major offensive to recapture those positions. The attack began in June 1916, but the Russians thwarted this thrust and even captured the strategic locality of Erzingyan.[4] By August the Turks had not attained their goals, while the Russians were themselves too exhausted to follow up their victories.[5]

Both sides, seriously under supplied and under nourished, then consolidated their lines. But then winter came earlier than usual towards the end of 1916 and a stalemate descended upon the eastern Anatolian front.

TOWNSHEND SURRENDERS AT KUT-EL-AMARA

While the defeated Allied troops at Gallipoli returned to Egypt, the beleaguered British garrison continued to hold out at Kut-el-Amara. Fresh forces were brought in from France, and combined with troops based in Basra, the Commander-in-Chief General Sir John Nixon ordered further British attempts to relieve the besieged forces. These attempts failed.[6]

Two further large scale British attacks took place in April – but these also failed. The relief forces did all they could possibly do to reach the besieged force at Kut – but failed.

With supplies almost non-existent, soldiers starving and all hope of relief gone, General Townshend surrendered on 29 April. 'They were' wrote Knight 'the victims of an incompetence, indifference, and ineptitude on the part of the Government, its expert advisors, and those in chief command of

---

3   Von Sanders, ibid, pp. 132-33.
4   Knight, ibid, Vol. VII, p. 115.
5   Von Sanders, ibid, pp. 127-9.
6   Von Sanders, ibid, p. 132.

the expedition, such as had hardly been equalled in the whole history of the wars of the British Empire.'[7]

This British defeat was a tremendous loss of prestige, coming so soon after the defeat and withdrawal from Gallipoli.

Many of the Allied prisoners thereafter died from sickness and deprivation. They weren't alone in succumbing to sickness On 6 April Field Marshal von der Goltz also died from sickness.

Goltz's successor, the Turkish General Halil Pasha, did not quickly pursue the defeated British forces, who still controlled the area from Fellalieh southward to Basra.[8] Instead he led his Turkish troops into Persia to battle a small Russian force there. The Russians had entered Persia from the north, and Germany and Turkey both sent officers and advisors to assist the Persian army to oust them.

THE BRITISH CONSOLIDATE

Von Sanders requested the Turkish High Command to desist from over involvement in Persia and to utilise the Turkish forces to pursue the British and drive them out of Mesopotamia. His advice was not completely heeded and as a result the British consolidated their position south of Kut.

They built a railway from Basra along the Tigris River to Korna and beyond. Fresh forces also arrived, led by a worthy replacement for Townshend in Major-General Frederick Maude, who was one of the few commanders to have emerged unscathed from the Suvla Bay landings. Maude was content to wait until his force was ready before renewing the offensive.

In late September 1916 CIGS Robertson informed Maude that his task was to defend Basra and 'the oilfields and pipeline of the Anglo-Persian Oil Company.'[9] But in October, through the exertions of General Monro, (C-in-C of India) Robertson relented somewhat, and gave permission to Maude 'to maintain an aggressive front', but within 'the defensive policy by which he had been instructed.'[10]

---

7   Knight, W. *The History of the Great European War,* (London), Vol. VII, p. 92.
8   Von Sanders, ibid, p. 134.
9   Lloyd George, ibid, Vol. 2, p. 1025.
10   Lloyd George, ibid, Vol. 2, p. 1025.

By this stage the Turkish Empire, although having sustained some terrible defeats against the Russians, seemed to be holding the upper hand in their conflicts against the British Empire.

THE ASSYRIAN GENOCIDE

For those whose destinies depended upon a defeat of Turkey, the future seemed somewhat bleak by the middle of 1916. The situation for all the *dhimmi* communities was becoming progressively worse. Not only was the Armenian community being systematically destroyed, but so too was the ancient Assyrian community.

This ancient Christian community lived in some areas alongside the Armenians, as well as in the region bordering Turkey, Syria, Iraq and Iran. David Gaunt, an authority on the subject of the relationship between the Muslim and Christian minorities in the Turkish Empire during World War One, wrote:

> Of all modern genocides, that perpetrated on the Assyrian peoples of Kurdistan during World War I is one of the most obscure and little known. Somewhere between 250,000-300,000 Assyrians, about half the population, were killed or died from starvation and disease in a series of campaigns orchestrated by the Ottoman Turkish government.[11]

It would appear that there was only one real solution for the preservation of the minority groups in the Ottoman Turkish Empire from total destruction – the conquest of the entire region by the Allied forces. But at the end of 1916 this possibility was far from being actualised.

---

11   Gaunt, D, *The Assyrian Genocide 1915*, SEYFO Center 1915, www.seyfocenter.com. Material in Gaunt's article derived from: David Gaunt, *Massacres, Resistance, Protectors: Muslim-Christian Relations in Eastern Anatolia during World War I* (Piscataway, N.J.: Gorgias Press 2006). Another to have written on the subject is Travis, Hannibal. *Genocide in the Middle East: The Ottoman Empire, Iraq, and Sudan.* (Durham, NC: Carolina Academic Press, 2010). In 2007 the International Association of Genocide Scholars officially recognized that what happened to the Assyrians, was, like what happened to the Armenians and Greeks in Asia Minor, a genocide. www.genocidescholars.org

§

First blood in the Sinai

THE WORK OF THE EEF

The initial role of the EEF was to protect the railway as it was being constructed from Kantara (also spelled Qantara) north-eastwards towards the oases region, where the 5th Yeomanry Brigade was based. In April Chauvel brought the Anzac Mounted Division to Salhia, just west of Kantara, where he was to consolidate his force before permanently moving them to the east of the Canal, where the 5th Yeomanry Brigade would then come under his command.

Much time was spent patrolling into the Sinai. On 13 April the 3rd Light Horse Brigade encountered a Turkish patrol in the region of Jif-jaffa, location of huge water wells which Von Kressenstein had developed as part of his strategy of attacking the Suez Canal through the interior of the Sinai. Signaller Henry Bostock wrote of another long trip: 'During this period we made several very long patrols across the desert. Our first was to locate a lost plane and airman ... We rode all day, camped and skirmished the desert next morning and then were ordered back to camp.'[1]

---

1 Bostock, H. *The Great Ride*, (Perth, 1982), p. 33.

FIRST ASSAULT - APRIL

Colonel Von Kressenstein was observing all of these EEF moves, and realised that he would need to strike before the EEF became too firmly ensconced in their new positions east of the Suez Canal. His attack was delayed as German and Austrian reinforcements had not arrived in time.[2] When these specialised forces did arrive, and when it became apparent that the British were speeding up the movement of forces from Egypt to Europe, it was decided to quickly attack.[3]

The 5th Yeomanry Brigade were placed in small isolated groups in the oases area. Meanwhile a small but efficient force under the command of Von Kressenstein moved forward towards these isolated British forces. The Royal Flying Corps (RFC) spotted this force and informed GHQ on 22 April. Chauvel ordered Ryrie to send troops forward – but they did not reach the forward lines in time.

Taking advantage of an early morning fog, the Turco-German force attacked the 5th Yeomanry Brigade on 23 April 1916, first at Oghratina, then at Katia and finally at Dueidar. The isolated British forces were outnumbered and suffered many casualties.

Although Ryrie's brigade was already moving forward, Chauvel ordered other regiments to head eastwards to the battle zone. Idriess recalled receiving the order to mount up and move into the desert and of then galloping over the metalled road leading out of Kantara.[4]

For the most part, though, the ANZAC mounted men arrived too late - at Hill 70 they were confronted by the sight of hundreds of dead Bedouins and Turkish and British soldiers, mostly of the 5th Yeomanry Brigade.

CONSOLIDATION IN ROMANI-KATIA AREA

The Turkish force may not have made it to the Suez Canal, but they exposed the vulnerability of small isolated British units. Murray quickly adapted his

---

2   Von Sanders, ibid, p. 141.

3   Von Sanders, ibid, p. 142.

4   Idriess, ibid, p. 10.

strategy. Chauvel was then commanded to take command of the EEF forces east of Hill 70, and the depleted 5th Yeomanry came under his command. They were soon joined by Lieutenant Wilson, who wrote:

> After an eventful journey I reached the Regiment and found them in rather a state of depression. Only a few weeks before my arrival they had lost a complete Squadron except for about seven survivors.[5]

In time, infantry of the British 52nd Lowland (Scottish) Division also moved forward, and established a trench line from Romani through to the Sinai coast. From the time that Chauvel moved forward to take command of the region he began sending the 2nd Light Horse Brigade and Chaytor's New Zealanders deep into the Sinai, looking for water supplies, and destroying supplies established by Von Kressenstein.

In the following months, as the summer heat intensified, Chauvel constantly sent out patrols. Walters wrote: 'Anzac Day 25th April. We are preparing to move out and meet our enemy the Turk in a day or 2, but perhaps as usual it will blow over.'[6]

On another occasion Walters wrote of a trip out to destroy the water wells at Jif-jaffa: 'We are out here at the well' he wrote on 10 June 1916 'and have just about pumped her dry preparatory to destroying it … It was rather peculiar, after travelling so many miles over a desert to strike this beautiful well.'[7] The following day the wells were completely destroyed – thereby destroying any hopes Von Kressenstein had of again attacking the Suez Canal through the mid-Sinai route.

The Turkish force was not idle during this period either. They constantly sent out cavalry patrols, while German planes, *Taubes*, were constantly bombing and photographing EEF positions. Wilson, who was slowly becoming accustomed to life in the desert, wrote to his brother Ted from his base at Kantara on 9 July 1916 about planes in the desert:

---

5   Wilson, ibid, p. 42.
6   Walters.
7   Walters.

"… there are a lot of our airmen here, it is very interesting to see them turn out when an enemy is reported. The De Haviland, the best of the lot, went after a Fokker about a fortnight ago, just caught him up over the Australians who promptly plugged our man's petrol tank and fetched him down. The Pilots often dine with us and they say they'd sooner fly over Turks than Colonials."[8]

While Chauvel's forces were busily readying themselves, and while they continued to adjust to the somewhat different characteristics of each other, Von Kressenstein continued his task of moulding his German expertise with his Turkish soldiers, and being as best prepared as he could be for mounting a second and larger attack upon the Suez Canal.

Chauvel and his ANZAC forces were looking forward to having another encounter with 'Johnny' Turk – and they were very eager to make up for their great loss at Gallipoli.

8   Wilson, ibid, p. 43.

§

CHAPTER 53

The 'Sykes-Picot' Agreement

THE NEGOTIATIONS ARE RENEWED

No major military movement in the Sinai (except for protecting the Suez Canal) could occur until a political agreement had been made with the French concerning the future of the region.

While in Paris, Picot persuaded his superiors to agree 'to include the four Arab towns of the Syrian hinterland in the Arab zone to be self-administered, but under French influence.'[1]

Although they recognized it would be a challenge to administer the inland region, they mostly desired direct rule over the coastal region and Lebanon, and to control the inland region through puppet Arab rulers.[2]

From the French perspective it was imperative to ensure that they ruled over the Lebanon region. 'Picot argued', wrote Fromkin, 'that Christian Lebanon would not tolerate even the nominal rule of the Emir of Mecca, while Paul Cambon, the French ambassador in London, warned that French rule would be necessary to avert the outbreak of a religious war.'[3] Cambon

---

1 Friedmann, ibid, p. 105. For another source on the Anglo-French negotiations see James Barr, *A Line in the Sand*, (London, 2011).
2 Friedmann, ibid, p. 105.
3 Fromkin, ibid, p. 192.

stated: 'It is enough to know the intensity of rivalries between the various rites and religions in the Orient to foresee the violence of the internal strife in Lebanon as soon as no external authority is there to curb it.'[4]

The French desire was for an extended area from the Mediterranean through to the region of Mosul (northern Mesopotamia). Part of this actually matched what the British (that is, Kitchener) wanted. The British actually wanted the French to have Mosul, so that the French would then be interposed between the British zone in the south (from Haifa southwards) and Russia in the north. Britain was willing to give up the potential oil resources of Mosul in order for France to be the buffer against Russia.[5]

There were several other significant modifications from the original hard-lined French approach. Amongst these was for a special enclave to be formed around Jerusalem 'with boundaries still to be defined'; while 'the position of Haifa and Acre as a Mediterranean outlet for the British in Mesopotamia were left open.'[6]

THE ISSUE OF PALESTINE

When Sykes joined the negotiations several key matters had still to be clearly ascertained, one of these being the region of Palestine. From the outset Sykes held a strong view that it was in Britain's best interests that apart from a 'Jerusalem enclave' Britain should administer the Mediterranean coast south of Acre.[7]

In the initial discussions between Sykes and Picot the French proposal was that, wrote Antonius, 'Jerusalem and Bethlehem with their immediate surroundings should form a separate enclave to be subjected to a special regime of international control to suit its sacred character, but that the rest of Palestine should continue to form an integral part of Syria.'[8]

4   Andrew, C & Kanya-Forstner, A. *The Climax of French Imperial Expansion 1914-1924*, (Stanford, 1981), cited in Fromkin, ibid, p. 192.
5   Fromkin, ibid, p. 191.
6   Friedmann, ibid, p. 106.
7   Stein, ibid, p. 254. While in Cairo in 1915 he heard concerning Picot's trip there that the French would be willing to give up the coast south of Acre. Leslie, S. *Mark Sykes – His Life and Letters*, p. 241.
8   Antonius, ibid, p. 247.

Concerning Palestine, consideration had to be given to the interest of Muslims, Christians and Jews in this country; and concerning the Jewish people, it was noted that 'the members of the Jewish community, throughout the world, have a conscientious and sentimental interest in the future of the country.'[9]

Sykes fought to retain this coveted land, or as much of it as possible, for Britain, as it would then be contiguous to British holdings further south, in Egypt. France conversely desired it for themselves.

If Britain was to administer only the region around Haifa and Acre, then it was important that the beginning of the French administered area was pushed as far north of Haifa as possible.

Ultimately it was agreed that in exchange for France gaining the port of Alexandretta (which was Kitchener's first choice), Britain would gain the region of Acre and Haifa, which would offer them their Mediterranean port. From Haifa they would construct a railway through to Mesopotamia – and hence have direct communications between the Mediterranean and the Persian Gulf (although Alexandretta would have been shorter).

Apart from this region, the remainder of the strategic 'land between empires' would be administered by some form of international body, the term used being – *internationalisation* - a compromise which France reluctantly conceded to Britain.[10] This was to be regarded as the Brown Area. The finer details concerning its form and administration would need to be determined following discussions with her Allies, primarily Russia, as well as Italy, and an Islamic representative.[11]

The French, though, never completely gave up on the desire to administer this land. They knew that this 'agreement' first had to be accepted and endorsed by the Russians, and they hoped to be able to get the Russians to endorse their desire to control the 'Holy Land.'[12]

---

9   Friedmann, ibid, p. 107.
10   Stein, ibid, p. 234.
11   Friedmann, ibid, p. 107.
12   Stein, ibid, p. 260.

THE REMAINING AREAS

Apart from Palestine, the remaining areas not being directly administered by the British or French would form an Arab state, albeit associated with zones of economic interest from either of the major powers. In this region the areas covered by the large towns Aleppo, Hama, Homs and Damascus would permit for such an entity – but be subject to French and not to British influence.[13]

The entire region, including the intended Arab national entity (outside of the Arabian Peninsula), would be divided into 'British and French commercial and administrative spheres of influence.'[14]

Sykes in pursuing this line believed he was doing what the key men in Cairo, especially Clayton and Storrs, actually wanted when they spoke of Arab 'independence'. But what they actually meant was Arab 'independence' under British influence and guidance.[15] These men felt that Arab 'independence' would better develop under British administration, whereas under French administration all things French would be imposed upon the population.[16]

But, as David Fromkin states, what these British 'Arabists' in Cairo really desired was an expanded area of influence for Cairo to administer, and now that very area had been surrendered to the French.[17]

An initial agreement was reached on 3 January 1916. Picot and Cambon had no faith at all in Hussein being able to fulfil his commitment, and they counselled their Foreign Minister to conclude the agreement with the British as soon as possible.[18]

Prime Minister Briand presented the interim agreement to the French Cabinet on 4 January. As could be expected they were deeply perturbed. Poincare represented their views by stating that it was a reversal of the 1912 'agreement.'[19]

---

13 Fromkin, ibid, p. 193.
14 Friedmann, ibid, p. 106.
15 Fromkin, ibid, p. 193.
16 Fromkin, ibid, p. 194.
17 Fromkin, ibid, p. 194. For one of the best descriptions of this period, see Fromkin.
18 Fromkin, ibid, pp. 192-3.
19 Poincare, ibid, Vol. VIII, p. 8.

The French Government, though, were caught in a bind. Their bargaining position was weak, and they needed to get what they could - as quickly as possible. Their bargaining position was weak due to two main factors:

- They were totally reliant upon Britain and the forces of the British Empire to stave off defeat by the Germans in France.
- Soldiers of the British Empire (namely British, Australian and New Zealander) were poised in the Sinai and could potentially capture the region under question. As no French troops were involved, or would potentially be involved, then the British were in a far superior position to the French.

Discussions continued on the minor points in the meantime, but in February 1916 both the British and French Cabinets accepted the agreement. Under the final agreement there were to be six distinct regions:

1. That under direct French rule, including the coastal region of Lebanon. This was the Blue Area.
2. That under direct British rule, mostly the *Vilayets* of Basra and Baghdad. This was the Red Area.
3. That under Arab rule but with French economic and administrative influence. This was Area A.
4. That under Arab rule but with British economic and administrative influence. This was Area B.
5. The area around Haifa and Acre, which would be part of the British Red Area. The details concerning the rail link to Mesopotamia were still to be determined.
6. The Jerusalem enclave, which basically encompassed most of Palestine. This was the Brown Area. This was the internationalised zone, the administration of which was still to be determined.

Sykes desired a quick acceptance of the Agreement so that the campaign in Syria could commence (initially to be in southern Cilicia or Alexandretta).

He still believed that this would then 'spark al-Faruqi's promised Arab revolt.'[20] As Hirtzel was later to state: 'Without the British offensive there could have been no Arab revolt; and without the Sykes-Picot Agreement there would have been no British offensive.'[21]

The needs to, firstly fire up the Arab revolt, and secondly obtain a diplomatic agreement with the French, were interrelated. The fulfilment of the conditions of this Agreement would depend upon active Arab involvement. A decision by an Interdepartmental Committee on 4 February 1916 stated that 'the co-operation of the Arabs' was to be secured and that they were to 'fulfil the conditions and obtain the towns of Homs, Hama, Damascus and Aleppo ...' In addition to such *active* Arab involvement, the consent of Russia was also required before the Agreement could be implemented.[22]

WHO WOULD ADMINISTER THE 'INTERNATIONALISED' ZONE?

By now the major question to be considered was: 'Who would administer the Brown Area, the 'internationalised' zone?' One very interesting proposal to this question was presented in a Memorandum written by William Hall, head of the Intelligence Department at the Admiralty, who wrote on 12 January 1916: 'In the Brown area the question of Zionism, and also of British control of all Palestinian railways ... [will] have to be considered.'[23]

Hall was fully aware of the possible, and even natural, blending of Britain's geo-political interests, and the Jewish national aspirations.

Until this point Sir Mark Sykes MP had little knowledge of Zionism and of the Jewish desire to establish a national entity in Palestine. He had been so focussed upon trying to appease both the Arab and French aspirations, that this important component was neglected.

Following the initial agreement, and before Sykes travelled to Petrograd to discuss the Anglo-French Agreement with the Russians, Sykes was alerted

20   Fromkin, ibid, p. 195.
21   FO 608/107, p. no. 2256, French Claims to Syria' Memorandum by Sir A. Hirtzel, 14 Febraury 1919, cited in Friedmann, ibid, pp. 108-9.
22   FO 371/2767/938, 'Arab Question, 4 February 1916, cited in Friedmann, ibid, p. 112.
23   'Memorandum on the Proposed Agreement with the French', 12 January 1916 by William Hall, War Department Secret Series, cited in Friedmann, ibid, p. 111.

to these Jewish aspirations by Hall's memo and statement,[24] that the Jewish people might oppose the 'promises' made to the Arabs. Hall also stated that the 'British should land troops in Palestine, for only then would the Arabs come over to the Allies.'[25]

It was at this point that Sykes understood that in the discussions concerning the future status of Palestine, both he and Picot had neglected to consider 'that Jews might be concerned about the political future of Palestine.'[26]

As a result of this awakening, Sykes established contact with Herbert Samuel and thus began his association with the Jewish nationalist aspirations. In time he saw the great opportunity of synthesizing British objectives in Palestine with those of Zionism.

HOW TO CAPTURE AMERICAN JEWISH SUPPORT?

Hall's suggestion was merging with another emerging dynamic – American public opinion. Early in 1916 Zev Jabotinsky met Lord Newton, the Minister of Propaganda, and spoke to him about the concept of a Jewish Legion as a means of negating the opposition of the American Jews to the Triple Alliance.[27]

The vast majority of the Jewish population of the United States came originally from regions under the control of Russia, and were forced to leave due to the 1881-2 and 1905 state inspired *pogroms.*

Thus, for the majority of American Jews, Russia was synonymous with rampant anti-Semitism and the Czarist regime was the epitome of evil. Any sympathy many may have had for Britain and the Allies was negated by them being allied to Russia. Adopting a positive position concerning Jewish national aspirations in Palestine and establishing a Jewish Legion were two such ways to change this attitude.

On 16 December 1915 Lucien Wolf, the foreign secretary of the Conjoint Committee,[28] submitted a Memo at the invitation of Lord Robert Cecil in

---

24 Fromkin, ibid, p. 196.

25 Fromkin, ibid, p, 196.

26 Fromkin, ibid, p. 196.

27 Jabotinsky, V. *The Story of the Jewish Legion,* (New York, 1945), pp. 65-66.

28 The Conjoint Foreign Committee was composed of representatives of the Board of Deputies of British Jews and the Anglo-Jewish Association.

the Foreign Office,[29] concerning the make-up of the American Jewish community – and an analysis of how best to encourage them to adopt a more
positive attitude towards the Allied war effort. Although not a Zionist, Wolf
himself stated:

> ... in any bid for Jewish sympathies to-day very serious account must
> be taken of the Zionist Movement. In America the Zionist organiza-
> tions have lately captured Jewish opinion ... This is the moment for
> the Allies to declare their policy in regard to Palestine... What they
> especially want to like to know is that Great Britain will become mis-
> tress of Palestine. This may be difficult to say in view of French claims
> ...[30]

Then in February 1916 the Conjoint Foreign Committee sent an official
Memorandum to the Foreign Office calling upon the Allies to 'authorize
a public statement on the Palestine question, giving certain assurances
to the Jews.'[31] Another similar proposal came in the same month – from
McMahon in Cairo. Earlier in February, Edward Suares, the President of
the Jewish community in Alexandria, had made a statement concerning the
need for Britain to take a more positive role concerning Jewish aspirations
in Palestine. This perspective found its way to McMahon, who accordingly
forwarded it to the Foreign Office, where it was read by Harold Nicholson
on 23 February.[32]

These initiatives were indicative of a growing groundswell of interest
and involvement among Jewish people, particularly in Britain and America,
concerning a future Jewish national entity in Palestine – under British protection. This was now within the context of who would administer the 'internationalised' zone; combined with a growing desire to capture American
and in particular Jewish American support for the Allied war effort.

29   Lord Cecil and Lord Crewe were now taking a more prominent role in the Foreign Office, due to Grey's deteriorating health.
30   Stein, ibid, pp. 220-1.
31   Stein, ibid, p. 221. The Conjoint Foreign Committee was comprised of representatives of the Board of Deputies
of British Jews and the Anglo-Jewish Association.
32   FO 371/2671, cited in Sanders, R. The High Walls of Jerusalem, (New York, 1983), p. 333.

This perspective was no doubt discussed in a meeting between Colonel William House, President Wilson's envoy to the Allied Powers, at a function in London on 14 February, between House, Asquith, Lloyd George, Grey and Balfour.[33]

Wolf then submitted an official proposal to the British Foreign Office on 3 March 1916 stating, in part: 'In the event of Palestine coming within the sphere of influence of Great Britain and France at the close of the War, the Governments of those Powers will not fail to take account of the historic interest that country possesses for the Jewish community.'[34]

Interestingly at this time Gerald Fitzmaurice in the Foreign Office commissioned Hugh O'Beirne to also write a Memorandum, suggesting 'that if we could offer the Jews an arrangement as to Palestine which would strongly appeal to them we might conceivably be able to strike a bargain with them as to withdrawing their support from the Young Turk Government which would then automatically collapse.'[35] There were numerous other similar proposals and remarks at the time, including from Lord Cecil, who stated: 'I do not think it is easy to exaggerate the international power of the Jews.'[36]

The Foreign Office acknowledged receipt of Wolf's memo on 9 March and already on 11 March they had informed their ambassadors in Paris and Petrograd: 'it has been suggested to us that if we could offer to the Jews an arrangement in regard to Palestine completely satisfactory to Jewish aspirations, such an offer might appeal strongly to a large and powerful section of the Jewish community throughout the world.'[37]

The message, drafted by Lord Crewe, then continued: '... the Zionist idea has in it the most far-reaching political possibilities, for we might hope to use it in such a way as to bring over to our side the Jewish forces in America, the East, and elsewhere, which are now largely, if not preponderantly, hostile to us.'[38] The message concludes:

---

33 Sanders, ibid, pp. 334-5.

34 'Suggested Palestine Formula', FO 371/2671, cited in Stein, ibid, p. 222.

35 FO 371/2671, cited in Sanders, ibid, p. 334. Fitzmaurice, a former employee in the British Embassy in Constantinople believed there was a Jewish conspiracy behind the Young Turk Revolt.

36 FO 371/2671, cited in Sanders, ibid, p. 326.

37 CFC 1916/206, cited in Stein ibid, p. 223.

38 Stein, ibid, p. 223.

We consider, however, that the scheme might be made far more at-
tractive to the majority of Jews if it held out to them the prospect that
when in course of time the Jewish colonists in Palestine grows strong
enough to cope with the Arab population they may be allowed to take
the management of the internal affairs of Palestine (with the exception of Jerusalem and the Holy Places) into their own hands.[39]

PICOT AND SYKES IN RUSSIA

Sykes, meanwhile had joined Picot in Russia at the beginning of March,
where they hoped to obtain Russian consent for the agreement. Russia, naturally, stuck to her original request for incorporation of Constantinople, the
Bosphorus and Dardanelles into the Russian Empire.

When viewing the remainder of the Anglo-French agreement, Sazanov
saw that the zone of French influence in the region of Cilicia actually included some of the regions of the Armenian *vilayets*, which the Russians were in
the process of capturing from the Turks. Russia was unwilling to concede
these areas to the French.[40]

The French sought compensation elsewhere. This new initiative now
provided the French with a natural opportunity of 'regaining' Palestine.
France now put forth a proposal that they be compensated for the loss of
territory in the Cilicia-Armenia region, by having Palestine incorporated
into her administered region in Syria.

Then followed a political discussion which incorporated modern politics and ages-old traditions. Initially it seemed that Sazanov was willing to
accede to the French request. In a memorandum to his colleagues 'he suggested ... that in regard to Palestine, Russia would be prepared to concern
herself solely with the Holy Places and to agree, accordingly, to the cutting
down of the area to be internationalised.'[41]

While these discussions were taking place Ambassador Buchanan informed Sykes about the Foreign Office telegram of 11 March, which includ-

---

39   FO 371/2671, pp. 20-23, cited in Sanders, ibid, p. 342.
40   Stein, ibid, p. 260.
41   Adamov, No. 77, cited in Stein, ibid, p. 260.

ed the proposals of Lucien Wolf and O'Beirne.[42] When the matter was introduced to Picot, he reacted very negatively.[43]

Sykes, though, soothed the way, outlining a proposal for a Jewish Chartered Company in Palestine, to which Picot could see some merit, as 'it might materially help in the war.'[44] Picot was willing to concede something for at that point the terrible Battle of Verdun was raging and the French needed all the help from Britain that they could muster[45] - and any international Jewish support as well! Picot, though, was totally opposed to any such Zionist entity being under the protection of Britain.[46]

When Sykes enthusiastically wrote back to the Foreign Office about his ideas and discussion with Picot, he was instructed to tone down his enthusiasm. Grey, who was now back at the helm after a period out due to ill-health, asked that Sykes expunge from his memory Samuel's Palestine Memorandum. Grey had only one matter in mind – not to upset the French.[47]

The Russians also offered him very little sympathy on the matter.[48] Sazanov, wrote Stein 'would agree to any arrangement providing adequate guarantees for the Orthodox Church and its establishments and would be prepared in principle to raise no objection to the settlement of Jewish colonists.'[49] But when it came to the Zionist proposal, Sazanov 'objected that there was no room in Palestine for all the Jews of Russia.'[50] Sykes was not put off by this negative attitude, and when he left on 16 March he was determined to do his utmost to find a workable solution.

On 26 March Paleologue asked Sazanov about the Russian position concerning Palestine, and thanked him 'for having intimated in conversation' that, provided Britain accept that Palestine be included in French Syria, then Russia would not object.[51] Sazanov in his reply was more cautious on

---

42   The telegram from the Foreign Office also included the proposal of Hugh O'Beirne, of the Foreign Office, who had made a similar proposal.

43   Friedmann, ibid, p. 113.

44   Friedmann, ibid, p. 115.

45   Sanders, ibid, p. 351.

46   Friedmann, ibid, p. 115.

47   Sanders, ibid, p. 349. Samuel, incidentally, had re-circulated his memorandum on 16 March to the new members of the War Cabinet, seeing as the issue of Palestine was now on the agenda.

48   Stein, ibid, p. 229. Fromkin, ibid, p. 197.

49   Stein, ibid, p. 229.

50   Stein, ibid, p. 229.

51   Stein, ibid, p. 260.

this occasion, adding a qualification, 'that Russia would have to insist … that not only the Holy Places, but all towns and localities in which there were religious establishments belonging to the Orthodox Church, should be placed under an international administration, with a guarantee of free access to the Mediterranean coast.'[52]

'Russia' wrote Antonius 'had schools and convents and holy sites in her care all over the Holy Land, notably in Nazareth, Nablus and Hebron, far beyond the limits of the small enclave proposed by France. At first she attempted to stake a claim to a Russian protectorate over the Holy Land, but that was resisted by both Great Britain and France. Then, seeing the wisdom of dropping that claim for the time being, she declared her willingness to consent to a regime of international control provided it applied to the whole of the Holy Land in such a way as to include all the Russian establishments and sites within the zone of international administration.'[53]

According to what Sykes and Picot had worked out, Palestine would be administered by an international regime, the character of which was yet to be determined. Although the French most definitely did not like this arrangement, the British could push for this due to Russian interest in the Holy Places and thereby Russia's reluctance to see France administer the Holy Places exclusively.[54]

But the French Premier Briand had held secret negotiations with the Russians, whereby it was agreed that the so-called international regime was impractical, and that the French should in fact administer Palestine (except the Holy Places) as well.[55]

The initial formal aspect of the Anglo-French agreement, having now gained the consent of the Russians, occurred when on 26 April 1916 Sazanov and Paleologue exchanged notes which related to the Russian component.[56]

---

52   Stein, ibid, p. 261.
53   Antonius, ibid, pp. 247-8.
54   Stein, ibid, pp. 236-7.
55   Fromkin, ibid, p. 197.
56   Antonius, ibid, p. 428.

FRENCH AND BRITISH CONFIRM THE AGREEMENT

Upon his return to London Sykes pursued the Zionist idea, and again met with Samuel. Samuel in turn introduced him to the Chief Rabbi of the Sephardic community, Rabbi Moses Gaster.

Impressed with what he heard, Sykes then arranged a meeting between Gaster, Samuel, Picot and himself, the object being to persuade Picot that the British and French 'should work together as patrons of Arabs and Jews.'[57] Picot was not interested in helping either Jewish or Arab nationalist ambitions. This rebuttal meant that there was no way of altering the Agreement as it then stood.

The British and French Governments then completed their negotiations, and the final agreement was confirmed between Grey and Cambon on 16 May 1916. Although officially it was the Anglo-French Agreement, it became better known as the 'Sykes-Picot' Agreement.

Despite the late interest in the national aspirations of the Jewish people, there seemed little apparent opportunity that such aspirations were to be fulfilled within this scheme. The only way such a concept as a Jewish national entity in Palestine could occur would be if Britain and not France administered the internationalised Brown Area, and that the Jewish concept would be integrated into the Brown Area. For this to happen, though, there would need to be some quite drastic political and military changes, and in May 1916 these seemed improbable.

---

57 Fromkin, ibid, p. 197.

ANGLO-FRENCH ('SYKES-PICOT') AGREEMENT

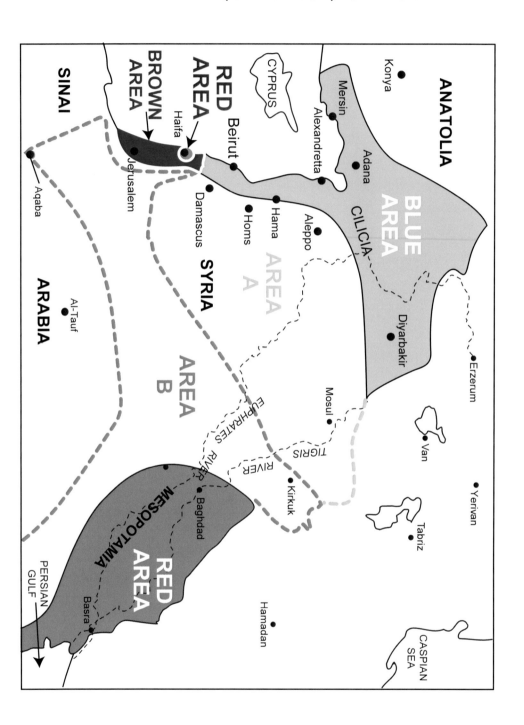

§

CHAPTER 54

The Hejaz offensive 'begins'

SHERIF HUSSEIN PROMPTED TO IGNITE THE FIRE

While Zev Jabotinsky was busily raising awareness for a Jewish Legion to be actively involved in the conquest of *Eretz Yisrael*, Sherif Hussein of the Hejaz finally decided to join in the war against Turkey.

In the early part of 1916 Feisal was in Damascus at Djemal's request and it was while there that Djemal convicted a number of key Arab leaders of treason and had them executed.[1]

During this same period Djemal was preparing to send 'fresh Turkish forces to the Southern Hejaz'. Cyril Falls states that this move precipitated the Arab revolt.[2] This Turkish force was composed of some 3,500 special-ised soldiers and included a German field mission led by Major Frieherr Othmar von Stotzingen.[3] Falls wrote: 'Stotzingen was charged with setting up a wireless station on the coast to communicate with the Germans in East Africa and also with the direction of propaganda in Somaliland, Abyssinia, the Sudan and Darfur.'[4]

---

1 Antonius, ibid, p. 191. Hussein was greatly perturbed by this act.
2 Falls, ibid, Vol. 1, p. 220.
3 Antonius, ibid, p. 191; Falls, ibid, Vol. 1. p. 228.
4 Falls, ibid, Vol. 1. p. 229.

Storrs stated: 'At last Husain, alarmed by Turkish activities and the Stotzingen Mission, took the plunge. On May 23rd, 1916, a message was telegraphed to Sir Henry MacMahon from Port Sudan: "Sharif's son Abdallah urgently requires Storrs to come to Arabian coast to meet him. Movement will begin as soon as Faisal arrives at Mecca."'[5]

Hussein understood that Djemal and the Turkish leadership was intent on bringing the Hejaz (and Yemen) into line, and that if he was ever going to activate a fight against the Turks it had to be now – before this new Turkish force arrived. Yet he first needed to await Feisal's return to the Hejaz so he would not be held captive by Djemal. Feisal left Damascus about 8 May.[6]

Storrs, Hogarth and Cornwallis of the Arab Bureau set out from Cairo on 28 May 1916. When these British representatives arrived at Qaddima on the Hejaz coast, Storrs received confirmation from the Foreign Office on 2 June 1916: "Foreign Office has approved payment of 10,000 pounds to Abdallah and 50,000 pounds to Sharif of Mecca. But this latter payment only in return for definite action and if a reliable rising takes place."[7] This was just the first of numerous such payments over the following years. The Arab revolt was going to be fuelled by British gold.

The British delegates were supposed to meet Abdullah, but instead Zaid the youngest son was sent, bearing letters from both Sherif Hussein and Abdullah. Abdullah stated in his message: "… My only request of you is to start operations in Syria to the best of your ability. God is our guide. Later will be our real meeting."[8]

The Arab revolt was due to begin simultaneously on Saturday 10 June, with attacks upon the Turkish garrisons at Medina, Mecca, Taif and Jeddah. The issue of the offensive in Syria was of great importance to Sherif Hussein, for, Zaid stated, even if 'the revolt went off as we hoped, was it not certain that the Turks, who had 80,000 men with guns in Syria, would descend upon them and wreak a terrible vengeance?'[9]

---

5   Storrs, ibid, p. 15; Falls, ibid, Vol. 1, p. 221.
6   Antonius, ibid, p. 193.
7   Quoted in Storrs, ibid, p. 156.
8   Quoted in Storrs, ibid, p. 156.
9   Quoted in Storrs, ibid, p. 159.

Zaid, on his father's request, also requested that al-Faruqi and 'whatever other Syrian officers might be chosen by the High Commissioner' be off Jeddah on 10 June.[10]   A further request for money and material was then made and these were promptly despatched by Wingate to Jeddah.[11]

Interestingly the man who initially sanctioned this relationship, Lord Kitchener, died at this very time. On 5 June 1916 Kitchener boarded *HMS Hampshire* at Scapa Flow to be taken to the Russian port of Archangel. At about 1930 hours it struck a mine and sunk shortly afterwards, taking Kitchener with it.

THE ARAB REVOLT 'BEGINS'

The timing of the revolt depended to an extent upon when the new Turkish force arrived in Medina. This force had to be stopped from proceeding from Medina to Mecca.   On 5 June 1916 Feisal and Ali deserted Medina with hundreds[12] of Turkish trained Arab recruits 'and sent a letter to the Turkish commanding officer saying that they were breaking off relations with the Turks on their father's orders and declaring a state of war.'[13]

Then on 10 June Hussein 'pushed a rifle through the window of his house in Mecca … and opened fire on the Turkish barracks, thus signalling the start of the Arab Revolt.'[14] The Turks in the barracks surrendered on 13 June, followed by Jeddah 16 June (although the fight there was supported by a bombardment from *HMS Fox*); while Taif surrendered on 22 September.[15]

Medina, under the command of Fakhri Pasha, held out until the end of the war and periodically this garrison force went out and pursued Feisal and Ali's forces.

NEWS OF THE REVOLT

News of the revolt spread quickly. The Turks and the Germans tried to deny it, while some in Egypt tried to promote it as British propaganda. Many

---

10   Quoted in Storrs, ibid, p, 160.
11   Falls, ibid, Vol 1, p. 221.
12   Figures vary, between 500 to 1500.
13   Knightley, P and Simpson, C. *The Secret Lives of Lawrence of Arabia*, (London, 1969), p. 51.
14   Knightley and Simpson, ibid, p. 51.
15   Many of the soldiers captured at Taif were Arabs and many of these then volunteered for the fight against Turkey. Falls, ibid, Vol. 1, p. 227.

viewed Hussein as a traitor to the Khalifa – the Caliphate.[16] When proof of the revolt became obvious, the Porte appointed Sharif Ali Haidar as the new Sherif of Mecca in place of Hussein. Haidar, though, was never able to get to Mecca.[17]

Muslims in India were not overly impressed, as they were more committed to the Sultan of Turkey as the legitimate Caliph of Islam.[18] According to George Antonius numerous Arab leaders, though, including Ibn Saud, met in Kuwait on 20 November and gave support to the revolt.[19] These leaders did not include Ibn Rashid and the Imam of Yemen 'who had already cast their lot with the Turks.'[20]

The initial success, due as much to British arms and finances as to Arab fighting skills, created a new problem for the British. For the revolt to be ongoing there would need to be a proper administration to liaise between the British and the Sherif of the Hejaz. The ideal location would be Jeddah, the major port on the Red Sea. Colonel Wilson of the Sudan Service then took on this responsibility.[21]

The French were not going to be left out of this new venture, and in September they despatched Colonel Edouard Bremond to head up their military mission to the Hejaz.[22]

THE IMPORTANCE OF RABEGH

The new designated Sherif of Mecca, Ali Haidar, was at Medina 'ready to make a triumphal entry into Mecca.'[23] The easiest journey to Mecca was via the port of Rabegh. This small location then became of vital military importance. If the Turks could capture Rabegh they would be in a good position to move on to Mecca.

---

16   Storrs, ibid, pp. 163-64.

17   Storrs, ibid, p. 164.

18   Antonius, ibid, p. 205.

19   Antonius, ibid, p. 205.

20   Antonius, ibid, p, 205.

21   One of his staff members was 'Husain Ruhi' who wrote: '... Muhammad Nasif... told me that Faruqi and Jamil were exerting their zeal to let the people here hate the English ... I wish one could get hold of Faruqi's bags and take a copy of his cipher book so that we may know all that is going on between him and his chief. He puts his cipher book in his small yellow bag which can easily be taken to a locksmith to be opened in F.'s absence. I think he is a rascal.' Storrs, ibid, p. 165.

22   Barr, ibid, p. 40.

23   Falls, ibid, Vol. 1, p. 232.

Suggestions were made to send a British brigade there, but these were vetoed by General Murray who 'considered that though the Sherif frequently spoke as if desirous of such support, the appearance of Christian troops so near the Holy Places would alienate the sympathies of the Arabs.'[24] That this concern was valid, is revealed by the fact that Sherif Hussein actually was unwilling to formally request the despatch of British troops in writing.[25]

In October 1916 there were signs that the Turks were planning to capture Mecca, execute Hussein, and end the revolt.[26] To achieve this they would need to first capture Rabegh. The British now had no choice but to send substantial aid to bolster the Sherif's faltering revolt, before the Medina expedition succeeded in reaching Rabegh.

WINGATE TAKES COMMAND

General Sir Reginald Wingate now took over command of the Hejaz operations from the British side.[27] This command was kept secret lest 'the fact that British officers were directing operations in the Holy territory of the Hejaz should create anti-Christian propaganda in Moslem countries and reflect adversely on the Sherif.'[28]

The irony is that Muslim Arabia needed the help of 'Christian' Britain to oust Muslim Turkey from a territory where non-Muslims were not permitted to reside! This situation raises a very interesting question: how would Christians and other non-Muslims fare in the territories further north if and when the rulers of the Hejaz, the custodians of Islam, ultimately held control over those regions?

LAWRENCE JOINS STORRS IN THE HEJAZ

Storrs returned to the Hejaz in October, writing in his diary on 12 October: 'On the train from Cairo little Lawrence my super-cerebral companion.'[29]

---

24 Falls, ibid, Vol. 1, p. 233. It seems that T.E. Lawrence had also cautioned against this, in a report he sent. See Wingate to Colonel Wilson, 23 November 1916, Wingate Papers, cited in Knightley and Simpson, ibid, p. 61.

25 Falls, ibid, Vol. 1, p. 234.

26 Knightley and Simpson, ibid, p. 59.

27 Falls, ibid, Vol. 1, p. 227. He was also *Sirdar*, commander of the Egyptian forces.

28 Falls, ibid, Vol. 1, p. 228. Wingate's representative was Wilson based in Jeddah.

29 Storrs, ibid, p. 171.

This was Thomas Edward Lawrence, who joined Storrs in his capacity as a staff member of the Arab Bureau in order to discern how best to ignite the revolt.

Storrs arrived in Jeddah on 16 October and then shortly afterwards, accompanied by Wilson and Lawrence, met Abdullah. Wilson then read out the letter from the *Sirdar* (Wingate) that the previous promise of a Brigade of men and aeroplanes was being withdrawn.[30] Abdullah was not very pleased with this information.[31]

Abdullah insisted that the British had promised they 'would do everything possible to help the Arabs' and included information from Maxwell pertaining to have 'considerable portions of the British Army' at their disposal. Abdullah also insisted that the British 'were becoming colder to the Arabs and trusting them less.'[32]

That evening the British representatives dined with Colonel Bremond, who stated, Barr wrote, that it was not in the interests of either Britain or France for the Arab uprising to succeed.[33] Bremond elaborated by stating: 'the partisans for a great Arab kingdom seek afterwards to act in Syria, and in Iraq, from where we – French and English – must then expel them.'[34]

The following day Storrs spoke with Said Pasha, the Hejazi Minister of War, who reinforced the unreliability of the Arabs, adding: 'that many, having received their rifles and ammunition from the Sharif, disappeared into the desert, to be seen no more.'[35] At a subsequent meeting Abdullah gave a report from Feisal that 'two Turkish aeroplanes had begun to operate, to the dismay bordering upon panic of the Arabs. He said that unless these were driven off or in some way checked, the Arabs would disperse.'[36]

Lawrence at this point spoke up and explained that 'few Turkish aeroplanes last more than four or five days.'[37] This comment, and subsequent

---

30 Storrs, ibid, p. 174.
31 Storrs, ibid, p. 174.
32 Storrs, ibid, p. 174.
33 Barr, ibid, p. 41.
34 Bremond to Quai d'Orsay, 20 October 1916, cited in Barr, ibid, p. 41.
35 Storrs, ibid, p. 176.
36 Storrs, ibid, p. 176.
37 Lawrence to Clayton, 17 October 1916, cited in Storrs, R. *Lawrence of Arabia, Zionism and Palestine*, (London,

comments and observations, seemingly impressed Abdullah. Storrs was then able to procure letters of introduction for Lawrence to proceed to Bir Abbas and to meet with Feisal and Ali.[38]

During this meeting Sherif Hussein constantly telephoned and interfered in the discussions. Later Abdullah met alone with Storrs. Abdullah, Storrs wrote, expressed his deep 'disappointment that I had been unable to bring the 10,000 pounds requested in his telegram.' Storrs explained that he thought the very generous subsidy given to the Sharif would suffice also for the sons.[39]

In a telegram to Clayton, Lawrence summated the situation and recorded Aziz el-Mazri as having stated that the: '… only way to bring sense and continuity into operation is to have English staff at Rabugh dealing direct with Sahrif [sic] Ali and Sharif Faisal without referring detail to Sharif of Mecca of whom they are all respectfully afraid.'[40]

Lawrence then departed first to Rabegh to meet Ali, who then took him to Feisal's camp – leaving at night so that no-one knew he was leaving.[41] Lawrence later wrote about his meeting with Feisal: 'I felt at first glance that this was the man I had come to Arabia to seek – the leader who would bring the Arab Revolt to full glory.'[42] Lawrence saw in Feisal someone who could potentially lead the revolt northwards – and ultimately oust 'the French out of all hope of Syria.'[43]

Several days later Lawrence returned to Yenbo, and then continued on to Jeddah where he joined Admiral Wemyss (the Naval C-in-C East Indies) with whom he sailed to Port Sudan. Wemyss was travelling to Khartoum to meet with Wingate – with whom Lawrence also needed to report.[44]

1941), p. 11. Lawrence provides a somewhat different scenario in *Revolt in the Desert*, (New York, 1927), p. 3.

38   Storrs, *Lawrence*, p. 12; Lawrence, T.E. *Revolt in the Desert*, p. 4.

39   Storrs, ibid, p. 177. Here was another example of the huge amounts of British gold which Hussein and his sons were demanding of the British for their involvement in the Arab revolt.

40   Lawrence to Clayton, ibid, p. 11.

41   Lawrence, *Revolt*, p. 8.

42   Lawrence, *Revolt*, p. 18.

43   Barr, ibid, p. 43.

44   Lawrence, *Revolt*, p. 28.

Wingate was pleased with Lawrence's optimistic report and advice that all that was required would be for regular British officers 'professionally competent and speaking Arabic' who could be attached 'to the Arab leaders as technical advisors.'[45] Lawrence then returned to Cairo. His task, seemingly, had been completed.

HUSSEIN PROCLAIMS HIMSELF AS 'KING OF THE ARAB COUNTRIES'

While in Jeddah, Storrs was made aware of Sherif Hussein's desire to be known as 'King of the "Arab Nation."' Storrs insisted that this title not be adopted just yet. There were numerous reasons for this, one being that such a move would need to be accepted by other Arab leaders, particularly Ibn Saud.

Hussein, nevertheless, announced himself as 'King of the Arab Countries' on 2 November 1916. On that day there was a traditional 'ceremony of *bai'a*, the traditional Arab custom in which the investiture is accompanied by formal declarations of allegiance.'[46] Storrs was upset when he later heard that Hussein had adopted the Arabic title of *Jalala* or *Malek* – King.[47]

Britain and France regarded the announcement 'as an untimely and injudicious step.'[48] It was blatantly obvious that the move was unwise and confrontational. Ultimately a compromise was arrived at, whereby he was entitled 'King of the Hejaz.'

LAWRENCE AND STORRS AGAIN IN THE HEJAZ

Wingate had been impressed by Lawrence's report, and following a suggestion from London on 11 November that there be a British officer acting alongside the Arab force, Lawrence was recommended.[49] Lawrence returned to the Hejaz shortly afterwards.

Storrs then made a fourth trip to the Hejaz, and met Sherif Hussein on 11 December 1916, in order to discuss the crucial military situation at Medina

---

45   Lawrence, *Revolt*, p. 29.
46   Antonius, ibid, p. 213.
47   Storrs, ibid, p. 185.
48   Antonius, ibid, p. 213.
49   Knightley and Simpson state that Lawrence was almost overlooked by Wingate due to a bureaucratic slipup. Knightley and Simpson, ibid, p. 61.

and the nearest coastal town of Rabegh. He saw the need for a competent Arab officer to lead the revolt, under Sherifian family direction. Storrs then mentioned the appropriateness of Aziz al-Masri.[50] Sharif Hussein agreed to this proposal. The Sherif also confided to Storrs that he was dissatisfied with al-Faruqi and desired another Cairo representative.[51]

En-route back to Egypt Storrs stopped at Yenbo, the closest port to Medina, where he requested a meeting with Feisal. At that time Turkish forces were closing in on Yenbo, and the Arab soldiers had deserted the trench defending the town, and many notables had boarded the British warship *HMS Hardinge*.[52]

Storrs finally met Feisal on 13 December, who immediately began to complain about the delay in supplying the 'Artillery requested four months ago.' Storrs then retorted: '... after the recent retreats, the courage of the Arab tribesmen stood in some need of vindication in the eyes of the world; even if they were for the moment unable to face their foes in the open field; their intimate knowledge of their own mountainous country should surely render them redoubtable enemies in guerrilla warfare.'[53]

Feisal requested a guarantee from Storrs that the British would protect Rabegh and Yenbo, for, he stated, 'with these two as bases upon which to fall back he would not hesitate to advance again upon the Turks and to take Wajh; it was the dread of being cut off that paralyzed his strength.'[54] Storrs concluded:

> The incoherent and spasmodic nature of Arab organization and operations is an additional proof, if such were needed, of the necessity of one supreme and independent control of the campaign: and as there appears to be no other Moslem who unites the various qualifications of Aziz Ali Bey, it is to be hoped that the Sharif will have the courage and self restraint to make his appointment a reality.[55]

50   Storrs, ibid, p. 184.
51   Storrs, ibid, p. 185. H.M.G. = His Majesty's Government.
52   Storrs, ibid, p. 186.
53   Storrs, ibid, p. 187.
54   Storrs, ibid, p. 187.
55   Storrs, ibid, p. 187.

By the end of 1916 it was not apparent if the revolt would actually succeed – despite the immense investment of gold bullion and arms by Britain. Storrs and others had noted the need for a leader who could co-ordinate the overall Arab forces. Aziz el-Masri ultimately did not attain to this position, but Ja'far Pasha el Askari became overall Arab field commander.[56]

Lawrence, meanwhile, adjusted to his new position, and following the disaster at Yenbo, he and Feisal began to strategize for an attack on another coastal town of Wejh, north of Yenbo. The success or failure of the Hejaz operations would be determined by the outcome of this attack.

---

56   Falls, ibid, Vol. 1, p. 235. Ja'far had fought with the Senussi and had been captured by the British.

CHAPTER 55

§

Romani to El Arish

PREPARATIONS FOR THE AUGUST OFFENSIVE

At the War Committee meeting on 6 July 1916 (which was attended by Sykes) it was decided that CIGS Robertson was to inform Murray, 'to prepare to occupy El Arish and Aqaba.' This move was also to 'encourage Syrian Arabs.'[1]

In conjunction with the above mentioned move, the railway was to continue towards El Arish, and the 'Naval C-in-C East Indies' was to prepare for the capture of Aqaba.[2] This decision was later vetoed as Hussein did not want any British forces landing there.

British infantry forces now moved forward to the area around Romani, and about 20 July Lieut. Wilson's squadron also moved forward and became attached to the 42nd Division at Pelusium.[3]

Chauvel utilised this waiting time to condition his men and horses to desert work. Idriess relates of one journey into the desert where each man had only one water bottle. Some of the men, he related, went 'raving' while others managed to return to camp only barely conscious, upon horses whose eyes were bulging out.[4]

---

1   Falls, ibid, Vol. 1, p. 231.
2   Falls, ibid, Vol. 1, p. 231.
3   Wilson, ibid, p. 43.
4   Idriess, ibid, p. 69.

New Zealander George Harper wrote that during one desert journey the heat descended upon them like a wave. The men's water then ran out and they were beginning to collapse. At that point, the Turks attacked. Thankfully, Harper recalled, the Turks too were suffering from the heat and they withdrew. Harper then collapsed himself, fell from his horse, and had to be revived.[5]

Following one such reconnaissance journey, when the temperature reached 120 degrees, General Murray signalled to Chauvel:

> The Commander-in-Chief wishes to convey to General Chauvel and troops of the Anzac Mounted Division his appreciation of the excellent work done in the arduous reconnaissance yesterday. The Commander-in-Chief does not think that any other troops could have undertaken this operation successfully in the present weather.[6]

In his preparations Von Kressenstein also had to contend with the heat of summer, including having to march over the sandy desert, at the hottest period of the year. But this he did. At the end of July 1916 his men marched for seven consecutive nights from El Arish, and reached the vicinity of Romani, forty kilometres east of the Suez Canal.

THE BATTLE OF ROMANI

The oncoming Turkish force was spotted on 19 July by Chaytor on a reconnaissance flight. During the next two weeks skirmishes between the two sides increased. Chauvel then began to put into place General Lawrence's plan for drawing the attacking force into a trap.

While the EEF men prepared, Von Kressenstein's force finally reached Katia oasis on the night of 2-3 August. Chauvel rightly predicted they would attack the following night. Just after midnight the forward Turkish troops

---

5   King, M. *New Zealanders at War*, (Auckland, 1981), p. 144.
6   Hill, ibid, p. 71.

collided with Australian soldiers and then regrouped. Then about 0100 hours they attacked again – in force.

The Turkish infantry outnumbered the Australians, who slowly withdrew from their position on Mount Meredith, being sprayed with German machine gun fire in the process. These troops then moved to nearby Wellington Ridge, where their position in time became vulnerable, with the Turks moving to outflank them. At that point Chauvel himself led his staff and the 2nd Light Horse Brigade forward at a canter and joined the 1st Light Horse Brigade.[7]

Superiority of numbers forced the Light Horse to withdraw from those two positions. Much of this was in accordance with General Lawrence's plan. As the sun then rose and the day became warmer, the Turkish infantry slowed their momentum, yet by 0800 hours they were still pressing in upon the Anzac soldiers. Communications with Lawrence had been cut, so Chauvel had to make quick decisions. He wanted to go onto the counter-attack, but had to wait until the New Zealanders arrived.

With the arrival of the New Zealanders, the tide was turned and the Turkish thrust was halted. Chauvel's men then counter-attacked – and won the crucial battle at Romani.[8] This victory was a turning point, effectively turning a defensive campaign into an offensive one.

Reg Walters experienced his baptism of fire at Romani. He wrote: 'Temperature is anything over 100… Poor old Jim Frost was shot dead. We rode up to a slope, dismounted and all but the horse holders had orders to advance in small rushes … the bullets were pinging around us like hailstones from 2 machine guns the Turks had. We had to crawl on our stomachs for 50 yds pushing little ridges of sand up in front of us as we went ½ way up. I was next to Jim Frost and … he was shot through the arm and heart.'[9]

Wilson wrote of his involvement in the battle:

7   Hill, ibid, p. 76.
8   The EEF lost some 1,100 casualties, including 202 killed, many of whom were ANZAC'S. Hill, ibid, p. 82; Wavell, *The Palestine Campaigns*, p. 50.
9   Walters.

On August 4th our Squadron was at Pelusium about twenty five miles from the Canal, on the Army railway. The Turks attacked at a place called Romani about another seven miles out, which was strongly fortified by us. About nine thousand attacked Romani and two thousand came straight on to Pelusium to cut the railway and water supply. This is the lot our Squadron (one hundred men) met and held till the rest of the Brigade came up, plus a regiment of New Zealanders. Then we drove them right back on to our forts at Romani and any that were alive or unwounded held up a white flag. Our Regiment also captured a battery of guns and we are trying to claim them to put in Gloucester.[10]

THE PURSUIT

The object of General Lawrence's plan after having halted the Turkish offensive at Romani, was to pursue them – back towards El Arish. The ensuing fighting in the heat of the day forced many Turks to surrender, while the remainder continued their retreat eastwards. Concerning events on 5 August Wilson wrote:

… we moved out in pursuit … at dawn and found them entrenched at Qatia… It was here that I spent the most exciting moments of my life. It was impossible for Infantry to cross the plain so they said we had to go – that was our Brigade and three Anzac Brigades – what a sight! We all extended over about three and a half miles and started quietly off for the low ridge, the only cover to be seen, and only just high enough to hide the horses. At that shells began to arrive but we didn't break out of a walk - as we wanted to do a bit of a burst at the finish – and when we got to about half a mile off we started off at the gallop. Bullets and shrapnel seemed to be everywhere and we were all very glad to reach the ridge. Well, there we stopped for about five hours and couldn't go any further. Then the order came to retire a

---

10   Wilson, ibid, p. 48.

troop at a time … However, we managed to get back again alright …
We went out again next morning but Johnny Turk had gone.[11]

With the victory at Katia, Chauvel's men, be they ANZAC or British
Yeomanry, were exhausted by the evening of 5 August. Although Chauvel
had to retire that evening, he was determined to pursue the retreating
Turkish force as soon and as ruthlessly as he could.

Concerning the battle Von Sanders wrote:

> The Turco-German attack failed completely, because the force used
> was too small, because its approach was known to the British, and
> because the expeditionary corps was completely exhausted when it
> reached the enemy.
>
> Instead of turning the enemy's flank, the flank of the expeditionary
> corps was turned by the skilfully led British cavalry, and by the rein-
> forcements arriving from Kantara by rail. In the end the corps suc-
> ceeded in breaking away from the enemy, who at first pursued hotly.
> In the attack and in the retreat to El Arish the corps lost about one-
> third of its strength.[12]

PURSUIT TO BIR EL ABD AND MAZAR

Chauvel mustered those of his mounted troops which had not endured the
bulk of the fighting, and continued the pursuit. Ahead of him were possibly
6,000 Turco-German troops. The EEF force approached Bir el Abd on the
evening of 8 August and began to attack the following day.

As Chauvel's troops neared Bir el Abd the Turkish forces were ready and
put up a very determined fight. The fighting raged throughout 9 August,
this time exhausting Chauvel's force of 3,000 to such an extent that he had
to call off the pursuit and begin an orderly retreat. Wilson wrote: 'We have
been hard at it, day and night … We haven't averaged two hours sleep a
night and have often had forty winks when the lead was flying … we have

---

11   Wilson, ibid, pp. 48-49.
12   Von Sanders, ibid, p. 144.

been hunting them out of the country, which meant about three more lively scraps each of which I very much enjoyed …'[13]

TOWARDS EL ARISH

The Turkish force then withdrew further eastwards. Although there were numerous more engagements between the two sides over the following months including at Mazar in September, the Turks withdrew back to a new defensive line from El Arish to Maghdaba. The Turks meanwhile were also continuing their efforts to construct the railway line south from Beersheba, first to Kossaima, with the object of going through the central Sinai – to the Suez.

When the British intelligence became aware of this move they increased reconnaissance into the central Sinai, primarily through the Imperial Camel Corps.[14] The Imperial Camel Corps (ICC) was commanded by Lieut-Colonel C.L. Smith V.C, and was composed of ten Australian, six British and two New Zealand companies.

During this period the EEF was strengthened with the arrival of more British infantry and Romani became the main camp for the Sinai Campaign.

As the EEF moved progressively eastwards towards El Arish, the railway inched along at the rate of about one kilometre per day. 'It was possible to calculate when this railroad would reach the Turco-Egyptian frontier east of El Arish' wrote Von Sanders. 'It was expected in January 1917.'[15]

Von Sanders had wanted more Turkish soldiers in order to forestall this British movement eastwards, but this was not possible, as many Turkish troops were fighting elsewhere in Galicia, Roumania, Macedonia, the Caucasus and in Iraq (Mesopotamia).[16]

CHANGE OF COMMAND STRUCTURE

Until mid-1916 General Murray commanded all the forces in the Sinai, as well as having responsibility over the troops at Salonika (the Levant Base)

13 Wilson, ibid, p. 47.
14 Powles, Lieut-Col C.G. *The New Zealanders in Sinai and Palestine*, (Auckland, 1922), p. 46.
15 Von Sanders, ibid, p. 145.
16 Von Sanders, ibid, p. 145.

and in Egypt. To adequately oversee this huge region he was forced to move his HQ from Ismailia back to Cairo.

Murray then placed all forces to the east of the Suez Canal under the command of General Sir Charles Dobell, and this force henceforth was known as Eastern Force. The vanguard of Eastern Force was known as the Desert Column, which was formed into a Corps under the command of Lieutenant-General Sir Philip Chetwode. The Desert Column was composed of the ANZAC Mounted Division (AZMD); the 42nd and 52nd British Infantry Divisions; and the Imperial Camel Corps (ICC).

This combination of British, Australian and New Zealand troops was bound to create some interesting dynamics – both ways. Often times the British troops viewed the ANZAC's as mere colonials, while the ANZAC's looked at the British, especially the officers, as pompous. Chetwode on one occasion said to Chauvel: 'Not only do your men fail to salute me when I ride through your camps, but they laugh aloud at my orderlies.'[17]

Despite such internal dynamics the orders for this new formation remained the same for all: for the best defence of the Suez Canal the Turkish force was to be forced back to El Arish. All of the planning had until this point hinged upon this dictum.

But this dictum was soon to change.

17   Gullet, H.S. *The AIF in Sinai and Palestine*, (1984), p. 207.

NORTHERN SINAI 1916

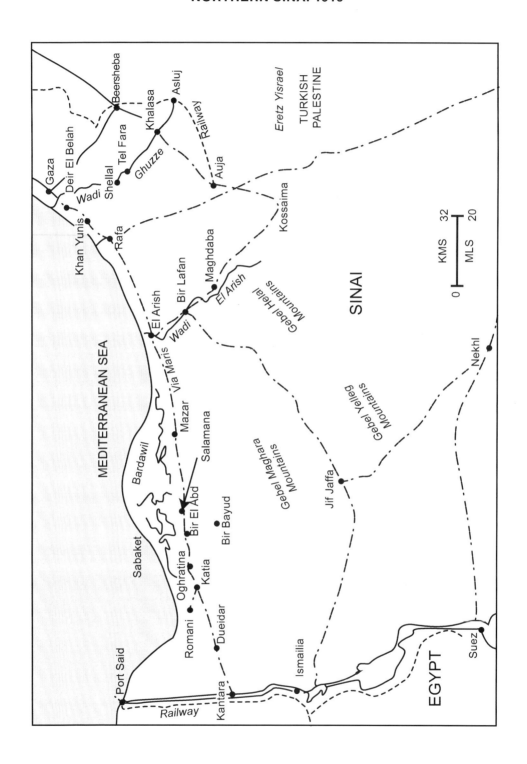

§

CHAPTER 56

Jabotinsky and Aaronsohn

JABOTINSKY MEETS PATTERSON

While Wolf, Samuel, Weizmann and Sykes were in their different ways encouraging the political interest in a Jewish national entity in Palestine, Jabotinsky continued with his quest for the Jewish Legion.

In the middle of 1916 he met Colonel Patterson, who had been discharged from hospital in London following his Gallipoli sickness. Patterson then introduced Jabotinsky to a number of British officials who could be interested in his concept of a Jewish Legion. Some of these men had heard about the Zion Mule Corps and of their involvement at Gallipoli. Such positive comments caused Jabotinsky to confess to Trumpeldor, when he saw him, that he had been right in the formation of this unit.

In late autumn of 1916 the 120 men of the Zion Mule Corps who remained in the British Army and who had re-enlisted in the 20th Battalion London regiment, arrived in London. Trumpeldor invited Jabotinsky to visit them in their London barracks. Upon hearing of the presence of these 120 Jewish men from Zion, one British official, Colonel Leopold Amery, said to Jabotinsky that this would become the nucleus of his proposed Jewish Legion.[1]

Thus by the end of 1916, and despite numerous obstacles, Jabotinsky and others were still optimistic that a Jewish fighting force would assist in the capture of *Eretz Yisrael.*

At that time, though, the conquest of Palestine was not part of the official British policy. By the end of 1916 the Asquith Government was prepared to secure the Sinai Peninsula up to the border with Palestine as the buffer zone to the Suez Canal; and to pump in whatever was needed to get the Arab revolt alight and moving.

SYKES DEVELOPS HIS IDEAS

When he returned from Russia Sykes began developing his scheme to merge all the various agreements of the Middle East together into something workable. It was going to be mammoth task in view of the false foundation on which it was built, as David Fromkin states:

> It was because Cairo, taken in by al-Faruqi's hoax and believing fully in the potency of Arab secret societies, had persuaded London that Hussein of Mecca could tear down the Ottoman Empire that all of these commitments, mortgaging the future of the postwar Middle East, had been made by the Asquith coalition.[2]

Sykes met with Samuel, Weizmann, Sokolow and Gaster, and on different occasions expressed his plan, which was a 'French-English condominium in Palestine, Arab Prince to conciliate the Arabs, and, as part of the Constitution a Charter to Zionism for which England would stand guarantor...'[3]

As a result of these meetings, and their feedback, Sykes continued to grow in his understanding of Zionism. He also saw the potential of merg-

---

1   Jabotinsky, ibid, p. 78.

2   Fromkin, ibid, p. 199.

3   *Gaster Diaries*, April 16 1916, cited in Sanders, ibid, p. 362; Stein, ibid, p, 278.

ing the Jewish nationalist concept with Britain's geo-political goals in the region. Towards the end of the year his understanding of this grew even further following meeting with a vibrant young Zionist from *Eretz Yisrael*, named Aaron Aaronshon.

AARONSOHN AND THE *NILI*

The deteriorating situation in Syria further confirmed to the group of potential Jewish espionage workers that they needed to act. Aaron Aaronsohn in particular had no faith at all in the regime of Djemal Pasha. By early 1916 the British had made no contact with the small group based at Atlit. This caused Feiberg to attempt to reach Egypt on camel, posing as a Turkish officer. He was captured near El Arish and tortured and interrogated at Beersheba – but did not divulge the reasons for his attempt at reaching Egypt.[4]

Realising that to attempt this again was fool-hardy, Aaron Aaronsohn, with the encouragement of Leonard Woolley, then set out in July 1916 to establish contact with the British, via Damascus, Constantinople, Berlin, Denmark and then on to London.[5] His goal was to get the British authorities, especially in Egypt, to understand that *NILI* could offer credible military intelligence. In his absence he asked his sister Sarah to continue collecting relevant information which could be of use for the British.

Aaronshohn was a renowned scientist and one whom Djemal Pasha trusted. By the middle of 1916 the Turkish Governor was aware that his war machine was lacking in oil. Aaronsohn convinced him that fuel was obtainable from sesame seeds, but to best achieve this he would need to travel to Sweden and speak there to other scientists.[6]

After a circuitous journey Aaronshon finally reached Britain on 22 October 1916, where he was duly 'arrested' – as being a Turkish national, and was taken to London. There his first meeting was at Scotland Yard, after which he was conveyed to the War Office.[7] Now, finally, there was hope that

---

4   Alexander Aaronsohn, *'The "Nili" or "A" Organisation*, cited in Verrier, ibid, p. 98.
5   Verrier, ibid, p. 99.
6   Verrier, ibid, p. 100.
7   Verrier, ibid, p. 187.

the offers of the *NILI* would be taken seriously. Indeed the information he provided the War Office matched their intelligence, and he was accepted as *bona fide*.

On 30 October he was invited to speak to Brigadier Walter Gribbon, who served under Major-General George Macdonough, the Director of Military Intelligence.[8] Also in attendance were Mark Sykes and Gerald FitzMaurice. In the following days Aaronsohn had numerous meetings with those actively involved in Middle East affairs.

Meanwhile others were devoting their time and efforts to furthering the cause of Zion. Harry Sacher wrote a booklet entitled *Zionism and the Jewish Future*, which Lord Cromer wrote a review of in *The Spectator*. Lord Cromer said that the Zionist dream 'is rapidly becoming a practical issue and before long politicians will be unable to brush it aside as the fantastic dream of a few idealists.'[9]

Herbert Sidebotham of the *Manchester Guardian*, also began writing favourable articles. James de Rothschild now became actively involved, and pressured Weizmann and Sokolow to put together a proposal which could be sent to the Government for consideration.[10]

AARONSON DEPARTS FOR EGYPT

After four weeks in London, Aaronsohn was asked by the War Office to travel to Cairo in order to establish contact with the personnel there. He was given the cover name of William Macks, for if at any time his cover was 'blown' it would mean certain difficulty for his family back in Palestine.[11]

Aaronshon arrived in Egypt on 16 December 1916 not knowing how he would be received by the British authorities, and if they were interested in the information he offered. If the British were content just with encouraging the Arab revolt by sending in lots of precious gold bullion, as well as staying in the Sinai and proceeding no further, then what he and *NILI* had to offer would be of little relevance.

8　Verrier, ibid, p. 101.
9　*The Spectator,* 12 August 1916, cited in Stein, ibid, p. 301.
10　Stein, ibid, pp. 296-305.
11　Aaronsohn's Diary, 12 December 1916, cited in Verrier, ibid, p. 224.

But an event occurred in Britain while he was en-route to Egypt which would greatly enhance the possibility of a British military presence in Palestine – an event which could place value upon what he had to offer. This event was the formation of a new Government – led by David Lloyd George.

§

CHAPTER 57

Lloyd George and the 'Promised Land'

ASQUITH OUT – LLOYD GEORGE IN

By late 1916 it was clear that the War was not going well for the Allies. The Asquith Government was coming under considerable pressure. David Lloyd George and others were encouraging Asquith to re-organize the running of the War, but party politics and personality clashes became involved.

Ultimately on 5 December 1916 Asquith resigned as Prime Minister, and after others, for one reason or another, could not accept the post, it was offered to David Lloyd George. According to his *Memoirs*, he took the position reluctantly.[1] One of the first moves that Lloyd George made was to offer Arthur Balfour the position of Foreign Secretary.[2]

It did not take Lloyd George long to begin to revamp the British policy in the Eastern Mediterranean. He stated the policy as it stood when he took over office:

---

1 Lloyd George, D. *Memoirs*, (London, 1938) Vol. I, p. 596.
2 Lloyd George, ibid, p. 597.

When I formed my Government, the instructions under which Sir Archibald Murray was operating charged him to confine himself to the defence of Egypt and the Canal, in maintaining which he was recommended if possible to advance as far as El Arish on the eastern side of the Sinai Peninsula – still within the Egyptian frontier – and maintain his front from there.[3]

He then writes of his first move:

I at once raised with the War Office the question of allowing him to embark on a further campaign into Palestine when El Arish had been secured, and on my instructions Sir William Robertson wired to Murray on 9th December, 1916, asking him to submit plans for an advance beyond El Arish, and state what additional troops he would require to execute them.[4]

Lloyd George stated in his memorandum to the War Cabinet concerning 'the proposal for a Palestine campaign' that its objective would be 'the capture of Jerusalem.'[5] Robertson then sent the following message to Murray on 9 December:

"To-day Prime Minister mentioned to me desirability of making your operations as successful as possible. I am in entire agreement. Wire précis of action proposed beyond El Arish, stating what additional troops you would require for advance, if any. I cannot help thinking that in view of importance of achieving big success on Eastern Front, and the effect this will have, you might risk having fewer troops on Western. A success is badly needed, and your operations promise well."[6]

---

3   Lloyd George, ibid, Vol. II, p.1081.
4   Lloyd George, ibid, Vol. II, p.1081.
5   Lloyd George, ibid, Vol II, p. 1083.
6   Robertson to Murray, 9 December 1916, cited in Lloyd George, ibid, Vol. II, pp. 1081-82. Lloyd George pointed out

Murray responded the following day and stated that: 'after taking El Arish he proposed to advance to Rafah, on the Syrian frontier, complete the clearing of the Sinai Peninsula, and then, if circumstances permitted move against Beersheba, where the enemy's main concentration appeared to be. He asked', Lloyd George continued, 'if he could have two divisions from Mesopotamia and any spare mounted troops there were in Mesopotamia or India, assuming that nothing could be spared from France.'[7]

CIGS Robertson replied that the Prime Minister wishes "you to make maximum possible effort during the winter. Until the spring we cannot send any troops from Mesopotamia, and if you need reinforcements before then they must be drawn either from France or Salonika ..."[8]

Murray had wanted a division for a move against Beersheba for mid-February. This request concerned the War Office, as it would require extra forces for the Spring offensive on the Western Front, and Robertson had to remind Murray to make do with what he had.

THE CAPTURE OF EL ARISH

Encouraged by the support of the new government Murray set his sights upon El Arish. Reg Walters was at the base camp at Mazar on 20 December and wrote in his diary: 'We were going to have our Christmas Dinner today. In fact I had an invite over to the Engineers ... where a great dinner of Turkeys etc was being prepared. We have just been issued with tin fruits galore, plum puddings ... and then we all got the order to move at 11 a.m.' Walters and his mates then picked up their food and took it with them as they rode – eastwards.[9]

On 21 December Walters wrote again: 'We have been travelling since yesterday dinner time and are now 4 miles from "El Arish" and I think we will attack this morning. Maybe it has been evacuated.'[10]

that reference to 'Western' indicates western front in Egypt and not the Western Front in France.

7   Murray to Robertson, 10 December 1916, cited in Lloyd George, ibid, Vol. ii, p. 1082.
8   Robertson to Murray, no date provided, cited in Lloyd George, ibid, Vol. ii, p. 1082.
9   Walters.
10 Walters.

Early in the morning of 21 December the Desert Column surrounded El Arish. Lieutenant Wilson recalled that: 'As soon as it got light we peeped over a hill and there were these Turkish trenches, but no sign of Johnny Turk … they had all cleared out in the night.'[11]

Indeed the Turkish garrison had withdrawn and not a shot had been fired by the Desert Column, who then entered the small oasis town as victors. 'The praise for this bloodless victory', wrote Guy Powles, 'was in a measure due to the horses, for the Turk was beginning to feel a wholesome dread of the speed and wide striking range of our mounted arm.'[12]

The bloodless victory and tranquil surroundings were, unfortunately, soon disturbed. Two Gallipoli veterans had strolled down to the beach and were examining a sea mine when it exploded, killing them both.[13]

BATTLE OF MAGDHABA

The Turkish garrison at El Arish had withdrawn to two other Turkish positions, Rafa on the coast and Magdhaba some twenty-three miles (thirty-five kilometres) south-east on the Wady El Arish. Chetwode had come to El Arish by boat and decided it was imperative to quickly strike at the Turkish garrison at Magdhaba. The ANZAC horsemen were instructed to quickly saddle up again and move towards the object during the night. As they moved forward they rode for forty minutes, then led the horses for ten minutes in order to warm themselves up, and then had ten minutes rest.[14]

The Desert Column horsemen reached their destination at 0350 hours, which was well illuminated by camp fires. The Turks were not anticipating an attack. At 0630 hours planes of the 1st Squadron Australian Flying Corps (AFC) bombed the Turkish camp. The Turkish fire then gave their positions away to the Anzac horsemen. Many of the pilots of the AFC were in fact former Light Horsemen.

At first light the attack began, with the New Zealanders and 3rd Light Horse Brigade advancing in order to cut off the Turkish retreat. The ICC

11 Wilson, ibid, p. 59.
12 Powles, ibid, p. 50.
13 Walters.
14 Powles, ibid, p. 50.

was released directly at the centre of the Turkish camp, while the 1st Light Horse Brigade was kept in reserve.

The battle continued throughout the hot and thirsty day. The longer the battle lasted, the better it was for the Turks, who held the water supplies, while the Desert Column had to rely upon supplies being brought to them. Meanwhile the engineers were drilling for water at Bir Lahfan, but were unsuccessful and by 1300 hours the Desert Column position became desperate.

By mid-afternoon with no victory in sight Chauvel advised Chetwode that they were about to call the attack off. When General Cox of the 1st Light Horse Brigade received this message, he instructed his orderly to take the message away and return with it later. Cox subsequently unleashed his horsemen against the Turkish stronghold – and the first scent of victory was in the air. The other regiments quickly followed.

Reg Walters wrote: 'At 2 p.m. the order came for all to advance and then the fun began. We practically surrounded the Turks who were strongly resisting. All fixed bayonets and it was a grand and exciting sight to see all our horsemen galloping … small bodies of Turks were holding up their hands and of course we quickly made them prisoners.'[15]

'By 3.30 pm' Powles recalled 'the New Zealanders with fixed bayonets were swarming over the trenches … and the Turks were surrendering in all directions.'[16] By 1630 hours Magdhaba was captured.[17]

Although not a large fortification, the capture of Magdhaba was significant as it resulted in the clearing of the Turks out of the Sinai. Chetwode stated of this victory: '… the mounted men at Magdhaba had done what he had never known cavalry to do in the history of war: they had not only located and surrounded the enemy's position, but they had got down to it as infantry and carried fortified positions at the point of the bayonet.'[18]

---

15 Walters.
16 Powles, ibid, p. 53.
17 Hill, ibid, p. 89.
18 Idriess, I. The Desert Column, p. 165.

THE RETURN TO EL ARISH

The captured water supply was not sufficient for the needs of the EEF attacking force – as well as the Turkish prisoners. While some troops remained behind at El Magdhaba, the majority of the force now began the agonizing return to El Arish on a ration of one water bottle. Their situation is summed up by Powles: 'They had been marching and fighting for 30 hours without pause and for most of them it meant the third night without sleep. To pass one night without sleep is trying; two nights is absolutely painful; but the third night without sleep after heavy fighting with all the added strain and excitement that it means – is almost an impossibility.'[19]

Throughout that night ride men and horses collapsed through utter exhaustion. Hundreds of soldiers experienced hallucinating dreams. Some saw large buildings well lit up; two, including Chauvel, thought they saw a fox and presuming to be in a fox hunt, galloped off into the desert after it; others saw weird looking soldiers riding next to them; while others saw flower covered fields.

'Many discussions have followed these happenings' wrote Powles, and our wise ones laid it down that the brain had temporarily lost certain of its powers of endurance, which sleep alone could restore.'[20]

Walters wrote from El Arish the following day: 'We arrived back here at 9 a.m. this morning. It was a particularly rough job on the horses … The men are all dead beat & are at this moment sleeping just as they laid down in the lines. We have had 3 night rides during the last 4 nights. So can say we all feel a bit weary.'[21]

CHRISTMAS 1916

At this point the winter rains descended upon the men, drenching the weary troops. Their tents were still far behind the front line, and despite some supplies coming in from Cyprus, firewood was much in demand. With

---

19   Powles, ibid, p. 54.
20   Powles, ibid, p. 152.
21   Walters.

Christmas only a few days away, the main concern was, 'How were the Christmas dinners to be cooked?'

A telegraph line stretched along the Sinai coastline from Kantara into Palestine, the poles of which were made of iron – and wood. This line was essential for future communication purposes, and strict orders had been given for these poles not to be touched. Yet with Christmas dinners beckoning and no wood supplies in sight, such order were bound not to be heard.

Disguised as Signallers, some members of the Camel Brigade, dismantled a few of these poles, and brought the wood back to El Arish. The ploy worked well – until mid-afternoon on 25 December, when it was discovered. By this time, however, the Christmas dinners had not only been cooked, but well and truly digested. His Majesty's Signallers were now, unfortunately, minus eight kilometres of essential telegraph line![22]

THE NEXT MOVE

After the festive season and accompanying rainfall had passed by, and a new year descended upon them, the men were anticipating their next move. By this time many of them had spent close to a year in the Sinai, and they were anticipating a change of scenery. A major clue as to their next move would be the progression of the railway, which had been slowly creeping along the Sinai coast during 1916. '… many and anxious were the eyes directed upon the railway line' wrote Powles 'as it crept up to El Arish. The great question of the day – a question which caused as much speculation as the Melbourne Cup – was "would it cross the wadi?" … Then one joyful day,' he continued 'a patrol was ordered as escort to the surveying engineer … who went across the wadi; and we said, looking into each other's eyes, "It seems too good to be true, we *are* for the Promised Land after all!"'[23]

When it became clear that entrance into the 'Promised Land' was eminent, Lloyd George was pressured by the French to allow French forces to be involved. The Prime Minister was against this idea, and at the Anglo-French Conference in London on 28 December 1916, he communicated this to the

---

22 Powles, ibid, pp. 58-9.
23 Powles, ibid, p. 64.

French Prime Minister Ribot. Lloyd George would only permit a French Political Mission, and token French and Italian forces to be involved.[24]

The capture of the 'Promised Land' was to be undertaken primarily by soldiers from Britain, Australia and New Zealand.

AARONSOHN'S ACTIVITIES

While the EEF soldiers were anticipating entering into the 'Promised Land', Aaronsohn made his first journey back home since arriving in Egypt. On 24 December he boarded a small trawler and headed for the area of Atlit in order to establish contact with members of *NILI* there.

Although the trip basically failed, as they couldn't land due to bad weather, it was nevertheless the beginning of a venture which in the forth-coming months would provide the EEF commanders with much valuable intelligence information by which they were to conduct their up-coming incursion into the 'Promised Land.'[25]

24   Lloyd George, ibid, Vol. II, p. 1085.
25   Aaronsohn Diary, ibid, Verrier, ibid, pp. 227-8.

CHAPTER 58

§

First strikes – Rafa and Wejh

TOWARDS RAFA

Murray's next move was the conquest of Rafa, thereby clearing the Sinai completely of Turkish troops. A combined force of ANZAC and British mounted troops, the Imperial Camel Corps and artillery set out on the forty-eight kilometre journey to Rafa on 8 January 1917. The movement of this force prompted Powles to write:

> There are Australians among them and Yeomen from the British Isles and our own New Zealanders, and following them a band of tall, silent, swarthy Sikhs on huge Indian camels. There are Hong Kong and Singapore Mountain Battery, who so ably serve the Camel Brigade.[1]

During the night march the horses munched on green grass - for many it was the first time they had done so since leaving the Nile Delta many months before. The advance went smoothly, until they neared the border, when they were spotted by the Bedouin, who in their customary fashion alerted the Turks.

---

1 Powles, ibid, p. 68.

At 0600 hours on 9 January the Auckland Regiment in advance reached the boundary marker between Egypt and Palestine. The commander then 'rode forward alone' past the Boundary Pillar,' wrote Powles 'and taking off his hat, there thanked Almighty God that he had at last been permitted to enter the Holy Land (and was the first New Zealander to do so!)'[2]

THE BATTLE OF RAFA

Shortly after arriving at the outskirts of Rafa on 9 January, the battle began in earnest. The main line of defence around Rafa was a hill named El Magruntein to the west of the town. Lieut. Wilson wrote of that day: 'We had twenty-nine miles of desert to ride and had to be ready to rush the position, if possible, at dawn. However the Turks and Germans were expecting us and heavy fighting broke out as soon as it was light enough to see.'[3]

The Turco-German force stubbornly held their ground against every move by the EEF. 'The New Zealanders', wrote Bostock, 'had the toughest job. They were attacking the toughest position.'[4] 'The battle was proceeding', Wilson recalled, 'when I was told to take a message to the Commanding Officer of the Warwickshire Yeomanry who were in action about half a mile to our right.' Some minutes later he started to approach the ridge where they were engaged. 'Suddenly I thought I had been blown to smithereens,' he wrote, 'something hit me with such terrific force that, although I was running forward as fast as I could, I did a complete somersault backwards.'[5] Although only lightly wounded he had to return to base camp with other wounded.[6]

By mid-afternoon the New Zealanders had captured the Police Station, thereby opening a way for the other EEF forces. Aerial reconnaissance then revealed large Turkish troop formations coming from Shellal (some sixteen kilometres away) and Khan Yunis (closer by). By 1630 hours the ammuni-

2 Powles, ibid, p. 69.
3 Wilson, ibid, p. 60.
4 Bostock, ibid, p. 55.
5 Wilson, ibid, p. 60.
6 Wilson, ibid, p. 61.

tion was getting low and the horses were in desperate need of water. General Chetwode then gave orders to withdraw. Before this order came into effect though, 'the New Zealand Mounted Brigade', wrote Archibald Wavell, 'cleared the central keep by a fine bayonet charge. A little later the Camel Corps carried one group of works by assault. After this', Wavell continued, 'the remainder of the defences soon fell and as darkness came, victory was complete.'[7]

This New Zealand assault, as successful as it was, caused one family great grief that day. One section was composed of four brothers, three in the firing line and one being the horse holder for the day. 'In the final attack on the trenches' wrote Bostock 'the Turks surrendered and white flags went up. However, just as the New Zealanders were a few yards from the trenches,' Bostock wrote, 'a German machine-gunner opened fire, killing the three brothers. The New Zealanders then took no prisoners.'[8]

Wilson and the other wounded he was leading arrived at the Australian Field Hospital at 0300 hours and were met, wrote Wilson, by a 'great bearded Australian … who took me to a tent with one bed in it, with white sheets, and handed me some pyjamas. He never asked me what was the matter but gave me a bottle of port and said: "Get that inside you Digger, and you'll be right in the morning" which was quite true. I woke about 6 am and looked out of my tent, just in time to see the rest of the troops returning. Nearly every other man was asleep in the saddle.'[9]

'Among the prisoners', wrote Wilson, 'was a German Major who was in charge of their machine guns, a magnificent well—dressed figure. I said "Good morning," to him and he replied in perfect English "Good morning to you – wasn't that a damn good scrap?" He had been at Oxford for three years just before the war broke out.'[10]

---

7   Wavell, A.P. *The Palestine Campaigns*, (London, 1931), p. 66.
8   Bostock, ibid, p. 55.
9   Wilson, ibid, p. 62.
10   Wilson, p. 63.

A 'damn good scrap' it may have been to this German officer, but it came at a cost in human lives. This first battle for the conquest of the 'Promised Land' cost the EEF 71 men killed and 415 wounded.[11]

WEJH – THE FIRST MAJOR ARAB VICTORY

While the British, Australian and New Zealand soldiers had been fighting and dying in the Sinai and Rafa, the British High Command was becoming concerned by the lack of movement in the Hejaz. A small British force was retained at Suez for possible despatch to Rabegh, but the issue remained of 'Christian' soldiers being present on Arabian soil. Hussein would not commit his request in writing.[12]

Accordingly the British withdrew these forces from Suez in January 1917, and in turn despatched a small military mission to Jeddah led by Lieut-Col. S. Newcombe.[13] T.E. Lawrence was also part of this specialized force.

A plan was then developed for a two-pronged attack upon Wejh, north of Yenbo. If Wejh could be captured the Turkish garrison in Medina would be reluctant to advance upon Rabegh, as Medina could then effectively be attacked by this Arab force.

The plan devised by Lawrence and Feisal was for Feisal and Abdullah to advance north along the coast, while the British Navy would land troops closer to Wejh. Feisal's group of 10,000 headed out of Jeddah on 18 January, but before they reached Wejh, about 600 Arab and British men were landed by the British on 23 January and captured the small Turkish garrison.[14] This victory was a major psychological boost for the cause of the revolt.

Medina now became the southernmost point of the Turkish line of communication, and both Mecca and Rabegh were secure. The Turks were now forced to concentrate troops at several other major positions north of Medina, especially at Tebuk and Ma'an, in order to protect the Hejaz railway.

---

11   Wavell, ibid, p. 66.

12   Eastern Report 10 January 1917, CAB 24/143/18. The Eastern Report, which was prepared in London with information coming from the Arab Bureau for the War Cabinet, also stated that 'King Hussein had to guarantee the safety of Christian soldiers being in Arabia.'

13   Newcombe had previously worked with the PEF and had been involved in mapping and surveying the Sinai Peninsula.

14   Falls, ibid, Vol. 1, p. 237. British aerial reconnaissance also assisted. Barr, ibid, p. 43.

The capture of the Red Sea ports permitted the British Navy to transfer about 700 Arab POW's who had been captured fighting for the Turks in Mesopotamia, and who now chose to join the struggle against the Ottoman regime. These men were joined also by Muslim soldiers from French North Africa, and well as other Muslims from Egypt and India.[15]

During the following months, the British officers, as well as some French soldiers based at Jeddah under Colonel Bremond, worked with the Arabs training them how to destroy the railway line. The purpose behind this strategy was to completely isolate and ultimately capture the Turkish garrison at Medina.

But then in April 1917 a tribal leader from the region some 300 miles (480 kilometres) north of Wejh, inland from Aqaba and below Maan, visited Feisal's camp in Wejh. Auda abu Tayi, sheikh of the Howeitat tribe, indicated that an area where he roamed, the Wadi Sirhan, could become a springboard for the capture of Aqaba and expansion northward.[16] This news provided Lawrence and Feisal the opportunity to develop a plan for the capture of Aqaba. This small port was important for supplying the Arab force for future operations.

While these preparations were taking place in the Hejaz, the EEF prepared for their next move – against Gaza.

VICTORIES IN MESOPOTAMIA

While these plans were taking shape, General Maude launched a renewed British offensive in Mesopotamia in late 1916. His force slowly inched north along the Tigris River, and on 9 January 1917 the 3rd Lahore Division attacked the Turkish forces at Kut-el-Amara. Kut, the scene of a great tragedy for the British, finally fell on 3 February.

Thereafter other key positions were taken by the British-Indian force, and by 25 February all of the Turkish positions along the Tigris River in the vicinity of Kut had been captured.

15   Murphy, D. *The Arab Revolt 1916–1918*, (London, 2008), p. 17.
16   Lawrence, Revolt in the Desert, pp. 63- 65; Barr, ibid, p. 44.

Maude was bound by his previous instructions to protect the *Vilayet* of Basra. On 24 February he had contacted CIGS Robertson asking if the Government 'in any way desire to modify their instructions.'[17] Lloyd George was keen to capture Baghdad, but Robertson was reluctant. Finally Lloyd George and others of like-mind in the War Cabinet persuaded the War Office to permit Maude to capture this most historical of Eastern cities.[18]

The Turkish High Command now realized that Baghdad was imperilled. They quickly withdrew their remaining forces from the south, as well as ordering troops based in Persia back to protect this strategic city.

The key MEF breakthrough occurred on the night of 26 February 1917 when the British-Indian force broke through the Turkish Eighteenth Army Corps line. The surviving Turkish forces then retreated to Selman Pak, just south of Baghdad. The Mesopotamian Expeditionary Force now consolidated its force at Azizie prior to a last push on to Baghdad.

The fight for Baghdad effectively began on 6 March, and continued unabated until the night of 10-11 March, when, Von Sanders stated: 'Baghdad was lost by the Turks.'[19] 11 March 1917 marked one of the key dates in the entire campaign against Turkey.

Baghdad was such an important Islamic city that the British needed to be very cautious concerning their actions there. A proclamation was put together, which Mark Sykes had much to do with, and was issued to the general populace.[20] 'The language of the proclamation was guarded', wrote Lloyd George, 'as while we had no desire to annex Mesopotamia, we could not yet be sure what its ultimate government would be.'[21]

It was hoped at this stage that the MEF would link up with the Russian forces. This, however, did not occur as Russian troops then began to be withdrawn – as a result of the revolution then occurring in Russia. The withdrawal of Russian troops from the Caucasus in turn released those Turkish troops which had been fighting against the Russians in that region.

---

17 Lloyd George, ibid, Vol. II, p. 1078.
18 Lloyd George, ibid, Vol. II, pp. 1078-9.
19 Von Sanders, ibid, p. 163.
20 Leslie, S. *Mark Sykes: His Life and Letters*, (London, 1923), pp. 259-61.
21 Lloyd George, ibid, Vol. II, p. 1079.

It was reasonable to expect that some of those Turkish soldiers would now be released to fight against the British both in Mesopotamia and in Syria. The British now had to consolidate their presence in and around Baghdad, as well as quickly capture Palestine – particularly Jerusalem – before these Turkish troops arrived. But before Jerusalem could be captured, they first had to capture Gaza.

PREPARATIONS FOR GAZA

By early March, Wilson had recovered from his wounds and was back at the front line, at El Burg. While there he wrote, 'the Turks have gone right back to Jerusalem now – at least, that is the latest information – and we expect to get into Palestine a bit, and then sit down. I don't think the French want us to invade Palestine.'[22]

Wilson was right on the matter of the French not really wanting the British to take control over Palestine. Lloyd George, however, was pushing for a quick capture of Jerusalem and the entire land. The capture of Jerusalem had now become the fulcrum of his strategy in the East. The road to Jerusalem, though, was via Gaza.

Von Sanders recorded for the period of early March: 'At the beginning of March strong British cavalry felt its way to Chan Junis (Khan Yunis) and occupied the place on March 8th. Soon they assembled a considerable force in the region El Arish-Tell Rifah. On March 22nd numerous British scouting parties advanced against Wadi Razze (Ghuzze or Gaza), and in the ensuing days the enemy observed was assembling large forces near Chan Julis (Khan Yunis).'[23]

THE IMPORTANCE OF *NILI*

It was during this period that the British desperately needed dependable intelligence. Much of this they acquired through the work of Aaronsohn and the *NILI*. Aaronsohn during this period had to constantly battle against the arrogance and suspicion of many of the British officers. This was in part

---

22   Wilson, ibid, p. 72.
23   Von Sanders, ibid, p. 164.

due to the prevailing 'world-view' within the Arab Bureau and British establishment in Cairo, which did not see any place for Zionism and a Jewish national entity in Palestine. Yet two men with whom he did have a good relationship were Wyndham Deedes and William Ormsby-Gore.

Aaronsohn's tasks included assisting with drawing up detailed maps and supplying other bits of relevant information, and periodically making trips on small trawlers to the coast near Atlit in order to collect information from the *NILI* agents.

In his diary for 12 March he recorded: 'Heard good news at 9 o'clock. Lt-General Maude had occupied Baghdad. Hurrah!'[24] On the same day he was visited by Captain Graves, who stated: 'They had reasons to believe that the Turks would offer some resistance on the Gaza-Tell Sherita [sic]-Djemamch line.' Graves wanted details from Aaronsohn 'on the nature of the ground and the possibility of movements for the troops.' Aaronshon provided five points which they should adopt in planning their campaign in the vicinity of Gaza, one of which was to: 'Make a military demonstration at Bir Seba [Beersheba] via the South … (Water reservoirs have been destroyed by the Turks in their retreat "but not thoroughly.")'[25]

Later on 3 April, following a conversation with Clayton, Aaronsohn wrote how Clayton stated of 'my strategy concerning Jerusalem': "You have sound logics and thorough local knowledge. You interested me immensely."[26] It seemed that finally his knowledge and information was indeed of value. Aaronsohn's urgency to get to Jerusalem, though, would have to wait, as they first had to capture the gateway in to 'the land between empires' from the south – Gaza.

24 Aaronsohn Diary, 12 March, cited in Verrier, ibid, p. 247.
25 Aaronsohn Diary, 12 March, cited in Verrier, ibid, p. 247.
26 Aaronsohn Diary, 12 March, cited in Verrier, ibid, p. 252.

CHAPTER 59

§

Disaster in Gaza

TOWARDS GAZA

While Lloyd George was battling with his 'westerner' generals and the French concerning the proposed advance into Palestine, General Murray now began moving towards Gaza. With this strategic location captured, he would have a perfect launching pad for the proposed autumn offensive.

Meanwhile General Chaytor captured Khan Yunis, which lay between Rafa and Gaza, on 23 February. This forced Von Kressenstein to withdraw his remaining forces in the region north of the Wadi Ghuzze (Wadi Gaza or the ancient Nahal Besor).[1] The EEF also captured other smaller Turkish positions in the Sinai and southern region, thereby effectively negating any potential Turkish thrust inland through the central Sinai and coming in behind the EEF force.

By the beginning of March 1917 Eastern Force was composed of the Anzac Mounted Division; the newly formed Imperial Mounted Division (composed of the 3rd and 4th Australian Light Horse Brigades and the 5th and 6th British Mounted Brigades, and commanded by Major-General H.W. Hodgson); the Imperial Camel Corps (ICC); the 52nd, 53rd, and 54th British

---

1 In 1 Samuel 30: 9 it is referred to as the 'Brook Besor' in the King James Version.

Infantry Divisions; RHA (Royal Horse Artillery); and other auxiliary troops. Eastern Force was now more British in composition than ANZAC.

One ANZAC who was now present was Lieutenant Hugo Throssell VC. Following his exploits at Hill 60 at Gallipoli in August 1915, Throssell had a period of convalescence, and a recruiting trip to Australia. He arrived back on 17 March in preparation for the upcoming battle.

Murray decided to come forward to El Arish to oversee the battle of Gaza, despite the close proximity of both Dobell and Chetwode. Secrecy though was still of the essence for this operation. For this reason they decided to strike while railhead was still not at the front. Another component of surprise, as well as entertaining the troops, was a large race meeting which was held on the Rafa battleground on 21 March, entitled the *Desert Column First Spring Meeting.*

'The course was excellent going' Powles commented, 'and with natural grassy slopes for lawn and grandstand, the spectators were happily provided for. The "fields"' he continued 'were good and races keenly contested among the Yeomanry, Australians and New Zealanders.' The *Promised Land Stakes,* Powles was proud to declare, was won by the New Zealand horse, 'Maori King.'[2]

THE BATTLE BEGINS ON 26 MARCH 1917

Gaza, the southern gateway into the 'land between empires', was protected on its south by a large mound named Ali Muntar. Murray proposed launching his main attack there with the 53rd Welsh Division. There would also be diversionary attacks elsewhere. The Anzac Mounted Division was to encircle Gaza to the north and cut the Gaza-Jaffa road. The Imperial Mounted Division was to move behind them and cut off other access roads from Gaza. The ICC and 54th East Anglia Division were to cut and cover the route from Gaza to Beersheba. The 52nd Lowland Division was kept in reserve.

Early in the morning of 26 March 1917 the troops began moving to their allotted positions. While the Anzac Mounted Division was heading

2 Powles, ibid, p. 84.

north they captured a Turkish divisional commander. By mid-morning the cordon around Gaza was complete, aided greatly by a thick fog which had drifted in from the sea. The infantry attack on Ali Muntar, however, had not commenced, as the same thick fog had blanketed their vision – as well as there being some human error.

As soon as the encirclement of Gaza began other major Turkish formations at Huj, Hariera, Sheria and Beersheba were immediately informed, but as Von Sanders rather caustically stated, 'with the customary Turkish delay in starting, the march for the relief of Gaza was delayed into the afternoon hours.'[3]

THE FIGHT FOR ALI MUNTAR – HEIGHT 83

Finally around noon Welshmen of the 53rd Division, who had previously seen action at Gallipoli, began moving towards their objective under heavy artillery, rifle and machine-gun fire. One of those who observed this move was Ion Idriess, who wrote: 'The poor Welshmen, coming up the open slopes towards the redoubts were utterly exposed to machine-gun and rifle-fire... Some thousands of the poor chaps bled on Ali Muntar that day.'[4]

Ali Muntar, or Height 83 to the Turco-German command,[5] witnessed some intense fighting, where hundreds of young Welsh soldiers paid the supreme sacrifice.

THE ENTRY INTO GAZA FROM THE OTHER DIRECTIONS

Anxious for a speedy victory, Chetwode also commanded the Anzacs[6] to move into Gaza from their positions in the north. Von Sanders recorded how the 'British entered the city from the north, east and south-east. Every hedge, every house was fought for.'[7]

After heavy hand-to-hand fighting, the British infantry and dismounted Anzacs had linked hands by 1800 hours. Tala Bey, the Turkish commander

---

3 Von Sanders, ibid, p. 165.
4 Idriess, ibid, p. 192.
5 Von Sanders, ibid, p. 165.
6 When referring to the men of the Anzac Mounted Division, I will use lower case.
7 Von Sanders, ibid, p. 165.

of Gaza was then preparing to blow up the water wells and wireless station, while the civic leader of Gaza was actually preparing a feast to welcome the British and ANZAC victors.

Unfortunately, the British commanders weren't completely aware of the success of their forces in the town. Also, according to a preconceived plan, if the town had not been captured by nightfall, the EEF forces would withdraw so as to water the horses, and also for fear of the arrival of strong Turkish reinforcements.

General Dobell, unaware of the fall of Ali Muntar and the presence of forces in the town, announced a withdrawal in the late afternoon. Chauvel protested vigorously, "But we have Gaza!" Dobell replied: "Yes; but the Turkish reinforcements are all over you."[8]

So withdraw they did. Some of the Anzacs had to hike six kilometres through narrow streets and cactus hedges to retrieve their horses before making the journey back to the Wadi Ghuzze.

Ultimately the news of the capture of Ali Muntar and the centre of the town reached Dobell, and he ordered an immediate re-seizure of the position. But it was too late. The Turco-German force, surprised at their reprieve, had quickly re-established themselves. While Dobell was left to rue his mistake, the Turkish commander Tala Bey was exultant in his good fortune.

As the EEF withdrew from Gaza in defeat to the south of Wadi Ghuzze, they left behind them on the battlefield some 523 men killed, 2,932 wounded and 512 missing, mostly captured.[9]

CONSEQUENCES

This first EEF attack had, like the naval assault at Gallipoli, warned the Turks of the Allied intentions. Colonel von Kressenstein and Tala Bey now set about modifying the Turkish front line. They maintained a solid defence line between Gaza and Tel Hariera, and thereafter established strong points at Tel Sheria and Beersheba.

---

8   Gullett, H.S. *The AIF in Sinai and Palestine*, (1984), p. 294.

9   Wavell, ibid, p. 80. Von Sanders stated that they buried some 1,500 British dead; Von Sanders, ibid, p. 165.

News of a disastrous defeat was not initially received in London. The War Cabinet wanted good reports from the 'minor theatres', as there was nothing but a bloody quagmire on the Western Front. The capture of Baghdad by General Maude was one good report, while the overthrow of the Czar was initially seen as a positive development. News therefore of a *near* victory at Gaza was not good enough.

When it was clear that in a second assault the EEF was likely to break-through, the War Cabinet met on 2 April 1917 and 'devoted the afternoon', wrote Lloyd George, 'to an examination of the prospects in Palestine. We realized' he continued, 'the moral and political advantages to be expected from an advance on this front, and particularly from the occupation of Jerusalem.'[10] The War Cabinet then passed a resolution authorizing CIGS Robertson to inform Murray that '... we were very anxious to exploit the successes already achieved to the utmost possible extent, and to capture Jerusalem; ...'[11]

Lloyd George was of the opinion at this point that Turkey was on the verge of collapsing, and thereby he wanted to encourage Murray. In Mesopotamia General Maude was moving north from Baghdad, while it was being planned that Grand Duke Nicholas would move through Armenia, and into northern Mesopotamia. Thus an aggressive campaign in Palestine and Syria could well force Turkey to sue for peace.

There was another factor why Lloyd George desired to defeat Turkey. He wrote:

For the British Empire the fight with Turkey had a special importance of its own ... The Turkish Empire lay right across the track by land or water to our great possessions in the east – India, Burma, Malaya, Borneo, Hong Kong, and the Dominions of Australia and New Zealand.[12]

---

10 Lloyd George, ibid, Vol 2, p. 1086.
11 Lloyd George, ibid, Vol. 2, p. 1086.
12 *War Memoirs of Lloyd George*, Vol 4, 1917 (Boston, 1934), pp. 66-67, cited in Fromkin, ibid, p. 282.

Lloyd George (like other members of the present British Cabinet), had one main matter on his mind: the preservation of the link to the Eastern Empire. His thoughts as to how this would be achieved are evident when he and Lord Curzon met with Sykes on 3 April 1917, prior to Sykes' departure to Egypt where he was to join the EEF as political advisor. Sykes was instructed to: (1) Make every effort to ensure that Turkish Palestine fell within the British and not the French area after occupation. (2) To ensure that no pledges concerning Turkish Palestine be given to the Arabs. (3) Not to prejudice the Zionists and their possible future involvement alongside Britain in the political future of Turkish Palestine.[13]

The Jewish nationalist movement was now, *finally*, in the plans for the future destiny of the 'land between empires.'

THE GAZA FRONT

While the War Cabinet encouraged and bolstered Murray's efforts, the Turks too strengthened their position in and near Gaza. The Turkish position was bolstered by the overthrow of the Czar. Tired of the War the Russians then withdrew their forces from the Caucasus. Some 25,000 Turkish troops were now released for service elsewhere - some of whom came south.

The Turkish fortifications around Gaza were substantially improved, full use being made of the high ground and the abundance of the cactus plants in the area. This time there was to be no opportunity for the mounted troops to encircle Gaza as had happened in the first battle. There was now a solid defensive line stretching from Gaza through to Tel esh Sheria, half way to Beersheba, and then further deployments through to Beersheba, rendering an EEF breakthrough very difficult.

INCREASED OPPRESSION AGAINST THE LOCALS

The possible British breakthrough increased Turkish sensitivity towards any potential fifth-column operating within the country. Many people were expelled from their homes.

---

13 Fromkin, ibid, p. 287.

Additionally many suspected Arab nationalists were hanged by the Turkish authorities. But pressure also mounted now against any group suspected of being sympathetic to the Allies. The entire Jewish community now found itself in this category, and the first Jewish community to bear this collective punishment was Jaffa/Tel Aviv. Aaronshohn recorded in his dairy on 19 April: 'I heard of looting [plunder] of Jewish Jaffa Two Yemenites hung on trees are all the Jews that remained in the city. Everything Jewish was plundered ... Djemal Pasha cynically asserted that he was driving the Jews away for their own good.'[14]

'Refugees arrived from Gaza and Jaffa in a destitute condition,' wrote Marie James from Safed in April 1917, 'as they were not allowed to bring any food and scarcely any clothing. After their houses had been plundered by the Turkish soldiers, many died on the way.'[15] Only intervention by the German Foreign Ministry hindered Djemal Pasha from expelling the remainder of the Jewish community of Jerusalem.

The general situation in the land became desperate. Miss James continued: 'An eyewitness who returned from Salt' she wrote, 'said she saw twenty five carriages from the train filled with women and children and with little clothing, and men were carrying old women on their backs.'[16] The situation was reminiscent of the collective punishment meted out against the Armenians, Greeks and Assyrians, in 1915 and 1916.

William Ormsby-Gore wrote while compiling the Eastern Report on 3 May: 'The tale of executions, deliberate starvation, and deportations by the latter [Djemal Pasha] is already a heavy one. His latest victims have been the Palestinian Jews; and the Jews of Jaffa and Haifa are now receiving the same treatment as was meted out to the Armenians by the C.U.P leaders earlier in the war. The inhuman barbarities of the present rulers of Turkey call for speedy vengeance. These new pogroms in Palestine should awaken some previous supporters of the Young Turks to their real character... '[17]

---

14 Aaronsohn Diary, cited in Verrier, ibid, p. 255.
15 Diary of Marie James, quoted in *JMI*, 1919, p. 69.
16 Diary of Marie James, ibid, pp. 69-70.
17 CAB 24/143/18, Eastern Report, 3 May 1917.

The activities of the *NILI* were now seriously endangered, and if un-covered could potentially endanger the remaining Jewish community in Palestine. Sarah (Sariti) Aaronsohn had joined Aaron in Cairo at that time, but despite understanding the dangers, realized that for the benefit of their goal (a British military takeover) she had to return to Palestine.

THE SECOND BATTLE OF GAZA

The only way the suffering of the civilian, mostly non-Muslim, population could be alleviated would be by a quick and decisive capture of the land. This could only occur if Gaza was first captured.

On 17 April the 52nd Lowland and 54th East Anglia Divisions, including five newly arrived tanks, moved out from the shelter of Wadi Ghuzze to their forward positions. Then on 19 April 1917 a heavy EEF artillery barrage began at 0500 hours aimed at the 3rd Turkish Division in Gaza. This attack was supplemented by fire from Allied warships off shore. Von Sanders re-corded that: 'The principal attack was directed against the positions of the 53rd [Turkish] Division between Gaza and Tell Sheria, and designed to break the Turkish front.'[18]

The British infantry divisions, as well as the 53rd Welsh Division, at-tacked directly in front of Gaza, while the Imperial Mounted Division made a dismounted assault further east. The Anzac Mounted Division protected the far eastern flank.

The fighting throughout that first day was very intense as it occurred along a wide front. Reg Walters wrote: 'Wednesday … we moved out in darkness to take up a position. We dismounted and then marched a consid-erable distance. About daylight we were down in a hollow when the Turks at short range opened up on us… Meanwhile our artillery and Navy got going and I will never forget that bombardment. One could hardly hear himself speak.'[19]

Shortly afterwards, with the completion of the bombardment, Walters continued: 'We were ordered to fix bayonets and charged. But the Turks

---

18 Von Sanders, ibid, p. 166.
19 Walters.

rushed back onto the next ridge. After popping it into them about 50 sur-rendered, so on again we went in small rushes about ½ mile. Turks seemed to be everywhere – I could see we had a nasty job on.'

Walters then continued: 'Turkish shrapnel began to come onto us. I was about twenty yards from Will with shrapnel falling all round us... It was about 1 P.M. that we got it hot and horrible The Turks were down in a waddy [sic] about ½ mile away and to get to it we had to advance over open country with no cover. I had been through a fair bit of fire one way or another but the Lord save us from going through such a hell again. The shrapnel shells just formed one continual screech [sic] and the shrapnel just fell around us like hail. How many of us got to the Waddy [sic] I don't know. But the order came to advance so we just had to face it ... Men were falling around me ... It will always remain a nightmare to those of us who got through.'[20]

Walters and his unit managed to hold off the Turks for several hours. Then he noticed Turkish reinforcements moving to try and outflank his group, and was able to gratefully record: 'The Yeomanry relieved us shortly after and we were told to retire.' That was the good news. The bad news was that they had to retire the same way they had come. 'We were all dead beat when we got over the ridge' he recalled. But then, he continued 'the General came galloping up and told us to advance again in another direction. Many of the chaps were hit in this advance with machine gun fire and shrapnel. A huge explosive shell burst a few yards away from me and a great junk [sic] of iron flew past my body about ½ a yd [yard] away.'[21]

Nearly every unit of Eastern Force suffered terribly that day. Von Sanders recorded concerning the end of the first day of intense fighting: 'On the whole the enemy had been thrown back to his initial positions or had withdrawn to them on his own accord.'[22]

---

20   Walters.
21   Walters.
22   Von Sanders, ibid, p. 167.

ANOTHER FAILURE

The intense fighting continued into the following day, but the Turco-German force held its ground. Not even the new instrument of war, the tank, could dislodge them. The EEF was ordered to fall back to the south side of Wadi Ghuzze and to fortify their position there, dig in, and await the expected Turkish counter-attack. The counter-attack never happened, and the two sides ended up facing each other: the EEF line running just to the south of Wady Ghuzze and the Turco-German line to the north, in an elevated area.

The battle that was supposed to mark the beginning of the end for the Turks and to climax with the capture of Jerusalem, had failed, and it failed at a great cost. The EEF suffered some 6,444 casualties, including 509 confirmed killed. Falls maintains that most of the 1,576 missing were killed, and whose bodies remained unburied in no-man's land.[23] One of those killed was Ric Throssell, whose well-known brother Hugo, VC, was again wounded.[24]

This second major defeat in Palestine, coupled with the larger defeat at Gallipoli, now placed much pressure upon both the British generals and politicians to develop a plan for the ultimate capture of the 'Holy Land' and for its political future. It was imperative that a solution would need to be favourable to Britain considering the huge cost in lives the campaign against Turkey had so far cost her. At this stage British and ANZAC casualties were into their tens of thousands.

In view of this high casualty rate it was now imperative that Britain press on and secure a victory. Although the battles of Romani and Rafa were significant, until this point the soldiers of the Turkish Empire and won all three of the major battles against the soldiers of the British Empire – at Gallipoli and now twice at Gaza. A victory was now essential if Jerusalem was to be captured by Christmas.

---

23   Falls, ibid, Vol. 1, p. 348.
24   Hamilton, ibid, pp. 268-9.

§

CHAPTER 60

Jewish hopes raised

CONSEQUENCES OF THE VICTORY IN THE 'PROMISED LAND'

U ntil early 1917 much of the work of the Zionist movement had
been purely hypothetical – *when* a sympathetic power gains control of *Eretz Yisrael* we shall seek their endorsement for our vision!
Until early January 1917 much of the work of the British strategists had been
hypothetical – *when* we ultimately gain control over Palestine we shall make
it a secure buffer zone for the Suez Canal.

The victory of the EEF at Rafa changed the entire situation from the hypothetical to the real. Britain was now on the move in the 'Promised Land'.
This being so it was now imperative that the British Government firmly determine its policy regarding the land of Israel, vis-à-vis the French, and it
was imperative now for the Zionist movement to obtain a firm commitment
from the British Government concerning their part in the future. If such a
commitment was not received now, then perhaps the opportunity would be
irretrievably lost.

On 17 February a distinguished group of men met at the home of Dr.
Gaster, which included Gaster, Weizmann, Lord Rothschild, Samuel, James
de Rothschild, Sokolow and Sykes. It was what Weizmann termed: 'The first
full-dress conference leading to the Balfour Declaration.'[1]

---

1 Weizmann, ibid, Vol. 2, p. 188.

At this meeting it was agreed that they did not want the condominium proposal (dual British-French administration), or internationalisation, in Palestine, due to what Weizmann stated were 'all the complications, rivalries, inefficiencies, compromises and intrigues which that would entail, to the detriment or perhaps complete paralysis of our work. What the Zionists wanted' he continued, 'was a British protectorate with full rights according to the terms of the memorandum.'[2] However, those present did not want 'any jurisdiction over the Holy Places, which they want to be internationalized.'[3]

The group understood clearly that the establishment of a Jewish national entity in Palestine was the consensus of Zionists everywhere, especially in America, where the Zionist leader, Justice Louis Brandeis, was advisor to President Wilson on Jewish affairs.

At this meeting Sykes was frank about the difficulties which lay ahead in achieving this goal, particularly with the French, as well as with the emerging Arab nationalist movement. But, Sykes stated, they could receive Arab support 'particularly if they received Jewish support in other matters.'[4] Throughout this, and other meetings with the Jewish leaders, Sykes not once mentioned the Agreement with the French.

Following this meeting Sokolow was entrusted with the task of 'modifying the attitude of the French' as well as gaining the support of Italy and the Pope.[5] Brandeis would be called upon to enhance exposure throughout America, while work would also need to be done in Russia among both the Zionist and non-Zionist millions there.[6]

Weizmann meanwhile was meeting with Sykes and Picot – who was, as usual, very obstructionist, and was still agitating for French control in Palestine. A meeting with Balfour on 22 March produced a fresh thought, that of a joint Anglo-American protectorate over Palestine.[7]

---

2 Weizmann, ibid, Vol. 2, p. 188.
3 Weizmann, ibid, Vol. 2, p. 188.
4 Weizmann, ibid, Vol. 2, p. 189.
5 Weizmann, ibid, Vol. 2, p. 189.
6 Stein, ibid, pp. 378-9.
7 Weizmann, ibid, Vol. 2, p. 190.

There was now somewhat of an urgency in the matter from a Jewish perspective. When Baghdad had fallen, the proclamation by the British Government (which Sykes had helped put together) emphasized Arab aspirations – while not a word was said about the Jewish people, despite the fact that there were at least 50,000 Jewish people living in Baghdad.[8]

Now with the EEF poised to attack, and seemingly win, at Gaza, and then enter into Palestine proper, it was more than urgent to elicit some form of commitment from the British Government.

JEWISH HOPES RAISED

On the morning of 3 April 1917 Lloyd George met with Weizmann and C.P. Scott, and the Prime Minister informed them of his desire to capture Palestine. At the same meeting Lloyd George was reminded of the desire of forming a Jewish unit to serve in the liberation of *Eretz Yisrael*, and of the presence of the 120 former Zion Mule Corps men now training at Winchester. Lloyd George commented that these men should be sent to the front where their knowledge of the terrain would be invaluable for the campaign.[9]

Several days later Jabotinsky, serving as a private in the 20th Battalion London Regiment, was summoned to a meeting by Lord Derby, the War Secretary, and General Woodward, the Director of Organisation, in London.[10]

The Lord and the General were somewhat intrigued when confronted by 'a private in a British infantry battalion', but they nevertheless asked for details about the 'Jewish unit scheme.' When they asked Trumpeldor and Jabotinsky if they could expect many Jews to join up, Trumpeldor replied: "If it is to be just a regiment of Jews – perhaps. If it will be a regiment for the Palestine front – certainly. If, together with its formation, there will appear a government pronouncement in favour of Zionism – overwhelmingly."[11] The conversation then touched upon other matters, including the role of

---

8   For details of conversations and communications between Weizmann, Sykes, Sokolow and others at that time, see Stein, ibid, pp. 378-9.

9   Stein, ibid, p. 383.

10   Jabotinsky, ibid, pp. 82-83.

11   Jabotinsky, ibid, p. 83.

the Zion Mule Corps and Trumpeldor at Gallipoli – which was positively acknowledged.

Jabotinsky later met with General Geddes, the Director of the Recruiting Department. Together they determined that the name of the prospective Jewish unit would be – the Jewish Regiment. It was to have a menorah as its insignia, together with the Hebrew word *Kadimah* – forward.

When asked who should command this Jewish Regiment, Jabotinsky recalls having mentally recited all the Jewish candidates – Lionel Rothschild, Major Schonfield, James Rothschild, Fred Samuel, Eliezar Margolin (who, Jabotinsky wrote, 'had been in my thoughts ever since our first days in the Gabbari camp in Alexandria, and was somewhere on the Flanders front with the Australians.'[12]).

'But' he continued 'with all my feelings of respect to every one of them, I considered then, and consider still today, that this historic privilege had been faithfully won by another: by the man who had not been ashamed to undertake the leadership of the Mule Drivers and who had converted them into a corps for which the War Minister had profound respect; the man who in hospital and convalescent home has us ever in his thoughts … writing his book, *With the Zionists in Gallipoli*; the man who believed in us when we were laughed at and ridiculed… There is only one nominee. Even though he is not a Jew, he must be our Colonel and I hope one day he will be our General: Patterson.'[13]

JEWISH HOPES CHALLENGED

Despite this positive development Weizmann and the Zionist leaders soon received a reality check when on 16 April they became aware of the Anglo-French ('Sykes-Picot') Agreement.

A distraught Weizmann then met with Lord Cecil, Associate-Secretary of the Foreign Office on 25 April and discussed the entire matter. He stated that the Zionists only wanted to come under a British protectorate, and not a French one. Weizmann pointed out to Cecil, 'that a Jewish Palestine would

---

12 Jabotinsky, ibid, p. 88.
13 Jabotinsky, ibid, p. 89.

be a safeguard to England, in particular in respect to the Suez Canal.' Cecil then suggested 'that it would help a great deal if the Jews of the world would express themselves in favour of a British protectorate.'[14]

Shortly afterwards Balfour visited America and met Justice Brandeis and they spoke about the Zionist initiative. Brandeis then promulgated the concept of a Jewish Palestine throughout the United States America, and not just Jewish America, was now more attuned to the events in the Middle East. On 2 April President Wilson had asked both Houses of Government to sanction a declaration of war upon Germany, which was agreed on 6 April. Although the United States never declared war on Turkey, being now an Ally of Britain and France, America would henceforth be more actively involved in all matters involved in the War effort.[15] President Wilson was also opposed to secret treaties and European imperialism, having been informed of the 'Sykes-Picot' Agreement.

With the 'Sykes-Picot' Agreement now becoming known, the British Government began to look at ways in which it could be modified to best suit their interests. The interests of Britain and those of Zion were now converging – just as hundreds of British Christians and some British strategists had been advocating for some 300 hundred years! Blanche Dugdale, Balfour's biographer, wrote: 'By the end of April [1917] the Foreign Office recognized, with some slight dismay, that the British Government was virtually committed.'[16]

FRENCH APPREHENSIONS AND BRITISH RE-ASSESSMENT

While Britain was moving towards modifying the 'Sykes-Picot' Agreement, France, aware of Britain's intentions, was looking at how best to counteract these British moves. Sykes had already alerted Picot to the proposal of a British administration in Palestine[17], and then while in Paris on 6 April enroute to the East, he met again with Picot. Sykes wrote to the Foreign Office on 6 April how he (Sykes) 'impressed on him [Picot] importance of meeting

---

14   Weizmann, ibid, Vol. 2, p. 192.
15   It was at this time that Morgenthau was entrusted with a task from Wilson to seek a separate peace with Turkey. The effort failed almost as soon as it began.
16   Cited in Weizmann, ibid, Vol. 2, p. 194.
17   Sykes to Picot, 28 February 1917, cited in Stein, pp. 386-8.

Jewish demands and expressed my opinion strongly that it would be advantageous to prepare French mind for idea of British suzerainty in Palestine by international consent.'[18] Sykes also spoke of a joint British-American administration, which the French also dismissed.[19]

All of these deliberations and suggestions ultimately convinced President Poincare, 'that in London our agreements are now considered null and void. British troops will enter Syria from the south and disperse our supporters.'[20] Poincare's comments echoed those of Lloyd George, who had stated to Ambassador Bertie also in April that, wrote Kedourie, 'the French would have to accept a British protectorate in Palestine.'[21] Lloyd George stated: 'we shall be there by conquest and shall remain.'[22]

Following their meetings in Paris both Sykes and Picot left for the East. Picot was sent to Egypt to act as *French High Commissioner for Occupied Territories in Palestine and Syria.* He was instructed to ensure the retention of French interests in Syria, and to be considerate towards the Jewish colonies in the region. This was in accordance with a new tactic now being adopted by the French. Realizing that the Jewish appeal was gaining in popularity, the French were endeavouring to support it – and by so doing hoping to divorce it from being a purely British idea.

The presence of Picot, like that of Sykes, in the Middle East, was based upon the assumption that the EEF would defeat the Turks at the second battle of Gaza and quickly conquer the land. When this did not happen, the politicians, like the commanders, then had time to re-evaluate their relative positions.

The British and Zionist leaders could now garner world-wide support for the idea of a British-Jewish protectorate in Palestine.

---

18   Sykes to Foreign Office, 6 April 1917, Sledm, No. 42, cited in Stein, ibid, pp. 388-9.
19   Sykes to Foreign Office, 8 April 1917, Sledm, No. 49. cited in Stein, ibid, pp. 388.
20   Poincare Diary, 7 April 1917, cited in Poincare, Vol. IX, p .109.
21   Kedourie, ibid, p. 159.
22   Lady Algernon Gordon Lennox (ed.), The Diary of Lord Bertie of Thame, 1924, vol. II, p. 123, cited in Kedourie, ibid, p. 159.

ACTIVE INVOLVEMENT OF THE JEWISH PEOPLE

Despite the military set-back at Gaza, Balfour and Brandeis continued spreading the word in the United States. Sokolow travelled to Italy in late April 1917, meeting both the Pope and the Italian Prime Minister. Both seemed sympathetic towards Zionism, yet they had reservations about the future of the 'Holy Places' and of a British-sponsored protectorate in Palestine.[23] Pope Benedict XV stated to Sokolow, concerning the return of the Jewish people to Palestine: 'It is providential; God has willed it.'[24]

From Italy Sokolow travelled to France and met with Prime Minister Ribot. Ribot assured him of French support and sympathy, a sentiment which became official when the French issued a written Memorandum of support on 4 June 1917.[25]

This French Memorandum predated any official British position of support for Zionism, and was a desperate French attempt to steer the Zionist cause away from a purely British concern.[26] Interestingly this extra interest in Zionism was also due to a German interest in supporting the Jewish nationalist movement.[27]

On 20 May 1917 a Conference was convened in London consisting of delegates from the various Zionist entities in Britain.[28] Weizmann, who was now the President of the Zionist Federation gave a cautionary address, stating that: 'States must be built up slowly, gradually, systematically, and patiently.'[29] He also warned about complacency in light of the overthrow of the Czarist regime. His greatest warning though, in his speech, related to opposition within the Jewish world against the very notion of a Jewish national entity.[30]

The Conjoint Foreign Committee responded with a counter-statement which was printed in the *Times* on 24 May 1917. This statement basically

---

23   Stein, ibid, pp. 406-415.
24   Sokolow to Weizmann, 12 May 1917: *Ch. W.P.*, cited in Stein, ibid, p. 408.
25   This was done through a letter from Foreign Minister Cambon to Sokolow on 4 June 1917, cited in Stein, ibid, pp. 416-7.
26   Stein, ibid, p. 418.
27   Stein, ibid, pp. 516-7.
28   Weizmann, ibid, Vol. 2, p. 200.
29   Weizmann, ibid, p. 201.
30   Weizmann, ibid, p. 201.

expressed the view that not all British Jews favoured the proposed British-Zionist protectorate proposal.

This statement in turn upset the British Government, which was now endeavouring to garner world-wide support for the proposal of taking Palestine and providing the Jewish people with a protectorate there. An intense debate then permeated the British Jewish community, culminating in the resignation of those on the Conjoint Committee who were strongly opposed to the Zionist proposal, and a number of changes within the Jewish Board of Deputies.

This open attack against the Zionist objective prompted Weizmann to meet with Balfour on 15 June, together with Sir Ronald Graham, in order to ascertain from him the official Government stance regarding the Zionist initiative.[31]

Balfour suggested that the Zionist Federation should: 'submit to him a declaration which would be satisfactory to us, and which he would try and put before the War Cabinet.'[32] The Political Committee of the Zionist Federation, headed up by Sokolow, then began working on a draft proposal to be presented to the British Government.

THE BATTLE FOR RUSSIAN JEWISH SUPPORT

Ironically at the very time when the Allied leaders were showing some public sympathy towards Zionism, internal Jewish debates over the matter escalated. By this stage, following the March Revolution, there was a possibility that Russia might sign a separate peace treaty with Germany. The Allies were desperate to avoid this occurring. Thus all avenues which could favourably dispose the Russian people, or at least large numbers of them, towards the Allied cause, were being explored.

One of the most vocal groups in Russia calling for a Russian withdrawal from the War and signing a peace treaty with Germany were left-wing, socialist agitators. These agitators also called for a withdrawal from all Czarist-regime agreements, including those with Britain and France. Many

---

31 Weizmann, ibid, p. 203.
32 Weizmann, ibid, p. 203.

of these agitators were Jewish, and members of the newly formed Jewish socialist movement, named the *Bund*. The *Bundists* dreamed of a socialist society in Russia, where Jewish and non-Jewish Russians could be equal. They believed a Jewish-Zionist entity in Palestine, under a British protectorate contradicted this *Bundist* ideology.

The Russian Zionists therefore were quite ambivalent about this new concept of a Jewish-British relationship in Palestine. Although many favoured partnership with the British, others were hesitant, fearing repercussions upon the two and half million Jewish people living under Austro-German control. They were also aware of the policy of the Berlin Zionist Executive at the beginning of the War, which declared for neutrality, and which opposed any sanctions aimed against Turkey.

At the All-Russian Zionist Conference held in early June 1917 there was no clear Russian Zionist consensus concerning the deliberations now beginning between the Zionist movement and the British Government. The British and American Zionists had to proceed virtually alone.

THE FORMAL REQUEST

When rumours spread that the Germans were making approaches to the Zionists, the British interest in Zionism intensified.[33] They promptly requested the Zionist leadership to quickly submit their requests. Lord Rothschild, representing the Zionist movement, submitted a formal letter to the British Government on 18 July 1917, outlining the Zionist proposal for a Jewish national home in Palestine.

By early August all the Cabinet members had seen this letter. Some were very favourably inclined towards the proposal, some were indifferent – and several were opposed. The most outspoken opponent was Edwin Montague, who in mid-July, had become the Secretary of State for India. Montague, a cousin of Herbert Samuel, represented that section of British Jewish society to whom Zionism was a threat to their position as assimilated British Jews.

At a Cabinet meeting in mid-September Montague strongly voiced his opposition to the Zionist proposal, which resulted in the 'withdrawal of the

---

33   Fromkin, ibid, p. 296.

item from the agenda.'[34] This caused both Weizmann and Rothschild to meet with Balfour. Balfour informed Weizmann, 'that his sympathies had not been changed by the attitude of Montague.'[35]

Weizmann spoke to Jan Smuts on 21 September 'and obtained from him the expected reiteration of his loyalty.'[36] He then spoke to Lloyd George on 28 September, who agreed to place a memorandum on the agenda for the War Cabinet meeting scheduled for 4 October 1917.[37]

FINALLY – A JEWISH LEGION

The Zionist proposal was closely associated with Jabotinsky's efforts to establish a Jewish Legion. At the end of August the Government announced the formation of the Jewish Regiment, complete with the Star of David insignia. The *London Gazette* on 23 August 1917 announced its formation. Part of the reason for its formation was due to an effort by the Government to enlist foreigners, mostly of Russian citizenship, who were residing in Britain. Following the Russian Revolution of March 1917 an agreement was reached with the Kerensky Government whereby these men would return and fight for Russia. Alternatively, though, they could now join this all Jewish unit and fight for the liberation of *Eretz Yisrael*.[38]

The unit was officially formed on 24 August 1917. John Patterson was commissioned as the commander, Jabotinsky was commissioned as an officer, while Trumpeldor, because of his disability, failed to be enlisted.

Once it became known that this unit was destined for *Eretz Yisrael,* more volunteers enlisted. 'It was a visiting Rabbi who conducted a Sabbath service,' wrote Private Rubinstein from Britain who was then serving in France, 'who brought to my notice that a Jewish Regiment was being formed for service in Palestine and said to me: "Who knows, this may be the beginning of a National Home for our Jewish People."'[39]

---

34   Weizmann, ibid, p. 204.
35   Weizmann, ibid, p. 204.
36   Weizmann, ibid, p. 204.
37   Weizmann, ibid, p.   .
38   Gouttman, ibid, pp. 73-4.
39   Freulich, R. *Soldiers in Judea*, (New York, 1964), p. 25.

Its formation, however, was greeted by a hail of opposition, mostly from the very same group who opposed Zionism. British Jews, these opponents stated, should be serving in regular British units.[40]

The War Cabinet met on 3 September and the first item on the agenda was the supposed Jewish Regiment. It was noted that a deputation of influential British Jews had met with the Secretary of State for War, and stated that some 40,000 Jews had served with distinction with the British forces, and it would be unfair to them that the reputation of British Jewish soldiers be pinned to this new Jewish Regiment.[41]

It was agreed, therefore, to drop the term Jewish Regiment, and the battalions of Jewish soldiers would receive numbers like any other unit in the British Army. The Minute concluded: 'It was generally agreed that there was a close connection between this subject and the question of the attitude to be taken up towards the Zionist movement as a whole.'[42]

The former members of the Zion Mule Corps, as well as new recruits, such as Jabotinsky, would be formed into the 38th Battalion Royal Fusiliers, and would not carry any distinctive Jewish insignia.

Another early recruit was Lieutenant Eliazar Margolin. Margolin had fought in numerous battles on the Western Front and distinguished himself at the attack on Mouquet Farm on 29-30 August 1916.[43] In June 1917 he temporarily commanded the 14th Battalion in Belgium, before returning to his 16th Battalion. He was badly injured in the Battle of Passchendale in September 1917 and returned to hospital in England in order to recover quickly – so he could return to the field.[44]

The Australian Army, however, had different ideas, and in view of his age (forty-two) they would not permit Margolin to return to active service. It was while languishing in a convalescent home in this semi-depressed state that Jabotinsky heard of his presence in Britain, and located him in late 1917.[45]

---

40   CAB 23/4, 3 September 1917.
41   CAB 23/4, 3 September 1917.
42   CAB 23/4, 3 September 1917.
43   Gouttman, ibid, p. 50, Note 49.
44   Gouttman, ibid, pp. 50-51.
45   Gouttman, ibid, p. 51.

Despite initial reservations, Margolin agreed to join, and after the Australian Army agreed to his transfer, Margolin became the commander of the second Jewish battalion, the 39th Battalion Royal Fusiliers.[46]

Other Jewish soldiers followed. Although there had been a movement in the United States to enlist Jewish volunteers in the British Army, this had not received the support of the American Government, as the United States at that stage was still not at war against Turkey. Yet many such volunteers awaited the call, including, surprisingly, David Ben Gurion and Yitzchak Ben Zvi.

MONTAGUE'S LAST DITCH EFFORT

At its meeting on 3 September 1917 the War Cabinet discussed the correspondence between Lord Rothschild and Balfour, 'on the question of the policy to be adopted towards the Zionist movement.' At this juncture Montague produced a statement entitled: 'The Anti-Semitism of the present Government' which expressed his view that 'the phrase "the home of the Jewish people" would vitally prejudice the position of every Jew everywhere.'[47]

Suggestions to postpone the Zionist question were opposed by Balfour, who pointed out, 'this was a question on which the Foreign Office had been very strongly pressed for a long time past.'[48] It was agreed that no further overtures would be made to the Zionist organisation until the views of President Wilson and the United States Government had been ascertained.[49]

So while Wilson and the Americans pondered over the proposed alliance between Britain and the Zionist movement, Montague was busy arguing to change the wording of the proposed agreement, from 'Palestine being *the* Jewish national home', to, there being *'a* Jewish national home in Palestine.'

Weizmann and Lord Lionel Rothschild sent a fresh memorandum to the War Cabinet on 3 October 1917 in which they emphasized that British help towards Zionism was necessary, and that 'Imperial interests' were in-

---

46 Jabotinsky, ibid, p. 102.
47 CAB 23/4, 3 September 1917.
48 CAB 23/4, 3 September 1917.
49 CAB 23/4, 3 September 1917.

volved.[50] The War Cabinet which met on 4 October was now even more sympathetic towards Zionist ambitions due to fresh news of German sympathy towards Zionism. At this meeting Leopold Amery and Lord Milner had produced a redrafted text of Rothschild's original proposal. A copy of this was sent to President Wilson, from whom no clear answer had as yet been received from the previous correspondence. Copies of this redraft were also sent for comment to both pro and anti-Zionist camps in Britain. At the 4 October meeting Montague argued strongly against the Zionist proposal.[51]

The opponents felt it was unwise to state that Palestine was to be *the* Jewish homeland. Also, it was felt that as a result of the Armenian massacres by the Turks, and by the uncovering of the *NILI* espionage network in Palestine, it would be very detrimental to the lives of Jewish people living in Palestine if a statement was released revealing Britain's commitment towards a Jewish national entity there.

Yet there were several key supporters at this point, including the Chief Rabbi and Herbert Samuel. Samuel was firmly of the opinion that if the Turks remained in control of Palestine then it would ultimately fall under German influence, or the influence of another European nation. Britain's presence in Egypt would then be threatened. Samuel had no hesitation in stating that the best safeguard would be for a strong Jewish presence in Palestine, and that a policy of support by the British Government would win for her immeasurable support throughout the world. Samuel also added that such a declaration of support would need to be made when the military situation in Palestine was suitable.[52]

Emanating from the 4 October meeting, though, was a revised version of the original memorandum presented by Rothschild to Balfour on 19 July. In this amended version the wording was changed, from stating the Jewish National Home, to a Jewish National Home in Palestine.[53]

---

50   Stein, ibid, p. 519.
51   Weizmann, ibid, p. 206.
52   Stein, ibid, p. 528.
53   Weizmann, ibid, p. 206.

Several days later Weizmann communicated this information to Brandeis and stated that it was 'essential to have not only President's approval of text, but his recommendation to grant this declaration without delay.'[54] Weizmann concluded his message to Brandeis: 'Your support urgently needed.'[55]

Apprehensions concerning German intentions mounted during October, as important elements of the German press were favourable towards Zionism. The Berlin Zionist Executive had actually submitted Memorandums to the German Foreign Office during the previous months, suggesting that Germany and Turkey provide some encouragement towards Zionism. They were anxious lest a British-French-Zionist policy be adopted, which would then threaten and prejudice the Jewish people living within the Ottoman Empire. This possible German connection influenced the British Foreign Office which was determined now to pre-empt any such German move.[56]

The German Government, however, was reluctant to provide support, fearful lest the Turks suspect her of having ulterior motives. The British position was then made easier when a positive response to a British-Zionist alliance was received from Colonel House, representing President Wilson, on 16 October 1917. The final obstacle had been removed, and the British War Cabinet could now make an official decision upon the Zionist proposal – for the establishment of a Jewish national entity in *Eretz Yisrael*.

---

54   Weizmann, ibid, p. 206.
55   Weizmann, ibid, p. 206.
56   Stein, ibid, pp. 516-7.

§

CHAPTER 61

Enter Allenby

CHANGE OF COMMAND

The failures at Gaza as well as the Allied spring offensive in France seriously affected the public confidence in the running of the War. A decisive Allied victory, somewhere, was essential. With this view in mind the War Cabinet decided at their 23 April meeting to press on vigorously with the campaign in Palestine. They also decided to introduce new leadership. Murray's achievements were significant, but after two large failures new blood was required.

The position was offered to that great South African, General Jan Christian Smuts. But after serious contemplation, Smuts rejected this offer.[1] The War Cabinet, though, wanted him to be involved, and shortly after Smuts came onto the War Cabinet as the Imperial representative.

The position of commander for the EEF was later accepted by General Edmund Allenby, then the commander of the Third British Army at Arras, and who had much experience as a cavalry commander. Prior to his departure, Lloyd George met him (together with CIGS Robertson), and, wrote the Prime Minister: 'I said the Cabinet expected "Jerusalem before Christmas."'[2]

---

1 He was confronted with serious political challenges in South Africa and felt he could not remain involved there and at the same time hold down a permanent position on the field.
2 Lloyd George, ibid, Vol. II, p. 1090.

GENERAL BEAUVOIR DE LISLE AND ALLENBY

The reference to Jerusalem was also the chief topic in another discussion he had prior to departure. One of the few commanders to survive unscathed from the Gallipoli campaign was Major-General Beauvoir de Lisle, who had commanded the 29th Division following General Hunter-Weston's departure.

De Lisle returned to service in France with the 29th Division following withdrawal from Gallipoli. In his book *Reminiscences of Sport and War*, de Lisle wrote:

In June 1917 I was on leave for ten days in London and saw in *The Times* that Allenby had been selected as Commander-in-Chief Egypt. Knowing he was at the Grosvenor Hotel, my wife and I went there to congratulate him on his appointment.

"No cause for congratulation," said Allenby in his gruff way. "Had to give up a jolly fine army and to take over a rotten show. Archie Murray is a good man and if he could not succeed, I don't see how I can."

"My dear Allenby," I replied, "you are on velvet. You may make all the mistakes in tactics and strategy, but nothing can prevent you being in Jerusalem by the 31st December."

"How do you make that out?" he asked. I told him of the book *Light for the Last Days* written by Dr. Grattan Guinness in 1886, in which he stated that the interpretation of the three prophecies in Daniel, Ezekiel and Revelation all pointed to the same year, 1917, as the end of the Gentile Times, a period of 1260 years – "Time, times and half a time."

"At the same time," I added, "don't forget your big guns."

"That is all very well," said Allenby, "but I am told the reinforcement of heavy artillery has been sunk and is now at the bottom of the Mediterranean."

"Well," I replied, "you can go to the War Office and say you refuse to accept this command unless the guns are replaced." To this he agreed and said he would follow this advice the same afternoon.

As we said goodbye and wished him all good luck, I added: "When you get to Jerusalem, Allenby, I hope you will not ride in state, for that is reserved in the future for One higher than you."[3]

This conversation no doubt would have both intrigued and encouraged the incoming Commander-in-Chief of the EEF!

SYKES ARRIVES AND MEETS AARONSHOHN

On the same day as the War Cabinet made the important decision of proceeding in Palestine, Sykes, who had just arrived in Cairo, met with Aaronsohn and said to him: "Since you left London your Zionistic activities have made tremendous progress."[4] Also on 23 April Wyndham Deedes said to him: "You know also that we have never received such fine reports as those sent in by your organisation."[5]

Prior to his departure from the EEF Murray stated to Aaronsohn: "I want to tell you personally and privately how deeply I am moved by incidents in Palestine. I shudder when I think of the Jews meeting with the same fate as the Armenians."[6]

By May 1917, at the time when Major Ormsby-Gore departed to London where he became personal assistant to Lord Milner and an associate of Sykes on the War Cabinet Secretariat,[7] numerous British officials were finally recognizing the important role being played by the *NILI*.

---

3   De Lisle, B. *Reminiscences of Sport and War*, (London, 1939), pp. 229-230, cited in Guinness, P. Hear O Israel, (New York, 1983), pp. 97-8.

4   Aaronsohn Diary, 23 April 1917, cited in Verrier, ibid, p. 258.

5   Aaronsohn Diary, 23 April 1917, cited in Verrier, ibid, p. 258.

6   Aaronsohn Diary, 22 May 1917, cited in Verrier, ibid, p. 267. Knowing that Aaronsohn, like Jabotinsky, was keen to get a Jewish Legion formed, he then went on to explain that at that time a Jewish Division was not needed – but more fully trained soldiers.

7   Stein, ibid, pp. 294-5. In these capacities Ormsby-Gore edited the Eastern Report, which was an overview of all the Intelligence reports from the East and which kept the War Cabinet abreast of such developments.

CHETWODE DEVELOPS A PLAN

Prior to Allenby's arrival General Sir Philip Chetwode replaced Dobell as commander of the Eastern Force. Chauvel now took over command of the Desert Column Corps, the first Australian to attain to the rank of Lieutenant-General. Chaytor took over command of the Anzac Mounted Division. To bolster the efforts of the EEF, the War Cabinet then decided to send troops from the Salonika front.

Chetwode set about devising a plan to break through the Turkish front line. One solid trench system from the coast at Sheik Ajlin inland for some seven kilometres to Sheik Abbas was established. From Sheik Abbas the line moved south to Tel el Jemmi, atop the Wadi Ghuzze, and then followed the Wadi Ghuzze to Shellal. It continued along the Wadi to Tel el Fara, and then onto Gamli. Between these positions there were detached posts. Due to the lack of suitable water, the area east of Gamli was covered by mounted patrols operating out from the main posts. In his planning he utilised much of the intelligence supplied by the *NILI*.[8]

Meanwhile Chetwode continued with those projects initiated by Murray: the railway and pipeline. Both of these veered away from the coast and headed inland to Shellal, where there were also some springs. A large reservoir was constructed at Shellal and this became the main base camp. Wherever possible other water sources were sought and wells restored.

The mounted patrols moved both north and south-east of Wadi Ghuzze in the general direction of Beersheba, the extreme south-eastern end of the Turkish line. The Turks were also active, sending out patrols to monitor the EEF activities. Contact between the rival patrols was common. '… we have been doing supports and front line duty' Walters wrote, 'between Gaza and Beersheba. Turkish cavalry in full view on the ridges.'[9]

Although on most occasions the two sides merely observed each other, occasionally they clashed. Trooper Malone of the 16th ICC Company was attached to the 5th Light Horse Regiment, and wrote on 8 May 1917:

---

8   Aaronsohn Diary, 10 & 12 May 1917, cited in Verrier, ibid, pp. 264-5.
9   Walters.

Pushed onto ridge W of Auja from which we observed a train lying on track with men picking up rails. With 3 others advanced to within 400 yds of track – train moved out and as it went [we] opened fire on another patrol to our left, but was then out of range ... caught a Bedouin and 2 Turks ... This railway runs as far as Kossiami.[10]

The Turks were pulling up the railway track they had previously built extending south of Beersheba, by which they intended reaching the Suez Canal via the central route of the Sinai. It had reached Kossaima (Nitzanna) when the EEF captured El Arish and Magdhaba, and work had then stopped. But now its rails could be pulled up and used for another line they were constructing behind Gaza in order to quickly bring supplies and reinforcements there.

THE RAID ON 22 MAY

Chetwode decided to destroy the railway and stop the Turks from re-using those valuable resources. The plan was for two groups to set out and to blow up each individual rail link, and the bridges, thereby hindering any further movement of trains along the line.

On 22 May 1917 one group of engineers accompanied by men from the 1st Light Horse Brigade set out from Shellal for the station of Asluj. Another group of engineers, accompanied by the ICC set out from Rafa and aimed for Auja. The Imperial Mounted Division, including Lieutenant Robert Wilson, made a strong reconnaissance in the direction of Beersheba as a decoy on the same day.

Altogether some twenty-two kilometres of railway were destroyed, as well as a number of arched bridges, including one of eighteen arches at Asluj. During the operation, engineers also surveyed the water wells in the region. Ancient wells particularly at Asluj (Park Golda) and Khalasa (Haluza) were inspected, and their findings determined that with some work those wells could sustain two mounted divisions.

---

10 Malone Diary, ibid.

The existence of these wells was determined by General R.E.M. Russell, the Chief Engineer, who had discovered their existence from reading the findings of the Palestine Exploration Fund (PEF). The PEF had previously written that in antiquity large communities, particularly Nabateans, had lived at these locations. Interviews with local Bedouin confirmed the view that large water supplies were located south of Beersheba. Chauvel states that the Intelligence Department only disclosed water to be present at Bir es Esani, but that, Chauvel stated was too far west for their plan.[11] Aaronsohn's information was also vitally important.

These findings as well as information gathered from numerous patrols, helped Chetwode to formulate his plan. Towards the end of May 1917 he wrote up his 'Notes on the Palestine Campaign'.

Through various intelligence sources, primarily from the *NILI*, he had determined the approximate strength of the Turkish forces, and their general areas of deployment. He deduced that another frontal assault upon Gaza was not possible, while an assault upon the centre of the Turkish line would not be practical due to its proximity to Turkish reinforcement centres (namely Tel el Sheria and Huj). The Turks, if pressed hard could easily fall back to predetermined lines of defence, keeping in touch with their water and supply lines, and in the process draw the EEF further away from their supply lines.

Only one option remained - so Chetwode surmised – an attack against the extreme Turkish left flank at Beersheba. Such a move was contrary to both logic and history. No force had conquered the land with an assault and victory from that direction, due primarily to the lack of sufficient water to the south of Beersheba.

To succeed, two components were required: secrecy and a shortened supply line. Construction of the railway line from El Arish thereafter quickened, a branch of which deviated north-east towards Shellal.

---

11   Chauvel's Private Papers, PR00535, Folio 2, p. 33. Chauvel gives the impression that the PEF Journal was procured by Russell, and that he read about the water sources at Khalasa and Asluj.

ALLENBY ARRIVES

Chetwode's plan was enhanced with the arrival of fresh troops from Salonika, initially the 7th and 8th Mounted Yeomanry Brigades, and later the 60th London Division. Other units from India, Aden and Egypt later arrived, and from them the composite 75th Infantry Division was formed. Small French and Italian units were also on the way, both insignificant as fighting forces, but important political expressions of the French and Italians.

The new commander, General Edmund Allenby, arrived in Egypt on 28 June 1917. He carried with him a special message from the Prime Minister, who 'wanted Jerusalem as a Christmas present for the British nation.'[12] Upon arrival Allenby moved his HQ from Cairo to Rafa. Another who arrived at that time was Richard Meinertzhagen, who came to inspect the Intelligence Service. Following contact with Aaronsohn, Meinertzhagen became aware of the Zionist cause.[13]

Allenby's presence was quickly felt on the front line, for within days he was at his advanced HQ. He made an early effort to familiarise himself with the various units, often making quick surprise visits to the camps. Other meetings were more formal, as Wilson wrote of one such review:

… we sat on our horses for three hours without moving an eyelash with drawn swords which ultimately weighed about five ton – whilst he rode around. This was after three hours of forming up and getting into shape - a battle is a picnic compared to a show of this sort.[14]

Aaronsohn met Allenby on 17 July in Cairo, and the C-in-C stated to the Zionist from *Eretz Yisrael* that he 'had been informed that I was thoroughly acquainted with the country' and asked many questions.[15]

---

12 Wavell, ibid, p. 96.
13 Meinertzhagen told Leonard Stein that it was Aaronsohn who first 'made him alive' to the concept of a Jewish National Home. Stein, ibid, p. 294, footnote 37.
14 Wilson, ibid, p. 83.
15 Aaronsohn Diary, 17 July 1917, cited in Verrier, ibid, p. 283.

YILDERIM – 'LIGHTNING FORCE'

The Turkish losses in Erzerum and Baghdad caused a re-evaluation of how Germany co-operated with the Turks. Instead of being involved in training the Turkish Army, and being mere adjuncts to it, as was the case from 1913-1917, a new structure was now found necessary – the *Yilderim* (Lighting). Von Sanders wrote:

> Jilderim was erected on an entirely different basis. At the head of Jilderim there was to be a staff organized like that of a German army group, consisting almost exclusively of German officers, with a German general at the head.
>
> The army group was to consist of Turkish armies, to which various German troops and numerous German auxiliary formations were to be attached. For an effective conduct of the war in the Turkish theaters with their enormous difficulties of supply, Jilderim received special German funds … to the amount of 5,000,000 pounds.[16]

General von Falkenhayn, the former Chief of the German General Staff until 1916, was placed in command of the *Yilderim* formations, which were hereafter technically known as 'Army Group F.' Attached to the *Yilderim* were crack German troops, known as *Asien Korps*. This new formation was formally decreed on 2 July 1917,[17] and its initial main objective was the recapture of Baghdad.

Another new formation was the Seventh Turkish Army, composed of various divisions from other Turkish army groups. The initial command was offered to Mustapha Kemal. Kemal refused the offer and it was given to Fewzi Pasha. The Seventh Army was initially sent to Aleppo from where they were to be deployed further south.

Military activity in Mesopotamia was limited during the summer of 1917. During that period numerous Turkish reinforcements arrived in

---

16 Von Sanders, ibid, p. 174.
17 Von Sanders, ibid, p. 174.

Mesopotamia. The *Yilderim* were not amongst these reinforcements, although that was the intention.

Although the main Turkish positions were on the Tigris River, other formations were located on the Euphrates. On 28 September the forces of the Mesopotamian Expeditionary Force (MEF) attacked the Turkish position at Romadi and won a major victory

Due to the furthering of the revolution in Russia there was no longer any Russian military presence in the region. Regardless of this disadvantage the MEF continued to edge forward, and on 6 November 1917 they captured Tekrit, some 150 kilometres north of Baghdad.[18] Their next objective was the oil rich region of Mosul.

The fact that British-Indian forces and not Arab forces had captured Baghdad was a concern for King Hussein, as it was one of the principle Arab cities that he coveted to rule over. Damascus now became even more important for the Arabs.

The movement of British-Indian forces north from Baghdad towards Mosul was also apt to give more angst to the French – as this region was earmarked as Area A to be administered by the French according to the Anglo-French Agreement.

At this time important facts were being established on the ground.

---

18   Von Sanders, ibid, p. 182.

VILAYETS OF BAGHDAD & BASRA

CHAPTER 62

§

Movements in the Arab sector

SYKES MEETS KING HUSSEIN

The presence of Picot in Cairo, and Colonel Bremond in Jeddah, unnerved King Hussein of the Hejaz. The British officials in Cairo then realized it was time to expose the Anglo-French Agreement to King Hussein. The first move was when Sykes and Picot met three Muslim Syrian representatives about 25 April, and presented the outline of the 'Sykes-Picot' Agreement to them.[1]

Prior to Sykes' departure to the Hejaz, the Foreign Office telegrammed Wingate on 28 April with clear instructions of what Sykes was to communicate, which were: '(1) to explain that, whilst the Allies were determined to support Arab race aspirations, the authority of King Hussein could not be imposed upon peoples who did not desire it, and the extension of his dominion must be dependent on its acceptance by the natives concerned; (2) to make it clear that in Baghdad and its district, whilst desirous of promoting Arab culture and prosperity, we should retain that position of military and political predominance which our strategical and commercial interests

---

1 Kedourie, ibid, p. 161.

required; (3) to reassure King Hussein in regard to the French aims in the interior of Syria.'[2]

Sykes met with Feisal on 2 May at Wejh, and then wrote to Wingate: 'explained to him the principle of the Anglo-French [Agreement] in regard to Arab confederation.'[3] This was followed by a meeting with King Hussein on 6 May, the gist of which Sykes wrote and which was recorded in the Eastern Report:

> In the course of the interview the King insisted on two points, both of which are important and worthy of consideration and sympathy: -
> 1. That if France annexed Syria he would be open to the charge of breaking faith with the Moslems of Syria by having led them into a rebellion against the Turk in order to hand them over to a Christian Power.
> 2. That if Arab independence be not assured he feared that posterity would charge him with assisting in the overthrow of the last Islamic power without setting up another in its place.

'Sir Mark Sykes explained fully,' Ormsby-Gore continued in the Report 'in accordance with his instructions, the agreement regarding the Arab confederation or State. The King seemed relieved, as the agreement of the Powers if realised would dispose of his two points. He also impressed on the King the importance of the Franco-Arab settlement, and at last got him to admit that it was essential to Arab development in Syria, but only after a very lengthy argument.'[4]

Sykes also wrote a message to Wingate on 6 May to be relayed to Picot: 'I am satisfied with my interviews with Sherif Feisal and King of the Hijaz, both of whom now stand at the same point as was reached at our last joint meeting in Cairo with the three Syrian delegates …'[5]

---

2   Cab 24/143/18 , Telegram No 472. Eastern Report, 3 May 1917.
3   Cab 24/143/18, Eastern Report 10 May 1917, from telegram from Wingate on 7 May 1917 [no 496] relaying message from Sykes of 6 May.
4   CAB 24/143/18, Eastern Report, 10 May 1917.
5   FO 371/3054, 93335/86256, Wingate telegram No. 496, Cairo 7 May repeating Sykes telegram from Jeddah of 6 May 1917, cited in Kedourie, ibid, p. 164.

Hussein also indicated that he would like to meet with Picot, together with Sykes, so arrangements were then set in motion for Picot to come to the Hejaz. In the meantime Sykes left Jeddah and en-route to Cairo he stopped in Wejh and there met with Lawrence on 7 May. In this brief meeting Sykes informed Lawrence of the 'Sykes-Picot' Agreement, and, seemingly, Lawrence was not happy to hear of it.[6] Lawrence, probably, wished he had never heard of it, as it went against his own desires – as it went against the desires of most in the Arab Bureau. But hear of it he did.

His attitude towards this news is perhaps best expressed by James Barr in his book *A Line in the Sand:* 'Lawrence, who had repeatedly stressed that his government wanted to see the Arabs claim Damascus for themselves, now realised that Sykes's deal with Georges-Picot meant that he had inadvertently been lying. If the Sykes-Picot agreement survived the war, reaching Damascus would have no consequence at all …'[7]

MOVEMENT TOWARDS AQABA

Several days after these meetings, on 9 May 1917, Lawrence and others including Sheikh Auda, left Wejh.[8] Arriving at Wadi Sirhan the Arab chieftains set about securing co-operation with other tribes of the region. It was uncertain if these tribes would accept the authority of the Sherifians of Mecca – another indication that not all Arabs would follow King Hussein of the Hejaz.[9]

Lawrence then reportedly set out on an 800 kilometre journey to Baalbek, beyond Damascus.[10] Lawrence's goal was to determine which tribes in that vast eastern region would join the uprising.[11] Many said they would

---

6   Barr, J. *A Line in the Sand*, (London, 2011), p.37.

7   Barr, ibid, p. 45.

8   Lawrence, Revolt in the Desert, ibid, p. 69.

9   Lawrence, ibid, p. 79.

10   There is some discrepancy if this trip was actually undertaken at all, or if perhaps only part of it was undertaken. See Knightley and Simpson, ibid, pp. 80-2.

11   Lawrence was helped in his journeys and overall work with the Arab tribes by quite an amazing woman named Gertrude Bell. Miss Bell had lived and worked among the Arab people for many years and had written extensively about them, and her information was invaluable to Lawrence. See Wallach, J. *The Extraordinary Life of Gertrude Bell, Advisor to Kings, Ally of Lawrence of Arabia*, (London, 1997).

join <u>once</u> operations began in the Transjordan region.[12] One of those tribes was the Beni Sakr tribe, of whom we will hear more about later.[13]

Once again the faulty foundation upon which the entire Arab revolt had been founded was evidenced, for by now it was all too apparent that al-Faruqi and Sherif Hussein's initial statements of a general uprising were unfounded. Such a revolt, if it was really going to happen, would depend much upon British involvement – and British gold, lots of British gold.[14]

SYKES AND PICOT MEET KING HUSSEIN

The ship transporting Sykes and Picot called into Wejh on 17 May, allowing Picot to meet Feisal. Together they then continued on to Jeddah.[15] On 18 May Sykes and Picot met with King Hussein and Feisal as well as Fu'ad al Khattib, the Hejazi Foreign Minister.[16]

Hussein emphasised the necessity for the close co-operation of the French and British in the realisation of Arab aspirations, and the incapacity of the Arabs to achieve anything without their united help.

Picot then read a message from the French President in which reference was made to the Syrian littoral, on which the conversation then turned. Hussein repeated that 'he could not be a party to proceeding which would have as their purpose the handing over of a Moslem population to the direct rule of a non-Moslem state.'[17]

Sykes then withdrew for half an hour, and on his return the conversation changed to the question of having British and French advisors in the Arab administered areas. Hussein admitted the necessity of European advisors to be heads of departments, and Sykes 'urged the essential importance of such advisers having executive authority, an idea which the King naturally disliked; Fuadd said that it would mean the end of Arab independence. ...'[18]

---

12 Falls, ibid, p. 239.

13 In the second volume, in connection to the failed second battle in Transjordan in May 1918.

14 See Knightley and Simpson, ibid, pp. 82-3.

15 Sykes to Wingate, 23 May 1917, Sykes Papers, MEC, St, Anthony's College.

16 Sykes wrote a report to Wingate from Aden on 24 May, which was furthered to Ormsby Gore who wrote a report in the Eastern Report on 31 May 1917.

17 Sykes to Wingate, 23 May 1917, Sykes Papers, MEC, St. Anthony's College.

18 Cab 24/143/18, EASTERN Report No 18. Author W Ormsby-Gore. 31 May 1917.

According to Sykes the meeting then ended most inconclusively, and that Picot was unfavourably impressed by the King. The following day they met again, aboard the British flagship, at which Colonel Wilson was also in attendance. Ormsby-Gore summarised Sykes telegram of this meeting:

The King read an answer to the message from the French President, in the course of which he stated that, as he had confidence in Great Britain, he should be content if the French Government pursued the same policy towards Arab aspirations on the Syrian littoral as the British did in Baghdad. M. Picot received the King's message very well, and relations became cordial.[19]

Afterwards Feisal gave Sykes a message from the King to the effect that they were ready to co-operate to the fullest extent with France in Syria and with England in Mesopotamia, but they asked for help from England with Idrisi and Ibn Saud, begging that an endeavour might be made to induce them to recognize King Hussein's position as leader of the Arab movement, without in any way infringing on their independence.[20]

What is very interesting in this communication is mention of the problems of getting Ibn Saud and Idrisi to accept Hussein's leadership – just as numerous British officials in London had previously warned!

Another very telling statement by Hussein are his words; 'that he could not be a party to any proceedings purposing to hand over Moslems to the direct rule of a non-Moslem State.' Being a custodian of Islam, and from the very region where non-Muslims were forbidden to live, these sentiments would be expected. Herein lies another reason why most if not all of the *dhimmi* peoples of Syria, Mesopotamia and Palestine would not want to be under any form of control emanating from the Hejaz.

19   Cab 24/143/18, EASTERN Report No 18. Author W Ormsby-Gore. 31 May 1917. Also FO 371/3054, 104269/86256, Sykes telegram to Wingate, Aden 24 May 1917, Sykes Papers, MEC.
20   Cab 24/143/18, EASTERN Report No 18. Author W Ormsby-Gore. 31 May 1917. Also FO 371/3054, 104269/86256, Sykes telegram to Wingate, Aden 24 May 1917, and Sykes to Sir. P Cox, Baghdad, 21 May 1917, in Sykes Papers, MEC, St. Anthony's College. Sykes wrote to Cox: 'Visited Jeddah with purpose of introducing French Commissioner to King of Hejaz and giving him an outline of Anglo-French policy in regard to Arab area. Interview fairly satisfactory.'

The most important outcome of this meeting, though, was that King Hussein and Feisal were now made aware of the terms of the Anglo-French Agreement. Picot wrote: 'In sum, the King now knows our agreements which has not upset him as much as had been feared.'[21] Fu'ad al-Khatib was also present in these meetings, and he too testified that the 'Sykes-Picot' Agreement had been told to Hussein.[22]

However, as Kedourie in particular points out, (see Kedourie, ibid, pp. 164-184) the Anglo-French Agreement may have been disclosed, but it was still subject to different interpretations by the British, French and Arabs, as represented by Sykes, Picot and King Hussein. It was, as Kedourie states, a 'game of mutual bluff.'[23]

This matter of the King 'bluffing' Picot in particular is borne out in a letter from Clayton to Sykes on 31 July. Clayton had just chatted with Fu'ad al-Khatib, the outcome of which Clayton wrote:

… from conversations with him it appears almost certain that the King has not at all understood the situation, as explained to him by you and M. Picot, regarding the future of Syria and Iraq. He seems under the fixed impression that both will fall to him unconditionally, and has given this out publicly. Of course he may be bluffing, but when it comes to the point he will inevitably maintain that his version of the interview is the correct one, and we have never given him anything in writing to the contrary. It is a matter for consideration whether we should not put this right by giving the King an *aide-memoire* of what you actually told him…'[24]

Mutual bluff it may have been, but at least the King, and Feisal, were now aware of the existence of the Anglo-French Agreement. Yet theorizing about the defeat and dismemberment of the Turkish Empire was of no avail to any of the three parties at that time. Except for the British successes in

---

21 *A.E. Guerre 1914-1918*, Vol. 877, Picot's telegrams nos 13-18, via Aden 24 May 1917, cited in Kedourie, ibid, p. 165.
22 Kedourie, ibid, p. 166.
23 Kedourie, ibid, p. 182.
24 Clayton to Sykes, 31 July 1917, CAB 24/143/18, Eastern Report XXVII, 2 August 1917.

Mesopotamia, the Turks still controlled the region, holding up the British behind a defensive line from Gaza to Beersheba, while the Arabs were still bottled up inside the Hejaz. It was now time for establishing facts on the ground.

CAPTURE OF AQABA

The first fact on the ground for Feisal's force was Aqaba, which he considered 'indispensable in order to encourage the Beni Sakhr and Huweitat, and to ensure their hearty co-operation.'[25]

On about 19 June, after Lawrence's return, the Arab force numbering some 500 men set out for their next objective – to capture the small Red Sea port of Aqaba. Their first objective was the Turkish garrison at Aba el Lissan, which protected the route from Ma'an to Aqaba.

This position was attacked by a camel charge on 2 July – and captured. While some 300 Turkish soldiers were killed, the Arabs lost just two men killed.[26] Devoid of its main outer defence, Aqaba surrendered on 6 July 1917 – and the Arabs marched in with some 600 Turkish (and one German) prisoners.[27]

Following this success Lawrence rode across the Sinai and arrived in Cairo, reporting, he later wrote, first to Clayton, and then to General Allenby[28] (although he was still theoretically under Wingate's command). Thereafter his exploits began to be taken more seriously by the British High Command. Allenby interviewed Lawrence, who spoke at length about the campaign in the east, to which Allenby replied, so Lawrence stated: "Well, I will do for you what I can."[29]

Supplies and 16,000 pounds in gold sovereigns (for buying the support and loyalty of the Arab tribes) were quickly despatched to Aqaba.[30]

---

25 Clayton to Wingate, 30 May 1917, Sykes Papers, MEC, St. Anthony's College. In this same message Clayton also stated that if the Arabs captured Aqaba they might want to claim it 'hereafter', which could be a problem, for after the war 'it might be of considerable importance to the future defence scheme of Egypt.'

26 Falls, ibid, p. 240.

27 Falls, ibid, p. 240.

28 Lawrence, T. E. *Revolt in the Desert*, pp. 120-21.

29 Lawrence, ibid, p. 122.

30 Lawrence, ibid, p. 121.

In August 1917 the operations of Feisal and Lawrence were detached from Wingate's authority, and brought under that of General Allenby. This move, wrote Wingate, 'moved Feisal [and Lawrence] from the restricted and defined field of military operations for the freedom of the Hejaz, to the far wider and more complicated territory of world war and world politics.'[31]

Allenby immediately recognized the potential in developing the operations in the eastern sphere. But changes were imperative if Feisal's Arab Northern Army (ANA) was to play any meaningful role in the impending campaign. More British supplies were required, as well as the support and allegiance of the Arabs and Bedouin tribes in Syria and Transjordan.

Large quantities of supplies, including armoured cars, were then dispatched to Aqaba, where Lieut-Colonel P. C. Joyce became the base commander. Now the Arab Northern Army would be composed of three major components: a regular Arab force under the command of Jaffer Pasha el Askeri; the British force under the command of Joyce; and a small French force under the command of Captain Pisani.

Although the Arab Northern Army (ANA) would play only a secondary role in the upcoming campaign, at least it was now active, and the conquest of the Turkish Empire would not have to be carried out entirely by the soldiers of Britain, Australia, New Zealand and India.

These soldiers of the British Empire, incidentally, were soon to have one of their biggest challenges yet – a daring attack upon the desert town of Beersheba.

---

31   Wingate, R. *Wingate of the Sudan*, (London, 1955), cited in Knightley and Simpson, ibid, p. 82.

CHAPTER 63

§

Towards Beersheba

CHETWODE'S PLAN ADOPTED

Allenby basically accepted Chetwode's plan to strike at the extreme left of the Turkish line at Beersheba. One of the main components in adopting this plan was the availability there of water.[1]

To achieve a thorough and complete victory he required more infantry and artillery – and received most of what he requested. With the arrival of these new forces he abolished Desert Column, and formed three distinct Corps:

- The Desert Mounted Corps (DMC), under the command of Chauvel, and composed of the Anzac Mounted Division (AZMC); the newly formed Australian Mounted Division (AMD); the Yeomanry Mounted Division; and associated RHA artillery.
- The 20th Army Corps, under the command of Chetwode, and composed of the 53rd (Welsh) Division; 60th (London) Division; 74th (Yeomanry) Division. The 10th (Irish) Division arrived later.
- The 21st Army Corps, under the command of Lieutenant-General Bulfin, and composed of the 52nd (Lowland) Division; 54th (East Anglia) Division; and 75th (British-Indian) Division.

---

1 Verrier, ibid, p. 102. 'Aaronsohn and *NILI* not only confirmed that there was water in and near Beersheba: they provided detailed information on the capacities and conditions of the wells.'

- Other units coming under direct HQ command included the Imperial Camel Corps (ICC); 7th Mounted Brigade; Imperial Service Cavalry Brigade and 20th Indian Infantry Brigade.[2]

Chauvel now became commander of one of the largest mounted forces in the annuls of the British Empire. It had been a position aspired to by Chetwode, who wrote to Chauvel on 12 August 1917:

> I shall always be proud of having had such a fine body of men under my command, as your Anzac mounted troops, & grateful to you for the able way in which you have led them.
>
> I cannot say how much I envy for the command of the largest body of mounted men under one hand – It is my trade – but fate has willed otherwise.
>
> I wish you and my old Command every success and further laurels on their standards.[3]

Impressive preparations were taking place behind the Wadi Ghuzze as both supplies and fresh troops were brought forward and placed at strategic locations. All efforts had to be made to deceive the Turco-German High Command into anticipating a diversionary attack upon Beersheba and a main British-led thrust against Gaza. Allenby's strategy was the exact opposite.

THE *NILI* UNCOVERED

Much of the planning for operations behind the Turkish front line was based upon accurate information supplied by *NILI*.[4] However as the military situation became more desperate Djemal Pasha took more drastic moves against

---

2 Wavell, ibid, pp. 101-2.

3 Chetwode to Chauvel, 12 August 1917, in Chauvel's Private Papers, Series 2, PR00535, AWM.

4 As evidenced in words spoken by Allenby following Aaronsohn's death several years later: 'The death of Aaron Aaronsohn deprived me of a valued friend and of a staff officer impossible to replace. He was mainly responsible for the formation of my Field Intelligence organisation behind enemy lines ... His death was a loss to the British Empire and to Zionism, but the work he has done can never die.' Original, in Allenby's own handwriting, in Aaronsohn Archives, Zichron Yaacov, and cited in Stein, ibid, p. 294.

any potential 'fifth columnists', and again the minority groups and Arab nationalists bore the brunt of his cruel measures.   Any known or suspected Arab nationalists also received cruel treatment by the Turkish authorities, and some were hanged outside Jaffa Gate in Jerusalem. In such an environment the operations of *NILI* became progressively more dangerous.

Through a series of unfortunate incidents the entire *NILI* ring was uncovered in September 1917. While Aaron was in Egypt, many of the twenty-three operative agents and some of the twelve passive members, were arraigned and severely tortured, and some were executed. Sarah was tortured and interrogated for five days, and then shot herself, but lingered in severe agony for several days before dying.   Her sixty-eight year old father also died under duress.

In such an environment Djemal Pasha could have enacted revenge upon the wider Jewish community. Some timely intervention by Talaat Pasha and the Germans, though, mollified him.

In view of such events, it was essential that any public announcement of sympathy towards Zionism by the British Government had to be coupled with a military breakthrough – otherwise the entire Jewish community in Palestine would be endangered.

A speedy British-led breakthrough was now awaited with great anticipation by many of the local inhabitants of Palestine. Could Allenby deliver what the people so desperately wanted?

DECEIVING THE ENEMY

There were numerous methods utilised by the Intelligence Department to trick the Turks concerning where the main attack would occur. Chauvel wrote:

Various simple devises were adopted to further delude the Turk. For instance, on one occasion a haversack was allowed to be dropped by a Light Horseman during a reconnaissance. It contained amongst the usual paraphernalia, what purported to be an unfinished letter to his girl in Australia, describing what a bad time they were having, doing these long reconnaissance's on the hot summer days, without any other object than to deceive the enemy into thinking we were going to attack Beersheba, where as the real attack was to be at Gaza, where the Light Horse would not have a show![5]

The haversack, which also contained information about the inability of a large British-led assault against Beersheba due to the water and transport problem, was picked up by a pursuing Turkish patrol, and as Chauvel wrote: 'It was afterwards discovered from enemy documents, that the letter was found by them, & served its purpose in helping to deceive the Turkish High Command.'[6]

Although Ismet Bey, the Turkish commander at Beersheba, was sceptical about this information, Von Kressenstein was convinced of its genuineness. He removed a division of reinforcements from Beersheba, which had only just recently arrived there. Von Kressenstein was adamant that a large force could not approach Beersheba from the waterless south and east. Ismet Bey, still not convinced, nevertheless strengthened his defences to the west, south and east of Beersheba.

TROOPS BEING PREPARED

While all these preparations were in progress, the troops were rested as much as possible. The mounted forces had a three way rotation: one month patrolling the desert, one month resting near the beach (not really a rest when horses had to be constantly cared for) and one month of intensive training.

The rest period nevertheless did offer a break from the desert and from the skirmishes. Occasionally leave was granted to Kantara, or even Port Said. Trooper Malone wrote of one of his experiences while on furlough:

5 Chauvel's Private Papers, PR00535.003, Series 3.2, p. 34.

6 Chauvel's Private Papers, PR00535.003, Series 3.2, p. 34. See also Falls & Becke, Part 1, p. 31, which states the date as 10 October. They also state: 'The officer who planned and carried out this ruse has requested that his name should not be made public.' Although Richard Meinertzhagen in his book '*Middle East Diary*' claims to have orchestrated this operation, there are others who claim that he fabricated his involvement. See Brian Garfield, *The Meinertzhagen Mystery*, (Washington, 2007), pp. 14-36. According to Garfield, the idea was conceived by Lieut-Col. James Belgrave, principal intelligence officer with the EEF, and the bag was dropped by Major Arthur Neate, an intelligence officer with the Desert Mounted Corps.

Sept 16.   Arrived Kantara & then entrained to Port Said. There are immense stacks of war materials of every description stacked here, guns, rations, tractors, light engines and mortars ...

Sept 17.   Sailed on harbour. Ran down a boat load of Australians & got chased down the harbour – but succeeded in escaping.[7]

Malone's entries reflect the emphasis now being given to this campaign, as revealed by the immense quantities of supplies, and the sporting relationship between the ANZAC forces. But for him and all the other soldiers, after a few days leave it was back to the front – and to the ordeals of life in the desert during the hot summer.

Heat, dust and constant patrolling was the routine. 'For nearly three weeks now we have been on a flying stunt' William Johns wrote to his niece in Auckland, '... have not seen a blanket & only got my boots off once or twice. Though the days are so hot, the nights', he concluded, 'are as cold as charity.'[8]

On 19 October 1917 Wilson wrote:

... We haven't done any fighting but frequently have big reconnaissances out Beersheba way, one of which was what the Turks called a victory and you mentioned in your last letter. They always claim to have driven us back but we simply go back just to go to bed...

When on a small patrol one morning I was fortunate enough to capture a Turkish cavalry officer. What attracted my attention to him were his stirrups and irons, as they are called. His spurs and the horse's bit were all made of shining brass and I had never seen this, before or since, so I decided to take possession of them. The other thing that took my fancy was a beautiful pair of Zeiss field glasses hanging around his neck, and I relieved him of that burden as well.'[9]

---

7   Diary of Trooper Malone, ibid.
8   Johns, William Henwood 1891-1917. Letters to iris, 1915-1917. Auckland War Memorial Museum Library, MS 1392.
9   Wilson, ibid, p. 91.

'Finished up a 24 hours stunt yesterday', wrote Reg Walters, '… Had a long ride out to within 6 miles of Beersheba. Met slight opposition. We left here at 6 A.M. In position at 2 P.M. Stayed there until 10 P.M. & arrived back here just after 4 A.M. Consequently we are all pretty dopy this morning.'[10]

THE PLAN

The EEF plan called for a heavy diversionary naval and artillery bombardment of Gaza during the last days of October 1917, and the actual attack was designated to begin on 31 October. The basic plan was for:

- The infantry attack upon Gaza, the 'feint' would be carried out by Bulfin's 21st Infantry Corps.
- The attack upon Beersheba would be carried out by the 20th Infantry Corps who would assault the Turkish trench system to the south-west and west of Beersheba.
- The Anzac and Australian Mounted Divisions would approach Beersheba from the east, having swung well to the south in the previous days.
- The 7th Yeomanry Brigade would connect the region between the 20th Corps and the Australian and New Zealand mounted forces.
- The Yeomanry Mounted Division would cover the region between Gaza and Beersheba (in conjunction with the 10th Irish Division).
- A column of cameliers under the command of Lieut-Colonel Newcombe, coming up from Aqaba, was to make a feint north towards Hebron.
- Simultaneous to all of the activities, the Arab Northern Army (ANA) of Feisal and Lawrence was to attack Turkish positions further to the east in the Transjordan region (particularly the destruction of a railway bridge in the Yarmuk Valley), and these were to climax by 5 November.

---

10 Walters.

The Turco-German forces too had been preparing for battle. Although the *Yilderim* force had been instructed to move south from Aleppo, they had still not arrived. General Von Falkenhayn was only able to set up his HQ in Jerusalem on 5 November. At that point the HQ of the Turkish 7th Army was at Jemmameh, north of Gaza, and of the Turkish 8th Army at Hebron.

Aerial superiority of the Royal Flying Corps (RFC) and the Australian Flying Corps (AFC) hindered German planes from doing any reconnaissance flights behind the EEF lines. The success of the operation depended entirely upon secrecy, concealment and quick movement.

The troops began moving out to their positions in late October. The Desert Mounted Corps was to move south-east along the Wadi Ghuzze towards Asluj and then turn north and then north-east before veering westwards towards Beersheba early in the morning of 31 October.

MOVING FORWARD

The Desert Mounted Corps under General Harry Chauvel and the 20th Infantry Corps under General Sir Philip Chetwode, began slowly moving from camps near the Mediterranean Sea, inland on 20 October 1917. This move was made as much as possible during the nights, and made in secrecy.

Simultaneously the engineers began moving towards the isolated water wells in the area further east, while camels also transported huge amounts of water to some future watering places, such as Esani. The railway was also developed rapidly at this stage, having already crossed the Wadi Ghuzze, at Shellal, and was heading towards Karm in the direction of Beersheba.

Trooper Walters wrote again on 21 October: 'The past week has been a busy one doing outposts & patrols. The big push seems very near now.'[11] Indeed the big push was very near.

On 24 October the 2nd Light Horse Brigade under General Ryrie, moved from its base position at Esani (near Ze'elim) to the south-east along Wadi Asluj to Asluj. They rode during the night in order to pass as much as possible undetected.

---

11 Walters.

This move in many ways was a risk, for despite the need for utmost secrecy, the success of this manoeuver depended heavily upon the large water wells at both Asluj and Khalasa being fully repaired and operative. Contrary to common belief, the men and horses did not go without water for three days prior to the battle at Beersheba.

The first major move in the forthcoming Third Battle of Gaza was made on 25 October. Men of the 8th Light Horse Regiment captured some low ridges near Wadi Hanafish (Nahal Ofakim) which was on the Beersheba side of Wadi Ghuzze.

This position was intended to protect the railway line as it crossed the Wadi Ghuzze at Shellal and continued to Karm (in the region between Shellal and Beersheba) and which was to be the absolute forward position for the 20th Infantry Corps advance on Beersheba.

This area had previously been in no-man's land, and this move was the first attempt to permanently possess it by either side. Shortly after taking this key position the Australians withdrew and the Middlesex Yeomanry of the 8th Mounted Brigade took over.

The Light Horse arrived at Asluj early in the morning of 25 October and began working immediately on clearing the wells. They had lots of physical work to do and not much time to complete the task. At this point the horses of two regiments were sent back to Khalasa for watering.

On this day the War Cabinet met in London, but because of pressing matters they never discussed the Zionist proposal. Chaim Weizmann waited outside 10 Downing Street to hear of the outcome. For this meeting however there was no outcome – it would be discussed at the next meeting scheduled for 31 October.

Early in the morning of 27 October a large Turkish force composed of two cavalry regiments and some 2,500 infantry attacked the isolated British positions, mostly of the 8th Yeomanry Mounted Brigade. Several positions were quickly overrun and several held out for the remainder of the day. The determined British defence enabled the 53rd Welsh Division and the 3rd Light Horse Brigade time to come and relieve the position, and at their arrival the Turks withdrew.

Seventy-nine British soldiers were killed in this battle, including Major Alex Lafone of the London Yeomanry, who was awarded the Victoria Cross posthumously, and a Jewish officer named Captain Van Den Bergh of the Middlesex Hussars.

During the night of 28 October both mounted divisions, the Anzac and Australian, set out from their camps, mostly in and around Tel el Fara and headed in the direction of Esani, Khalasa and Asluj. This column was some ten kilometers long.

The horses were fully-fed and watered, and the men carried supplies for three days. Trooper Jim Henderson of the 4th Light Horse Brigade recalled how they packed a blanket, greatcoat and emergency rations.[12]

Meanwhile at Asluj men of the 2nd Light Horse met Colonel Newcombe and a detachment of irregular Arabs, known as 'Newcombe's Column'. This unit was to operate further to the east of the ANZAC's and detour towards Hebron when the attack on Beersheba actually took place. The remaining men of the Anzac Mounted Division moved this morning to Khalasa.

The wells at Asluj were sufficiently repaired on 29 October and water began to be pumped into huge canvas reservoirs and troughs. The same was happening at Khalasa, but there the wells were not in need of the same amount of repair. During the night time the Anzac Mounted Division headed for Asluj arriving early in the morning.

General Chauvel arrived at Asluj on 30 October and set up the Desert Mounted Corps Headquarters. During the day time the horsemen rested up and hid in the surrounding *wadis* (dry river beds). That evening the Anzac Mounted Division was to ride some forty kilometres, while the Australian Mounted Division was to ride some fifty-six kilometres, in order to be ready for their operations on 31 October.

'We only moved at night' recalled Henderson 'and hid as best we could in cracks and crannies in the wadis or in the shadow of our brownish horses in the daytime, while we tried to sleep … After torturing nights … we still

---

12   Diary of Jim Henderson, *Mountain Views,* (Healesville local newspaper), 19 April 1993, p. 2.

had no idea where we were or where we were going, or whether this was just another toughening up routine.'[13]

The 53rd, 74th and 60thDivisions of the 20th Infantry Corps were beginning their long march over rocky terrain to the western approaches of Beersheba. The Irish 10th Division remained in reserve, filling the gap to the west of the 53rd Division.

The 7th Yeomanry Brigade was preparing for a move to fill the flank between the infantry on the southern side of Beersheba and the Anzac and Australian mounted forces further east.

With the 7th Light Horse Regiment in the vanguard the Anzac Mounted Division set out from Asluj at 1800 hours on 30 October, while the Australian Mounted Division set out from its watering hole at Khalasa. All the troops of the EEF were heading in the direction of Beersheba.

Beersheba and Balfour [B]-Day was fast approaching.

---

13   Diary of Jim Henderson, ibid.

§

CHAPTER 64

Beersheba and Balfour Day

BEERSHEBA AND ENVIRONS – THE MORNING OF 31 OCTOBER 1917

The Anzac Mounted Division (AZMD) reached Bir Arara about 0200 hours, and then headed towards their destination north at Bir Salim Abu Irgeig (adjacent to the present Beersheba-Dimona road).

Their main task in the upcoming battle was to capture the positions of Bir es Sakaty and cut off the road to Hebron; and capture Tel el Saba, which commanded the plain leading into Beersheba from the east.

The Australian Mounted Division was held in reserve, and they headed for Khasm Zanna, due east of Beersheba about five miles (eight kilometres) - adjacent to the present day Beersheba-Dimona Road. Chauvel was to set-up his headquarters near Khasm Zanna, hereafter known as Chauvel's Hill.

As these horsemen were riding through the low lying hills towards their positions, the British infantry were walking over many kilometres of rough terrain towards their destinations. This combined EEF force numbered some 58,000 men and 242 artillery guns, while III Turkish Corps facing them numbered about 4,400 men and 28 artillery guns.[1]

Then once all the infantry and artillery were in place, the British artillery opened fire on the Turkish trenches to the south-west and west of

---

1 Jones, I. 'Beersheba: The light horse charge and the making of myths,' in *Journal of the Australian War Memorial*, No. 3, October 1983, pp. 29.

Beersheba at about 0555 hours. The artillery 'commenced to bombard the enemy's positions on a front of some 4,500 yards. Some 100 field guns and howitzers took part in the bombardment, while twenty heavy guns were engaged mainly in counter-battery work.'[2]

Being the end of summer the area, 'was dry as powder and bare of vegetation; there was no breath of wind; so that after an hour's bombardment the Turkish defences were screened in a dense cloud of dust.'[3]

This intense artillery bombardment stopped for forty five minutes at about 0700 hours, 'to permit the murk to clear a little and the observers to locate their targets. Visibility did not much improve during the pause, but', wrote Falls, 'from what could be seen of the wire it was by no means all cut.'[4]

Then at 0800 hours the British infantry led by the 181st Brigade of the 60th London Division attacked the forward Turkish positions and aimed for the strongly defended Hill 1070 to the south of Beersheba. Also at about 0800 hours 'the Anzac Mounted Division reached Bir el Hammam and Bir Salim abu Irgeig, their first objective, with only slight opposition.'[5]

There was a timetable for the fighting this day and it was very important that it was strictly adhered to. Beersheba had to be captured in one day, in order to maximise the element of surprise, and also due to the need for water. The bulk of the hard fighting was to be by the British infantry against the heavily fortified Turkish trenches, and it was imperative that these were captured early so the mounted men could complete the capture of Beersheba from the east - and to obtain the precious water wells intact.

RENEWAL OF INFANTRY ASSAULT

Although visibility was not completely cleared, Brigadier-General Da Costa nevertheless received permission from Major-General Shea (GOC 60th Division) at 0820 hours to continue the assault. It was preceded by a ten

---

2   *A Brief Record of the Advance of the Egyptian Expeditionary Force, July 1917 to October 1918,* London, 1919, p. 122.

3   Falls, C. *Military Operations – Egypt and Palestine, From June 1917 to the End of the War,* (London, 1930), Part. 1, p. 48.

4   Falls, C. ibid, p. 48.

5   A Brief Report, ibid, p.122.

minute artillery barrage. Then at 0830 hours the 181st Brigade of the 60th London Division 'advanced' wrote Falls, 'to the assault of Point 1070,[6] an advanced enemy work which was captured within ten minutes. The guns now moved forward in order to cut the wire of the enemy's main line of defence.'[7] The loss of this position greatly demoralised the Turks.[8]

While the artillery was firing, two London battalions inched forward, and 'the wire-cutting parties cut the necessary gaps while the barrage was still upon the Turkish trenches'[9] just thirty or so metres ahead.

Shortly afterwards the Londoners captured the forward Turkish trenches after sustaining about 100 casualties of their own, at about 0845 hours.[10] New Zealander, Trooper Malone, observed the British assault and wrote: 'Oct 31. Stand to. Shells bursting on ridge SW of Beersheba. Guns on all sides belching forth shells of all sizes & descriptions until whole sky was hidden under pall of smoke ... Infantry advanced on trenches in front.'[11]

Now the artillery could be brought forward over the rough terrain to these newly captured strategic positions. The artillery began firing at the stronger Turkish defences with the idea of cutting the wire. The huge clouds of dust produced by the shells bursting, however, made it impossible to determine the success of this barrage.

THE MOVE TOWARDS BIR ES SAKATY

While the British infantry were attacking the trenches, phase two of the battle began at 0930 hours. Ryrie and the 2nd Light Horse Brigade set off at the trot across the plain towards Bir es Sakaty, with the 7th Light Horse Regiment in the vanguard. Glad of the open space, the horses were soon going at the gallop. At this sight the Turkish artillery in hills to the north of Beersheba opened fire, but the Light Horse did not sustain one casualty. Unfortunately, though, they galloped straight through a Bedouin camp, and some of the Bedouins were hit by shrapnel.

---

6   Falls states it as Point 1069.
7   A Brief Record, ibid, p. 122.
8   Falls, ibid, p. 50.
9   Falls, ibid, p. 48.
10 Falls, ibid, p. 48.
11 Diary of Trooper Malone, ibid.

The Light Horse quickly reached the Beersheba-Hebron road, captured a convoy of ten wagons, and then after some fighting approached Bir es Sakaty. However the enemy artillery now zoned in on them, and they were pinned down, finding shelter in some nearby *wadis*. They were bitterly disappointed that after having gained so much ground at speed, and being so close to the enemy artillery, they were impinged from going any further. Any attempt would have been suicidal for man and horse. Nevertheless their presence there meant that no reinforcements would be able to get through along the Hebron Road.

THE ATTACK BEGINS OF TEL EL SABA

At 1000 hours Chaytor released the New Zealand Mounted Rifles Brigade and the 1st Light Horse Brigade towards Tel el Saba. These men had the advantage of artillery support, with the Somerset Battery coming forward and firing from about 3,000 yards (or about three kilometers.)

Tel el Saba is wedged between Wadi Khalil (Hebron) on one side and Wadi Saba on the other and the Turks held a great advantage by being on the high ground. The New Zealanders attacked across a large front from the east; while the Australians attacked from the south with the goal of crossing Wadi Saba and scaling the heights. The fighting for this strategic position ensued for the following five hours.

Meanwhile, despite being slowed down by Turkish machine-gun fire, at 1040 hours the 231st Brigade, 74th Division, closed to within about 500 metres of the Turkish front line.[12] The Londoners and the 74th Division advanced along their front, all the time sustaining further casualties.

The intense fighting of the British infantry was observed by the Australian Mounted Division which at 1100 hours 'reached Iswaiwin.'[13] Trooper Reg Walters recorded: 'We came right around Beersheba ... Meanwhile Jacko had his hands full watching the infantry who were making the frontal attack.'[14]

---

12   Falls, ibid, p. 49.
13   A Brief Report, ibid, p. 122.
14   Walters.

BEERSHEBA – THE AFTERNOON OF 31 OCTOBER 1917

While Walters and his mates observed, Chetwode, with Hill 1070 captured and satisfied that the wire had been cut at the next line of trenches, then gave the order at about 1215 hours for the attack against those Turkish trenches to begin. The 179th and 181st Brigades of the 60th Division and 230th and 231st Brigades of the 74th Division went forward.[15]

The 74th Division however came under very heavy fire, of which Falls writes: 'The two Welch Fusilier battalions of the 231st Brigade met with stout resistance. In one post which fought to the last, Corporal John Collins … bayonetted fifteen Turks. These two battalions suffered nearly two-thirds of the casualties of the whole corps and took three-quarters of the prisoners.'[16]

'All the 60th Division's objectives', wrote Falls, 'were in its hands before 1 p.m.'[17] This meant all the positions between the Khalasa-Beersheba Road and Wadi Saba. The 74th Division soon afterwards captured their positions north of the Wadi Saba, and so by 1330 hours 'all objectives had been gained and soon after an outpost line was established.'[18]

The Australian historian Gullett wrote: 'The work of the infantry had been brilliantly and completely successful, and the day was still young. All now depended on Chauvel.'[19] Indeed the British infantry had done their job, and had done it magnificently. The final capture of Beersheba now depended upon Chauvel. His task, however, very much depended upon a swift capture of both Bir es Sakaty and Tel el Saba.

LONDON – NOON ON 31 OCTOBER 1917

At about noon in London (1400 hours at Beersheba), at about the time when the British infantry had completed their allotted task, the members of the British War Cabinet were congregating at 10 Downing Street in London. The last issue on the agenda for this day's crucial meeting was entitled: *The Zionist Movement*. These men were about to discuss and decide upon a mat-

---

15 *A Brief Report*, ibid, p. 122.

16 Falls, ibid, p. 50. In the footnotes from Falls, he mentions that Collins also 'repeatedly carried wounded men back to cover' as well as other activities, and was awarded the Victoria Cross.

17 Falls, ibid, p. 50.

18 *A Brief Report*, ibid, p. 122. British casualties for the day's fighting were 136 men killed, 1,010 wounded and 5 missing. Falls, ibid, *From June 1917 to the end of the War*, Part 1, p. 52.

19 Gullett, ibid, p. 387.

ter that could change the destiny of Britain, the Jewish people, the Middle East and the world.

Apart from Lloyd George and Balfour the other members were: Bonar Law (who had been born in Canada); Alfred Milner (born in Germany); George Barnes (born in Scotland); Arthur Henderson (born in Scotland); Lord George Curzon (born in England); Edward Carson (born in Dublin); Jan Christian Smuts (born in the Cape Colony in South Africa). Edwin Montagu, the only Jewish person in the Cabinet, was in India, but his views on the subject were known.

This assorted group represented a cross stream of Britain and the Empire. If we count Bonar Law as a Canadian (he did live there for the early years of his life), then with the presence of Smuts representing South Africa, the major components of the Empire were present except Australia and New Zealand. Their contribution for the 31 October, however, was not to be in the Cabinet room in London, but on the field of war in Beersheba.

CHALLENGES FOR CHAUVEL'S MEN

The final Turkish positions around Bir es Sakaty were captured by the 2nd Australian Light Horse Brigade at about 1300 hours.[20] They then moved to take control of the Hebron Road, which they achieved by 1350 hours.[21]

The Turks, meanwhile, were holding firmly to the high ground of Tel el Saba, and kept the Anzac soldiers pinned down by their concentrated machine-gun fire. Although the Inverness and Somerset batteries were present, the Turks were so well entrenched in places that the artillery fire was mostly ineffective. Desperate for a breakthrough Chauvel then released the 3rd Light Horse Brigade towards Tel el Saba at about 1400 hours.

Throughout the day's fighting several German *Taubes* were operative and dropped bombs on the EEF troops, and about 1430 hours a bomb severely wounded the commander of the 8th Light Regiment, Lieutenant-Colonel Maygar, VC. He later died of his wounds.[22]

---

20   *A Brief Report*, ibid, p. 122.
21   *A Brief Report*, ibid, p. 122.
22   Gullett, ibid, p. 406.

Despite this interference, the 3rd Light Horse Brigade continued to move forward. But then the dismounted Auckland Brigade moved in towards the ancient *tel* about 1410 hours and after a series of rushes with the bayonet, had within half an hour cleared the east side of Tel el Saba.

As Allenby later reported: 'The strongly held position of Tel es Saba was captured by the New Zealand Mounted Rifles Brigade, assisted by the 1st Australian Light Horse Brigade by 1500.'[23]

With the capture of this strategic position the surviving Turks retreated westwards towards Beersheba. Simultaneous to the work of the New Zealanders, the Tasmanians and Victorians of the 3rd Light Horse Regiment had crossed the Wadi Saba and captured that part of the *tel*, and then began pursuing the retreating Turks.

With the capture of Tel el Saba by Chaytor's men the approach into Beersheba from the east was now open. The problem now though was that time was running short and it would soon be dark. According to the battle plan, Chauvel's men were to complete the capture by this point.

CHAUVEL'S DILEMMA

Indeed time was running out for Chauvel and he needed to make a quick decision as to how he was going to make the knock-out punch. Allenby was messaging him and urging a quick strike. At that time General Hodgson, commander of the Australian Mounted Division, Brigadier-General M.W Fitzgerald, commander of the 5th Mounted (Yeomanry) Brigade, and probably also Brigadier-General William Grant, commander of the 4th Light Horse Brigade were together at Chauvel's headquarters at Khasm Zanna.

There was a lengthy discussion about the next move. If Tel el Saba had fallen earlier as anticipated, then a dismounted assault on the town as was customary for the Light Horse, would probably have eventuated. Time, however, was now of the essence. It was obvious that Chauvel was contemplating doing something 'different' – a frontal mounted assault.' Chauvel turned to

---

23 *A Brief Report*, ibid, p. 122; Powles, ibid, p. 138.

Hodgson and instructed him to release Grant.[24] Fitzgerald protested, but Chauvel's decision was final.[25]

Although there were various opinions as to why Chauvel would choose Australian mounted infantry as opposed to British cavalry, perhaps it was because Chauvel knew instinctively that for this something 'different' was needed. Chauvel's biographer, Alec Hill alludes to another interesting dynamic that was possibly exercising upon Chauvel's mind on this occasion: 'There was also the nagging thought that Chetwode, whose objectives had been captured, might rush some of his own troops into the town.'[26]

Chauvel's basic plan was for the 4th Light Horse Brigade to charge into Beersheba across the plain; the Anzac Mounted Division, plus the 3rd Light Horse Brigade from their positions to the north of Beersheba to move southwards towards Beersheba; the 7th Mounted (Yeomanry) Brigade to move up the Beersheba-Khalasa Road; while the 5th Mounted Brigade and 11th Light Horse Regiments would come behind in reserve.

Brigadier-General Grant then relayed the informed to his regimental commanders some time after 1530 hours, and they in turn informed the squadron commanders.[27] The Brigade War Diary states: 'Verbal orders received from Division to attack and capture BEERSHEBA as quickly as possible.'[28]

By this stage the horses and been unsaddled and were widely spread over the area of Iswaiwan. The men had to be informed, their horses saddled, and all other preparations necessary had to be made.

Jim Henderson of the 4th Regiment from Victoria recalled that the squadron commanders began arousing the men from where they had been resting: 'With half an hour of daylight left, things began to happen! With a sudden order to mount, the regiment packed forward into a valley in the foothills at the edge of the plain.'[29]

---

24   Chauvel to his wife, 1 November 1917, Chauvel Papers, Series 4 PR 00535, Folder 11.

25   For further details about this conversation see Falls, ibid, p. 58, Footnote 1. For one of the best descriptions of the charge at Beersheba, see Ian Jones, 'Beersheba: The light horse charge and the making of myths,' in *Journal of the Australian War Memorial*, No. 3, October 1983, pp. 26-37.

26   Harry Chauvel to H.S. Gullet, Notes on Chapter 23, *Sinai and Palestine*, cited in Hill, ibid, p. 127.

27   The 4th Light Horse Brigade War Diary, Volume 1, p. 58, states the time as 1630 hours. See also Jones, ibid, p. 30.

28   4th Light Horse Brigade War Diary, AWM, Volume 1, page 58.

29   Diary of Jim Henderson, *Mountain Views*, Healesville Local paper, Victoria, 19-4-1993.

The squadron leader then informed Henderson and his fellow men 'Beersheba is … across the plain. All packs to the rear. We are going to ride straight into the Turkish position in extended order. It has never been done before! There is no barbed wire, we think, thank God!'

The men, waiting in expectation the whole day, hearing the artillery and shooting, and observing the slow progress in capturing Tel el Saba, were now excited. The horses no doubt picked up on the atmosphere and also began to sense an important event was about to happen.

As the Australian horsemen were preparing themselves to charge into Beersheba, the Turks were in the process of evacuating the town. Light Horse historian Ian Jones stated: "a general retirement had been ordered by Ismet Bey *before* the charge was launched. At the same time he had ordered the 27th Divisional Engineer Company 'to destroy the water supply.'"[30]

LONDON - APPROXIMATELY 1400 HOURS (1600 IN BEERSHEBA)

About this time in London the discussions on the Agenda item *The Zionist Movement* began. Until this point opinions had differed on the concept of a Jewish national entity in Palestine. Edwin Montagu, the only Jewish member of the Cabinet had been strongly opposed and Lord Curzon moderately opposed. Carson initially had been mildly opposed. Three members in particular were strongly in favour, Lloyd George, Balfour and Smuts. The others - Bonar Law, Henderson, Barnes and Milner - were mildly in favour.

Then Curzon suddenly offered his support. Following further discussion, Lord Balfour stated, 'that he gathered that everyone was now agreed that, from a purely diplomatic and political point of view, it was desirable that some declaration favourable to the aspirations of the Jewish nationalists should now be made. The vast majority of Jews in Russia and America, as, indeed, all over the world, now appeared to be favourable to Zionism.'[31]

Balfour reiterated that there had been two main arguments against Zionism, (a) That Palestine was inadequate to form a home for either the

---

30   Jones, *Beersheba*, ibid, p. 34. Italics in the original.
31   CAB 23/4, War Cabinet meeting, 31 October 1917, Item, 12.

Jewish or any other people. And (b) The difficulty felt with regard to the future position of Jews in Western countries.

Concerning the first issue Balfour understood:

> … that there were considerable differences of opinion among experts regarding the possibility of the settlement of any large population in Palestine, but he was informed that, if Palestine were scientifically developed, a very much larger population could be sustained than had existed during the period of Turkish misrule. As to the meaning of the words "national home," to which the Zionists attach so much importance, he understood it to mean some form of British, American, or other protectorate, under which full facilities would be given to the Jews to work out their own salvation and to build up, by means of education, agriculture, and industry, a real centre of national culture and focus of national life. It did not necessarily involve the early establishment of an independent Jewish State, which was a matter for gradual development in accordance with the ordinary laws of political evolution.[32]

Lord Curzon, although sympathetic to the Zionist position, still held certain reservations about the optimism of some of the others present concerning the future of a Jewish homeland in Palestine. He also stated the necessity of retaining the Christian Holy Places in Jerusalem and Bethlehem, and remarked, 'if this were to be effectively done, he did not see how the Jewish people could have a political capital in Palestine.' Yet despite his reservations, Curzon concluded, that 'some expression of sympathy with Jewish aspirations would be a valuable adjunct to our propaganda.'[33]

THE CHARGE TO CAPTURE BEERSHEBA

Lieutenant-Colonel M. Bouchier, commander of the 4th (Victorian) Light Horse Regiment and Lieutenant-Colonel D. Cameron, commander of the

---

32 CAB 23/4, ibid.
33 CAB 23/4, ibid.

12th (New South Wales) Light Horse Regiment drew their men up behind a ridge 1200 metres behind Hill 1280.[34]

The two regiments drew up a squadron at a time, the Victorians on the right and the New South Welshmen on the left, in three lines, with about 500 metres between each line. The machine gun squadron was on the left of the 12th Regiment.[35]

As they had neither sword nor lance, they drew their bayonets. This was the finale of the day's fighting. The hard fighting of the British infantry and Anzac Mounted Division plus 3rd Light Horse Brigade depended upon this attack in order to preserve the water wells from being destroyed.

The men came out from behind the hills and in front of them lay Beersheba off to the west. The sun was beginning to get low and shone directly into the men's faces. It was about 1630 hours.[36] They then set off at the trot. The trot soon developed into a gallop.

The 4th Brigade War Diary stated: 'The Bde [Brigade] went in at the gallop capturing the lines of trenches on the plain about one mile E [East] of the town.'[37]

The leading squadrons were led by Major J. Lawson and Major E.M. (Eric) Hyman. The Turks observed this movement and quickly positioned their artillery to fire on the galloping Australians. Hyman and Lawson in the front line experienced the brunt of the Turkish fire. They kept going, and soon came to a shallow and thinly manned Turkish trench which they easily jumped over. They then came to a more heavily manned second trench. Here a number of Australians died, while the remainder dismounted and thus ensued a close quarters hand to hand fight.

Meanwhile Hyman's squadron rode more to the south of the trench system, and although Hyman and some of his men charged into the Turkish trenches, others found a breach in the trench system. Two squadrons led by

---

34   The exact number of men who charged is not known, but it would have been less than 800.

35   4th Light Horse Brigade War Diary, ibid.

36   12th Light Horse Regiment War Diary, AWM, October 1917, p. 37. The 4th Light Horse Regiment War Diary (AWM, October 1917, Volume X, p, 7) states the time was 1600 hours.
4th Light Horse Brigade War Diary, ibid.

37   4th Light Horse Brigade War Diary, ibid. Jones states (*Beersheba*, ibid, p. 26) that the number of men who ultimately engaged the enemy was between 4-500 men.)

Captain R. Robey and Captain J. Davies headed towards Beersheba with the objective of quickly surrounding it.

One of the major objects of the operation was the swift capture of the water wells before they could be destroyed. By a stroke of good fortune the German engineer responsible for the destruction of the wells was on leave in Jerusalem at that time. His replacement was in the process of detonating the explosives at random in the switchboard of a central building when the Light Horsemen rode in. He was hindered from accomplishing his task by the decisive action of Troopers Bolton and Hudson.[38]

Had the German officer succeeded and those valuable water wells destroyed, then the victory would have been sour indeed. Historian Ian Jones stated: 'while Beersheba would have fallen without the charge, all indications are that a substantial part of its water supply would have been lost until wells and pumping equipment could be repaired.'[39] Allenby's strategy of a swift movement to Jaffa and Jerusalem would have been postponed.

The Turks who had already been ordered to make an orderly retreat, now bolted for the only accessible means of escape, directly north into the hills above Beersheba.

The Light Horse in the north-east then began moving from their direction in pursuit of these Turkish soldiers, as too did some of the 4th Light Horse Brigade as they wound their way through Beersheba.

This movement, though, was interrupted when at about 1700 hours a German *Taube* dropped bombs on the attacking force. Thirteen men from the mostly South Australian 9th Light Horse Regiment were killed.[40] Sam Eedle writes: 'The Westminster Dragoons were themselves engaged, and lost one man dead and seventeen wounded in the fray.'[41]

Despite this incident, by about 1730 hours[42] with the sun setting to the west, Beersheba had been captured, and the 4th Light Horse Brigade had

---

38 Jones, *Beersheba*, ibid, p. 34.
39 Jones, *Beersheba*, ibid, p. 34.
40 Gullett, ibid, p. 405.
41 Eedle, ibid, p. 11. One of those involved that day was trooper Archie Newton.
42 12th Light Horse Regiment War Diary, ibid.

completed what the British infantry and Anzac Mounted Division had set up for them.

All that remained now was for the mopping up operations, in which the Yeomanry, various infantry units and ANZAC forces were all involved.[43]

The official record of the day stated: '... the 4th Australian Light Horse Brigade moved forward to attack Beersheba. The brigade galloped over successive lines of trenches in the face of severe machine-gun and rifle fire, and succeeded in occupying the town by about 1800.'[44]

Allenby stated in his report:

> ... attempts to advance in small parties across the plain towards the town made slow progress. In the evening, however, a mounted attack by Australian Light Horse, who rode straight at the town from the east, proved completely successful. They galloped over two deep trenches held by the enemy just outside the town, and entered the town at about 7 p.m., capturing numerous prisoners.
>
> The Turks at Beersheba were undoubtedly taken by surprise, a surprise from which the dash of the London troops and Yeomanry, finally supported by their artillery, never gave them time to recover. The charge of the Australian Light Horse completed their defeat.[45]

When describing the charge of the Light Horse, Wavell stated: 'The moral results of the charge were even greater than the material gains. It set the pace for the whole campaign, inspiring the brigade which carried it out with immense confidence and all the other mounted troops with a spirit of rivalry and emulation. And this demonstration of the power of mounted men to ride home on their infantry undoubtedly shook the nerve of the Turks.'[46]

---

43 A Brief Report, ibid, p. 122, and Falls, ibid, p. 50.

44 A Brief Report, ibid, p. 122. The Light Horse lost 31 men killed in the charge, one of whom was stretcher-bearer, Albert 'Tibby' Cotter. Cotter played 21 cricket Tests for Australia. Total ANZAC casualties for the day were 53 men killed and 144 men wounded. Falls, ibid, Part 1, p. 60.

45 Dispatch of General Allenby, 16 December 1917, in *The Advance of the Egyptian Expeditionary Force*, p. 3.

46 Wavell, ibid, p. 126. Lieut. Wilson was not at the forefront of the fighting on 31 October, but wrote on 6 November 1917: '... You will see by the address that we have taken Beersheba, it was a great show, we galloped it from behind whilst the Infantry came at the front. We took their guns, eight hundred horses and no end of prisoners and we have now paved the way for our comrades to do the same with Gaza and I'm thankful to say they won't be able to use us there ... ' Interestingly he makes no mention of the charge of the Australian Light Horse! The best way to understand the capture of Beersheba is that it was a team effort by the British, New Zealand and Australian troops, finished off by the charge at the end of the day.

Despite the fact that only two of the water wells had been destroyed there was not the water necessary for the 58,500 thirsty and weary men who now poured into Beersheba – let alone the horses and other animals. These men and animals would require some 1,800,000 litres of water, while the amount available in the wells was only about 400,000 litres. A number of men therefore had to be sent back to Karm in order to water.

THE BALFOUR DECLARATION IS FINALIZED

Part one of the important outcomes of 31 October 1917, the capture of Beersheba, had now been attained. All that was now required was the real-isation of part 2 – the political solution for the future of 'the land between empires.' This depended solely upon a vote now taking place in London.

At about 1700 hours (1500 hours in London), the members of the War Cabinet concluded their discussion and debate. Balfour then said a few words, and then the vote was taken. Nine were in favour of having a Jewish national entity in Palestine once it had been captured from the Turks, and one, Montagu (in absentia), was opposed.

Finally the War Cabinet authorized –

The Secretary of State for Foreign Affairs to take a suitable opportuni-ty of making the following declaration of sympathy with the Zionist aspirations:-

"His Majesty's Government views with favour the establishment in Palestine of a national home for the Jewish people, and will use its best endeavours to facilitate the achievement of this object, it being clearly understood that nothing shall be done which may prejudice the civil and religious rights of existing non-Jewish communities in Palestine, or the rights and political status enjoyed by Jews in any other country."[47]

Balfour was authorized to inform Weizmann, and the leading Zionists of the acceptance of their proposal, albeit one substantially altered from the

---

47   CAB 23/4, ibid.

original. Weizmann was waiting outside while the Cabinet met, and Sykes then came outside and said: "Dr Weizmann, it's a boy."[48]

As the initial proposal had been submitted in a letter from Lord Rothschild to Balfour in July, Balfour was now to formally write to Rothschild of the Government's decision. On 2 November 1917 Balfour wrote to Rothschild, beginning by stating: 'I have much pleasure in conveying to you, on behalf of His Majesty's Government, the following declaration of sympathy with Jewish Zionist aspirations which has been submitted to, and approved by, the Cabinet.' Then followed the Declaration, as endorsed on 31 October by the War Cabinet, which was henceforth known as the 'Balfour Declaration.' Balfour concluded his letter by stating: 'I should be grateful if you would bring this declaration to the knowledge of the Zionist Federation.'

A similar attempt at a British-sponsored Jewish restoration was made by Palmerston in 1840. That attempt failed primarily because of four reasons:

- The lack of sufficient troops in the land to effect the idea.
- Opposition from other European powers to such a concept.
- Britain then had an 'alliance' with Turkey, which because of its Islamic status could not condone the presence in *dar al Islam* of a non-Muslim (*dhimmi*) national entity.
- The lack of any tangible Jewish institution which could work together with Britain for the implementation of such a concept.

In October 1917 all of these factors were lined up in Britain's favour. But now that the first victory on the ground had been attained, and the political position verified, it was still necessary for the remainder of the land to be captured, and captured quickly, before the Turks could enact any retribution upon the surviving Jewish community in *Eretz Yisrael*.

The next goal in this quest was Jerusalem.

---

48 Weizmann, ibid, Vol. 1, p. 208.

THIRD BATTLE OF GAZA

(BATTLE OF BEERSHEBA)

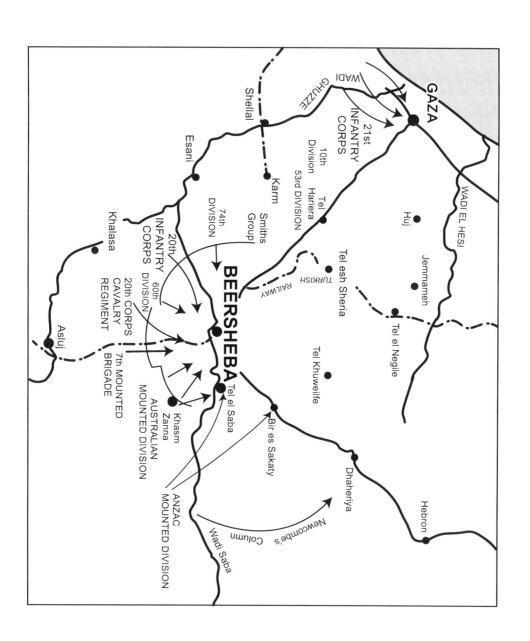

§

CHAPTER 65

Onto Jaffa and Jerusalem

FEINT TOWARDS HEBRON AND FIGHTING IN GAZA

Allenby now wanted to roll back the Beersheba-Gaza line, surround the Turkish forces and move up the plain of Philistia and take Jerusalem as quickly as possible. But even with the wells of Beersheba he was severely handicapped by the lack of water. In addition the hot *khamsin* wind began to blow, quickly drying the throats of man and animal.

Despite these set-backs preparations were made after several days for the next objective: breaking the centre of the Turkish line at Tel esh Sheria (near present day Kibbutz Mishmar HaNegev). This objective was dependent upon consolidation of the ground to the north of Beersheba, and another, successful, strike at Gaza.

As troops began moving north of Beersheba on 1 November, Newcombe and his cameliers were engaging the Turks near Hebron. Australian patrols also reached as far as El Dhaheriya, between Beersheba and Hebron. Idriess wrote: '... our mobile regiment was detached for reconnaissance up the Hebron road down which old man Abraham had travelled to Beersheba. Although without sleep we rode cheerfully into the Judean hills.'[1]

---

1 Idriess, ibid, p. 253.

Von Kressenstein and the Turco-German staff resolved to recapture Beersheba. They were diverted from this objective, however, by the news of the raiding parties at Hebron and El Dhaheriya. They believed these moves were a major EEF thrust towards Jerusalem, and so they diverted the forces intended for Beersheba and sent them towards Hebron.

They confronted the EEF forces at a dominating mound, about sixteen kilometres north of Beersheba named Tel Khuweilfeh (Kibbutz Lahav). Other Turkish forces also surrounded Newcombe's force, killing some and capturing the survivors, including Newcombe.

Meanwhile the third attempt to capture Gaza, led by the 21st Infantry Corps, began during the night of 1 November. The defences at Gaza, subdued by a continuous bombardment since 27 October, were softened up before the troops of the 54th Division began their assault. The following days witnessed much hand-to-hand fighting, primarily in the vicinity of Ali Muntar, and already by 4 November the British had lost 441 men killed and 1,963 men wounded.[2]

FIGHTING AT TEL KHUWEILFEH

Allenby suffered two set-backs to his goals in early November. Lawrence was to engineer a diversionary attack in Transjordan. He and a small number of Arab troops were to destroy part of the railway running down the Yarmuk River between Deraa and Semack. This move was aimed at hampering the Turks from reinforcing and supplying their forces facing the EEF. The attack, though, basically failed and only part of their objective was achieved.

The other set-back was the movement of Turkish troops towards the Hebron road. No pursuit could be possible while this large Turkish force remained around Tel Khuweilfeh, which was strategically important as well as the location of large water wells.

Intense fighting took place in and around this location from 2-7 November, as well as the nearby Ras el Nagd. New Zealander Malone re-

---

2   Falls, ibid, p. 74.

called: 'Bullets falling everywhere. Lay in all day under fire.'[3] Due to the lack of water, the longer the engagement lasted, the worse the position became for the EEF.

An all-out offensive was planned against both Gaza and Tel Khuweilfeh on 6 November. In addition the first major move was to be made against the centre of the Turkish line, especially at Tel esh Sheria and Tel Hariera. The fighting at all these locations was extremely intense.

Malone's entry for 6 November at Tel Khuweilfeh read: 'Filluel hit in chest & died of wounds. Friend killed – hit in stomach. Gorrie hit in head – killed.'[4] All units suffered terrible casualties. In the centre, the 10th, 74th and 60th Divisions contended throughout 6 November against the strategically located Turkish Kauwukah and Rushdi trench systems which were located between Tel Hariera and Tel esh Sheria. The Australian Mounted Division was now engaged, and as they charged, they had to evade the dead and wounded Londoners.

The intense fighting continued into 7 November. Walters in the central sector also recorded on 7 November: 'Had a pretty rough time the last few days. You would not recognize us for dirt. We had just had a quick move this morning & are now at or near SHARIA. The news had just come through that GAZA has fallen. Jacko is getting a nasty knock right along the line.'[5]

GAZA AND THE CENTRE OF THE LINE CAPTURED

After a week of intense fighting the men of the 21st Infantry Corps gained the summit of Ali Muntar at dawn on 7 November. Gaza at the third attempt was finally in the hands of the EEF. The cost, once again, had been high, with hundreds of British soldiers paying the supreme sacrifice.

Also in the early hours of 7 November Tel esh Sheria fell to the London 60th Division, while shortly afterwards the 10th Irish Division captured Tel Hariera. The Turkish forward line had finally been broken, with the excep-

---

3   Diary of Malone, ibid.
4   Diary of Malone, ibid.
5   Walters.

tion of a few menacing rear-guard actions. Towards the end of 7 November Tel Khuweilfeh also fell to the EEF.

Upon being informed of all these losses, General Von Falkenhayn, recently ensconced at his headquarters at the Augusta Victoria Hospice in Jerusalem, ordered Von Kressenstein to withdraw from the Gaza line and establish a new defensive line on the northern side of Wadi el Hesi (Nahal Shiqma). As the Turkish troops quickly moved back to this new line, they were pursued by the British-Anzac troops, who were equally determined to quickly surround them before they escaped and reached this new line.

UP THE PLAIN OF PHILISTIA

Allenby's strategy was for the mounted troops to move quickly up the plain of Philistia. At this point the emphasis was upon rapid movement of these mounted troops. The next Turkish line of defence ran from the mouth of Wadi el Hesi on the coast through to the village and fortifications near the village of Huj (Har Hoga and Kibbutz Dorit); Jemmameh (Har Jemmameh near Kibbutz Ruhama) and Tel el Nejile (Tel Nagila).

Progress on 7 November, however, was disappointing, due primarily to the lack of water and menacing rearguard actions.   Progress, though, improved on 8 November. Walters recorded that this was a 'Red Letter day' for his unit, as they ran into a position of thousands of Turkish troops. 'Of course', he stated, 'we had to face a fair amount of Gun and Machine Gun fire but completely demoralised the enemy … What a great victory we are having. Jacko is getting back [moving back] for his life.'[6]

THE YEOMANRY CHARGE AT HUJ

The key position in the centre of this defensive line was Huj, location of a large Turkish camp. On 8 November as the London infantrymen were approaching they came under Turkish fire, as well as Austrian artillery fire. The mounted troops were called upon to charge this position, and this was carried out by the 5th Mounted Brigade. Led by men from Worcestershire

---

6 Walters.

and Warwickshire, these men and horse gallantly rode in against entrenched Turkish infantry and Austrian artillery and captured the position.

Wilson's Gloucestershire Regiment was in reserve and arrived shortly after. He later wrote:

> The first man I saw was a friend of mine in the Worcester Yeomanry whose horse had been killed under him and who had been killed by a bayonet obviously before he had a chance to put up a fight…. The only section of the enemy force to stand their ground were the gunners, mostly Austrians; the guns were manned and fired to the last second by these green uniformed fellows. The Turkish infantry was still scuttling away… We buried those splendid yeomen at dawn and, for the first time, realised the wicked waste of war.[7]

In this brief encounter, twenty-nine Yeomen were killed and forty-six wounded, while 100 of 170 horses were also killed. But by late on the evening of 8 November, the 52nd Division, after sustaining heavy losses, had gained all the positions along the Wadi el Hesi.

PURSUIT BY THE MOUNTED FORCES

Now the door was opened for the mounted forces, and all three divisions, the Anzac, Australian and Yeomanry, set off in hot pursuit of the Turks, who were now retreating to their next line of defence, the Wadi Surar (Nahal Sorek). This Wadi ran from the Mediterranean coast inland over the coastal plain past the ancient Biblical site of Bet Shemesh and the Jewish village of Hartuv (Artouf) and then into the Judean Hills to the vicinity of Jerusalem.

The most strategic part of this line from the coast to the foothills of the Judean hills, was the Mughar-Katrah Ridge. Another important location was Junction Station, on the Jaffa-Jerusalem railway line. From here the spur down to Beersheba began. If this location was captured, the Turks could no longer use the Jaffa-Jerusalem railway.

---

7 Wilson, ibid, p. 94.

Over the following days the ANZAC and British horsemen captured position after position. They were greatly aided by the men of the Royal and Australian Flying Corps (AFC) who continually hassled and bombed the retreating Turkish force, and provided invaluable intelligence information.[8]

CAPTURE OF JUNCTION STATION AND MUGHAR

At this point Allenby determined to split the Turkish force into two, force a wedge between them, and then mount a two-pronged attack: one in the direction of Jaffa and the other in the direction of Jerusalem. The crucial position in the thrust towards Jerusalem was Junction Station. If the Turks lost this position, then their next line of defence was beyond the Jaffa-Jerusalem railway line. For Allenby, any hope of reaching Jerusalem before the winter rains set in depended upon a speedy break through at this point.

Troops began moving into their positions on 12 November, and the battle began in earnest on 13 November. The fighting ensued along the entire line. British Yeomanry dashed at the strategic Mughar Ridge and after courageous fighting from them and the infantry, the position was captured, as too was the nearby Katrah position. Evelyn Rothschild, the nephew of Baron Edmund, was killed in the clash at Mughar. The following day the 75th Division captured Junction Station. The way to Jerusalem was now further opened.

BATTLE OF AYUN KARA

The way to Jaffa was blocked by a strong Turkish force ensconced near the village of Ayun Kara, which was adjacent to the Jewish colonies of Rishon-le-Zion and Rehoboth. This key position was attacked on 14 November by the New Zealand Mounted Rifles.

The attacking New Zealanders were heavily outnumbered by the Turks. At one point, during a Turkish counter-attack, the fighting was so intense that every available soldier, including signallers, gallopers and batmen from the Regimental Headquarters, was rushed forward until reinforcements ar-

---

8   One pilot in the AFC was Frank McNamara, who had recently been awarded the Victoria Cross for gallant actions on 20 March 1917.

rived from the 3rd Squadron. This Squadron then advanced, dismounted under the command of Major Twistleton, and came to within a few metres of the Turkish line.[9]

The heavily outnumbered New Zealanders at one point were rushed by the Turkish infantry. They stood their ground and then counter-attacked with the bayonet. The Turks were no match for the tough New Zealanders, and leaving hundreds of their dead and wounded behind them, they fled. This was the last Turkish attempt to maintain the Jaffa-Jerusalem line on their right flank.

The New Zealanders lost 44 men killed and 141 wounded in this fierce encounter. Some of their men died afterwards of their wounds.[10]

THE TURKISH ARMY SPLIT

The fighting of 13 and 14 November effectively sealed the fate of the Turkish Army. The Turkish 7th Army now retreated into the Shephelah and Judean Hills, while the 8th Army retreated towards Jaffa, and the defensive line running to the north of the Jerusalem-Jaffa railway. The British-ANZAC force remained in hot pursuit. On 14 November Walters recorded: 'The last few days have been very strenuous. Shell fire every day … We have now joined up with the Inf. [infantry] & are near the junction of Jerusalem-Jaffa Line.'[11]

Jerusalem and Jaffa now beckoned. The next objective in the move to Jerusalem was the area around Latrun and nearby Arab village of Yalo as well Tel Jazar, the Biblical Gezer. Tel Jazar and the associated ridge controlled the Valley of Ajalon, and the land route from Jaffa to Jerusalem via Ramle. Latrun, further to the east, marked the point at where the Gaza-Jerusalem and Jaffa-Jerusalem routes converged. Two main routes to Jerusalem went out from Latrun, one via Bab el Wad and the other via Bet Horon.

On 15 November the EEF moved towards these objectives. In the process they liberated more Jewish colonies, as well as the Arab towns of Ramle and Ludd (Lod), and captured hundreds of Turks.

---

9   Powles, ibid, p. 148.

10   For further information on the role of the New Zealand Mounted Rifles, see Kinloch, T. *Devils on Horses*, (Auckland, 2007).

11   Walters.

WELCOME BY THE LOCALS

It was a great relief for the Jewish colonists to see Allied soldiers. The EEF soldiers, likewise, were pleased to see these signs of civilisation. Walters wrote:

> It seemed strange to ride through decent villages with stone build-ings and tiled roofs inhabited by Jews who in some cases could speak English and who were mighty glad to see the Red, White & Blue in place of the Turkish Crescent. We fared pretty well in these villages for brown bread and fruit, which was very acceptable after the weeks of tinned dog and biscuits. The Oranges particularly are a boon. We buy them here at the rate of 30 for 1/- [shilling]. They come from Jaffa and Ramley. The Jews have plenty of bread to sell and we have con-sumed a good bit of it, but they charge an unreasonable price for sale. i.e. 1/- for a small loaf that a man can eat for one meal. In nearly every village one finds a fine engine and pumping plant and if not blown up by the retreating Turks is of immense value for drawing water for our horses.[12]

A certain degree of homesickness was felt by some of the soldiers when see-ing these villages, and the 'mimosa hedges in full bloom.' One interesting event occurred in the village of *Nahalat Reuven* (Inheritance of Reuben) which Powles wrote of:

> The lane led out into an open space where crowds of white men, wom-en and children welcomed us with loud cries of "Shalome, Shalome" and much talking in Yiddish. Suddenly came a clear cut question in excellent English from a woman, "Do you know a soldier of the name of _____?" An audible smile went down the little column and the Staff Officer leading suggested that there doubtless were many soldiers of that name in the Division, but that if she knew his regi-ment enquiries could be made. Quickly the answer came, "Yes, he is

12 Walters.

a New Zealander and is in the N.Z. Mounted Regiment, but I do not know which. I would much like to find him because he is my son." And before any further answer could be given a burly policeman, who had been riding behind the Provost Marshal and who had been chosen by that officer quite haphazard that morning from the Divisional Mounted Police as his horse holder for the day, rode forward and said he had a letter for a Mrs_____ which had been given to the Divisional Police by Trooper_____ of the Auckland Regiment about a year ago with the request that all enquiries be made for his mother in the villages of Palestine. And here we found her after riding 200 miles through an alien land: and she was the first white woman we had spoken to in all that ride.

Needless to say that Trooper_____'s C.O. was at once communicated with, and the son was given leave to go to his mother.[13]

There was a very warm welcome for the EEF liberators. At Rishon-le-Zion, the inhabitants lined the streets in order to, wrote Idriess, 'stare at these brown, sleeveless soldiers. We must have seemed queer fighting men to them', he continued, 'for they stared as if they had expected to see supermen, not rough-clad Australians. I don't think they could realize that we actually were the men who had driven back their taskmaster of centuries. They seem also to be on the verge of something they cannot believe, cannot understand: they tremble when they whisper Jerusalem. It appears there is some prophesy, centuries old, that one day Jerusalem will fall and will be taken from the Turk or from whatever infidel holds it.'[14]

Wilson wrote on 22 November 1917: '... Have been too busy to write anything till now, but at last we are more or less settled down. Our Squadron is now doing escort to Corps Head Quarters which is an ideal job – we are at present living in a modern Jewish village built by Rothschild, the people are all fruit farmers and we buy practically anything we want. We have a roof

---

13 Powles, ibid, p. 155.
14 Idriess, ibid, p. 284.

over our heads which is a great advantage as the winter is in full sway and we get very heavy rains.'[15]

Several days later Wilson again wrote: '… we are still living in the Jewish colony… This civilisation comes as a great relief to us as it is the first we have struck in the two hundred miles between here and Egypt which has taken us nineteen months to cover…'[16]

Chauvel set up his HQ in Khirbat Deiran (Rehoboth) on 16 November – in the home of Lazar Slutzkin, who had been expelled in 1914-15.

JAFFA CAPTURED

Following the capture of Ayun Kara the Anzac Mounted Division and 21st Infantry Corps peeled off towards Jaffa. On 16 November the New Zealanders liberated Jaffa, and then quickly moved on to occupy the south-ern bank of the Nahr Auja (Nahal Yarkon).

The liberated towns and villages were now placed under the jurisdiction of representatives of 'Occupied Enemy Territory Administration (OETA)'. The Royal Navy arrived off Jaffa on 19 November, and began landing large quantities of supplies, some of which came from the various relief agencies which now came in order to assist the impoverished local population.

Jaffa, including the new Jewish colony of Tel Aviv, was only a shadow of its former self. Only some 10,000 of its pre-War population of 50,000 remained. Many residents, especially Jewish, had been expelled in 1914-15; many had been drafted into the Turkish Army; many had died of starvation and deprivation; while many had been expelled by Djemal Pasha at the time of the initial attacks upon Gaza.

Within days of Jaffa's liberation many of these residents, who had some-how survived, returned. They came, wrote Powles, 'on camel back and on donkeys and on foot, with all the worldly goods they still possessed packed upon camels, mules and donkeys. It was a motely crowd,' he continued, 'that arrived day after day and it showed many signs of the privations of war. Food had been exceedingly scarce and many had actually starved to death.'[17]

---

15 Wilson, ibid, p. 97.
16 Wilson, ibid, p. 98.
17 Powles, ibid, p. 158.

The fate which had befallen Jaffa was now being felt by many other towns and villages still under Turkish control. Marie James, in her last diary entry, wrote from Safed in November 1917: 'The Government is prosecuting its search for spies with increased vigour. We have been secretly warned to destroy all letters and papers, especially those written in English, as the Turks are more suspicious of what they do not understand. It is therefore necessary for me to bring "Life in Safed during the War" to an abrupt conclusion, trusting that deliverance will soon come to this unhappy country through Him Who is the "Prince of Peace."'[18]

CAPTURE OF LATRUN AND PREPARING FOR JERUSALEM

Deliverance was indeed on the way, but Safed would not taste it until September 1918. Meanwhile the Australian Mounted Division captured the area around Latrun and Yalo on 16 November, thereby opening the way to Jerusalem. With this victory the Turks had now been completely cleared out from the plain of Philistia.

But this gain had come at a considerable cost. In the period from 31 October, the EEF had suffered some 10,000 casualties. That was a heavy price to pay and many more British, Australian and New Zealand families were bereft of their loved ones.

This high cost, though, also ensured the preservation of life and property of the local population in that region who had managed to survive Djemal Pasha's harsh regime. Deliverance preserved them from suffering a fate similar to that of the Armenians, Greeks and Assyrians and other minority groups within the Turkish Empire.

The goal was now to rigorously continue the campaign and to deliver more people from the intolerable Turkish regime. The next stage was for the conquest of the city associated with the Prince of Peace - Jerusalem.

---

18 Diary of Marie James, ibid, p. 70.

TO JAFFA AND JERUSALEM

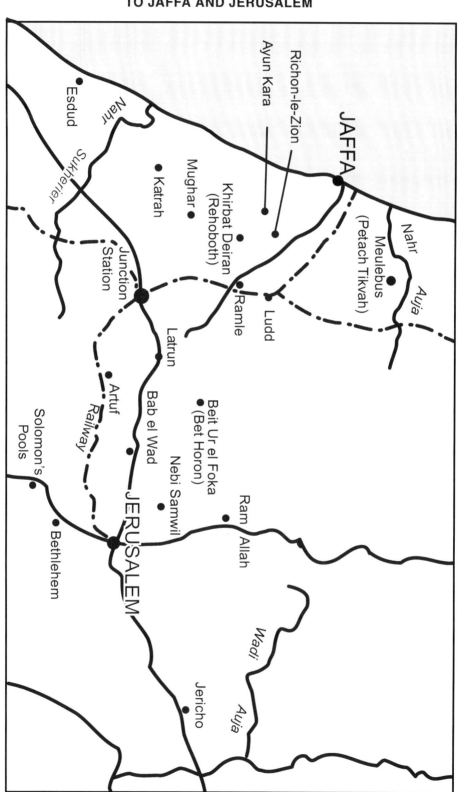

CHAPTER 66

§

The hills surrounding Jerusalem

MOVE INTO THE JUDEAN HILLS

History has revealed the danger involved in foreign armies pressing an attack through the Judean hills to Jerusalem. Yet despite the history lessons and lack of adequate supplies Allenby chose to proceed. He wanted to take advantage of the Turkish disorganisation and the psychological edge his troops now held over the Turks.

Allenby's strategy was to establish a firm line along the Nahr Auja (Yarkon River) over the Samarian hills north of Jerusalem and running down to the Jordan River some sixteen kilometres north of Jericho. From this platform he could cross the Jordan River, take Transjordan, cut the Hejaz railway, and move northwards to Damascus. His initial objectives were to capture first Jerusalem, and then Jericho.

The EEF made its entry into the Judeo-Samarian range along three routes on 18 November. The 75th and 52nd Divisions of 21st Corps headed towards Jerusalem in the region of the main route from Latrun and Bab el Wad, while the Yeomanry Division headed towards the Bet Horon route further to the north.

But as the troops began moving out, the clouds finally burst, drenching the land, men and animals. It now became clear that this was difficult terrain for horses to operate effectively in and thereafter the operation was primarily one for the infantry – or dismounted horsemen.

The EEF soldiers now began to suffer from the elements, as well as from strategically entrenched Turkish troops. Most of the EEF soldiers were still wearing their summer uniform, and lacked warm clothing.

Heavy resistance was encountered from the Turks in the region between Latrun and Bab el Wad, on the main road to Jerusalem. Walters recorded: 'Started off last night along the road to Jerusalem, but it came on to pour rain ... The road winds in between great hills (very beautiful and inspiring). Horses & men are dead here and there along the track from the Turkish sniper who is busy.'[1]

On 20 November the 75th Division captured the strategic ridge upon which Saris (today near junction of Jerusalem-Moshav Shoresh road) and Kuryat el Enab (Abu Ghosh) were located. Further to the north the dismounted Yeomanry Division was hindered from gaining its objective by fierce fighting at the Zeitoun Ridge (just north of present day Givat Zeev). This ridge controlled the Beth Horon route – and delayed any advance towards the Jerusalem-Nablus road. The 75th Division moved forward to assist the Yeomanry.

While moving in this direction, on 21 November, the 75th Division came under fire from Turkish troops located near the strategically located Nebi Samwil mosque, located atop a commanding ridge which dominated the approaches to Jerusalem. It was here that Richard the Lion Heart's quest for the capture of Jerusalem was thwarted during the Crusades. But this time the British soldiers succeeded where King Richard had failed.

One brigade of the 75th Division attacked and captured this strategic height. Seeing this location as holding the key to the capture of Jerusalem, the 75th Division thereafter adopted the key as their divisional symbol. Subsequent Turkish counter-attacks failed to recapture the summit of this position.

---

1 Walters.

Lieutenant Wilson wrote of this time, on 22 November 1917: 'We have done a lot of fighting since my last letters and all has gone well – we have not actually taken Jerusalem but last night we had driven them out of all their trenches and the town itself was under rifle fire so we expect any minute to hear that it has fallen.'[2]

Jerusalem did not fall as Wilson expected, or as Allenby desired, due to tough Turkish resistance. Just to the north of Nebi Samwil, between that strategic ridge and Zeitoun, lay the village of El Jib, which remained in Turkish hands. The EEF, therefore, could not attain its goal of reaching and cutting off the Jerusalem-Nablus Road north of the city.

By 24 November a stalemate had developed in the hills surrounding Jerusalem. Allenby then called for a cessation of further advances and a consolidation of his line. Over the following days the exhausted 75th and 52nd and Yeomanry Divisions were replaced by the 60th, 10th and 74th Divisions of the 21st Infantry Corps.

The ANZAC mounted men were mostly based back in various locations on the plain, except for the 10th Light Horse Regiment which was stationed at the Jewish colony of Artuf (Hartuv). From there they patrolled daily into the Judean hills, venturing up to villages on the outskirts of Jerusalem, including Ein Karem (traditional birthplace of John the Baptist), Setaf and other locations.

While these men were probing around in the hills surrounding Jerusalem, the politicians in London were tackling some thorny issues associated with the ultimate capture and future status of Jerusalem.

THE POLITICS OF JERUSALEM

Jerusalem now became a major issue for the War Cabinet, which had declared that upon its capture a proclamation would be issued assuring the Muslim world that the British forces were the protectors of the Muslim Holy Places. At a meeting on 26 November 1917 a message was read from Allenby who was inquiring about what flags were to be hoisted in Jerusalem. The

---

2   Wilson ,ibid, p. 97.

War Cabinet replied: 'In view of the unique character of the city and of the many difficult political and diplomatic questions that were raised in connection with it, General Allenby should be informed that no flags should be hoisted in the event of the occupation of the city by Allied troops.'[3]

Apart from these Cabinet meetings, other deliberations were held in Cairo, especially between Sykes (until his replacement as Government liaison officer by Gilbert Claydon), and Wingate. The Foreign Office was concerned lest friction arise 'in connection with Holy Places in the event of an occupation of Jerusalem by the British forces', wrote to Wingate in Cairo on 16 November 1917 making a number of proposals for safeguarding especially the Christian and Muslim Holy Places. 'In general,' the Memo continued, 'Jerusalem should be kept under martial law so as to avoid Franco-Italian complications ...'[4]

Wingate in his reply on 19 November, stated that he and Allenby had decided it best to place picked Christian guards at the Christian Holy Places, and picked Muslim, probably Indian, guards at the Muslim Holy Places. A Military Governor for Jerusalem had also been selected, Colonel Borton, the Postmaster General in Egypt. 'This arrangement' wrote Wingate, 'will effectually prevent political interference on the part of interested Powers by maintaining a purely military administrative system entirely under General Allenby until the military situation becomes much clearer than it is at present.'[5]

Wingate went on to say that Borton had been instructed by him and Allenby to deal with the various representatives of the Christian, Muslim and Jewish Holy Places and communities, and to assure them that little change would be presently made, 'pending the re-establishment of a purely civil Government which is not possible as long as any enemy forces are in being in Palestine.'[6]

Despite these British plans the French were determined to be politically involved in the conquest of Jerusalem. Wingate sent an urgent telegram to

---

3   CAB 23/4, WC 282, 26 November 1917.
4   FO 371/3061, No. 21308, 16 November 1917, p. 383.
5   FO 371/3061, ibid, p, 403.
6   FO 371/3061, ibid, pp. 403-4.

the Foreign Office on 21 November, stating that he had been informed that since Picot could not 'arrive in time at Allenby's headquarters Monsieur de France has been instructed to proceed there as soon as possible in order to enter Jerusalem with the British troops.' Wingate also wrote: 'The French Government further request that if Borton Pasha [Colonel Borton] is appointed Governor of Jerusalem he [i.e. Monsieur de France] should receive similar instructions with regard to French participation in the administration of Jerusalem.'[7]

On the same day, 21 November, Allenby received instructions from the CIGS Robertson at the War Office, concerning his actual entrance into Jerusalem. His every move was being dictated by the Government planners, in which Sykes again played a major role. Allenby was informed in these instructions that he was to enter Jerusalem on foot.[8]

Meanwhile in a letter to the Foreign Office dated 24 November 1917, Wingate (with Allenby's concurrence), was becoming concerned about the French position. The French Government was insisting that Picot, who was now on the scene, be involved in the official entry into Jerusalem. Wingate and Allenby were strongly of the opinion that a military administration should be created for the conquered areas of Palestine 'so long as military operations are in progress.'[9]

Picot, however, was 'sticking to his guns', and at a subsequent meeting with Wingate he, 'expressed his dissatisfaction with these arrangements which he considered would be strongly resented in France.' 'Picot declared', Wingate stated, that 'over a year ago it was agreed between British and French Governments that pending final settlement of peace terms, any conquered portions of Palestine should be jointly administered by us and the French, exclusive of the Italians or other nationalities.' Picot claimed that it was this understanding that warranted French officers being placed beside the British officers in the future administration of Palestine.[10]

---

7   FO 371/3061, ibid, p. 410.
8   FO 371/3061, ibid, p. 420.
9   FO 371/3061, ibid, pp. 430-1.
10   FO 317/3061, ibid, p. 435.

The agreement referred to by Picot was a Memorandum between Grey and Monsieur Cambon on 16 May 1916, concerning the future administration of Palestine, but Wingate thought this to be quite flimsy evidence to demand such an important position of authority. The Foreign Office found that their hands were tied, and instructed Wingate on 26 November 1917 that both Picot, representing the French Government, and Clayton representing the British, could enter Jerusalem with Allenby, but that both would then 'enter upon their full duties at once under General Officer Commanding.'[11] This ensured that the final word concerning the role of Picot in Jerusalem would be entrusted to General Officer Commanding – General Allenby.

Despite Britain's promise to the Jewish people as stated in the Balfour Declaration, and despite the presence of a large British-led army in the land, the French were not going to easily surrender any controlling interest in the 'Holy Land.'

EEF AND TURKISH OFFENSIVES IN LATE NOVEMBER

To hinder the Turco-German command from disrupting his objectives in the Judean hills, Allenby attacked across the Nahr Auja (Yarkon River), north of Jaffa on 24 November. The Turks counter-attacked the following day, and drove the British and New Zealanders back over the river.

Some quite intense fighting occurred along the entire front line from near the coast through to the foothills. 'Fronting us' recalled Idriess, 'the country was dotted with villages, one very pretty Jewish one, Muleubis, being all smoke from bursting shells.'[12] Despite such battle conditions Idriess managed to discover a point in common with his native land:

> Groves of dark green gums were everywhere. The inhabitants are very jealous of each individual tree. They import Australian "sucker" gum, the gum that out pastoralists find almost impossible to kill by ring-barking... When I was "suckering" in Australia I little dreamt that one day I would be in a strange land where people would treasure

---

11   FO 371/3061, ibid, p. 433.
12   Idriess, ibid, p. 292. Muleubis is Petach Tikvah.

as more precious than gold, the very trees that we sought so hard to kill as pests.[13]

Idriess never had an opportunity of seeing more of this Jewish agricultural village as he was then wounded in this action. He, like many of the other wounded, was then transported back to Cairo. His involvement in the war against Turkey, which took him to Gallipoli, the Sinai, Gaza, Beersheba and now Judea, was over.

While Allenby had his strategy for planning this general attack, the Turco-German command also had offensive plans at this time. They wanted to disrupt the change-over of the EEF forces in the Jerusalem hills. Between 27 November and 3 December they attacked with the *Yilderim*, which had finally arrived in the region, along the entire EEF line from Beth Horon to the coastal plain.

One position which was quite severely hit was where the Yeomanry Division was located in the region of Zeitun and Beitunia Ridge, where they sustained many casualties. Another location heavily attacked was El Burj (near Modiin). Here a numerically superior *Yilderim* force nearly overwhelmed the 8th and 9th Light Horse Regiments and several British units, but they managed to hold the attacking force off.

This desperate Turkish attempt to wrest back the initiative failed. It lacked the necessary penetration and their gains were minimal compared to their losses. Hereafter they were again on the defensive, while the EEF now went fully on to the offensive - with Jerusalem now firmly in its sights.

---

13 Idriess, ibid, p. 292.

CHAPTER 67

§

The capture of Jerusalem

PREPARATIONS

While the Turkish counter-attack had further exhausted their Seventh Army, the EEF had become re-invigorated, and was now fully prepared for a second attempt to capture Jerusalem. Plans for the assault were slightly complicated by orders not permitting intense fighting near the Old City. The plans were basically to surround Jerusalem and compel the Turks to withdraw. In this operation the RFC played a vital role by surveying Turco-German troop movements, and dropping countless propaganda pamphlets calling upon the Turks to surrender.

The plan called for:

- The 60th and 74th Divisions to move towards Jerusalem from the west, and then circle to the north of Jerusalem and cut the Jerusalem-Nablus Road near El Jib, the Biblical Gibeah. The 10th Division was to operate to the north of the 74th Division.
- A composite force known as 'Mott's Detachment' (commanded by Major-General S. Mott) would move by degrees to Hebron along the Patriarchs Road, then capture Bethlehem and enter the southern outskirts of Jerusalem. It was to then skirt to the east and cut the Jerusalem-Jericho Road. This force was composed of the 53rd Division and

various other units, including a cavalry regiment, the Westminster Dragoons.

• Linking the two infantry thrusts in the hilly area either side of Wadi Surar (Sorek Valley) would be the mounted forces of the 10th Light Horse Regiment and the Worcestershire Yeomanry Regiment.

All the plans for the capture of Jerusalem were much dependent upon the weather and transport. The Jerusalem-Jaffa railway was repaired as far as Ramle, enabling supplies to be taken from Jaffa port to Ramle. They were then taken to the front line by the Egyptian labour Corps (ELC) teams, which included some 2,000 donkeys and scores of camels.

PRELIMINARY MOVES

The first major move in this second battle of Jerusalem was on 4 December when 'Mott's Detachment' moved into the Judeo-Samarian hills, to a location south of Hebron. By 5 December some troops were already in position north of Hebron.[1]

Lieutenant A. Banham, commander of 'C' Squadron, the Westminster Dragoons, wrote that: 'having been sent on to Hebron with my troop, we adopted the rather unusual proceeding of riding through the town with drawn swords as I did not like the look of some of the characters lurking thereabouts.'[2]

By 7 December 1917 preparations were going well. On that same day the Jewish people were beginning the festival of *Hanukkah*, which recalled their liberation from Greek-Syrian tyranny under Emperor Antiochus Epiphanes IV in 165 BC.[3]

During the evening of 7 December 1917 the clouds burst and the rain descended upon the awaiting troops. Yet despite these discomforts, the feel-

---

1   Falls, ibid, *From June 1917 to the end of the War*, Vol. 1, p. 240; *A Brief Record of the Advance of the Egyptian Expeditionary Force,* ibid, December 5.

2   National Army Museum Archives, Access No: 7503-31-15. Copied from a handwritten letter in the Westminster Dragoons Archives by Sam Eedle and given to the author. See also Rowe, Major E. *2ⁿᵈ County of London (Westminster Dragoons) Yeomanry,* p. 90.

3   This festival, also known as the festival of lights, is celebrated over an eight day period.

ings of the soldiers were attuned to a higher matter. '... all ranks of the 10th Light Horse Regiment,' wrote Brigadier-General L.C. Wilson, 'had been engaged in continuous duties for many days and nights, during which time wind and rain squalls prevailed. The thoughts of entering Jerusalem,' he concluded, 'counteracted all personal discomforts.'[4]

The personal discomforts that night and the following day though were great. Falls wrote that: 'The troops passed a wretched night in cold, driving rain ... Camels fell with their legs splayed outwards ... and had to be bundled off the road after their loads had been taken off. Several of their Egyptian drivers died from exposure.'[5]

THE FINAL OFFENSIVE BEGINS

The final offensive for the capture of Jerusalem began with an artillery barrage at 0200 hours on 8 December 1917. The 60th and 74th Divisions then headed towards Jerusalem along the old Jerusalem-Jaffa Road, or moved down from the heights of Nebi Samwil. These soldiers had a daunting task, combatting both the elements and entrenched Turkish infantry.

One particularly important position was the village of En Karem, the traditional birthplace of John the Baptist. The 159th Brigade of the 60th Division finally captured this position, but lost 57 men killed in the process.[6] Most of the objectives of the 60th Division were captured by 0700 hours.

The 74th Division was to pivot from the north of the Jerusalem-Jaffa Road and head north-east and cut off the Jerusalem-Nablus Road north of Jerusalem. Most of their initial positions were captured by 0730 hours.

Neither of these two Divisions could continue, however, due to the slow progress of 'Mott's Detachment.' The 53rd Division, making its way from the south, was slowed by the presence of a thick fog. The two mounted regiments operating between had numerous skirmishes as they attempted to reach the Jerusalem-Bethlehem Road.

---

4   Wilson, Brig-Gen, L.C. *Operations of the Third Light Horse Brigade*, (no publishing details), p. 19.
5   Falls, ibid, p. 243.
6   Falls, ibid, pp. 245-6. Later a nearby village of Malha was captured by the 10th Light Horse.

'A' Squadron of the 10th Light Horse, under the command of Major Charles Dunckley, was ordered to take the village of Malha, to the east of En Kerem and half way to the Patriarch's Road, and to patrol that region until the 53rd Division arrived.[7]

When the Welsh Division arrived at Bethlehem it was found to be deserted by the Turkish troops, and it was captured on the evening of 8 December. All the units then consolidated their positions. The Westminster Dragoons moved to Beit Jala, just to the south of the position held by the 10th Light Horse. Lieutenant Banham recalled: 'The country is wild and rugged; the weather was cold, with driving rain ...'[8]

By the evening of 8 December the three front line infantry divisions and the mounted forces were all poised on the outskirts of Jerusalem, ready for a final offensive on the morrow.

ANXIETY WITHIN THE CITY

While soldiers from Britain and Australia were preparing for the final attack upon Jerusalem, excitement coupled with fear and anxiety gripped the inhabitants of the 'Holy City.'

On the morning of 8 December Djemal Pasha had sent instructions that a large number of the inhabitants of Jerusalem, including 'the remaining religious chiefs', were to be expelled. They were informed by the police to be ready for immediate departure. This order was especially hard for the Armenian community, from whom 300 individuals from their small community of 1400 were ordered to leave. Of all the community groups the Armenians best understood the implications of this order.

There were, however, insufficient vehicles to take these people out. This logistical problem was telegraphed back to Djemal Pasha in Damascus. His response was 'that they and theirs must walk.' The official publication of the EEF of this campaign, the *Brief Report*, recorded of this situation:

7   Browning and Gill, *Gallipoli to Tripoli*, (Osborne Park, 2011), p. 322. Dunckley came from Bruce Rock (Gullett, ibid, p. 518, footnote), the same district as the author.
8   Banham, ibid.

The fate of countless Armenians and many Greeks has shown that a population of all ages suddenly turned out to walk indefinite distances under Turkish escort is exposed to outrage and hardship which prove fatal to most of them…'[9]

Fortunately the lack of vehicles saved these poor people from death and duress. The delay in telegraphing Djemal Pasha and receiving his response had eaten up precious time, and it was by now too late in the day to put the order into effect. The *Brief Report* stated, 'the Turk's power to destroy faded with the day.'[10]

Once news filtered through that the EEF troops were poised on the outskirts of Jerusalem, panic overcame the Turkish troops in the forward positions. The *Brief Report* stated that: 'at 1700 civilians were surprised to see a Turkish column galloping furiously cityward along the Jaffa road. In passing they alarmed all units within sight or hearing, and the wearied infantry arose and fled, bootless and without rifles, never pausing to think or fight.'[11]

Excitement now gripped the population, and, stated the *Brief Report*: 'a great enthusiasm arose among the Jews. There was a running to and fro; daughters called to their fathers and brothers concealed in outhouses, cellars and attics, from the police, who sought them for arrest and deportation. "The Turks are running," they called ; "the day of deliverance has come". The nightmare was fast passing away …'

Yet the Turks still remained in Jerusalem, so the residents had to restrain their emotions. 'In the evening' the *Brief Report* continues, 'he [the Turks] fired his guns continuously, perhaps heartening himself with the loud noise … perhaps to cover the sound of his own retreat. Whatever the intention was, the roar of the gunfire persuaded most citizens to remain indoors, and there were few to witness the last act of Osmanli authority.'[12]

---

9   *Brief Report*, ibid, December 8.
10   *Brief Report*, ibid, December 8.
11   *Brief Report*, ibid, December 8.
12   *Brief Report*, ibid, December 8.

JERUSALEM FALLS - 9 DECEMBER 1917

About midnight on 8 December the Turkish Governor, Izzet Pasha, went to the Post Office, dismissed the staff, and then destroyed the telegraphic equipment. Then, the *Brief Report* states:

> At 0200 on Sunday tired Turks began to troop through the Jaffa gate from the west and south-west, and anxious watchers, peering out through the windows of the Grand New Hotel to learn the meaning of the tramping, were cheered by the sullen remark of an officer, 'Gitmaya mejburuz' ("We've got to go"), and from 0200 to 0700 that morning the Turks streamed through and out of the city, which echoed for the last time their shuffling tramp.[13]

The last Turkish soldiers left the vicinity of the Old City about 0700 hours in the morning of 9 December, mostly retreating to the Mount Scopus ridge to the north of the Old City. The final Turkish representative to depart was the Governor. He wrote a letter of surrender and then departed down the Jericho Road.

The liberation of Jerusalem from the despotic Turkish regime now gave the Jewish people a double reason for celebrating *Hanukkah,* as well as giving all the citizens of Jerusalem, particularly the minority groups, great cause to celebrate.

INITIAL MOVEMENT OF TROOPS INTO JERUSALEM

The advance troops coming from the south, namely the Westminster Dragoons, 10th Light Horse and Worcestershire Regiment, all moved towards Jerusalem early in the morning of 9 December.

The 'B' Squadron of the 10th Light Horse moved to a high point between Bethlehem and Beit Jala at 0430 hours. Then at first light, 'A' Squadron moved to the Arab village of Beit Saffafa on the outskirts of Jerusalem adjacent to the Patriarch's Road (today Hebron Road).

---

13   *Brief Report*, ibid, 8 December; Falls, C & MacMunn, General Sir G. *Military Operations: Egypt and Palestine,* (London, 1928), pp. 280-1.

The Westminster Dragoons began to move out at 0530 hours and by 0800 hours they had passed Mar Elias Monastery (almost the halfway point between Jerusalem and Bethlehem). 'A' Squadron (which included Archie Newton) then made towards the village of Beit Saffafa where, wrote Banham, 'I came across a patrol of 3 or 4 men of the 10th Australian Light Horse.'[14]

While the mounted men moved towards the Old City, reports came in between 0800 to 0900 hours from the 179th Brigade (60th Division) that there was no resistance on the En Kerem-Jerusalem Road, and also from the 231st Brigade from 74th Division, that there was no resistance in their vicinity.[15]

THE SURRENDER OF JERUSALEM – PART ONE

While these EEF troops were making their way cautiously into the outer suburbs of Jerusalem, there was activity of another kind near the Old City. Early in the morning of 9 December 1917 the Mayor of Jerusalem, Hussein Salim el-Husseini, holding Izzet Pasha's letter of surrender and the symbolic keys of Jerusalem and accompanied by a few others, made his way towards the western suburbs of Jerusalem in search of the forward British forces in order to surrender the city. Their efforts though were more complicated than anticipated.

The delegation initially met two mess cooks, Private H. E. Church and Private R. Andrews from the 2/20th Battalion, 180th Brigade, 60th Division, who were actually lost. They declined the honour of accepting the surrender.[16] Then two outpost sergeants, F. G. Hurcombe and J. Sedgwick of the 2/19th Battalion, met the delegation, which was now displaying a flag of truce. They too felt unworthy of receiving the surrender, but not before having their photograph taken with the delegation.[17] This meeting took place several hundred metres from Lifta (behind the present Central Bus station where a memorial marks the spot).

Then, on the third attempt, the delegation met Major F. Barry and Major W. Beck of the 60th Division Artillery (RFA), who quickly left in order

14   Banham, ibid; Rowe, ibid, p. 91; Falls, ibid, p. 257.
15   Falls, ibid, p. 256.
16   Falls, ibid, p. 252. There are other versions as to why the two privates were in that location.
17   Falls, ibid, p. 252. The Mayor had with him Lewis Larsson, a photographer from the American Colony in Jerusalem.

to relay the information to their superiors. At this point Lieutenant-Colonel H. Bailey, 303 Brigade RFA, met the delegation, and was informed by the Mayor: "I am the Mayor of Jerusalem, and I desire to surrender the City to the British General."

Bayley then sent one of his men, Major F. Price, back to their HQ to telegraph General Shea. This telegram went out at 0855 hours and read: 'Jerusalem has surrendered. Colonel Bayley, R.F.A., is now with the Mayor awaiting any General Officer to take over the City.'[18]

Colonel Bayley then sent Major Cooke with an Arab policeman to take control over the Post Office, while he himself proceeded with the Mayor and the delegation down Jaffa Road towards the Old City.

FIRST EEF TROOPS TO REACH THE OLD CITY

Meanwhile 'C' Squadron of the Westminster Dragoons continued along the Hebron (or Patriarch's Road) through Katamon, and were then joined by 'A' Squadron, and at 0845 hours 'the advanced guard was at the walls of Jerusalem.'[19] One of these men was Archie Newton and another was the regimental doctor, E. S. Massiah (also pronounced 'Mashiach'). Before departing in the morning Massiah had been instructed to join the Dragoons vanguard, being told 'there would probably be a job for him the other side of the City.'[20]

As Captain Rowe and his men rode adjacent to the walls of the Old City, they soon approached Jaffa Gate and David's Tower (Citadel), where, Rowe wrote:

> … the riders met with a demonstration of welcome such as never could have had a parallel. Men, women and children, their tears mingling with their cheers: olive branches waving and being thrown down to be ridden over: men and women pressing forward to touch the riders

---

18   Falls, ibid, p. 253.
19   Falls, ibid, p. 257.
20   Rowe, ibid, p. 91.

and express their joy as they rode past, it was all an experience never
to be forgotten.[21]

This was indeed an experience that neither the rider nor the observer would
have forgotten. But for one person this incident must have been very san-
guine indeed. Rowe adds:

> Had they but known that of those riding past – men looked on as their
> deliverers – was one by the name of Massiah it can be imagined their
> emotions would have been even more deeply disturbed.[22]

THE SURRENDER – PART TWO

Meanwhile on the western side of the city, Brigadier-General Watson commander of the 180th Brigade, 60th Division, read the telegram sent at 0855
hours, then quickly mounted a horse and made haste to meet the mayor, to
assure him that the surrender would be officially accepted.

Chetwode was then informed of the impending surrender, and he del-
egated General Shea, commander of the 60th Division, to officially accept
it. While all this activity was taking place, and while Shea prepared himself, General Watson and Lieutenant–Colonel Bayley, with an escort of ten
gunners (artillerymen) were escorted to Jaffa Gate (joining the Westminster
Dragoons horsemen), 'and walked through the gap beside it made for the
German Emperor's entrance.'[23]

At Jaffa Gate General Watson accepted the surrender and received the
keys of the City as he wanted to reassure the people that all was well, and
to apprehend any possible lawlessness, as looting had already begun. He
then placed a guard of two gunners on Jaffa Gate until other units arrived
in force.[24]

---

21   Rowe, ibid, p. 91.

22   Rowe, ibid, p. 91.

23   Falls, ibid, p. 254.

24   Falls (page. 254) states this was the 2/17th London Battalion, while Rowe (page. 93) gives the impression that it was 'C'
Squadron of the Westminster Dragoons.

One of those to greet Watson inside the Jaffa Gate was Bertha Spafford Vester of the American Colony.[25]   She wrote of General Watson's entrance into the city: '… suddenly there came a subdued shout, for people were still afraid to show their joy. *"Aju Aju* (They've come)" came the shout, and Brigadier-General Watson was sighted escorted by Hassain Effendi, Mr Salameh, and a crowd of followers.'

It was indeed an emotional time for all who observed this historic occasion. 'For us the joy of that hour,' Mrs Vester continued, 'was indescribable. I rushed down and kissed the general's stirrup and rushed back. I feel quite sure that he never knew who the person was who did that impulsive act.'[26]

Shortly afterwards the Westminster Dragoons horsemen continued to ride around the walls and passed Damascus Gate. Then at the north-west corner of the walls they were stopped by Turkish machine-gun fire coming from the Mount of Olives. The men dismounted and their horses were taken back to Herod's Gate, and they then encountered the Turkish resistance. In the ensuing firefight several men were hit, and while Corporal Richer died, Corporal Hawkins was saved from certain death by the efforts of Dr. Massiah![27]

At some time afterwards Mrs Vester, her husband and brother-in-law then invited General Watson into the nearby hospital where three EEF wounded were located. 'It would be hard to find words to describe the joy of these men at seeing their brigadier general again' wrote Mrs Vester. 'Poor Roberts, in his weak mental state, upbraided the general for having left him to suffer so long. But the general soothed him with kind words.'[28]

At some time after 1100 hours General Shea finally arrived in order to formally receive the surrender and the keys of Jerusalem, Watson having previously returned them to the mayor. Ernie Meyer, a British soldier, stated of this event: 'Fresh cheering in the streets announced the arrival of the

---

25   Falls wrote: 'Inside the walls there was no disturbance of any sort; in fact, they were greeted by some American ladies, overjoyed at their arrival.' Falls, ibid, p. 254.

26   Vester, B. *Our Jerusalem*, (Jerusalem, 1981), p. 275.

27   Rowe, ibid, pp. 91-2.

28   Vester, ibid, p. 275.

divisional commander in his car, accompanied by a glittering staff.'[29] The official surrender then took place again at Jaffa Gate.[30]

While all these deliberations were taking place, the EEF troops began filtering into Jerusalem. 'My goodness, the people of Jerusalem gave us a warm reception,' recalled Private Alec Wilson of the 60th Division of that eventful morning.

It was to be expected that these soldiers would be given a saviour's welcome. Cyril Falls states it well: 'The haste of their flight saved many of the principal Christian and Jewish citizens, who had been ordered to leave with their families and walk ... to Nablus. The inhabitants received Major-General Shea with wild enthusiasm.'[31]

FIGHTING TO THE NORTH OF THE CITY

Yet Wilson, like many of his fellow soldiers, was unable to savour this welcome. 'We marched up Jaffa road,' he recalled, 'past Damascus Gate and took up positions near Shuafat, to protect Jerusalem from the expected counter-attack from the north.'[32]

Meanwhile Chetwode, when informed that there was no Turkish resistance to the south and south-west of Jerusalem, ordered all units at 1030 hours to continue towards their initial objectives.[33] This movement was now hampered again by the onset of heavy rain.

The men of the 60th Division then renewed fighting against the Turks at 1345 hours on Mount Scopus. Here the British infantry were encountering stiff resistance from a Turkish rear guard, who finally were defeated after a bayonet charge. The retreating Turks were being hassled along the road leading north out of Jerusalem by the RFC, especially near Shuafat, where Alec Wilson was heading.

The aircraft also bombed the Jerusalem-Jericho Road to the east of Jerusalem, which eased the movement of the 53rd Division as they circum-

---

29 Meyer, E. 'With Allenby' in *Jerusalem Post Magazine*, 15 December 1978, p. 16.
30 According to Rowe this took place at 1300 hours, while according to Raymond Savage *Allenby of Armageddon*, (London, 1925), p. 231, it was about 1100 hours.
31 Falls, ibid, p. 254.
32 Meyer, ibid, p. 17.
33 Falls, ibid, p. 256.

vented Jerusalem from the south. The 53rd Division then cut the Jericho Road, and moved to link up with the 60th and 54th Divisions on the Mount of Olives Ridge.

Other men of the 60th Division pressed on and captured Tell el Ful several kilometres to the north of Jerusalem, where they linked up with men of the 74th Division. The encirclement of Jerusalem had been completed.

THE ENTRANCE OF ANZAC HORSEMEN

The 10th Light Horse and Worcestershire Yeomanry began moving into Jerusalem in the early afternoon.[34] These men represented the Desert Mounted Corps which had fought every battle and skirmish from Suez through to Jerusalem, while the 10th Light Horse represented the ANZACs who had fought every battle from Gallipoli to Jerusalem. Not one soldier who entered Jerusalem for the first time, Gullet wrote, was left unmoved by the touch of the Saviour Jesus. In the midst of the grossness of war, he concluded, each man came close to that 'pure and trusting' faith of his childhood.'[35]

Major Dunckley and the 'A' Squadron led the way, followed by the other squadrons, including 'C' Squadron, commanded by Throssell, under the overall command of Lieutenant-Colonel Todd.[36]

As these representative ANZACs rode in 'with their emu plumes stirring in the breeze,' Gullet wrote, 'they were rushed by the populace, who marvelled at the size of their big, long-tailed horses.'[37] Walters recalls of that day: 'Was just on the outskirts of Jerusalem. People welcomed us offering wine, fruit etc ... Plenty to eat.'[38]

'The people' Walters continued, 'who seemed a very mixed race, with Jews in the ascendancy were mighty glad to see the British troops take con-

---

34   Contrary to the statement of H.S. Gullet, ibid, the 10th Light Horse Regiment was not the first EEF mounted force to enter Jerusalem.

35   Gullett, ibid, p. 519.

36   Gullett, ibid, pp. 518-9.

37   Gullet, ibid, p. 519.

38   Walters.

trol of their Holy Town. In fact at first they were jumping all over themselves to give us anything and do anything for us.'[39]

The villagers on the outskirts of Jerusalem 'were coming along', recalled Henry Bostock, 'with anything to sell, but mostly it was wine.' One of Bostock's mates, Dinnie Connaughton, was determined not to upset their hospitality, and, Bostock continues, Dinny 'made them to understand that he was there to sample the wine to see if it was fit to be sold.' Whether Dinnie found some to his liking, or overdid the sampling, we are not told, but Bostock does tell us that 'when it came to mount and ride into Jerusalem, I had to help him onto his horse.'[40]

'We passed a house' Bostock recalls, 'where the occupants were holding a dance in what appeared to be a large verandah with glass sides and well lit. Truly a sight to remember on such a memorable night.'[41] Yet serious and exciting as that day was, it was not without its lighter side. 'Dinnie', Bostock recalled, 'after all his wine sampling, fell off his horse.' Some people in a nearby house, who were watching the parade of Australian horsemen, saw Dinnie fall, and 'took him inside, gave him a nice meal and a bed for the night.' Most of the remaining Australians, meanwhile, continued into Jerusalem and located other less glamorous lodgings.

But the Light Horsemen too could not long savour the delight of victory. In the mid-afternoon Lieutenant-Colonel Todd received orders for 'B' Squadron to proceed north of Jerusalem and join in the fighting alongside the British infantry and Westminster Dragoons, to hold and secure the northern approaches to the city.

While most of the horsemen sought billets in the City, Walters and some other Light Horsemen had to return to Artuf, of which he wrote: 'Had a wet night riding home but stayed in a Jews House at ARTUF. Good bed and food. Thought I was home again. Indeed the Jewish inhabitants enjoyed the news they [the Light Horsemen] brought.'[42]

---

39   Letter of Reg Walters to his family. Copy in author's possession.
40   Bostock, ibid, p. 110.
41   Bostock, ibid, p. 113.
42   Walters.

'We were the first to bring tidings of <u>Jerusalem falling</u> to this village', Walters wrote to his family, 'and they <u>were</u> pleased. One old Jew came in and asked us if it was quite correct and when we told him it was he threw his hat down on the floor packed up his goods ... and [was] off to <u>Jerusalem</u>.'[43]

Although Chauvel could not be present at the capture of Jerusalem, he was able to announce its fall to a large Jewish audience at a *Hanukkah* banquet in Khirbat Deiran (Rehoboth). Indeed as far as a symbolic date for the liberation of Jerusalem was concerned, it could not have been more appropriate.

THE DAY AFTER

Allenby's major concerns following the capture of the city were, firstly to establish law and order in the city, and secondly to protect it against any possible Turkish counter-attack.

On 10 December all the troops of the EEF were involved in consolidating the region to the north of Jerusalem. Also on that day the new Military Governor of Jerusalem, Colonel Borton, arrived.[44] Borton immediately began the transfer and re-organization of the civil administration. Jerusalem, like the remainder of the captured area, came under OETA.

In the midst of these two important factors, Allenby had to ensure that everything went according to plan for the major event about to happen on the morrow – the official surrender, the centrepiece of which would be his entrance into the 'Holy City.'

This event was the culmination of the campaign, the goal set by Lloyd George early in the year when he stated that he wanted Jerusalem captured by Christmas. This goal was achieved, but at considerable loss of life to the EEF.[45]

The last act in this dramatic victory was scheduled to occur at noon on 11 December. This event was organized down to the smallest detail by the

---

43   Letter of Reg Walters to his family. Copy in author's possession.
44   Borton later had to resign from this position and on 28 December 1917 Colonel Ronald Storrs became the Governor of Jerusalem. Storrs, ibid, p. 285.
45   EEF casualties in the capture of Jerusalem amounted to 1,667 (Wavell, ibid, p. 167), while during the period from the beginning of the Third Battle of Gaza until 15 December, the casualties were 2,509 men killed, 14,698 men wounded, and 1,721 men missing (Falls, ibid, p. 262).

Foreign Office and communicated to the GHQ of the EEF. On 10 December EEF GHQ then relayed these final details to each person who was to participate in the procession and proclamation from the Citadel of Jerusalem.[46]

The eyes of the entire world were now focussed upon Jerusalem.

---

46   GHQ EEF to General Officer Commanding 20 Corps and Military Governor of Jerusalem, 10 December 1917. EEF War Diary, December 1917.

THE BATTLE FOR JERUSALEM

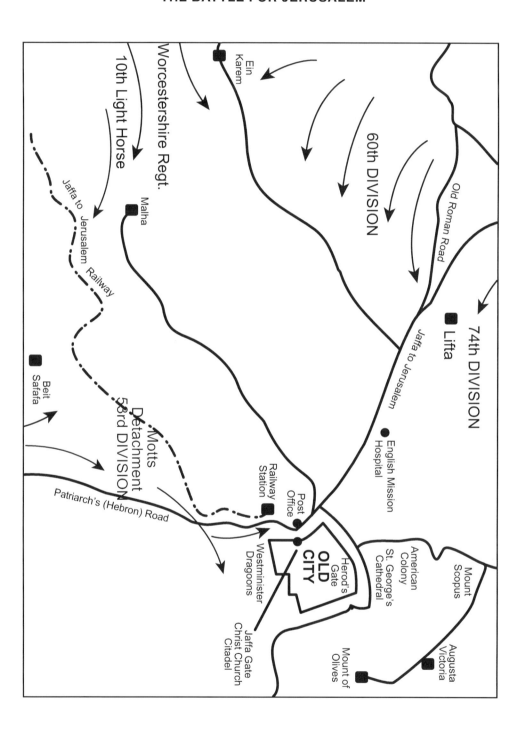

CHAPTER 68

§

Allenby's entry

THE PROCESSION AND PROCLAMATION

The entry of General Allenby into Jerusalem, to officially end 400 hundred years of Ottoman Turkish rule, was scheduled for 11 December. Allenby drove that day from his HQ at Junction Station, in a motorcade of eleven vehicles according to Wyndham Deedes who was part of the group.[1]

It is not exactly clear where the party alighted, but it could have been at General Shea's HQ, which at this stage seemed to be at the hospital belonging to the London Jews Society (English Mission Hospital) on Prophets Street.[2] In the weeks prior to the capture of Jerusalem this location had been used by the Turks for their General Staff Headquarters.

Allenby then mounted a horse at some point and rode along Jaffa Road towards the Old City.[3] Most of the inhabitants of Jerusalem came out to witness this historic occasion. 'I saw Allenby on a beautiful horse,' recalled Rivka Amdursky-Buxbaum, a young Jewish eyewitness. 'They told us he

---

1 Wyndham Deedes to his mother, 11 December 1917, GB 165-0079, MEC, St Anthony's.

2 *The English Mission Hospital* (Jerusalem Press ltd, 1944), no page numbers; *English Mission Hospital,* (Jerusalem, 1947), p. 4; *Jerusalem Hospital,* (CMJ, no date), p. 10; *Jewish Intelligence,* (London, January 1945), p. 12; Bradnack, B. *Anglican International School,* unpublished booklet, p. 13. Cyril Falls, however, states that Shea's HQ was 'at the British Ophthalmic Hospital of St. John on the Jaffa Road.' Falls, ibid, p. 254. The Ophthalmic Hospital was located to the south of Jerusalem, on Hebron Road, while the English Mission Hospital was on Prophets Street, adjacent to Jaffa Road, on the western side. It would be more likely that this was in fact the location of Shea's HQ, although later he could have transferred to the other British hospital.

3 Deedes states that this was some 200 yards from Jaffa Gate, Deedes, ibid. Interestingly Falls, p. 259, makes no mention of Allenby riding a horse.

was a king. And everyone said: "Let's go out and see the king." It even seemed to Amdursky-Buxbaum that Allenby was more than just a king. Perhaps, she concluded 'it was the Messiah.'[4]

Outside Jaffa Gate Allenby in compliance with his instructions from the Government, and in complete contrast to the German Kaiser's ostentatious entrance into Jerusalem on 31 October 1898, then dismounted and proceeded to walk into Jerusalem's Old City. Lining the entranceway were fifty British soldiers from England, Scotland, Ireland and Wales on one side[5], while on the other side were thirty-four New Zealanders,[6] and thirty-one Australians of the 10th Light Horse Regiment, led by Captain Hugo Throssell, VC.[7]

He was officially welcomed by Governor Borton, and then proceeded towards the entrance of the Old City, followed by an entourage of numerous diplomatic and military representatives, including Francois Picot. Colonel T. E. Lawrence was also present, as Staff Officer for Brigadier-General Clayton. Lawrence wrote that this ceremony 'was the supreme moment of the war.'[8]

The large wooden door at Jaffa Gate was opened, and the entourage then entered into the Old City, passing between a guard of honour composed of twenty French soldiers on the right side and twenty Italian soldiers on the left side of the gate.[9]

The four groups of soldiers then 'fell in behind the procession in column of fours',[10]and followed the procession to the steps leading into the ancient Citadel where they were greeted by the 'notables of the City.'[11] The entourage then ascended up the steps. The soldiers from the guard of hon-

---

4   Lossin, Y. *Pillar of Fire*, (Jerusalem, 1983), p. 57.

5   GHQ EEF to General Officer Commanding 20 Corps and Military Governor of Jerusalem, 10 December 1917. EEF War Diary, December 1917. Other sources state there were 110 British soldiers. See *New York Times Mid-Week Pictorial*, (New York, December 1917), no page numbers.

6   Kinloch, ibid, p. 237.

7   Olden, Lieut-Col. A. *Westralian Cavalry*, (Melbourne, 1921), p. 203.

8   Lawrence, T.E. *Seven Pillars of Wisdom*, (London, 1935), Vol. II, p. 464; *Revolt in the Desert*, ibid, p. 192.

9   GHQ EEF to General Officer Commanding 20 Corps and Military Governor of Jerusalem, 10 December 1917. EEF War Diary, December 1917; Falls, ibid, pp. 259-60.

10   Falls, ibid, p. 260.

11   Falls, ibid, p. 260.

our then formed a semi-circle in front of the platform, immediately adjacent to the buildings of the London Jews Society at Christ Church.[12]

A proclamation of martial law was then read out to the population in Arabic, Hebrew, English, French, Italian, Greek and Russian, which was later posted on the walls around the city. The proclamation read:

> To the inhabitants of Jerusalem the Blessed and the people dwelling in its vicinity.
>
> The defeat inflicted upon the Turks by the troops under my command has resulted in the occupation of your city by my forces. I therefore here and now proclaim it to be under martial law, under which form of administration it will remain so long as military considerations make it necessary.
>
> However, lest any of you should be alarmed by reason of your experience at the hands of the enemy who has retired, I hereby inform you that it is my desire that every person should pursue his lawful business without fear of interruption. Furthermore, since your city is regarded with affection by adherents of three of the great religions of mankind, and its soil has been consecrated by the prayers and pilgrimages of multitudes of devout people of these three religions for many centuries, therefore do I make known to you that every sacred building, monument, Holy spot, shrine, traditional site, endowment, pious bequest, or customary place of prayer, of whatsoever form of the three religions, will be maintained and protected according to the existing customs and beliefs of those to whose faiths they are sacred.[13]

The ceremony was watched by as many as could squeeze into the Old City buildings. 'During the ceremony', wrote Bertha Vester, 'I was on the balcony of the Grand New Hotel … I knew I was fortunate indeed to be witnessing one of the great events of history. I realized that the whole Christian

---

12   Christ Church Compound. Today the London Jews Society is known as CMJ.
13   GHQ EEF to General Officer Commanding 20 Corps and Military Governor of Jerusalem, 10 December 1917; Falls, ibid, pp. 260-1.

world outside of Germany and Austria was jubilant. People in the streets were crying at their deliverance. I saw a Jew embrace a Greek priest, and his tall clerical hat went askew in the exuberance of fraternal feeling. Truly we could sing with the Psalmist, "Then were our mouths filled with laughter and our tongue with smiling... The Lord hath done great things for us, therefore we are glad."[14]

Following the public event on the steps of the Citadel, Allenby and his entourage proceeded to the nearby Turkish barracks (today's Kishleh Police Station) where the community leaders of Jerusalem were individually introduced to him.

ALLENBY AND PICOT

Following the formal ceremony Allenby then exited from Jaffa Gate and was driven to Shea's HQ for lunch. Shea, Picot and Lawrence too were in attendance. Lawrence was basically interested in Allenby's next military move, and how this would affect him. Allenby explained that operations would probably have to be curtailed until February, when a push down to Jericho would be made. Lawrence meanwhile was asked to keep a close eye on the traffic of food up the Dead Sea for the Turkish forces.[15]

Francois Picot, though, was in quite a belligerent mood. He was incensed that the notables of Jerusalem had not been introduced to him (nor even to the other French and Italian representatives).[16] He was determined to make a point for the French, and stated, as Lawrence recorded: 'And tomorrow, my dear General I will take the necessary steps to set up a civil government in this town.'

Everyone in attendance were, according to Lawrence, aghast at this bold statement. 'Salad, chicken mayonnaise and foie gras sandwiches hung in our wet mouths unmunched, while we turned to Allenby and gaped. Even he seemed for the moment at a loss.' After regaining his composure Allenby then related the content of his instructions: 'In the military zone the only authority', he stated firmly, 'is that of the Commander-in-Chief – myself.'

---

14 Vester, ibid, p. 280.
15 Lawrence, T.E. *Revolt in the Desert*, (USA, 1927), p. 192.
16 Storrs, ibid, p. 279.

Picot began to protest: 'But Sir Grey, Sir George Grey …' He could not complete his statement, which referred to previous 'agreements' between the former British Foreign Secretary and the French Government concerning a dual civil administration over the conquered areas of Palestine. 'Sir Edward Grey referred to the civil government', Allenby concluded, 'which will be established when I judge that the military situation permits.'[17]

There was nothing more to be said. Picot may have disagreed with this off-handed response from Allenby, but there was nothing he could do about it. The British-ANZAC forces were in possession of Jerusalem and Judea and not the French, and the area was under British military administration through OETA.

This was one of the final nails driven into the 'Grey-Poincare' under-standing and 'Sykes-Picot' Agreement concerning French involvement in the administration of Palestine – and Jerusalem.

ALLENBY'S REPORT

With the official activities over, Allenby then returned to his HQ near Junction Station. Then he compiled his official report to the Government as requested:

> I ENTERED this city officially at noon to-day with a few of my staff, the commanders of the French and Italian detachments, the heads of the Picot Mission, and the military Attaches of France, Italy, and the United States of America. The procession was all on foot. At the Jaffa Gate I was received by guard representing England, Scotland, Ireland, Wales, Australia, New Zealand, India, France and Italy.'

Allenby then alluded to each of the stipulations laid down in his instruc-tions: 'The population received me well' ; 'Guards have been placed over the Holy Places' ; and that the Latin and Greek representatives had been con-

---

17   Lawrence, *Seven Pillars of Wisdom*, p. 455. I have only managed to verify this happening from Lawrence's writings.

tacted concerning Christian Holy Places, and Indian Muslim soldiers and officers had been placed around the Muslim Holy places.[18]

By the time Allenby's report reached London, the world was just beginning to hear about the great events which had transpired during the last three days: that Jerusalem had been liberated – from four hundred years of Turkish rule, and during the festival of liberation, *Hanukkah*.

Additionally it had been liberated just before Christmas, as Prime Minister Lloyd George had requested. Lloyd George's desire was not only geo-political, it was also so there would be a morale booster for the peoples of the British Empire.

But the capture of Jerusalem was much more than just a morale lifting booster for the people of the British Empire – its capture had effects and consequences of world-wide and long-term significance.

---

18 CAB 23/4, WC 296, p. 247.

§

CHAPTER 69

The Significance of Jerusalem's capture

LLOYD GEORGE'S ASSESSMENT OF THE CAPTURE OF JERUSALEM

News of the capture spread quickly throughout the world. It was just as Lloyd George and the War Cabinet had anticipated. A simple entrance, in complete contrast to the Kaiser's grandiose entrance on 31 October 1898, had greatly increased British prestige throughout the world. It was the same German Emperor they were fighting against in 1917 – and the British desired for the world to know of this contrast.

Thereafter whatever Britain proposed concerning the status of Jerusalem and the 'Holy Land' stood a good chance of acceptance.

Many peopled viewed the capture of Jerusalem, together with the capture of Beersheba and the Balfour Declaration on 31 October 1917, as linked. What purpose would there be if a national home for the Jewish people was established without Jerusalem as its political and cultural capital? Jerusalem had been, after all, either in practice or in theory the Jewish capital for almost 3,000 years!

Others viewed the capture as an important event, distinct from the Jewish connection, while some were relieved that the 'Holy City' had been liberated from Islamic control.

Still others viewed the capture as a combination of many factors – the above stated, and more. Lloyd George for instance also saw it as a complete contrast to the indiscriminate carnage and loss of life on the Western Front. He wrote:

> The achievement was of immense importance, alike on military and on sentimental grounds… Our 600,000 casualties in the fiasco on the Western Front had so depleted our resources in men that we could no longer exploit victory on any front, but the moral effect of the victory was tremendously important. It cheered our own people at a critical time, when defeatist elements were making their influence felt among us. It greatly encouraged our American Allies. And among that great international fraternity, the Jewish race, it was an earnest of the fulfilment of the Balfour Declaration … that we favoured "the establishment in Palestine of a national home for the Jewish people."[1]

Indeed, after a year in which the British Empire suffered some 600,000 casualties in achieving very little by way of long term gain, here was a victory of much greater short and long term significance - but for only a small percentage of the casualties compared to the Western Front.

THE EASTERN REPORT'S RESPONSE

The Eastern Report (which provided the War Cabinet with up-to-date information about the military and political proceedings in the eastern sphere), for 13 December 1917, provided possibly the most comprehensive analysis of the significance of the capture of Jerusalem.[2] Under the heading THE RETAKING OF JERUSALEM, it stated:

> The surrender of Jerusalem is politically speaking the most important military event that has yet been recorded in the Eastern Report. It

---

1   Lloyd George, ibid, Vol. II, p. 1091-2.
2   CAB 24/144/21, Report No 46, 13 December 1917.

is, in certain aspects, a decisive action since, whatever else may happen, unless we are evicted by force from Jerusalem during hostilities, it would appear hardly possible for Jerusalem to be handed back to Turkish control, *as the sense of the whole world would be against such an action.*[3]

The Report then provided an analysis of the effects of the Balfour Declaration and capture of Jerusalem upon numerous entities.

THE VATICAN'S RESPONSE

The Vatican was very upbeat by Jerusalem's capture. The Vatican Secretary of State, Count de Valvis, stated to the Foreign Office on 12 December (quoting the official organ, the *Observatore*) that, 'the entry of British troops into Jerusalem had been received with satisfaction by Catholics who cannot but rejoice that the Holy City should be in the possession of a Christian power', and that there 'is every hope that interests and rights of the Catholic Church will be respected.'

The statement concluded with these startling words: '*They add that they thank Providence for not allowing Jerusalem to fall into the hands of Government of the Czar* [sic].'[4]

THE FRENCH RESPONSE

Under the heading *The Future from a French Point of View* the Eastern Report quoted from a telegram from Lord Bertie, the British ambassador in Paris on 11 December. Lord Bertie was quoting from *Le Temps*, the foremost French newspaper of the time, which wrote that it 'awaits with the deepest interest the congratulatory message which the Pope will assuredly send to the King on the conquest of Jerusalem.' The paper then declared 'that England is not following a selfish object in Palestine. The Holy Places will be under international authority. The aspirations of the Israelites will be respected. France applauds these results all the more cordially because

---

3 CAB 24/144/21, Eastern Report No. 46, 13 December 1917. Italics mine.
4 FO 371/3061, 21308, p. 480. Italics mine.

she also has an important and disinterested mission in the East. It is impossible that the inhabitants of the Lebanon, Syrian Arabs, or Armenians of Cilicia and the neighbouring regions can remain subject to the Turkish regime, which has starved, persecuted, or massacred them.'[5]

There was also another French perspective, as epitomised by the attitude of Francois Picot. This significant group, although rejoicing in the Allied victory, was nevertheless perturbed that French ambitions for either controlling Jerusalem itself, or together with Britain, were now appearing more improbable.

French ambitions then became focussed upon Syria proper, and especially Damascus.

THE IMPACT UPON THE *DHIMMI* GROUPS

The *La Temps* newspaper made a very insightful statement when it referred to those who had been 'starved, persecuted, or massacred' by the Turkish regime.

The Turkish decision to enter the War alongside the Central Powers gave her an ideal cover under which to carry out her brutal policies against the subject or *dhimmi* people groups. It would appear from the sources that in excess of 1.5 million Christians (primarily Armenian, Greek and Assyrian) were killed since late 1914. Thousands of Jewish people, primarily from Palestine were also killed or died of deprivation during the War.

In addition there were also thousands of Arab people, especially in Syria, who died of deprivation, and many were executed for nationalist activities.

Those Christians, and other *dhimmi* groups, who survived the War, needed to be placed in a more tolerable environment. The EEF victories gave the opportunity for safer environments to be established.

THE JEWISH RESPONSE

Irrespective of whether a Jewish person was committed to political Zionism or not, the vast majority of the Jewish people were surely gladdened to hear

---

5   CAB 24/144/21, Eastern Report No. 46, 13 December 1917, citing from telegraph No. 1455. *La Temps* was perhaps too kind to 'the English', for indeed there were self-serving geo-political factors involved in Britain's decision to capture Jerusalem.

the news of the capture of Jerusalem. Jerusalem was the heart of both their national and cultural aspirations.

The Eastern Report also stated:

> So much has been said about Zionism lately that it is unnecessary to expand on the effect of the capture of Jerusalem on world Jewry. ... that wherever there are Jews there are Zionists, in theory at least, and that no matter what views these may have held about the war till now, henceforth the goal of their ambitions rests in Entente[6] hands.

A very large number of Jewish people indeed viewed the events of 31 October and 9-11 December as two parts of a whole. The Eastern Report mentioned a very special event which occurred in Odessa, in the Crimean region of Russia. Under the heading of *Zionism*, it stated: 'there was a crowd of 150,000 Jewish people who paraded for two hours in front of the British Consulate in Odessa when they heard news of the Balfour Declaration. The then British Consul then came out and gave a speech to them, after which they proceeded then to the American Consulate.'[7]

THE RESPONSE IN THE UNITED STATES OF AMERICA

Michael Oren, who wrote the seminal book *Power, Faith and Fantasy: America in the Middle East 1776 to the Present* alluded to the above mentioned event, and wrote:

> In spite of its ambiguities and disclaimers, the Balfour Declaration was widely interpreted as a commitment to ensure Jewish statehood and as an unqualified triumph for Zionism. Jews throughout the world believed that it could not have been formulated without Wilson's consent. A crowd of 100,000 Jews reportedly danced in gratitude outside the U.S. consulate in Odessa, with smaller demonstrations occurring

---

6 Entente = Triple Alliance, or the Allies.
7 CAB 24/144/21, Eastern Report No. 46, 13 December 1917.

in front of legations in Greece, China, and Australia. Telegrams of thanks billowed into the White House.[8]

The Zionist movement in the United States was naturally very enthusiastic about the combination of the Balfour Declaration and capture of Jerusalem. 'But', wrote Oren, 'American Jews were not alone … restorationist Protestants also demanded a presidential endorsement of Zionism.'[9] Teddy Roosevelt stated: 'It seems to me that it is entirely proper to start a Zionist State around Jerusalem.'[10]

Although there was initially a degree of concern by Wilson about the close connection between Zionism and Britain, on 6 September 1918 he 'officially identified Zionism with the foreign policy of the United States.'[11]

There were, of course, opponents of the British-Zionist connection in the United States, as indeed there were in most countries.

CHRISTIAN SYMPATHY FOR THE CAPTURE

The Eastern Report also mentioned the importance of the fall of Jerusalem to Bible-believing Christians, and continued by adding: 'and our success will have a considerable moral effect in America.'[12]

Apart from the Jewish people, no other group was as excited by the events in Palestine and Jerusalem, from the perspective of future hopes, than the strong evangelical Christian movement. The following statement by the Anglican-based London Jews Society is perhaps representative of the attitudes and opinions of many, in Britain, North America – and throughout the world:

With one step the Jewish cause has made a great bound forward. For centuries the Jew has been downtrodden, depressed, hated and unloved by all nations. For 2,000 years now the Jew has suffered

---

8   Oren, M. *Power, Faith and Fantasy*, (New York, 2007), p. 362-3.
9   Oren, ibid, p. 359.
10 Oren, ibid, p. 359.
11 Oren, ibid, p. 365.
12 CAB 24/144/21, Eastern Report No. 46, 13 December 1917.

as no other nation on the earth's surface in his restless wanderings. Wherever he has gone he has been ill-treated, but now there is at least a prospect of his settling down once again in his own country, and of becoming in the eyes of men a Nation amongst the Nations, in place of being a wanderer in every clime. He is now to have a home for himself in his God-given land. The day of his exile is to be ended.

What does all this mean for us Christians? In the light of prophetic Scripture we recognize that such an action on the part of our Government and on the part of the Allied Powers, in being united in their resolve to reinstate the Jew in his own land, is full of significance. Our Lord, when asked the question, 'What shall be the signs of Thy coming and of the end of the age', gave one of the signs, in Luke 21: 24, to be that 'Jerusalem shall be trodden down of the Gentiles (nations) until the times of the Gentiles (nations) be fulfilled.' Ever since A.D. 70 Jerusalem and Palestine have been under Gentile domination, and now we seem to be on the very verge of a literal fulfillment of the last prediction, and it is certainly a distinct warning to us that the Lord 'is near, even at the very doors.' (St. Matt 24: 33).[13]

Additionally the Eastern Report mentioned the positive effect upon the Roman Catholic world, as well as in Russia, where the Greek Orthodox Church, it stated, 'is very strongly attached to Jerusalem, and to the places of pilgrimage.'

THE RUSSIAN REACTION

The Russian Government also communicated with the British Government on 12 December, not so much offering congratulations, but 'suggesting that a special provincial Russian agent might be allowed to proceed to Jerusalem to assist in the administration of the various Russian institutions in that city.'[14] The British Foreign Secretary replied, that he 'has the honour to state

---

13   *JMI*, 1917, pp. 129-30.
14   FO 371/3061, ibid, p. 486.

that as Jerusalem is in military occupation the presence of foreign agents is in the opinion of the British military authorities undesirable.'

'The General-Officer-Commanding', Balfour continued, 'has however been asked to render any protection to Russian institutions which he may render desirable.'[15] Any Russian thoughts of getting actively involved in the jurisdiction of Jerusalem were firmly squashed by this message from the British Government. The British had no intention of allowing the Russians to gain from her hard fought political and military victories.

It was vital for the Jewish people that no other European power received any political benefit in Jerusalem and Palestine. The British Government had made its commitment via the Balfour Declaration and all Jewish hopes lay firmly with that commitment – and they did not want any French or Russian interference there.

THE ISLAMIC WORLD'S RESPONSE

Considering the Islamic world, the Eastern Report stated:

> The Dome of the rock [sic], which was the point of prayer to which Mohommad himself turned before he established Mecca,[16] gives Jerusalem a special sanctity to Moslems of all sects. The various Christian shrines of Calvary, the Holy Sepulchre, and Bethlehem are also regarded by the Moslems with great reverence. The effect of the fall of Jerusalem will therefore be considerable among Moslems as a whole, and have a tendency to produce Anglophile sentiments, and to lessen the malignant power of political Pan-Islamists.

Somewhat contrary to what the Eastern Report stated, however, 'the malignant power of political Pan-Islamists' did not dissipate under British rule. A major change had, in fact, occurred to the status of Muslims in Jerusalem. Until that point, with the exception of the Crusader period, Islam had con-

---

15   FO 371/3061, ibid, p. 486.

16   The Dome of the Rock was not then in existence, but what Ormsby-Gore probably meant was the location where the Dome of the Rock was later built, which was the very location where the First and Second Jewish Temples had once existed.

trolled the Temple Mount, Jerusalem, and the land of Israel – and the destinies of all those who lived there.

The conquest of Jerusalem and the region of Judea by a Christian nation, and the promise of this region being entrusted to the Jewish people, created an intolerable situation for most Muslims.

Islam basically determined that Muslims could not live under the control of non-Muslims, be they Christian or Jewish, who are *dhimmis*, second class citizens.

For those *dhimmis*, though, who for centuries had to live under Islamic suzerainty (often in difficult circumstances), this new period offered a totally new, and liberating, reality.

THE IMPACT UPON THE TURKISH EMPIRE

The capture of Jerusalem was going to have considerable impact upon Turkey, as the Eastern Report highlighted:

> The loss of Jerusalem will certainly result in an access of unpopularity to the C.U.P. and the Germans in Turkey. The C.U.P. itself will be furious at having lost a great asset and a hold over the Zionists, the Germans will know that they have to take the blame for the loss. Anti-Germanism and anti-Enverism will from now on be a growing force in Turkey, and it is well to remember that the loss of Jerusalem will be a constant source of irritation, and will not pass away with a few weeks.[17]

As will be seen in the following volume, the loss of Jerusalem and later other regions of the Ottoman Empire, merely provoked the Young Turk leadership to make more concerted efforts to Turkify the remainder of their Empire – and even to expand eastwards into other Turco-centric regions of Asia.

---

17 CAB 24/144/21, Eastern Report No. 46, 13 December 1917.

THE ATTITUDE OF THE ARAB NATIONALIST MOVEMENT

The Eastern Report stated, concerning the Arab nationalist movement:

It is less satisfactory to consider that our adoption of Zionism and our capture of Jerusalem will tend to a certain extent to somewhat abate Arab enthusiasm. As matters stand the King of Hejaz will feel that Jerusalem has passed from al Islam[18] owing perhaps to his co-operation, and that the only definite result has been a declaration in favour of the Jews. This, however, may only be of transient effect if we take an early opportunity of showing that we are behind the Arabs, appreciate their assistance, and desire their liberation. There is no doubt, however, that this aspect of the situation requires careful consideration and attention, otherwise the enemy will not be slow to profit by this event.

The goal of Feisal and Lawrence, and indeed the Syrian-based nationalists, had always been more focussed upon Damascus than anywhere else. From December 1917 Damascus became the main goal of the Arab Northern Army. It was also the goal of the French, and by the end of 1918 a major clash loomed between these two entities – and the British were often caught in the middle of what became an ugly situation.

During the following years the British Government tried to encourage the Arab nationalists to accept the presence of the Jewish national entity – albeit with the purpose of bettering her own geo-political goals in the region. But almost from the beginning it encountered great difficulties in trying to achieve such a reconciliation. On other occasions the British authorities in the region actually tried to undermine the policy of the British Government and to thwart the promise of a national home for the Jewish people in Palestine.

The core issue at hand in this inability of the Arab nationalist movement to accept the existence of the Jewish nationalist movement, though, was not about the merits or demerits of Jewish and Arab nationalism. The

---

18 *Dar al Islam* – the area of Islam.

core issue revolved around a non-Islamic entity having political control over Muslims within the region of *dar al Islam*.

A NEW ZEALAND SOLDIER'S BOLD ACTION

Meanwhile as all these reactions and responses were coming to the fore, a young New Zealand soldier named Louis Salek, who was serving with the 6th Light Horse Regiment, visited Jerusalem. Salek had a Jewish nationalist flag given to him by Jewish people in Cairo prior to his departure from there for *Eretz Yisrael*. He entered into the Old City, probably through Jaffa Gate, and ascended to the top of the Citadel (or Tower of David) where he daringly flew the Star of David flag to be seen by all.

It was greeted with enthusiasm by the Jewish observers, but with disdain and anger by the Muslims, and was ordered to be quickly taken down by the British authorities.[19]

This was quite an amazing little episode - a New Zealander, from the uttermost ends of the earth, flying a Jewish flag from the Citadel of David. According to Josephus Flavius the Jewish/Roman historian, parts of the Citadel were the only buildings left standing by the Romans when they destroyed Jerusalem in 70 AD. The Romans made this decree in order for those mammoth buildings to be a testimony of the power and might of Rome – that not even those large buildings could stop us!

The Citadel in many ways was a representative of that time when Rome triumphed, the Jewish people were defeated, and Jewish national life in the land of Israel ended.[20] Thereafter Jewish national life was mostly associated with the *galut*, the diaspora (or dispersion) when they were scattered amongst the nations.

A process of restoration, though, had been underway for just over a century. That process of restoration in many respects became tangible in 1798

---

19   'The flag waved free', *Jerusalem Post Magazine*, 23 May 1990. Thus far I have only read of this account from one primary source. But the late Ruth Stark related the same incident to the author in an interview in 1997. The flag is now located at the Jerusalem City Museum located in the Citadel.

20   Although there was a second revolt against Rome in 132-135 AD, yet the destruction of Jerusalem and of the Temple in 70 AD signifies to most Jewish people the end of their national life in *Eretz Yisrael*.

when Napoleon invaded the region. From that period the modern geo-political battle for control over the 'land between empires' began in earnest.

During the following century numerous events occurred as part of this dynamic, a dynamic which was played out between two geographical locations: the Bosphorus/Dardanelles Straits in the north, and the Isthmus of Suez in the south.

Throughout that very same period Jewish hopes and desires for a national restoration slowly developed. But in order to achieve such a restoration they would need the help of a sympathetic empire, which would be a modern day Cyrus nation.[21]

All the events from 1798 began to climax at the beginning of 1915 with the Gallipoli Campaign, and then came to a logical conclusion at Beersheba on 31 October and Jerusalem between 9-11 December 1917. By that time Britain had indeed become that modern day Cyrus nation.

THE ROAD FROM GALLIPOLI DID INDEED LEAD TO JERUSALEM

Many tracks converged at Gallipoli in 1915. Those tracks then became a road, and that road led from Gallipoli to the Suez, to the Sinai, to Gaza, to Beersheba – and finally to Jerusalem.

Although at that time there was also a road which led from Basra to Baghdad, and another which began in Mecca and was aiming for Damascus, it was the road to Jerusalem which had most world-wide significance.

Jerusalem in 1917 was a place of great importance for people all over the world – and not just for those who faithfully adhered to the faiths of Judaism, Christianity and Islam.

In view then of the carnage and futility of the First World War on both the Western and Eastern Fronts, there was no greater prize to be won than the capture, or liberation, of Jerusalem.

---

21   The emperor of Persia (Iran) who permitted the Jewish people to return to *Eretz Yisrael* following their exile to Babylon in the 6th century BC.

With its capture those sentiments of Trumpeldor at the time of the formation of the Zion Mule Corps, and the words of John Monash on his way to Gallipoli, now had definite substance.

Gallipoli indeed was the beginning of a road which led to Jerusalem.

* * *

Epilogue

JERUSALEM TO SAN REMO - AND BEYOND

The capture of Jerusalem in 1917 wasn't the end of the road. It was merely a significant stopping point in the journey. That journey continued into 1918, and resulted in the capture of Jericho, Megiddo (Armaggedon), Amman, Semack (the Sea of Galilee), Damascus, Homs, Hama – and Aleppo.

On 30 October 1918 Turkey and Britain signed an armistice. By that time the combined forces of the British Empire (Britain, Australia, New Zealand and India) had paid quite a hefty price in defeating the Ottoman Empire.

According to the figures of the War Office put together in 1922 those nations lost 31,737 men dead in the Dardanelles Campaign; 37,408 dead in the Mesopotamian Campaign and 19,005 dead in the Egypt Campaign.[1] This was a total of 88,150 mostly British, Indian, Australian and New Zealand soldiers who had died liberating the region from the Turkish regime.[2]

This was no small sacrifice. The number of Arab men who died fighting with the Arab Northern Army by comparison was very small.

At the conclusion of the War there began the very complicated and often-times messy business of unravelling and implementing the various agreements made during the War. On numerous occasions the British and

---

1 Although some of these would have been against the Senussi, the vast majority died fighting against the Turkish Empire, from the Suez through to Aleppo. *Statistics of the Military Effort of the British Empire during the Great War*, War Office, March 1922.

2 Many Jewish soldiers were included in this number, either as being part of those national forces, or in the Zion Mule Corps or the 'Jewish Legion' battalions.

the French were at loggerheads with each other; while the French and the Arab nationalists physically battled against each other.

The first step in the rebuilding after the War was the Peace Conference in Versailles which began in February 1919. One important outcome of this Peace Conference was the formation of the League of Nations.

The Versailles Conference, though, was primarily concerned with coming to peace terms with Germany and the Austro-Hungarian Empires. Another Conference was convened in order to settle peace terms with the Turkish Empire. This Conference was convened at San Remo in Italy, in April 1920.

There the representative powers proposed the establishment of mandates for the region of Turkey-in-Asia, in order to prepare those regions for eventual self-government. They offered a mandate to France to administer the region of Syria and Lebanon; a mandate to Britain to administer the region of Mesopotamia; and another mandate to Britain to administer the region of Palestine, which would incorporate the Balfour Declaration. The vote for endorsing these proposals was taken on 25 April 1920. The road from Jerusalem had now led to San Remo.

The British Government accepted the offer of the Palestine Mandate, but then they modified it by slicing off some 77% of the allotted territory in order to placate French and Arab nationalist ambitions and desires. That 77% then became Transjordan, and later the Hashemite Kingdom of Jordan.

The area for the national home of the Jewish people was then to be encompassed within the remaining 23%, an area totalling about 3% of the land mass of Turkey-in-Asia – excluding Arabia.[3] In July 1922 all fifty-one member nations of the League of Nations voted for Britain to administer the Palestine Mandate, and to prepare it for being a national home for the Jewish people.

In time five sovereign independent nations evolved from the area encompassed in these mandates, the area which the Turkish Empire had once

---

3   In 1947 that area was considerably reduced ever further.

ruled in Asia; these being the Arab nations of Iraq, Syria, Lebanon, Jordan – and the Jewish nation of Israel.

Another Arab nation also came into being after World War One – Saudi Arabia. Ibn Saud ousted King Hussein of the Hejaz in 1925, united the regions of Nejd and Hejaz, and founded the Kingdom of Saudi Arabia.

The Jewish presence in *Eretz Yisrael* was always fraught with danger, not just from Arab opponents, but also from British opponents – those who had another vision for the Middle East, a vision which did not include a national home for the Jewish people in Palestine. In 1939 the combined forces of opposition resulted in the British Government effectively rescinding the Balfour Declaration.

Undaunted by all the opposition, the Jewish people persevered and by the eve of World War Two some 550,000 Jews resided in *Eretz Yisrael*.

Although the crucible of the Nazi-inspired Holocaust occurred in Europe, the Nazis (with local Arab sympathizers), also had a plan to annihilate the Jewish people in the Middle East. Thankfully this plan never eventuated, mostly because of British, Australian, New Zealand, South African, Indian and other Allied soldiers who stopped the German-led thrust at Tobruk in 1941 and El Alamein in 1942.[4]

Despite the murder of some six million of their people in the Holocaust, the Jews miraculously survived, both in Europe and in the Middle East. Only one thing mattered to them now, only one hope – to establish a national entity where Jewish people could live freely and could defend themselves.

Finally, some twenty-seven years after the San Remo Conference, that hope became a reality. The first stage of this reality was a decision by the United Nations (which replaced the League of Nations), meeting at Flushing Meadows in New York on 29 November 1947, to establish two new states in the region of Palestine west of the Jordan River – a Jewish State **and** an Arab State.

Although being strategically very vulnerable, the Jewish leadership accepted this United Nations offer. In what can only be described though

---

4 Those other soldiers came from Poland, Greece, the Netherlands, Belgium, Czechoslovakia (Czech Republic and Slovakia), Rhodesia (Zimbabwe), Crete, Jewish soldiers from Palestine, and other groups. For further information see Crombie, K. *El Alamein: Halting an Impending Holocaust in the Middle East,* (Perth, 2012).

as one of the most ill-conceived (and saddest) decisions of the century, the Arab leadership **did not** accept the offer of the United Nations to have their own state. They chose instead to attempt to destroy the impending Jewish State.[5]

They did not succeed, and the Jewish leadership, headed up by David Ben Gurion and Yitzhak Ben Zvi, proclaimed the State of Israel on 14 May 1948. Five Arab nations invaded the fledgling Jewish State the following day – but Israel miraculously survived.

The State of Israel then opened its doors to those Jewish people who had survived the European Holocaust. Additionally it also opened its doors to more than 500,000 Jewish refugees who were forced to leave Arab and Islamic countries. Israel became a sanctuary to many who were regarded as second-class citizens in the lands where they had lived.

Indeed if there was anything positive, any light at all to come out from the quagmire and darkness of the First World War (and also of the Second World War) it was this – that British, Australian, Indian and New Zealand soldiers had aided in laying the foundations for the establishment of a national home for the Jewish people.

Perhaps then, when looking at the events which transpired since the Gallipoli Campaign began, those profound words of Winston Churchill - *'in fulfilment of a destiny as yet not understood by mortal man'* – indeed may have referred to the establishment of modern Israel.

---

5   Had the Arab leadership accepted the United Nations offer, then there is every likelihood that the travesty which was the Palestinian refugee situation might have been averted, or, would at least not have been as drastic as it was.

Selected Bibliography

Books

A Brief Record of the Advance of the Egyptian Expeditionary Force, July 1917 to October 1918, (London, 1919).

Adam-Smith, P. *Anzacs,* (Melbourne, 1991).

Akcam, Taner. *A Shameful Act: The Armenian Genocide and the Question of Turkish Responsibility.* (Henry Holt and Co.. Kindle Edition).

Antonius, G. *The Arab Awakening,* (Beirut, 1938).

Aspinall-Oglander, C. *Military Operations Gallipoli.* Volume II: May 1915 to the Evacuation, (IWM & Battery Press 1992), www.wikipedia.com

Balakian, P. *The Burning Tigris,* (Harper-Collins e-books, Kindle).

Barnett Smith, G. *The Life of the Right Honourable William Ewart Gladstone,* (London, 1880).

Barr, J. *A Line in the Sand,* (London, 2011).

Bicheno, J. *A Glance at the History of Christianity and of English NonConformity,* (London, 1798).

Bostock, H. *The Great Ride,* (Perth, 1982).

Browning and Gill, *Gallipoli to Tripoli,* (Osborne Park, 2011).

Bullock, D. *Allenby's War,* (London, 1988).

Carmel, A. *Activities of the European Powers in Palestine 1799-1914,* Asia and Africa Studies 19 (1985), (Institute of Middle Eastern Studies, University of Haifa).

Clark, C. *The Politics of Conversion,* (Oxford, 1995).

Clark, C.M.H. *Select Documents in Australian History 1788-1850,* (Sydney, 1950).

Crombie, K. *Three Sons of Abraham,* (Perth, 2013).

Dadrian, Vahakn N. *The History of the Armenian Genocide: Ethnic Conflict from the Balkans to Anatolia to the Caucasus,* (Oxford, 1995).

De Haas, J. *Theodor Herzl,* (Chicago, 1927).

Dolan, H. *36 Days – The Untold Story of the Anzac assault on 25th April 1915,* (Macmillan, Australia, 2010, Kindle Book, 2010).

Durie, M. *The Third Choice,* (Deror Books, 2010).

Earl of Oxford and Asquith, *Memories and Reflections,* (Boston, 1928).

Eedle, S. *Archie Newton – His Service with the 2nd County of London (Westminster Dragoons) Yeomanry*, (Tewkesbury, 1997).

Eliav, M. *Britain and the Holy Land, 1838-1914: Selected Documents from the British Consulate of Jerusalem*, (Jerusalem, 1997).

Eliav, M. *Eretz Israel and its Yishuv in the Nineteenth Century (1777-1917)*, (Jerusalem, 1978) [Hebrew].

Ellern, H and B. *Herzl, Hechler, the Grand Duke of Baden and the German Emperor, 1896-1904*, (Tel Aviv, 1961).

Encyclopaedia Judaica.

Encyclopaedia Britannica, 1975.

Facey, A.B. *A Fortunate Life*, (Melbourne, 1981).

Falls, C. *Military Operations – Egypt and Palestine, From June 1917 to the End of the War*, (London, 1930), Part 1.

Falls, C. *Military Operations – Egypt and Palestine, From June 1917 to the End of the War*, (London, 1930), Part 2.

Finn, J. *Stirring Times*, (London, 1878), Vol 1 and 2

Frankel, J. *The Damascus Affair: "Ritual Murder," Politics and the Jews in 1840*, (Cambridge, 1997).

Freulich, R. *Soldiers in Judea*, (New York, 1964).

Friedmann, I. *The Question of Palestine*, (New Brunswick, 1992).

Fromkin, D. *A Peace to End all Peace*, (New York, 1989).

Gabriel, M. *Islam and the Jews,* Lake Mary, (Florida, 2003).

Garfield, B. *The Meinertzhagen Mystery*, (Washington, 2007).

Gawler, Colonel G. *Observations and Practical Suggestions in Furtherance of the Establishment of Jewish Colonies in Palestine*, (London, 1845).

Gilbert, M. *Winston S. Churchill*, Vol. 3: 1914-1916, *The Challenge of War*, (Boston, 1971).

Gordon, Dr. H.L. *The Jewish Legions in the British Army during the First World War (1914-1918)*, (New York, 1940).

Goren, H. *Germany and the Middle East: Past, Present and Future,* edited by Haim Goren, (Jerusalem, 2002).

Goren, H. *Dead Sea Level: Science, Exploration and Imperial Interests in the Near East*, (London, 2011).

Gouttman, R. An *Anzac Zionist Hero*, (London, 2006).

Guinness, P. *Hear O Israel*, (New York, 1983).

Gullet, H.S. *The AIF in Sinai and Palestine*, (1984).

Hamilton, General Sir Ian. *Gallipoli Diary*, (New York, 1920), www.gutenberg.org.

Hamilton, J. *The Price of Valour*, (Sydney, 2012).

Hechler, W. *The Jerusalem Bishopric*, (London, 1883).

Herold, J. Christopher. *Bonaparte in Egypt*, (London, 1963).

Hill, A.J. *Chauvel of the Light Horse*, (Melbourne, 1978).

Hodder, E. *The Life and Works of the Seventh Earl of Shaftesbury*, (London, 1886).

Hopwood, D. *The Russian Presence in Syria and Palestine, 1843-1914: Church and Politics in the Near East*, (Oxford, 1969)

Hourani, A. *Syria and Lebanon*, (Oxford, 1946).

Hughes, R. *The Fatal Shore*, (London, 1987).

Hyamson, A. *British Consulate in Jerusalem in relation to the Jews of Palestine 1838-1914*, (London, 1939).

Idriess, I. The Desert Column, (Australia, 1973.,

Israel Pocket Library. *Zionism*, (Jerusalem, 1973).

Israel Pocket Library. *History from 1880*, (Jerusalem, 1973).

Jabotinsky, V. *The Story of the Jewish Legion*, (New York, 1945).

Johnston, R.M. *The Corsican: A Diary of Napoleon's Life in His Own Words*, (London, 1910).

Kedourie, E. *In the Anglo-Arab Labyrinth*, (London, 2000).

Kedourie, E. *The Chatham House Version and other Middle Eastern Studies*, (London, 1970).

Kett, H. *History the Interpreter of Prophecy*, (London, 1799).

Kinloch, T. *Echoes of Gallipoli*, (Auckland, 2005).

Kinloch, T. *Devils on Horses*, (Auckland, 2007).

King, M. *New Zealanders at War*, (Auckland, 1981).

Kinross, Lord. *Between two Seas*, (New York, 1969).

Knight, W. *The History of the Great European War*, (London).

Knightley, P and Simpson, C. *The Secret Lives of Lawrence of Arabia*, (London, 1969).

Kobler, F. *The Vision Was There: A History of the British Movement for the Restoration of the Jews to Palestine*, (London, 1956).

Laffin, J. *The Dagger of Islam*, (London, 1979).

Lawrence, T.E. *Revolt in the Desert*, (New York, 1927).

Lawrence, T.E. *Seven Pillars of Wisdom*, (London, 1935).

Leslie, S. *Mark Sykes – His Life and Letters*, ((London, 1923).

Lewis, B. *The Middle East and the West*, (New York, 1964).

Lieber, S. *Mystics and Missionaries, The Jews in Palestine, 1799-1840*, (Salt Lake City, 1992).

Lloyd George, D. *War Memoirs*, (London, 1939). Volumes 1 and 2.

Lossin, Yigal. *Pillar of Fire*, (Jerusalem, 1983).

Lowenthal, M. *The Diaries of Theodor Herzl,* (New York, 1956).

Macmunn, Lt-Gen Sir G & Falls, Capt. C, *Military Operations – Egypt and Palestine. From the Outbreak of War with Germany to June 1917,* (London, 1928).

Mango, A. *Ataturk,* (London, 1999) Kindle e-Book edition.

McCleod, G. *Anzacs,* (North Ryde, 1985).

Milton, G. *Paradise Lost – Smyrna 1922,* (London, 2009).

Monson, J. *The Land in Between,* (Jerusalem, 1983).

Moorehead, A. *Gallipoli,* (Illustrated Edition, South Melbourne, 1975).

Moorhouse, G. *Hell's Foundations: A Town, Its Myths & Gallipoli,* (United Kingdom, 1992).

Morgenthau, H. *Ambassador Morgenthau's Story,* (1918), www.net.lib.byu.edu

Morice, J. *Six Bob A Day Tourist,* (Australia, 1985).

Murphy, D. *The Arab Revolt 1916–1918,* (London, 2008).

Murray, I. *The Puritan Hope,* (Edinburgh, 1971).

Olden, Lieut-Col. A. *Westralian Cavalry,* (Melbourne, 1921).

Orchard, S. *English Evangelical Eschatology, 1790-1850,* unpublished thesis (Cambridge, 1992).

Oren, M. *Power, Faith and Fantasy,* (New York, 2007).

Paleologue, M. *An Ambassador's Memoirs,* edited by F.A. Holt, (New York, 1925), www. net.lib.byu.edu

Parkes, J. *Whose Land?* (Britain, 1970).

Patterson, J. *With the Zionists in Gallipoli,* (London, 1916).

Powles, Lieut-Col C.G. *The New Zealanders in Sinai and Palestine,* (Auckland, 1922).

Pragai, M. *Faith and Fulfilment: Christians and the Return to the Promised Land,* (London, 1985).

Pugsley, C. *Gallipoli: The New Zealand Story,* (Auckland, 1990).

Ridley, J. *Lord Palmerston,* (London, 1970).

Rowe, Major E. *2nd County of London (Westminster Dragoons) Yeomanry,* (London, 1962).

Sacher, H. *A History of Israel,* (New York, 1976).

Samuel, H. *Memoirs,* (London, 1945).

Sanders, R. *The High Walls of Jerusalem,* (New York, 1983).

Savage, R. *Allenby of Armageddon,* (London, 1925).

Schetman, J. *Jabotinsky – Rebel and Statesman,* (New York, 1956).

Schwarzfuchs, S. *Napoleon the Jews and the Sanhedrin,* (London, 1979).

Scult, M. *Millennial Expectations and Jewish Liberties,* (Leiden, 1978).

Selected Letters of T.E. Lawrence, edited by David Garnett, (London, 1941).

Shadbolt, M. *Voices of Gallipoli,* (Auckland, 1988).

Sokolow, N. *History of Zionism,* (London, 1919).

Stein, L. *The Balfour Declaration*, (London, 1961).

Storrs, R. *Orientations,* (London, 1945).

Storrs, R. *Lawrence of Arabia, Zionism and Palestine*, (London, 1941).

Teveth, S. *Ben Gurion: The Burning Ground, 1886-1948*, (Boston, 1997).

The Annual Register, (London, 1798).

Tibawai, A.L. *British Interests in Palestine*, (Oxford, 1961).

Toynbee, A. *Armenian Atrocities: The Murder of a Nation*, (London, 1915).

Toynbee, A. *The Western Question in Greece and Turkey,* (London, 1992).

Trevelyn, G. *The History of England*, (London, 1948).

Tuchman, B. *Bible and Sword*, (New York, 1956).

Tuchman, B. *The Guns of August*, (New York, 1962).

Verete, M. *The Restoration of the Jews in English Protestant Thought 1790-1840*, Middle East Studies, (London, January 1972).

Verete, M. 'A Plan for the Internationalization of Jerusalem', in *From Palmerston to Balfour: Collected Essays of Mayir Verete*, (Frank Cass, London).

Verrier, A. *Agents of Empire*, (London, 1995).

Vester, B. *Our Jerusalem*, (Jerusalem, 1981).

Viscount Bryce, *The Treatment of Armenians in the Ottoman Empire 1915-16*, (London, 1916).

Von Sanders, *Five Years in Turkey*, (United States Naval Institute, 1927).

Wallach, J. *Germany and the Middle East 1835-1939*, (Tel Aviv, 1975).

Wavell, *The Palestine Campaign,* ((London, 1931).

Weizmann, C. *Trial and Error,* (Philadelphia, 1949). 2 Volumes.

Weldon, Captain L. B. *Hard Lying*, (London, 1925).

Wilkinson, P. *For Zion's Sake*, (Paternoster, 2010).

Wilson, Brig-Gen, L.C. *Operations of the Third Light Horse Brigade*, (no publishing details).

Wilson, R. *Palestine 1917*. Edited by Helen Millgate. (Tunbridge Wells, 1987).

Winter, J. 'Under Cover of Darkness', in *America and the Armenian Genocide 1915*, edited by Jay Winter, (New York, 2003).

Wolf, L. *Notes on the Diplomatic History of the Jewish Question.* (London, 1919).

Yaari, A. *The Goodly Heritage*, (Jerusalem, 1958).

Yeor, Bat, *Islam and Dhimmitude*, (Cranberry, NJ, 2002).

Ye'or, Bat, *Understanding Dhimmitude: Christians and Jews under Islam and the Actualization of History*, (RVP Publishers, Kindle Edition).

Other Materials

Numerous files from the Foreign Office (FO), and War Office (WO) and British Cabinet (CAB) at the National Archives in Kew, London.

The 4th Light Horse Brigade War Diary, (Australian War Memorial, AWM), Volume 1.

12th Light Horse Regiment War Diary, AWM, October 1917.

4th Light Horse Regiment War Diary, AWM, October 1917, Volume X.

Diary of Jim Henderson, *Mountain Views,* (Healesville local newspaper), 19 April 1993.

Egyptian Expeditionary Force Diary, Oct and December 1917.

Johns, William Henwood 1891-1917. Letters to Iris, 1915-1917. Auckland War Memorial Museum Library, MS 1392.

Chauvel's Private Papers, PR00535.003, AWM.

Diary of John Nicolayson, Conrad Schick Library.

Jewish Chronicle, 12 March 1915.

Jewish Chronicle, 30 April 1915.

Jewish Chronicle, 22 January 1915.

Diary of Trooper Reg Walters, 10th Light Horse Regiment.

(Unpublished, copy in author's possession).

New York Times Mid-Week Pictorial, (New York, December 1917), no page numbers.

Statistics of the Military Effort of the British Empire during the Great War, War Office, (March 1922).

Diary of Marie James, quoted in *JMI,* 1919.

Journal of the Australian War Memorial. April, 1984; October 1983; April 1991.

LJS Report, (London, 1833),

The St. James Chronicle (or British Evening Post), from Thursday, July 12 to Saturday July 14, 1798.

The Courier, 19 June 1798. British Library (Newspaper House).

Jewish Expositor, (London, 1825).

Jewish Intelligence, (London, 1826).

The Gentleman's Magazine, September 1799.

Jewish Chronicle, 30 April 1915.

Winter, D. 'The Anzac Landing – the Great Gamble', *Journal of the Australian War Memorial,* April 1984.

Daily Express, 4 October 1915.

Jones, I. 'Beersheba: The light horse charge and the making of myths,' in *Journal of the Australian War Memorial,* No. 3, October 1983.

Meyer, E. 'With Allenby' in *Jerusalem Post Magazine,* 15 December 1978.

R. W. Greaves, 'The Jerusalem Bishopric 1841' in *English Historical Review,* 64, 1948.

Skinner, J. *The Three Anglican Bishops in Jerusalem,* in 'Church Quarterly Review', July 1884.

Temperley, H. *Near East: Disraeli and Cyprus,* English Historical Review, XLVI, (April, 1931).

Levine, S. 'The Flag Waved Free', in the *Jerusalem Post*, 23 May 1990.

Selected website sources

Australian War Memorial, *Gallipoli*, www.awm.gov.au

The Long, Long Trail, www.1914-1918.net.

www.wikipedia.com. (Used on numerous occasions).

Gaunt, D, *The Assyrian Genocide 1915*, SEYFO Center 1915, www.seyfocenter.com.

Gabriel Mitchell, 'Ataturk, Ben Gurion, and Turkey's Road Not Taken', *The Tower*, Issue 8, November 2012, in www.thetower.com.

Chris B. Rooney, "The International Significance of British Naval Missions to the Ottoman Empire, 1908-1914," *Middle Eastern Studies,* Vol. 34, no. 1 (January 1998), cited in www.mthdyoke.edu

Kifner, J. *The Armenian Genocide of 1915: An Overview,* in www.nytimes.com.

www.genocidescholars.org

Southern Poverty Law Centre, *State of Denial*, Intelligence Report, Summer 2008, Issue No. 130, www.splcenter.org.

Archives

Australian War Memorial, Canberra.

Bodleian Library, Oxford.

British Library, London.

Central Zionist Archives, Jerusalem.

Conrad Schick Library and Archive, Christ Church, Jerusalem.

Imperial War Museum, London.

Jabotinsky Institute, Tel Aviv.

Kings College Archive, London.

National Archives, Kew, London.

Middle East Centre, St. Anthony's College, Oxford.

Queen Elizabeth II War Memorial, Waioru, New Zealand.

Yad Ben Zvi Archives, Jerusalem.